Cocoon

DEVELOPER'S HANDBOOK

Lajos Moczar
Jeremy Aston

Developer's Library

201 West 103rd Street, Indianapolis, Indiana 46290

Cocoon Developer's Handbook

International Standard Book Number: 0-672-32257-9

Library of Congress Catalog Card Number: 2001090437

Printed in the United States of America

First Printing: December 2002

05 04 03 02 4 3 2 1

Trademarks

All terms mentioned in this book that are known to be trademarks or service marks have been appropriately capitalized. Sams Publishing cannot attest to the accuracy of this information. Use of a term in this book should not be regarded as affecting the validity of any trademark or service mark.

Warning and Disclaimer

Every effort has been made to make this book as complete and as accurate as possible, but no warranty or fitness is implied. The information provided is on an "as is" basis. The authors and the publisher shall have neither liability nor responsibility to any person or entity with respect to any loss or damages arising from the information contained in this book.

Acquisitions Editor
Shelley Johnston

Development Editor
Heather Goodell

Managing Editor
Charlotte Clapp

Project Editor
Matthew Purcell

Copy Editor
Cheri Clark

Indexer
Erika Millen

Proofreader
Suzanne Thomas

Technical Editors
Luca Morandini
Ben Shapiro
Vadim Gritsenko

Team Coordinator
Amy Patton

Interior Designer
Gary Adair

Cover Designer
Alan Clements

Page Layout
Juli Cook

Graphics
Steve Adams
Tammy Graham
Oliver Jackson
Laura Robbins

Contents at a Glance

Table of Contents

About the Authors

Jeremy Aston has been developing commercial software solutions since 1988 and has been involved in Web application development since 1995. He has extensive experience in developing multilingual, branded Web applications and specializes in e-learning, having developed content and learning management solutions since 1997. He spends most of his development time building XML/XSLT/Java solutions that try to get as close to a pure content/logic/presentation separation as possible.

He lives with his wife and young family on the south coast of England, rides a motorbike every day, and will be glad to be able to go to bed now.

Lajos Moczar has worked in IT for the past 13 years. After getting his start in C/C++ development, he moved on to database administration, IT architecture, and project management. His experience in Java goes back to its inception. Since getting involved in Java, Lajos has gradually focused his career on Web application development. During one such project, in which he had to write his own XML publishing engine, he discovered Cocoon and was hooked. Since then, he has used Cocoon on various projects and has become a frequent contributor to the Cocoon users mailing list. In early 2002, he put his expertise to work by offering the first available full-length Cocoon training classes. On his site, `www.galatea.com`, Lajos maintains a pre-integrated packaging of Apache, Tomcat, and Cocoon called Az. Through his company, Galatea IS, Inc., Lajos specializes in helping developers make effective use of open source software for Web application development.

Ben Shapiro has been creating Web-based publishing systems since 1997 and is well-versed in both Java and Microsoft technologies. He is an open source advocate, and leverages open source software whenever possible to design and implement robust, creative, and low-cost solutions to technology challenges. He has worked with many large companies on XML-based publishing tools using best of breed technologies such as XML, XSLT, Apache Cocoon, Apache Tomcat, JSP, and Apache Struts.

Dedication

To Little, Littlest, and Littler still...

—Jeremy

To Mariah, to whom I owe much more than this book. AdInA

—Lajos

Acknowledgments

Jeremy Aston

Writing this book has been a real dichotomy of pleasure and pain. It has consumed far more time and been far more pressured than I ever thought it would be; but it has also been a very rewarding experience, and I hope that you, the reader, gain something from the effort that has been put in by the whole production team.

With this in mind, I have to thank my co-author Lajos. We have never met (yet) but without his willingness to get involved, this book may never have made it. Over the many email and phone conversations we had, it was good to know that we shared a common vision of what we wanted the book to be. Many thanks to Ben Shapiro for contributing much in the way of leg work to help make the vision a reality. A massive thank you must go to Shelley Johnston at Sams. She has put up with much but given much with a smile. The same is true of Heather Goodell and Matt Purcell—together with Shelley they make a great team and are just as (if not more) responsible for getting this book done as the authors. Thanks must also go to the technical editing team of Luca Morandini and Vadim Gritsenko, who have done a top job of making sure the technicalities are spot on.

As for my erstwhile nocturnal companion, I must pay respect to Jamaican Blue Mountain coffee—the best beans in the world. Alongside coffee, I must also mention some of many artists whose music accompanied my writing sessions, including Aphex Twin, Plastikman, Leftfield, The Orb, Future Sound of London, Faithless, The Verve, Alabama 3, Feeder, Kraftwerk, Happy Mondays, Massive Attack, Mazzy Star, Pop Will Eat Itself, The Grid, KLF, Underworld, Chemical Brothers, and more. I recommend them all for anyone else who has to do something like this.

For their (sometimes unknowing) support and help, thanks go out to Roach, Doghair, SASManPete, Piers, the KP development team, David Brent, Edward and Tubbs, Dave Gorman, my Triumph Speed Triple, and the whole Cocoon development community.

Last but not least, I must say a big thank you to Sophie and Ellie, who let me do this and would have seen even less of me if I had worked sensible hours.

Now where did I put my bedroom?

Lajos Moczar

My name would not be on this book without the support of Mariah, who not only managed a house full of rowdy kids while I wrote, but enabled the meeting of my deadlines despite various disruptions of our lives and my occasional self-doubts. Her help and advice also made possible the Cocoon training classes that I gave this year and whose material has proven invaluable to this work.

This book is the fruition of the past three years I've worked with Cocoon and watched it mature from a simple XSLT servlet to a feature-laden application development platform. Chief among those whose material contributions I must acknowledge are the tireless contributors to the project whose ideas and innovations have benefited all of us users. Another big thanks must go to those manning the cocoon-users mailing list and whose help not only has proved invaluable to beginners and experts alike, but has thereby significantly contributed to the growing adoption of Cocoon as a mature product. To those who helped with the book: our technical editors, Luca Morandini, who deserves a medal for all those tiny errors he uncovered in my listings, and Vadim Gritsenko, who should be known as the "cocoon auto-responder" for his timely and accurate responses on the Cocoon users mailing list, as well as Ben Shapiro. I must naturally commend my co-author Jeremy Aston for his work, as well as his overall vision for the book. Finally, I would like to acknowledge the tremendous effort on the part of those of the Sams staff who I know were involved in getting this book on the shelf: Shelley Johnston, Heather Goodell, Matt Purcell, and Cheri Clark. I had no idea how much behind-the-scenes work goes into a book like this.

We Want to Hear from You!

As the reader of this book, *you* are our most important critic and commentator. We value your opinion and want to know what we're doing right, what we could do better, what areas you'd like to see us publish in, and any other words of wisdom you're willing to pass our way.

You can e-mail or write me directly to let me know what you did or didn't like about this book—as well as what we can do to make our books stronger.

Please note that I cannot help you with technical problems related to the topic of this book, and that due to the high volume of mail I receive, I might not be able to reply to every message.

When you write, please be sure to include this book's title and author, as well as your name and phone or email address. I will carefully review your comments and share them with the authors and editors who worked on the book.

Email: opensource@samspublishing.com

Mail: Mark Taber
Associate Publisher
Sams Publishing
201 West 103rd Street
Indianapolis, IN 46290 USA

Reader Services

For more information about this book or others from Sams Publishing, visit our Web site at `www.samspublishing.com`. Type the ISBN (excluding hyphens) or the title of the book in the Search box to find the book you're looking for.

INTRODUCTION

Introduction from Lajos Moczar

Back in 1999, I was working on yet another Java-based Web application. This particular application was a database-driven reporting system, something I'd made a sort of specialization of over the previous couple of years. Those of you who have done the same thing probably have painful memories of using JDBC, custom connection pooling, and HTML wrappers around your result set data. My experience was no different. In our frustration with this particular project, our team had already created a suite of Java objects that created basic HTML elements—page, body, table, and so on. It worked, but the process was still not as easy as I needed it to be.

About that same time, I'd been playing around with various Java implementations of XML and XSL parsers. Hoping that this technology might offer a solution for our reporting-tool woes, I coded up a program that took a database result set as input, applied an XSL stylesheet, and returned the result to the servlet. What joy! No longer did I have to struggle with the mess of HTML, logic, and data within a servlet. Rather, I finally had a realistic way to separate presentation logic from my data and its subsequent processing.

While I was proudly showing off the revised application, a colleague downloaded something from the Apache Software Foundation site called Cocoon. Immediately, it became apparent that this took the separation I'd just achieved to another level. It provided not only an elegant way to separate the presentation from data, but both from logic. This concept (which has come to be known as Separation of Concerns), and its implementation in Cocoon, was probably the thing that sold us on the technology. It gave us a new paradigm for dividing up the tasks of building and maintaining our application. For the future, it helped ensure that those who inherited our application actually stood a chance of understanding it.

Within a few weeks of finding Cocoon, I'd converted our application to Cocoon. The results were everything we wanted. Our colleagues were impressed, our management was impressed, and we were able to complete our application to spec. For the next year or so, the application ran perfectly, happily serving up HTML and PDF reports.

Shortly thereafter, we started hearing about the 2.0 version of Cocoon that was just starting development. Like true tech junkies, we downloaded the new stuff and built a version of our app with it. Some of you might remember the days of these alpha versions of Cocoon 2.0, when you needed to write pipelines backward, with the serializer first and the generator last! We had quite a few bugs to fix back then to make the thing work, but it was rather exhilarating to be involved with something that we knew was going to be big. And it has been big. Since these early days, I have watched Cocoon become an impressive piece of work. From a simple XSL transformation servlet, Cocoon has evolved into what you could only call a Web application development platform.

There has been, however, one negative side effect of Cocoon's growth, and that is its complexity. For the beginner, Cocoon can be somewhat daunting, with its dazzling array of features and ground-breaking technologies. At the same time, as is common with OSS projects, documentation has lagged somewhat behind the development. Unfortunately, this combination has the potential to hinder widespread adoption in the marketplace. In early 2002, after going through a difficult learning curve myself with some features in the new version of Cocoon, I decided to offer what would be the first available courses devoted to Cocoon. Even though I considered myself well-versed in the software, I learned quite a bit more preparing for these courses! However, not only were my courses a success, but their material came in handy when, a few months later, I found myself writing this book.

If there is one thing that is needed for someone trying to work with Cocoon, it is a clear "big picture" introduction—something that gives you a map of this complex technology and a sense of where you are within it. As with anything in this crazy world of information technology, having this map or picture can be the difference between success and failure. I had to come to my own "big picture" understanding before I could make effective use of Cocoon. In this book, Jeremy and I have tried to present this understanding in a way that can benefit both beginners and experts alike. We hope our readers can use this book to learn not only what Cocoon can do, but also how to use it effectively to build mission-critical Web applications. This is what we have done in our years working with Cocoon, and we hope that this book shows you how to do the same.

Introduction from Jeremy Aston

In the summer of the year 2000, I was running a team of developers working on the next version of a Web application that would manage learning and training resources in an organization. In the couple of years leading up to that point, we had spent considerable time working on technologies that allowed the abstraction of the page data with presentation logic; however, a number of shortcomings were apparent that we wanted to fix. The application was moving to be a hosted service, offering a low-cost, customized e-learning portal. We had customers who wanted their own look and feel, text, and even language variants. The existing architecture was not easy to change and relied on a lot of expensive development resources. The goal was to find an alternative that would help disperse some of the editorial control to Web editors and nontechnical users.

During various research and development efforts, we looked at several solutions. Our application was already J2EE based and used servlets and enterprise beans. Naturally, we looked at JSP as a possible solution; however, we had problems with being able to quickly repurpose the application from servlets to JSP without creating code that was even more unmanageable.

The possibilities offered by transforming XML seemed to be a much more "pure" way to go, and we had significant success writing proof of concepts that merged XML data streams with XSLT stylesheets. What proved more difficult was developing an architecture that was fast, scalable, and resilient. In the end, time constraints meant that we made some minor improvements to the existing, proven architecture and lived with that for some considerable time.

During this time, however, I did take notice of a project that seemed to reflect a state of mind that we had reached. During my R&D phases, I had looked at various initiatives being undertaken as part of the Apache project. One specific area caught my eye. The guys working on a code base called "Cocoon" had concluded that page tagging languages such as ASP, JSP, PHP, and CFM had some major design limitations that would prove to be real barriers to separating content from logic. XML and XSLT were core technologies in their solution. This mentality was spot on with the feelings of the team and myself. Unfortunately, Apache Cocoon (to give it its proper title—but for the sake of brevity it's known as plain old Cocoon from here on in) was not much more than some beta code, and we could not justify the risk we would take to implement a solution based on the architecture.

It was not until I changed jobs and started working for an e-learning content development company that I started to look at Cocoon again. I was brought in to help drive the adoption of technologies that would increase productivity and reduce the amount of reinvention that was endemic to the production process. I spent some time looking at various third-party tools, all of which had some major limitations. Nothing was flexible, nothing was user oriented, nothing was customizable, and very little was anywhere near open or based on really open standards.

As a result, my new team and I started to look at creating a set of tools that would help increase our efficiency. The key areas of change were clear—e-learning content is basically a set of raw data in the form of instructional text, graphics, animations, user interactions, audio, video, and so on, combined with presentational logic that displays the data to the end user. This problem was perfect for being solved by an XML/XSLT-based solution. If the data was described in XML, we could really easily merge it with XSLT presentation templates and churn out our final content.

After developing some simple proof of concepts that worked on a batch basis, we started to consider the prospect of developing a really user-friendly application that would empower nontechnical users to be able to create and publish e-learning content. In response to this need and some complementary needs within our customer base, we started to design and build such an application. When considering how we should build it, my mind went back to the Cocoon project, and I revisited the site.

While there, I realized how far Cocoon had come. Version one was production code and version two was well along. After a short tryst with version one, we looked at version two and were completely bowled over. This was clearly the way forward.

Since then we have started development in earnest and found where Cocoon is great and where it is not so great. Part of this process involved my writing some basic notes for developing in Cocoon for new members of my team. These notes developed into "ctwig"—the Cocoon Two Idiots Guide—which is now part of the Cocoon distribution.

This book is a natural progression. It is the result of being on the Cocoon learning curve; it is the distilled knowledge base of experience that has come from developing a real-world application using Cocoon. Some things may be missing, some may lack some detail; but the important stuff is all here. No doubt, as you develop your own applications, you will find solutions to problems that Lajos and I have not encountered. We are sure you will find better solutions to problems that we have raised. What we aim to do in this book is help you resolve the basics, avoid common but expensive mistakes, and move on to really extending your knowledge.

Lajos and I sincerely hope you find this book useful and wish you all the best as you use Cocoon to develop powerful and flexible Web applications.

Who Should Read This Book?

Simply stated, the book is intended for anyone who wants to design and develop applications using Cocoon. Web application developers and architects will find this book useful not only for the technical detail about implementing solutions using Cocoon but also for the background information on separation of concerns, real-world multitier architectures, and internationalization. HTML-based Web authors will no doubt find much help in coming to grips with the possibilities offered by transforming XML using XSLT. Webmasters and Web site publishers will gain from understanding how the Cocoon publishing framework supports the more effective and efficient unification of the process and technology camps within their business. Finally, those individuals particularly interested in content management and e-learning content development will hopefully gain some ideas from some of the principles contained in the real-world code examples presented.

Scope

So what does this book cover? For readers new to Cocoon, it covers everything one needs to know to be able to create Web applications. For the more experienced developer, it hits on ways that Cocoon can be used more effectively, presents alternative ways of achieving a particular result, and details the pros and cons of each method. We would not state that this book is the definitive guide to Cocoon—after all, it is a constantly progressing product—however, we believe that this book does provide something for every reader, regardless of experience with Cocoon or Web application development.

Consideration is given to issues and methodologies generic to application development. A firm foundation is quickly developed. Finally, deeper topics are discussed and reference material is provided.

The book can be read sequentially or used as a "just in time" reference manual to be dipped into and out of as needed.

How This Book Is Organized

The book is divided in to three main parts. The first part introduces Cocoon, why it should be used, how to install it, its architecture, and the basics of how Cocoon works. Part II develops the theme and discusses key aspects of Cocoon that are used throughout the development of an application. This is illustrated using a sample application. Part III delves deeper into more advanced Cocoon development features. Part IV discusses how all of this can be brought together as a well-structured application. Part V of the book provides extended reference material on some particularly important Cocoon components, especially the sitemap. All of this is backed up in Part VI with a comprehensive set of appendixes that provide a practical reference manual.

Looking at each chapter in more detail, what do we find?

At the start of Part I, Chapter 1 introduces Cocoon and explains why it is a solid technology on which to develop Web applications.

Chapter 2 discusses the Avalon framework that is the foundation on which it is built.

Chapter 3 explains how Cocoon works, and its processing model.

Chapter 4 introduces possibly one of the most important aspects of Cocoon: the sitemap.

Moving into Part II of the book, Chapter 5 provides an overview of the sample application, its design, and how it will be put together.

Chapter 6 covers how Cocoon is installed.

Chapter 7 looks at the basics of creating static pages, introducing the practical side of pipeline processing concepts.

Chapter 8 introduces dynamic content using the easily understood XSP technology.

Chapter 9 starts a series of chapters that cover the major Cocoon components, starting with generators.

The next component to be discussed is transformers, and these are covered in Chapter 10.

Chapter 11 looks at what matchers and selectors are, how they work, and which ones to use in which circumstances.

Chapter 12 covers how actions can be incorporated into an application and the benefits of doing so. This chapter also covers the closely associated topic of form handling.

Chapter 13 explains how you can use Cocoon to handle browser implementation issues simply and easily.

Chapter 14 provides a suitable close to Part II by covering internationalization of content.

Part III is introduced with Chapter 15. This chapter looks at how Cocoon can be extended by implementing new components.

Chapter 16 examines more details of database interaction within Cocoon.

Chapter 17 looks at Web services and SOAP.

Chapter 18 covers how Cocoon integrates with the wider J2EE infrastructure.

Chapter 19 explains how the Lucene search technology has been integrated into Cocoon and how this can be used in your own applications.

Chapter 20 investigates the hot topic of portal development, something Cocoon is ideally suited to achieve.

Chapter 21 introduces Part IV and discusses the design factors to take into consideration when developing an application with Cocoon.

Chapter 22 expands on the preceding chapter and demonstrates practical examples of how an application can be developed.

The whole topic of application deployment, management, and tuning is covered in Chapter 23, which closes Part IV.

Part V aggregates material from the rest of the book into chapters that form a reference tool. This is quickly demonstrated through Chapter 24, a detailed breakdown of the whole sitemap and how to use every single component that can be contained within it.

Chapter 25 demonstrates how to use entity catalogs to make resource resolution more effective.

Chapter 26 covers what you need to do to implement a parent component manager.

Chapter 27 discusses the resources that are available to Cocoon developers, especially the documentation and online support. It also encourages participation in the Cocoon project.

Finally, in Part VI the appendixes provide reference information on XSP and logicsheet commands.

Source Code

As is the fashion nowadays, there is no CD-ROM to accompany this book. The source code can be obtained, however, from the Sams Web site, `www.sams.com`. The material is also available from the authors' Web sites, `www.pigbite.com` and `www.galatea.com`.

PART I

Introduction to Cocoon

CHAPTER

CHAPTER 1

Introduction to Cocoon

This chapter introduces Cocoon and explains why Cocoon is a solid technology on which to base Web application development. It covers several areas:

- A quick overview of the history of Cocoon
- The principles of multitier Web applications design
- What possibilities XML offers
- How Cocoon exploits these possibilities

This chapter is intended not to form a comprehensive reference to the concepts behind multitier Web application design, but rather to provide sufficient technical discussion to prime the new user and support a reasonable case for the use of Cocoon over alternative technologies. If you want to jump straight into Cocoon itself, please collect $200 and advance to Chapter 2!

The History of Cocoon

Cocoon is an XML publishing framework. At its core it manages the delivery of XML data streams, processing and transforming them as appropriate. Cocoon started life as a servlet that performed XSLT transformations on streams of XML data, with the Apache Cocoon project gaining momentum from way back in early 1999. Its creator, Stefano Mazzocchi, developed the first version of Cocoon as a way of realizing some ideas for better Web publishing technologies. The early inclusion of Cocoon into the Apache XML project reaped many benefits through the proven open source development method.

By the middle of 2000, the first production release of Cocoon had gained a significant following and had evolved into something much more powerful than a mere servlet. By this time as well there had been many advances in the understanding of what would be required by the next generation of powerful publishing frameworks, as well as a clear picture of the technology requirements in the light of concrete standards. Cocoon One was a self-confessed "proof of concept," limited by enforced design decisions and its own success.

The second version of Cocoon was a rewrite of the code base used in version one. The architecture was changed to support SAX processing instead of the DOM-based system inside version one. This had the immediate effect of improving the performance and processing potential of Cocoon Two. The processing steps were also refined to create an extensible framework. Supporting this was another new key concept, the "sitemap"—effectively a configuration file for the processing chain, or "pipeline," required to serve responses to requests from the client.

By the middle of 2001, Cocoon version two had matured to the release candidate stage. The open source community had contributed a large amount of code, refinements to the architecture, and significant testing resource. Eventually, in November 2001, release candidate two became the full production release of Apache Cocoon 2.00.

But why is Cocoon so important? What does it offer that other well-established Web development approaches do not? Why should every Web application developer and site publisher consider using Cocoon as his or her core technology? The answer to these important questions lies in an understanding of the links between the business processes and technology of Web publishing.

The Rise of Scripting Technologies

When HTTP and HTML were invented and the World Wide Web was born, the first Web servers included an interface that allowed a program to capture the HTTP request, interpret the request, and dynamically build a response. This interface was the Common Gateway Interface, CGI, and was the foundation for virtually all Web applications for some time. Most CGI applications were written using languages such as Perl or C. However, after a time new scripting methods started to find their way into the toolset of the Web developer.

These new methods were based around the idea of embedding proprietary tags into what otherwise looked like a normal HTML page. A request to a CGI component or proprietary interface would parse the page and replace the proprietary tags with the relevant data. Tags would perform various functions such as database queries and variable substitution. Tags were introduced that handled traditional computer language constructs such as conditional processing, loops, and exception handling. Typical examples of these scripting languages are ASP, JSP, CFM (ColdFusion), Python, PHP, and others.

These scripting technologies have gained a vast user base, because they are simple to learn, are well supported, offer rapid development potential, and, for a long time, were the only real choice. In addition, APIs like Java servlets permit the use of a traditional language (obviously Java in this case) as a gateway development language. As the use of object-oriented development techniques has increased, so too have the capabilities of scripting languages to reflect reuse and component-based design. JSP permits the calling of tags held in a tag library, as well as separate objects held as "beans." Microsoft extended its desktop Component Object Model (COM) to permit the calling of components across the network from within ASP files. COM objects can be built in languages like Visual Basic or C++, offering greater performance and integration with the Windows platform.

So why do we need yet another method for publishing information on the Web? In my book it comes down to two main drivers, one technical and the other nontechnical. Let's deal with the nontechnical one first.

Like most things in life, Web development has become far more complex. Gone are the days when one or two people with a reasonable HTML knowledge and an image editing package could create a commercial site. We are in an age when running a Web site wizard to get your "funky corporate" (or whatever) look is simply not good enough. Web sites are no longer static, electronic versions of printed brochures. They are media rich and incorporate highly technical features such as e-commerce and database back ends. They have to cater to a global audience. Content needs to change very regularly, perhaps even every second. The Web site might be the primary method for the customer to interface with the organization. Even more so—the Web is not the only electronic channel. Both mobile and interactive TV access to content is part of the network offering, and in some cases more attractive than a Web browser on a PC.

To achieve this requires the effective pooling of multiple skills and resources. Graphics artists, animators, editors, developers, copy writers, project managers, marketing experts, and more all need to get together to create and maintain a site. This simply cannot be achieved by funneling all the work through HTML coders. Capability needs to be passed around the chain and processes need to be automated. How does Cocoon help with this? Let's discuss that after we have considered the key technical driver for needing another Web publishing technology.

This driver is centered on the developments in application architecture design over the recent past and is known as the "model-view-controller," or MVC, architecture.

The MVC Architecture

Anyone who has been in software development for many years or has had to maintain old code will have come across software that handles data access, business logic, and presentation all in one big bucket of code. This is almost justifiable if the software is accessed by only one type of client. In the modern world of enterprise applications and multiple types of clients, however, a new approach was needed.

For some time, developers had been used to writing software with a three-tier client/server architecture. As illustrated in Figure 1.1, the bottom tier would contain the data, the middle tier would include business logic that accessed and served the data according to the system's rules, and a final top tier would present the data to the user and handle user input.

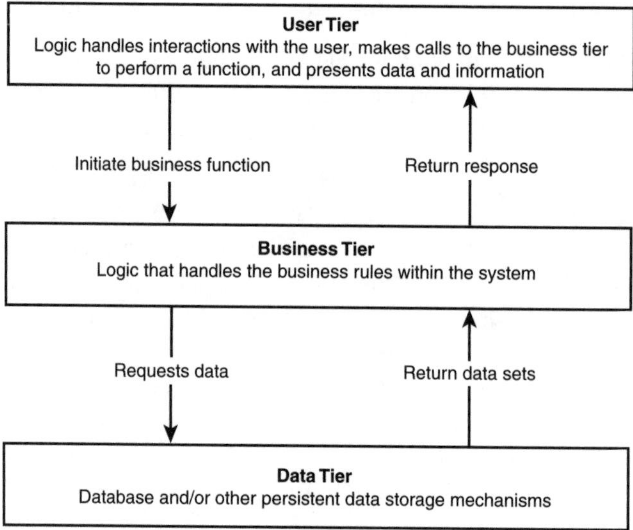

Figure 1.1
Three-tier client/server architecture.

The recent past has seen a move to applications with multiple, "n-tier" architectures. The number of layers has increased as abstraction, object orientation, and functional decomposition of a problem has become more widespread. In an enterprise Web application it is not uncommon to have at least four tiers. In addition, the technologies contained within each tier have increased. For example, a typical application may have several data sources, an enterprise application server, a browser-based front end, a fat client interface, wireless capabilities, and so on.

Throughout this architectural evolution, developers have had to face practical challenges in implementing n-tier solutions. In theory the lines between the tiers are clear, but in practice they very quickly get blurred. Business process rules very easily get mixed up with application logic, which is further mixed with the specifics of managing the user interface.

The MVC architecture is a design pattern that helps solve some of the problems generated by defining an approach to handling the relationships among the data, application, and presentation. The architecture has its roots in Smalltalk, and through its object-oriented (OO) foundation, it has been successfully migrated as a pattern generic enough for implementation with almost any technology.

More About MVC

If you want to know more about MVC, there are plenty of Web sites and books on the design pattern: `http://java.sun.com/blueprints/patterns/j2ee_patterns/model_view_ controller/index.html_is a great start.`

In MVC the *Model* represents application data and the fundamental business rules that determine how the data can be accessed and maintained. Typically, this is the area of the application that is reflecting, or modeling, a real-world business process.

The *View* manages the presentation of the model. It accesses the data and renders it accordingly. The view needs to maintain consistency with the state of the model. To do this it can either request an update on the current state or receive change notifications from the model. If the state has changed, it can then interact with the controller to resolve the changed data and render it correctly. With an MVC architecture you can have multiple views on a model.

The final part of the MVC architecture is the *Controller*. It is responsible for picking up the user interactions, converting those into actions for the model to handle, and then changing the view accordingly.

Figure 1.2 illustrates the components of the MVC architecture and how they relate to each other.

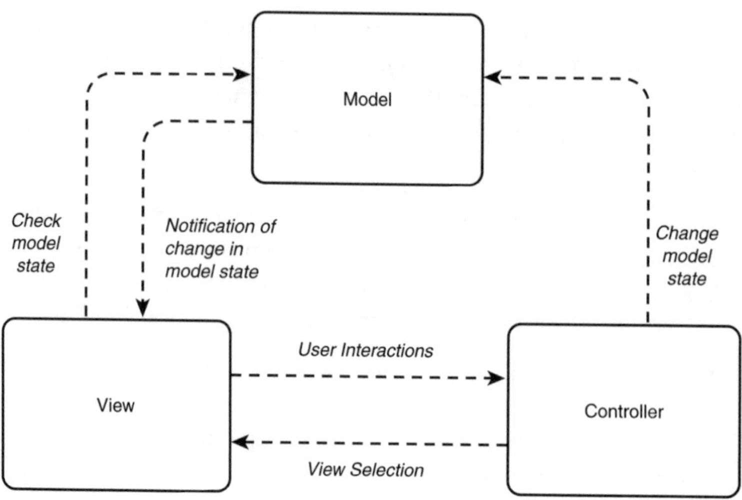

Figure 1.2
MVC architecture.

The MVC architecture can be illustrated by considering almost any real-world application. Take, for example a stock-price-monitoring application that sits on your desktop and keeps you up-to-date with your portfolio status. To do that, the application user interface, or view, must be reflecting the latest price data that the market has. The trading data is encapsulated by the model, in this case probably a database. Changes in the trading data such as volume and price fluctuations are changes in the model state. Either the view can regularly initiate, or *pull*, a request to the model to see whether the state has changed, or the model can flag, or *push*, state change notifications to the view.

Either way, the view knows that the model has changed and it needs to be updated. It can now ask its controller to go and do what it needs to do to update the view. The controller handles communicating with the model to get the latest data and then packaging it up in a way that is contextually relevant for the view. The controller may decide it needs to change the view—perhaps the price has gone to an alert level or the market has closed, and the interface is changed accordingly.

The user may also choose different views. The user may be looking at a summary screen and then want to see a three-month price/volume graph. These are two different views, with two different controllers. Each controller can interact with the model in just the way it needs to so as to obtain the right data, perform any presentation-oriented logic, and make sure that the view is updated.

The MVC approach applies a conceptual realization, that is, that there is a difference between the logic applied to coding business rules and the logic applied to building a user interface. This might seem like common sense, but I know from my own experience in large client/server development projects the lines very quickly become blurred when a business rule seems absolutely intertwined with how a user engages that rule.

The benefit of the MVC architecture to the modern application developer is that it helps to separate the system logic from the presentation logic. It is this separation that enables the production of multiple client interfaces, employing multiple technologies, that service interaction with a supporting business system and data. Implementing an MVC design pattern is easy with Cocoon and thus makes it an excellent platform for building on.

Common Issues for the Modern "Web" Application Developer

Indeed, the adoption of a technology such as Cocoon and design patterns like MVC can help overcome various issues that the modern Web application developer faces. The following list documents some of the most common areas of concern for most Web-oriented application development projects:

- Multiple delivery channels
- Multiple data sources
- Multilingual capabilities
- Personalization
- Branding and customization
- Content syndication
- Distributed data and application management
- Poorly executed use of scripting languages

This list is by no means exhaustive and does not even touch on platform issues such as scalability, resilience, and performance. Let's take a more in-depth look at these issues.

Marshaling Multiple Data Sources and Multiple Delivery Channels

It is probably a semantic error to suggest that the preceding issues are faced by a *Web* application developer. It would be more correct to suggest that an application is developed and there are a number of interfaces to that application, a primary one typically being via a

Web browser. This is not the only variable that the enterprise application designer must consider; there is also the likelihood of needing to obtain data from numerous sources. In some scenarios these sources may be a number of databases residing within the enterprise. This can present a significant challenge in itself; however, in the world of the Web, the problem can be compounded by the need to access data from other organizations. The data also may not be easily accessible.

For example, a portal offering information about a city may have several external data sources. They may want to get a national news feed, a news feed filtered for local news, weather data, local listings, classifieds, and so on. Much of this data may not be accessible via direct links into suppliers' databases. The data may be fed in the form of data files or via a SOAP-type gateway.

When you then look at how this data might be presented, there are many options. Clearly, the Web would be a primary channel. WAP would be another likely contender. The data could also drive the content of a printed local area guide. Content could be syndicated to other third parties as data files or via a network interface. Another consideration of how the data might be presented is the need for personalization. This could encompass not just individual preferences but also more significant aspects such as multilanguage capabilities. Not to be forgotten would be capabilities to allow administrative users to manage the data.

As Figure 1.3 illustrates, scenarios such as these can present a hefty challenge to system designers and developers over the problems to be resolved in writing a single interface to a single database.

How can content be aggregated from multiple sources and marshaled down publishing routes to multiple channels? There is, unfortunately, not one simple answer to this question. Different problems require different solutions. Some problems might require the use of a very scalable component-based approach such as Enterprise JavaBeans. The use of particular technologies at the back end may be out of the hands of the designer for commercial or legacy reasons.

The key point to make, though, is that whatever the technology is that handles this, it must do the following:

- Encapsulate the data into structures that can be used by different delivery mechanisms
- Keep business logic separate from presentation logic
- Keep the final presentation tier as simple and logic free as possible

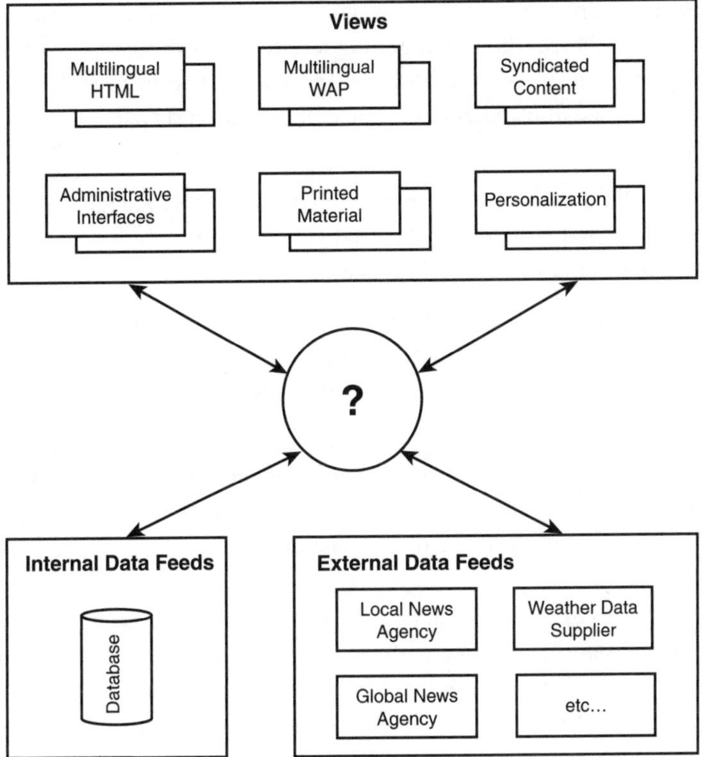

Figure 1.3

The data source to delivery channel marshaling question.

Multilingual Capabilities

One of the successes of the Internet, the Web in particular, has been the opportunity for reaching a global audience. If an organization wants to make the most of its global Web presence, it is important that the site be available in more than one language. What major issues should be considered?

Firstly, there is actual *translation* of the content. Is this something that can be done in-house, or should it be performed by a third-party agency? How often does it get done? Are all the language version sites going to reflect the same content, or are they almost like separate versions? How will changes in the major or base site language version be flagged for synchronization with the rest of the sites? An interesting point here is that if an outside agency is used, automated processes can be set up to transfer source content and receive the translated results. You can then add these as an extra delivery channel and data source to the list of possibilities given previously.

Translation alone is not enough; *localization* is vital. Localization refers to the tuning of content to suit a culturally specific audience. Generally this is thought of as being geared toward country-specific optimizations; however, it could be that even with one country, content is localized for specific audiences. Typical localization scenarios would include the following:

- Use of local spelling conventions when using a common language. For example, in the U.S. "color" is spelled without the "u" that is used within the UK ("colour"). Localization takes note of these differences.
- Cultural conventions. For example, in some countries certain colors, images, or phrases may be unacceptable or have different connotations than that intended in the original content. A localized site would take notice of these conventions.
- Poorly translated words. Some words or phrases that may be common in one language may have no direct translation into another language. Other words, especially product names, may be used without translation but mean something completely different. When a site is localized, these factors are accounted for.

Clearly it is unrealistic to expect to be able to handle these issues though pure automated software. Machine translation can cope with a certain amount of localization; however, most of this type of content needs to be proofread by people. These things need consideration at the design phase. With a dynamic site, then, third parties are almost invariably involved to be able to manage the changes that take place. What is important, though, is that the architecture makes it easy to create localized language variants and supports the automated processing of content changes.

Another area that is affected by language is the *user interface*. Some of the points in localization are applicable here; however, one of the most common implications is the change in the length of words. Conversions from English to German are a really good example. For instance, the word "hovercraft" in English is rendered as "Luftkissenfahrzeug," literally "air cushion vehicle." Although perhaps not a common word in most Web sites, it does illustrate the point that menu options and general-content text can dramatically increase in length. Some languages read from right to left and others use very different character sets. A poorly designed interface can need substantial rework to support another language. Global corporate identities can be damaged by having to redesign sites for each language. Well-designed interfaces, coupled with well-architected software, can dramatically reduce the time needed to rework interfaces and get new variants up and running.

Personalization

Most sites you visit these days offer some kind of personalization capability. It may be as simple as offering the user a "welcome" message with his or her name tagged on the end, or it may be that the user can choose what content appears on the pages and how it is presented. Many sites, such as Amazon.com, monitor how users navigate the site, what they buy, and so on. On each visit the user can be proactively targeted with items that have a higher probable level of interest to that user. Advertising can be targeted.

Much of this functionality might be managed through components of a good e-commerce solution. The rules might be contained in a bespoke personalization engine. Again, the important point is that the publishing engine can handle content in a component-based fashion, so it can be "sliced and diced" as required.

Branded Customization and Syndication of Content

A few years ago, a lot more was heard of two phrases in reference to e-commerce: "B2B" and "B2C." B2B refers to the business-to-business trade, and B2C means business-to-consumer. B2C e-commerce covers any situation in which an individual makes a purchase as a general consumer. B2B covers trade in which businesses sell the supply of service or product to other businesses. Some of the resources that can be sold by organizations cover data. Internet companies can sell technology or databases such as search engines. News and financial agencies can sell news and finance data. Weather organizations can sell weather data and so on.

A quick way for a company to augment its Web content is to buy some of the data and incorporate it on its site. This might be done just through the offline transfer of data. It can even go to the point where one part of a Web page is actually being supplied, in real-time, by another company. For example, a recruitment site will clearly have a database of jobs that are available. To add value to the offering, the site can also provide help on building a CV, interview techniques, or training material to bridge skill gaps. Obviously, much of this might be beyond the resources of a small team but could be bought in. If the supplier of training material has a site, they can provide that content for inclusion on the recruitment site or they can offer a branded site, customized to the needs and look of the recruitment site.

This is realistically possible only if the training provider built the site so that it can be syndicated, content sent on, look and feel customized, and so on. If this was done, a complex set of B2B opportunities can be opened up, as illustrated in Figure 1.4.

Simpler scenarios here might be these:

- A large corporation might want to provide intranet pages that have a common look and feel but permit the branding elements to be configured for different business divisions.
- A supplier may provide information pages to the customer base. Each customer page may be branded to reflect that customer and have options specific to the customer.

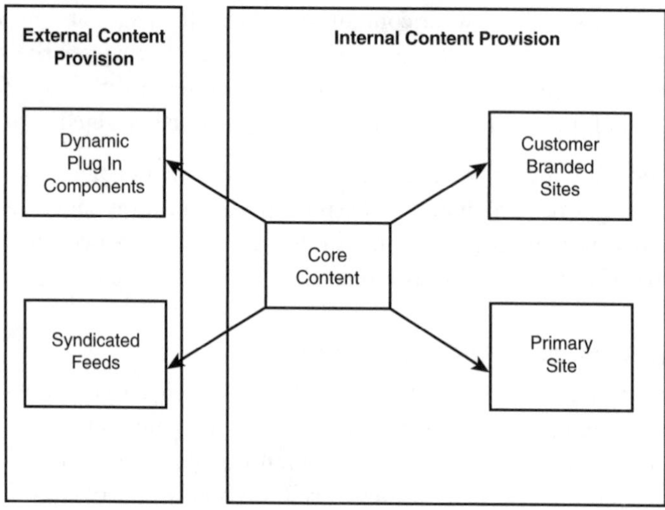

Figure 1.4
Internal and external options for content provision.

Of course, to be able to effectively support these functions, the content and data need to be very separate from the presentation itself.

Distributed Data and Application Maintenance

One of the reasons that many more applications have Web browser-based interfaces is that it is simple to give people access to systems. Many applications are remotely managed by people; data entry and maintenance can be distributed, as can work associated with administrative duties.

In the world of highly dynamic sites, it is especially important that good *content management* functions be available to all the contributors. Not that long ago, any site changes would have to either come from a database or be hand-coded by HTML developers. Nowadays, the creators of the content need to be empowered to make that content available as quickly and as easily as possible. They need to be able to access templates that let them enter content as quickly as possible, review how it looks and feels, and then publish. This process may be undertaken by a number of people, go through an editorial review process, and so on. What should be taken out of the production cycle as much as possible is the need to rely on a technical person to turn the content into HTML and publish it.

If content is to be delivered down multiple channels, it must be able to be captured and encapsulated in one way that can be handled by each of the views onto the data.

There are several content management products around that allow this to be done—at a price. Some have to be used to deliver the site and thus are not suitable for the production of content that is viewable offline. Another possible shortcoming is the capability of specific products to sit in the middle of multiple data sources and delivery channels. Given these potential shortcomings, there is still plenty of reason to look at other publishing options such as Cocoon.

Poorly Executed Use of Scripting Languages

Poor execution of scripting languages is perhaps one of the key drivers for the use of a publishing framework like Cocoon. What do I mean by this statement? As highlighted earlier, scripting languages such as ASP, JSP, PHP, and CFM have been used to create Web sites. Many have been developed without regard for the issues discussed previously, such as separation of presentation and content. Few have been designed to be maintainable. Although information is available on implementing the MVC design pattern using these technologies, relatively few designers and developers have practical experience in implementing solutions. What we are left with are too many applications that are highly difficult to maintain. Consider the following basic example and ask yourself how many sites you know that are similar.

Consider the following JSP code fragment:

```
<html>
<head>
<title>A basic JSP example page</title>
</head>

<body>
<h1>A basic JSP example page</h1>

<%

int i = 10;
String s = "Hello";

%>

<p><%=s %></p>
<p>The number is <%=i %>.

<% if ( i < 10 ) { %>
    <br>This is less than 10
<% } else { %>
```

```
    <br>This is more than or equal to 10
<% } %>
</p>
</body>
</html>
```

Obviously this code is not very complex; however, it manifests various problems that make it very difficult to maintain or to use if solving some of the problems discussed so far.

Firstly, there is the mixing of logic with presentation. Even in this small example this leads to a segment of code that is highly unreadable. The `if...then...else` construct is hidden in between script markers. Logic follows presentation follows logic. As page complexity grows, so does the difficulty in trying to work out what is happening.

Now consider what I would need to do if this page needed to be rendered in French, German, Spanish, and Italian. I could make copies of this page and translate into each of the languages. There are now five versions of this page I have to maintain, each equally difficult to read. What happens if the test limit is changed from 10 to 11? I must go into five pages, find the code to change (three lines in this case), and change it.

This problem can be compounded if the page needs to be customized for individual business customers. If I have 10 customers who each have a customized site (each with just one language), I now have 15 copies of the same page—with all its content and logic.

What about the maintenance? What if the marketing department (who owns the page) wants to change the string from "Hello" to "Welcome"? Fifteen pages to change, four translations to make. A software developer has to be engaged to do the work; try explaining to a nontechnical person how to safely edit, test, and publish a JSP page.

Compound this problem further by replacing the preceding example with a real-world page (all those database queries!), think of the translation headache, and place the page into a dynamic situation where not just that page but many others have to be changed daily. Clearly this would be a highly challenging environment.

There are various ways that pages such as this can be better constructed to reduce some of these problems. In the case of JSP, for example, the use of tag libraries and beans could abstract some of the logic. A multitier, MVC-based JSP and servlet framework could be used to separate logic and content further. Cascading style sheets could be employed to ease formatting modifications. The fact remains, though, that there are a vast number of Web applications that are made up of pages riddled with a mishmash of content and logic. Some scripting languages are more prone, usually through the profile of the developer, to these kinds of issues. If you are not a JSP user, just replace the earlier code with a similar example in the language you know and love.

The point that should be crystal clear from this brief examination of some of the issues facing application developers is that consideration must be given to how an application can be built that reduces these issues. Even if your application does not need to be multilingual, will it have to be presented in several versions? Quite possibly. Will content be required to be presented down different delivery channels? If not now, then you can bet your salary that it will within a few months.

In considering these problems, many designers and developers have been looking at the opportunities offered by using XML-based technologies.

The Opportunities Offered by XML

So what can XML do to help? In itself it is no panacea. The real key is that an application be well designed to take into account the various requirements that are its raison d'être. A suitable architecture could be designed without the use of XML and work quite happily. What XML does do, however, is offer a flexible and convenient method for representing encapsulated data, coupled with a powerful method of transforming that data via XSLT (*eXtensible Stylesheet Language for Transformations*) and XPATH.

This section is not intended to be a tutorial on XSLT, but rather a brief summary is appropriate. An XSLT stylesheet *transforms* a *source tree* into a *result tree*. The source tree *has* to be well-formed XML, and the result tree can be well-formed XML but can equally be other output formats such as HTML.

An XSLT stylesheet matches *patterns* with elements in the source tree. When a pattern is matched, a *template* is called to produce the output code. The pattern matching is achieved using XPATH expressions. To perform a transformation, the source XML file must be parsed with the XSLT stylesheet in a parser. Some browsers (for example, IE 5) contain a parser, or you can use parsers that are standalone or embedded in other applications.

The earlier JSP page could be constructed by an XML/XSLT transformation. The relevant files could be constructed as shown in Listing 1.1 and Listing 1.2.

Listing 1.1 *XML Content File—content.xml*

```
<?xml version="1.0"?>
<page>
    <title>A basic JSP example page</title>
    <value>10</value>
    <string>Hello</string>
    <comparison>
```

Listing 1.1 *(continued)*

```
        <less>This is less than</less>
        <more>This is more than or equal to</more>
    </comparison>
</page>
```

Listing 1.2 *Stylesheet—stylesheet.xsl*

```
<?xml version="1.0"?>
<xsl:stylesheet xmlns:xsl="http://www.w3.org/1999/XSL/Transform" version="1.0">

<xsl:template match="page">
    <html>
        <head>
        <title><xsl:value-of select="title"/></title>
        </head>

        <body>
            <h1><xsl:value-of select="title"/></h1>

            <![CDATA[<%]]>

            int i = <xsl:value-of select="value"/>;
            String s = <xsl:value-of select="string"/>;

            %>

            <p><![CDATA[<%]]>=s %></p>
            <p>The number is <![CDATA[<%]]>=i %>.

            <![CDATA[<% if ( i < ]]> <xsl:value-of select="value"/> ) { %>
                <br/><xsl:value-of select="comparison/less"/> <xsl:value-
                                of select="value"/>
            <![CDATA[<%]]> } else { %>
                <br/><xsl:value-of select="comparison/more"/> <xsl:value-
                                of select="value"/>
            <![CDATA[<%]]> } %>
            </p>
        </body>
    </html>
</xsl:template>
</xsl:stylesheet>
```

Listing 1.1 is an XML file that contains all the content and variables as elements. The page title is there, as are the number and text strings that are used.

Listing 1.2 is a sample style sheet that will transform the XML file into the JSP presented in Listing 1.1. Using an XML editor, such as Cooktop, will allow you to load the XML and XSLT files and preview them. The XSLT stylesheet has a single template that is looking for the `<page>` element in the XML file. After it has this, it can start building the JSP code. It uses the `<title>` element to set the title tag and a level-one heading tag, and replaces the variable assignments with the data contained in the `<value>` and `<string>` elements. It then uses the `<value>` data and the two comparison strings (`<comparison>/<less>` and `<comparison>/<more>`) in place of the hard-coded text from the original JSP source.

> **Editing XML and XSLT Files**
> XML files and XSLT stylesheets can be created using almost any text-editing tool, including old favorites like VI or Notepad. There are also many specialist editors around that are geared toward supporting XML more fully, having DTD and Schema support, links to data sources, and built-in transformation engines. An excellent MS Windows-based freeware product is Victor Pavlov's Cooktop. You can download this free from `http://xmlcooktop.com`.

The listing is complicated slightly by the use of the `<![CDATA[ ]]>` construct. This is used to wrap up the JSP `<%` tag so that the XSLT parser is not confused.

Using this method already has some advantages in comparison to the original JSP:

- There only has to be one XSLT stylesheet file. This is now a template for all the others.
- There can be multiple XML data files that contain the language- and branding-specific data, but they can all be rendered using a single template.
- If the master file changes, the others can easily be edited by a nontechnical user or a third-party translation organization to effect updates.
- The new JSP files can be created at the push of a button via a batch process that parses the files, thus helping to ensure that updates are quickly implemented.

There a still some issues with this solution as it stands, however:

- The XSLT stylesheet is not particularly readable.
- If the amount of the `<value>` element needs to be changed, every XML file must be changed.
- Distribution of content management capability has been extended but is not significantly better.

In spite of some of these concerns, the XML/XSLT combination is an extremely powerful one. This was not lost on the developers of Cocoon as they implemented the XML publishing theory.

Cocoon—Implementing the XML Publishing Theory

The Cocoon project has taken the concepts of publishing using XML/XSLT and implemented them in an effective platform. This has been achieved by not only providing the transformation capabilities but also looking at some of the wider issues of the separation of logic and presentation, along with multichannel delivery.

The whole way that Cocoon has been architected provides a firm foundation on which to provide publishing platform and develop applications that are highly flexible. Cocoon has taken the basic XML/XSLT transformation functions and added to them through a key set of enhancements:

- Configurable management of the request/response process
- *eXtensible Server Pages* (XSP), an XML-based scripting language that supports the separation of logic from presentation using *logicsheets*
- Extendable handlers for each stage of the request/response process

Inherent to the design of Cocoon is cognizance of how Web sites and applications are managed from a business perspective. Through the early history of the Web, the owners of information were also generally the creators/maintainers of the information via HTML pages. As the Web grew in popularity and Web-site complexity increased, so too did the separation of skills. Information owners no longer created or maintained the HTML. Coders also had to start to implement designs produced by other parties (for example, graphic artists). As we have already noted, HTML and traditional scripting languages are ill-suited to support this. They do not provide enough technical support for the number of "contracts" between contributing parties.

Even the preceding XML/XSLT example does not support the right number of contracts between the parties. Although the content and the presentation may be separate, the logic and presentation are not. More help is needed.

Cocoon, by embracing and extending the XML/XSLT model, increases the technical support for these contracts. The Apache XML Project describe this as the "pyramid model of Web contracts," as illustrated in Figure 1.5.

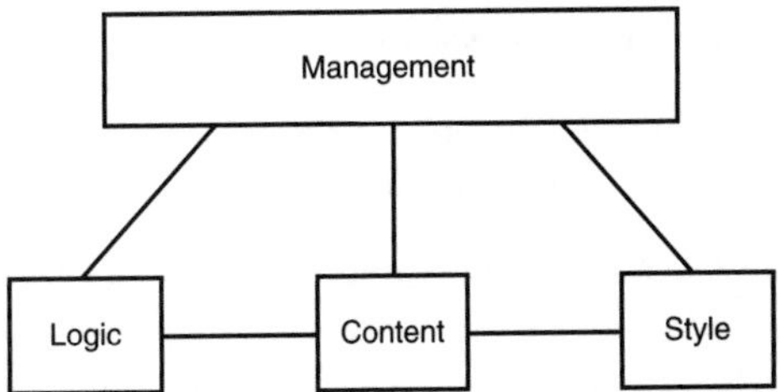

Figure 1.5
The pyramid model of Web contracts (as defined by the Apache XML Project).

In the diagram the rectangles represent specific parties:

- *Management* refers to the decision makers, those people who determine what is going onto the site and how it should appear.
- The *logic* role defines the people who are responsible for developing the code that accesses databases, encapsulates business rules, and so on.
- The *content* box contains the people who are responsible for creating and owning the raw site content.
- The final box—the *style* role—covers the people who are responsible for presenting the content, its look and feel, and so on.

The lines between the boxes represent the contracts between the parties. The intent is that each party can perform all its tasks without overlapping into other boxes. Where there needs to be an interaction, a contract is provided to enable that to occur. The Cocoon architecture provides the infrastructure to enforce these contracts. It is interesting to note that there is no contract between the style and logic boxes. This is because these two areas should never have a direct connection. As you shall see through the subsequent chapters, Cocoon routes application design down a path that enforces this separation, thus ensuring that we get maintainable, flexible, and robust applications.

Summary

In this chapter we have reviewed the use of scripting technologies in Web application development and discussed some of the weaknesses. We have reviewed the MVC architecture and established the following points:

- There are solid reasons for n-tier design.
- There is a need to embrace the concepts of the separation of logic for specific purposes, namely business and presentation.
- Most importantly, there is a need to separate that logic from the presentation itself.

Finally, we have looked at the strengths of an XML/XSLT-based approach over pure scripting.

With all of this in hand, we are now well placed to look at the specifics of Cocoon and how we can go about developing applications using it.

CHAPTER 2

Avalon

Although this is a book about Cocoon, it is good to spend a little time looking at Avalon. If you have not come across Avalon, you may not know that it is another part of the Apache Project, falling under the Jakarta umbrella. Interestingly enough Cocoon and Avalon share a common heritage in that Stefano Mazzocchi was instrumental in getting both projects going. It is no surprise, then, that Avalon and Cocoon are closely related from a technical perspective; thus, for any Cocoon developer it is very useful to have an understanding of what Avalon is all about and what the relationship to Cocoon development is.

What Is Avalon?

Avalon is actually a parent project for several subprojects:

- Framework
- Excalibur
- LogKit
- Phoenix
- Cornerstone

Note

Apache Avalon is found at `http://jakarta.apache.org/avalon`. With the exception of Cornerstone, you can download archived source or binary files as well as being able to access the latest code via the CVS repository. At the time of writing, Cornerstone was not an official release and therefore available only via CVS.

The combination of each of these subprojects is an infrastructure for Java server technology. This came out of work that was being done on the Apache JServ (the original Apache Java servlet engine) as the development team realized the generic possibilities of many of the code functions that were being implemented. For example, most server applications need to perform logging of events, and developers will spend time writing log functionality. More often than not, this functionality will not just cover simple message writing but allow more complex details to be stored. Various levels of logging may be implemented so that the range of errors can be controlled, or perhaps stack traces are sent to a log device. Another common function of a server application is database connectivity. Many lines of code are repeated by coders building chunks of code that create a connection to a database, perform queries, or manage pools of connections.

The reach of abstract and concrete functions that are typical of a Java-based server-side application goes beyond tasks such as logging and database connectivity. You could consider messaging, services, security, and so on. Avalon seeks to cover these bases by combining a number of complementary code libraries. These are organized into the project specified previously.

The whole Avalon concept is based on some key design principles. The two most relevant to this discussion are *Inversion of Control* and *Separation of Concerns*.

Inversion of Control

Inversion of Control (IOC) basically means that a component of a system is configured and managed by the entity that creates it. A component can make use only of functions that its creator has explicitly defined and told the component about. This has the benefit that components cannot go off and do something that the controlling object does not know about. When considering a generic yet flexible system this is very important because it means that the controlling object can determine what capabilities the component has. The parameters of the component's universe are set by the controlling object. This is important for Cocoon because it means that when a new Cocoon component (for example, a generator) is created, the new generator class can determine exactly what methods it will allow to work. No hidden functionality will get called; thus, control, power and security are placed in the hands of the creator.

Note

Generators are covered in more detail in Chapter 8, "Content Logic: Generators."

Separation of Concerns

Separation of Concerns (SOC) means that the components of a system are dealt with as discrete entities. For example, for a car to function it needs to have an engine, wheels, a chassis, a steering mechanism and so on. Although each of these parts of the car are interdependent, they can be considered as black boxes when viewed from another part of the car "system". For example, a transmission system must interact with the engine so that the wheels can turn, but how many cylinders the engine has, its source of fuel, and the combustion mechanism are irrelevant. What is important is that the interface (that is, the gearbox) between the engine and the transmission works in a way that is complementary to both systems. The same is true when you consider how Cocoon separates the management/logic/content/style concerns—each one being concerned only with the necessities of self-support, with interfaces that provide a contract between the concerns.

The principle is affected in Avalon by the way a component implements functionality. In line with the inversion of control principle, the methods that the component instantiates are set by the creating object; however, the actual functionality of the method is unknown to the creating object—it simply knows that it can communicate with a component method using a predefined interface.

Avalon Framework

Avalon Framework is the core Avalon subproject. The framework is a collection of interfaces, the rules (or contracts) that they must work under, and some default implementations.

Roles

Avalon uses a theatrical analogy to help contextualize the way it works and how you should think of components. If you imagine a play or film, there are roles that actors play. The actor must learn a script that goes with the role, and only then will the actor know what to say, when to say it, and where he should be on the stage. Avalon components are the same. A component has a *role*, which in turn has defined methods, properties, and rules—the script. Each component is there to fill a specific task, maintaining a database connection pool, for example.

Component Lifecycle

Utilizing IOC and SOC, the Avalon framework separates out the various actions that a component may want to perform into stages that the component implementation can choose to implement or ignore. Each stage is called by the framework in a known order, each of the stages being grouped into one of three predefined phases. This combination of phases and stages is termed the component *lifecycle*. These are the lifecycle phases:

- *Initialization*—Occurs once at the beginning of the component lifecycle.
- *Active Service*—Occurs multiple times during the component lifecycle.
- *Destruction*—Occurs once at the end of the component lifecycle.

The stages that occur in each of the phases are triggered by the calling of a particular method in an interface. If the component does not implement the stage, it will not extend the interface. Each of the stages is called using the method and in the order detailed in Table 2.1. This table also identifies the interface that must be extended by the component to trigger the call.

Table 2.1 *Component Lifecycle Stages*

Phase	Stage	Interface
Initialization	`enableLogging()`	`LogEnabled`
	`contextualize()`	`Contextualizable`
	`compose()`	`Composable`
	`configure()`	`Configurable or`
	`parameterize()`	`Parameterizable`
	`initialize()`	`Initializable`
	`start()`	`Startable`
Active Service	`suspend()`	`Suspendable`
	`recontextualize()`	`Recontextualizable`
	`recompose()`	`Recomposable`
	`reconfigure()`	`Reconfigurable`
	`resume()`	`Suspendable`
Destruction	`stop()`	`Startable`
	`dispose()`	`Disposable`

Contracts

An Avalon *contract* basically describes the rules that govern which interfaces a component needs to implement and how the component then interacts with those interfaces. For example, every single component must implement the `Component` interface and must handle any configuration through either the `Configurable` or the `Parameterizable` interface. In another example, if the component uses other components, it must implement the `Composable` interface. The only method that the `Composable` interface has is `compose()`, which must be called only once during the lifecycle of the component.

Avalon Excalibur

Avalon Excalibur is a collection of several component implementations. Whereas Avalon Framework provides the interfaces and contracts that components must use, Avalon Excalibur takes those interfaces and provides key functionality that is common to servers. Components exist for many tasks, all of which are available via the Avalon API documentation.

Avalon LogKit

Avalon LogKit is a toolkit of functions that are specifically there to provide advanced logging capability such as variable log format and error level handling.

Avalon Phoenix

This part of the Avalon infrastructure provides a solid foundation for the hosting of services that a server provides. Server components are deployed in packages made up of *blocks*, code libraries that contain the actual server functionality. In simple terms, if Avalon Framework is a component framework, then Avalon Phoenix is a server framework. Of course, components that are deployed on Avalon Phoenix do have their basis on Avalon Framework.

Avalon Cornerstone

Avalon Cornerstone is a set of predefined blocks that can be deployed on a Avalon Phoenix–based server.

How Does Cocoon Use Avalon?

Cocoon actually uses only part of the Avalon infrastructure—namely, Framework, Excalibur, and LogKit. All the Cocoon core components are based on Avalon components so that they can easily make use of the infrastructure provided. For example, Cocoon components need to perform logging at some stage so that they all extend the `AbstractLoggable` class. Base components are extended by subclasses and implement other Avalon Framework interfaces such as `Component`, `Composable`, and `Configurable`.

The fundamental roles that Cocoon defines for its components are configured in a file called `cocoon.roles`, which can be found in the `org/apache/cocoon` folder of the source tree. This file is really used only to configure the roles and is not used to configure components, hence it is compiled into the runtime cocoon.jar. Another, far more relevant, file is `cocoon.xconf`. This file is used to provide specific configuration data for components. You can find `cocoon.xconf` in the `WEB-INF` folder. Here you will find parameters for configuring database connection pool sizes, the logicsheets that are available to the system, memory pool sizes, sitemap configuration, and so on.

Summary

In this chapter we have taken a brief look at the Avalon infrastructure to see what it is and how it relates to Cocoon. Avalon is an important part of Cocoon and having an awareness of it should help make your understanding of Cocoon application development more well-rounded.

CHAPTER 3

The Cocoon Processing Model

There are two ways of describing the Cocoon architecture—one simple, the other complicated. The simple description is that Cocoon is a servlet. Easy enough, but this is such an oversimplification that it becomes an untruth! To truly describe the architecture of Cocoon requires that we look at various aspects of how Cocoon is put together.

Although Cocoon is typically thought of as a servlet, this is really an incorrect stance. The typical way Cocoon is accessed is via a servlet, but strictly speaking, that is simply providing an access interface to a powerful publishing mechanism. Cocoon was designed to be interfaced to in a flexible way. As an example, Cocoon also provides a command-line interface; in fact, this is the method that is used to generate the documentation via the Ant build process.

Cocoon is similar to most modern-day applications in that it is made up of layers of processing technology. Avalon forms part of the core infrastructure on which Cocoon sits; however, Cocoon is much more than an implementation of Avalon components. It should come as no surprise to discover that Cocoon is made up of layers of technology (see Figure 3.1) that gradually focus in on the ultimate purpose: running *your* code in *your* application.

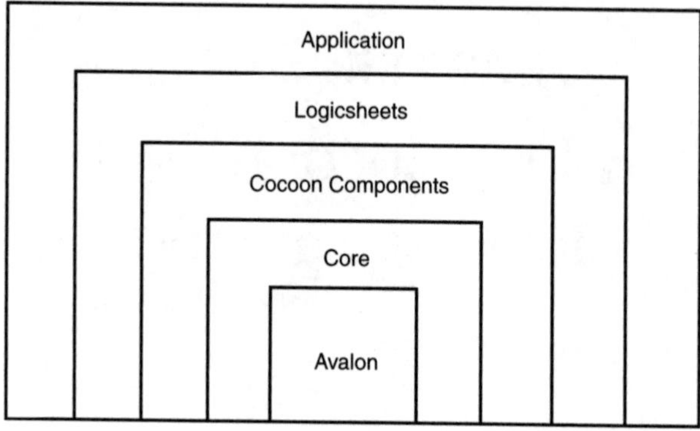

Figure 3.1
Cocoon Component Architecture.

Framework Layer

Cocoon's base layer provides the wrapper around Avalon, contextualizing the infrastructure for the bespoke requirements of Cocoon.

Avalon

At the heart of Cocoon is Avalon. As discussed in the preceding chapter, Cocoon makes use of the infrastructure and core components that Avalon provides. This foundation provides the staple logic for the rest of Cocoon such as logging, database connection pooling, configuration management, thread handling, and object pooling.

Caching Mechanism

Just above the Avalon components is the Cocoon caching mechanism. Cocoon takes care of caching the responses to requests, thus speeding up multiple accesses to the same page. The mechanism is based on the Avalon caching components but is extended to meet the specific needs of Cocoon. In addition, Cocoon can pool components to support better performance. Again, this is a specific implementation of the interfaces that Avalon supplies.

The Pipeline

The pipeline is a key aspect of Cocoon. If you consider a Web server processing a request for an HTML page, the server will get the request, find the file, and serve the response back. This can be made more complex if, for example, the response is dynamically formed using something like PHP. In this case, the request is passed to another block of code that handles the generation of the PHP.

Cocoon is more complex than this, requiring the generation and transformation of XML streams. The number of steps between request and response can be many; therefore, the pipeline is designed to act as a "marshall," defining the steps and controlling the entry and exit from one to another—basically coordinating the steps. The pipeline is controlled through a configuration file known as the sitemap. We will cover the sitemap in more detail in the next chapter.

Program Generation and Base Component Classes

As the pipeline is processed, base components are used to handle, generate, compile, load, and execute logic. Components exist to manage the generation of XML data streams, transform these streams, and serialize the result into whatever format is required. The base components extend Avalon components and form the key classes and interfaces for specific components to be built on. The base component classes also include component management functions that support the administration of component selection and lifecycle. This is done using the principles of Inversion of Control and Separation of Concerns, thus following the patterns promoted by Avalon.

Processing Layer

The processing layer is where you will find code that manages the components dealing with processing the request/response cycle. It is split into two parts: the sitemap components and logicsheets.

Sitemap Components

Sitemap components are called by the pipeline mechanism as it handles the processing of a request. The sitemap components include the various generators, transformers, and serializers that are needed to deal with XML streams. They also include logical components such as selectors, matchers, and actions. All of these components are dealt with in detail in the next chapter.

Logicsheets

As part of Cocoon's implementation of the model-view-controller (MVC) pattern, libraries of code have been developed that provide access to typical functions that the Web application developer needs. These can be called from the application code and are called logicsheets. Future chapters on how to create content with Cocoon cover the exact nature of logicsheets in more detail; however, their existence provides a highly useful bed of reusable functionality for the developer.

Implementation Layer

As we near the top of the Cocoon processing tree, we find machinery that comes as part of the implementation of the user application. These are the files that provide the configuration and login specific to the application.

Configuration Files

A Cocoon application has several configuration files. These have many purposes, including the following:

- Define what components are used by the application
- Configure the components
- Set up data sources and connection pools
- Tune Cocoon and the application
- Configure what debugging data is collected

The two most important configuration files are `cocoon.xconf` and `web.xml`, both of which can be found under the `WEB-INF` folder of the Web application.

Custom Components

If a developer has extended Cocoon and added his or her own components, these form part of the implementation layer. For example, components that handle the generation, transformation, and process flow of a response are all likely to be components that have forms bespoke to the application. These will provide processing capability that is specific to the application, reflecting business rules and requirements that are not indigenous to Cocoon itself.

Even if the developer has not extended the Java-based components themselves, it is highly likely that the application will utilize XSP, the XML-based server-side scripting language that is part of Cocoon. This logic effectively is part of the custom components because XSP files are compiled into generator components for execution.

Custom Logicsheets

If the developer develops libraries of code as logicsheets, these too are included in the implementation layer.

Content Layer

The highest level of the Cocoon processing model is the content layer. This is where the source material to feed the application can be found. The content typically can be found in many formats: as XML, relational and object databases, HTML, graphic formats, and so on. Whatever form it takes, however, there will be logic in the implementation layer that extracts the content, processes it, and presents it in whatever form is required for consumption by the end user.

Summary

In this chapter we have reviewed the layers that Cocoon is made up of, progressing from the wrapping of the Avalon infrastructure through to where user logic and content can be found. These layers provide the developer with a flexible route to developing an application without compromising the ability to take advantage of proven design patterns and a robust superstructure.

The one critical part of this processing model that we have not looked at in depth is the pipeline mechanism, expressed through the sitemap. Let's do that right now.

CHAPTER 4

Introduction to the Sitemap

One of the most important concepts of Cocoon to understand is the way it processes requests. To provide a high level of flexibility and separation of concerns, Cocoon uses a *pipeline processing* model. This basically means that a request goes through a sequential chain of events to generate a response. The chain of events that takes place is configured via a configuration file—the *sitemap*. This chapter is intended to explain the fundamentals of pipeline processing and what can be found in the sitemap.

Pipeline Processing

Based on the number of messages on the Cocoon user lists, it seems that for most people new to Cocoon, pipeline processing and the sitemap are new concepts and, for some, relatively hard to grasp. So the big question is, Why is it done this way?

Take, for example, a two-step chain—the transforming of some XML data with an XSLT stylesheet. If you were publishing to a Web browser such as IE5, you could perform the transformation at the client side. To do so, you would use the WC3 method of including a processing instruction that specifies the stylesheet to use *within* the XML file:

```
<?xml version="1.0"?>
<?xml-stylesheet type="text/xml" href=http://localhost/somestylesheet.xsl?>
<title>Page Title</title>
```

What is wrong with this? Well, what happens if you want to use a different stylesheet to transform this XML file? You are forced to change the source XML. That might not be a major issue if you are dynamically creating the XML on-the-fly; however, it is a big problem if the XML files are static, cached, or otherwise nondynamic.

The preceding scenario also presents application architecture issues, namely the separation of application logic separate from presentation logic. Even assuming that the XML is dynamically built, there would have to be a close relationship between the code that is grabbing the data from the model and the code that determines what stylesheet to use to transform the XML.

Cocoon One suffered with this problem because it used the preceding processing instruction to advise the transformer which stylesheet to use. Developers were left to work out some quite creative solutions so that they could vary the stylesheets to use on a single XML data source. What was clear was that this situation was not really meeting the core principles of Cocoon.

The pipeline processing model inside Cocoon Two provides a neat solution to this problem. Inside the pipeline, a clearly defined sequence of basic steps has been identified that apply to the processing of requests:

1. *Request Matching and Selection.* The first step is to identify the incoming request and match it to a sequence of interactions that can handle the request (the pipeline).
2. *SAX Generation.* The generation step generates a stream of SAX events from a data source. This may be a file or some other source such as database.
3. *Transformation.* Many, but not all, streams require transformation. A transformer takes the stream from the generator and turns it into another stream of SAX events. Typically, the transformation process involves the application of an XSLT stylesheet.
4. *Serialization.* The final step in the pipeline process is the serialization of a stream of SAX events into the response. Obviously, this needs to be in a form that can be rendered by the client. Cocoon contains various serializers that handle clients wanting HTML, WML, XML, PDF, and so on.

Although the preceding steps form the core functions offered by the pipeline, the pipeline is capable of several other interventions on the processing stream:

- *Request redirection.* Just as with standard request redirection, this permits the application to change what resource is being requested. This effectively reenters the pipeline matching and selection process, thus permitting the redirection to another Cocoon-generated resource.
- *Action handling.* Actions are self-contained chunks of code that can be used to perform operations on the request. Typical action tasks include session authentication, database interaction, form handling, and so on. This enables repeated logic to be removed from the generation of a page, thus simplifying the process and providing a cleaner separation of concerns.
- *Aggregate content.* This allows the construction of a single stream of SAX events to be generated from several source streams. For example, multiple files could be brought together to form a single document.
- *Views.* These enable you to have different views of a resource. By configuring specific element attributes on particular points in the sitemap, you can set triggers that cause a response to be generated from another set of transformation and serialization processes. This is an extremely effective alternative to creating multiple matchers in a pipeline.

The Sitemap

The sitemap is the name of the file that contains the configuration information for the pipelines that an application requires. The main Cocoon sitemap file is found in the root of the Cocoon Web application folder and is called `sitemap.xmap`. If you examine the Cocoon distribution, you will note that the root sitemap also contains links to sub-sitemaps that configure specific parts of the Cocoon distribution such as different samples. A sub-sitemap is another `sitemap.xmap` that is in the root of its own application folder. This enables you to build a sitemap that is specific for your application and can be distributed without the need for complex changes to the core Cocoon sitemap, other than to "mount" it in the core sitemap.

The sitemap is used to resolve requests for resources. It firstly *matches* a request to a set of processing commands inside a pipeline. The processing steps that the pipeline defines use various *components* that actually do their bit of the work to handle the request and generate a response.

The sitemap is undoubtedly one of the main sources of confusion within Cocoon; however, it is not that difficult to use after its structure is understood and a few examples have been considered. So, to start with, what is to be found in the sitemap?

Components

The first section of the sitemap defines the components that can be used in the pipelines. This sits in between the `<map:components>...</map:components>` element. Inside this element are to be found additional elements that configure each component. Components can fall into various categories, as defined in Table 4.1. Each of the components is covered in a little more depth in this chapter and in detail in separate chapters later in the book.

Table 4.1 *Component Categories*

Component	Description
`<generators/>`	Generates a stream of SAX events from a source such as an XML file, class, or database.
`<transformers/>`	Transforms the stream of SAX events from the generator to another stream of SAX events.
`<readers/>`	Generates and serializes in one go, bypassing the SAX event mechanism. Readers are really useful for handling binary files or other files that do not need to be subjected to the full pipeline processing chain.
`<serializers/>`	Final component in a pipeline processing chain. Readers take a stream of SAX events and turn it into a character stream.
`<matchers/>`	Matchers are used to parse the request that comes into Cocoon and work out which part of a pipeline should be used to handle the request. Matchers work like an `if` statement.
`<selectors/>`	Selectors extend the capabilities offered by matchers to something more analogous to a `switch` statement. Again, like matchers, they can be used to test the request for particular elements and pick the correct part of the pipeline to use.
`<actions/>`	Actions are used to handle complex logic associated with handling a request. Typical examples of actions' usage would be database interoperability or authentication handling. Actions can be used to direct flow within a pipeline processing chain.

Note

Note that the component elements within the table are prefixed with the map: prefix in the sitemap file.

Views

After each of the components has been specified, the sitemap can specify any views it uses. Views are contained within the `<map:views>...</map:views>` element and define processing chains. A view processing chain can be used to provide an alternative to how a resource is generally handled. For example, you may have a pipeline that takes an XML file and transforms it to HTML. A view could be used to enable you to serialize the XML file directly, thus providing a method for obtaining the raw content.

Resources

The sitemap can then optionally contain resources, specified in between the `<map:resources>...</map:resources>` element. A resource is a reusable pipeline processing chain and can be called from multiple pipeline matches.

Action Sets

Another sitemap section that makes more effective use of other parts of the sitemap is action sets. These are defined in between the `<map:action-set>...</map:action-set>` element and allow the collection of actions together.

Pipelines

The final part of the sitemap is the `<map:pipelines>...</map:pipelines>` section. This element contains one or more pipelines that contain the specific commands for matching requests and handling them. The root Cocoon sitemap contains several pipelines; however, a typical application would have only a single pipeline. Having multiple pipelines does allow sub-sitemaps to be mounted and also permits separate error handling to be configured.

Basic Request Handling

Within the pipeline, one or more matches for requests will be defined. Matches are contained within the `<map:match>...</map:match>` element. The match element will always specify a `pattern` attribute that is used to define the search pattern. For example:

```
<map:match pattern="index.html">
...
</map:match>
```

would examine the request to see whether the requesting agent was requesting `index.html`.

Patterns can also contain wildcards. For example, the pattern

```
<map:match pattern="*.html">
...
</map:match>
```

would match any request for a resource with a `.html` extension. This pattern would work only from the application root folder; however, the addition of a double asterisks (`**`) will match any request, even if preceded by a folder hierarchy. Therefore,

```
<map:match pattern="**.html">
...
</map:match>
```

will match requests to page.html, level1/page.html, and level1/level2/page.html, and so on.

After a request has been matched, the rest of the pipeline can be processed. The minimum steps that must be taken include source generation and serialization. Take the following example:

```
<map:match pattern="page.source">
    <map:generate type="file" src="page.xml"/>
    <map:serialize type="xml"/>
</map:match>
```

The first thing that happens here is the matching. The pipeline will be executed if Cocoon gets a request for page.source. This resource does not exist as a physical file; the response is built by firstly generating a stream of SAX events from an XML file called page.xml. The type attribute of the <map:generate> element is specifying that a generator component with a name of file is used to stream an XML file into SAX events. The generator name and Cocoon to use are specified in the <map:components> section of the sitemap.

The subsequent SAX events stream is then passed to a serializer for conversion to the final character stream. Again, the <map:serialize> element has a type attribute that specifies the actual serializer to use. In this instance the sitemap is specifying that we serialize the SAX stream to XML. As with the generator, the mapping of the serializer name reference to a component occurs upstairs in the <map:components> section.

The final result of this operation is a stream of character data that reflects the XML contained within page.xml. Of course, the user does not know that page.source does not exist as a physical resource, nor does the user know any of the components that are used to generate the response to the request for page.source.

In most cases, XML source streams would have some kind of transformation applied to them. Otherwise, there would not be much point in using Cocoon—after all, a Web server will serve raw XML files with a lot less overhead than Cocoon! To achieve this, a transformation step can be added between the generation and serialization steps:

```
<map:match pattern="page.html">
  <map:generate type="file" src="page.xml"/>
  <map:transform type="xslt" src="stylesheets/xml2html.xsl"/>
  <map:serialize type="html"/>
</map:match>
```

It should be fairly obvious that the <map:transform> element follows the <map:generate> and <map:serialize> elements by specifying a type and source file for the transformer. In the preceding example, the pipeline will use the XSLT transformation component and apply the stylesheet specified in the src attribute. This will take the SAX event stream from the generator and transform it to another SAX event stream for the serializer to handle. The serializer type has changed to "html" because the transformer is sending HTML as its SAX event stream.

We saw earlier that the pattern attribute can accept wildcards. How is this handled in the subsequent generate/transform/serialize process? The answer is that you can use tokens to replace each wildcard used in the pattern.

The tokens are specified as {*<n>*}, where *<n>* is the index of the wildcard in the pattern string. For example:

```
<map:match pattern="*.html">
  <map:generate type="file" src="{1}.xml"/>
  <map:transform type="xslt" src="stylesheets/xml2html.xsl"/>
  <map:serialize type="html"/>
</map:match>
```

will take whatever is used in place of the * wildcard in the request and use it wherever the {1} token is found. So a request for page1.html will result in the generator looking for page1.xml, and a request for page2.html will cause the generator to look for page2.xml as its source.

If more than one wildcard is specified, you simply use a suitably numbered token to effect the substitution. For example:

```
<map:match pattern="**/*.html">
    <map:generate type="file" src="{1}/{2}.xml"/>
    <map:transform type="xslt" src="stylesheets/xml2html.xsl"/>
    <map:serialize type="html"/>
</map:match>
```

will serve requests for /level1/page.html and /level1/.../levelx/page.html, just as long as /level1/page.xml and /level1/.../levelx/page.xml exist. Note that this will not serve any content in the root. If you want to do this, the following pattern and token substitution will work:

```
<map:match pattern="**.html">
    <map:generate type="file" src="{2}.xml"/>
    <map:transform type="xslt" src="stylesheets/xml2html.xsl"/>
    <map:serialize type="html"/>
</map:match>
```

The great advantage of this pipeline processing capability is the opportunity it offers to drive different output from the same source content. Consider the following sitemap fragment:

```
<map:match pattern="page.xml">
    <map:generate type="file" src="page.xml"/>
    <map:serialize type="xml"/>
</map:match>

<map:match pattern="page.html">
  <map:generate type="file" src="page.xml"/>
    <map:transform type="xslt" src="stylesheets/xml2html.xsl"/>
  <map:serialize type="html"/>
</map:match>

<map:match pattern="page.wml">
    <map:generate type="file" src="page.xml"/>
    <map:transform type="xslt" src="stylesheets/xml2wml.xsl"/>
    <map:serialize type="wap"/>
</map:match>
```

This sample is setting up handlers for three different requests: `page.xml`, `page.html`, and `page.wml`. The first handler is simply churning out the XML file. The second handler uses the same XML file but transforms it to HTML. The final handler transforms the same source XML document into WML for delivery to a WAP-enabled device. Of course, these examples could be made even more powerful by the use of wildcards and token substitution.

What the earlier examples should illustrate is that even at its most basic, the sitemap and pipeline processing architecture offers a highly flexible and powerful method for handling the publishing of requests.

Default Components

Because the Cocoon architecture is such that new components can be developed and used extremely easily, the sitemap includes a method to mark a particular component as a default for a given component category. In each of the component grouping elements, a `default` attribute can be specified that indicates which component is to be treated as the default:

```
<map:generators default="file">
    <map:generator
         name="file"
         src="org.apache.cocoon.generation.FileGenerator"/>
    <map:generator
         name="serverpages"
         src="org.apache.cocoon.generation.ServerPagesGenerator"/>
```

```
    <map:generator
         name="request"
         src="org.apache.cocoon.generation.RequestGenerator"/>
    <map:generator
         name="status"
         src="org.apache.cocoon.generation.StatusGenerator"/>
</map:generators>
```

The preceding sitemap sub-section configures the various generators that can be used. The `default` attribute is specifying that the `file` generator should be used wherever a `<map:generate>` element is used without a `type` attribute.

Matchers

Request matching is not limited to wildcards. Besides the wildcard matching on resource name capabilities described previously, various other matchers have been created, as described in Table 4.2.

Table 4.2 *Cocoon Matchers*

Matcher	Description
`WildcardURIMatcher`	Allows the type of matching given in the earlier examples. This is usually the default matcher.
`RegexpURIMatcher`	Allows matching of a request URI using regular expressions instead of wildcards.
`RegexpHeaderMatcher`	Matches a request header against a regular expression. This, for example, can be used to look for specific header variables such as referer.
`RegexpHostMatcher`	Matches the target host header against a regular expression.
`RegexpRequestAttributeMatcher`	Matches a request attribute against a regular expression.
`RegexpRequestParameterMatcher`	Matches a request parameter against a regular expression.
`RegexpSessionAttributeMatcher`	Matches a session attribute against a regular expression.
`RequestAttributeMatcher`	Searches for a request attribute.
`RequestParameterMatcher`	Searches for a request parameter.
`SessionAttributeMatcher`	Allows a basic match to be made against a session attribute.
`WildcardHeaderMatcher`	Matches a request header against a wildcard.

Table 4.2 *(continued)*

Matcher	Description
`WildcardHostMatcher`	Matches the target host header against a wildcard.
`WildcardRequestAttributeMatcher`	Matches a request attribute against a wildcard.
`WildcardRequestParameterMatcher`	Matches a request parameter against a regular expression.
`WildcardSessionAttributeMatcher`	Matches a session attribute against a regular expression.

The clear differences here are the method used for matching and what the match is performed against. Matchers that use regular expressions (`regexp`) can be very useful and powerful alternatives to wildcard matches. For example:

```
<map:match type="regexp" pattern="^(en|de|fr)-(.*)$">
    <map:generate type="file" src="{1}/{2}.xml"/>
    <map:transform type="xslt" src="stylesheets/xml2html.xsl"/>
    <map:serialize type="html"/>
</map:match>
```

will match requests starting with `en` or `de` or `fr`, followed by the `-` character, followed by any string of characters to the end of the line. The generator will then take the result of the first expression (`(en|de|fr)`) to form a folder name, and then append `.xml` to the result of the second expression (`(.*)`) to form its source filename. So a request for `en-login` would resolve to `en/login.xml`.

Regular Expressions
A whole chapter could be devoted to regular expressions, but because I want to concentrate on Cocoon, I will not be writing one. If you want to know more, there are loads of sites that cater to all levels. A great tutorial can be found at `http://www.zvon.org/other/PerlTutorial/Output/index.html`.

To make a matcher available for use in the sitemap, it must be declared as a component. The following sitemap fragments illustrate how this is done:

```
<?xml version="1.0"?>
<map:sitemap xmlns:map="http://apache.org/cocoon/sitemap/1.0">
    <map:components>
        ...
        <map:matchers default="wildcard">
            <map:matcher name="wildcard"
                src="org.apache.cocoon.matching.WildcardURIMatcher"/>
            <map:matcher name="regexp"
                src="org.apache.cocoon.matching.RegexpURIMatcher"/>
```

```
            <map:matcher name="request"
                 src="org.apache.cocoon.matching.RequestParamMatcher"/>
        </map:matchers>
        ...
    </map:components>
    ...
</map:sitemap>
```

The preceding fragment uses three matchers, `WildcardURIMatcher`, `RegexpURIMatcher`, and `RequestParamMatcher`. These are given the respective names `wildcard`, `regexp`, and `request`. It is these names that are then used in the `<map:match>` element; for example:

```
<map:match type="regexp" pattern="(.*)/(en|fr)/(.*)$">
    ...
</map:match>
```

would pick the matcher identified by the name `regexp` for use. Note also that the fragment sets the `wildcard` matcher to be the default if no `type` attribute is present in the `<map:match>` element.

Selectors

Closely related to matchers are selectors. Where selectors differ is that they can be used like a Java `switch` construct to test for several conditions. The standard selectors included with Cocoon are detailed in Table 4.3.

Table 4.3 *Cocoon Selectors*

Selector	Description
`BrowserSelector`	Allows tests to be made against the user-agent data in the request header.
`HeaderSelector`	Allows tests against request header data.
`HostSelector`	Allows selector actions against the results of tests on the request host parameter.
`ParameterSelector`	Performs matches against the request parameter values.
`RequestAttributeSelector`	Allows tests to be made against request attributes.
`SessionAttributeSelector`	Allows tests to be made against session attributes.

To illustrate how selectors are used, consider the following example. It uses the `BrowserSelector` to pick a suitable stylesheet to render some content dependant on the user's browser type:

```
<map:match type="regexp" pattern="^(en|fr|de)-(.*)$">
    <map:generate type="file" src="{1}/{2}.xml"/>
    <map:select type="browser">
        <map:when test="explorer">
            <map:transform type="xslt" src="stylesheets/ie/xml2html.xsl"/>
        </map:when>
        <map:when test="netscape">
            <map:transform type="xslt" src="stylesheets/ns/xml2html.xsl"/>
        </map:when>
        <map:otherwise>
            <map:transform type="xslt" src="stylesheets/standard/xml2html.xsl"/>
        </map:otherwise>
    </map:select>
    <map:serialize type="html"/>
</map:match>
```

This segment shows how the pipeline can be routed to use transformers specific to a browser. As can be seen, selectors have an `otherwise` clause that gets called when none of the specific tests resolves.

As with matchers, the selectors available in the pipeline and their configuration are set up in the `<components>` section of the sitemap:

```
<?xml version="1.0"?>
<map:sitemap xmlns:map="http://apache.org/cocoon/sitemap/1.0">
    <map:components>
        ...
        <map:selectors default="browser">
            <map:selector name="browser"
                 src="org.apache.cocoon.selection.BrowserSelector">
                <browser name="explorer" useragent="MSIE"/>
                <browser name="pocketexplorer" useragent="MSPIE"/>
                <browser name="handweb" useragent="HandHTTP"/>
                <browser name="avantgo" useragent="AvantGo"/>
                <browser name="imode" useragent="DoCoMo"/>
                <browser name="opera" useragent="Opera"/>
                <browser name="lynx" useragent="Lynx"/>
                <browser name="java" useragent="Java"/>
                <browser name="wap" useragent="Nokia"/>
                <browser name="wap" useragent="UP"/>
```

```
                <browser name="wap" useragent="Wapalizer"/>
                <browser name="mozilla5" useragent="Mozilla/5"/>
                <browser name="mozilla5" useragent="Netscape6/"/>
                <browser name="netscape" useragent="Mozilla"/>
            </map:selector>
            <map:selector name="parameter"
                 src="org.apache.cocoon.selection.ParameterSelector"/>
            </map:selectors>
            ...
    </map:components>
    ...
</map:sitemap>
```

Generators

Generators are the first of the components that the pipeline uses to actually serve the content. A generator creates a stream of SAX events from one or more sources. There is an almost infinite number of sources that can be envisaged, but typical ones would be the generator itself, a file, databases, a Web service, and so on.

The generators that ship with Cocoon at the time of writing include those listed in Table 4.4.

Table 4.4 *Cocoon Generators*

Generator	Description
`DirectoryGenerator`	Generates an XML representation of a directory listing, passing the XML down the chain as a series of SAX events.
`FileGenerator`	Reads an XML file and passes it down the chain as a series of SAX events. This is typically configured as the default generator because most of the time you will want to return a response that has been sourced from an XML file.
`FragmentExtractorGenerator`	Works with the `FragmentExtractorTransformer` to extract particular nodes from a SAX stream and handle them separately. It is especially used when creating images from an SVG file.
`HTMLGenerator`	Reads an HTML document and uses the Jtidy library to turn it into well-formed XHTML.

Table 4.4 *(continued)*

Generator	Description
`ImageDirectoryGenerator`	This is an extension of the directory generator and lists specifically image files, adding information to the XML regarding image dimensions.
`JspGenerator`	This is a neat generator that interacts with a servlet engine to capture the results of a request for a JSP and present them as SAX events to the rest of the processing chain.
`MP3DirectoryGenerator`	Extends `DirectoryGenerator` to handle the specifics of MP3 files.
`NotifyingGenerator`	Creates a SAX event stream representing the current system notification message. This can be used during error handling to get an easily parsed description of the problem.
`PHPGenerator`	This generator is included in Cocoon only as an option but will create a SAX stream based on a PHP page.
`ProfilerGenerator`	Creates a stream based on the profiler data.
`RequestGenerator`	Builds a stream of XML as SAX events that represents the request header data.
`ScriptGenerator`	Can be configured to handle scripts in various dialects and pass them around as SAX events.
`SearchGenerator`	Performs a search through a given set of one or more resources and streams the result through.
`StatusGenerator`	Generates information about the status of Cocoon. This is presented as a SAX event stream driven from XML.
`StreamGenerator`	Reads data from the input stream of an HTTP request. The data must be presented as XML in the POST message.
`VelocityGenerator`	Takes a Velocity template file, converts to XML, and streams as SAX events.
`XMLDBGenerator`	Reads XML data streams from an XML:DB-compliant source and passes them on as SAX events.
`XMLDBCollectionGenerator`	Generates a collection of XML:DB resources in a hierarchy. This "directory" of the structure of the XML:DB source can be used for navigation.

Generators are configured in the `<components>` section of the sitemap:

```
<?xml version="1.0"?>
<map:sitemap xmlns:map="http://apache.org/cocoon/sitemap/1.0">
```

```
    <map:components>
        ...
        <map:generators default="file">
            <map:generator
                name="file"
                src="org.apache.cocoon.generation.FileGenerator"/>
            <map:generator
                name="serverpages"
                src="org.apache.cocoon.generation.ServerPagesGenerator"/>
            <map:generator
                name="request"
                src="org.apache.cocoon.generation.RequestGenerator"/>
            <map:generator
                name="status"
                src="org.apache.cocoon.generation.StatusGenerator"/>
        </map:generators>
        ...
    </map:components>
    ...
</map:sitemap>
```

Transformers

Transformers are an optional part of the pipeline, but in most cases when the source is an XML file, you will find that they will be used.

A transformer takes an input SAX event stream, does something with it, and then passes it on as another SAX event stream. Typically, this is achieved using XSLT in the form of a stylesheet; however, various other transformers are shipped with Cocoon, as described in Table 4.5. As with the rest of the Cocoon architecture, transformers are flexible and new ones can be developed by anyone to suit a particular need.

Table 4.5 *Cocoon Transformers*

Transformer	Description
`CachingCIncludeTransformer`	Is basically the same as the `CInclude Transformer` but implements caching.
`CIncludeTransformer`	Is used to action a `<cinclude:include>` element and embed a subsequently specified XML resource within another XML stream.

Table 4.5 *(continued)*

Transformer	Description
`FilterTransformer`	Is used to filter out unwanted elements from the source stream, thus limiting the number of elements passed down the chain.
`FragmentExtractionTransformer`	Works with the `FragmentExtractorGenerator` and is generally used for image creation with SVG.
`I18nTransformer`	Is used to perform language translation and localization on a stream. It works by defining a dictionary and then applying definitions to matching elements in a stream.
`LDAPTransformer`	Handles input from an LDAP source. (This is an optional transformer.)
`LogTransformer`	Takes input from a specified log file and makes it available as XML via the SAX stream.
`ReadDOMSessionTransformer`	Works on a specified session variable that contains a DOM object. It then transforms the DOM object to SAX events for further processing.
`RoleFilterTransformer`	Filters a SAX event list based on user roles. This can be used, for example, to dynamically configure form display.
`SQLTransformer`	Queries a database, passing the result back in the SAX event stream.
`WriteDOMSessionTransformer`	Takes a SAX stream and turns into a DOM object, stored in the session. This operates along with the `ReadDOMSessionTransformer`.
`XIncludeTransformer`	Performs an include using the `XInclude` specification.
`TraxTransformer`	Is usually specified as the default transformer in a sitemap and is aka the `XSLTTransformer`. It is used to apply an XSLT stylesheet to the SAX event stream.
`XTTransformer`	Permits XSLT transformations to be done using the XT transformer library rather than Trax. (This is another optional component.)

One of the key points of transformers is that the pipeline can contain more than one transformer, and thus you can chain the results of one transformation into another. This is a really important concept and is critical to some transformers. For internationalization you will want to generate your source, pass it through the I18n transformer to substitute dictionary phrases, and then transform the result with an XSLT transformation ready for rendering. Another scenario could be that you use a browser selector to pick a transformer that will generate browser-specific code, but you use a common format across the variants and then use a single stylesheet to handle the final rendering process.

The architectural benefits that this approach offers are also much more beneficial than those of other scripting technologies. Source content can go through a number of steps to reach a final publishing stage, thus providing a practical framework to support separation of concerns. Key transformation steps can remain "black boxes" that accept only a particular data model regardless of the capabilities of a generator. If the stream created by the generator does not fit a particular transformer, an intermediate transformer can be used to provide compatibility rather than having to modify the generator or transformer.

The following example shows how transformers are configured in the sitemap:

```
<?xml version="1.0"?>
<map:sitemap xmlns:map="http://apache.org/cocoon/sitemap/1.0">
    <map:components>
    ...
    <map:transformers default="xslt">
        <map:transformer
            name="xslt"
            src="org.apache.cocoon.transformation.TraxTransformer">
            <use-store>true</use-store>
            <use-request-parameters>false</use-request-parameters>
            <use-browser-capabilities-db>false</use-browser-capabilities-db>
        </map:transformer>
        <map:transformer
             name="i18n"
             src="org.apache.cocoon.transformation.I18nTransformer"/>
        <map:transformer
             name="xinclude"
             src="org.apache.cocoon.transformation.XIncludeTransformer"/>
        <map:transformer
             name="cinclude"
             src="org.apache.cocoon.transformation.CIncludeTransformer"/>
        </map:transformers>
        ...
    </map:components>
    ...
</map:sitemap>
```

Serializers

The final key component of the request-response mechanism is the serializer. This component is responsible for taking a stream of SAX events and turning it into a format suitable for final delivery. As much as we would like all the clients that Cocoon serves to be able to handle XML, the fact is that they don't: browsers (in the main) still like poorly formed HTML, other applications want comma-separated values, and so on. The serializer does the job of providing the native format that the requesting client needs, and, as Table 4.6 shows, Cocoon is rich with packaged and optional serializers.

Table 4.6 *Cocoon Serializers*

Serializer	Description
`FOPSerializer`	The FOP serializer takes care of turning a stream of Formatting Objects (FO) compliant XML into PDF, PostScript, and PCL formats. This provides a super way of building high-quality documentation that is suitable for electronic or hard-copy distribution from the same data sources that drive an application.
`HTMLSerializer`	Usually defined as the default serializer in most applications, this component turns XHTML into HTML.
`LinkSerializer`	This produces links from an input stream.
`SVGSerializer`	This takes Scalable Vector Graphics (SVG) XML definitions and turns them into XML, JPG, or PNG formats. The same serializer is used separately to configure each potential output format based on mime type.
`TextSerializer`	Like the `SVGSerializer`, the `TextSerializer` can be used to format specific types of text content based on mime type configurations. VRML and raw text are supported.
`XMLSerializer`	Again, the `XMLSerializer` is a multipurpose beast that can handle different specific XML schemas. It is used for simple XML and WML (WAP).

The following sitemap segments reflect how the same serializer can be configured to handle variations on a theme:

```
<?xml version="1.0"?>
<map:sitemap xmlns:map="http://apache.org/cocoon/sitemap/1.0">
    <map:components>
    ...
    <map:serializers default="html">
        <map:serializer name="vrml"
            mime-type="model/vrml"
            logger="sitemap.serializer.vrml"
            src="org.apache.cocoon.serialization.TextSerializer"/>
```

```
<map:serializer name="wml"
    mime-type="text/vnd.wap.wml"
    logger="sitemap.serializer.wml"
    src="org.apache.cocoon.serialization.XMLSerializer">
    <doctype-public>-//WAPFORUM//DTD WML 1.1//EN</doctype-public>
    <doctype-system>http://www.wapforum.org/DTD/wml_1.1.xml</
     doctype-system>
    <encoding>ASCII</encoding>
    <omit-xml-declaration>yes</omit-xml-declaration>
</map:serializer>
<map:serializer name="svgxml"
    mime-type="image/svg-xml"
    logger="sitemap.serializer.svgxml"
    src="org.apache.cocoon.serialization.XMLSerializer">
    <doctype-public>-//W3C//DTD SVG 20000303 Stylable//EN</
     doctype-public>
    <doctype-system>http://www.w3.org/TR/2000/03/WD-SVG-20000303/</
     doctype-system>
</map:serializer>
<map:serializer name="text"
    src="org.apache.cocoon.serialization.TextSerializer"/>
    logger="sitemap.serializer.text"
    mime-type="text/text"
<map:serializer name="fo2pdf"
    src="org.apache.cocoon.serialization.FOPSerializer"
    logger="sitemap.serializer.fo2pdf"
    mime-type="application/pdf"/>
<map:serializer name="fo2ps"
    src="org.apache.cocoon.serialization.FOPSerializer"
    logger="sitemap.serializer.fo2ps"
    mime-type="application/postscript"/>
<map:serializer name="fo2pcl"
    src="org.apache.cocoon.serialization.FOPSerializer"
    logger="sitemap.serializer.fo2pcl"
    mime-type="application/vnd.hp-PCL"/>
<map:serializer name="svg2jpeg"
    src="org.apache.cocoon.serialization.SVGSerializer"
    logger="sitemap.serializer.svg2jpeg"
    mime-type="image/jpeg"/>
<map:serializer name="svg2png"
    src="org.apache.cocoon.serialization.SVGSerializer"
    logger="sitemap.serializer.svg2png"
    mime-type="image/png"/>
```

```
        </map:serializers>
        ...
    </map:components>
    ...
</map:sitemap>
```

Views

As discussed previously, views can be defined and used to provide an alternative way of presenting some content. The initial objective was to provide a way of presenting the raw content of a resource to search engines. Because the processing chain will at some stage have the content in a raw form, it makes sense to enable that stream to be presented to a search engine in a raw form. Why? Because by the time the stream has gone through the preferred rendering process, it is likely to have been augmented with a lot of irrelevant information (for example, navigation, ads, presentation) and even be in a form that is not easily machine readable by a search engine.

What a view does is allow the stream to be captured and transferred to an alternative processing chain. A simple view would capture the generator stream and serialize that to XML; more complex views might capture the results of a transformation or aggregation.

The principle of views can be extended and offer ways of debugging applications by capturing raw output at various stages of processing.

Readers

Readers are used as combined generators and serializers. They are used when a resource just needs to be served without any possibility of transformation. Typical examples are binary files such as images, plug-ins, and raw text. These are served with the `ResourceReader`. Cocoon also has readers to handle JSP and database sources.

Content Aggregation

A pipeline can gather source data from multiple sources and collate, or aggregate, it before passing it on down the chain. The neat part of this is that the sources can, if needed, be generated by other parts of the pipeline. Here's an example:

```
<map:match pattern="index.html">
    <map:aggregate element="page">
        <map:part src="cocoon:/topbar.xml" element="topbar"/>
        <map:part src="cocoon:/menu.xml" element="menu"/>
        <map:part src="cocoon:/index.xml" element="main"/>
    </map:aggregate>
    <map:transform src="stylesheets/xml2html.xsl"/>
    <map:serialize/>
</map:match>
```

What this example does is firstly specify an aggregation. The resultant stream will have a root element of `page`. The aggregation is made up of three separate sources. Each source has its own root element (`topbar`, `menu`, and `main`), and each source is to be found by looking in the current sitemap. This is specified by the use of `cocoon:/` as a pseudo protocol. The resultant stream is then sent en masse to a transformer and serialized.

Pseudo Protocols
Just as `http://`, `ftp://`, or `mailto://` at the beginning of a URI indicates a particular protocol, Cocoon also understands its own pseudo protocols. `cocoon:/` refers to a pipeline in the current sitemap, and `cocoon://` refers to a pipeline in the root sitemap. If you want to refer to a resource relative to the current servlet context, use the `context://` pseudo protocol. The `resource://` pseudo protocol will find a resource using the context classloader, thus enabling the storage of resources on the classpath. The `xmldb://` pseudo protocol will access XML:DB managed resources.

Actions

Actions provide a powerful mechanism for structuring application-specific logic. They can be used to perform tasks that must occur on every request, such as session authentication. Form handling and database interaction can be a breeze with actions. When actions are combined with the closely related matchers and selectors, you have a powerful arsenal of techniques for separating out business logic from presentation. Examples of actions are provided throughout the book.

Summary

In this chapter we have looked in a lot more detail at pipeline processing and how it is implemented in Cocoon through the sitemap. The structure of the sitemap and the components therein have been examined, along with examples of how these might be used.

The scene is now set to move into developing an application with Cocoon.

Part II

Getting Started with Cocoon

Chapter

CHAPTER 5
Designing the Sample Application

The goal of this chapter is to introduce the sample Web application that will be our mechanism for explaining the various features and strengths of Cocoon. We will start by providing an overview of the problem, using a scenario involving a fictitious client. Based on the requirements that we can extract from the problem, we will produce a high-level design for the solution. In the chapters following, we will show how we can use Cocoon to build an application that fulfills all the business requirements. Each chapter will deal with a specific set of Cocoon concepts which will be demonstrated by adding layers of complexity to our application. Our goal here is not to produce a complete application that you can immediately put into production. Rather, we'll work off these scenarios to introduce various Cocoon components and features. At the conclusion of this section, you should have a good idea of the basics of building a Cocoon application. In the section following this one, we'll get into more complex Cocoon functions.

The Problem

Our Web application begins its life as a business problem at the corporate meeting room of the fictional ABC Software Company. The ABC Software Company is a major software company ready to launch its new high-end HR software, AbcApp. AbcApp is targeted to a Fortune-500 customer base—clients that the ABC Software Company has worked hard to acquire and will work even harder to keep.

Although everything is set to go with the software, management is in a quandary—they were supposed to have an AbcApp support Web site months ago, but it is not ready. The purpose of the site is to provide a way for the company's high-end customers to submit support requests, track trouble tickets, communicate with technicians, view support costs, and so forth. Originally, the site was based on static HTML pages and a handful of JSPs communicating with a back-end database. A team of contractors had been bought in for the project, and had created a spiffy-looking site tuned to traditional browser clients.

The problem began when the support staff wanted to change the ticket submission forms so that customers could be more detailed in their requests. From that idea came the requirement to actually create portals personalized to each customer so that not only could customers access their own data, but targeted information could be fed to the pages they browsed. The problem became compounded when the board insisted that the site support both a U.S. and a European customer base. The final blow to the original design came when a phone-happy executive wanted to be able to access the key areas of the site on his WAP-enabled phone.

The new requirements have generated copious numbers of emails and empty coffee cups, but the Web support team is no closer to a solution. The original Web site designer is long gone, and the team is now well aware that it would do no good to simply follow the original design. Moreover, the release of AbcApp is only two weeks away, giving the team a virtually impossible task. It is at this critical step that we are called in.

Approaching the Problem

Before we see what Cocoon can do to solve this problem, let's lay out the requirements. The support Web site for AbcApp consists of the following main areas:

- The "front gate" or authentication area.
- The informational area, where customers can access PDF documentation about AbcApp.
- The trouble ticket area, where customers submit trouble tickets and view status of open tickets. New tickets are stored in a database and the support staff is alerted by email.
- The contract area, where customers can view the status of support contracts.

Looking across these areas, we can extrapolate the following elements that our design must handle:

- Static data pages rendered as HTML and WML
- PDF documentation
- Security and authentication
- Forms
- Email generation
- Database operations
- Internationalization: the site must handle character sets and localization for the U.S. and various European countries
- Personalization
- Aggregation of data from multiple sources

Finally, there are some other requirements that must be considered so that this design can be used well into the future and will not repeat the mistakes of the previous site:

- Easy maintenance of data files
- Easy maintenance of forms
- Capability to handle multiple people/teams working on the site
- Fast implementation

So how do we go about using Cocoon to handle all of these requirements?

Application Design Preparation

To design our Web site, we must first break our requirements down into two groups: process flows and process requirements. In general, this is sound design philosophy. When using Cocoon it is especially important, because Cocoon is loaded with numerous features. To use Cocoon well, knowing the basic processing flows that our application must support will enable us to lay out the broad framework of our application. After we do that, we can look at the requirements that affect each part of the processes.

Cocoon Application Design
We'll deal more with the principles of designing Cocoon-based applications in general in Chapter 21, "Designing Cocoon Applications."

Process Flows

We start by extracting the core processing flows from the business requirements. There are four main processes:

- Presentation of status data pages—welcome page, information pages, and so on
- Presentation of database-driven pages: Trouble Ticket status, contract status
- Presentation and processing of forms
- Authentication

Figure 5.1 shows the basic unidirectional flow of data that produces HTML, WML, and PDF pages. Here we can see how clients receive data from static data files. Now if our fictional scenario were real, someone would have to extract data out of the original HTML and JSP pages and reformat it into XML. We will assume, of course, that the erstwhile Web team has already done this for us.

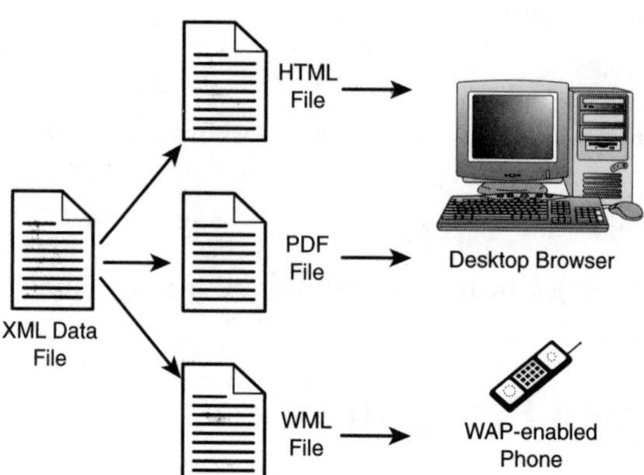

Figure 5.1
Process: static file to rendered page.

Figure 5.2 shows a slightly more complex flow. Here, the database is our primary data source. However, we also will be combining this data with data from various static XML pages and presenting it in the right format to the user.

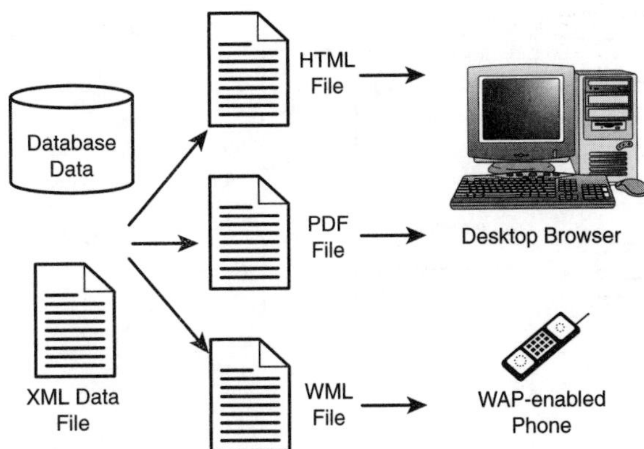

Figure 5.2

Process: Static file plus database data to rendered page.

Figure 5.3 shows the basic form processing model. Forms are defined as data definitions, which are presented to the client in the appropriate format (HTML or WML). When the user submits a completed form, this data must be processed and turned into both emails and database inserts.

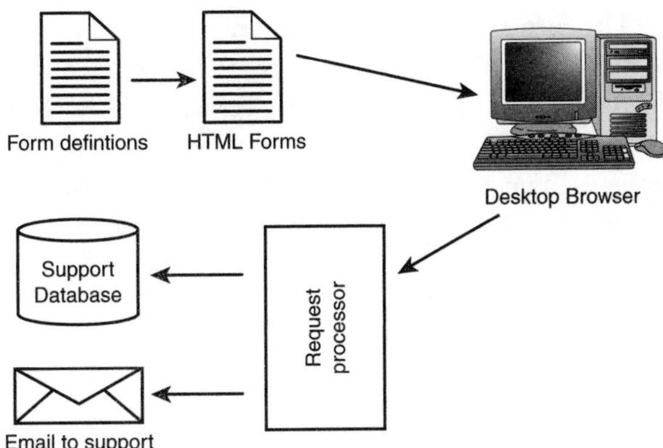

Figure 5.3

Process: Form processing.

In Figure 5.4, we see the authentication model. This model relies on a database-driven login and must include robust protection of restricted pages from non-authenticated users. This model should also implement some sort of tracking.

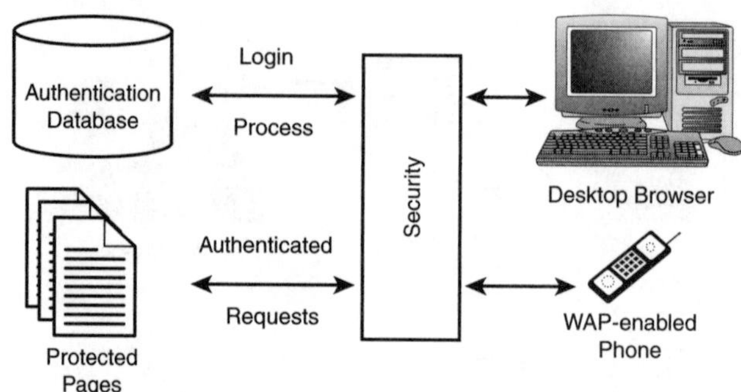

Figure 5.4
Process: Authentication.

Process Requirements

Now that we know what processes our application must support, let's consider the various specific requirements.

Client-Side Requirements

We have already noted that we are supporting two primary clients: traditional browsers and WAP-enabled phones. The former will receive some pages as HTML and some as PDF. While we are at it, we might as well consider support for PDAs, such as the Palm Pilot, for which we can use HTML but must take into account screen real estate. Another client-side requirement is internationalization. Both the site pages and the documentation pages will be written in various languages. The pages that are rendered to the browser clients must therefore be able to support the proper character sets. In addition, the pricing pages will be expected to support various currency formats. Finally, we must implement personalization so that content is defined by who the customer is.

Server-Side Requirements

On the server side, we have several things to consider. We have bidirectional database operations to deal with, as well as email generation. We must implement security so that customers can log in and view just the data that pertains to them. We also should take care to implement good site manners, like graceful handling of non-existent pages or page errors.

Designing the Application

Now that we have a basic idea of what our application must do, let's consider the design as we will implement it with Cocoon. We have already reviewed the basic Cocoon concepts and components in Chapter 2, "Avalon." Let's now see how we will make use of them.

Process Flows

In Figure 5.5, we see which Cocoon components will support the data flow from static XML files to the client. As discussed before, data extraction is handled in Cocoon by Generators, so-called because they generate SAX events out of the input XML data. In this flow, the XML data will be read by the `FileGenerator`, which transforms it into SAX events and passes them to the next component in the pipeline, the `TraxTransformer`. This is the mechanism whereby input SAX events are transformed or processed in some way as specified by XSLT definitions, or XSL files. At the other end, the now-transformed data must end up in HTML, PDF, or WML. To accomplish this, we will use three Serializers: the `HTMLSerializer`, `XMLSerializer`, and `FOPSerializer`. We also need to consider how to differentiate between traditional browsers and WAP-enabled phones. To accomplish this task, we will make use of the `BrowserSelector`.

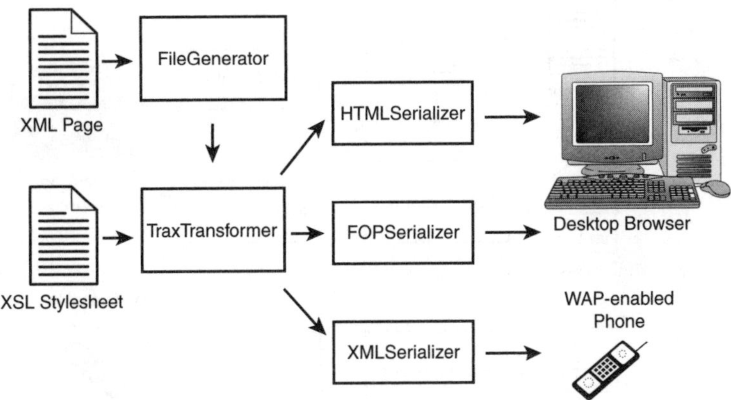

Figure 5.5
Process: Static file to rendered page.

Figure 5.6 shows how data will be extracted from a database and presented to the client. For the `Generator` component, we will be using eXtensible Server Pages (XSPs) and logicsheets. The XSPs are actually compiled into `Generator` components by the `ServerPagesGenerator`. We will use the `HTMLSerializer` and `FOPSerializer` for the client rendering.

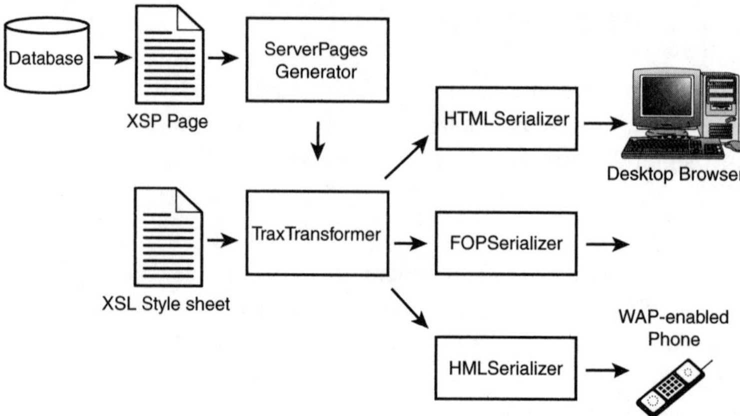

Figure 5.6

Process: Database data to rendered page.

In Figure 5.7, we see combined database and static data sources. We'll use aggregation for this operation, along with an XSP and `FileGenerator`.

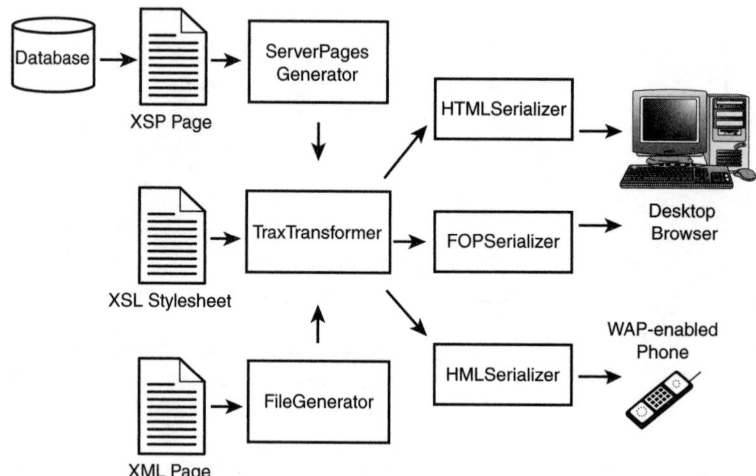

Figure 5.7

Process: Database plus static data to rendered page.

Figure 5.8 shows an example of how Cocoon will handle form processing. There are several components of this process we need to account for: form validation, database inserts, and email generation.

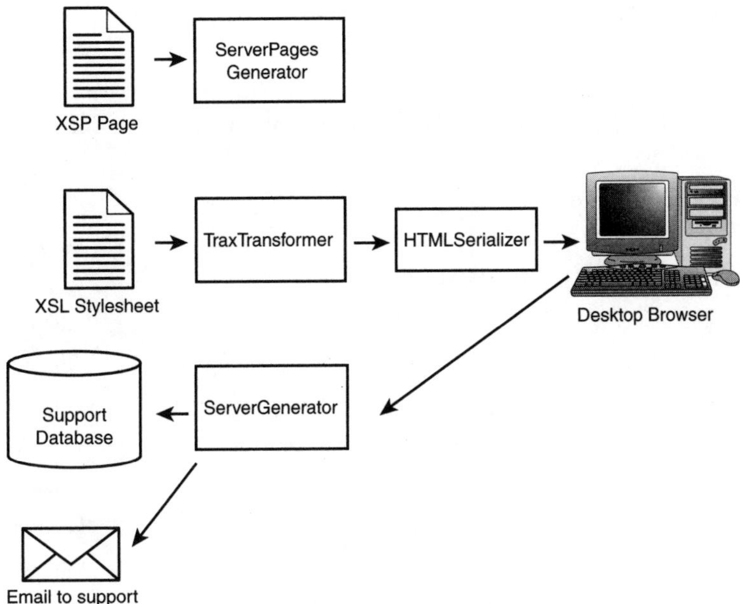

Figure 5.8
Process: Form processing.

Preparing for the Application

Because our problem involves a database, we'll need to set up a database that we can access from Cocoon. In our example, we'll use MySQL, but you can use any database you want to, provided that your have a jar file that provides JDBC access to it.

You can find MySQL at `http://www.mysql.com`, in both source and binary form. Be sure to download the MySQL JDBC access library, which does not come with the database archive file.

Another prerequisite is having the Java Development Kit (JDK) installed on our machine. We can use anywhere from JDK 1.2.2 to JDK 1.4, but JDK 1.3.1 is preferred. Cocoon will probably not support JDK 1.2.2 after version 2.0.3. Cocoon does support JDK 1.4, but there are some bugs that we'd rather not deal with.

In the next chapter, we'll start off by downloading, building, and installing Cocoon into a Tomcat servlet container.

Quick Reference

If you'd like to jump ahead to an example of a particular function that we'll demonstrate with this application, Table 5.1 shows which functions are demonstrated in which chapters.

Table 5.1 *AbcApp Functionality by Chapter*

Function	Location
Serving static pages in HTML, PDF, WML	Chapter 7
Accessing trouble tickets via XSPs	Chapter 8
Accessing trouble tickets via SQLTransformer	Chapter 10
Implementing customized pages using transformer-based aggregation	Chapter 10
Implementing customized pages using sitemap-based aggregation	Chapter 11
Implementing protected area using pipelines	Chapter 11
Implementing protected area using actions	Chapter 12
Implementing authentication using XSPs	Chapter 8
Implementing authentication using actions	Chapter 12
New ticket submission form and process	Chapter 12
Alternatives for multibrowser support	Chapter 13
Implementing internationalization	Chapter 14

Summary

In this chapter, we've had a chance to look at requirements for a support Web site. In the next eight chapters, we will build this site using Cocoon. In Part IV, "Techniques for Building Cocoon Applications," we'll come back to the subject of designing, developing, and deploying Cocoon-based applications, and see how this exercise can help us come up with a set of principles that we can use for other applications. For now, let's get started with building the application.

CHAPTER 6
Installing Cocoon

In this chapter, we will learn how to build, install and start Cocoon. We'll cover the differences between binary, CVS and source distribution builds. Finally, we'll review the contents of the Cocoon web application.

Path/Environment Variable Conventions
Although we provide instructions for building Cocoon on both Windows and Unix, we will generally refer to paths and environment variables using Unix conventions. To understand Unix environment variables in Windows terms, bracket the variable name with percent signs. Thus, `$CATALINA_HOME` on Unix is equivalent to `%CATALINA_HOME%` on Windows. To understand Unix path names in Windows terms, simply replace forward slashes with backward slashes. Thus, `$CATALINA_HOME/webapps/cocoon` on Unix becomes `%CATALINA_HOME%\webapps\cocoon` on Windows.

Downloading Cocoon

Cocoon can be called in two ways: one as a command-line application, the other as a Java servlet. In our application, we will be using the latter, because we are building a Web application. When Cocoon is accessed as a servlet, it must run inside a servlet container that conforms to the Java Servlet Specification 2.2 or greater. There are many servlet containers available to use: Apache Tomcat, WebLogic, JBoss, JRun, Orion, iPlanet, and others. Depending on your choice, and the OS you are running on, Cocoon can be easy or hard to install. For our purposes, we will use what is arguably the easiest (and cheapest!) environment, Apache Tomcat. The application in this book was tested on version 4.0.5 of Tomcat on Windows 2000, Windows XP, and Red Hat Linux 7.2.

Installing Cocoon in Other Containers
The installation page in the Cocoon documentation is generally very helpful in getting you started in various servlet containers: `http://xml.apache.org/cocoon/installing/index.html`.

In our application, we will be using the current stable release of Cocoon, which is 2.0.3.

Prerequisites

Because Cocoon is, after all, a Java application, you must have a JVM installed somewhere on your system. Cocoon will run on Java 1.2 or greater.

There are no hard and fast rules for memory and disk space, but you will run into problems if your machine lacks sufficient quantities of either. In general, Cocoon seems to function well with at least 60MB of memory available to the JVM (we'll discuss this more in Chapter 23, "Cocoon Administration"). Because Cocoon uses temporary disk space for various purposes, you should have at least 200MB free *after* you install Cocoon but before you start your servlet container.

If you are running on Unix, you must have an X server running. Probably the biggest cause of problems for beginners is starting Cocoon without an X server. The libraries that Cocoon uses for graphics operation use the Java AWT library, which in turn relies on a running X server. Although it is possible to build Cocoon so that it doesn't use these libraries, that is an advanced topic which is not considered here.

If you have a headless Unix server that does not have an X server, you have four options (you'll find these described in more detail in Chapter 22, "Techniques for Developing Cocoon Applications"):

- Install Xvfb, a Virtual X Server, which is available from `http://www.xfree86.org` and which does not require actual display hardware to run on.
- Use Java 1.4, which does not require an X server for AWT. The disadvantage here is that some Cocoon components fail under Java 1.4.
- Install an alternative version of AWT, called PJA, from `http://www.eteks.com`. Check the specific instructions in `http://xml.apache.org/cocoon/installing/index.html` on using this software.
- If you don't have a need for SVG or FOP, remove the batik jars from the Cocoon build and the references to `SVGSerializer` and `FOPSerializer` from the sitemap.

Where to Find Cocoon

Cocoon is a subproject of the Apache XML Project group. The group project index page is at `http://xml.apache.org`, and Cocoon's own homepage can be found at (funnily enough) `http://xml.apache.org/cocoon`. Cocoon is available in several formats:

- As a stable release binary
- As a stable release source distribution
- As a snapshot of the current CVS code
- Directly from the CVS file store

Any of these formats includes all the files you need in order to be able to compile and run the application. This is not just the source files but also the libraries that it uses, such as the Avalon classes, Xerces and Xalan. The choice of which one you use really comes down to how far into the world of bleeding-edge code you want to be.

The stable release code will be the stuff that has been through enough testing to consider it production quality. Versions of libraries that are used may not be the latest, and there is less chance of your hitting on bugs as a result. Using a stable release also ensures that a project development team and their customer can be sure that there is a baseline for testing code.

Using a CVS development snapshot or using the CVS file store directly amount to pretty much the same thing: You will be using code that could be anywhere in the development/test lifecycle, from just-written code to something that is ready for inclusion in a release. That clearly entails some risk because code may not work properly, need refinement, be removed, or change name or convention. The advantage is that you can get the latest updates and collaborate as part of the project through developing, refining, and testing code that becomes part of the core product. Using CVS is clearly the choice if you want to get involved in the project because it is the only way of ensuring that you have all the very latest code.

There is another choice, and that is to have a foot in both camps. You can use the latest release as the base installation for development but maintain a CVS source-code base as well. You can then include any parts of the latest code that you might require. Of course, this approach has some inherent risks and caveats, but it can be effective if managed carefully.

The files for the latest official release can be found in `http://xml.apache.org/dist/cocoon`. This folder contains both the absolute latest release and the most recent previous release in both binary and source formats. Each of these is compressed as either a Windows-compatible .zip file or a gzipped tar archive for Unix. The naming convention of these files is pretty obvious, with the Cocoon version number starting the filename. After that comes an indicator to show whether the distribution is a binary or source release. Naturally, use of `src` in the filename indicates that it is the Cocoon source, and `bin` indicates that the file is the binary distribution, containing the prebuilt `.WAR` (Web application archive) file for deployment straight into a servlet container.

One point to note here is that beginning with version 2.0.3, the binary distribution of Cocoon has been packaged for use with either JDK1.2/1.3 or JDK1.4 virtual machines. The reason for this is that there are differences in the way the different JDKs package components such as those for JDBC and XML parsing. If no JDK version is indicated in the binary download filename, the WAR was compiled for execution under a JDK1.2/1.3 virtual machine. Use of `vm14` shows that the binary needs to be executed under a JDK1.4 virtual machine.

The source distribution contains all the files required to build Cocoon from scratch. For the build, you can choose what exactly to build and whether to package it up into a WAR file. During development of an application, you are going to want to be able to quickly add files, and you do not want to have to package them into a WAR every time just to test them.

Although we won't cover the subject in more detail, the binary distribution contains the documentation and a WAR file. The WAR file can be deployed within a servlet container without further configuration. The binary distribution is there really for ease of deployment, and for developers the source distribution is a more effective choice.

Downloading the Cocoon 2.0.3 Release

Now that you know how Cocoon is distributed, let's get the source distribution and compile. You will find the source for 2.0.3 at `http://xml.apache.org/cocoon/dist/cocoon-2.0.3-src.tar.gz` or `http://xml.apache.org/cocoon/dist/cocoon-2.0.3-src.zip`. Download the appropriate archive and unpack it somewhere on your hard drive. That's it! Now you can skip down to the section on Compiling Cocoon.

Getting a CVS Release

If you are daring enough, or desperate for bleeding-edge features, you'll want to get the latest CVS release. CVS, which stands for Concurrent Versioning System, is the version control system of choice for open source projects. Besides knowing how to do the basic CVS commands, one important thing to know is that CVS is organized by branches, or revision tags. The branches represent different development efforts—there are usually one for the current release and one or more for future releases. Often, developers limit certain releases to a particular feature set, and then create new branches for more bleeding-edge code.

The revision tags that are available for Cocoon can be found by viewing the CVS repository online. Clicking on the Code Repository link from the main Cocoon project welcome page at `http://xml.apache.org/cocoon` will take you to the `xml-cocoon2` repository. From this page you will see a drop-down box that shows all the revision tags that are available, as illustrated in Figure 6.1.

The most relevant branches for Cocoon are `HEAD`, which represents the latest 2.1 development version, and `cocoon_2_0_3_branch`, which represents bug fixes and minor enhancements to the 2.0.3 release. It is possible that the `cocoon_2_0_3_branch` will eventually become the 2.0.4 release, but no release schedule has been posted at the time of writing.

Using CVS on the Command Line

If you are on Unix, or are running Cygnus Tools on Windows, follow these instructions.

First, change the directory to the place where you want to download and build Cocoon. Then you have to log in to the CVS repository:

```
cvs -d :pserver:anoncvs@cvs.apache.org:/home/cvspublic login
```

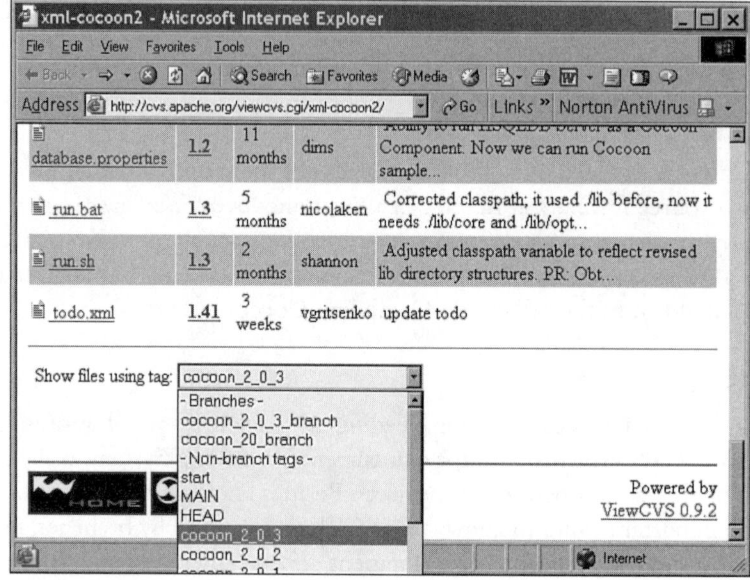

Figure 6.1

CVS revision tags in the online repository.

You will be prompted for a password, which is `anoncvs`.

Next, decide which branch to download. The default is the `HEAD` branch, or the 2.1 version. If that is what you want, just type this:

```
cvs -d :pserver:anoncvs@cvs.apache.org:/home/cvspublic checkout xml-cocoon2
```

If you prefer to get the `cocoon_2_0_3_branch` (or another named branch), type the following:

```
cvs -d :pserver:anoncvs@cvs.apache.org:/home/cvspublic checkout -r
➥ cocoon_2_0_3_branch xml-cocoon2
```

Any of these checkout commands will give you a directory called `xml-cocoon2` at the location from which you ran the checkout. Within this directory, you will find all the directories and files described in the next section. If you are ready, skip to that section and we'll discuss building Cocoon.

One thing you'll have to do, if you want to stay somewhat current, is to update your local CVS repository with the latest and greatest. This is fairly simple.

First, change the directory to the existing `xml-cocoon2` directory that contains the original checkout code. Next, log in as shown previously. Finally, issue an update command. To update a `HEAD` branch, just type this:

```
cvs -d :pserver:anoncvs@cvs.apache.org:/home/cvspublic update -d -P
```

To update a `cocoon_2_0_3_branch`, type the following:

```
cvs -d :pserver:anoncvs@cvs.apache.org:/home/cvspublic update
➥ -d -P -r cocoon_2_0_3_branch
```

Finally, whenever you are done with CVS, logout with this:

```
cvs -d :pserver:anoncvs@cvs.apache.org:/home/cvspublic logout
```

Using WinCVS

If you are on Windows, and would like a nice GUI interface to CVS, download WinCVS from `http://cvsgui.sourceforge.net/download.html`. Install and start it according to the directions.

First, you need to tell WinCVS what to connect to. Choose Admin->Preferences, and for the Enter the CVSROOT field, type this:

```
:pserver:anoncvs@cvs.apache.org:/home/cvspublic
```

In the Authentication section, choose Passwd File on the CVS Server. Then click OK to save the changes.

Now you can log in. Choose Admin->Login and, when prompted, type `anoncvs` for the password.

Next, choose Create->Checkout module. Enter the module name to checkout, `xml-cocoon2`, in the Checkout Settings tab. Then go to the Checkout Options tab, check the By Revision/Tag/Branch check box, and enter the identifier in the text box, as per the example shown in Figure 6.2.

For the latest 2.1 branch, enter `HEAD`. For the latest 2.0.3 branch (really 2.0.4), enter `cocoon_2_0_3_branch`.

Click OK, and WinCVS will begin the download. Wait until it is finished, and then go to the next section to learn about compiling Cocoon.

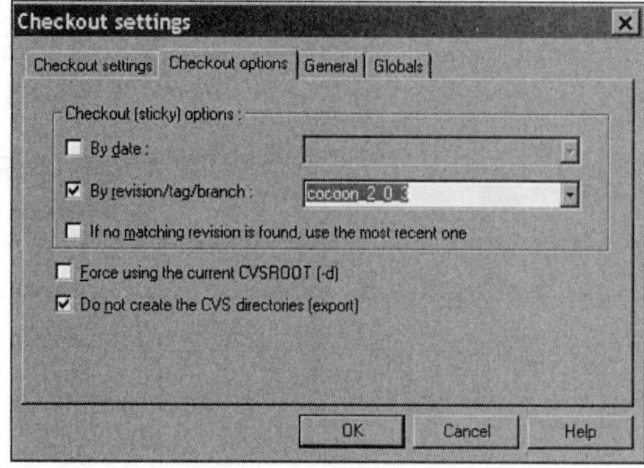

Figure 6.2
Selecting a tag identifier in WinCVS.

Building Cocoon

In this section, we'll cover building Cocoon. Although we will focus specifically on the latest release, 2.0.3, the instructions should apply to other releases, such as 2.1. If you have downloaded Cocoon from the CVS repository, you'll need to change directory to the `xml-cocoon2` directory.

The Cocoon Source Directory Structure

The Cocoon source directory structure is outlined in Table 6.1. From now on, we will refer to this folder as `$COCOON_SRC`.

Table 6.1 *Cocoon Source Directory Structure*

Folder	Description
(root level)	Among other things, the root level contains the build script and configuration file (`build.xml`).
`docs`	HTML documentation. This is precompiled from the XML-based source documents that can be found with the rest of the source. Not present in CVS versions.
`legal`	License files for all the libraries that Cocoon uses.
`lib`	Contains the jars used by Cocoon.
`lib/core`	Required Cocoon libraries (won't run without them).

Table 6.1 *(continued)*

Folder	Description
`lib/local`	Folder for any user-specific libraries. For example, you might put your database-specific Jar files here so that they can be built into the `webapp`.
`lib/optional`	Optional Cocoon libraries.
`src`	Complete source files for Cocoon.
`src/documentation`	Source files for the Cocoon documentation.
`src/java`	Java source files.
`src/resources`	Source graphics, including logos and "powered by" images.
`src/scratchpad`	Area used for new code and non-core examples.
`src/test`	Temporary source files (CVS source only).
`src/webapp`	Web application source files.
`tools`	Contains the Ant distribution and some supporting files.

When looking at the `documentation` folder, you will note that the bulk of the files are XML based and there are `sitemap.xmap` and `cocoon.xconf` files. This is because the documentation is rendered using Cocoon and forms an excellent example of how to configure a publishing mechanism using Cocoon.

The Cocoon Scratch Pad

The Cocoon scratch-pad area is an ever-changing store of work in progress that is likely to make it into the main build. Over time the scratch pad has been home to most of the code, and it is almost inevitable that you will want to look at what is going on in the scratch pad on a regular basis. Most, if not all, of the new Cocoon components such as generators and transformers will get peer reviewed and tested in the scratch pad before being rolled up to the main application on the next release. Major sample applications such as the SunSpot portal lived in the scratch pad while being honed and turned into code that was deemed stable enough to become part of the core distribution.

With Cocoon version 2.0.3 you can get all the scratch-pad files pulled into the WAR package by using the `installscratchpadwar` Ant build target. This build target asks for a destination folder for the final WAR but will always put a copy in the `build/cocoon` folder.

The Cocoon 2.0.3 scratch-pad contents have some extremely interesting components that will hopefully make it into version 2.1. Among them is XMLForms, an extension that seeks to make the creation of form-based Web applications more simple. Another interesting application is the sample <slash-edit/> XML editor that can be used to modify XML content. This illustrates the use of `SourceWritingTransformer` to write content.

Caution
Be very careful if you decide to deploy scratch-pad components in a production environment because the scratch-pad content is there precisely because it is liable to change and is effectively being debugged and reviewed. It is not uncommon for component names to change or even to disappear, so it is safest to treat the scratch pad as an area of interest but not as a source for production-quality, long-term components.

The Cocoon webapp Source Folder

The Cocoon `webapp` folder contains all the source files that can be accessed as samples and examples from your Web browser. This area is very rich in quality sample code that shows how to achieve many of the tasks you may want to perform in your own applications.

The `docs/samples` subfolder has many of the more programmatical examples, such as JSP handling, session state management, SOAP, SQL access, and XSP.

The `i18n` folder contains the code that supports the internationalization examples. As discussed elsewhere in the book, the `mount` folder is there so that new applications can be quickly and easily added. The `protected` folder contains resources that can be accessed only after an element of user authentication has taken place and that from the sample files for the relevant sample. A related folder of interest is the `sunspotdemo` application folder. This is a basic customizable portal that illustrates many aspects of Cocoon application development, including authentication, personalization, complex pipeline configuration, and more.

Another key folder in the core distribution is the `mount` folder. Any sub-sitemaps that are placed in a folder structure under this folder are automatically mounted by the root sitemap. If the scratch-pad examples are built, these are placed under the `mount` folder.

As far as Web application deployment goes, much of the most important information can be found under the `WEB-INF` folder. Directly in `WEB-INF` are `cocoon.xconf` and `web.xml`. Cocoon application configuration is achieved through changes to settings in `cocoon.xconf`, and the Web application operational parameters can be affected by editing settings inside `web.xml`. All the Cocoon library files (`.jar` files basically) are found in the `lib` folder. This `lib` folder in the build Cocoon Web application is a union of the core libraries, any optional libraries that are used, and the "local" libraries required by the specific application. Files that are not deployed in `.jar` library files can be placed in the `WEB-INF/classes` folder. There is also a folder called `db` that contains the sample database data relevant to the Cocoon tutorial and sample applications.

In a production environment you will also find that the `WEB-INF` folder contains a `logs` subfolder. This is where the Cocoon log files can be found.

The Cocoon Java Source Folder Hierarchy

The `src/java` folder within the top-level Cocoon source folder contains (unsurprisingly) the Java source code for Cocoon. It is very simply organized with everything sitting in the `org.apache.cocoon` package. Building the Cocoon javadocs is worthwhile if you want to understand the package hierarchy and gain some insight into the underlying code.

Under the `org/apache/cocoon` folder are the major subdivisions of components. Generators, transformers, matchers, sitemap management classes, and so on are all found in appropriately named packages off `org/apache/cocoon`. In many of the package folders you will also find interfaces, resolvers, and factory classes that form the basis of each Cocoon component.

The `servlet` folder contains the key `CocoonServlet` class that acts as the servlet interface into the Cocoon engine. The main engine entry point, found in the `Cocoon` class, sits in `org/apache/cocoon`.

As you look through the various folders under `org/apache/cocoon`, you will see some non-Java files, such as `cocoon.roles`, various `.xmap` files, and others. All of these files are used for the configuration of components both at compile and at runtime.

Compiling Cocoon

For building a distribution, Cocoon utilizes the Ant build tool. To make things really easy, the relevant Ant library is included with Cocoon.

> **Jakarta Ant**
> Ant is a flexible and powerful build utility that was developed as part of the Apache Jakarta project. If you ever suffered through makefiles or custom build scripts, chances are you will love Ant. I personally consider Ant one of the five best open source applications. You can read more about Ant at `http://jakarta.apache.org/ant/`.

Ant is invoked via the `build.bat` (`build.sh` on Unix) file, and it gets its build information from the `build.xml` file. Both of these files are in the root `$COCOON_SRC` folder.

Before you can do any building, you need to tell the build process where it can find Java. You do so by setting an environment variable called `JAVA_HOME` that points to the root folder of the Java Development Kit on your build machine. On Windows, at a command-line prompt you need to type

```
SET JAVA_HOME=<d>:\<path>
```

where

d is the drive letter of the drive where the JDK is, and

path is the folder path to the root folder of the JDK.

This would look something like the following:

```
SET JAVA_HOME=c:\java\jdk1.3
```

On Unix the command to enter is

```
JAVA_HOME=/<path>
```

where

path is the path to the root directory of the JDK.

Setting JAVA_HOME Permanently

It is, of course, easier if JAVA_HOME is set permanently, because you need it set not only for the Cocoon build, but for the running of your servlet engine as well. On Unix, JAVA_HOME is typically set in /etc/profile or user .profiles. On Windows 2000/XP/NT, you can set JAVA_HOME under Control Panel, System, Advanced, Environment Variables. On Windows 95/98/ME, you can set JAVA_HOME in c:\autoexec.bat.

After the JAVA_HOME environment variable has been configured, you are ready to do a build. For the basic build, make sure you are in the $COCOON_SRC top-level folder and then enter the following:

On Windows:

```
.\build.bat -Dinclude.webapp.libs=yes webapp
```

On Unix:

```
./build.sh -Dinclude.webapp.libs=yes webapp
```

The build process then kicks off and will go about compiling, copying, and configuring Cocoon. In just a few minutes (unless you are on a 386!) you will find a new folder called build/cocoon (which we will refer to as $COCOON_BUILD) under the $COCOON_SRC folder, which contains a number of subfolders. In $COCOON_BUILD itself, you will see the cocoon.war file. This is the packaged application ready for simple deployment onto Tomcat or whatever servlet engine you are using. You will also see a webapp folder. This contains the Web application before it is packaged in the WAR.

Building CVS Versions

Because Cocoon versions pulled straight from CVS will change from day to day, you are not guaranteed a perfect build. If you run into problems, you have three choices: (1) post the problem on the mailing list and hope someone has figured it out already; (2) find and fix the problem yourself; (3) wait a day or two or switch back to a release version.

The build process can be told to build a couple of other useful things as well. Table 6.2 details some other build targets that can be specified in the format `.\build.bat target` (`./build.sh target` on Unix); just replace *`target`* with the text in the Target column of the table.

Table 6.2 *Build Targets*

Target	Description
`docs`	HTML versions of the documentation. Normally these are held in XML files that conform to the Docbook DTD and served dynamically, but generating them in HTML format can be useful for static delivery.
`javadocs`	An absolute must for developers, this will generate the Javadoc documentation for all the classes in Cocoon.
`printer-docs`	Printer-friendly HTML versions of the documentation.

Installing Tomcat 4.0.5

In case you don't already have Tomcat 4.0.5, you can find binary distributions for most platforms at `http://jakarta.apache.org/builds/jakarta-tomcat-4.0/archives/v4.0.5/bin/`. We won't cover the installation of Tomcat here, but you can find everything you need to know at `http://jakarta.apache.org/tomcat/tomcat-4.0-doc/RUNNING.txt`. We will refer to the directory of your Tomcat installation as `$CATALINA_HOME` (or `%CATALINA_HOME%` for Windows).

Cocoon and Other Versions of Tomcat

Cocoon will of course run on the other versions of Tomcat, from 3.2 to the current 4.0.5 and 4.1.12. Some of these versions, however, have particular issues that affect the Cocoon installation. We picked Tomcat 4.0.5 because you can just drop in `cocoon.war`, restart Tomcat, and be off and running. For full details on the various other Tomcat versions, consult `http://xml.apache.org/cocoon/installing/index.html`.

Installing cocoon.war in Tomcat

The simplest way to install Cocoon in Tomcat is to take the `cocoon.war` file and copy it into `$CATALINA_HOME/webapps` (Unix) or `%CATALINA_HOME%\webapps` (Windows). Obviously, unless you defined `$CATALINA_HOME`, replace it with the actual location of Tomcat on your machine. And that's it! Either start Tomcat, if it's not running, or stop and restart it. Tomcat will automatically deploy `cocoon.war`. After Tomcat has started, you will find a `cocoon` directory under the `webapps` directory.

Testing the Installation

You can test your Cocoon installation by entering the following into a browser:

```
http://localhost:8080/cocoon
```

Clearly, if your servlet container is running on a different port, you need to change "`8080`" to whatever port is relevant.

If Cocoon is working properly, you should see a screen similar to the one shown in Figure 6.3.

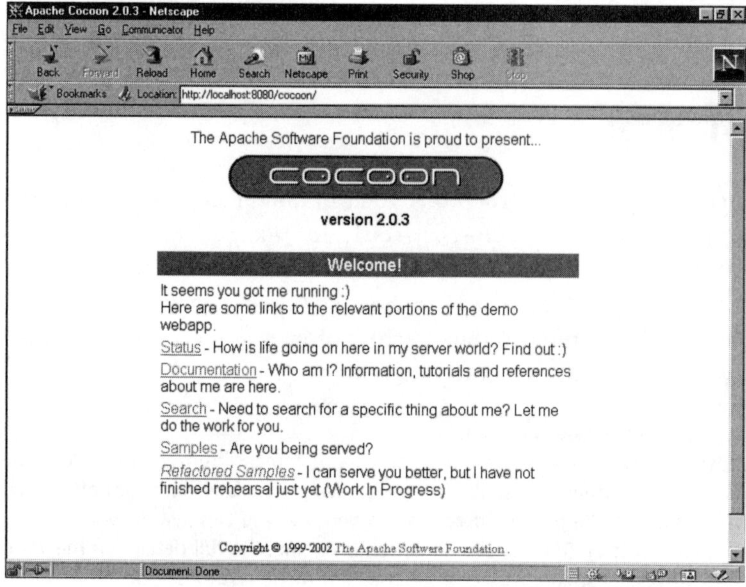

Figure 6.3
The Cocoon welcome page.

Cocoon Samples

If you are interested in browsing through the built-in samples, click on the Samples link in the welcome page and you'll be taken to `http://localhost:8080/cocoon/welcome`, which is shown in Figure 6.4.

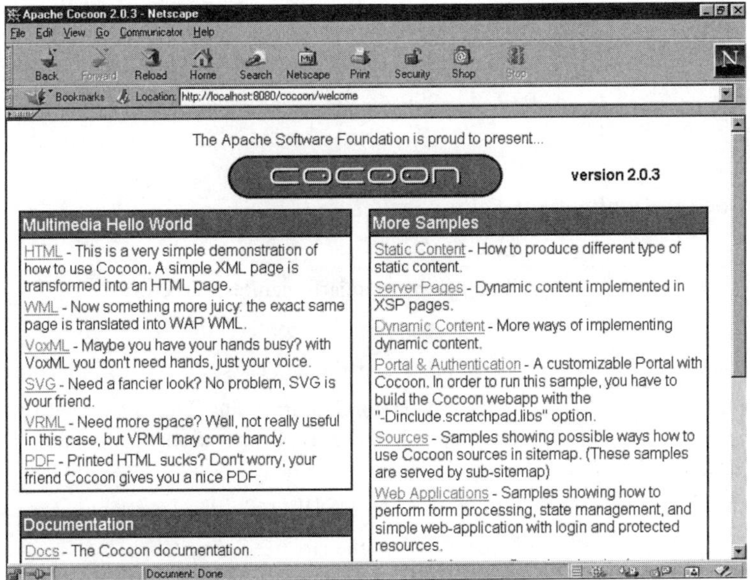

Figure 6.4
The Cocoon samples page.

This page has several sections of interesting samples.

The first section contains multiple views of a "Hello!" page. HTML, WML, VoxML, SVG, VRML, and PDF versions of the same data are all there and clearly show how multiple delivery channels can be configured.

The documentation section offers links to the documentation and supporting introductory information.

The system section demonstrates some HTTP request and environment handling.

The samples section has some additional and more complex samples covering static and dynamic content generation, XSP generation, and a very basic Web application that highlights action handling and database interaction.

One way of really learning to understand how these many samples work is to study the source files and the sitemaps that are used to generate them. The sitemap is perhaps the place to start because it will help point you to the actual source files that are used. The sitemap can be examined at `$CATALINA_HOME/webapps/cocoon/sitemap.xmap`. Some of the samples utilize sub-sitemaps, and you can view these in the folders under `$CATALINA_HOME/webapps/cocoon`.

Cocoon Directory Structure

Let's quickly look at the directory structure of the expanded Cocoon `webapp` that is now located at `$CATALINA_HOME/webapps/cocoon`. Table 6.3 lists the main directories and files you should be aware of.

Table 6.3 *Cocoon Deployment Folder Structure*

Folder	Description
`META-INF`	The jar/war-standard manifest directory.
`WEB-INF`	The Web application configuration directory.
`WEB-INF/classes`	Location of user-defined classes that are not included in any jars.
`WEB-INF/cocoon.xconf`	The Cocoon configuration file. This file is processed once, at startup. It defines various operational parameters as well as the logicsheets.
`WEB-INF/db`	Location of the HSQLD files used for some of the samples.
`WEB-INF/lib`	Location of all the jars needed by Cocoon.
`WEB-INF/logkit.xconf`	Configuration file for the Avalon logging functions that Cocoon utilizes.
`WEB-INF/logs`	Location of Cocoon log files.
`WEB-INF/web.xml`	Web application definition file. Here is where the Cocoon servlet is defined, along with various startup parameters.
`cocoon.xconf.moved`	Old location of `cocoon.xconf`. Prior to Cocoon 2.0.3, it lived here. You can delete this file.
`docs`	Part of the samples.
`documentation`	
`logicsheets`	Part of the samples.
`mount`	Part of the samples.
`protected`	Part of the samples.
`resources`	Part of the samples.
`samples`	Part of the samples.
`search`	Part of the samples.
`sitemap.xmap`	File defining Cocoon components and pipelines.

Table 6.3 *(continued)*

Folder	Description
`stylesheets`	Part of the samples.
`sub`	Part of the samples.
`sunspotdemo`	Part of the samples.
`templates`	Part of the samples.
`tutorial`	Part of the samples.
`welcome`	Part of the samples.

Understanding the Sitemap Engine

One important thing to mention here is that Cocoon has two sitemap engines: a compiled version and an interpreted version. Both are defined in the Cocoon configuration file, `cocoon.xconf`. This file is located in the `$CATALINA_HOME/webapps/cocoon/WEB-INF` directory. The compiled version, the default, operates by taking the sitemap, compiling it into an object and executing it. To handle changes, Cocoon can monitor sitemaps and reload them when they have changed. When it goes to reload a sitemap, it can do so either synchronously or asynchronously. Synchronous reloads take place as explained here:

1. A request is received by Cocoon.
2. Cocoon detects that the sitemap has changed since the last request, and starts a task to recompile the sitemap.
3. The request must now wait until this task completes.
4. When the sitemap has been recompiled, the request is then processed and the results are returned to the client.

Asynchronous reloads have a slightly different process flow:

1. A request is received by Cocoon.
2. Cocoon detects that the sitemap has changed since the last request and starts a background task to recompile the sitemap.
3. The request is processed using the old sitemap, and the results are returned to the client.
4. New requests continue to be processed by the old sitemap until the recompilation is complete, at which point the new sitemap is used.

The difference between synchronous and asynchronous reloading is important when you're developing. In general, you want to make sure that Cocoon utilizes synchronous reloading. Otherwise, you might make changes to the sitemap and not see them reflected immediately. Depending on the size of your sitemap or the speed of your processor, this can be several minutes. However, you should also be aware that with synchronous reloading you might get a Cocoon error page while the sitemap is being recompiled, instead of your browser simply hanging until the recompilation is complete. For a beginner, this can be rather unnerving! It can also be confusing, because it is not easy to tell whether the error occurs because the recompilation is still going on or because you have some error in your pipeline or data file.

Both the flag that tells Cocoon to check for sitemap changes and the reload method can be found in the `<sitemap>` tag in `cocoon.xconf`. By default, the `check-reload` parameter is set to `yes` and the `reload-method` is set to `synchron`. This will be what you want for development. However, if you are using an older distribution, you might have to edit `cocoon.xconf` to get the settings you want.

The interpreted sitemap is faster than the compiled engine, because it does not bother with compiling and executing a sitemap object. By default, it is commented out (you can have only one at a time). If you want, you can uncomment it, and comment the compiled version. Problem is, there is a bug with Cocoon 2.0.3 in which sub-sitemaps do not inherit component definitions from the parent sitemap. This will be a problem for us, because we will be building projects with sub-sitemaps in this book. This bug is fixed in the 2.0.4 development version, also known as the `cocoon_2_0_3_branch` in CVS.

If you want to use the interpreted engine, you'll have to build Cocoon from the `cocoon_2_0_3_branch` in the CVS repository. Alternatively, you can do this. Download the Cocoon 2.0.3 source release and the `cocoon_2_0_3_branch` from CVS. Then, copy the file `xml-cocoon2/src/java/org/apache/cocoon/components/ExtendedComponentSelector.java` from the CVS source to the release source tree. Then build Cocoon from the release directory as described previously. Alternatively, you can edit the file `src/java/org/apache/cocoon/components/ExtendedComponentSelector.java` and add the following method at the end of the file, before the last closing brace:

```
public boolean hasComponent(Object hint) {
    boolean exists = super.hasComponent( hint );
    if ( !exists && this.parentSelector != null ) {
        exists = this.parentSelector.hasComponent( hint );
    }
    return exists;
}
```

Summary

In this chapter, we've covered various ways of downloading Cocoon. The fastest way to get started is actually with a binary distribution, but as we've seen, building Cocoon is simplicity itself. Having built and installed Cocoon, we are now ready to work on our own application. In the next eight chapters, we'll implement the functionality we designed in Chapter 5, "Designing the Sample Application," and start to see the power of Cocoon.

CHAPTER 7
Creating Static Pages

We are finally ready to begin our Cocoon development project. In this chapter, we will start by setting up our project and creating a static page that can be displayed in a few different formats. We'll write our first pipelines and get a taste of how easy it is to use Cocoon.

First, let's just review where we stand with our Cocoon installation:

- We have Tomcat installed on our machine. The place where Tomcat is installed is known as `$CATALINA_HOME` (Unix) or `%CATALINA_HOME%` (Windows).
- The directory where the Cocoon Web application resides is `$CATALINA_HOME/webapps`.
- We have built Cocoon 2.0.3, installed the `cocoon.war` file in `$CATALINA_HOME/webapps`, and started or restarted Tomcat. The Cocoon Web application is located in `$CATALINA_HOME/webapps/cocoon`.
- Tomcat is currently running on port 8080. All our URLs will therefore start with `http://localhost:8080`. Because we installed our Cocoon Web application in the default `$CATALINA_HOME/webapps/cocoon`, that gives us a URI base of `http://localhost:8080/webapps/cocoon`. If you edited `$CATALINA_HOME/conf/server.xml` and changed

either the server name (the default is `localhost`) or the port (the default is `8080`), you will have to translate our URLs to what is appropriate for your installation.

As mentioned in Chapter 6, "Installing Cocoon," you are free to name your Cocoon webapp anything you want. However, for this book we will be following the default name of `cocoon`.

Building a Subproject

To start with, we have to create a subproject for our sample application. It is an extremely sound principle of developing with Cocoon to mount your projects as subprojects off the main sitemap. What this means is that each project or application you develop will live in its own directory under the main Cocoon webapp and will have its own sitemap, called a sub-sitemap (first mentioned in Chapter 4, "Introduction to the Sitemap"). A sub-sitemap does not have to define any of the components that the top-level sitemap defines. All it needs to contain is project-level components and pipelines, along with reference to top-level components. This tremendously facilitates the process of administering Cocoon projects, because you end up with a series of small sitemaps instead of one huge one (like the sitemap that comes with Cocoon, for example). We will cover this point more in Chapter 15, "Extending Cocoon Components."

Nesting Sitemaps
We've covered this topic before, but it is worth repeating. You can nest sitemaps as much as you want to. What we call the "top-level" sitemap is simply the one at the root of the application. Whatever components are defined here can be utilized by sitemaps lower in the hierarchy without their needing to be redefined.

Creating the Project Directory

First, let's create our project directory. We'll call it simply `abc`, in honor of our fictitious client. Simply change directories to `$CATALINA_HOME/webapps/cocoon` and create a directory called `abc`. We'll also create some subdirectories to contain our content, logic, and stylesheets. This is not a required layout, but it is a good one to consider when developing with Cocoon. We will deal with this subject more thoroughly in Chapter 15. Here's what to do:

On Unix:

```
cd $CATALINA_HOME/webapps/cocoon
mkdir abc
mkdir abc/content
mkdir abc/images
mkdir abc/style
```

```
mkdir abc/logic
mkdir abc/xsp
```

On Windows:

```
cd %CATALINA_HOME%\webapps\cocoon
mkdir abc
mkdir abc\content
mkdir abc\images
mkdir abc\logic
mkdir abc\style
mkdir abc\xsp
```

Directory Structures
There is no rule for how you create deployment directories in Cocoon. You can put everything in the project directory, if you want to. However, for the sake of maintenance it is a good idea to separate logic, content, and style in some way, as we've done here.

Creating a Sub-sitemap

A sub-sitemap generally lives at the root of the project directory. At its minimum, a sub-sitemap only needs to reference the top-level components and define project-specific pipelines, or processing paths.

We will start with a super-simple sitemap. In the `abc` directory, create a file called `sitemap.xmap` with your favorite editor. As you type, remember that the sitemap is an XML file, so you must pay attention to opening and closing tags, quotes, and all the other little syntactical elements you would with a regular XML file.

Listing 7.1 shows what should be in your `sitemap.xmap`.

Listing 7.1 *Basic Sub-sitemap (sitemap.xmap—Version 1)*

```
<?xml version="1.0"?>

<map:sitemap xmlns:map="http://apache.org/cocoon/sitemap/1.0">

 <map:components>
  <map:generators default="file"/>
  <map:transformers default="xslt"/>
  <map:readers default="resource"/>
  <map:serializers default="html"/>
  <map:selectors default="browser"/>
```

Listing 7.1 *(continued)*

```
  <map:matchers default="wildcard"/>
 </map:components>

 <map:pipelines>
  <map:pipeline>
  </map:pipeline>
 </map:pipelines>
</map:sitemap>
```

Let's analyze this a bit. The first line is simply the traditional XML header tag. The rest of the lines are Cocoon-specific tags belonging to the `map` namespace, as indicated in the second line. The lines between `<map:components>` and `</map:components>` provide a reference to the components in the top-level sitemap. All we are doing here is indicating what our default is for each type of component, as you learned in Chapter 4. A default means that if we use a component without specifying its `type` attribute, the defined default type will be applied. For example, according to this sitemap, our default serializer is `html`. This means that whenever we want to use the `html` serializer, we can omit the `type` attribute. Although this is permissible, *it is highly recommended* that you always define component types for the sake of readability and maintainability. Just think what will happen if you always rely on the defaults but one day forget and change the `default` attribute for one of the components—oops!

The processing paths of our applications are defined in the block delimited by `<map:pipelines>` and `</map:pipelines>`. At a minimum, this block will contain a single `<map:pipeline>` block. There are reasons we would want to have multiple `<map:pipeline>` blocks, but we will cover this later, in Chapter 9, "Using Content Logic: Generators."

As it stands, this sitemap does nothing, because no pipelines are actually defined. We will start adding pipelines in the next section, but first we must tell the main sitemap about this one.

Mounting the abc Sub-sitemap

To tell the main sitemap about our new sitemap, we have to add a pipeline to the former so that any URI patterns for our Web application will be directed to our sitemap.

In the `<map:pipelines>` section of the main sitemap, we insert the following:

```
<map:pipeline>
  <map:match pattern="abc/**">
    <map:mount uri-prefix="abc" src="abc/sitemap.xmap" check-reload="yes"
➥reload-method="synchron"/>
  </map:match>
</map:pipeline>
```

Because this is the first time we've actually seen a working pipeline, let's look at it closely. Any pipeline starts by defining what URIs it should handle. We use a `Matcher` for this purpose. In this case, this `Matcher` is looking for any URI that starts with `abc/`, regardless of what follows. (We'll discuss `Matchers` in more detail in Chapter 11, "Using Sitemap Logic: `Matchers` and `Selectors`.") If such a URI is encountered, Cocoon is directed by the `<map:mount>` tag to pass the URI to the `sitemap.xmap` in the `abc` directory for processing. The `<map:mount>` tag has several attributes, as shown in Table 7.1.

Table 7.1 *<map:mount> Attributes*

Attribute	Description	Required
`uri-prefix`	This tells Cocoon what uri-prefix is handled by the sub-sitemap. In general, though not required, the uri-prefix is the same as the `Matcher` pattern (minus the wildcard characters) and the same as the directory name.	yes
`src`	The parameter for this attribute indicates where the sub-sitemap is. In this example, we provide the file location relative to the current location (`$CATALINA_HOME/webapps/cocoon`). However, it is also acceptable to provide just the directory name, assuming that there is a file called `sitemap.xmap` inside.	yes
`check-reload`	Same as the parameter in `cocoon.xconf`. `check-reload` tells Cocoon to check on each matching URI to see whether the sub-sitemap has changed since the last time it was used. If so, the sub-sitemap will be recompiled. You generally set this attribute to no (the default) for production, to save time. Otherwise, leave it as yes.	no
`reload-method`	Defines the reload method—either `asynchron` (default) or `synchron`.	no

Automated Sitemaps

There is a special convention for specifying auto-mounted sitemaps. This means that you can create a project directory in the auto-mount area and put a sitemap in it, and it is immediately available to Cocoon. The default Cocoon webapp has such an area defined: the `mount` directory off the main webapp directory. Take a look at the main sitemap to see how the `<map:mount>` tag is defined for this example. What you'll see is a pipeline like this:

```
<map:pipeline>
  <map:match pattern="mount/*/**">
    <map:mount check-reload="yes" src="mount/{1}/" uri-prefix="mount/{1}"/>
  </map:match>
</map:pipeline>
```

The key to this pipeline is the `*/**` in the `<map:match>` tag. We'll discuss how these wildcard characters work in Chapter 11. For now, however, just know that if we put our `abc` directory under the `mount` directory, it would be automatically mounted by Cocoon, and we would not have to go through the steps in the earlier section. We won't be taking advantage of this feature with our project, however, but we will for other samples later in the book.

Creating Our First File

It is now time to start coding. You'll remember from our sample specification that we had a requirement to transform XML files to a format that various types of browser clients could understand. For starters, we'll work on getting our XML data converted to HTML for traditional browsers. Then we'll look at other formats. The process of this conversion is called transformation, and the particular type of transformation we'll be using here is XSLT, or XSL Transformation.

Creating the XML File

To see this transformation in action, we first need an XML file, which we will call `main.xml`, and which will live in the `abc/content` directory. This file, which you'll find in Listing 7.2, will contain a simple message, welcoming the user to ABC Software.

Listing 7.2 *Simple XML page (main.xml)*

```
<?xml version="1.0"?>

<page>
 <title>Welcome to ABC Software</title>
 <content>
  <paragraph>
   Welcome to the ABC Software support website. On this site, you will be able
to submit support requests, track open requests and view your support contract
bills.
  </paragraph>
 </content>
</page>
```

Creating the XSL File

There is nothing remarkable about our XML file. We just made up some tags to encapsulate a title and a couple of welcome sentences. But for this data to be useful, we need an XML stylesheet, or XSL file, that tells Cocoon how to transform it into HTML. We'll call this file `main.xsl`, and put it in the `style` directory. It is shown in Listing 7.3.

Listing 7.3 *HTML Stylesheet (main.xsl)*

```
<?xml version="1.0"?>

<xsl:stylesheet version="1.0" xmlns:xsl="http://www.w3.org/1999/XSL/Transform">

  <xsl:param name="view-source"/>

  <xsl:template match="page">
   <html>
    <head>
     <title>
      <xsl:value-of select="title"/>
     </title>
    </head>
    <body bgcolor="white" alink="red" link="blue" vlink="blue">
     <xsl:apply-templates/>
    </body>
   </html>
  </xsl:template>

  <xsl:template match="title">
   <h2 style="color: navy; text-align: center">
         <xsl:apply-templates/>
   </h2>
  </xsl:template>

  <xsl:template match="paragraph">
   <p align="left">
    <xsl:apply-templates/>
   </p>
  </xsl:template>


</xsl:stylesheet>
```

We will assume that you have some knowledge of XSL, in order to understand this. Essentially, an XSL file defines processing sets or templates that match particular source tags. You'll see in our file that we match several tags that were in `main.xml`: `<page>`, `<title>`, and `<paragraph>`. The processing instructions that follow each match tell Cocoon what HTML data to output. For example, when the XSLT processor encounters a `<paragraph>` tag in our input file, it will output the standard `<p>` tag, followed by the content of the `<paragraph>` source tag.

If you've been following along with our examples, you should have the following files in the `abc` directory:

```
abc/sitemap.xmap
abc/content/main.xml
abc/style/main.xsl
```

Adding a Pipeline

Now we need to tell Cocoon how to recognize our brand-new files. We do so by editing our sitemap and adding our first pipeline. It looks like this:

```
<map:pipeline>
 <map:match pattern="index.html">
  <map:generate type="file" src="content/main.xml"/>
  <map:transform type="xslt" src="style/main.xsl"/>
  <map:serialize type="html"/>
 </map:match>
</map:pipeline>
```

Note that you should replace the empty `<map:pipeline>/</map:pipeline>` pair in your original sitemap with this entry.

Let's examine this for a moment. The start of the pipeline is the `Matcher`. In this case, the `Matcher` is looking for the pattern `index.html`. If the `Matcher` encounters a URI with this pattern, it hands the URI over to the pipeline for processing. The pipeline itself has three steps. First, it reads our `main.xml` file using a `FileGenerator`. This component turns the XML data from the file into SAX events. Then, the SAX events are sent to a `TraxTransformer` for processing. The `TraxTransformer` will convert the SAX events to HTML using the XSL file we created, `main.xsl`. Finally, the HTML data will be sent to the browser using an `HTMLSerializer`.

It can be confusing to think that the `TraxTransformer` is doing conversion to HTML, while the `HTMLSerializer` is responsible for writing the data to the client. Remember that a pipeline is nothing more than a series of components that deal with SAX events. The SAX events that represent the input data are transformed by the `TraxTransformer` into output SAX events based on the rules defined in the XSL file—in this case, rules that result in HTML. These output events still constitute XML data, although now they are actually well-formed HTML. What the `HTMLSerializer` does is to write the HTML SAX events out to the socket that the browser is reading from. In the process, this serializer adds the correct mime-type so that the browser knows what to do with the data.

One important thing to note is that there is no inherent correlation between filenames and URI patterns. In Cocoon, you can map any kind of URI pattern to particular files because the `Matchers` are based on what you define in the sitemap, rather than filenames. We can name our file `stupid.xml` but still map it to the URI pattern of `index.html`, and the users will never know. This feature of Cocoon is another example of the split between logic, content, and style. In a large project, various people can create the XML and XSL files for the application according to whatever conventions they follow, and the project integrator will put it all together as a coherent whole using the sitemap as the "glue" for everything. We'll see this in action as we develop our application further.

More About Matchers
In this and the following chapters, we'll create a literal `Matcher` for each example. You might get the impression that any Web page you want to define must have its own pipeline. That is not the case! It is much more convenient to use wildcard characters and group pipelines by their processing flow or stylesheet. However, we are going to leave this subject for Chapter 11, so read on!

The pipeline components `map:generate` and `map:transform` share a common set of attributes, shown in Table 7.2. Table 7.3 shows the attributes of `map:serialize`.

Table 7.2 *<map:generate> <map:transform> Attributes*

Attribute	Description	Required
`type`	Defines what type of component to use. Defaults to whatever is set to default in the `map:components` section of the sitemap.	no
`src`	Defines the path for the data or XSL file.	yes
`label`	Optional handle so that we can access this component from a view.	no

Table 7.3 *<map:serialize> Attributes*

Attribute	Description	Required
`type`	Defines what type of component to use. Defaults to whatever is set to default in the `map:components` section of the sitemap.	no
`mime-type`	Defines the mime-type to be sent back to the client. Defaults to the mime-type defined for the `type`.	no
`status-code`	The status code to be returned to the clients. Useful for handling errors.	no

Viewing Our First File

If you have been following along, you should be able to view this file by pointing your browser to `http://localhost:8080/abc/cocoon/index.html`. Hopefully, you will get something like what's shown in Figure 7.1.

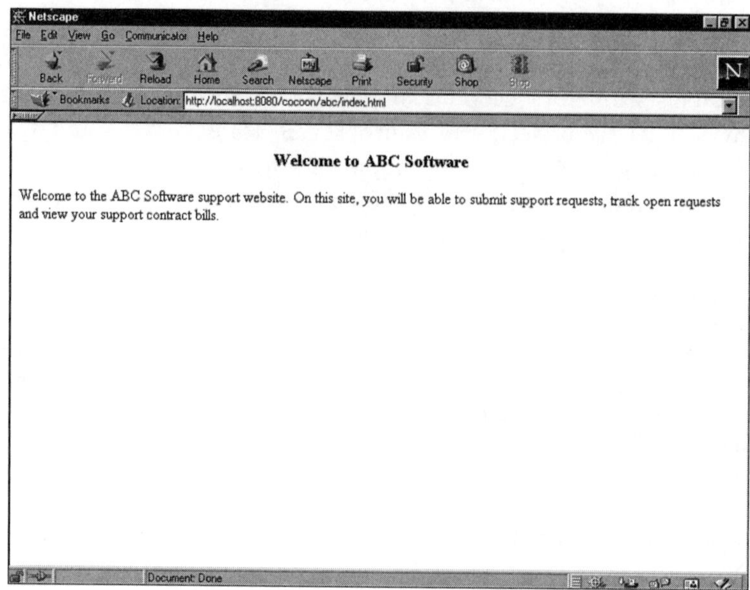

Figure 7.1
Welcome to ABC Software.

If you don't see this page as expected, double-check `main.xml`, `main.xsl`, and `sitemap.xmap`. If these are all correct, try reloading the page in your browser. The first time, you might have caught Cocoon in the middle of recompiling the sitemap.

Now that we have generated our first HTML page, let's take the same data and view it in WML, for our WAP-enabled phone, and PDF. To do this, we will need to create new XSL files and new pipeline entries.

Creating a WML Page

Wireless Markup Language (WML) is an XML-based meta language that is used for WAP-compliant devices, typically mobile phones, PDAs, and so on. Although similar to HTML, WML differs in that instead of being based on pages, it has a *deck* of *cards*. A WAP device can display only one card at a time, but by placing each card in a deck, the device can preload several cards and avoid latency problems that would be there if each card were loaded on demand. A final point is that because WML is XML based, it must be as well formed as any other XML document.

To see our index page in WML, we can keep the same source XML file, replace the transforming stylesheet with one that creates WML, and use a WML serializer.

Writing the XSL

First, we'll create a new XSL file that contains the rules to transform the `main.xml` file into WML. In the `abc/style` directory, we'll create `main-wml.xsl` as shown in Listing 7.4.

Listing 7.4 *WML Stylesheet (main-wml.xsl)*

```
<?xml version="1.0"?>

<xsl:stylesheet version="1.0" xmlns:xsl="http://www.w3.org/1999/XSL/Transform">

 <xsl:template match="/page">
  <wml>
   <card id="index">
    <xsl:attribute name="title">
     <xsl:value-of select="title"/>
    </xsl:attribute>
    <xsl:apply-templates/>
   </card>
  </wml>
 </xsl:template>

 <xsl:template match="page-title">
   <p><big>
     <xsl:apply-templates/>
   </big></p>
 </xsl:template>

 <xsl:template match="title">
 </xsl:template>

 <xsl:template match="paragraph">
   <p>
     <xsl:apply-templates/>
   </p>
 </xsl:template>

</xsl:stylesheet>
```

This is an extremely simplistic XSL file. All we are essentially doing is capturing any <paragraph> tags from our source file and displaying them in a single card on our WAP phone.

Adding a Pipeline Entry

We must now tell Cocoon how to handle the WML page. We do this by adding the following after the existing <map:match>/</map:match> pair:

```
<map:match pattern="index.wml">
 <map:generate type="file" src="content/main.xml"/>
 <map:transform type="xslt" src="style/main-wml.xsl"/>
 <map:serialize type="wml"/>
</map:match>
```

This pipeline looks very much like our first. The two main differences are that we are using a different XSL file and we are using a different serializer. In this case, although the type attribute is set to wml, we are actually using the XMLSerializer. If you look at the serializer definitions in the main sitemap ($CATALINA_HOME/webapps/cocoon/ sitemap.xmap), you will see that the <map:serializer> entry that has the name attribute of wml is using the XMLSerializer object along with a defined mime-type of text/vnd.wap.wml. This is because WAP-enabled devices actually speak XML but must have the correct mime-type so that they can recognize the WML tags.

Just to make sure that your sitemap looks like ours, Listing 7.5 shows what it should look like.

Listing 7.5 *Basic Sub-sitemap (sitemap.xmap—Version 2)*

```
<?xml version="1.0"?>

<map:sitemap xmlns:map="http://apache.org/cocoon/sitemap/1.0">

 <map:components>
  <map:generators default="file"/>
  <map:transformers default="xslt"/>
  <map:readers default="resource"/>
  <map:serializers default="html"/>
  <map:selectors default="browser"/>
  <map:matchers default="wildcard"/>
 </map:components>
```

Listing 7.5 (continued)

```
 <map:pipelines>
  <map:pipeline>
   <map:match pattern="index.html">
    <map:generate type="file" src="content/main.xml"/>
    <map:transform type="xslt" src="style/main.xsl"/>
    <map:serialize type="html"/>
   </map:match>

   <map:match pattern="index.wml">
    <map:generate type="file" src="content/main.xml"/>
    <map:transform type="xslt" src="style/main-wml.xsl"/>
    <map:serialize type="wml"/>
   </map:match>
  </map:pipeline>
 </map:pipelines>
</map:sitemap>
```

Testing the WML Example

To test this example, you will need access to a WML browser. Various mobile device development kits from the major mobile telephone manufacturers contain device emulators, or you could use Web-based ones, such as Yahoo!, if your Web server faces the public Internet. The quickest solution, however, is to use a tool such as WinWap (`http://www.winwap.org`). It is possible to download this tool and use it on a trial basis; however, please be sure to register the product for use beyond the trial period.

> **Other WML Browsers**
> My favorite WML-capable browser is the OpenWave SDK, available at `http://www.openwave.com`. Users of the Opera browser will also be able to view WML files natively. Opera is available at `http://www.opera.com`.

After you have your browser up, type `http://localhost:8080/cocoon/abc/index.wml` into the location bar. You should see something like that shown in Figure 7.2.

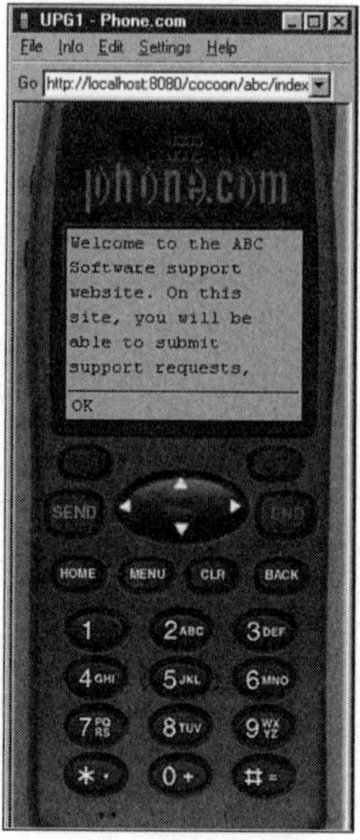

Figure 7.2
Welcome to ABC Software – WML Version.

Creating a PDF Page

Portable Document Format is the file format used by Adobe Acrobat documents. It is, as its name suggests, highly portable and is often used to present electronic documentation that is likely to be printed.

Cocoon is able to produce PDF documents from XML because part of the XSL specification includes a section covering *Formatting Objects*, more commonly known as XSL:FO. This defines elements that control presentation. The nice people at Apache have developed a practical tool that takes XSL:FO-compliant stylesheets to drive the production of files that are compatible with binary formats, including as PDF. This is known as the Formatting Objects Processor, or FOP.

> **Note**
> You can find out more about the XSL:FO specification at the W3C site under `http://www.w3.org/TR/2001/REC-xsl-20011015`. FOP is available as part of the Apache XML project and can be found at `http://xml.apache.org/fop`. The FOP libraries are included as part of the Cocoon distribution, so you don't have to do anything else to be able to use FOP. Another excellent resource in learning about FO is Chapter 18 of Elliotte Rusty Harold's *XML Bible*, which can be found online at `http://www.ibiblio.org/xml/books/bible2/chapters/ch18.html`.

Using FOP, you can build a stylesheet that transforms the source content into a set of XSL:FO elements that are then serialized into the required binary file format.

Writing the XSL

Our new XSL file will contain the rules to transform the `main.xml` file into PDF. In the `abc/style` directory, create a file called `main-pdf.xsl` that contains what's shown in Listing 7.6.

Listing 7.6 *PDF Stylesheet (main-pdf.xsl)*

```
<?xml version="1.0"?>
<xsl:stylesheet version="1.0"
  xmlns:xsl="http://www.w3.org/1999/XSL/Transform"
  xmlns:fo="http://www.w3.org/1999/XSL/Format"
>
  <xsl:template match="page">
    <fo:root xmlns:fo="http://www.w3.org/1999/XSL/Format">
      <fo:layout-master-set>
        <fo:simple-page-master master-name="page"
            page-height="29.7cm" page-width="21cm"
            margin-top="1cm" margin-bottom="2cm"
            margin-left="2.5cm" margin-right="2.5cm">
          <fo:region-before extent="3cm" />

          <fo:region-body margin-top="3cm" />

          <fo:region-after extent="1.5cm" />
        </fo:simple-page-master>

        <fo:page-sequence-master master-name="all">
          <fo:repeatable-page-master-alternatives>
            <fo:conditional-page-master-reference
                master-reference="page"
                page-position="first" />
          </fo:repeatable-page-master-alternatives>
        </fo:page-sequence-master>
      </fo:layout-master-set>

      <fo:page-sequence master-reference="all">
        <fo:static-content flow-name="xsl-region-after">
          <fo:block text-align="center"
              font-size="10pt" font-family="Courier"
```

Listing 7.6 *(continued)*

```
            line-height="14pt">Page
          <fo:page-number />
          </fo:block>
        </fo:static-content>

        <fo:flow flow-name="xsl-region-body">
          <xsl:apply-templates />
        </fo:flow>
      </fo:page-sequence>
    </fo:root>
  </xsl:template>

  <xsl:template match="title">
    <fo:block font-size="36pt" font-family="Helvetica" space-before.optimum=
      "24pt" text-align="center">
      <xsl:apply-templates />
    </fo:block>
  </xsl:template>

  <xsl:template match="paragraph">
    <fo:block font-size="12pt" font-family="Times" space-before.optimum="12pt"
      text-align="center">
      <xsl:apply-templates />
    </fo:block>
  </xsl:template>

</xsl:stylesheet>
```

At first glance, this stylesheet may seem more complex than the others we have looked at. However, it follows pretty much the same structure.

The `<xsl:template match="page">` section sets up the overall rules for how the content is to be rendered. Page sizes and margins are configured as page sequencing rules. In this case, the stylesheet defines a page footer in the `<fo:static-content flow-name="xsl-region-after">` section.

Outside of the root match, we have matches that handle the `<title>` and `<paragraph>` elements. These set up some font size and type rules that will govern the display of these particular elements. You will note that the stylesheet uses three font types: Helvetica, Times, and Courier. These correspond to particular types that are allowed by the PDF specification, but FOP allows the extension of these to include other fonts.

Adding a Pipeline Entry

We must now tell Cocoon how to handle the PDF page. We do this by adding the following after the other `<map:match>` tags in our sitemap:

```
<map:match pattern="index.pdf">
 <map:generate type="file" src="content/main.xml"/>
 <map:transform type="xslt" src="style/main-pdf.xsl"/>
 <map:serialize type="fo2pdf"/>
</map:match>
```

Once again, our pipeline defines a generator, transformer, and serializer. This time, we are using the `FOPSerializer` to send the data to our browser.

Testing is simple. Point your browser to `http://localhost:8080/cocoon/abc/index.pdf` and you should see what's shown in Figure 7.3.

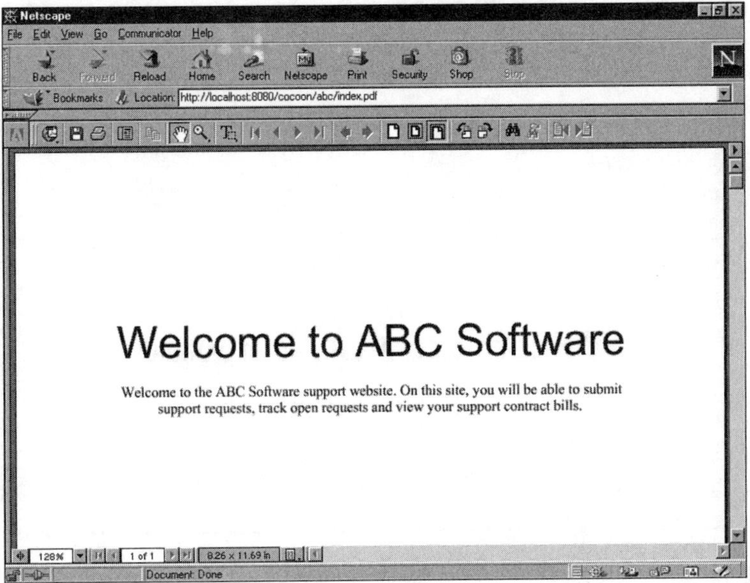

Figure 7.3
Welcome to ABC Software – PDF Version.

To be able to view the PDF, you of course need to have the Adobe Acrobat Reader application for your platform.

Viewing the Page in Postscript

We can also view the same file in Postscript by changing the serializer in our pipeline. The output from XSL:FO can be used to drive both Postscript and PDF documents. Let's rewrite our last pipeline as shown here:

```
<map:match pattern="index.ps">
  <map:generate type="file" src="content/main.xml"/>
  <map:transform type="xslt" src="style/main-pdf.xsl"/>
  <map:serialize type="fo2ps"/>
</map:match>
```

Figure 7.4 shows the output. The Postscript output is being viewed using the GSview from Ghostgum Software (`http://www.cs.wisc.edu/~ghost/`).

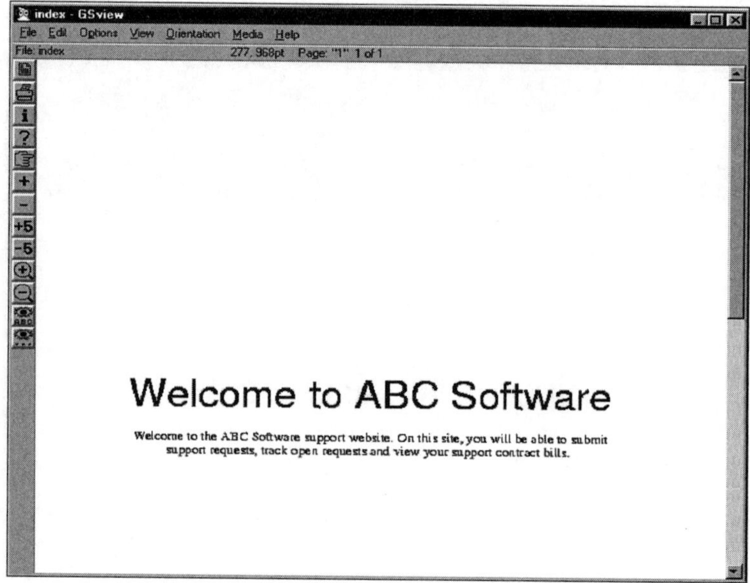

Figure 7.4

Welcome to ABC Software - Postscript Version.

Summary

Congratulations! You now have created your first Cocoon file and can view it in four ways: HTML, WML, PDF, and PS. Let's review what we did.

First, we created our XML data file, `main.xml`. This is where our content lives, the "model" component in MVC terms, and where we go when we want to make changes to our title or the verbiage that will be displayed to the user. Obviously, if this were a real site, we would have much more in the way of content and tags. The important thing, however, is that nothing in the file is concerned with style or the presentation of the data.

The presentation job is handled by means of the XSL files we created. In them, we told the `TraxTransformer` what output tags to generate as it encountered various input tags. All three stylesheets, for example, had instructions on what to do with `<title>` and `<paragraph>` tags. Again, all our examples were simple. Production stylesheets can get quite complex. XSL is in a sense a mini–programming language that can take quite a while to master. The upside of its complexity is that you can pretty much do anything you want to with XSL.

Finally, we hooked everything together by defining processing paths or pipelines in our sitemap. At this point, you might question why we need so much code in our pipelines to define the relatively simple process of XSL transformation. Indeed, if all we use Cocoon for is XSLT, there are arguably easier alternatives. However, we have only just touched on some of the things Cocoon can do. In the next few chapters, we will add logic to our application and see how well Cocoon can handle that.

CHAPTER 8
Using Content Logic: XSPs

In this chapter, we will extend our application by adding content-side logic. Here is where we will start to see exactly how Cocoon goes beyond simple XSLT transformation.

We can broadly generalize logic in Cocoon as either sitemap logic or content logic. Sitemap logic refers to processing rules that are implemented in pipelines using Cocoon components such as matchers, selectors, views, and actions. We'll see these in action in Chapter 11, "Using Sitemap Logic: Matchers and Selectors," and Chapter 12, "Using Sitemap Logic: Actions and Forms."

Content logic refers to logic that is implemented at the data collection or data processing step. In this chapter, we'll look at XSPs and logicsheets as ways to implement content logic. In the next two chapters, we'll cover generators and transformers as other mechanisms for content logic. We won't explicitly cover this subject, but you can also implement content logic in the data source. A stored procedure, for example, is a good way of handling logic within the data source. Another example is an EJB that encapsulates various rules and provides data to Cocoon after applying those rules. We'll discuss this in Chapter 18, "Cocoon Interfaces: J2EE."

A good example of content logic is when user-specific data is being retrieved from a database (as we will cover in this chapter). Here, the actual data that is retrieved could depend on the identify of the user, as established during an authentication process. Another example is a process that performs certain actions and responds with certain data depending on the request parameters submitted from a form. We'll cover that one too.

eXtensible Server Pages

One implementation of content logic is in *eXtensible Server Pages*, or *XSPs*. XSPs are an innovation of the Cocoon project and are in some ways analogous to Java Server Pages (JSPs). In its most basic form, an XSP is an XML file that contains embedded code. Cocoon reads XSPs using the `ServerPagesGenerator`. The latter executes the embedded logic and combines the output with the XML content in the rest of the file. The resulting SAX events are sent to the next component in the pipeline for processing. Figure 8.1 demonstrates this processing flow.

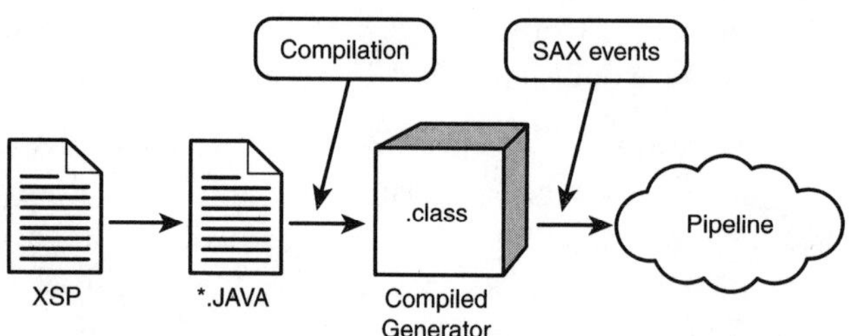

Figure 8.1
Basic XSP processing flow.

When an XSP is processed, it actually gets turned into a Java object, content and all. Cocoon does this by creating a `.java` file, compiling it, and executing it. This Java object itself is actually a `Generator` object that produces SAX events just like we saw the `FileGenerator` do with `main.xml`.

Starting Out with XSPs

To understand how this all works, let's look at a simple XSP. We'll take our `main.xml` file (created in Chapter 7, "Creating Static Pages"), rewrite it as an XSP, and add a bit of logic that spits out the current date and time.

We'll start as simply as possible, by creating a file called `content/main.xsp`, shown in Listing 8.1.

Listing 8.1 *Simple XSP (main.xsp - Version 1)*

```
<?xml version="1.0"?>

<xsp:page language="java" xmlns:xsp="http://apache.org/xsp">

<page>
 <title>Welcome to ABC Software</title>
 <content>
  <paragraph>
   Welcome to the ABC Software support website. On this site, you
   will be able to submit support requests, track open requests and
   view your support contract bills
  </paragraph>
</content>
</page>

</xsp:page>
```

As you can see, we just encapsulated the entire content of `main.xml` with an `<xsp:page>` tag block. The `<xsp:page>` tag has two attributes: The first defines the language, Java, and the second defines the XSP namespace. The namespace declaration is important, because it tells the `ServerPagesGenerator` that it must handle the tags that begin with `xsp`. An important point is that in XSPs, the top user tag is referred to as the "user root." The root of the XSP itself is `<xsp:page>`, and the user root in our example is `page`.

As it stands, this simple XSP does the same as `main.xml`, but adds more processing overhead. To make it worthwhile, let's add some logic so that it looks as shown in Listing 8.2.

Listing 8.2 *Simple XSP (main.xsp - Version 2)*

```
<?xml version="1.0"?>

<xsp:page language="java" xmlns:xsp="http://apache.org/xsp">

<xsp:structure>
 <xsp:include>java.util.Date</xsp:include>
</xsp:structure>
```

Listing 8.2 *(continued)*

```
<xsp:logic>
  Date now = new Date();
</xsp:logic>

<page>
 <title>Welcome to ABC Software</title>
 <content>
  <paragraph>
   Welcome to the ABC Software support Website. On this site, you
   will be able to submit support requests, track open requests and
   view your support contract bills
  </paragraph>
  <paragraph>
   By the way, today's date is <xsp:expr>now</xsp:expr>.
  </paragraph>
</content>
</page>
</xsp:page>
```

The first new tags are in the `<xsp:structure>` block. This block contains one or more `<xsp:include>` tags, which equate to `import` statements in Java. They tell Cocoon what Java packages, or parts thereof, we intend to use. Many XSPs won't need an `<xsp:structure>` block at all, but if it is used, it must precede any user tags. Note: In this example, importing of `java.util.Date` is not necessary because XSPs always import `java.util.*`; we're showing the import just to illustrate the usage of the `<xsp:structure>` tag.

The second new block is the `<xsp:logic>` block. This is where we can basically do anything we want in Java. This block could contain pages and pages of code, though this would not be a good design idea. In our case, we are defining a `Date` object that is automatically set to the current `datetime` on initialization.

The final new element is the `<xsp:expr>` tag, which enables us to access the value of a variable in the midst of our XML content. In this case, we want to print the current `datetime`. All we have to do is put the `now` variable name inside the `<xsp:expr>` tags, and when Cocoon processes it, it will automatically call the `toString()` method on the `now` object and insert the resulting string in place of the entire expression. Thus,

```
<paragraph>
 By the way, today's date is <xsp:expr>now</xsp:expr>.
</paragraph>
```

gets expanded by the `ServerPagesGenerator` to

```
<paragraph>
 By the way, today's date is Wednesday, May 29, 2002 13:11:00 MDT
</paragraph>
```

or whatever the current date and time are.

Adding a Pipeline Entry

Our final step is to tell Cocoon about our new page:

```
<map:match pattern="index.xsp">
 <map:generate type="serverpages" src="content/main.xsp"/>
 <map:transform type="xslt" src="style/main.xsl"/>
 <map:serialize type="html"/>
</map:match>
```

You can see that this is very similar to the pipeline for `index.html` created in Chapter 7. We are using the `ServerPagesGenerator` to process `content/main.xsp`, but the stylesheet and serializer are the same.

Testing the XSP

To see the XSP in action, point your browser to `http://localhost:8080/cocoon/abc/index.xsp` and you should see what's shown in Figure 8.2.

Adding a Logicsheet

Earlier, we talked about how Cocoon helps separate content from logic, and both from style. However, XSP actually integrates content and logic! Doesn't this violate this basic principle? Yes it does, but in fact, when you think about it, it is impossible to separate content from logic. What we really want to avoid is combining content with *presentation* logic, as is done in HTML. But content will almost always need some logic in order to handle dynamic situations. Where we can go terribly wrong is when logic begins to take over an XSP page like fungus. When you can no longer find your content, you know you have a problem.

Fortunately, Cocoon has a solution: logicsheets. Logicsheets are to XSPs what taglibs are to JSPs. Logicsheets are actually XSL files that associate logic blocks with tags. Each logicsheet also must declare its own namespace. This means that we can take logic out of our XSP, store it in the logicsheet, and reference by custom tags. This makes the XSP much neater.

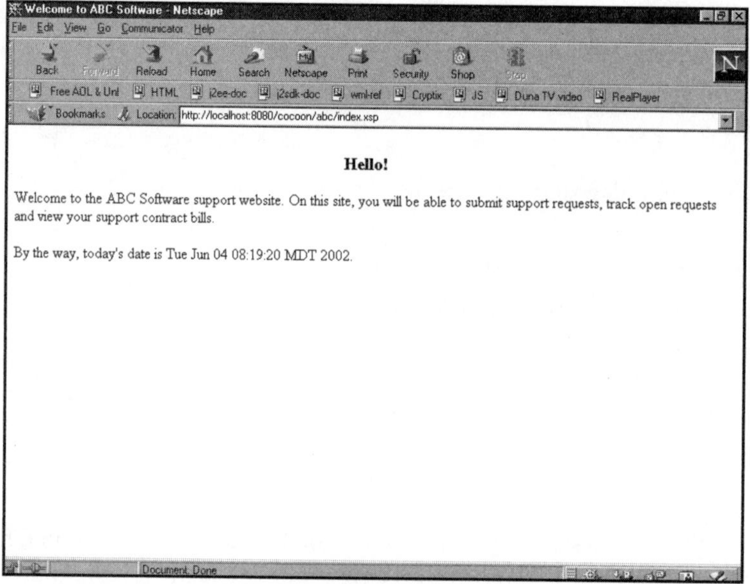

Figure 8.2
Welcome to ABC Software.

Figure 8.3 shows how logicsheets fit into the XSP processing model shown previously.

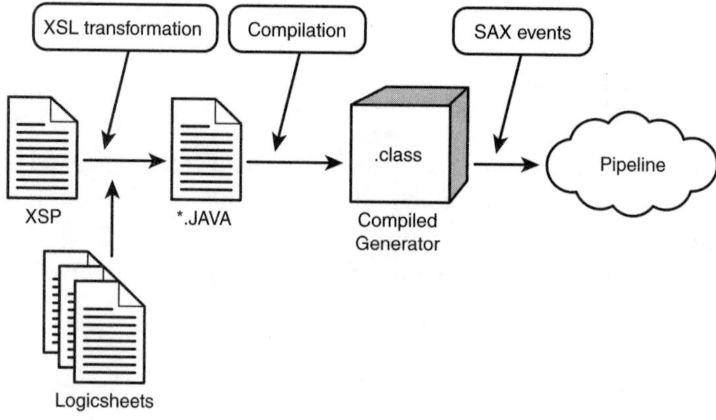

Figure 8.3
XSP flow with logicsheets.

As you can see, an XSP is first run through an XSLT process whereby any logicsheet tags are replaced with the content defined in the logicsheet itself. In other words, the XSP, being of course a valid XML file, is transformed by however many logicsheets are defined in the `<xsp:page>` tag. The resulting file is then turned into Java, compiled, and executed.

Cocoon comes with some built-in logicsheets that are defined in `$CATALINA_HOME/webapps/cocoon/WEB-INF/cocoon.xconf` and physically live in the cocoon jar file. In fact, we've already met one of them, `xsp.xsl`. That's right, the `xlmns` attribute in the `<xsp:page>` tag tells Cocoon that this page uses the XSP logicsheet. The entry in `cocoon.xconf` looks like this:

```
<xsp-language logger="core.markup.xsp" name="xsp">
      <parameter name="prefix" value="xsp"/>
      <parameter name="uri" value="http://apache.org/xsp"/>
```

Following this entry, you will find two sets of logicsheets: Java and JavaScript. We'll deal primarily with the Java logicsheets—the JavaScript versions are discussed briefly at the end of this chapter.

```
<target-language name="java">
        <parameter name="core-logicsheet" value="resource://org/apache/cocoon/
           ➥components/language/markup/xsp/java/xsp.xsl"/>

         <!--Java logicsheets go here -->

      </target-language>

      <target-language name="js">

         <!--JS logicsheets go here -->

</target-language>
```

Table 8.1 shows the elements of the XSP logicsheet.

Table 8.1 *XSP Logicsheet Tags*

Tag	Description
`xsp:page`	Is the root tag of any XSP. During transformation, this tag is replaced with Java import statements and the class skeleton.
`xsp:structure`	Defines program-level declarations, such as `<xsp:include>`.
`xsp:include`	Is equivalent to the `import` statement in Java.
`xsp:logic`	Embeds logic in an XSP.
`xsp:content`	Embeds XML content inside a `<xsp:logic>` block.

Table 8.1 *(continued)*

Tag	Description
`xsp:expr`	Returns the output of the `toString()` method of an object or wraps primitive Java types to their `String` representation as a `Text` node.
`xsp:element`	Builds an XML tag named by the given name attribute.
`xsp:attribute`	Adds an attribute to a given `<xsp:element>`. Can contain either text or `<xsp:expr>` tags.
`xsp:pi`	Dynamically builds a processing instruction named by the `target` attribute.
`xsp:comment`	Creates an XML comment.

Let's now go through the process of creating our own logicsheet.

Creating a Logicsheet

Remember, a logicsheet is an XSL stylesheet. What we'll do is create a logicsheet that provides a single tag to get the current date and time. This will enable us to eliminate the `<xsp:structure>` and `<xsp:logic>` tags we had in our XSP. Listing 8.3 shows a simple logicsheet.

Listing 8.3 *A Simple Logicsheet (abc.xsl)*

```
<?xml version="1.0"?>
<xsl:stylesheet
  xmlns:xsl="http://www.w3.org/1999/XSL/Transform"
  xmlns:xsp="http://apache.org/xsp"
  xmlns:abc="http://samspublishing.com/abc/1.0"
  version="1.0">

<xsl:template match="xsp:page">
  <xsp:page>
    <xsl:apply-templates select="@*"/>
    <xsp:structure>
      <xsp:include>java.util.Date</xsp:include>
    </xsp:structure>
    <xsp:logic>
      Date now = new Date();
    </xsp:logic>
    <xsl:apply-templates/>
  </xsp:page>
</xsl:template>
```

Listing 8.3 *(continued)*

```
<xsl:template match="abc:datetime">
  The current time is <xsp:expr>now</xsp:expr>
</xsl:template>

<xsl:template match="@*|node()">
  <xsl:copy>
    <xsl:apply-templates select="@*|node()"/>
  </xsl:copy>
</xsl:template>

<xsl:template match="text()">
  <xsl:value-of select="." />
</xsl:template>

</xsl:stylesheet>
```

In this example, we declare a single tag for the logicsheet, `abc:datetime`:

```
<xsl:template match="abc:datetime">
  The current time is <xsp:expr>now</xsp:expr>
</xsl:template>
```

We must also declare the namespace for the logicsheet, which we do in the `<xsl:stylesheet>` tag as `abc`. That means that any tag prefixed with `abc:` should be handled by this logicsheet.

> **Namespace Declarations**
> If you are new to namespaces, they can be confusing. The main thing to remember is that a namespace *does not define a physical file*. Rather, it is a unique URI that serves *only* as an identifier for the set of tags supported by a particular logicsheet. Typically, you put in a domain name that tells the reader something about where the namespace originated. In this example, we're using our publisher's domain name, but don't go looking for `abc/1.0` on their site—it isn't there. We could have just as easily used `http://www.galatea.com/abc/1.0` or `http://www.pigbite.co.uk/abc/1.0`. What is important, however, is that anywhere we define our namespace, we use the *same* URI. We'll see this in the following discussion.

Remember that we had to use an `<xsp:include>` statement in our original XSP. In this logicsheet, we make sure to put this at the beginning by catching the `<xsp:page>` tag and inserting the `<xsp:structure>` block inside. Because it is also a good place to declare our `Date` object, we put it there as well, inside the `<xsp:logic>` block. The only tag we actually define for our logicsheet is something called `datetime`. We are telling Cocoon that anytime an XSP uses our `<abc:datetime>`, it should substitute the text `The current time is` plus the value of the `now` variable. Note: Again, importing of `java.util.Date` is redundant, because `java.util.*` is already imported.

You're probably wondering about the last two templates in `abc.xsl`: that for `@*|node()` and that for `text()`. These are necessary in any logicsheet, because we need to make sure that any tags that we don't want to handle (that is, any tags that are not part of our namespace) are passed on verbatim. These could include user tags (XML data) or tags for other logicsheets to process. If you don't include these last two templates in your logicsheet, you will encounter rather unexpected results!

Defining the Logicsheet

We can put the `abc.xsl` logicsheet in the `$CATALINA_HOME/webapps/cocoon/abc/style` directory. Now we must tell Cocoon about it so that Cocoon can map any tag with the `abc` namespace to our file. It doesn't actually matter where we put our logicsheet, as long as we tell Cocoon where it is. We could also jar it up and stick the jar in the `WEB-INF/lib` directory if we wanted to.

As mentioned previously, logicsheets are defined in `$CATALINA_HOME/webapps/cocoon/WEB-INF/cocoon.xconf`. If you open this file, look for the `<target-language name="java">` line, under which are a series of `<builtin-logicsheet>` blocks. We'll add the following at the end of the series:

```
<builtin-logicsheet>
  <parameter name="prefix" value="abc"/>
  <parameter name="uri" value="http://samspublishing.com/abc/1.0"/>
  <parameter name="href"
    value="file:///c:/apps/jakarta-tomcat-4.0.1/webapps/cocoon/abc
    ➥/style/abc.xsl"/>
</builtin-logicsheet>
```

Table 8.2 describes each parameter in more detail.

Table 8.2 *Logicsheet Definition Parameters*

Parameter	Description
`prefix`	Tells what tag prefix this logicsheet covers. For ours, the prefix is `abc`.
`uri`	The namespace URI. This must match *exactly* what we defined in the logicsheet file.
`href`	The physical location of the logicsheet. Here, we give the full path to the file. The usual way is to put it in a jar file and provide the full package name, such as `resource://com/samspublishing/cocoon_book/abc.xsl`. We'll learn about the `resource://` protocol in Chapter 11.

The last step to making the new logicsheet available to Cocoon is to restart our servlet container so that Cocoon can reread `cocoon.xconf` and know that our new namespace maps to the `abc.xsl` logicsheet.

Using the Logicsheet

With the logicsheet in place, and Cocoon restarted, we can rework our XSP to look like as shown in Listing 8.4.

Listing 8.4 *XSP with the Logicsheet (main.xsp - Version 3)*

```
<?xml version="1.0"?>

<xsp:page language="java"
   xmlns:xsp="http://apache.org/xsp"
   xmlns:abc="http://samspublishing.com/abc/1.0"
>

<page>
 <title>Welcome to ABC Software</title>
 <content>
  <paragraph>
   Welcome to the ABC Software support website. On this site, you
   will be able to submit support requests, track open requests and
   view your support contract bills
  </paragraph>
  <paragraph>
    <abc:datetime/>
  </paragraph>
</content>
</page>

</xsp:page>
```

Isn't that much simpler? We don't have to define any `<xsp:structure>` or `<xsp:logic>` blocks, because they will be added by Cocoon during processing. The net result will be the same as our previous example, but we have a cleaner XSP to deal with. Also important is the fact that we could reuse this logicsheet in another page, and not have to rewrite the logic. As long as we define the namespace, so that Cocoon will load the correct logicsheet, we have full access to all associated tags.

Now that we've introduced XSPs and logicsheets, we are ready to get into some more complicated code than simply showing the current date. We'll use one of the requirements for the fictitious ABC Software support Web site. This requirement is one in which users need to be able to view their own trouble ticket data on the Web site.

Handling Authentication

The first component of this requirement is authentication—users need to first be identified and authenticated before proceeding to the personalized support section. For simplicity's sake, users will log in using a simple HTML form. When the form is submitted, the target will be an XSP that will handle the actual authentication and, if it is successful, put the userid into the session object. Finally, data for the authenticated users will be retrieved from the database. Figure 8.4 shows the basics of this process.

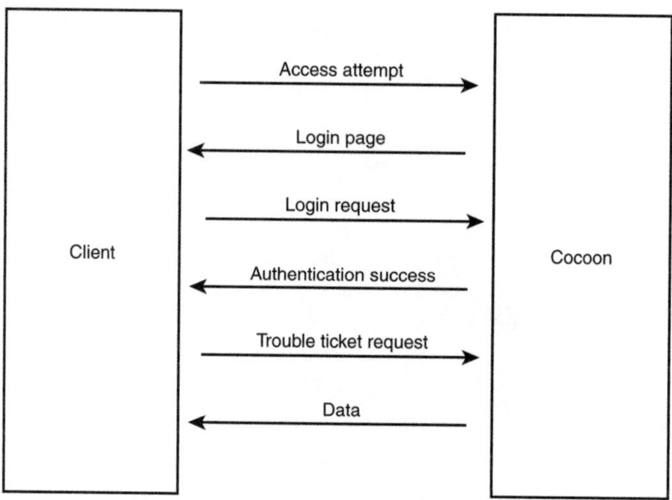

Figure 8.4
Status tracking process flow.

To make our job easier, and cut down on the amount of code we need to put in our XSPs, we'll make use of several logicsheets: `esql`, `xsp-session`, and `xsp-request`.

Login Page

The login will be handled by an extremely simple login page, shown in Listing 8.5. This file will be called `login.html` and will reside in `$CATALINA_HOME/webapps/cocoon/abc/content`.

Listing 8.5 *Simple Login Form (login.html)*

```
<html>
 <head>
  <title>Please login</title>
  <style type="text/css">
   <!--
    body { font-family: verdana, helvetica, sans serif; font-size: 10pt; }
    td { font-family: verdana, helvetica, sans serif; font-size: 10pt; }
   -->
  </style>
 </head>

 <body>
  <br/>
  <center>
   <h3>Please login to access your trouble ticket information</h3>
   <br/>

   <form action="login" method="post">

   <table>
    <tr>
     <td align="right">User:</td>
     <td align="left"><input type="text" name="user"/></td>
    </tr>
    <tr>
     <td align="right">Password:</td>
     <td align="left"><input type="password" name="pass"/></td>
    </tr>
    <tr>
     <td colspan="2" align="center"><input type="submit" value="Login"/></td>
    </tr>
   </table>

   </form>

 </body>
</html>
```

Now you might think we can access this directly with our browser, but that is not the case. Cocoon intercepts and resolves *all* requests to its URI base, so we must create a pipeline to handle our login form. But, you ask, `login.html` is not XML nor do we need any conversion, so how do we define it? Fortunately, Cocoon has a component that enables files to be "passed through" the pipeline unprocessed: a Reader. Let's look at the syntax, and add the following pipeline to our `sitemap.xmap`:

```
<map:match pattern="login.html">
 <map:read mime-type="text/html" src="content/login.html"/>
</map:match>
```

The attributes for `map:read` are shown in Table 8.3.

Table 8.3 *<map:read> Attributes*

Attribute	Description	Required
`mime-type`	Defines the mime-type Cocoon will use to describe the resource as it is returned to the client.	yes
`src`	Location of the resource to be read.	yes
`type`	Type of resource to read: either `jsp` for `*.jsp` files, or `resource` for everything else.	no

Login Handling XSP

In `login.html` we defined the action for the form to be something called `login`, and which we expect to handle the parameters `user` and `pass`. Now we will write an XSP to handle this process, and we will create a pipeline entry that will match the URI `login`.

The authentication XSP is shown in Listing 8.6. The path to this file in our webapp is `$CATALINA_HOME/webapps/cocoon/abc/xsp/login.xsp`. For now, we'll just match the supplied userid and password with hard-coded values. Obviously, a more robust model would use a database or another external source to validate the login. However, we want to keep things simple for now. As we go along in the next few chapters, we'll see other ways of implementing authentication.

Listing 8.6 *Simple Authentication XSP (login.xsp)*

```
<?xml version="1.0" encoding="ISO-8859-1"?>

<xsp:page language="java"
  xmlns:xsp="http://apache.org/xsp"
  xmlns:xsp-request="http://apache.org/xsp/request/2.0"
  xmlns:xsp-session="http://apache.org/xsp/session/2.0"
  create-session="true"
>
```

Listing 8.6 *(continued)*

```
<page>

<xsp:logic>
 String msg = "";
 String user = <xsp-request:get-parameter name="user"/>;
 String pwd = <xsp-request:get-parameter name="pass"/>;

 if (user.equals("BigCorp") &amp;&amp; pwd.equals("secret")) {
   msg = "User '" + user + "' has been authenticated" +
      " - you can now proceed to the support page.";
   <xsp-session:set-attribute name="user">
    <xsp:expr>user</xsp:expr>
   </xsp-session:set-attribute>;
 } else {
   msg = "Login failed";
 }

</xsp:logic>

 <title>Login results</title>
 <content>
  <title>Login results</title>
  <paragraph>
   <xsp:expr>msg</xsp:expr>
  </paragraph>
 </content>
</page>

</xsp:page>
```

Let's review this section by section.

Namespace Declarations

In addition to declaring the XSP namespace, we must also declare that of `xsp-request` and `xsp-session`. We need `xsp-request` so that we can access the request parameters set by `login.html`. We need `xsp-session` so that we can set a session variable called `user`. This variable will be needed when we access the trouble ticket data.

Remember: The namespace declaration you use in your XSP *must match* what's defined in `cocoon.xconf`. If there is a mismatch, Cocoon won't be able to load the right logicsheet.

You'll also notice that the `create-session` attribute in `<xsp-page>` is set to `true`. As it stands, the user coming to this page has no session. The `create-session` attribute tells Cocoon to create a `Session` object, which we can then interact with via the session logicsheet. Without this attribute, your first call to the session logicsheet would result in a null pointer exception.

Access Session and Request Objects Directly
There is an alternative to the `xsp-request` and `xsp-session` logicsheets. Any XSP has access to both `Session` and `Request` objects. We'll discuss how to use these at the end of this chapter.

Extracting the Request Parameters

It might look odd to mix XML with Java code, until you recall that an XSP is first passed through an XSLT transformation involving all defined logicsheets and is then compiled into a Java object. The `<xsp-request:get-parameter name="user">` tag will be replaced by valid Java code during this transformation. So assigning the value of this tag to a `String` object called `user` is entirely correct, though a bit funny-looking at first.

Note also that we must put any calls to the `xsp-request` or `xsp-session` logicsheets *after* the root user tag, in this case `<page>`.

AND Operator

You might have noticed the tags `&&` in place of the boolean `AND` operator in the `if` statement. Because an XSP must still be valid XML, the normal `&&` that you would expect will cause the XML parser to throw an exception. Thus, we replace it with the `&&`.

Setting a Session Attribute

To set a session attribute, we use the `<xsp-session:set-attribute>` tag. This means that the value of the attribute, in this case the value in the `user` variable, is stored in the `Session` object, which will persist for the duration of the session (or until we remove it). It is important to note when setting session attributes that the data between the tags will be interpreted as a literal. If we simply wrote

```
<xsp-session:set-attribute>user</xsp:session:set-attribute>
```

we would be setting the value of the `user` attribute to the literal `user`. However, by surrounding `user` with the `xsp:expr` tags, we are in effect saying: Substitute this for the string value of the `user` variable. Because the XSP logicsheet is applied before the `session` attribute, the `<xsp-session:set-attribute>` tags will end up surrounding a literal.

Adding the Pipeline Entry

Let's make sure we have a pipeline to handle our login XSP:

```
<map:match pattern="login">
 <map:generate type="serverpages" src="xsp/login.xsp"/>
 <map:transform type="xslt" src="style/main.xsl"/>
 <map:serialize type="html"/>
</map:match>
```

This should need no explanation, because it is similar to what we did for `main.xsp`.

Testing the Login Page

Now we are ready to try out our login page. We'll first pull up the login form at `http://localhost:8080/cocoon/abc/login.html` and then enter the hard-coded values of `BigCorp` for the userid and `secret` for the password. After pressing the Login button, we should see what's shown in Figure 8.5.

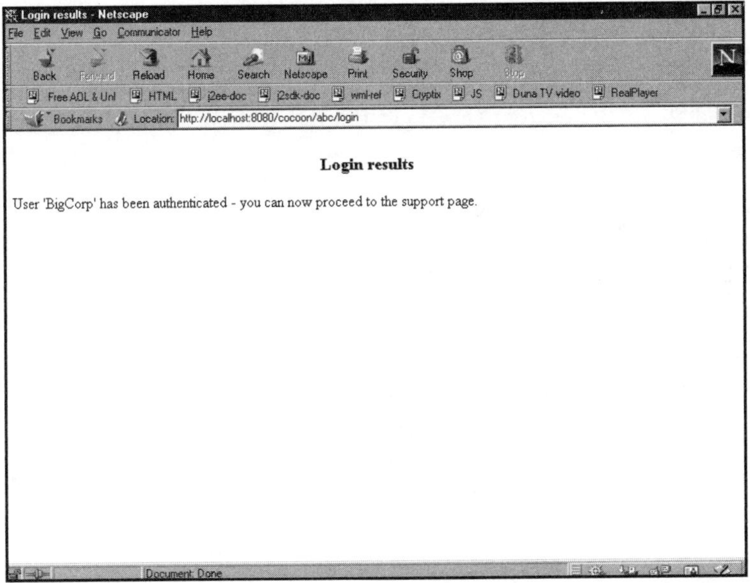

Figure 8.5
Login succeeded.

Now we are ready to work on the Ticket Tracking page.

Cocoon and Databases

Thanks to the Avalon component Excalibur, Cocoon has robust database connection pooling capabilities. For this next example, we will show how to create a pool of MySQL connections. You can, of course, use your database of choice. The only requirement is that you have a JAR file available containing the JDBC driver for that database. After we have set up our connection pool, we will write an XSP that uses the ESQL logicsheet to do a database select. The ESQL logicsheet provides tags that encapsulate the JDBC commands necessary for database operations. As you will see, this turns out to be much simpler than directly using the JDBC commands themselves.

Setting up a database connection pool in Cocoon involves three steps:

1. Make the JDBC JAR available to Cocoon.
2. Instruct Cocoon to preload the JDBC driver.
3. Define the connection pool.

Making the JDBC JAR Available to Cocoon

For a MySQL database, the current version of the JDBC driver is contained in a JAR file called `mm.mysql-2.0.11-bin.jar`.

> **Obtaining the MySQL JDBC Driver**
> The current version of this driver is available at `www.mysql.com/downloads/api-jdbc.html`.

There are three options in making a JAR file available to Cocoon, as shown in Table 8.4.

Table 8.4 *Possible Location of External JAR Files*

Location	Notes
`$JAVA_HOME/jre/lib/ext`	Use this if you want all Java applications on the machine to have access to the JAR.
`$CATALINA_HOME/common/lib`	Use this if other Web applications on this server will need access to this JAR.
`$CATALINA_HOME/webapps/cocoon/WEB-INF/lib`	Use this if you want the JAR available only to Cocoon.

For our example, we'll place our jar in $CATALINA_HOME/common/lib, because we might have another Web application that will need access to MySQL.

Preloading the JDBC Driver

Preloading the JDBC driver means that Cocoon will save time by loading the class at startup. We define these classes in $CATALINA_HOME/webapps/cocoon/WEB-INF/web.xml, in an <init-param> tag:

```
<init-param>
  <param-name>load-class</param-name>
  <param-value>
    <!-- For IBM WebSphere:
    com.ibm.servlet.classloader.Handler -->

    <!-- For Database Driver: -->
    org.hsqldb.jdbcDriver

    <!-- For parent ComponentManager sample:
    org.apache.cocoon.samples.parentcm.Configurator
    -->
    org.gjt.mm.mysql.Driver
  </param-value>
</init-param>
```

Here, we've added the org.gjt.mm.mysql.Driver JDBC driver to the other defined classes. Two of these are actually commented out; the org.hsqld.jdbcDriver is used for the Hypersonic SQL (HSQLDB) database, which the Cocoon samples use. If you don't need the Cocoon samples, you can comment out this class as well.

Defining the Connection Pool

Connection pools are defined in $CATALINA_HOME/webapps/cocoon/WEB-INF/cocoon.xconf. As with the JDBC drivers to load at startup, you can define as many connection pools as you need. Cocoon will manage them during operation according to the parameters you specify. The default Cocoon installation comes with a "personnel" connection pool defined for an HSQLDB database. Again, if you don't plan on using the samples, comment it out.

This is what connection pool for a MySQL database called abc might look like:

```
<datasources>
  <jdbc name="abc" logger="core.datasources.abc">
    <pool-controller min="5" max="10"/>
    <auto-commit>false</auto-commit>
```

```
    <dburl>jdbc:mysql://localhost/abc</dburl>
    <user>root</user>
    <password/>
  </jdbc>
  <!-- other connection pools go here -->
</datasources>
```

The <jdbc> tag has two attributes: the name, which is required because that is how we'll refer to the connection pool, and the prefix to use for log messages concerning the pool. We'll discuss logging in Chapter 23, "Cocoon Administration," but for now, suffice it to say that it is a good idea to give a unique name to the `logger` parameter so that you can easily search the logs and find any messages relating to the pool.

Table 8.5 goes over the tags beneath the <jdbc> tag.

Table 8.5 *Connection Pool Tags*

Tag	Description	Required
`pool-controller`	Defines the minimum (`min`) and maximum (`max`) connections Cocoon should create for this database. For Oracle databases, you must add a third attribute, `oradb`, and set it to `true`.	yes
`auto-commit`	Determines whether transactions are automatically committed. Default is `true`.	no
`dburl`	The JDBC URL for the pool database.	yes
`user`	The userid to use for database access.	yes
`password`	The password to use for database access.	yes

Implementing the Changes

With these three changes made—copying the database JAR to a location where Cocoon can access it, adding the JDBC driver to the list of classes the Cocoon will load on startup, and defining the connection pool—we can restart Cocoon. To see whether Cocoon properly loaded the class file, look in `$CATALINA_HOME/webapps/cocoon/WEB-INF/logs/access.log` and check for a line something like this (the example is for MySQL):

```
DEBUG   (2002-05-27) 18:29.57:100   [access] (Unknown-URI) Unknown-thread/Cocoon
Servlet: Trying to load class: org.gjt.mm.mysql.Driver
```

You'll see the other JDBC drivers listed here as well. Also, check `$CATALINA_HOME/webaps/cocoon/WEB-INF/logs/core.log` for error messages with the tag corresponding to the logger name as specified in the pool <jdbc> tag. If there were any problems in creating the pool, like when the database server is down, you'll see them here. As mentioned previously, we will cover the Cocoon log files in more detail in Chapter 23.

The Trouble Ticket Page

Now we are ready to create the XSP that will access a database and retrieve the trouble ticket information for the authenticated user.

Creating the Database

First, we need a database and some tables. Remember that when we defined the JDBC connection previously, we specified the database name as `abc`. Obviously, before the pool can be properly initialized, we should have created a database called `abc`. Listing 8.7 shows the script to create the database and the tables we need. This is MySQL-specific—you'll have to adapt this to your own database server if you are not using MySQL.

Listing 8.7 *Script to Create abc Database and Tables (abc.sql)*

```
create database abc;
use abc;

create table TroubleTickets (
Customer         varchar(20)     not null,
CustomerLocCode      varchar(3)     null,
TicketId         int             not null,
TicketDesc       varchar(250)    null,
TicketOwner      varchar(50)     not null,
TicketStatus     char(1)         not null,
TicketOpened     varchar(10)     not null,
TicketClosed     varchar(10)     null,
TicketNotes      varchar(250)    null
);

create table CustomerLocations (
Customer       varchar(20)    not null,
CustomerLocCode  varchar(3)     not null,
CustomerLocation varchar(64)  not null
);

insert into TroubleTickets values ('BigCorp', 'NYC', 1,
'Unable to start application on Windows XP', 'John G.', 'C',
```

Listing 8.7 *(continued)*

```
'5/30/02', '5/31/02', 'User missing libabc.dll');
insert into TroubleTickets values ('BigCorp', 'NYC', 2,
'Application crashed on Solaris 2.8 with message: Program aborted with error -33
', 'John G.', 'O', '6/03/02', '', '');
insert into TroubleTickets values ('BigCorp', 'BER', 3,
'Application crashed on Linux 7.2 with no error message',
'John G.', 'O', '6/03/02', '', '');
insert into TroubleTickets values ('BigCorp', 'BER', 4,
'User does not know how to start the application', 'John G.',
'C', '5/27/02', '5/27/02', 'User directed to the documentation');
insert into TroubleTickets values ('BigCorp', 'NYC', 5,
'User does not know how to start the application', '', 'O',
'6/11/02', '', '');
insert into TroubleTickets values ('BigCorp', 'NYC', 6,
'User does not know how to start the application', '', 'O',
'6/12/02', '', '');
insert into TroubleTickets values ('BigCorp', 'NYC', 7,
'User does not know how to start the application', '', 'O',
'6/13/02', '', '');
insert into TroubleTickets values ('BigCorp', 'NYC', 8,
'User does not know how to start the application', '', 'O',
'6/14/02', '', '');
insert into TroubleTickets values ('BigCorp', 'NYC', 9,
'User does not know how to start the application', '', 'O',
'6/15/02', '', '');
insert into TroubleTickets values ('BigCorp', 'NYC', 10,
'User does not know how to start the application', '', 'O',
'6/16/02', '', '');
insert into TroubleTickets values ('BigCorp', 'NYC', 11,
'User does not know how to start the application', '', 'O',
'6/17/02', '', '');
insert into TroubleTickets values ('BigCorp', 'NYC', 12,
'User does not know how to start the application', '', 'O',
'6/18/02', '', '');
insert into TroubleTickets values ('BigCorp', 'NYC', 13,
'User does not know how to start the application', '', 'O',
'6/19/02', '', '');

insert into CustomerLocations values ('BigCorp', 'NYC', 'New York, NY');
insert into CustomerLocations values ('BigCorp', 'BER', 'Berlin, Germany');
```

Writing the XSP

If you have ever written servlets or JSPs that retrieve data from a database, you know how many statements you actually need in order to write even a simple query. So you'll appreciate how much coding the `esql` logicsheet saves you. Let's look at our new XSP (see Listing 8.8), which we'll call `tickets.xsp` and which we'll put in the `xsp` subdirectory of our project folder.

Listing 8.8 *Ticket XSP (tickets.xsp)*

```
<?xml version="1.0" encoding="ISO-8859-1"?>

<xsp:page language="java"
  xmlns:xsp="http://apache.org/xsp"
  xmlns:esql="http://apache.org/cocoon/SQL/v2"
  xmlns:xsp-session="http://apache.org/xsp/session/2.0"
>

  <page>

   <title>Trouble tickets for <xsp-session:get-attribute name="user"/></title>

   <content>

   <esql:connection>
     <esql:pool>abc</esql:pool>
     <esql:execute-query>
       <esql:query>
        select * from TroubleTickets where Customer =
        '<xsp-session:get-attribute name="user"/>'
        order by TicketOpened
       </esql:query>
       <esql:results>
        <tickets>
         <esql:row-results>
           <ticket>
            <esql:get-columns/>
           </ticket>
         </esql:row-results>
        </tickets>
       </esql:results>
     </esql:execute-query>
   </esql:connection>
```

Listing 8.8 *(continued)*

```
    </content>
  </page>
</xsp:page>
```

First, notice that we added the namespace declaration for the ESQL logicsheet to the <xsp:page> tag. As in the other examples, this declaration must match what was used when the logicsheet was defined. Now let's go over the ESQL statements line by line.

```
<esql:connection>
```

This is the root ESQL tag; all our ESQL statements reside between these tags.

```
<esql:pool>abc</esql:pool>
```

This defines which connection pool we will be using. You can have multiple <esql:pool> tags inside an <esql:connection> block, each covering multiple queries or update statements. Obviously, the name of the pool must match one of the pools defined in $CATALINA_HOME/webapps/cocoon/WEB-INF/cocoon.xconf.

```
<esql:execute-query>
```

This tag encompasses a query. It will contain the SQL statement and, optionally, the result set.

```
<esql:query>
 select * from TroubleTickets where Customer =
 '<xsp-session:get-attribute name="user"/>'
 order by TicketOpened</esql:query>
</esql:query>
```

Here, we set up our SQL command. Remember that when the user is authenticated, the userid is placed in a session variable called user. We rely on this attribute to build this SQL statement.

```
<tickets>
```

This is a user tag; we use it to encapsulate the dataset returned from the query.

```
<esql:row-results>
```

This sets up the results—it creates a loop that will process each row of the result set. In other words, each row of data will be processed by the commands inside this tag.

```
<ticket>
```

This is another user-defined tag that defines a specific row.

```
<esql:get-columns/>
```

This tag retrieves all columns from each row. The command will cause Cocoon to create tags for each column using the column name as the tag name and containing the column value. This is the same as if we had written this:

```
<Customer><esql:get-string column="Customer"/></Customer>
<CustomerLoc><esql:get-string column="CustomerLocCode"/></CustomerLoc>
<TicketId><esql:get-string column="TicketId"/></TicketId>
<TicketDesc><esql:get-string column="TicketDesc"/></TicketDesc>
<TicketOwner><esql:get-string column="TicketOwner"/></TicketOwner>
<TicketStatus><esql:get-string column="TicketStatus"/></TicketStatus>
<TicketOpened><esql:get-string column="TicketOpened"/></TicketOpened>
<TicketClosed><esql:get-string column="TicketClosed"/></TicketClosed>
<TicketNotes><esql:get-string column="TicketNotes"/></TicketNotes>
```

Obviously, `<esql:get-columns/>` is easier to use. However, there are several reasons to use individual `<esql:get-string>` tags:

- If you want to programmatically select specific columns, as opposed to preselecting them in the SQL statement
- If you want to apply logic to the values to change them
- If you want to change the tags from the default column names to something else
- If you want to create a nested query using a specific column value

Modifying main.xsl

In the previous XSP, we defined two new user tags, `tickets` and `ticket`. We now need to modify our `main.xsl` stylesheet to handle these tags by adding the following lines at the end (before the `</xsl:stylesheet>` tag):

```
<xsl:template match="tickets">
  <table border="1">
   <xsl:apply-templates/>
  </table>
 </xsl:template>

 <xsl:template match="ticket">
  <tr>
   <xsl:for-each select="*">
```

```
      <td>
        <xsl:apply-templates/>
      </td>
    </xsl:for-each>
  </tr>
</xsl:template>
```

As we discussed in the preceding section, the `tickets` tag encapsulates the entire result set. We use it here to set up a table that will have one row for each database row. The `ticket` tag represents one row at a time, and contains tags for each of the columns. Hence, in the template for `ticket`, we can loop through all its children and put each child in its own table column.

Adding a Pipeline

And finally, we need to add a pipeline entry for our new XSP:

```
<map:match pattern="tickets">
 <map:generate type="serverpages" src="xsp/tickets.xsp"/>
 <map:transform type="xslt" src="style/main.xsl"/>
 <map:serialize type="html"/>
</map:match>
```

Testing the XSP

We can now test our XSP by re-authenticating and then pointing the browser to `http://localhost:8080/cocoon/abc/tickets`. You should see something like what's shown in Figure 8.6.

And that's it. With a few lines, we have created an XML file that extracts data from our database table and spits it back out as XML.

Expanding the XSP

The example we've given is pretty basic—let's change it slightly by using a nested query. Suppose that we want to group our result by the customer location, New York or Berlin, into separate HTML tables. We could, of course, sort the result set the way we want to and use XSL to split out the different locations into tables. But we could also do what's shown in Listing 8.9.

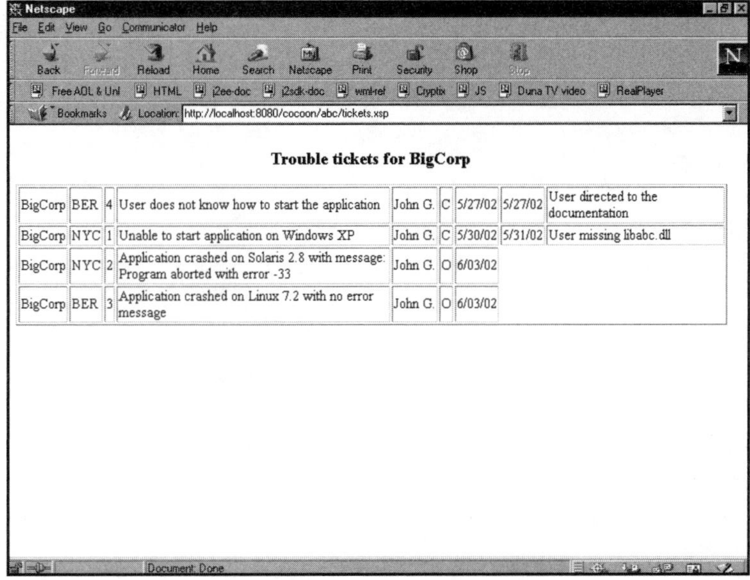

Figure 8.6
Trouble tickets for BigCorp.

Listing 8.9 *Revised Ticket XSP (tickets-b.xsp)*

```
<?xml version="1.0" encoding="ISO-8859-1"?>

<xsp:page language="java"
  xmlns:xsp="http://apache.org/xsp"
  xmlns:esql="http://apache.org/cocoon/SQL/v2"
  xmlns:xsp-session="http://apache.org/xsp/session/2.0"
>

  <page>

   <title>Trouble tickets for <xsp-session:get-attribute name="user"/></title>

   <content>

   <esql:connection>
     <esql:pool>abc</esql:pool>
     <esql:execute-query>
       <esql:query>
```

Listing 8.9 *(continued)*

```
        select * from CustomerLocations where Customer =
       '<xsp-session:get-attribute name="user"/>'
       order by CustomerLocation
      </esql:query>
      <esql:results>
       <locations>
        <esql:row-results>
          <location><esql:get-string column="CustomerLocation"/></location>

          <esql:execute-query>
           <esql:query>select * from TroubleTickets where Customer =
            '<xsp-session:get-attribute name="user"/>'
            and CustomerLocCode = <esql:parameter type="string">
            <esql:get-string ancestor="1" column="CustomerLocCode"/>
            </esql:parameter> order by TicketOpened
           </esql:query>
           <esql:results>
            <tickets>
             <esql:row-results>
              <ticket>
               <esql:get-columns/>
              </ticket>
             </esql:row-results>
            </tickets>
           </esql:results>
          </esql:execute-query>

        </esql:row-results>
       </locations>
      </esql:results>
    </esql:execute-query>
  </esql:connection>

  </content>
 </page>
</xsp:page>
```

The main point here is that we nest the second query inside the `<esql:row-results>` block. Because this block will get processed for every row in the result set, the nested query will be executed each time as well. The nested query is dynamic in that one of the parameters in the `where` clause depends on the value of the `CustomerLocCode` in each row.

We'll also need to add another template to `main.xsl`:

```
<xsl:template match="location">
  <br/> 
  <h3>Trouble tickets for <xsl:apply-templates/></h3>
 </xsl:template>
```

And finally, we need a new pipeline:

```
<map:match pattern="tickets-b.xsp">
 <map:generate type="serverpages" src="xsp/tickets-b.xsp"/>
 <map:transform type="xslt" src="style/main.xsl"/>
 <map:serialize type="html"/>
</map:match>
```

And when we access the page `http://localhost:8080/cocoon/abc/tickets-b.xsp`, we'll see what's shown in Figure 8.7.

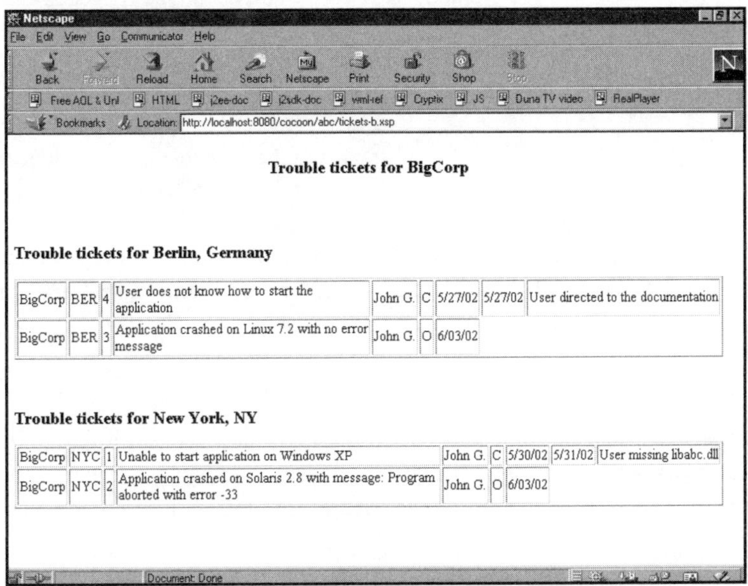

Figure 8.7
The revised trouble-ticket page.

XSP Internals

Before we leave this chapter, let's look "under the hood" of XSPs a bit.

When an XSP is converted into a Java file, it extends `org.apache.cocoon.components.language.markup.xsp.XSPGenerator` that has the following lineage:

```
java.lang.Object
  |
  +--org.apache.avalon.framework.logger.AbstractLoggable
        |
        +--org.apache.cocoon.xml.AbstractXMLProducer
              |
              +--org.apache.cocoon.generation.AbstractGenerator
                    |
                    +--org.apache.cocoon.generation.ComposerGenerator
                          |
                          +--org.apache.cocoon.generation.ServletGenerator
                                |
                                +--org.apache.cocoon.generation.
                                      ➥AbstractServerPage
                                      |
                                      +--org.apache.cocoon.components.language.
                                            ➥markup.xsp.XSPGenerator
```

As a `ServletGenerator`, an XSP has access to various objects in the environment as you would have in a servlet. Three of these are `Context`, `Request`, and `Response`. Through the `Request` object, an XSP also has access to a `Session` object.

Context

The `org.apache.cocoon.environment.http.HttpContext` object implements various methods of the `javax.servlet.ServletContext` class. You can use this to access the initialization parameters of the Cocoon servlet or find the full path of a given virtual path.

Request

The `org.apache.cocoon.environment.http.HttpRequest` object implements various methods of the `javax.servlet.http.HttpServletRequest` class. As with the latter, you can get request parameters, headers, and cookies. You can also get the `session` object, but it is `org.apache.cocoon.environment.http.HttpSession` instead of `javax.servlet.HttpSession`.

Response

The `org.apache.cocoon.environment.http.HttpResponse` object implements various methods of the `javax.servlet.http.HttpServletResponse` class.

If we wanted to, we could rewrite our `login.xsp` using the `Request` and `Session` objects instead of the `xsp-request` and `xsp-session` logicsheets, as shown in Listing 8.10.

Listing 8.10 *Rewritten Authentication XSP (login-b.xsp)*

```
<?xml version="1.0" encoding="ISO-8859-1"?>

<xsp:page language="java"
  xmlns:xsp="http://apache.org/xsp"
>

<xsp:structure>
 <xsp:include>org.apache.cocoon.environment.Session</xsp:include>
</xsp:structure>

<page>

<xsp:logic>
 String msg = "boo";
 Session session = null;
 String user = request.getParameter("user");
 String pwd = request.getParameter("pass");

 if (user.equals("abcuser") &amp;&amp; pwd.equals("secret")) {
   msg = "User '" + user + "' has been authenticated" +
      " - you can now proceed to the support page.";
   session = request.getSession(true);
   session.setAttribute("user", user);
 } else {
   msg = "Login failed";
 }

</xsp:logic>

 <page-title>Login results</page-title>
 <content>
  <title>Login results</title>
  <paragraph>
```

Listing 8.10 *(continued)*

```
    <xsp:expr>msg</xsp:expr>
    <xsp:expr>user</xsp:expr>
  </paragraph>
 </content>
</page>

</xsp:page>
```

Really, this is about as simple as using the logicsheets. In fact, it might be easier to read, especially for people who have a background in servlets and are used to working with the `HttpServletResponse`, `HttpServletRequest`, `HttpSession`, and `ServletContext` objects.

The one thing to be aware of is that for the integrity of the Cocoon processing model and for convenience, not all methods of the original objects are exposed by the Cocoon versions. If in doubt, check the documentation or the source code of the objects.

JavaScript Logicsheets

If you have a bunch of legacy JS code, you might be able to reuse it in Cocoon. Cocoon supports XSPs with embedded JavaScript or JavaScript logicsheets. There are three built-in JS logicsheets: `xsp-request`, `xsp-response`, and `xsp-session`. Functionally, they are the same as their Java counterparts.

> **Rhino**
> Cocoon uses the Rhino implementation of JavaScript, which is written entirely in Java and can therefore be compiled into a Java class. Rhino is available from `www.mozilla.org/rhino/` and is included in Cocoon.

To illustrate the use of JavaScript logicsheets, we can rewrite our original login XSP (shown previously in Listing 8.6). The revised page is shown in Listing 8.11.

Listing 8.11 *JavaScript-based login XSP (login-c.xsp)*

```
<?xml version="1.0" encoding="ISO-8859-1"?>

<xsp:page language="javascript"
  xmlns:xsp="http://apache.org/xsp"
  xmlns:xsp-request="http://apache.org/xsp/request/2.0"
  xmlns:xsp-session="http://apache.org/xsp/session/2.0"
>
```

Listing 8.11 *(continued)*

```
<page>

<xsp:logic>
 msg = "boo";
 user = <xsp-request:get-parameter name="user"/>;
 pwd = <xsp-request:get-parameter name="pass"/>;

 if (user.equals("BigCorp") &amp;&amp; pwd.equals("secret")) {
   msg = "User '" + user + "' has been authenticated" +
      " - you can now proceed to the support page.";
   <xsp-session:set-attribute name="user">
    <xsp:expr>user</xsp:expr>
   </xsp-session:set-attribute>;
 } else {
   msg = "Login failed";
 }

</xsp:logic>

 <page-title>Login results</page-title>
 <content>
  <title>Login results</title>
  <paragraph>
   <xsp:expr>msg</xsp:expr>
  </paragraph>
 </content>
</page>

</xsp:page>
```

The only difference between this and the previous version is the fact that the `<xsp:page>` tag has the language attribute set to `javascript` and that we are using JavaScript variables. However, before we can use this we need to tweak the pipeline slightly and add a parameter that tells Cocoon we are using JavaScript-based XSPs:

```
<map:match pattern="login">
 <map:generate type="serverpages" src="xsp/login-c.xsp">
  <map:parameter name="programming-language" value="js"/>
 </map:generate>
 <map:transform type="xslt" src="style/main.xsl"/>
 <map:serialize type="html"/>
</map:match>
```

The `<map:parameter>` tag is the key here. Without setting the `programming-language` key to `js`, Cocoon would compile this XSP using the Java compiler, and would generate errors for the variable syntax.

Summary

In this chapter, we have written and used several XSPs. We have used the `xsp-session` and `xsp-request` logicsheets and seen alternatives to them. We know how to create our own logicsheet and where to define it. We have seen how to enable database access in Cocoon and use the `esql` logicsheet. There are loads of other things we can do with XSPs. In Chapter 12, we will also make use of the `sendmail` and `form-val` logicsheets. But first we need to look into sitemap logic.

CHAPTER 9

Using Content Logic: Generators

In the preceding chapter, we discussed how to implement content logic using XSPs. While we're on the subject, in this chapter we'll cover some of the other generators that come with Cocoon. Strictly speaking, we are dealing more with content than logic, but there is enough customization possible with these generators that it fits well enough.

In previous chapters we have already met the `FileGenerator` and `ServerPagesGenerator`. In Chapter 19, "Searching with Cocoon," we'll deal with the `SearchGenerator`. Here are the generators that are covered in this chapter:

- `DirectoryGenerator` (with `ImageDirectoryGenerator` and `MP3DirectoryGenerator`)
- `ErrorGenerator`
- `HTMLGenerator`
- `JspGenerator`
- `RequestGenerator`
- `VelocityGenerator`

Note
If you are poking through the source code and are wondering about `XMLDBCollectionGenerator` and `XMLDBGenerator`, those two are deprecated and replaced by the `xmldb` pseudo protocol. We'll see that in action in Chapter 16, "Cocoon Interfaces: Databases."

The examples that we'll go through to illustrate these components will all be done within the `abc` project we created in Chapter 7, "Creating Static Pages." If you choose to put the files directly under the root directory of your Cocoon Web application, remember to remove the `abc` directory name from the URLs we provide.

DirectoryGenerator

This component is useful for producing a drillable directory listing from a given starting point. Using it couldn't be simpler. We'll start with two pipeline entries in `sitemap.xmap`:

```
<map:match pattern="dir-list/**">
  <map:generate type="directory" src="{1}"/>
  <map:transform src="style/dirlist.xsl"/>
  <map:serialize type="html"/>
</map:match>
```

The `<map:generate>` tag for the `DirectoryGenerator` tags one parameter, `src`, which specifies what directory to read. The generator will generate SAX events for each file or subdirectory in the named directory. All tags will belong to the namespace `"http://apache.org/cocoon/directory/2.0"`. To use the tags, we need only create a stylesheet as shown in Listing 9.1.

Listing 9.1 *Stylesheet for DirectoryGenerator (dirlist.xsl)*

```
<?xml version="1.0"?>

<xsl:stylesheet version="1.0"
 xmlns:xsl="http://www.w3.org/1999/XSL/Transform"
 xmlns:dir="http://apache.org/cocoon/directory/2.0">

  <xsl:template match="/">
   <html>
   <head>
    <title><xsl:value-of select="dir:directory/@name"/></title>
    </head>
    <body bgcolor="#ffffff">
```

Listing 9.1 *(continued)*

```
     <h1>Directory Listing of <xsl:value-of select="dir:directory/@name"/></h1>
     <table border="0">
      <tr>
       <td>
        <a href="../"><i>parent directory</i></a>
       </td>
      </tr>
      <tr>
       <td>
         
       </td>
      </tr>
      <xsl:apply-templates/>
     </table>
    </body>
   </html>
  </xsl:template>

  <xsl:template match="dir:directory/dir:directory">
   <tr>
    <td>
     <a href="{@name}/"><xsl:value-of select="@name"/></a>/
    </td>
    <td>
     <xsl:value-of select="@date"/>
    </td>
    <td>
     <xsl:value-of select="@lastModified"/>
    </td>
   </tr>
  </xsl:template>

  <xsl:template match="dir:file">
   <tr>
    <td>
     <xsl:value-of select="@name"/>
    </td>
    <td>
     <xsl:value-of select="@date"/>
    </td>
    <td>
```

Listing 9.1 *(continued)*

```
        <xsl:value-of select="@lastModified"/>
      </td>
    </tr>
  </xsl:template>

</xsl:stylesheet>
```

Note that each `dir:directory` or `dir:file` tag has three attributes: `name`, for the name of the directory or file; `date`, for the last modified time in MM/DD/YY HH:MM AM format; and `lastModified`, for the last modified time as number of milliseconds since the epoch.

When we invoke the URL `http://localhost:8080/cocoon/abc/dir-list`, we will see what's shown in Figure 9.1.

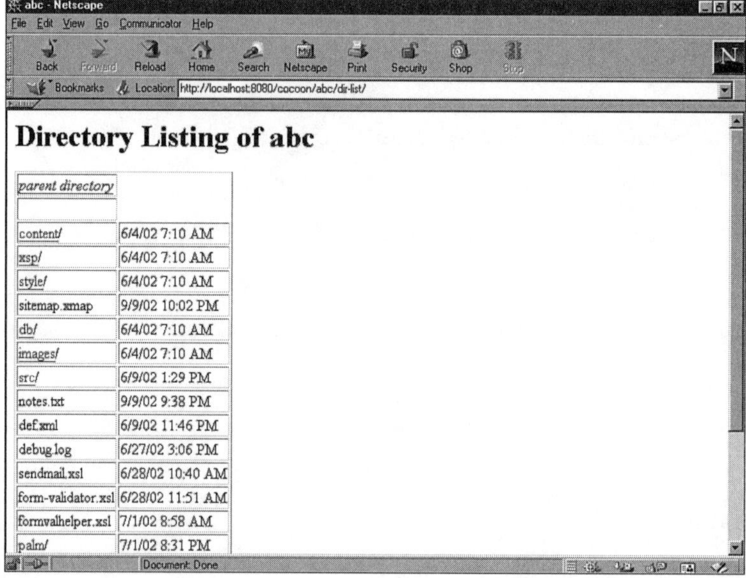

Figure 9.1
Output from DirectoryGenerator.

In case you are wondering, you can give this URL a fully qualified path, such as `http://localhost:8080/cocoon/abc/dir-list/c:/`. Just remember that any path you specify uses forward slashes, even on Windows.

One thing we can do to enhance this further is to have the file names link to a pipeline that invokes a `Reader` to display the content of the file as simple text. Remember from

Chapter 4, "Introduction to the Sitemap," that a `Reader` is a component that provides source content straight back to the client using the specified mime-type. A `Reader` does not do any XML operations on the data—just a simple pass-through.

Let's add the following pipeline:

```
<map:match pattern="file-reader/**">
 <map:read mime-type="text/html" src="{1}"/>
</map:match>
```

We also have to change the template for `dir:file` in `dirlist.xsl` to include the new links:

```
<xsl:template match="dir:file">
 <tr>
  <td>
   <a href="/cocoon/abc/file-reader/{@name}">
    <xsl:value-of select="@name"/>
   </a>
  </td>
  <td>
   <xsl:value-of select="@date"/>
  </td>
  <td>
   <xsl:value-of select="@lastModified"/>
  </td>
 </tr>
</xsl:template>
```

Now, for various reasons, two related generators are included in Cocoon: `MP3DirectoryGenerator`, which reads mp3 files and reports on mp3-related attributes, and `ImageDirectoryGenerator`, which reads GIF or JPEG files and shows attributes for width and height. To see these in action, we need to change our previous pipeline from

```
<map:generate type="directory" src="{1}"/>
```

to

```
<map:generate type="imagedirectory" src="{1}"/>
```

to use the `ImageDirectoryGenerator`, or

```
<map:generate type="mp3directory" src="{1}"/>
```

to use the `MP3DirectoryGenerator`. Then we need to modify our `dirlist.xsl` stylesheet to pick up the new attributes. For example, if we use the `ImageDirectoryGenerator`, we need to pick up attributes of `width` and `height`. Note that because both generators extend `DirectoryGenerator`, the attributes of `name`, `date`, and `lastModified` will always be available. Table 9.1 lists all the attributes of these three generators.

Table 9.1 *File/Directory Attributes Produced by Directory Generators*

Generator	Attribute	Description
DirectoryGenerator	name	Name of the file or directory
DirectoryGenerator	date	Last modified date in readable form
DirectoryGenerator	lastModified	Last modified date in milliseconds since the epoch
ImageDirectoryGenerator	width	Width of the image
ImageDirectoryGenerator	height	Height of the image
MP3DirectoryGenerator	frequency	Frequency of the file in KHz
MP3DirectoryGenerator	bitrate	Bitrate of the file in kilobits
MP3DirectoryGenerator	mode	Mode of the file, one of `stereo`, `joint stereo`, `dual channel`, `single channel`
MP3DirectoryGenerator	variable-rate	Set to `yes` if a VBR header is found
MP3DirectoryGenerator	title	Song title
MP3DirectoryGenerator	artist	Song artist
MP3DirectoryGenerator	album	Song album
MP3DirectoryGenerator	year	Song year
MP3DirectoryGenerator	comment	Song comments
MP3DirectoryGenerator	track	Song track number
MP3DirectoryGenerator	genre	Music genre

Using some of the MP3 attributes, we can modify the template for `dir:file` in `dirlist.xsl` as shown here:

```
<xsl:template match="dir:file">
 <tr>
  <td>
   <a href="/cocoon/abc/file-reader/{@name}">
    <xsl:value-of select="@name"/>
   </a>
  </td>
  <td>
   <xsl:value-of select="@date"/>
  </td>
```

```
  <xsl:if test="@album != ''">
   <td>Album: <xsl:value-of select="@album"/> </td>
  </xsl:if>
  <xsl:if test="@title != ''">
   <td>Title: <xsl:value-of select="@title"/> </td>
  </xsl:if>
  <xsl:if test="@artist != ''">
   <td>Artist: <xsl:value-of select="@artist"/> </td>
  </xsl:if>
 </tr>
</xsl:template>
```

We also must add the `MP3DirectoryGenerator` to our sitemap, because it is not included in the list of generators:

```
   <map:generator label="content,data" logger="sitemap.generator.mp3directory"
 name="mp3directory" src="org.apache.cocoon.generation.MP3DirectoryGenerator
"/>
```

After we change our `dirlist` pipeline from `directory` to `mp3directory`, we can check our `c:\My Music` directory. On my machine, the contents of this directory are as shown in Figure 9.2.

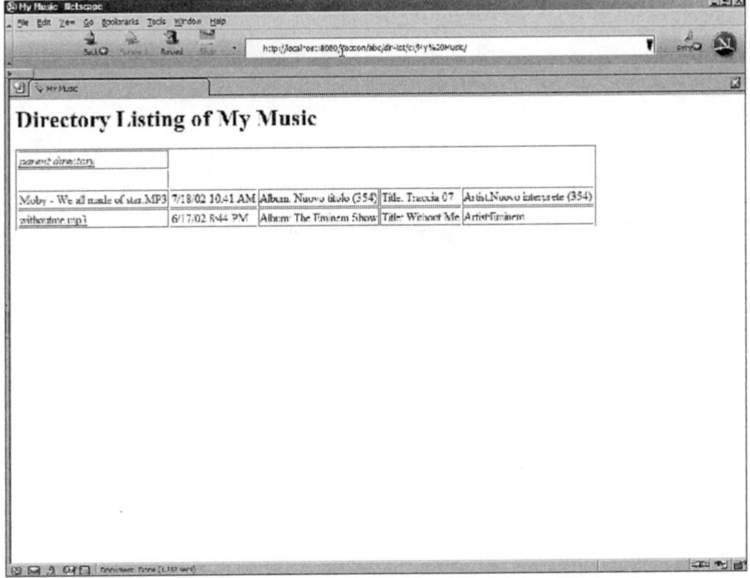

Figure 9.2
Output from MP3DirectoryGenerator.

ErrorGenerator

One problem Web site administrators is how to gracefully handle invalid URLs. Rather than let the Web server return a basic 404 error page, it is part of good site design to not just return a customized (and polite) error page, but log the error so that the administrator can make sure a page really isn't missing.

Cocoon provides a special pipeline tag called `<map:handle-errors>` that you can use to trap errors of a specific type. When you define a pipeline using this tag, Cocoon automatically generates the error tags using the `ErrorGenerator` and you just have to specify one or more `<map:transform>` steps and the `<map:serialize>` step. You won't find this generator in the usual source directory either. Its full name is actually `org.apache.cocoon.sitemap.ErrorNotifier` and it extends `org.apache.cocoon.sitemap.NotifyingGenerator`, which in turn extends `org.apache.cocoon.generation.ComposerGenerator`.

Let's add a pipeline at the end of our sitemap to handle 404 errors:

```
<map:handle-errors type="404">
 <map:transform src="style/error.xsl"/>
 <map:serialize/>
</map:handle-errors>
```

The stylesheet looks as shown in Listing 9.2.

Listing 9.2 *Stylesheet for ErrorGenerator (error.xsl)*

```
<?xml version="1.0"?>

<xsl:stylesheet version="1.0"
 xmlns:xsl="http://www.w3.org/1999/XSL/Transform"
 xmlns:error="http://apache.org/cocoon/error/2.0"
>

<xsl:template match="/">
 <html>
  <head>
   <title>Whoops</title>
  </head>

  <body bgcolor="#ffffff">
   <center>
    <h3>ABC Software</h3>
```

Listing 9.2 *(continued)*

```
    </center>

    <p>We're sorry, we couldn't find this page.</p>
    <p>The server message is: <xsl:value-of select="//error:message"/></p>
    <p>The description is: <xsl:value-of select="//error:description"/></p>
   </body>
  </html>
 </xsl:template>
</xsl:stylesheet>
```

Note the namespace for the tags coming out of the `ErrorGenerator`.

If we put in a bogus URI, we will see what's shown in Figure 9.3.

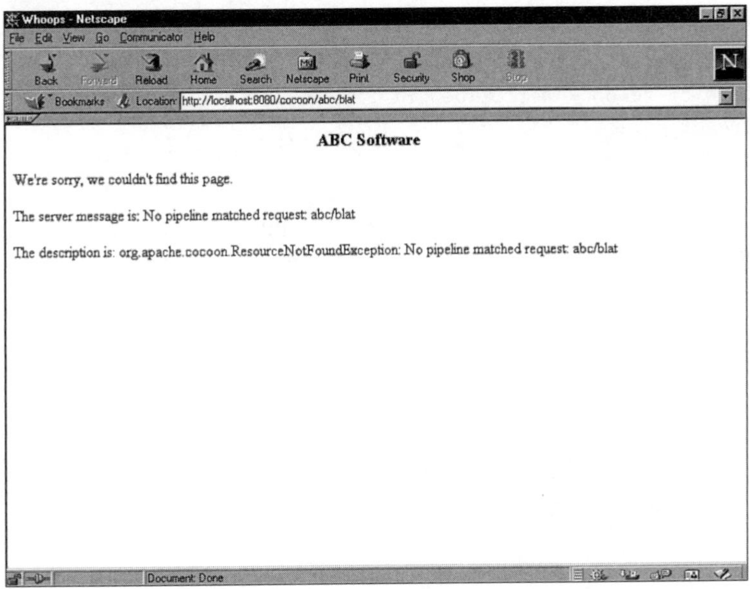

Figure 9.3
404 error.

Table 9.2 shows which tags are available from the `ErrorGenerator`. All these tags belong to the namespace `http://apache.org/cocoon/error/2.0`, which is indicated by the prefix `error`. The top-level tag of the group is `<notify>`.

Table 9.2 *Error Tags*

Tag	Description
`error:type`	Type of error: either "error" or "unknown"
`error:title`	Basic title: either "An error occurred" or "Object Notification"
`error:source`	Name of the exception class
`error:message`	A brief error message
`error:description`	The `message` part of the exception or "No details available"
`error:extra`	Detailed information

Multiples of these are possible. Each tag has a `description` attribute, which tells what kind of detail is being provided.

If we wanted to access the detailed information in the `extra` tags, we might add something like this to the `error.xsl`:

```
<xsl:for-each select="//error:extra">
 <h5><xsl:value-of select="@error:description"/></h5>
 <p><xsl:value-of select="."/></p>
</xsl:for-each>
```

Although we haven't covered it yet, a good use for this pipeline is to insert another `<map:transform>` step that would log the error to a database using the `SQLTransformer`.

HTMLGenerator

This is a useful component if you want to extract and process tags from legacy HTML files. The `HTMLGenerator` reads HTML documents, converts them to XHTML using JTidy, and pumps the resulting tags through the pipeline.

> **Note**
> JTidy is a nifty utility that checks HTML syntax and optionally fixes malformed HTML. JTidy can also do pretty printing of HTML. It is included by default in Cocoon, but if you want more information, you can find its home page at `http://sourceforge.net/projects/jtidy`.

Suppose we have a rather sloppy HTML file, as in Listing 9.3.

Listing 9.3 *Legacy HTML File (legacyhtml.html)*

```
<html>
<head>
  <title>This is a test</title>
</head>

<body>
  <center>
    <h3>Welcome to ABC Software</center></h3>
    <h5>This is a sloppy HTML page</h5>

  <br>
  <p>This is the first paragraph</p>
  <p>Whoops, we forgot to close this paragraph ...

</body>
</html>
```

Our closing `</center>` tag is in the wrong place, we used a `<br>` tag, and we forgot to close the last `<p>` tag.

Now we create a pipeline to handle this:

```
<map:match pattern="legacyhtml">
 <map:generate type="html" src="html/legacy.html"/>
 <map:serialize type="xml"/>
</map:match>
```

We've declared the output as `"xml"` so we can see how JTidy cleans up this code. If we point our browser to `http://localhost:8080/cocoon/abc/legacyhtml`, we'll get HTML like what's shown in Listing 9.4.

Listing 9.4 *Legacy HTML File After Cleanup (legacyhtml.xml)*

```
<?xml version="1.0" encoding="UTF-8"?>

<html xmlns="http://www.w3.org/1999/xhtml">

<head>
  <meta content="HTML Tidy, see www.w3.org" name="generator"/>
  <title>This is a test</title>
</head>
```

Listing 9.4 *(continued)*

```
<body>
  <center>
    <h3>Welcome to ABC Software</h3>
    <h5>This is a sloppy HTML page</h5>

   <br/>

   <p>This is the first paragraph</p>
   <p>Whoops, we forgot to close this paragraph ...</p>
  </center>

</body>

</html>
```

Now this is clearly a simplistic use of the `HTMLGenerator`. Besides an alternative to a reader, this generator can be used to clean up HTML files and extract specific tags. For example, if a site has large quantities of text embedded in HTML files, an XSL transformer could be used to extract the tags surrounding the desired content. The extracted content then can be passed to a custom transformer that can write the data back out to disk as XML files. Alternatively, another XSLT transformer can take the content and present it to the client using a new look and feel. This is a good way to convert a traditional site to a Cocoon-based site using a new look and feel but without rewriting the original files.

JspGenerator

Many sites have lots of legacy JSPs in addition to, or instead of, HTML files. The good news is that Cocoon lets you reuse these, either in the raw or as input XML. `JspGenerator` is the component that handles the latter. It reads a JSP containing well-formed XML and outputs SAX events to the pipeline. Closely related to this is the `JspReader`, which simply presents raw JSP files to the browser.

Fixing the JSP Components in 2.0.2

If you are using Cocoon 2.0.3 or greater, you can skip this section. However, if you are using Cocoon 2.0.2, you'll need to follow these instructions to fix both the `JspReader` and the `JspGenerator` because, sadly, they are broken in this version. Of course, this means that you must have the source distribution of 2.0.2 and must be read up on the building instructions we discussed in Chapter 6, "Installing Cocoon."

Patching JspReader

First, we have to patch the JSP reader component. Edit `$COCOON_EXTRACT/src/java/org/apache/cocoon/reading/JSPReader` and replace the following (lines 119–132). Replace

```
// KP: A hacky way of source resolving.
// Why context:// protocol returns not a string in URL format,
// but a system-dependent path with 'file:' prefix?
String contextDir = new File(httpContext.getRealPath("/")).toURL().t
oExternalForm();
src = this.resolver.resolve(this.source);
String url = src.getSystemId();
if(url.startsWith(contextDir)) {
    // File is located under contextDir, using relative file name
    url = url.substring(contextDir.length());
}
if (url.startsWith("file:")) {
    // we need a relative path
    url = url.substring(5);
}
```

with

```
String url = this.source;

// -- debug info --
src = resolver.resolve(url);
System.out.println("Resolved to: " + src);
java.net.URL resURL = httpContext.getResource(".");
System.out.println(". resource is: " + resURL);
// -- end debug --


// absolute path is processed as is
if (!url.startsWith("/")) {
    // get current request path
    String servletPath = httpRequest.getServletPath();
    // remove file part
    servletPath = servletPath.substring(0, servletPath.lastIndexOf('
/') + 1);
    url = servletPath + url;
}
```

Patching JspGenerator

Now we have to fix the JSP generator component. Edit `$COCOON_EXTRACT/src/java/org/apache/cocoon/generation/JspGenerator` and replace the following (lines 106–113). Replace

```
src = this.resolver.resolve(this.source);
String url = src.getSystemId();
// Guarantee src parameter is a file
if (!url.startsWith("file:/"))
    throw new IOException("Protocol not supported: " + url);

url = url.substring(5);
getLogger().debug("JspGenerator executing JSP:" + url);
```

with

```
String url = this.source;
// absolute path is processed as is
if (!url.startsWith("/")) {
    // get current request path
    String servletPath = httpRequest.getServletPath();
    // remove file part
    servletPath = servletPath.substring(0, servletPath.lastIndexOf('
/') + 1);
    url = servletPath + url;
}
```

Rebuilding Cocoon

Rebuild Cocoon with the appropriate command. On Windows, type

```
.\build.bat -Dinclude.webapp.libs=yes webapp
```

and on Unix type this:

```
./build.sh -Dinclude.webapp.libs=yes webapp
```

You don't have to copy over the entire `cocoon.war` to your runtime directory. Just copy `$COCOON_EXTRACT/build/cocoon/webapp/WEB-LIB/lib/cocoon-2.0.2.jar` to `$CATALINA_HOME/webapps/cocoon/WEB-INF/lib` and you're ready to go.

JSP Compiler

To handle JSPs, Cocoon needs to make use of a JSP compiler. The `JSPEngineImpl` forwards JSPs to this JSP engine. By default, Cocoon is set up to work with Jasper, the JSP engine that is part of Tomcat. Cocoon also can work with a different `JSPEngine` implementation, `JSPEngineImplWLS`, that can work with WebLogic's JSP compiler.

For our examples, however, we'll use Jasper. We don't need to change anything with Cocoon, but we do need to copy `$CATALINA_HOME/lib/jasper-compiler.jar` to `$CATALINA_HOME/webapps/cocoon/WEB-INF/lib`.

Testing JspReader

With the previous changes in place, and Cocoon bounced, we'll see how Cocoon can handle the JSP shown in Listing 9.5.

Listing 9.5 *Simple JSP (test.jsp)*

```
<%@ page import="java.util.*" %>

<html>

 <head>
  <title>Test JSP</title>
 </head>

 <body>
  <center>
   <h3>Let's see if Cocoon can handle this ... </h3>
  </center>

  <p>The current time is: <%=new Date()%></p>

 </body>
</html>
```

We need to add a pipeline to handle this:

```
<map:match pattern="rawjsp/*">
 <map:read mime-type="text/html" src="/abc/jsp/{1}.jsp" type="jsp"/>
</map:match>
```

One critical thing is that the `src` attribute *must* provide the path to the JSP file relative to the `cocoon` directory *and* it must start with a forward slash. Otherwise, Cocoon won't be able to find your file.

If all goes well, Cocoon will correctly display the JSP file as shown in Figure 9.4 when we point our browser to `http://localhost:8080/cocoon/abc/rawjsp/test`.

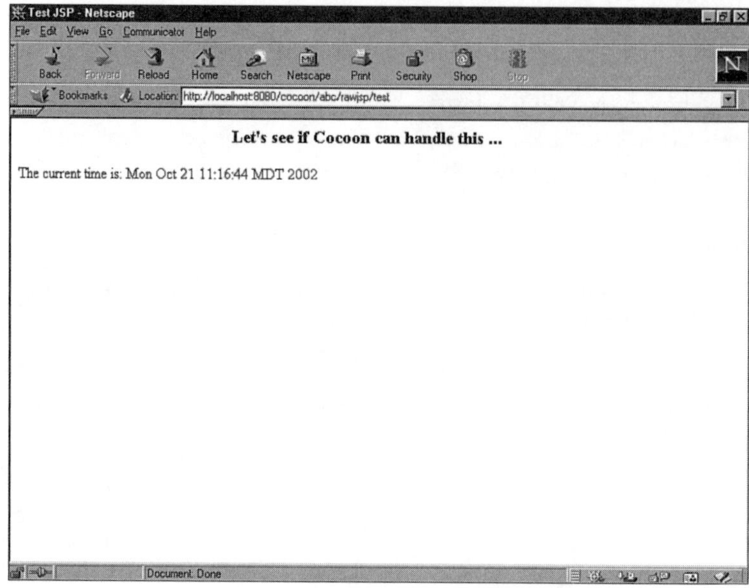

Figure 9.4
Test of JspReader.

Testing JspGenerator

Remember that the difference between these two components is that the `JspReader` serves up JSP files in the raw, whereas the `JspGenerator` parses them and converts them to SAX events (assuming they contain well-formed XML, of course). Listing 9.6 shows one such file.

Listing 9.6 *XML from JSP (hello.jsp)*

```
<%@ page import="java.util.*" %>
<page>
  <page-title>Test JSP</page-title>
  <content>
    <title>Hi there!</title>
    <paragraph>The current time is: <%=new Date()%></paragraph>
 </content>
</page>
```

And we need to add a pipeline to handle this:

```
<map:match pattern="jsp/*">
 <map:generate src="/abc/jsp/{1}.jsp" type="jsp"/>
```

```
 <map:transform src="style/main.xsl"/>
 <map:serialize type="html"/>
</map:match>
```

Note that the same rules for the `src` attribute apply here as well. Figure 9.5 shows the expected output from the URL `http://localhost:8080/cocoon/abc/jsp/hello`.

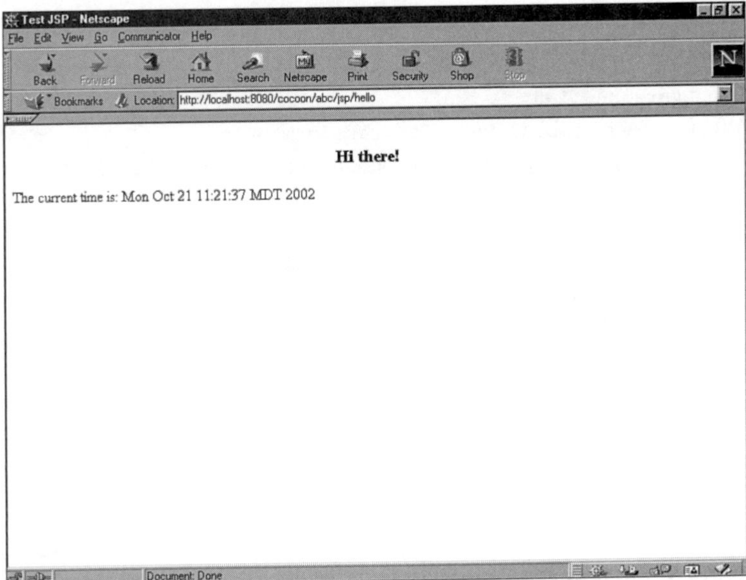

Figure 9.5
Test of JspGenerator.

RequestGenerator

This is another useful component. It takes whatever is in the request object and spits out corresponding tags, thus making such things as request parameters available to other components in the pipeline.

To see this in action, we will rewrite our login process in XSL. First, we define a new pipeline:

```
<map:match pattern="login3">
 <map:generate type="request"/>
```

```
 <map:transform type="xslt" src="style/dologin.xsl"/>
 <map:serialize type="html"/>
</map:match>
```

Listing 9.7 shows the contents of dologin.xsl.

Listing 9.7 *Login XSL (dologin.xsl)*

```
<?xml version="1.0"?>

<xsl:stylesheet version="1.0"
 xmlns:xsl="http://www.w3.org/1999/XSL/Transform"
 xmlns:request="http://xml.apache.org/cocoon/requestgenerator/2.0"
>

 <xsl:variable name="prefix">request:</xsl:variable>

 <xsl:template match="request:request">
  <html>
   <head>
    <title>Login results</title>
   </head>

   <body bgcolor="#ffffff">

   <xsl:variable name="user">
     <xsl:call-template name="get-parameter">
       <xsl:with-param name="name">user</xsl:with-param>
     </xsl:call-template>
   </xsl:variable>
   <xsl:variable name="pass">
     <xsl:call-template name="get-parameter">
       <xsl:with-param name="name">pass</xsl:with-param>
     </xsl:call-template>
   </xsl:variable>

   <xsl:choose>
     <xsl:when test="$user = 'BigCorp' and $pass = 'secret'">
      <p>Your login succeeded</p>
     </xsl:when>
     <xsl:otherwise>
      <p>Your login failed</p>
      <p><xsl:value-of select="$user"/></p>
```

Listing 9.7 *(continued)*

```
      <p><xsl:value-of select="$pass"/></p>
     </xsl:otherwise>
   </xsl:choose>

   </body>
  </html>
 </xsl:template>

 <xsl:template name="get-parameter">
   <xsl:param name="name"/>
   <xsl:value-of select="//request:parameter[@name=$name]/request:value"/>
</xsl:template>

</xsl:stylesheet>
```

In addition to request parameters, the RequestGenerator also provides request headers and sitemap parameters. For reference, the DTD for this generator is shown in Listing 9.8.

Listing 9.8 *RequestGenerator DTD (request-generator.dtd)*

```
<!ELEMENT request (requestHeaders, requestParameters, configurationParameters)>
<!ATTLIST request
  target CDATA #REQUIRED
  source CDATA #REQUIRED
>
<!ELEMENT requestHeaders ( header* )>
<!ATTLIST header
  name CDATA #REQUIRED
>

<!ELEMENT requestParameters ( parameter* )>
<!ATTLIST parameter
  name CDATA #REQUIRED
>
<!ELEMENT value #PCDATA>

<!ELEMENT configurationParameters ( parameter* )>
<!ATTLIST parameter
  name CDATA #REQUIRED
>
```

ScriptGenerator

Another useful generator is the `ScriptGenerator`, which allows you to make use of the Bean Scripting Framework, or BSF. Briefly, BSF is an architecture that allows you to incorporate scripting into a Java application. BSF supports any scripting language written in Java, including Netscape Rhino, VBScript, and JPython. There are actually two components to BSF: the BSF Manager, which is invoked by the application in order to access the scripting languages, and the BSF Engine, which is implemented by the scripting language in order for the latter to be accessible to the BSF Manager. An application using BSF has access to all the constructs of the various scripting languages that are available to the BSF Manager. In addition, the BSP Manager allows an application to make Java objects available to the scripting languages. These objects are called "beans," though they are not beans in the sense.

One thing to note is that because BSF does not actually compile the scripts, they will be parsed on every request. For large scripts, this can really slow down your pages. As an alternative way of using your existing JavaScript code, consider turning it into JavaScript XSP pages. These do get compiled and reused on subsequent requests, and so will be more efficient.

> **More About BSF**
> BSF is an IBM technology. Its official home page is now at `www-124.ibm.com/developerworks/projects/bsf`. The BSF distribution includes a well-written users guide in PDF.

The `ScriptGenerator` acts as the application in the BSF architecture, and is responsible for creating the BSF Manager. By default, this generator exposes the six objects, or beans, for use by the client scripts. These are shown in Table 9.3.

Table 9.3 *BSF Beans Exposed by the ScriptGenerator*

Object Name	Description
`resolver`	Resolver
`source`	Source
`objectModel`	`ObjectModelHelper` (allows access to Request, Response, Context)
`parameters`	Parameters object (holds list of sitemap parameters passed to the component)
`output`	`StringBuffer` object that holds the output
`logger`	Pointer to the `getLogger()` method

For our example, we'll re-implement our login process in JavaScript. Listing 9.9 shows our file.

Listing 9.9 *JavaScript Login (login.js)*

```
out      = bsf.lookupBean( "output" )
logger   = bsf.lookupBean( "logger" )
resolver = bsf.lookupBean( "resolver" )
source   = bsf.lookupBean( "source" )
objModel = bsf.lookupBean( "objectModel" )
params   = bsf.lookupBean( "parameters" )

request = objModel.get("request")
user = request.getParameter("user")
pass = request.getParameter("pass")
corp = params.getParameter("company")

out.append("<page><title>Login results</title><content>")
out.append("<paragraph>" + doLogin(user, pass) + "</paragraph>");
out.append("</content></page>")


function doLogin(u, p) {
   if (u == null && p == null) {
      return "Invalid request: expecting parameters of 'user' and 'pass'";
   } else {
      if (p == 'secret') {
        logger.debug("login.js: Login succeeded for " + u);
        return "Welcome " + u + ", you can now \
          enter the " + corp + " website";
      } else {
        logger.debug("login.js: Login failed for " + u);
        return "Oops " + u + ", your password is incorrect";
      }
   }
}
```

Although we are not using all the beans, we made references to them to illustrate the procedure. When you use a script in Cocoon like this, you must end up with well-formed XML. All output goes into the `StringBuffer` object that is provided by the `ScriptGenerator` and that will be used as the XML input source after the script has completed execution. You can also see how we can access the `HttpRequest` object using the `objModel` bean. We also are accessing a single sitemap parameter called `company`. Sitemap parameters are discussed in Chapter 11, "Using Sitemap Logic: `Matchers` and `Selectors`."

The pipeline to handle the preceding file looks like this:

```
<map:match pattern="script/*">
  <map:generate src="scripts/{1}" type="script">
   <map:parameter name="company" value="ABC Software"/>
  </map:generate>
  <map:transform src="style/main.xsl"/>
  <map:serialize type="html"/>
</map:match>
```

And the expected output, assuming that we pass in the right parameters, is as shown in Figure 9.6.

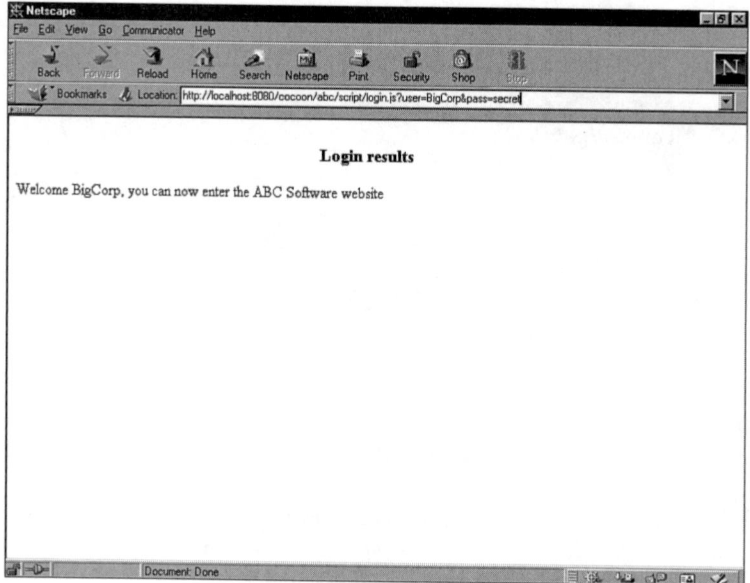

Figure 9.6
Output from login.js.

Supported Scripting Languages
By default, the `ScriptGenerator` supports Rhino JavaScript and JPython. To use Python, you must download JPython from `www.jython.org`, following the installation instructions, and copy `jython.jar` to `$CATALINA_HOME/webapps/cocoon/WEB-INF/lib`.

You can configure the ScriptGenerator to access other scripting languages by adding an <add-languages> block to the ScriptGenerator definition in the sitemap. For example, to add support for KawaScript, you might have something like this:

```
<map:generator label="content,data" name="script"
  src="org.apache.cocoon.generation.ScriptGenerator">

  <add-languages>
     <language name="kawa-scheme"
       src="org.gnu.kawa.bsf.engines.KawaEngine">
       <extension>scm</extension>
     </language>
  </add-languages>
</map:generator>
```

Naturally, the KawaScript jar file should be in the WEB-INF/lib directory of the Cocoon Web application.

VelocityGenerator

Our final generator of the chapter is the VelocityGenerator. Velocity is another Apache project, actually a subproject of the Jakarta project. If you are not familiar with it, Velocity is a Java-based template engine with which you can add Java logic to Web pages (or other types of files as well) without all the clutter of embedded code. In Cocoon, the Velocity Generator is responsible for initializing the Velocity engine, creating the Context object, and adding objects to it. Currently, VelocityGenerator adds five objects to the context, as shown in Table 9.4.

Table 9.4 *Objects Added to the Context by VelocityGenerator*

Object	Description
template	Relative path to the template file
request	HttpRequest object
response	HttpResponse object
context	HttpContext object
parameters	Parameters object containing any sitemap parameters being passed to the component

Let's rewrite (again!) our login process, this time as a Velocity template. Listing 9.10 shows the Velocity template.

Listing 9.10 *Velocity Template Login (login.vm)*

```
<?xml version="1.0"?>

#set($corp = $parameters.getParameter("company", ""))
#set($user = $request.getParameter("user"))
#set($pass = $request.getParameter("pass"))

<page>
 <title>Login results</title>
 <content>
  #if ($user && $pass)
    #if ($pass == 'secret')
     <paragraph>Welcome $user, you can now enter the $corp website</paragraph>
    #else
     <paragraph>Oops $user, your password is incorrect</paragraph>
    #end
  #else
     <paragraph>Invalid request: expecting parameters of 'user' and 'pass'
     </paragraph>
  #end

  <h3>Just for grins, here are the parameters we found:</h3>
  #foreach ($name in $request.getParameterNames())
   <paragraph>
    Parameter: $name = $request.getParameter($name)
   </paragraph>
  #end

  <paragraph>This template served by $template</paragraph>

 </content>
</page>
```

You'll notice that the first thing we do is set some variables: One points to a sitemap parameter and the other two point to request parameters. All the # statements are Velocity constructs. The # `foreach` construct illustrates how Velocity can access collections.

Our sitemap map entry is as follows:

```
<map:match pattern="velocity/*">
 <map:generate type="velocity" src="templates/{1}.vm">
   <map:parameter name="company" value="ABC Software"/>
 </map:generate>
```

```
  <map:transform type="xslt" src="style/main.xsl"/>
  <map:serialize type="html"/>
</map:match>
```

The output of a correct login using our Velocity template is shown in Figure 9.7.

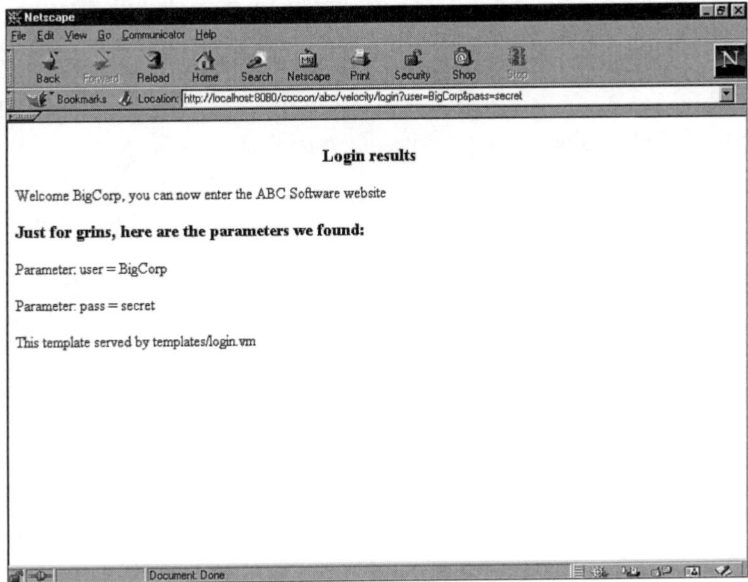

Figure 9.7
Output from login.vm.

More About Velocity
The Velocity home page is at `http://jakarta.apache.org/velocity`. If you are just getting started, this is a good introductory article: `www.javaworld.com/javaworld/jw-12-2001/jw-1228-velocity_p.html`.

Summary

Our discussion in this chapter has shown just how flexible Cocoon is. Rather than locking you into a specific technology, Cocoon allows you to incorporate other technologies into your application. In particular, the `HTMLGenerator`, `JspGenerator`, and `ScriptGenerator` are invaluable if you need to reuse older files or simply are more familiar with HTML, JSP, JavaScript, or Python. Generators like the directory generators show how anything can be used as an input source for XML data. As Cocoon grows, more and more of these components will be written, as developers seek to fulfill specific needs. In Part III, "Advanced Cocoon Features," we'll explore how to write one ourselves.

CHAPTER 10

Using Content Logic: Transformers

Whereas generators allow you to implement logic at the time data is collected, transformers allow you to implement logic on the data that is already collected by a generator. In some ways, transformers give you more options because you can chain them together to perform different operations on the input data.

We can categorize the places where logic can be implemented in a transformer in three ways (this is somewhat of a generalization, but it helps to understand what options exist with transformers):

- The transformer itself (that is, using the capabilities of the transformer)
- The input data to the transformer
- XSL stylesheets

Logic in a transformer refers to passing parameters to a transformer that affect its operation. Logic in input data means that you are specifying what the transformer should do by means of XML data from an earlier step. Logic in stylesheets can mean many things, from doing complex XSL operations to rather simple XLinks or XPointers. We'll explore the issue of logic in transformers by adding a few to our sample application.

TraxTransformer

First, we should mention a few more things about the default XSLT transformer, the `TraxTransformer`. There are some optional parameters that can be passed to this component in the sitemap that give you more options in your stylesheets. These parameters are

- `use-request-parameters`
- `use-browser-capabilities`
- `use-cookies`
- `use-session-info`
- `use-deli`

Essentially, any of these parameters, if present and no matter what the `value` attribute is set to, will cause the `TraxTransformer` to make various data sets available to the stylesheet as variables. There are pros and cons to this. It can be a good thing if you need to have access to all the request parameters from a form or perhaps various attributes in the session. However, the price is cacheability. By default, the `TraxTransformer` caches its output. When any or all of these parameters are used, this forces Cocoon to evaluate whatever data sets are specified to see whether the cached output is still valid. If something has changed in a request parameter or in the session, this will cause the output to be regenerated anew, even if perhaps the output didn't really change.

That being said, let's look at how we might use this information. In Chapter 8, "Using Content Logic: XSPs," we used `login.xsp` to process the output of `login.html`. If we wanted to, we could make the request parameters and session information available to the XSL that processes the login results page. Our sitemap entry would then look like this:

```
<map:match pattern="login">
 <map:generate type="serverpages" src="xsp/login.xsp"/>
 <map:transform type="xslt" src="style/login.xsl">
   <map:parameter name="use-request-parameters" value="true"/>
   <map:parameter name="use-session-info" value="true"/>
 </map:transform>
 <map:serialize type="html"/>
</map:match>
```

In our XSL, we declare a couple of variables:

```
<xsl:param name="user"/>
 <xsl:param name="pass"/>
 <xsl:param name="session-is-new"/>
 <xsl:param name="session-valid"/>
 <xsl:param name="session-id"/>
```

And then use them as we see fit:

```
<body bgcolor="#ffffff">
 <p>Your user name is <xsl:value-of select="$user"/></p>
 <p>Your password is <xsl:value-of select="$pass"/></p>

 <xsl:if test="$session-is-new = 'true'">
  <p>Your session is new</p>
 </xsl:if>
 <xsl:if test="$session-is-new = 'false'">
  <p>Your session is not new</p>
 </xsl:if>

 <p>Your session id is <xsl:value-of select="$session-id"/></p>
 <p>Your session validity is <xsl:value-of select="$session-valid"/></p>

 <br/>
 <xsl:apply-templates/>
</body>
```

In this example, we'll see something similar to what's shown in Figure 10.1.

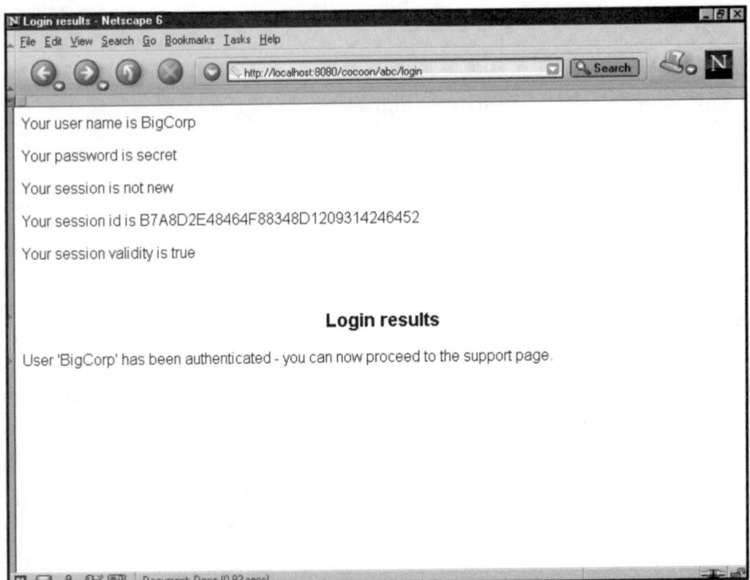

Figure 10.1
Login results with session/request information.

When the `use-request-parameters` attribute is set, the `TraxTransformer` will set a variable for each request parameter that is named with the parameter name. Similarly, when the `use-cookies` attribute is set, one variable will be created for each cookie and named with the cookie name.

Table 10.1 shows what variables are set by the `TraxTransformer` when the `use-session-info`, `use-deli`, and `use-browser-capabilities` attributes are set.

Table 10.1 *TraxTransformer Variables Set by use-session-info, use-browser-capabilities, and use-deli*

Category	Variable
use-session-info	session-available
use-session-info	session-is-new
use-session-info	session-id-from-cookie
use-session-info	session-id-from-url
use-session-info	session-valid
use-session-info	session-id
use-browser-capabilities	accept
use-browser-capabilities	user-agent
use-browser-capabilities	browser
use-browser-capabilities	browser-media
use-browser-capabilities	ua-capabilities
use-deli	deli-capabilities
use-deli	accept

SQLTransformer

The `SQLTransformer` is an example of implementing logic by means of input data. The `SQLTransformer` executes a specified query using a specified data source. The query and data source are typically set in an XML file that is read by a `FileGenerator`. The output of the `SQLTransformer` consists of tags that contain the results of the query and that belong to a predetermined namespace, `http://apache.org/cocoon/SQL/2.0`.

JDBC Driver Version

Be aware that the SQLTransformer expects that you will be using JDBC 1.2–compliant drivers. If you are not, you will need to change the definition of the component (in the <map:components> section of your sitemap) and add a <old-driver> attribute like this:

```
<map:transformer name="sql" logger="sitemap.transformer.sql"
src="org.apache.cocoon.transformation.SQLTransformer">
 <old-driver>true</old-driver>
</map:transformer>
```

In Chapter 8, we saw how to retrieve data from the `TroubleTickets` table using an XSP and the ESQL logicsheet. Let's see whether this is easier to do in the `SQLTransformer`.

Input File

The XML file that drives the operation of the `SQLTransformer` can contain any kind of user tags. The key is the `<execute-query>` block that contains the query (or subqueries) to be executed. Listing 10.1 shows this in action.

Listing 10.1 *Input File for SQLTransformer (tickets.xml - Version 1)*

```
<?xml version="1.0"?>

<page xmlns:sql="http://apache.org/cocoon/SQL/2.0">

 <title>Trouble tickets for BigCorp</title>

 <content>

  <execute-query xmlns="http://apache.org/cocoon/SQL/2.0">
   <query>
    select * from TroubleTickets where Customer = 'BigCorp'
    order by TicketOpened
   </query>
  </execute-query>

 </content>
</page>
```

As you can see, we retained our user tags but inserted the query inside the `<execute-query>` block. Note too that we had to declare the namespace for the `SQLTransformer` at the `<execute-query>` tag. Finally, it is a good idea not to have any whitespace between the `<query>` tags and their content as we do here for readability. Whitespace will often cause the `SQLTransformer` problems when it goes to execute the query.

Stylesheet

We'll have to define a new stylesheet (see Listing 10.2) for the output, because the returning tags are part of the SQL namespace.

Listing 10.2 *Stylesheet for SQLTransformer (tickets.xsl)*

```
<?xml version="1.0"?>

<xsl:stylesheet version="1.0"
  xmlns:xsl="http://www.w3.org/1999/XSL/Transform"
  xmlns:sql="http://apache.org/cocoon/SQL/2.0"
>

 <xsl:template match="/page">
  <html>
   <head>
    <title><xsl:value-of select="page-title"/></title>
   </head>

   <body bgcolor="#ffffff">
    <br/>
    <xsl:apply-templates/>
   </body>
  </html>
 </xsl:template>

 <xsl:template match="title">
  <center>
  <h3><xsl:apply-templates/></h3>
  </center>
 </xsl:template>

 <xsl:template match="sql:rowset">
  <table border="1">
   <xsl:apply-templates/>
  </table>
 </xsl:template>

 <xsl:template match="sql:row">
  <tr>
   <xsl:for-each select="*">
    <td>
```

Listing 10.2 *(continued)*

```
      <xsl:apply-templates/>
    </td>
   </xsl:for-each>
  </tr>
 </xsl:template>

</xsl:stylesheet>
```

Note how we declare the SQL namespace at the top of the stylesheet to match the declaration in `tickets.xml`. When the `SQLTransformer` executes, all the data it returns will be part of this namespace and will bear the prefix `sql`. The database set will be inside a `sql:rowset` block, and each row will be inside a `sql:row` block. Within this block, each column tag will be composed of `sql:` plus the name of the column. Note that we can change any of these things—the result set tag, the row tag, the namespace, or the prefix—by providing various input parameters to the `SQLTransformer`. Those parameters are listed later, in Table 10.2.

Defining the Pipeline

Finally, we need a pipeline to handle this:

```
<map:match pattern="tickets.html">
 <map:generate type="file" src="content/tickets.xml"/>
 <map:transform type="sql">
  <map:parameter name="use-connection" value="abc"/>
 </map:transform>
 <map:transform type="xslt" src="style/tickets.xsl"/>
 <map:serialize type="html"/>
</map:match>
```

In the pipeline, we have to pass a parameter to the `SQLTransformer` that tells it what connection pool to use. Here, we are using the `abc` pool we defined in Chapter 8. There are other parameters we could pass to this component, which we'll see in a minute. (Note: We'll deal more with sitemap parameters in Chapter 11, "Using Sitemap Logic: Matchers and Selectors.")

By typing the URL `http://localhost:8080/cocoon/abc/tickets.html`, we should get what's shown in Figure 10.2.

The full set of parameters that can be passed to the `SQLTransformer` is shown in Table 10.2.

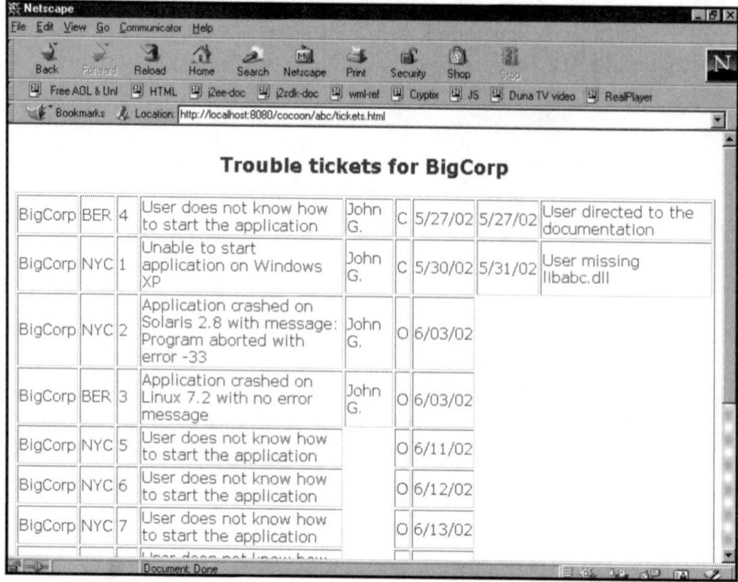

Figure 10.2
SQLTransformer output.

Table 10.2 *SQLTransformer Parameters*

Parameter Name	Description
use-connection	Name of the connection pool to use.
show-nr-of-rows	Set an attribute of the <rowset> tag called nrofrows that will be set to the number of rows returned. This is database driver dependent and may not always be set.
dburl	Database URL when not using a connection pool.
username	Username for the database login when not using a connection pool.
password	Password for the database login when not using a connection pool.
doc-element	Tag to use to surround the query results—defaults to rowset.
row-element	Tag to use to surround row results—defaults to row.
namespace-uri	Namespace—defaults to http://apache.org/cocoon/SQL/2.0.
namespace-prefix	Namespace prefix to use—defaults to sql.

There are also some other input tags that the `SQLTransformer` will recognize, besides `<execute-query>` and `<query>`. They are shown in Table 10.3.

Table 10.3 *SQLTransformer Input Tags*

Tag Name	Description
execute-query	Root tag of the input to SQLTransformer.
query	Contains the query to execute.
ancestor-value	Specifies a value from the previous result set to use in a nested query.
in-parameter	Specifies an input parameter to a stored procedure.
out-parameter	Specifies an output parameter from a stored procedure.
escape-string	In the query, replace single quote with two single quotes, and backslash with two backslashes.

Constructing Dynamic Queries

Most real-world applications will need to make use of dynamic queries. There are various ways to do this. Remember, we are not limited by an input XML file. We can use this file as a starting point, so to speak, and then use an XSL transformation to build our query.

Let's rewrite our XSP as shown in Listing 10.3.

Listing 10.3 *Input File for SQLTransformer (tickets.xml - Version 2)*

```
<?xml version="1.0"?>

<content>
  <dynamic-query/>
 </content>
```

We're not really putting anything here, except a placeholder for the query. What we'll do is run this XML through a `TraxTransformer` step in which the `use-request-parameters` attribute is set. In the XSL for this step, we can pick up a request parameter called `customer` and use it to build both a title and the query.

First, let's have a look at the sitemap:

```
<map:match pattern="tickets.xml">
 <map:generate type="file" src="content/tickets.xml"/>
 <map:transform type="xslt" src="style/tickets-prep.xsl">
   <map:parameter name="use-request-parameters" value="true"/>
 </map:transform>
 <map:transform type="sql">
  <map:parameter name="use-connection" value="abc"/>
 </map:transform>
```

```
 <map:transform type="xslt" src="style/tickets.xsl"/>
 <map:serialize type="html"/>
</map:match>
```

Listing 10.4 shows what `tickets-prep.xsl` looks like.

Listing 10.4 *Prep Stylesheet for SQLTransformer (tickets-prep.xsl)*

```
<?xml version="1.0"?>

<xsl:stylesheet version="1.0"
  xmlns:xsl="http://www.w3.org/1999/XSL/Transform"
  xmlns:sql="http://apache.org/cocoon/SQL/2.0"
>

 <xsl:param name="customer"/>

 <xsl:template match="/">
  <page>
   <title>Hello <xsl:value-of select="$customer"/></title>
   <content>
    <xsl:apply-templates/>
   </content>
  </page>
 </xsl:template>

 <xsl:template match="dynamic-query">
  <execute-query xmlns="http://apache.org/cocoon/SQL/2.0">
    <query>select * from TroubleTickets where Customer = '<xsl:value-of select="
$customer"/>' order by TicketOpened</query>
  </execute-query>
 </xsl:template>

</xsl:stylesheet>
```

Just as we showed in the discussion at the beginning of this chapter, the `TraxTransformer` will post any available request parameters to the stylesheet, which, in this case, is particularly interested in one called `customer`. Using this value, all the proper XML for the `SQLTransformer` is built and passed on. The latter then executes the completed query and returns the results to our last stylesheet. We can now call our new pipeline with the URL `http://localhost:8080/cocoon/abc/tickets.xml?customer=BigCorp`, and we will see entries for that customer.

More Options for Dynamic Queries

Some of the more curious readers will have looked at the source code for the `SQLTransformer` and seen that it has the capability to substitute values in the query using sitemap parameters. Unfortunately, this function is not available in Cocoon 2.0.3, which is why we aren't showing it here. You can find it, however, in Cocoon 2.1. Briefly, you can place `<substitute-value>` tags in the input query, each having a `name` attribute set to the name of the incoming sitemap parameter. When the `SQLTransformer` evaluates the query, it replaces each `<substitute-value>` tag with the value of the named sitemap parameter. If we are using Cocoon 2.1, therefore, we could write our query like this:

```
<query>
 select * from TroubleTickets where Customer =
 '<substitute-value name="customer"/>'
 order by TicketOpened
</query>
```

And we could define a pipeline entry like this:

```
<map:match pattern="tickets.xml">
 <map:generate type="file" src="content/tickets.xml"/>
 <map:transform type="sql">
  <map:parameter name="use-connection" value="abc"/>
  <map:parameter name="customer" value="BigCorp"/>
 </map:transform>
 <map:transform type="xslt" src="style/tickets.xsl"/>
 <map:serialize type="html"/>
</map:match>
```

Of course, the right way would be to set the sitemap parameter `customer` dynamically, with a value from either a `Matcher` or an `Action` (see Chapter 11 for information on doing this).

If you really need this kind of functionality, build Cocoon 2.1 and have a go at it!

FilterTransformer

There are many times when queries return too many rows to display at once. Cocoon provides the `FilterTransformer` that can be used for just such events. This component will allow only the specified number of tags starting from the specified position to pass through to the next step in the pipeline. Some databases, like Oracle, implement this same functionality with the `max-rows` and `skip-rows` settings. For those that don't, however, the `FilterTransformer` can be very useful.

Suppose we want to have a page that displays the contents of the `TroubleTickets` table in five row increments. At the top of the page are links for First, Previous, Next, and Last, just as we see with search-engine result pages.

We'll start by writing a new pipeline:

```
<map:match pattern="ticket-review">
 <map:generate type="file" src="content/ticket-review.xml"/>
 <map:transform type="sql">
  <map:parameter name="use-connection" value="abc"/>
 </map:transform>
 <map:act type="request">
  <map:parameter name="parameters" value="true"/>
  <map:parameter name="default.page" value="1"/>

  <map:transform type="filter" label="raw">
   <map:parameter name="element-name" value="row"/>
   <map:parameter name="count" value="5"/>
   <map:parameter name="blocknr" value="{page}"/>
  </map:transform>
 </map:act>
 <map:transform type="xslt" src="style/ticket-review.xsl"/>
 <map:serialize type="html"/>
</map:match>
```

We threw in an `Action` here, the `RequestParamAction`, just to make things work properly. We'll be discussing actions in Chapter 12, "Using Sitemap Logic: Actions and Forms," but for now the way this action works is that it makes any request parameters available to the subsequent components as sitemap parameters. We'll base the pagination on a request variable called `page`. Because a user might invoke the pipeline without specifying anything, we must set a default value for this parameter, which in this case is `1`.

The `FilterTransformer` takes three input parameters: the name of the element to count, in this case `row`; the total number of elements to let through (the group of elements is referred to as a "block"); and which block of elements to start with. Again, to make things dynamic, we will reference a sitemap parameter called `page` which is provided by the action that precedes the `<map:transform type="filter">` step.

The `ticket-review.xml` file, shown in Listing 10.5, just specifies a generic query with no `where` clause.

Listing 10.5 *Filter Transformer XML (ticket-review.xml)*

```
<?xml version="1.0"?>

<page>
 <title>Trouble tickets</title>
 <content>
  <execute-query xmlns="http://apache.org/cocoon/SQL/2.0">
   <query>select * from TroubleTickets order by Customer, TicketOpened</query>
  </execute-query>
 </content>
</page>
```

The output XSL, shown in Listing 10.6, is basically the same as the `tickets.xsl` that we saw earlier, but it has some new elements.

Listing 10.6 *Filter Transformer XSL (ticket-review.xsl)*

```
<?xml version="1.0"?>

<xsl:stylesheet version="1.0"
  xmlns:xsl="http://www.w3.org/1999/XSL/Transform"
  xmlns:sql="http://apache.org/cocoon/SQL/2.0"
>

 <xsl:template match="/page">
  <html>
   <head>
    <title><xsl:value-of select="page-title"/></title>
   </head>

   <body bgcolor="#ffffff">
    <br/>
    <xsl:apply-templates/>
   </body>
  </html>
 </xsl:template>

 <xsl:template match="title">
  <center>
  <h3><xsl:apply-templates/></h3>
  </center>
 </xsl:template>
```

Listing 10.6 *(continued)*

```
<xsl:template match="sql:rowset">
 <xsl:apply-templates/>
</xsl:template>

<xsl:template match="sql:block[count(sql:row) > 0]">
 <p>
  Page <xsl:value-of select="@sql:id"/> of
  <xsl:value-of select="count(//sql:block)"/>:  

 <xsl:if test="count(//sql:block) > 1">
  <xsl:if test="position() > 1">
    <a href="ticket-review?page=1">First</a>
     

    <a>
     <xsl:attribute name="href">
      <xsl:text><![CDATA[ticket-review?page=]]></xsl:text>
      <xsl:value-of select="position() - 1"/>
     </xsl:attribute>
     Previous
    </a>
     

  </xsl:if>

  <xsl:if test="position() != count(//sql:block)">
    <a>
     <xsl:attribute name="href">
      <xsl:text><![CDATA[ticket-review?page=]]></xsl:text>
      <xsl:value-of select="position() + 1"/>
     </xsl:attribute>
     Next
    </a>
     

    <a>
     <xsl:attribute name="href">
      <xsl:text><![CDATA[ticket-review?page=]]></xsl:text>
      <xsl:value-of select="count(//sql:block)"/>
     </xsl:attribute>
     Last
    </a>
     
```

Listing 10.6 *(continued)*

```
   </xsl:if>

  </xsl:if>

  </p>

  <table border="1">
   <xsl:apply-templates/>
  </table>

 </xsl:template>

 <xsl:template match="sql:row">
  <tr>
   <xsl:for-each select="*">
    <td>
     <xsl:apply-templates/>
    </td>
   </xsl:for-each>
  </tr>
 </xsl:template>

</xsl:stylesheet>
```

To understand this, we should explain what tags are coming back from the `FilterTransformer`. The following snippet shows the relevant tags:

```
<content>
  <rowset>
    <block id="1">
     <row>
       <!--  row data goes here -->
     </row>
     <row>
       <!--  row data goes here -->
     </row>
     <row>
       <!--  row data goes here -->
     </row>
     <row>
       <!--  row data goes here -->
     </row>
```

```
    <row>
      <!--  row data goes here -->
    </row>
   </block>
   <block id="2"/>
   <block id="3"/>
  </rowset>
</content>
```

The `FilterTransformer` inserts `<block>` tags inside the `<rowset>` tag that denotes the groups of rows. Only one block at a time will contain `<row>` elements. In this case, the first block contains five `<row>` elements, as if we had called this page for the first time. Using the `id` attribute of the `block` tags and by counting the total number of blocks, we can determine not only how many pages of data there are but also where we are in the set. In the XSL file, the key template is

```
<xsl:template match="sql:block[count(sql:row) > 0]">
```

which will catch only the `block` tag that actually contains `row` elements. After we enter this template, we can determine our position and set up the First, Previous, Next, and Last links.

Figures 10.3 through 10.5 show three pages of data.

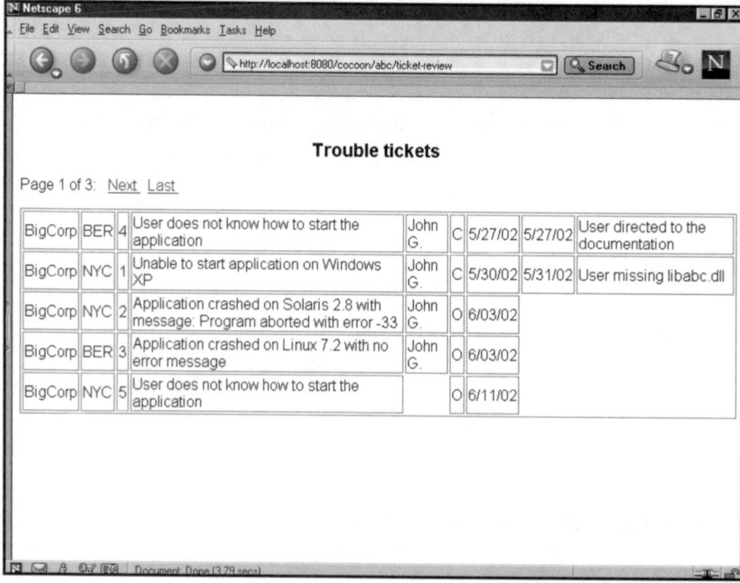

Figure 10.3
Filtered data from TroubleTickets table: page 1.

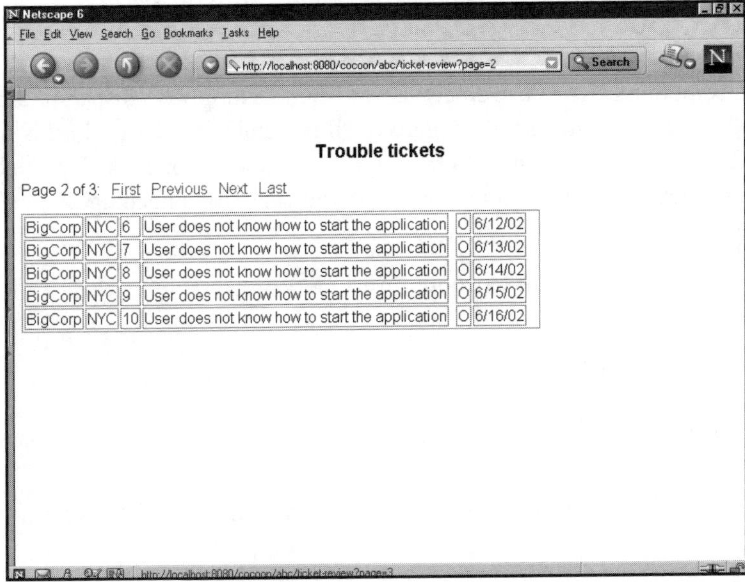

Figure 10.4
Filtered data from TroubleTickets table: page 2.

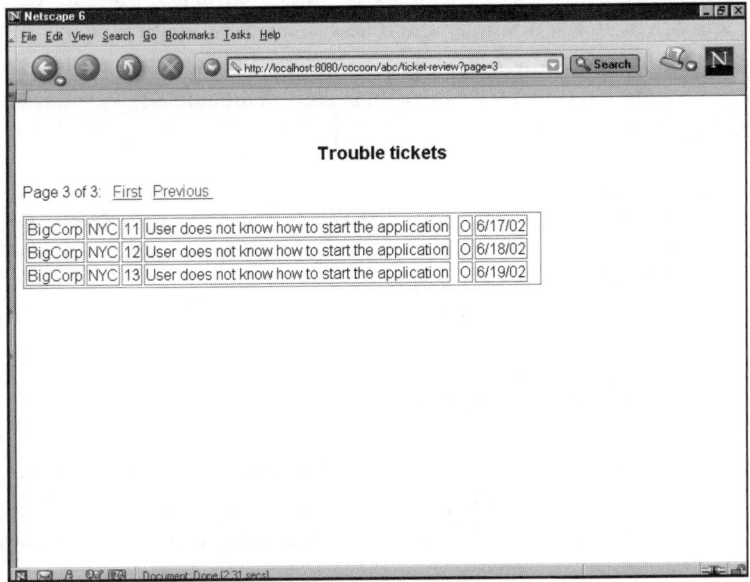

Figure 10.5
Filtered data from TroubleTickets table: page 3.

Transformer-Based Aggregation

Aggregation is something that is extremely useful when dealing with disparate data sources that need to be combined into a single page. We all remember trying to do this with complex servlets or JSPs that have to return rows from multiple database queries combined with data from one or more text files—you quite easily find yourself with a heaping plateful of spaghetti code.

You can implement aggregation in Cocoon in various ways:

- CInclude
- XInclude
- pipeline aggregation

In this chapter, we will take on the first two. In the next chapter, we'll cover pipeline aggregation.

CInclude and XInclude are rather similar. Both have `<include>` tags that are embedded into the source XML and point to the resources to include. However, there are some key differences. CInclude is first of all a Cocoon concept, whereas XInclude is an official W3C recommendation (`http://www.w3.org/TR/xinclude/`). CInclude provides caching capabilities, whereas XInclude does not. CInclude can also aggregate pipeline entries using the `cocoon:` pseudo protocol, whereas XInclude is limited to XML files referenced directly from the current working directory. On the other hand, XInclude allows the use of XPointer and can also include text content.

Cocoon Pseudo Protocols

We'll discuss the various Cocoon pseudo protocols in the next chapter. Briefly, these protocols give you a way to refer to pipelines as well as resources accessible from the servlet context or classloader.

Designing a Customer Home Page

To see transformer-based aggregation in action, we'll use as an example a new customer home page for our fictitious client. When we built the authentication pages in the preceding chapter, we ended up with a rather uninspiring page that simply provided the status of the authentication. Obviously, this is not going to impress Fortune 500 clients, so we need to rethink this part. Based on the requirements for our project, we have concluded that the best approach is to have a dynamically built home page for each customer. This page will contain a welcome message, a summary of current contract status, and various targeted (and tactful) advertisements for other ABC Software products.

We'll start simply. The new customer home page will contain three elements:

- Welcome message specifying the client name.
- One advertisement loaded from an XML file.
- Summary of current contract status: amount spent to date, amount remaining, and expiration date. This information will come from the database.

For now, we'll hard-code everything for the "BigCorp" customer. In Chapter 11, we'll see how to do more dynamic personalization.

The Advertisement Page

We will have two advertisement pages, `adv-xyz-01.xml` and `adv-xyz-02.xml`. Both are simple XML pages and will reside in `$CATALINA_HOME/webapps/cocoon/abc/content`. The first file (Listing 10.7) will be an ad targeted to customers who have a site license for AbcApp, and the second (Listing 10.8) will be for customers who have lesser licenses for the product.

Listing 10.7 *Advertisement Page (adv-xyz-01.xml)*

```
<?xml version="1.0"?>

<content>
  <ad-title>Get a 20% discount when you buy XyzApp</ad-title>
  <ad>
   We hope you like AbcApp, our award-winning HR app. We thought you'd like to
know about XyzApp, our new financials application. Since you already have a site
license for AbcApp, we are making XyzApp available to you at a 20% discount.
Please give your ABC Software rep a call!
</ad>
</content>
```

Listing 10.8 *Advertisement Page (adv-xyz-02.xml)*

```
<?xml version="1.0"?>

<content>
  <ad-title>Try XyzApp free for 90 days</ad-title>
  <ad>
```

Listing 10.8 *(continued)*

```
   We hope you like AbcApp, our award-winning HR app. We thought you'd like to
know about XyzApp, our new financials application. To give you the chance to try
it out, we will let you try XyzApp free for 90 days. Please give your ABC
Software rep a call!
  </ad>
</content>
```

Because these files will be read directly as XML, they don't need pipelines or stylesheets of their own.

The Contract Summary Page

This page will be an XSP employing the `esql` logicsheet to retrieve contract information from the database.

The database script we'll use is shown in Listing 10.9. Remember to adapt it to your database server if you are not using MySQL.

Listing 10.9 *Contract Table (abc-contracts.sql)*

```
use abc;

create table CustomerContracts (
Customer         varchar(20)      not null,
LicenseType      char(4)          not null,
ContractStart    varchar(20)      not null,
ContractEnd      varchar(20)      not null,
ContractAmount   float            not null,
ContractUsed     float            not null
);

insert into CustomerContracts values ('BigCorp', 'SITE',
 '09/30/01', '09/30/02', 10000.00, 5657.93);
```

Listing 10.10 shows `abc/xsp/contract-summary.xsp`.

Listing 10.10 *Contract Summary Page (contract-summary.xsp)*

```
<?xml version="1.0" encoding="ISO-8859-1"?>

<xsp:page language="java"
  xmlns:xsp="http://apache.org/xsp"
```

Listing 10.10 *(continued)*

```
  xmlns:esql="http://apache.org/cocoon/SQL/v2"
  xmlns:xsp-session="http://apache.org/xsp/session/2.0"
>

  <section>

   <title>Contract summary for <xsp-session:get-attribute name="user"/></title>

   <esql:connection>
     <esql:pool>abc</esql:pool>
     <esql:execute-query>
       <esql:query>select * from CustomerContracts where Customer = '<xsp-sessio
n:get-attribute name="user"/>' </esql:query>
       <esql:results>
        <contract-summary>
         <esql:row-results>
          <ends><esql:get-string column="ContractEnd"/></ends>
          <amount><esql:get-string column="ContractAmount"/></amount>
          <used><esql:get-string column="ContractUsed"/></used>
         </esql:row-results>
        </contract-summary>
       </esql:results>
     </esql:execute-query>
   </esql:connection>

  </section>
</xsp:page>
```

We also need to define a pipeline for the contract summary page that outputs XML:

```
<map:match pattern="support/contract-summary">
 <map:generate type="serverpages" src="xsp/contract-summary.xsp"/>
 <map:serialize type="xml"/>
</map:match>
```

Implementing the Customer Home Page with CInclude

With our design and individual pages complete, we are now ready to implement the new customer home page. First, we'll implement it using CInclude, which is done via the `CIncludeTransformer`. To do this, we need to write an XSP, add a pipeline entry, and write the accompanying XSL stylesheet.

XSP

To use the `CIncludeTransformer`, we need to write an XML or XSP file that contains the `cinclude` tags needed to pull in the advertisement and the contract summary. We will use an XSP, (see Listing 10.11), because we want to have access to the `user` session attribute.

Listing 10.11 *CInclude XSP (home-page.xsp - Version 1)*

```
<?xml version="1.0" encoding="ISO-8859-1"?>

<xsp:page language="java"
  xmlns:xsp="http://apache.org/xsp"
  xmlns:cinclude="http://apache.org/cocoon/include/1.0"
  xmlns:xsp-session="http://apache.org/xsp/session/2.0"
>

<page>
   <page-title>
    Welcome <xsp-session:get-attribute name="user"/> user!
   </page-title>

    <cinclude:include src="cocoon:/support/contract-summary"/>
    <cinclude:include src="content/adv-xyz-01.xml"/>
</page>
</xsp:page>
```

This is extremely neat and simple. We had to add the `cinclude` namespace declaration to the `xsp_page` tag. Note that we are not using the `context://` pseudo protocol to refer to `adv-xyz-01.xml`, because that is not supported by the `CIncludeTransformer`. We also took advantage of the session logicsheet to display a customized welcome page to the user.

Note that could have done the same thing in an XML file, as demonstrated in Listing 10.12.

Listing 10.12 *CInclude XML (home-page.xml)*

```
<?xml version="1.0"?>

<page xmlns:cinclude="http://apache.org/cocoon/include/1.0">
   <page-title>Welcome user!</page-title>
   <cinclude:include src="cocoon:/support/contract-summary"/>
   <cinclude:include src="content/adv-xyz-01.xml"/>
</page>
```

But then we wouldn't have access to the session attributes.

Pipeline Entry

The pipeline for this example is as follows:

```
<map:match pattern="home-page.xsp">
 <map:generate type="file" src="xsp/home-page.xml"/>
 <map:transform type="cinclude"/>
 <map:transform type="xslt" src="style/home-page.xsl"/>
 <map:serialize type="html"/>
</map:match>
```

There is nothing special about the `<map:generate>` tag, because we are using a standard XSP. However, we need to tell Cocoon to process the data from the XSP first by the `CIncludeTransformer`, in order for the aggregation to take place, and then by the regular XSLT transformer.

XSL

We also need an XSL file, to handle the aggregated content. You'll find this in Listing 10.13.

Listing 10.13 *CInclude XSL (home-page.xsl - Version 1)*

```
<?xml version="1.0"?>

<xsl:stylesheet version="1.0"
  xmlns:xsl="http://www.w3.org/1999/XSL/Transform"
>

 <xsl:template match="/">
  <html>
   <head>
    <title><xsl:value-of select="//page-title"/></title>
   </head>

   <body bgcolor="#ffffff">
    <table width="100%" cellpadding="0" cellspacing="0">
     <tr>
     <td align="left">
      <font face="arial"><b><xsl:value-of select="//page-title"/></b></font>
     </td>
    </tr></table>

    <br/> 
```

Listing 10.13 *(continued)*

```
    <table width="100%"><tr>
     <td width="75%">
      <xsl:apply-templates select="//title"/>
      <xsl:apply-templates select="//contract-summary"/>
     </td>
     <td width="25%">
      <xsl:apply-templates select="//ad-title"/>
      <xsl:apply-templates select="//ad"/>
     </td>
    </tr></table>

   </body>
  </html>
 </xsl:template>

 <xsl:template match="ad-title">
  <center>
  <h3>
   <font point-size="10pt"><xsl:apply-templates/>
  </font></h3>
  </center>
 </xsl:template>

 <xsl:template match="title">
  <center>
  <h3><font face="arial">
   Here is your contract summary:
  </font></h3>
  </center>
 </xsl:template>

 <xsl:template match="contract-summary">
  <table>
   <tr><td>
    Your contract ends on: <xsl:value-of select="ends"/>
   </td></tr>
   <tr><td>
    The amount of your contract is: <xsl:value-of select="amount"/>
   </td></tr>
   <tr><td>
    The amount used to date is: <xsl:value-of select="used"/>
```

Listing 10.13 *(continued)*

```
    </td></tr>
   </table>
  </xsl:template>

  <xsl:template match="ad">
   <p><font point-size="8pt"><xsl:apply-templates/></font></p>
  </xsl:template>

</xsl:stylesheet>
```

Figure 10.6 shows the expected output.

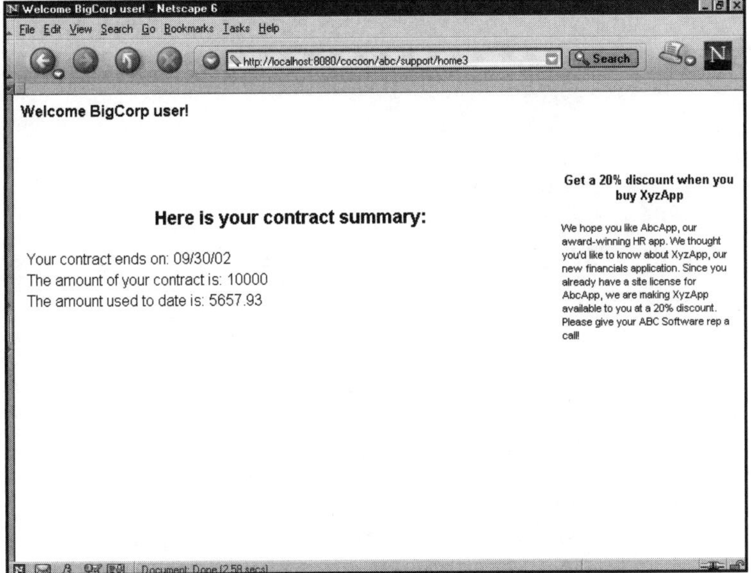

Figure 10.6
CInclude-based home page.

Using Namespaces with CInclude

When XML nodes from different sources are concatenated together as we have done here, you can run into problems if the different sources use the same tag but have different meanings for it. For example, if we had, for some reason, used the tag `contract-summary` in `adv-xyz-01.xml` but meant something different than in the contract summary XSP, we'd have problems.

To avoid this situation, we can add some other attributes to the `<cinclude:include>` tag. The full set of allowable attributes is shown in Table 10.4.

Table 10.4 *<cinclude:include> Attributes*

Attribute	Description
src	The data source
element	A user tag used to surround the content from this src
ns	The namespace to use for the included content
prefix	The prefix to use for each tag from the included content

With this in mind, we can rewrite our XSP as shown in Listing 10.14.

Listing 10.14 *CInclude XSP (home-page.xsp - Version 2)*

```
<?xml version="1.0" encoding="ISO-8859-1"?>

<xsp:page language="java"
  xmlns:xsp="http://apache.org/xsp"
  xmlns:cinclude="http://apache.org/cocoon/include/1.0"
  xmlns:xsp-session="http://apache.org/xsp/session/2.0"
>

<page>
   <page-title>Welcome user!</page-title>
   <cinclude:include src="cocoon:/support/contract-summary"
     ns="http://foo.bar.com/contract"
     prefix="contract"/>
   <cinclude:include src="content/adv-xyz-01.xml"
     ns="http://foo.bar.com/adv"
     prefix="adv"/>
</page>

</xsp:page>
```

Our stylesheet, shown in Listing 10.15, must account for these new prefixes.

Listing 10.15 *CInclude XSL (home-page.xsl - Version 2)*

```
<?xml version="1.0"?>

<xsl:stylesheet version="1.0"
  xmlns:xsl="http://www.w3.org/1999/XSL/Transform"
```

Listing 10.15 *(continued)*

```
  xmlns:contract="http://foo.bar.com/contract"
  xmlns:adv="http://foo.bar.com/adv"
>

 <xsl:template match="/">
  <html>
   <head>
    <title><xsl:value-of select="//page-title"/></title>
   </head>

   <body bgcolor="#ffffff">
    <table width="100%" cellpadding="0" cellspacing="0">
     <tr>
     <td align="left">
      <font face="arial"><b><xsl:value-of select="//page-title"/></b></font>
     </td>
    </tr></table>

    <br/> 

    <table width="100%"><tr>
     <td width="75%">
      <xsl:apply-templates select="//contract:title"/>
      <xsl:apply-templates select="//contract:contract-summary"/>
     </td>
     <td width="25%">
      <xsl:apply-templates select="//adv:ad-title"/>
      <xsl:apply-templates select="//adv:ad"/>
     </td>
    </tr></table>

   </body>
  </html>
 </xsl:template>

 <xsl:template match="contract:title">
  <center>
  <h3><font face="arial">
   Here is your contract summary:
  </font></h3>
  </center>
```

Listing 10.15 *(continued)*

```
</xsl:template>

<xsl:template match="adv:ad-title">
 <center>
 <h3>
  <font point-size="10pt"><xsl:apply-templates/>
 </font></h3>
 </center>
</xsl:template>

<xsl:template match="contract:contract-summary">
 <table>
  <tr><td>
   Your contract ends on: <xsl:value-of select="contract:ends"/>
  </td></tr>
  <tr><td>
   The amount of your contract is: <xsl:value-of select="contract:amount"/>
  </td></tr>
  <tr><td>
   The amount used to date is: <xsl:value-of select="contract:used"/>
  </td></tr>
 </table>
</xsl:template>

<xsl:template match="adv:ad">
 <p><font point-size="8pt"><xsl:apply-templates/></font></p>
</xsl:template>

</xsl:stylesheet>
```

The pipeline definition for this URI will not change, nor should the output. It should be exactly the same as the previous example, except you are assured that no tags will conflict between input sources.

Implementing the Customer Home Page with XInclude

If we wanted to use XInclude to build the new customer home page, then the transformer we'd use would be the `XIncludeTransformer`. However, because the `XIncludeTransformer` can include only physical files, we won't be able to redo the preceding example in its entirety. We can, however, create a test page with both advertisement files just to illustrate the use of the `XIncludeTransformer`. We'll start with the pipeline:

```
<map:match pattern="ads">
 <map:generate type="file" src="xsp/ads.xml"/>
 <map:transform type="xinclude"/>
 <map:transform type="xslt" src="style/ads.xsl"/>
 <map:serialize type="html"/>
</map:match>
```

Obviously, this is very similar to the `cinclude` example given previously. What is different, however, is the input file, which is shown in Listing 10.16.

Listing 10.16 *XInclude XML (ads.xml)*

```
<?xml version="1.0" encoding="ISO-8859-1"?>

<page xmlns:xi="http://www.w3.org/2001/XInclude">
 <page-title>These are all the ads on the site</page-title>
 <xi:include href="../content/adv-xyz-01.xml#xpointer(/content/ad)"/>
 <xi:include href="../content/adv-xyz-02.xml#xpointer(/content/ad)"/>
</page>
```

Not only are we using XInclude here, but we are taking advantage of XPointer syntax so that we pull only the part of the content we need. In this case, the XPath expression that is referenced by the `XPointer` function specifies the `ad` portion of the content, which eliminates the unnecessary tags that enclose it.

> **More About XPointer**
> XPointer is a mechanism for identifying XML fragments in XML source documents. It is another W3C recommendation that can be found at `http://www.w3.org/TR/xptr`. A good tutorial on XPointer can be found at `http://www.zvon.org/xxl/xpointer/tutorial/OutputExamples/frontpage.html`.

The stylesheet for this pipeline is shown in Listing 10.17.

Listing 10.17 *XInclude XSL (ads.xsl)*

```
<?xml version="1.0"?>

<xsl:stylesheet version="1.0"
  xmlns:xsl="http://www.w3.org/1999/XSL/Transform"
>
```

Listing 10.17 *(continued)*

```
 <xsl:template match="/">
  <html>
   <head>
    <title><xsl:value-of select="//page-title"/></title>
   </head>

   <body bgcolor="#ffffff">

   <xsl:apply-templates/>

   </body>
  </html>
 </xsl:template>

 <xsl:template match="ad-title">
  <center>
  <h3>
   <font point-size="10pt"><xsl:apply-templates/>
  </font></h3>
  </center>
 </xsl:template>

 <xsl:template match="ad">
  <p><font point-size="8pt"><xsl:apply-templates/></font></p>
 </xsl:template>

</xsl:stylesheet>
```

When we call this page, we will see what's shown in Figure 10.7.

LogTransformer

The `LogTransformer` can help in debugging pipelines. When inserted somewhere between `<map:generate>` and `<map:serialize>` tags, this component will pass SAX events through unchanged, but after first logging them to the specified file.

We can take the pipeline we used for the `CIncludeTransformer` example and add one more line:

```
<map:match pattern="home-page.xsp">
 <map:generate type="serverpages" src="xsp/home-page.xsp"/>
 <map:transform type="cinclude"/>
```

```
    <map:transform type="log">
      <map:parameter name="logfile" value="debug.log"/>
      <map:parameter name="append" value="false"/>
    </map:transform>
    <map:transform type="xslt" src="style/home-page.xsl"/>
    <map:serialize type="html"/>
   </map:match>
```

Figure 10.7

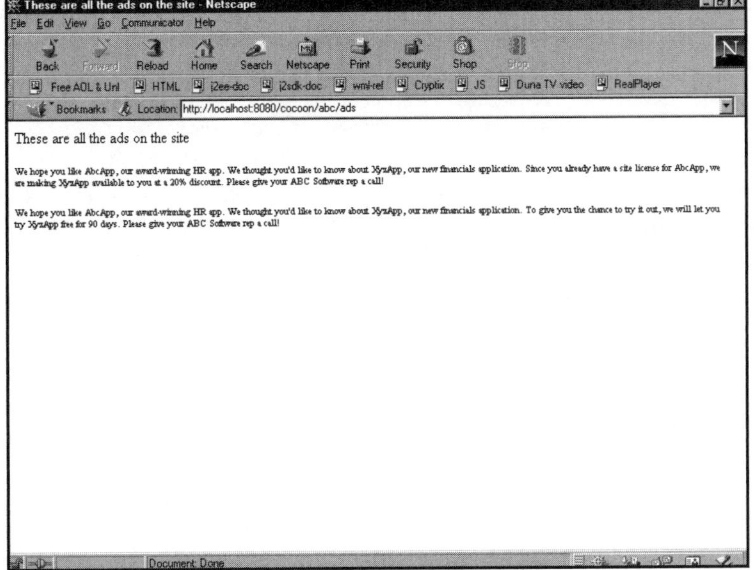

XInclude-based aggregation example.

The `LogTransformer` takes two input parameters. The required `logfile` parameter tells it where to write out all data that pass through it. The filename given is relative to the `sitemap.xmap`. Thus, the log file in this example will be at `$CATALINA_HOME/webapps/cocoon/abc/debug.log`. If the `append` attribute is present, no matter what the value is, data will be appended to the log file each time the pipeline is executed. Otherwise, the log file will be created anew for each execution. Note that the `LogTransformer` is not thread-safe, so if two clients are executing the pipeline at the same time, the log file will contain unexpected and potentially misleading information.

SourceWritingTransformer

In Cocoon 2.0.2 and 2.0.3, there is a transformer called `SourceWritingTransformer` in the scratchpad area. This component is in the main section in 2.1. The purpose of this transformer is to write XML out to some source. Currently, the only source type is a file, but eventually there will probably be more. If you've compiled Cocoon with the `-Dinclude.scratchpad.libs=yes` option on, as described in Chapter 6, "Installing Cocoon," or if you are using Cocoon 2.1, you can follow along with this example.

The first thing we need to do is define the `SourceWritingTransformer` in the sitemap. This is done as follows:

```
<map:transformer name="sourcewriter" logger="sitemap.transformer.sourcewriter"
src="org.apache.cocoon.transformation.SourceWritingTransformer"/>
```

This definition takes an optional attribute tag `<serializer>`, by which you can define the serializer that this transformer should use when outputting the XML. By default, the `XMLSerializer` is used.

To get the `SourceWritingTransformer` to work, all we need to do is bracket the desired output with a `<source:write>` block, as is done in Listing 10.18.

Listing 10.18 *SourceWritingTransformer XML*

```
<?xml version="1.0" encoding="ISO-8859-1"?>

<page
 xmlns:xi="http://www.w3.org/2001/XInclude"
 xmlns:source="http://apache.org/cocoon/source/1.0"
>
 <page-title>These are all the ads on the site</page-title>
 <source:write src="output/adsout.xml serializer="xml">
  <ads xmlns:ads="http://samspublishing.com/cocoon/ads">
   <xi:include href="../content/adv-xyz-01.xml#xpointer(/content/ad)"/>
   <xi:include href="../content/adv-xyz-02.xml#xpointer(/content/ad)"/>
  </ads>
 </source:write>
</page>
```

In this example, we designate that the content from the Xinclude'd files be sent to a file called `output/adsout.xml`. Note that the `SourceWritingTransformer` will automatically create the directory `output`, if it does not exist. We also had to define a serializer for the output, because we did not define one at the `<map:transformer>` level. Finally, we bracket all the output with a top-level tag `<ads>` that defines its own namespace.

The pipeline for this example is as shown here:

```
<map:match pattern="adsout">
 <map:generate type="file" src="xsp/ads.xml"/>
 <map:transform type="xinclude"/>
 <map:transform type="sourcewriter"/>
 <map:serialize type="xml"/>
</map:match>
```

The output file, `adsout.xml`, is shown in Listing 10.19.

Listing 10.19 *SourceWritingTransformer Output*

```
<?xml version="1.0" encoding="UTF-8"?>

  <ads xmlns:ads="http://samspublishing.com/cocoon/ads">
   <ad>
   We hope you like AbcApp, our award-winning HR app. We thought you'd like to
know about XyzApp, our new financials application. Since you already have a site
license for AbcApp, we are making XyzApp available to you at a 20% discount.
Please give your ABC Software rep a call!
  </ad>
   <ad>
   We hope you like AbcApp, our award-winning HR app. We thought you'd like to
know about XyzApp, our new financials application. To give you the chance to try
it out, we will let you try XyzApp free for 90 days. Please give your ABC
Software rep a call!
  </ad>
  </ads>
```

Be aware that all the content that is written to the output file will *not* make it past the `SourceWritingTransformer` step. What you will get, however, is a status message, shown in Figure 10.8.

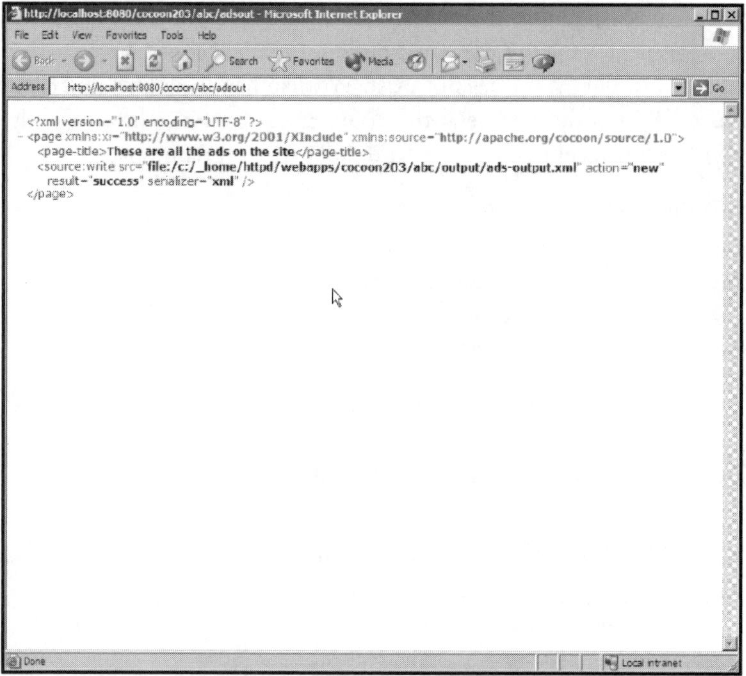

Figure 10.8
SourceWritingTransformer results.

Summary

In this chapter, we have seen that transformers can be extremely useful in either collecting data or modifying input data. We have seen some examples of how we can further modify data using stylesheets. Remember how the pipeline works: Input SAX events from the `Generator`, at the start of the pipeline move successively through each subsequent component until the output is rendered at the client. Because at any point we are dealing with SAX events, we can place a `Transformer` to act as a sort of filter to catch incoming data, modify certain tags, and spit the data back out for the next component to catch. We've also seen one example, the dynamic SQL pipeline, of chaining three transformers together to achieve the desired result. This is again one of the real benefits of Cocoon and one of the ways to separate content from logic from presentation.

In the next chapter we'll turn our attention to sitemap logic, that is, ways in which we can implement processing decisions in the sitemap.

CHAPTER 11

Using Sitemap Logic: `Matchers` and `Selectors`

In the preceding three chapters, we saw how to use content logic by means of XSPs, logicsheets, `Generators`, and `Transformers`. In this chapter and the next, we will see what we can do with "sitemap logic." What we mean by sitemap logic is implementing processing rules in pipelines. Hitherto, we have used pipelines purely to define the processing flow of our pages. Now, we will see how we can put logic into our pipelines.

When we talk about putting logic in the pipelines, we mean using sitemap components to implement conditional processing that determines what pipeline is used or what path is taken through a pipeline. There are five main components that we can use for this purpose: matchers, selectors, aggregates, views, and actions. In this chapter, we'll consider the first four; actions will be covered in the following chapter when we deal with forms.

Sitemap logic is based on the request and its associated information, such as the following:

- Request URI
- Request parameters
- Cookies
- Session information
- Session attributes

Sitemap parameters are an extremely powerful mechanism in Cocoon. The concept actually has two meanings, referring both to parameters that are passed to sitemap components, and to parameters that are returned by certain components. As used in the first sense, sitemap parameters are actually Avalon objects called `Parameters`. A `Parameter` object is basically equivalent to `java.util.Properties`, although there are some differences: `Parameters` are read-only and are created by specifying `<map:parameter>` tags in the sitemap. For example:

```
<map:parameter name="word" value="hello"/>
```

sets a parameter called `word` that contains the value `hello`.

As we said, you specify data to be passed to components in a pipeline using the `<map:parameter>` tag. When the sitemap executes the pipeline, it automatically creates a `Parameters` object and initializes it with the specified data. If there are no `<map:parameter>` tags, an empty object (`Parameters.EMPTY_PARAMETERS`) is passed to the component.

Now for the second meaning of the term. Most components can take sitemap parameters as just described. However, `Matchers` and `Actions` can do something else: They can return values to the sitemap. They do this by returning a `Map` object. A `Map` object is just a `java.util.HashMap` object.

When a request URI matches a pipeline, a new `Map` object is created by the `Matcher` (more precisely, the `Map` object is returned to the pipeline by the `Matcher`). This `Map` object contains a list of the substitution variables (see below), in order, starting with 1. Each time there is a new `<map:match>` or `<map:act>` tag, a new `Map` object is created that exists in the pipeline until the corresponding close tag. When a new object is created, it does not overwrite previous such objects; rather, it is added to a list of `Map` objects that the sitemap keeps for the pipeline. When a `</map:match>` or `</map:act>` tag is encountered, the `Map` object is removed from the list until the `</map:match>` at the end of the pipeline, at which time there are no more objects.

Using Matchers

All pipelines start with a `Matcher`. The `<map:match>` tag specifies what pattern the pipeline is meant to handle. After the `Matcher` matches a pattern, it returns a `Map` object. There are nine types of `Matchers`, but far and away the most common is the `WildcardURIMatcher`.

WildcardURIMatcher

The `WildcardURIMatcher Matcher` is the default `Matcher`, and the most popular. It is based on simple substitution and uses the traditional asterisk wildcard symbol to build URI matching patterns.

Using the WildcardURIMatcher

In Chapter 7, "Creating Static Pages," we defined the pipeline for our first page as follows:

```
<map:match pattern="index.html">
```

This means that the following pipeline can match only the URI `index.html`. Now that is not particularly useful, especially if the pipeline processing flow might be reused in another page destined to be rendered as HTML. So we can rewrite this pipeline in one way, like so:

```
<map:pipeline>
 <map:match pattern="*.html">
  <map:generate type="file" src="content/{1}.xml"/>
  <map:transform type="xslt" src="style/main.xsl"/>
  <map:serialize type="html"/>
 </map:match>
</map:pipeline>
```

Here, the use of the wildcard symbol means that this pipeline will handle any root URI request ending in `*.html`. By "root" URI, we mean any URI that is directly under the webapp name, or webapp + subproject name. For example, `http://localhost:8080/cocoon/index.html` would be handled by the preceding pipeline, were it in `$CATALINA_HOME/webapps/cocoon/sitemap.xmap`, because the base or root of that sitemap is `http://localhost:8080/cocoon/`. In the example we've been using, the base or root is `http://localhost:8080/cocoon/abc/`. So the preceding pattern will match any URIs beginning with the base and ending in `html`.

Note too that we've changed the `map:generate` line—instead of directly specifying the `main.xml` page, we use parameter substitution to specify that the actual XML file to be read by the `FileGenerator` is named with the value that was substituted for the first wildcard character. Remember, a `Matcher` is all about substitution. When it matches a URI, it replaces the wildcard characters with the literal that matches. In the example `http://localhost:8080/cocoon/abc/index.html`, the literal `index` is substituted for the wildcard character. These substituted variables are contained in the `Map` object returned by the `Matcher` and are keyed by numbers, starting with 1. Variables are referenced in the pipeline using the syntax {*x*}, where *x* is the number of the variable. You might wonder what `0` is: {`0`} refers to everything after the base URI. Thus, in this example, {`0`} holds `index.html`, whereas {`1`} holds `index`. The way this pipeline reads, then, this request will cause the `FileGenerator` to read the file `index.xml`.

The substitution variables not only are available to the `Generator`, but any other component has access to them as well. If we had a model in which each individual XML file had its own XSL file, we could write the `map:transform` line as follows:

```
<map:transform type="xslt" src="style/{1}.xsl"/>
```

Thus, `http://localhost:8080/cocoon/abc/index.html` would be directed to the file `index.html` and the stylesheet `index.xsl`.

There is yet another way to write our pipeline:

```
<map:pipeline>
 <map:match pattern="**.html">
  <map:generate type="file" src="content/{1}.xml"/>
  <map:transform type="xslt" src="style/main.xsl"/>
  <map:serialize type="html"/>
 </map:match>
</map:pipeline>
```

What this says is that this pipeline will handle any request starting from the URI base (`http://localhost:8080/cocoon/abc/`) and ending in `*.html` *regardless* of what is in between. Thus, this pipeline will match not only the preceding example, but also something like `http://localhost:8080/cocoon/abc/this/is/a/nested/folder/index.html`. Of course, you will then need to have all these directories actually existing under the `content` folder, because we are pointing the `FileGenerator` to the directory `content`, plus the value of `{1}`, plus the extension `xml`.

We can write our pipeline still another way:

```
<map:pipeline>
 <map:match pattern="**/*.html">
  <map:generate type="file" src="content/{2}.xml"/>
  <map:transform type="xslt" src="style/main.xsl"/>
  <map:serialize type="html"/>
 </map:match>
</map:pipeline>
```

This pipeline will do the same thing as the one before it. However, now we have separated some of the substitution variables. In the earlier example, the URL `http://localhost:8080/cocoon/abc/hello/world/index.html`, the variable `{1}` would hold `hello/world/index`. This might be good for some cases, but suppose we have pages that are *logically* nested but physically are all in the same folder? We can't tell the `FileGenerator` to resolve the file to `{1}.xml` because we don't have the `hello/world` directories. In this version of the pipeline, however, the variable `{1}` holds `hello/world` while variable `{2}` holds `index.html`. So this URL will cause Cocoon to read the file `content/index.xml` in our project directory.

Separating Processing with URI Patterns

Let's look at another example. If we have

```
<map:match pattern="*/*/*/*">
  <!—processing goes here →
</map:match>
```

and we put `http://localhost:8080/cocoon/abc/this/is/a/test` into our browser, the `Map` object that is returned by the `Matcher` will have the contents detailed in Table 11.1.

Table 11.1 *Matcher Map Object Contents*

Name	Value
0	this/is/a/test
1	this
2	is
3	a
4	test

This can be very useful in Cocoon because you can create logic simply by having extended URI patterns. Thanks to the pipeline concept, URIs are completely decoupled from underlying physical resources. With traditional Web servers, if you type `http://localhost:8080/cocoon/abc/this/is/a/test`, you'd better have all those directories created and have a file called `test` in the last one (unless, of course, you are using some sort of URL rewriting). In Cocoon, however, you don't need any directories at all, if you don't want them, but you can have directories in the URIs to separate processing. For example, you could use URI patterns to help choose processing paths for different users in different departments in a corporation. Let's say you have marketing and sales departments, each with a bunch of users. Each user has access to the same physical index page, `index.xml`. However, that page can be personalized (we'll show how in a bit) by who the user is and what department he or she is in.

Consider the following pipeline:

```
<map:match pattern="mycorp/*/*/*.html">
 <map:generate type="file" src="content/{3}.xml"/>
 <map:transform type="xslt" src="style/main.xsl"/>
 <map:serialize type="html"/>
</map:match>
```

The URL `http://localhost:8080/cocoon/mycorp/sales/mary/index.html` will produce a `Map` object with the contents detailed in Table 11.2.

Table 11.2 *Matcher Map Object Contents*

Name	Value
0	mycorp/sales/mary/index.html
1	sales
2	mary
3	index

In the pipeline, we use the key of `{3}` to find the right file, `index.xml`. The other values of `{1}` and `{2}`, however, can be passed to the XSL file and be used to personalize the contents. We'll see an example of this later.

Map Object Nesting

There is another important concept with `Matchers`, and that is nesting. We discussed earlier how for each `<map:match>` or `<map:act>` tag, a new `Map` object is created that exists until the corresponding close tag. When we have more than one `Map` object available in the pipeline, we refer to them using Unix-like path constructs. The most recent `Map` object is always referred to directly, such as `{1}` or `{myvalue}`. The `Map` object immediately before the current one (the parent) is referred to by prefixing the key name with `../` characters. The one before that (the grandparent) is referred to by prefixing the key name with an additional set of `../` characters. Suppose (and it will happen if you work with Cocoon long enough) you have a pipeline with three `Matchers` in it:

```
<map:match pattern="myarea/*">
   <map:match pattern="myarea/*.html">
     <map:match pattern="myarea/hello-*.html">
        <!—processing goes here →
     </map:match>
   </map:match>
</map:match>
```

Each `Matcher` produces a `Map` object with two parameters: `0` and `1`. If we try the URL `http://localhost:8080/cocoon/myarea/hello-world.html`, then any components under the third `<map:match>` tag will have access to all three `Map` objects, as shown in Table 11.3.

Table 11.3 *Matcher Map Object Contents*

Matcher	Name	Value	Reference
myarea/*	0	myarea/hello-world.html	{../../0}
myarea/*	1	hello-world.html	{../../1}
myarea/*.html	0	myarea/hello-world.html	{../0}
myarea/*.html	1	hello-world	{../1}
myarea/hello-*.html	0	myarea/hello-world.html	{0}
myarea/hello-*.html	1	world	{1}

Remember, the references in this table are from the standpoint of components operating within the third `<map:match>` tag.

Rewriting Our Sitemap

With this new understanding of `Matchers`, let's rewrite our sitemap and make it shorter and more reusable. First, Listing 11.1 shows the sitemap as we have developed it in Chapter 7, "Creating Static Pages," and Chapter 8, "Using Content Logic: XSPs."

Listing 11.1 *Original abc sitemap.xmap (sitemap.xmap)*

```
<?xml version="1.0"?>

<map:sitemap xmlns:map="http://apache.org/cocoon/sitemap/1.0">

 <map:components>
  <map:generators default="file"/>
  <map:transformers default="xslt"/>
  <map:readers default="resource"/>
  <map:serializers default="html"/>
  <map:selectors default="browser"/>
  <map:matchers default="wildcard"/>
 </map:components>

 <map:pipelines>
  <map:pipeline>

   <map:match pattern="index.html">
    <map:generate src="content/main.xml"/>
    <map:transform src="style/main.xsl"/>
    <map:serialize/>
   </map:match>
```

Listing 11.1 *(continued)*

```
    <map:match pattern="index.wml">
     <map:generate type="file" src="content/main.xml"/>
     <map:transform type="xslt" src="style/main-wml.xsl"/>
     <map:serialize type="wml"/>
    </map:match>

    <map:match pattern="index.pdf">
     <map:generate type="file" src="content/main.xml"/>
     <map:transform type="xslt" src="style/main-pdf.xsl"/>
     <map:serialize type="fo2pdf"/>
    </map:match>

    <map:match pattern="login.html">
     <map:read mime-type="text/html" src="content/login.html"/>
    </map:match>

    <map:match pattern="login.xsp">
     <map:generate type="serverpages" src="xsp/login.xsp"/>
     <map:transform type="xslt" src="style/main.xsl"/>
     <map:serialize type="html"/>
    </map:match>

    <map:match pattern="tickets.xsp">
     <map:generate type="serverpages" src="xsp/tickets.xsp"/>
     <map:transform type="xslt" src="style/main.xsl"/>
     <map:serialize type="html"/>
    </map:match>

  </map:pipeline>
 </map:pipelines>
</map:sitemap>
```

The strategy here is to reduce clutter and increase the reuse of pipelines. Right off the bat, we can see that we have two pipelines with the same XSP-based process, the one for `login.xsp` and the one for `tickets.xsp`. We can therefore substitute this for the last two pipelines:

```
<map:match pattern="*.xsp">
 <map:generate type="serverpages" src="xsp/{1}.xsp"/>
 <map:transform type="xslt" src="style/main.xsl"/>
 <map:serialize type="html"/>
</map:match>
```

We can also provide a more generic pipeline to handle `*.html` pages, as we showed previously. This makes our pipelines look like this:

```
<map:pipelines>
  <map:pipeline>

   <map:match pattern="login.html">
    <map:read mime-type="text/html" src="content/login.html"/>
   </map:match>

   <map:match pattern="*.html">
    <map:generate type="file" src="content/{1}.xml"/>
    <map:transform type="xslt" src="style/main.xsl"/>
    <map:serialize type="html"/>
   </map:match>

   <map:match pattern="*.xsp">
    <map:generate type="serverpages" src="xsp/{1}.xsp"/>
    <map:transform type="xslt" src="style/main.xsl"/>
    <map:serialize type="html"/>
   </map:match>

   <map:match pattern="index.wml">
    <map:generate type="file" src="content/main.xml"/>
    <map:transform type="xslt" src="style/main-wml.xsl"/>
    <map:serialize type="wml"/>
   </map:match>

   <map:match pattern="index.pdf">
    <map:generate type="file" src="content/main.xml"/>
    <map:transform type="xslt" src="style/main-pdf.xsl"/>
    <map:serialize type="fo2pdf"/>
   </map:match>

  </map:pipeline>
</map:pipelines>
</map:sitemap>
```

In this example, we've also eliminated a potential problem. The `login.html` page is supposed to be presented untouched to the browser—we don't need Cocoon to do any processing. However, the `Matcher` that handles `*.html` could be a problem except for the fact that Cocoon looks for matches in the sitemap from the top down. So if we put our original pipeline for `login.html` before that for `*.html`, we'll be fine. You will probably encounter this situation many times while working with Cocoon. As a general rule, try to put the more specific pipelines before the more general ones. This might help you avoid unexpected results.

Using Redirection

There is another problem with our revised sitemap. We originally specified that any URI ending in `index.html` would be handled by the page `main.xml`. Now, however, our more dynamic pipeline for `*.html` means that the URL `http://localhost:8080/cocoon/abc/index.html` will generate an error, because there is no corresponding `index.xml` file.

The solution is the `map:redirect-to` tag. Before any of the other pipelines, we can put the following:

```
<map:match pattern="">
 <map:redirect-to uri="index.html"/>
</map:match>

<map:match pattern="index.html">
 <map:redirect-to uri="main.html"/>
</map:match>
```

The first `redirect` sends any empty requests to `index.html`, and the second sends `index.html` to `main.html`, which we already know will be handled by the `*.html` pipeline. An empty request, by the way, is one that points to a Cocoon project but does not specify a page: `http://localhost:8080/cocoon/abc/` is an empty request (in fact, the only one that exists for our project).

This brings up a slight problem. What if our user types `http://localhost:8080/cocoon/abc`, omitting the trailing slash? What happens is that the main sitemap, the one in `$CATALINA_HOME/webapps/cocoon`, is going to try to handle this page. But if that sitemap doesn't have a match for `abc`, it will generate an error. The trailing slash does make all the difference. Remember the `map:mount` tag we put in the top-level sitemap:

```
<map:match pattern="abc/**>
  <map:mount uri-prefix="abc" src="abc/sitemap.xmap" check-reload="yes"/>
</map:match>
```

You can see that the Matcher is directing any URI starting with abc/, and ending with anything else, to the sitemap in our project folder. To handle http://localhost:8080/cocoon/abc, we'll have to add a map:redirect-to instruction before this mount:

```
<map:match pattern="abc">
 <map:redirect-to uri="abc/"/>
</map:match>
```

So when you type http://localhost:8080/cocoon/abc, you will be directed to the proper page and you'll see http://localhost:8080/cocoon/abc/ in your browser location bar.

Using Selectors

A Matcher implements a very simple logic: Either a URI matches or it doesn't. A Selector is more flexible. It operates within a pipeline as a switch statement. Using elements such as request parameters, session attributes, or sitemap parameters, a Selector directs processing to particular components.

SessionAttributeSelector

One of the requirements for our project was that pages are customized for particular customers. Let's suppose we have a stylesheet customized for BigCorp. This stylesheet will have a BigCorp logo and perhaps some tailored advertising or product announcements.

First, we need to create a new stylesheet. We'll copy abc/style/main.xsl to abc/style/BigCorp.xsl and replace the /page template with the following:

```
<xsl:template match="/page">
  <html>
   <head>
    <title><xsl:value-of select="page-title"/></title>
    <link rel="stylesheet" type="text/css" href="style/BigCorp.css"/>
   </head>

   <body bgcolor="#ffffff">
    <table width="100%" cellpadding="0" cellspacing="0">
     <tr>
     <td align="left">
      <font face="arial"><b>Welcome BigCorp user!</b>
     </font></td>
     <td align="right">
      <img src="images/BigCorp.gif" border="0"/>
     </td>
```

```
    </tr></table>

    <br/> 
    <xsl:apply-templates/>
   </body>
  </html>
 </xsl:template>
```

Notice that we've added both a CSS declaration and an image. However, without defining pipelines to handle these files, our page would error out. So we need to add pipelines for `*.css` and `*.gif` files:

```
<map:match pattern="*.css">
 <map:read mime-type="text/css" src="style/{1}.css"/>
</map:match>
<map:match pattern="**/*.css">
 <map:read mime-type="text/css" src="style/{2}.css"/>
</map:match>
<map:match pattern="*.gif">
 <map:read mime-type="image/gif" src="images/{1}.gif"/>
</map:match>
<map:match pattern="**/*.gif">
 <map:read mime-type="image/gif" src="images/{2}.gif"/>
</map:match>
```

We've declared two versions for each file type to handle relative paths. Suppose we have a URL like this: `http://localhost:8080/cocoon/abc/billing/private/bills.xml`. If we used the `BigCorp.xsl` stylesheet given previously, the browser will be looking for `http://localhost:8080/cocoon/abc/billing/private/images/BigCorp.gif` and `http://localhost:8080/cocoon/abc/billing/private/style/BigCorp.css`. By having a `Matcher` for `**/*.css` and `**/*.gif`, we ensure that any image or CSS, no matter what the URL says, will be loaded from the right directory. Also, it is a good idea to put these pipeline declarations at the front of the `sitemap.xmap` to ensure that no other `Matcher` accidentally catches these files.

The CSS file is shown in Listing 11.2.

Listing 11.2 *Customized CSS File (BigCorp.css)*

```
H3 {
    font-family: verdana, helvetica, sans serif;
    color: #0033ff;
    font-weight: bold;
```

Listing 11.2 *(continued)*

```
    font-size: 16pt;
}

P {
    font-family: verdana, helvetica, sans serif;
    color: #0033ff;
}

TD {
    font-family: verdana, helvetica, sans serif;
    color: #0033ff;
}
```

The image file, `BigCorp.gif`, can be found on the accompanying Web site.

Now we can implement our `Selector`. What we want to do is to look for the `user` attribute in the session. If it is equal to `BigCorp`, we will use `BigCorp.xsl;` otherwise, the pipeline will default to `main.xsl`:

```
<map:match pattern="*.xsp">
 <map:generate type="serverpages" src="xsp/{1}.xsp"/>

 <map:select type="session-attribute">
   <map:parameter name="attribute-name" value="user"/>

   <map:when test="BigCorp">
     <map:transform type="xslt" src="style/BigCorp.xsl"/>
   </map:when>
   <map:otherwise>
     <map:transform type="xslt" src="style/main.xsl"/>
   </map:otherwise>
 </map:select>

 <map:serialize type="html"/>
</map:match>
```

If you authenticate and go to `http://localhost:8080/cocoon/abc/tickets.xsp`, you should see what's shown in Figure 11.1.

Creating Protected Areas

The preceding example showed how we could customize processing based on session information. However, the pipeline we created for XSPs doesn't handle one situation:

unauthenticated users accessing our XSPs. We also have another little annoyance: the `.xsp` suffix that we've been adding on to everything to differentiate XSPs from other pipelines.

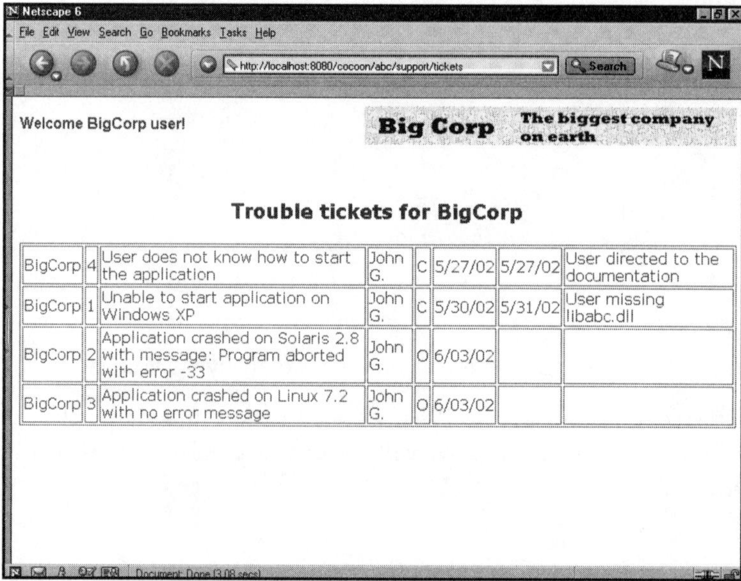

Figure 11.1
Customized Tickets page.

We can solve both of these problems by editing our sitemap once again, and this time using the `WildcardSessionAttributeMatcher`.

WildcardSessionAttributeMatcher

This `Matcher` allows us to choose pipelines based on a session attribute. In our example, the only session attribute we've been dealing with is the `user` attribute. So if we create a pipeline that relies on the `user` attribute, we are assured that it will be used only when that attribute actually exists.

Let's look at Listing 11.3 to see how this works.

Listing 11.3 *Implementing Protected Areas (sitemap.xmap)*

```
<?xml version="1.0"?>

<map:sitemap xmlns:map="http://apache.org/cocoon/sitemap/1.0">
```

Listing 11.3 *(continued)*

```
<map:components>
 <map:generators default="file"/>
 <map:transformers default="xslt"/>
 <map:readers default="resource"/>
 <map:serializers default="html"/>
 <map:selectors default="browser"/>
 <map:matchers default="wildcard"/>
</map:components>

<map:pipelines>
 <map:pipeline>

  <map:match pattern="*.css">
   <map:read mime-type="text/css" src="style/{1}.css"/>
  </map:match>
  <map:match pattern="**/*.css">
   <map:read mime-type="text/css" src="style/{1}.css"/>
  </map:match>
  <map:match pattern="*.gif">
   <map:read mime-type="image/gif" src="images/{1}.gif"/>
  </map:match>
  <map:match pattern="**/*.gif">
   <map:read mime-type="image/gif" src="images/{2}.gif"/>
  </map:match>

  <map:match pattern="">
   <map:redirect-to uri="index.html"/>
  </map:match>

  <map:match pattern="index.html">
   <map:generate src="content/main.xml"/>
   <map:transform src="style/main.xsl"/>
   <map:serialize/>
  </map:match>

  <map:match pattern="login.html">
   <map:read mime-type="text/html" src="content/login.html"/>
  </map:match>

  <map:match pattern="login">
   <map:generate type="serverpages" src="xsp/login.xsp"/>
```

Listing 11.3 *(continued)*

```
    <map:transform type="xslt" src="style/main.xsl"/>
    <map:serialize type="html"/>
   </map:match>

   <map:match type="sessionstate" pattern="*">
    <map:parameter name="attribute-name" value="user"/>

    <map:match pattern="support/*">
     <map:generate type="serverpages" src="xsp/{1}.xsp"/>

     <map:select type="session-attribute">
       <map:parameter name="attribute-name" value="user"/>

       <map:when test="BigCorp">
         <map:transform type="xslt" src="style/BigCorp.xsl"/>
       </map:when>
       <map:otherwise>
         <map:transform type="xslt" src="style/main.xsl"/>
       </map:otherwise>
     </map:select>

     <map:serialize type="html"/>
    </map:match>
   </map:match>

   <map:match pattern="support/**">
    <map:redirect-to uri="login.html"/>
   </map:match>

  </map:pipeline>
 </map:pipelines>

</map:sitemap>
```

We'll start with the line `<map:match type="sessionstate" pattern="*">` (`sessionstate` is the key name for the `WildcardSessionAttributeMatcher`). The way you use a `WildcardSessionAttributeMatcher` is to tell it what attribute you are switching on. We do this with the line immediately following:

```
<map:parameter name="attribute-name" value="user"/>
```

Now we really don't care about specific values of the `user` attribute—we just care that it is set. That is why the pattern in the `Matcher` is set to `*`. Cocoon will direct a URL to this pipeline only if the session attribute `user` is set. Once inside a pipeline, we'll look at the next `Matcher`, which is this:

```
<map:match pattern="support/*">
```

This means that the pipeline will handle only URIs that start with the directory `support` and end in anything else. As we did before, we'll use the substitution variable `{1}` to determine what XSP we use. Note that we are not relying on the suffix `.xsp` anymore; we built our application so that any request starting with `http://localhost:8080/cocoon/abc/support/` will be handled by this pipeline, which assumes that the request is to an XSP.

We also kept our previous `Selector` that determines what stylesheet to use, again based on the `user` session attribute.

One more gotcha that we had to consider in this revised sitemap: `login.xsp`. Because this XSP is the target of the form in `login.html`, we obviously need to access it when there is no previous session. Hence, we define a new pipeline just for `login.xsp` and put it before the `support` pipeline. Again, Cocoon takes the first match it finds as it traverses the sitemap from top to bottom, so `login.xsp` will always get processed correctly.

Finally, we have a catch-all pipeline after the protected area that catches any URI starting with `support` and redirects to the login page. This pipeline will be used only if the `user` attribute is not set in the session.

Protecting Pipelines with Actions

If you are wondering why we aren't using actions such as SessionValidatorAction and SessionInvalidatorAction, the answer is simple: that topic is covered in Chapter 12, "Using Sitemap Logic: Actions and Forms."

Using Pipeline Aggregation

Pipeline aggregation is a way to combine or aggregate data from multiple sources within the pipeline. We saw in Chapter 10, "Using Content Logic: Transformers," that we can do aggregation with the `CIncludeTransformer` and `XIncludeTransformer`. However, a very basic aggregation can be achieved in the pipeline.

When you use pipeline aggregation, you simply enclose multiple `map:part` tags within a `map:aggregate` block. The `map:part` tags point the pipeline to the XML sources to include (that is, sources that generate XML). Generally, the easiest way to do this is to set up pipelines as the XML sources and then reference them in the map:part tag. For example, let's look at the aggregation sample that comes in the Cocoon samples:

```
<map:match pattern="news/aggregate.xml">
 <map:aggregate element="page" ns="http://foo.bar.com/myspace">
  <map:part element="news" ns="http://foo.bar.com/slashdot"
    src="cocoon:/news/slashdot.xml"/>
  <map:part element="news" ns="http://foo.bar.com/moreover"
    src="cocoon:/news/moreover.xml"/>
  <map:part element="news" ns="http://foo.bar.com/xmlhack"
    src="cocoon:/news/ xmlhack.xml"/>
 </map:aggregate>
 <map:transform src="stylesheets/news/news.xsl"/>
 <map:serialize/>
</map:match>
```

This pipeline matches a request for news/aggregate.xml. The map:aggregate tag specifies that when the various parts are concatenated together, they will all reside under the root user tag page, and its associated namespace http://foo.bar.com/myspace. There are three map:part elements. Each one has a reference to another pipeline as defined in the src attribute. We know that the src is referring to another pipeline because it uses what is known as a "pseudo protocol."

Cocoon defines several extremely useful pseudo protocols that make it very easy to reference resources no matter where Cocoon is installed. Table 11.4 describes these in detail.

Table 11.4 *Cocoon Pseudo Protocols*

Tag	Description
cocoon:/	Refers to a pipeline in the current sitemap. There must be a pipeline that matches everything following the cocoon:/.
cocoon://	Refers to a pipeline in the root or top-level sitemap. There must be a pipeline that matches everything following the cocoon://.
resource://	Refers to a resource from the root of the context classloader. In other words, this resource can be in any jar file available in the classpath.
context://	Refers to a resource from the root of the servlet context, which is the root of the Web application. For our installation, this is $CATALINA_HOME/webapps/cocoon.
file://	Refers to a file resource using the full path.
xmldb://	Refers to an XML:DB-managed resource.
http://	Refers to a resource on a Web server—can be used to reference a resource on an external server, not necessarily the same server.

Now we can see this in action.

Revising the Customer Home Page

In the preceding chapter, we aggregated an advertisement and contract summary for a customer. We already have all the elements defined, although we are now going to put the contract summary into the protected area by using the match pattern `support/contract-summary`. Then, we simply need to define the aggregation and create a new stylesheet. We are going to do it two different ways: a simple way, and one that is slightly more complex. These pipelines, along with those beginning with `support`, are placed inside the restricted pipeline that matches the session attribute `user`. For the sake of clarity, let's see that entire pipeline:

```
<map:match type="sessionstate" pattern="*">
 <map:parameter name="attribute-name" value="user"/>

 <map:match pattern="support/home">
   <map:aggregate element="home">
     <map:part src="cocoon:/support/contract-summary"/>
     <map:part src="context://abc/content/adv-xyz-01.xml"/>
   </map:aggregate>
   <map:transform type="xslt" src="style/home-page.xsl">
     <map:parameter name="user" value="{../1}"/>
   </map:transform>
   <map:serialize type="html"/>
 </map:match>

 <map:match pattern="support/contract-summary">
  <map:generate type="serverpages" src="xsp/contract-summary.xsp"/>
  <map:serialize type="xml"/>
 </map:match>

 <map:match pattern="support/*">
  <map:generate type="serverpages" src="xsp/{1}.xsp"/>

  <map:select type="session-attribute">
    <map:parameter name="attribute-name" value="user"/>

    <map:when test="BigCorp">
      <map:transform type="xslt" src="style/BigCorp.xsl"/>
    </map:when>
    <map:otherwise>
      <map:transform type="xslt" src="style/main.xsl"/>
```

```
    </map:otherwise>
  </map:select>

  <map:serialize type="html"/>
 </map:match>
</map:match>
```

This is the simple version of pipeline aggregation, because we are not using namespaces or declaring the top-level tags for the `map:part` elements. We do, however, have to declare the top-level tag for the entire page, which we do as `home`. We are aggregating two sources here. The `cocoon:/support/contract-summary` reference points to the pipeline that matches `support/contract-summary`. Remember, the output of this pipeline is XML. The reference `context://abc/content/abc-xyz-01.xml` points to a physical file from the standpoint of the servlet context, which is `$CATALINA_HOME/webapps/cocoon`. We could also have written that line simply as

```
<map:part src="content/adv-xyz-01.xml"/>
```

but we wanted to demonstrate the use of the `context://` pseudo protocol.

After the aggregation itself, all that is necessary is to provide a stylesheet and define the right serializer. Listing 11.4 shows `style/home-page.xsl`.

Listing 11.4 *Home Page Stylesheet (home-page.xsl)*

```
<?xml version="1.0"?>

<xsl:stylesheet version="1.0"
  xmlns:xsl="http://www.w3.org/1999/XSL/Transform"
>

 <xsl:param name="user"/>

 <xsl:template match="/">
  <html>
   <head>
    <title><xsl:value-of select="page-title"/></title>
    <link rel="stylesheet" type="text/css">
      <xsl:attribute name="href">style/
       <xsl:value-of select="$user"/>.css
      </xsl:attribute>
    </link>
   </head>
```

Listing 11.4 *(continued)*

```
   <body bgcolor="#ffffff">
    <table width="100%" cellpadding="0" cellspacing="0">
     <tr>
     <td align="left">
      <font face="arial"><b>Welcome BigCorp user!</b>
     </font></td>

     <xsl:if test="$user = 'BigCorp'">
      <td align="right">
       <img src="BigCorp.gif" border="0"/>
      </td>
     </xsl:if>

    </tr></table>

    <br/> 

    <table width="100%"><tr>
     <td width="75%">
      <xsl:apply-templates select="//title"/>
      <xsl:apply-templates select="//contract-summary"/>
     </td>
     <td width="25%">
      <xsl:apply-templates select="//ad-title"/>
      <xsl:apply-templates select="//ad"/>
     </td>
    </tr></table>

   </body>
  </html>
 </xsl:template>

<xsl:template match="ad-title">
  <center>
  <h3>
   <font point-size="10pt"><xsl:apply-templates/>
  </font></h3>
  </center>
 </xsl:template>

 <xsl:template match="title">
  <center>
```

Listing 11.4 *(continued)*

```
  <h3><font face="arial">
   Here is your contract summary:
  </font></h3>
  </center>
 </xsl:template>

 <xsl:template match="contract-summary">
  <table>
   <tr><td>
    Your contract ends on: <xsl:value-of select="ends"/>
   </td></tr>
   <tr><td>
    The amount of your contract is: <xsl:value-of select="amount"/>
   </td></tr>
   <tr><td>
    The amount used to date is: <xsl:value-of select="used"/>
   </td></tr>
  </table>
 </xsl:template>

 <xsl:template match="ad">
  <p><font point-size="8pt"><xsl:apply-templates/></font></p>
 </xsl:template>

</xsl:stylesheet>
```

If you noticed, we passed a sitemap parameter called `user` to the `map:transform` step so that we can use it as an input parameter to the XSL. This parameter holds the value of the `Map` object returned by the `WildcardSessionAttributeMatcher`. Because we are actually inside a second `Matcher`, we need to make sure we get the right value out of the parent `Map` object. We use the `user` variable to find the right `*.css` file as well as to add the image for BigCorp. Note the syntax of the dynamically built `<link>` tag: there must be no whitespace between the `<xsl:attribute>` tag, the content insides, and the closing tag.

We can test this out by authenticating and browsing to `http://localhost:8080/cocoon/abc/support/home`. Figure 11.2 shows the expected output.

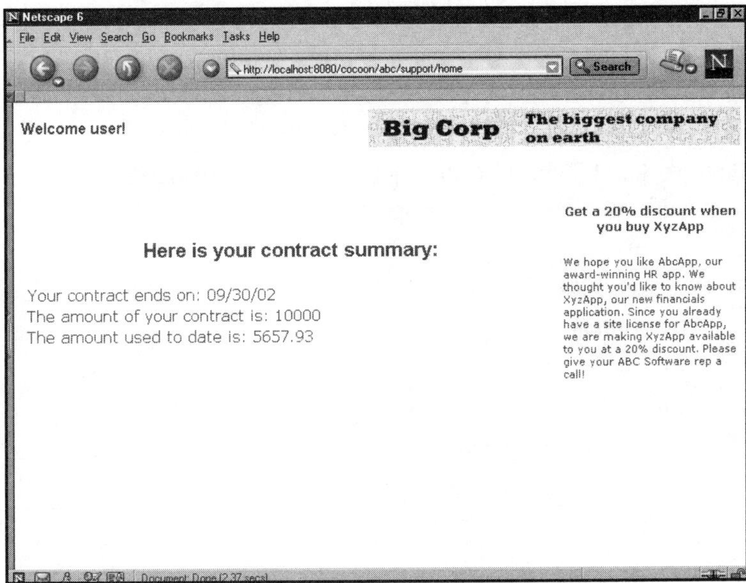

Figure 11.2
Customer home page.

As we did with the `CIncludeTransformer`, we can add namespace declarations to this pipeline and to the stylesheet to keep the tags from the different aggregated contents separate. This is the more complex version of pipeline aggregation, and the revised pipeline looks like this:

```
<map:match pattern="support/home">
  <map:aggregate element="home" prefix="home" ns="http://foo.bar.com/home">
    <map:part element="contract" prefix="contract"
      ns="http://foo.bar.com/contract"
      src="cocoon:/support/contract-summary"/>
    <map:part element="adv" prefix="adv" ns="http://foo.bar.com/adv"
      src="context://abc/content/adv-xyz-01.xml"/>
  </map:aggregate>

  <map:transform type="xslt" src="style/home-page.xsl">
    <map:parameter name="user" value="{../1}"/>
  </map:transform>
  <map:serialize type="html"/>
</map:match>
```

The `map:part` elements, as well as the top-level tag, all have associated namespaces. The value of the `element` attributes now becomes the prefix for the namespace. This means that all the tags from the contract summary page will be prefixed by the tag `contract:`, belonging to the namespace `http://foo.bar.com/contract`.

As reference, Table 11.5 and Table 11.6 show all the possible attributes for the `<map:aggregate>` and `<map:part>` tags, respectively.

Table 11.5 *<map:aggregate> Attributes*

Attribute	Description	Required
element	The root tag that will contain the aggregated tags.	yes
prefix	The prefix to use for all tags.	no
ns	Defines the namespace.	no
label	Provides a handle to a view.	no

Table 11.6 *<map:part> Attributes*

Attribute	Description	Required
src	The resource that this part points to.	yes
element	The root tag for the data coming from the source.	no
ns	Defines the namespace.	no
strip-root	Set to yes or true so that the root node of the data will be stripped off.	no
label	Provides a handle to a view.	no
prefix	The prefix to use for all tags.	no

Of course, we have to change our stylesheet to handle these tags, as shown in Listing 11.5.

Listing 11.5 *Home Page Stylesheet Using Namespaces (home-page-ns.xsl)*

```
<?xml version="1.0"?>

<xsl:stylesheet version="1.0"
  xmlns:xsl="http://www.w3.org/1999/XSL/Transform"
  xmlns:home="http://foo.bar.com/home"
  xmlns:contract="http://foo.bar.com/contract"
  xmlns:adv="http://foo.bar.com/adv"
>
```

Listing 11.5 *(continued)*

```
<xsl:param name="user"/>

<xsl:template match="/">
 <html>
  <head>
   <title><xsl:value-of select="page-title"/></title>
   <link rel="stylesheet" type="text/css">
     <xsl:attribute name="href">
      style/<xsl:value-of select="$user"/>.css
     </xsl:attribute>
   </link>
  </head>

  <body bgcolor="#ffffff">
   <table width="100%" cellpadding="0" cellspacing="0">
    <tr>
    <td align="left">
     <font face="arial"><b>Welcome user!</b></font>
    </td>

    <xsl:if test="$user = 'BigCorp'">
     <td align="right">
      <img src="BigCorp.gif" border="0"/>
     </td>
    </xsl:if>

   </tr></table>

   <br/> 

   <table width="100%"><tr>
    <td width="75%">
     <xsl:apply-templates select="//contract:title"/>
     <xsl:apply-templates select="//contract:contract-summary"/>
    </td>
    <td width="25%">
     <xsl:apply-templates select="//adv:ad-title"/>
     <xsl:apply-templates select="//adv:ad"/>
    </td>
   </tr></table>
```

Listing 11.5 *(continued)*

```
   </body>
  </html>
 </xsl:template>

 <xsl:template match="contract:title">
  <center>
  <h3><font face="arial">
   Here is your contract summary:
  </font></h3>
  </center>
 </xsl:template>

 <xsl:template match="adv:ad-title">
  <center>
  <h3>
   <font point-size="10pt"><xsl:apply-templates/>
  </font></h3>
  </center>
 </xsl:template>

 <xsl:template match="contract:contract-summary">
  <table>
   <tr><td>
    Your contract ends on: <xsl:value-of select="contract:ends"/>
   </td></tr>
   <tr><td>
    The amount of your contract is: <xsl:value-of select="contract:amount"/>
   </td></tr>
   <tr><td>
    The amount used to date is: <xsl:value-of select="contract:used"/>
   </td></tr>
  </table>
 </xsl:template>

 <xsl:template match="adv:ad">
  <p><font point-size="8pt"><xsl:apply-templates/></font></p>
 </xsl:template>

</xsl:stylesheet>
```

Notice that we have to tell the XSLT process what namespaces we are loading, and we have to prefix all our tags with the correct namespace prefix. This is generally the better practice, as opposed to our earlier example, because it ensures that tags from multiple sources won't clash.

So far, we have been using only the ad page `adv-xyz-01.xml`. You might wondering how we will target this to the right customers. We'll see that in the next chapter, but first we have a few more things to consider.

Using Views

A `view` is a way to "catch" XML output from any stage of a pipeline. That is, it provides a sort of alternative pipeline to generated XML data. This data does not have to come from the `map:generate` stage of a pipeline; it can come from any component.

The easiest way to understand this is to go back to our aggregate example. Suppose, for example, we had problems figuring out what the XML data looked like after the aggregation. With a view, we can actually capture this data and check it out.

We start by defining a view. `Views` go in the `map:views` section, which precedes `map:pipelines` in the sitemap. Our view is simple:

```
<map:views>
  <map:view from-label="beautify" name="beautify">
   <map:transform type="xslt" src="style/view.xsl"/>
   <map:serialize type="html"/>
  </map:view>
 </map:views>
```

What is defined here is a view called `beautify`, which takes the captured XML data and sends it through a transformer and serializer. The stylesheet that we will use is taken from `$CATALINA_HOME/webapps/cocoon/stylesheets/simple-xml2html.xsl`.

To use our view, we need to define the `label` attribute in the place where we want to capture the data. The value of the `label` attribute will contain one or more view names, comma or space delimited. In this example, we'll put a label in the `map:aggregate` line:

```
<map:aggregate element="home" label="beautify">
```

The way to actually use a view is to append `?cocoon-view=<view-name>` to the URL. Therefore, to see the raw XML after the aggregation of the contract summary and advertisement pages (the version in which we used namespaces), we type the following in our browser: `http://localhost:8080/cocoon/abc/support/home?cocoon-view=beautify`. The output is shown in Figure 11.3.

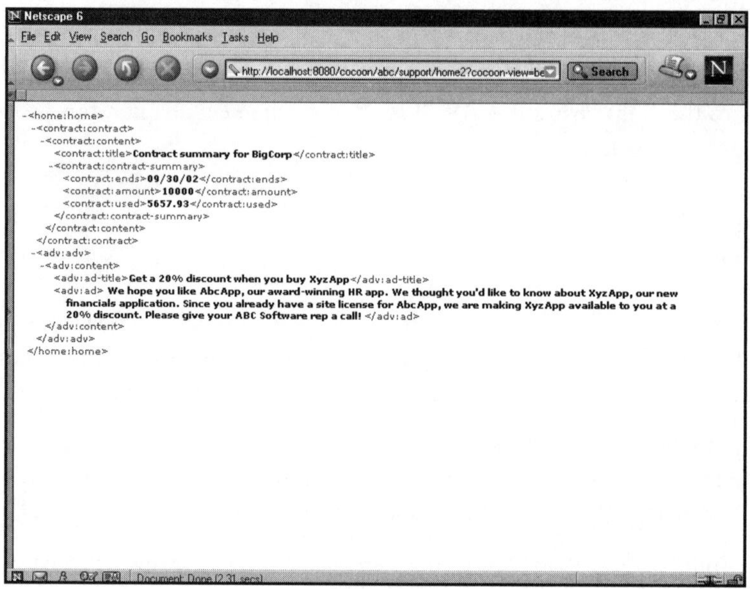

Figure 11.3

XML data after the aggregation.

This is a very good use of views, and it can save you much time when you are having problems with your stylesheet and need to see what tags are actually getting to it.

Another good use is when you want to extract part of the content of a page before it is combined with other data sources. For example, we might have had a contract summary page that displayed as PDF:

```
<map:match pattern="support/contract-summary.pdf">
  <map:generate type="serverpages"
     src="xsp/contract-summary.xsp" label="raw"/>
  <map:transform type="xslt" src="style/main-pdf.xsl"/>
  <map:serialize type="fo2pdf"/>
</map:match>
```

And we have a view called `raw` as follows:

```
<map:view from-label="raw" name="raw">
 <map:serialize type="xml"/>
</map:view>
```

By adding the `label` attribute to the `support/contract-summary.pdf` pipeline, we can now use this page in our aggregation by using the following `map:part` call:

```
<map:part src="cocoon:/support/contract-summary.pdf?cocoon-view=raw"/>
```

Now, without creating a new pipeline, we are assured that XML data is retrieved by the `map:part` call.

Protected Pipelines

In the aggregation examples, we've been using an XSP called `contract-summary.xsp`. In this chapter, we made sure that this file could be accessed only by an authenticated user by putting the pipeline inside the protected area. There is, however, another, easier way. We can set up a new `<map:pipeline>` block that has an attribute called `internal-only` set to `true`. Inside this block, we'll put the pipeline for the contract summary. We'll also change the URI pattern so that it doesn't accidentally get matched by anything else:

```
<map:pipeline internal-only="true">
 <map:match pattern="support-hide/contract-summary">
   <map:generate type="serverpages" src="xsp/contract-summary.xsp"/>
   <map:serialize type="xml"/>
 </map:match>
</map:pipeline>
```

The `internal-only` attribute makes any pipelines inside this `<map:pipeline>` block inaccessible from the outside. These pipelines can be used only from other pipelines. Therefore, we can freely call `support-hide/contract-summary` from our aggregated pipelines, but users cannot put that URI in their browsers and see anything. In general, it is a good principle to put anything in an internal pipeline that you don't want to have users see directly. Then you can include them from pipelines that are visible to the users.

Using map:resource and map:call

Closely related to the preceding topic is the definition of pipelines as "resources." Before the `<map:pipelines>` block of `sitemap.xmap`, we can define pipelines that are also inaccessible from the outside. These are enclosed inside `<map:resource>` blocks. For example, we could define our advertisement pages as shown here:

```
<map:resources>
  <map:resource name="ad1">
    <map:generate type="file" src="content/adv-xyz-01.xml"/>
    <map:transform type="xslt" src="style/adv.xsl"/>
    <map:serialize type="html"/>
  </map:resource>
  <map:resource name="ad2">
    <map:generate type="file" src="content/adv-xyz-02.xml"/>
    <map:transform type="xslt" src="style/adv.xsl"/>
    <map:serialize type="html"/>
  </map:resource>
 </map:resources>
```

Again, this comes before the `<map:pipelines>` block. As you can see, we don't define `Matchers` for these resources: we just name them and define the processing flow. Then, inside a regular pipeline, we can access a resource using the `<map:call>` tag:

```
<map:match pattern="adv-xyz-01">
 <map:call resource="ad1"/>
</map:match>
```

One thing to note is that when you invoke `map:call`, there is no returning to the pipeline from which you made the call. In other words, the `map:call` statement directs processing to the named resource, and execution will terminate at the end of the resource processing instructions.

Summary

In this chapter, we've covered a few ways to implement logic in pipelines. We learned about using the `WildcardURIMatcher` and saw various ways to implement aggregation. With views, we have an excellent tool for helping debug Cocoon projects (don't forget to take them out when you deploy!). Now we are ready to move on to even more logic with actions and sitemap parameters.

There are many cases in which you can implement the same thing in the sitemap or an XSP. By and large, the preferred approach is to take the sitemap solution, because it saves mixing of content and logic. Of course, many times you can't do this, such as when request or session parameters determine how a data source is accessed. But it is important to keep in mind that Cocoon is so flexible that although you will find yourself doing things in one way, there are other, simpler ways to do it.

CHAPTER 12

Using Sitemap Logic: Actions and Forms

In this chapter, we will continue our discussion of implementing logic in the sitemap. Now that we've covered `Views`, aggregation, `Matchers`, and `Selectors`, we'll make things more complicated by introducing actions. Because forms are closely linked with actions, we'll cover these as well, in the second part of the chapter.

Understanding Actions

An action is a Java component that can implement logic and interact with the sitemap via sitemap parameters. An action can get data from the sitemap via a `Parameters` object. Like a `Matcher`, it can also return data via a `Map` object. Actions also have an effect on the pipeline merely based on whether they return a `Map` object or a `null` object. If a valid object is returned, all steps inside the `<map:act>` block will get executed, with execution terminating after the last step. If a `null` object is returned, all steps inside the `<map:act>` block will be ignored, but all actions following it will be executed.

A minimal action that doesn't do anything is shown in Listing 12.1.

Listing 12.1 *Minimal action (min-Action.java)*

```
import org.apache.avalon.framework.parameters.Parameters;
import org.apache.avalon.framework.thread.ThreadSafe;
import org.apache.cocoon.Constants;
import org.apache.cocoon.environment.ObjectModelHelper;
import org.apache.cocoon.environment.Redirector;
import org.apache.cocoon.environment.Request;
import org.apache.cocoon.environment.Session;
import org.apache.cocoon.environment.SourceResolver;
import org.apache.cocoon.acting.AbstractAction;

import java.util.Enumeration;
import java.util.HashMap;
import java.util.Map;

public class TestAction extends AbstractAction implements ThreadSafe {

    public Map act( Redirector redirector, SourceResolver resolver,
      Map objectModel, String source, Parameters param )
        throws Exception
    {
    return null;
    }
}
```

This action extends `org.apache.cocoon.acting.AbstractAction`, which extends the `AbstractLoggable` Avalon object. The latter is useful because it provides access to the underlying logging mechanism. Any action must implement the `act` method defined in the `org.apache.cocoon.acting.Action` interface. This method takes five parameters, described in Table 12.1.

Table 12.1 *act Method Objects*

Object	Description
`Redirector` redirector	`SitemapRedirector` object that allows an action to perform a redirect
`SourceResolver` resolver	Provides access to the underlying `Environment` object
`Map` objectModel	Is used to access various objects in the calling environment, specifically `Context`, `Request`, `Response`
`String` source	The `src` attribute of the action
`Parameters` param	Contains any parameters being passed into the action from the sitemap

In our example, the `act` method just returns null. Of course, a real action can have all sorts of code, from simple parameter manipulation to complex calculations or processing.

Cocoon comes with various built-in actions, described in Table 12.2.

Table 12.2 *Built-in actions (Excluding sunShine actions)*

Action	Description
`DatabaseAddAction`	Adds or updates one or more database tables.
`DatabaseAuthenticatorAction`	Enables user authentication against a database table.
`DatabaseDeleteAction`	Deletes a record from a database table.
`DatabaseSelectAction`	Selects a record from a database table.
`DatabaseUpdateAction`	Updates a record in a database table.
`FormValidatorAction`	Validates request parameters against a definition file.
`HelloAction`	Checks to see whether a `Session` object has been created.
`HttpHeaderAction`	Adds specified HTTP headers to the response.
`LangSelect`	Deprecated—see `LocaleAction`.
`LocaleAction`	Obtains request locale information and sets it in the `Map` object.
`RequestParamAction`	Sets various request components in the `Map` object.
`RequestParameterExistsAction`	Checks to see whether one or more given request parameters exist. If they do, returns a `Map` of all parameters; `null` otherwise.
`ResourceExistsAction`	Returns an empty `Map` object if a given resource exists; `null` otherwise.
`ScriptAction`	Executes any script that can be run by the BSF.
`ServerPagesAction`	Executes an XSP to produce an XML result document.
`SessionInvalidatorAction`	Calls `invalidate()` method on the `session` object. Returns empty `Map` object on success; `null` otherwise.
`SessionIsValidAction`	Returns an empty `Map` object if a session exists and is valid; `null` otherwise.
`SessionPropagatorAction`	Sets given sitemap parameters in the session as attributes and returns them in the `Map` object.
`SessionStateAction`	Stores a given variable in a named session attribute to track session state.
`SessionValidatorAction`	Validates session attributes against a definition file.
`SetCharacterEncodingAction`	Sets the character encoding of request parameters.
`ValidatorActionHelper`	Passes the results of a form validation back to the sitemap.
`ValidatorActionResult`	Passes a result code back from a form validation.

As you can see, there are many things actions can do—and that's even before you write your own. We'll look at some of these as we develop our application further.

> **Database Actions**
> In this chapter, we'll cover the `DatabaseAuthenticatorAction` and the `DatabaseAddAction`, but the other three database actions (`DatabaseDeleteAction`, `DatabaseSelectAction`, and `DatabaseUpdateAction`) are covered in Chapter 16, "Cocoon Interfaces: Databases."

A Character-Counting Action

Before we examine some of the built-in actions, let's write a quick sample action to illustrate the use of sitemap parameters. Our action will return a count for the number of characters in a given word. Listing 12.2 shows the code for our action.

Listing 12.2 Character Counting Action *(CharCounterAction.java)*

```
package test;

import org.apache.avalon.framework.parameters.Parameters;
import org.apache.avalon.framework.thread.ThreadSafe;
import org.apache.cocoon.Constants;
import org.apache.cocoon.environment.ObjectModelHelper;
import org.apache.cocoon.environment.Redirector;
import org.apache.cocoon.environment.Request;
import org.apache.cocoon.environment.SourceResolver;
import org.apache.cocoon.acting.AbstractAction;

import java.util.Enumeration;
import java.util.HashMap;
import java.util.Map;

public class CharCounterAction extends AbstractAction implements ThreadSafe
{

    public Map act( Redirector redirector, SourceResolver resolver,
            Map objectModel, String source, Parameters param )
        throws Exception
    {
        Request request = ObjectModelHelper.getRequest(objectModel);
```

Listing 12.2 *(continued)*

```
        // First, see if a sitemap parameter was set
        String word = param.getParameter("word");

        if (word == null) {
            // Now see if it was set in the request
            word = request.getParameter("word");

            // Sorry, no "word" parameter set anywhere
            if (word == null) return null;
        }

        String chars = new Integer(word.length()).toString();

        getLogger().debug("CharCounterAction: word is " + word);
        getLogger().debug("CharCounterAction: word length is " + chars);

        Map map = new HashMap();
        map.put("count", chars);

        return(map);
    }
}
```

In this action, we're looking for a parameter called `word`. We first expect it in the `Parameters` object, which holds the sitemap parameters being passed to the action. If there is no such parameter, the action then looks in the request parameters. If there still isn't such a parameter, the action returns null. If a `word` parameter is found, the action computes the length of it and returns a `Map` object with a single parameter called `word`.

Note that we'll make our action part of a package called `test`.

Action Compilation

After we've written an action, we have to compile it and place it into the `$CATALINA_HOME/webapps/cocoon/WEB-INF/classes` directory. To compile an action, we need a few jars in the classpath. On Unix, we can compile our action with the script given in Listing 12.3.

Listing 12.3 *Action Build Script for Unix (build-Action.sh)*

```
export JAR_DIR=$CATALINA_HOME/webapps/cocoon/WEB-INF/lib
export CLASS_DIR=$CATALINA_HOME/webapps/cocoon/WEB-INF/classes

export CP=$JAR_DIR/avalon-excalibur-vm12-20020705.jar
export CP=$CP:$JAR_DIR/avalon-framework-20020627.jar
export CP=$CP:$JAR_DIR/cocoon-2.0.3.jar
export CP=$CP:$JAR_DIR/logkit-20020529.jar

javac -d $CLASS_DIR -classpath $CP:$CLASSPATH $1
```

And on Windows, we use the script shown in Listing 12.4.

Listing 12.4 *Action Build Script for Windows (build-Action.bat)*

```
@echo off

set JAR_DIR=%CATALINA_HOME%\webapps\cocoon\WEB-INF\lib
set CLASS_DIR=%CATALINA_HOME%\webapps\cocoon\WEB-INF\classes

set CP=%JAR_DIR%\avalon-excalibur-vm12-20020705.jar
set CP=%CP%;%JAR_DIR%\avalon-framework-20020627.jar
set CP=%CP%;%JAR_DIR%\cocoon-2.0.3.jar
set CP=%CP%;%JAR_DIR%\logkit-20020529.jar

javac -d %CLASS_DIR% -classpath %CP%;%CLASSPATH% %1%
```

To invoke these scripts on our action, type the following:

On Unix:

```
build.sh CharCounterAction.java
```

On Windows:

```
build.bat CharCounterAction.java
```

When compiled, the class file will be in the `$CATALINA_HOME/webapps/cocoon/WEB-INF/classes/test` directory. Next, we need to bounce our servlet container to make the action available to Cocoon.

Compiling actions via Ant
A better alternative to using these scripts is to use Ant to build your Cocoon project. A sample `build.xml` for just such an occasion is presented in Chapter 22, "Techniques for Developing Cocoon Applications."

Auto-Reloading in Tomcat
Tomcat has the capability to monitor webapps and automatically reload them when class files have changed. To enable this feature, define a context for Cocoon in `$CATALINA_HOME/conf/server.xml` that has the `reloadable` attribute set to `true`:

```
<Context path="/cocoon" reloadable="true"/>
```

Be aware, however, that sometimes continuous reloading of the Cocoon Web application will cause Cocoon or Tomcat to freeze up. This problem has been seen most notably on Windows 98, but it may have more to do with how much RAM you have than anything else.

Editing the Sitemap

We are still not ready to use our action. First, we need to define the action in the `<map:actions>` section of the sitemap, within the `<map:components>` block (which usually comes at the end of the former). You must define an action in this section before you can make use of it in a pipeline. Our actions section starts out small (don't worry, it'll grow throughout this chapter):

```
<map:actions>
 <map:action name="char-counter" src="test.CharCounterAction"/>
</map:actions>
```

Now we are ready to use it in a pipeline:

```
<map:match pattern="count/**">
 <map:act type="char-counter">
  <map:parameter name="word" value="{1}"/>
  <map:generate src="content/counter.xml"/>
  <map:transform src="style/counter.xsl">
   <map:parameter name="count" value="{count}"/>
   <map:parameter name="word" value="{../1}"/>
  </map:transform>
  <map:serialize/>
 </map:act>
  <map:generate src="content/main.xml"/>
  <map:transform src="style/counter.xsl"/>
  <map:serialize/>
</map:match>
```

Here we define a pattern `count/**`, which will invoke our action. We pass the `Matcher` substitution variable to the action as a parameter called `word`. The action will return a `Map` object that contains one parameter called `count`, set to the number of characters in the word. We're using the same `main.xml` file we've been using before, but we have a new stylesheet that takes two parameters: `count` and `word`. The source file, `counter.xml`, is a simple XML file with a root tag of `<page>` and a `<title>` tag inside:

```
<?xml version="1.0"?>

<page>
 <title>My first Action</title>
</page>
```

The Stylesheet

Let's look at the stylesheet, shown in Listing 12.5, because this is a good example of how sitemap parameters can be accessed by a stylesheet.

Listing 12.5 *Char Counter Stylesheet (counter.xsl)*

```
<?xml version="1.0"?>

<xsl:stylesheet version="1.0"
   xmlns:xsl="http://www.w3.org/1999/XSL/Transform"
>

 <xsl:param name="count"/>
 <xsl:param name="word"/>

 <xsl:template match="/page">
  <html>
   <head>
    <title><xsl:value-of select="title"/></title>
   </head>

   <body bgcolor="#ffffff">

    <xsl:apply-templates/>

    <xsl:if test="$count">
     <p>The number of characters in '<xsl:value-of select="$word"/>' is:
      <xsl:value-of select="$count"/>
     </p>
```

Listing 12.5 (continued)

```
    </xsl:if>
   </body>
  </html>
 </xsl:template>

<xsl:template match="title">
  <center>
  <h3><xsl:apply-templates/></h3>
  </center>
 </xsl:template>

 <xsl:template match="paragraph">
  <p><xsl:apply-templates/></p>
 </xsl:template>

</xsl:stylesheet>
```

The difference between this and our earlier stylesheets is the inclusion of the `<xsl:param>` tags, which are initialized by the `TraxTransformer` to hold the values we specified in the pipeline.

Testing the Action

If we type `http://localhost:8080/cocoon/abc/count/howlongisthisword` in our browser, we'll see what's shown in Figure 12.1.

We can also write an alternative pipeline in which we call our action with a request parameter holding the string to process:

```
<map:match pattern="count">
 <map:match type="request-parameter" pattern="word">
  <map:act type="char-counter">
   <map:parameter name="word" value="{1}"/>
   <map:generate type="file" src="content/counter.xml"/>
   <map:transform src="style/counter.xsl">
    <map:parameter name="count" value="{count}"/>
    <map:parameter name="word" value="{../1}"/>
   </map:transform>
   <map:serialize/>
  </map:act>
 </map:match>
</map:match>
```

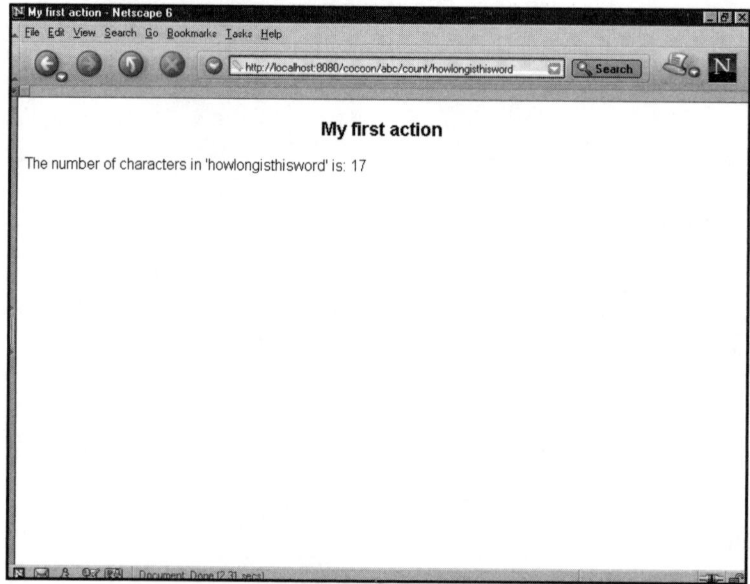

Figure 12.1
Char counter action.

Using Actions for Authentication

Now we are ready to use some of Cocoon's built-in actions. First, we'll show how actions can help create an alternative authentication mechanism for our support Web site. Remember, in Chapter 8, "Using Content Logic: XSPs," we used `login.xml` and `login.xsp` to implement authentication and protection of the support pages. Now, we can see whether actions can make this job easier.

Adding the Actions to the Sitemap

First, we have to start by defining several built-in actions in the `<map:actions>` block of our sitemap. Just as with any other Cocoon component, you still must define a built-in action before you can use it:

```
<map:actions>
 <map:action name="char-counter" src="test.CharCounterAction"/>
 <map:action name="session-validator"
   src="org.apache.cocoon.acting.SessionValidatorAction"/>
 <map:action name="session-invalidator"
```

```
  src="org.apache.cocoon.acting.SessionInvalidatorAction"/>
 <map:Action name="authenticator"
   src="org.apache.cocoon.acting.DatabaseAuthenticatorAction"/>
</map:Actions>
```

Creating the Descriptor File

You may remember, from our list of built-in actions at the beginning of this chapter, that the `DatabaseAuthenticatorAction` compares data with a database table. The particulars of this operation are defined in a descriptor file, which we'll call `auth-def.xml` and place in the `$CATALINA_HOME/webapps/cocoon/abc/content/defs` directory (which we'll have to create, because we haven't needed it yet). This file, which you can find in Listing 12.6, will define the connection pool to use, the table name, and the mapping between request parameters and column names.

Listing 12.6 *Authentication Descriptor File (auth-def.xml)*

```
<?xml version="1.0"?>

<auth-descriptor>
  <connection>abc</connection>
  <table name="Customers">
    <select dbcol="CustUserId" request-param="user" to-session="user"/>
    <select dbcol="CustPass" request-param="pass"/>
  </table>
</auth-descriptor>
```

The key lines are those with the `<select>` tags. In the first one, the value of the request parameter `user` will be matched to the table column `CustUserId`. If the validation is successful, the userid will be propagated in the session as an attribute named `user`. The second `<select>` tag matches the `pass` request parameter with the `CustPass` column, but doesn't propagate the value in the session.

Creating the Database Table

Let's not forget that we need to create the `Customers` table for this to work:

```
create table Customers (
CustUserId  varchar(10) not null,
CustPass    varchar(10) not null
);

insert into Customers values ('BigCorp', 'secret');
```

Creating the Authentication Pipelines

As with our authentication example in the preceding chapter, we need three pipelines to make this work. First, we need a pipeline for `login.html`, which we already have. Then we need a pipeline to handle the actual authentication, using the `DatabaseAuthenticatorAction`. For this, we'll redefine the pipeline for `login` that we used earlier, in Chapter 8. Finally, we need a pipeline to define the protected area; in our case, this will be the pipeline for `support/*` that we already defined.

All three pipelines are shown next:

```
<map:match pattern="login.html">
 <map:read mime-type="text/html" src="content/login.html"/>
</map:match>

<map:match pattern="login">
  <map:act type="authenticator">
   <map:parameter name="descriptor"
     value="context://abc/content/defs/auth-def.xml"/>
   <map:redirect-to uri="support/home"/>
  </map:act>
  <map:redirect-to uri="login.html"/>
</map:match>

<map:match type="sessionstate" pattern="*">
 <map:parameter name="attribute-name" value="user"/>

 <!--protected pipelines go here -->

</map:match>
```

Granted that our original login method (`login.xsp`) didn't use a database, this is still easier than writing an XSP. Of course, a real authentication mechanism would, in many cases, use a database, so this makes the `DatabaseAuthenticatorAction` a very useful component.

Using Actions for Forms

Forms can be the downfall of many a fine Web site. Often, the complexity of form validation results in gobs of JSP or JS code that becomes a maintenance nightmare. Although Cocoon might not be able to overcome all problems with form validation, many users will find that it can be a lifesaver in many situations.

In our support Web site, we need a form for customers to submit trouble tickets. We have a few fields to collect (shown in Table 12.3), each with various validation rules.

Table 12.3 *Form Elements*

Field	Rules
`Customer name`	Will be set to the value of the user session attribute (we don't have to display this)
`User name`	Must be filled in
`User email`	Must be valid email
`User telephone`	Must be valid telephone
`Product name`	Should be either AbcApp or XyzApp
`Product version`	Must be valid version number, of format *x.y.z*
`Problem description`	Must be filled out
`OS`	Must be one of Windows, Solaris, Linux, OSX
`Severity`	Must be 1, 2, or 3 for severity level (3 is most severe)

After a trouble ticket has been filled out correctly, the resulting data must be inserted into a database *and* emailed to a support email.

Clearly, we have our work cut out for us. We will use the following sitemap components to implement all this functionality:

- `FormValidatorAction`
- XSP with `xsp-formval` logicsheet
- `DatabaseAddAction`
- XSP with `sendmail` logicsheet

Note that we're introducing two new XSP logicsheets: `xsp-formval` and `sendmail`.

Let's get started.

Designing the Process

We'll put our form inside an XSP and use the `FormValidatorAction` to validate the user input. This action applies rules defined in an XML descriptor file against request parameters coming from a form submission. If all rules are met, the code inside the `<map:act>` block is executed. That is where we will place our code to insert the data into the database and email the support staff. The `DatabaseAddAction` that we'll use for the database insert part will use the same descriptor file to get the information to build the actual insert command.

If not all validation rules are met by the form, the request will be directed back to the form. However, we don't want the user to have to reenter all fields if just one was incorrect. We also want the user to know exactly what went wrong. We can accomplish both things using the `xsp-formval` logicsheet inside our XSP.

Writing the Form

First, we'll write the bare-bones form in an XSP, which we'll call `newticket.xsp`. This is shown in Listing 12.7.

Listing 12.7 *New Ticket Form (newticket.xsp - Version 1)*

```
<?xml version="1.0"?>

<xsp:page language="java" xmlns:xsp="http://apache.org/xsp"
  xmlns:xsp-session="http://apache.org/xsp/session/2.0"
>

<page>
 <page-title>New ticket form</page-title>
 <content>
  <title>New ticket submission form</title>
  <paragraph>
   Please fill out all fields as indicated.
  </paragraph>

  <form Action="newticket" method="post">
   <input type="hidden" name="customer">
     <xsp:attribute name="value">
      <xsp-session:get-attribute name="user"/>
     </xsp:attribute>
   </input>

   <table border="1">

     <tr>
      <td align="right">User name:</td>
      <td align="left">
        <input type="text" name="user_name"/>
      </td>
     </tr>
```

Listing 12.7 (continued)

```
<tr>
 <td align="right">User email:</td>
 <td align="left">
   <input type="text" name="user_email"/>
 </td>
</tr>

<tr>
 <td align="right">User telephone:</td>
 <td align="left">
   <input type="text" name="user_phone"/>
 </td>
</tr>

<tr>
 <td align="right">Product name:</td>
 <td align="left">
   <input type="text" name="product_name"/>
 </td>
</tr>

<tr>
 <td align="right">Product version:</td>
 <td align="left">
   <input type="text" name="product_version"/>
 </td>
</tr>

<tr>
 <td align="right">Product OS:</td>
 <td align="left">
   <select name="product_os">
     <option>Windows</option>
     <option>Solaris</option>
     <option>Linux</option>
   </select>
 </td>
</tr>
```

Listing 12.7 *(continued)*

```
      <tr>
       <td align="right">Problem description:</td>
       <td align="left">
         <textarea name="problem_desc" cols="30" rows="5"/>
       </td>
      </tr>
      <tr>
       <td align="right">Severity (1,2 or 3):</td>
       <td align="left">
         <input type="text" name="problem_severity"/>
       </td>
      </tr>

      <tr>
       <td align="center" colspan="2">
         <input type="submit" value="Submit"/>
       </td>
      </tr>

    </table>
   </form>

 </content>
</page>

</xsp:page>
```

All this is very straightforward and simple. We'll save use of the `xsp-formval` logicsheet for a bit later.

Modifying the Stylesheets

In the form in Listing 12.7, we put HTML tags right into the XSP (well-defined, of course, because we are dealing with XML here). We do this because there is really not much point in having some other user tags defined that will be mapped to `<table>`, `<tr>`, and `<td>` tags during the XSL transformer. Because we are technically violating the separation of content and style, however, purists may want to put the entire form in the stylesheet. There is a point to be made in their favor, although that implementation will involve a bit of XSL coding. For the purposes of learning, however, our method will suffice.

We do, however, have to make one small change to the stylesheets. The HTML tags in the XSP need to be passed through unaltered to the browser. By adding the following to our stylesheets (`main.xsl` and `bigcorp.xsl`), we can avoid any problems:

```
<xsl:template match="@*|node()" priority="-1">
  <xsl:copy>
    <xsl:apply-templates select="@*|node()"/>
  </xsl:copy>
 </xsl:template>
```

Writing the Descriptor File

The descriptor file used by the `FormValidatorAction` is an XML file describing the parameters to check. We'll also include the mapping information so that the `DatabaseAddAction` can build the insert statement. Listing 12.8 shows our descriptor file.

Listing 12.8 *New Ticket Descriptor File (newticket-def.xml)*

```
<?xml version="1.0"?>

<root>
  <parameter name="customer_name" type="string" max-len="20"
     nullable="no"/>
  <parameter name="user_name" type="string" max-len="54"
     nullable="no"/>
  <parameter name="user_email" type="string" max-len="60"
     matches-regex="^[\d\w][\d\w\-_\.]*@([\d\w\-_]+\.)\w\w\w?$"
     nullable="no"/>
  <parameter name="user_phone" type="string"
     min-len="10" max-len="20" nullable="no"/>
  <parameter name="product_name" type="string" max-len="20"
     nullable="no"/>
  <parameter name="product_version" type="double" min="1.0"
     max="3.0"/>
  <parameter name="product_os" type="string" nullable="no"/>
  <parameter name="problem_desc" type="string" max-len="255"
     nullable="no"/>
  <parameter name="problem_severity" type="long" min="1"
     max="3"/>

  <constraint-set name="add">
   <validate name="customer_name"/>
   <validate name="user_name"/>
```

Listing 12.8 *(continued)*

```
    <validate name="user_email"/>
    <validate name="user_phone"/>
    <validate name="product_name"/>
    <validate name="product_version"/>
    <validate name="product_os"/>
    <validate name="problem_desc"/>
    <validate name="problem_severity"/>
  </constraint-set>

  <connection>abc</connection>
  <table name="NewTickets">
    <values>
      <value param="customer_name" dbcol="Customer" type="string"/>
      <value param="user_name" dbcol="UserName" type="string"/>
      <value param="user_email" dbcol="UserEmail" type="string"/>
      <value param="user_phone" dbcol="UserPhone" type="string"/>
      <value param="product_name" dbcol="ProductName" type="string"/>
      <value param="product_version" dbcol="ProductVersion" type="double"/>
      <value param="product_os" dbcol="ProductOS" type="string"/>
      <value param="problem_desc" dbcol="ProblemDesc" type="string"/>
      <value param="problem_severity" dbcol="ProblemSeverity" type="int"/>
    </values>
  </table>
</root>
```

When a `FormValidatorAction` is used, it uses a file like this to validate input data, passed in as request parameters. Validation is defined either by a single `parameter` or by a set of parameters encapsulated in a `constraint-set`. The advantage of the latter is simply that you can validate more than one field at a time, a requirement of many forms you'll develop.

The `FormValidatorAction` can perform different validations on input data according to the datatype (actually, this is handled by the `AbstractValidatorAction`, which it extends). Constraints for datatypes `string`, `long`, and `double` are currently supported and are listed in Table 12.4.

Table 12.4 *Validation Constraints*

Parameter	Description	String	Long	Double
`nullable`	Field can't be null	yes	yes	yes
`matches-regex`	Regular expression	yes	yes	yes
`min-len`	Minimum length of the field	yes	no	no

Table 12.4 *(continued)*

Parameter	Description	String	Long	Double
max-len	Maximum length of the field	yes	no	no
min	Minimum value of the field	no	yes	yes
max	Maximum value of the field	no	yes	yes
equals-to	Literal that the field must match	yes	yes	yes
equals-to-param	Parameter whose value the field must match	yes	yes	yes

All constraints but the last two can be specified at the parameter or set level (in other words, they can be specified as attributes of either the `parameter` or the `validate` tag). The last two validation constraints can be specified only at the constraint set level. If a constraint is specified at both levels, those of the constraint set will prevail. Finally, you can also set a `default` attribute for a `parameter` tag and provide a default value for the field *if* the field allows nulls (`nullable="yes"`) *and* the request field really is null.

The definition also specifies how to insert the data into a database. This information will be used by the `DatabaseAddAction` and includes the connection pool name, the table name, and the mapping of request parameters to column names. It would be nice if all this information could be encapsulated in a tag that could be placed anywhere in the definition file, but under the current implementation of these files the `<connection>` and `<table>` tags must be under the root user tag (it doesn't have to be called `<root>`—call it whatever you want).

The `DatabaseAddAction`, like the other actions that use databases, extends `org.apache.cocoon.acting.AbstractDatabaseAction`, which provides the mechanism for reading and parsing these kinds of definition files. The latter recognizes the values in Table 12.5 for the `type` attribute of the `<value>` tag.

Table 12.5 *Datatypes Handled by AbstractDatabaseAction*

Type	Java Datatype	Notes
ascii	A CLOB	The value of the field is the path to the file that will be read using a `BufferedInputStream` to produce an ASCII input stream.
big-decimal	A `java.math.BigDecimal` object	
binary	A BLOB	The value of the field is the path to the file that will be read using a `FileInputStream` to produce a binary input stream.
byte	A `Byte` object	
string	A `String` object	

Table 12.5 *(continued)*

Type	Java Datatype	Notes
`date`	A `Date` object	Input data is converted to a `Date` object using the value of the optional `format` attribute as the format. If no `format` attribute is specified, the conversion will attempt to use the format "M/d/yyyy".
`double`	A `Double` object	
`float`	A `Float` object	
`int`	An `Integer` object	
`long`	A `Long` object	
`short`	A `Short` object	
`time`	A `Time` object	Input data is converted to a `Time` object using the value of the option `format` attribute as the format. If no `format` attribute is specified, the conversion will attempt to use the format "h:m:s a".
`time-stamp` the	A `Timestamp` object	Input data is converted to a `Time` object using the value of option `format` attribute as the format. If no `format` attribute is specified, the conversion will attempt to use the format "M/d/yyyy h:m:s a".
`now`	A `Timestamp` object initialized to the current date/time	
`image`	A BLOB	The value of the field is the path to the file that will be read using a `FileInputStream` to produce a binary input stream.
`image-width`	An `Integer` object	Actual column value is set to null.
`image-height`	An `Integer` object	Actual column value is set to null.
`image-size`	An `Integer` object	Actual column value is set to null.
`row-index`	An `Integer` object	Actual column value is set to null.
`image-mime-type`	An `Integer` object	Actual column value is set to null.
`array`	An `Array` object	
`row`	An `Object` object	
`object`	An `Object` object	

Setting Up the Database

If you are following along with this example, you'll now need a database table to hold the results of the form submission. The description is shown in Listing 12.9.

Listing 12.9 *New Ticket Database Table (newticket.sql)*

```
create table NewTickets (
Customer        varchar(20)     not null,
UserName        varchar(20)     not null,
UserEmail       varchar(60)     not null,
UserPhone       varchar(20)     not null,
ProductName     varchar(20)     not null,
ProductVersion  double          not null,
ProductOS       varchar(20)     not null,
ProblemDesc     varchar(255)    not null,
ProblemSeverity int             not null
);
```

Creating a Pipeline

To use the `FormValidatorAction` and `DatabaseAddAction`, we need to add them to the `<map:actions>` section, as shown here:

```
<map:actions>
 <map:action name="validator" logger="sitemap.Action.validator"
   src="org.apache.cocoon.acting.FormValidatorAction"/>
 <map:action name="insert" logger="sitemap.Action.insert"
   src="org.apache.cocoon.acting.DatabaseAddAction"/>
 <map:action name="request" logger="sitemap.Action.request"
   src="org.apache.cocoon.acting.RequestParamAction"/>
 <!-- other Actions -->
</map:actions>
```

Defining Actions in Sub-Sitemaps
You might be wondering whether every sub-sitemap has to define actions that are already defined in the main sitemap. You don't, actually. Although we are doing it here for the sake of explanation, it will suffice to simply define `<map:actions/>` in order to "inherit" all the actions of the main sitemap.

We can now define a pipeline to handle the submission of new trouble tickets. Note that we'll put this new pipeline in the protected area so that only authenticated users can access it.

```
<map:match pattern="support/newticket">
 <map:act type="validator">
  <map:parameter name="descriptor"
       value="context://abc/content/defs/newticket-def.xml"/>
  <map:parameter name="validate-set" value="add"/>
```

```
   <map:act type="insert">
    <map:parameter name="descriptor"
        value="context://abc/content/defs/newticket-def.xml"/>

    <map:generate type="serverpages" src="xsp/newticket-conf.xsp"/>
    <map:transform type="xslt" src="style/main.xsl"/>
    <map:serialize type="html"/>

   </map:act>
  </map:act>

  <map:generate type="serverpages" src="xsp/newticket.xsp"/>
  <map:transform type="xslt" src="style/main.xsl"/>
  <map:serialize type="xml"/>
 </map:match>
```

Remember, if an action returns a valid `Map` object, then everything inside that `<map:act>` block will be executed; otherwise, execution will fall outside the block. Our pipeline actually starts with the validation action. The first time through, because the form is new, validation will fail, and the pipeline will fall down to `newticket.xsp`, which displays the form. Each time the user submits the form incorrectly, the form will be redisplayed (we'll make sure in a minute that the user doesn't lose data in the process). Finally, when validation succeeds, the insert action takes place. Assuming that it succeeds (that is, the `DatabaseAddAction` returns a valid `Map` object), a confirmation page will be displayed.

Confirmation Page

Listing 12.10 shows a simple confirmation page. We'll add email logic later in the chapter.

Listing 12.10 *New Ticket Confirmation Page (newticket-conf.xsp - Version 1)*

```
<?xml version="1.0"?>

<xsp:page language="java"
 xmlns:xsp="http://apache.org/xsp"
 xmlns:xsp-request="http://apache.org/xsp/request/2.0"
>

<xsp:structure>
 <xsp:include>java.util.*</xsp:include>
</xsp:structure>
```

Listing 12.10 *(continued)*

```
<page>
 <page-title>Confirmation</page-title>
 <content>
  <title>Hello!</title>
  <paragraph>
   Your ticket has been submitted with the following values:
  </paragraph>
  <table border="1">
   <xsp:logic>
     Enumeration e = request.getParameterNames();
     while (e.hasMoreElements()) {
         String name = (String)e.nextElement();
         String value = request.getParameter(name);

         <xsp:element name="tr">
           <xsp:element name="td">
            <xsp:attribute name="align">right</xsp:attribute>
            <xsp:expr>name</xsp:expr>:
           </xsp:element>
           <xsp:element name="td">
            <xsp:expr>value</xsp:expr>
           </xsp:element>
         </xsp:element>
     }
   </xsp:logic>
  </table>
 </content>
</page>

</xsp:page>
```

This page also illustrates the use of some tags from the `xsp` logicsheet. To create the table of request parameters, we could have created several `<xsp:logic>` blocks and interspersed the HTML in between, just like in a JSP. However, it is cleaner and more readable to create the XML tags directly, using `<xsp:element>` and `<xsp:attribute>`.

If a user fills out the form correctly, as shown in Figure 12.2, they should see what is shown in Figure 12.3.

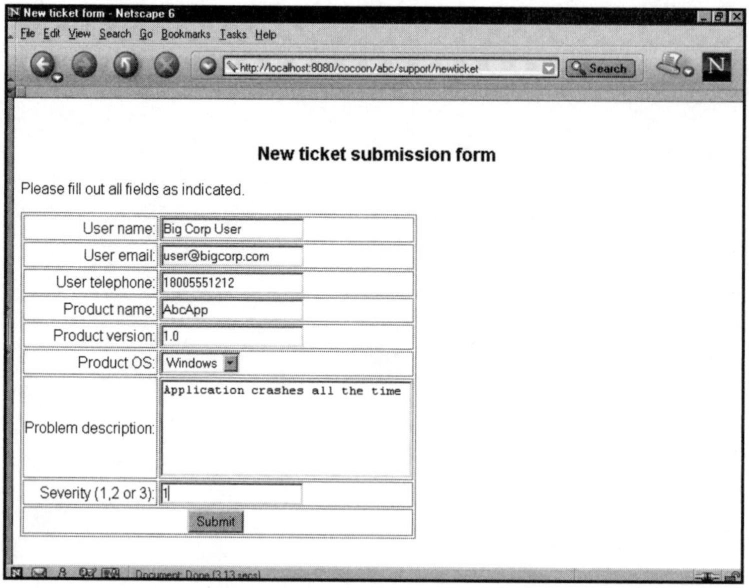

Figure 12.2
New ticket form.

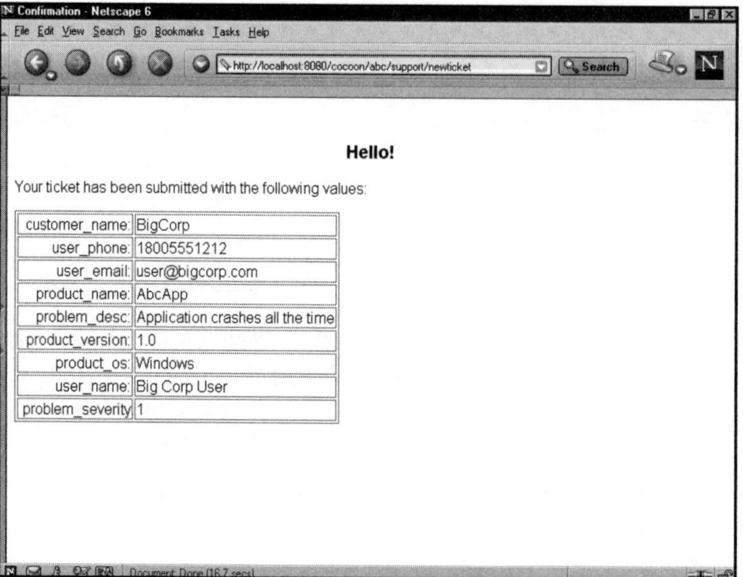

customer_name:	BigCorp
user_phone:	18005551212
user_email:	user@bigcorp.com
product_name:	AbcApp
problem_desc:	Application crashes all the time
product_version:	1.0
product_os:	Windows
user_name:	Big Corp User
problem_severity:	1

Figure 12.3
New ticket submission results.

Now if the user happens to miss a field in the form, something quite unintentional happens: The form is redisplayed, as we want, but all the other field values are missing! Moreover, there is no indication as to why the validation failed. Not much good for a production site, is it? We can solve this problem by using the `xsp-formval` logicsheet.

Enhancing the XSP with the xsp-formval Logicsheet

To use the `xsp-formval` logicsheet, we have to tell it where the definition file is. As stated previously, the definition file is the same that the `FormValidatorAction` is using. After we indicate the location of the definition file, we then have access to various tags that tell us what input data failed. We can also use other tags to snag the valid values that the user already filled out from the request object.

Portions of the rewritten `newticket.xsp` (Version 2, now) are shown here:

```
<?xml version="1.0"?>

<xsp:page language="java" xmlns:xsp="http://apache.org/xsp"
  xmlns:xsp-session="http://apache.org/xsp/session/2.0"
  xmlns:xsp-request="http://apache.org/xsp/request/2.0"
  xmlns:xsp-formval="http://apache.org/xsp/form-validator/2.0"
>

<page>
 <xsp:logic>
   boolean notnew = (<xsp-request:get-parameter name="visited"/> != null);
   boolean bad = false;
 </xsp:logic>

 <page-title>New ticket form</page-title>
 <content>
  <title>New ticket submission form</title>
  <paragraph>
   Please fill out all fields as indicated.
  </paragraph>

  <xsp-formval:descriptor
    name="context://abc/content/defs/newticket-def.xml"
    constraint-set="add">

  <paragraph>
   <xsp-formval:results/>
  </paragraph>
```

```
<form action="newticket" method="post">
 <input type="hidden" name="visited" value="true"/>
 <input type="hidden" name="customer_name">
   <xsp:attribute name="value">
    <xsp-session:get-attribute name="user"/>
   </xsp:attribute>
 </input>

 <table border="1">

   <tr>
    <td align="right">

     <xsp:logic>
       if (notnew &amp;&amp; <xsp-formval:is-error name="user_name"/>) {
          <font color="red">
           <xsp:text>*</xsp:text>

           <xsp-formval:on-null name="user_name">Name can't be null
           </xsp-formval:on-null>
           <xsp-formval:on-toolarge name="user_name">Max size is 2
           </xsp-formval:on-toolarge>
          </font>
          bad = true;
       }
     </xsp:logic>

     User name:
    </td>
    <td align="left">
      <input type="text" name="user_name">
        <xsp:attribute name="value">
          <xsp-request:get-parameter name="user_name" default=""/>
        </xsp:attribute>
      </input>
    </td>
   </tr>
   <!-- other form elements go here -->

   <tr>
    <td align="center" colspan="2">
      <input type="submit" value="Submit"/>
```

```
        </td>
       </tr>

     </table>
    </form>

    </xsp-formval:descriptor>

 </content>
</page>

</xsp:page>
```

We'll go through this piece by piece.

Namespace Declarations

To use the xsp-formval logicsheet, we must declare its namespace at the top of the XSP. We also need to include the xsp-request logicsheet because we will need to access request parameters.

Boolean notnew

We need some way of telling whether this is the first time the user has accessed the form. If it is the first time, there is no point in displaying validation errors. This variable is set to the value of a hidden form parameter called visited.

Descriptor File

Any use of the xsp-formval logicsheet must start with the <xsp-formval:descriptor> tag; in our case, this tag surrounds the <form> tag and all its contents. The name attribute points the logicsheet to the definition file that it needs in order to generate the validation statements. The constraint-set attribute specifies which validation set to use. Note that we do not have to use the same set as is used by the FormValidatorAction, but it wouldn't make much sense not to.

<xsp-formval:results>

This tag produces a string that contains all the failed validations. It is useful for debugging purposes, but not suitable to present to users (we are presenting it in the figures in this chapter only to show what it looks like).

User Name Validation

In this example, we just show the validation of the `user_name` element. As you can see, quite a lot of code is needed to see what failed. First, we check the `notnew` variable to make sure that this is not the first time the user has visited the form. Then we use the `<xsp-formval:is-error>` tag to see whether there were any errors for this element. If so, we set the font to red and then query the logicsheet to see exactly which validation failed. Because we specified in the definition file that the `user_name` field must be non-null and cannot be greater than 20 characters, we have to check both things using the corresponding `xsp-formval` tags. Now, in many cases, it might just be enough simply to see whether there were any errors, but in this case, we'd like to tell the user exactly what failed.

Filling in Field Values

Because we want to preserve whatever data the user entered for the field, we must set the `value` attribute of the field to the value of the corresponding request parameter. Note that in some situations, if a validation fails you might not want to reset the field to the bad value.

If we try to submit this revised form with a missing user name, we will see the page shown in Figure 12.4.

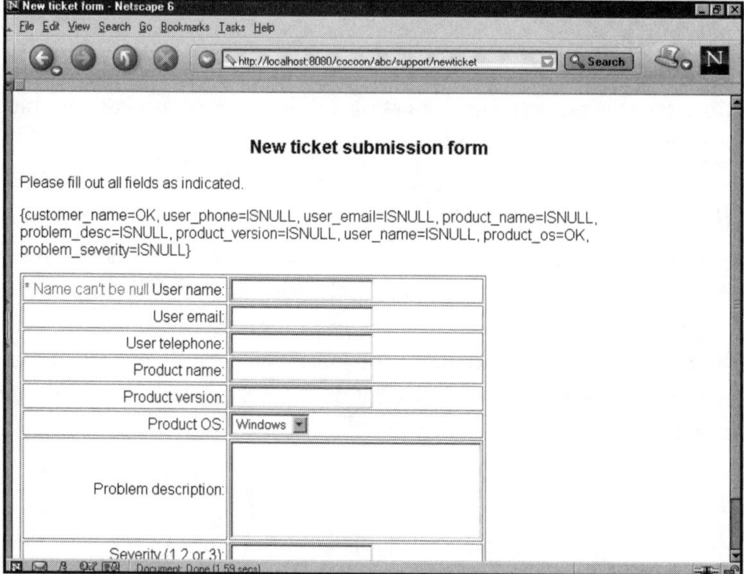

Figure 12.4

New ticket validation results.

Enhancing the Form Validation Process

As you have noticed, we can quite easily run into readability problems when using the `xsp-formval` logicsheet in XSPs. Even a simple form, like our example, will end up many times longer when it contains all the required form validation processing.

There is hope, however. Rather than tediously typing the processing commands for each form field, we can create a logicsheet that does the job for us. What we want is a logicsheet that can do the following:

- Provide all the necessary tags for a row in a form table
- If a field fails validation, provide the user with some sort of relevant message
- Preserve already entered data in fields that are valid

The logicsheet that we'll show is rather specific to our example; that is, it assumes that we have a form that has its fields arranged inside a table. We also will handle just text fields; the drop-down that we had for the Operating System field won't be supported in this example.

Writing the Logicsheet

We'll call our logicsheet `formvalhelper.xsl` and assign it the namespace `http://samspublishing.com/val-helper/1.0` with a prefix of `val-helper`. It is shown in Listing 12.11.

Listing 12.11 *Form Validation Helper Logicsheet (formvalhelper.xsl)*

```
<?xml version="1.0"?>

<xsl:stylesheet version="1.0"
  xmlns:xsl="http://www.w3.org/1999/XSL/Transform"
  xmlns:xsp="http://apache.org/xsp"
  xmlns:val-helper="http://samspublishing.com/val-helper/1.0"
  xmlns:xsp-formval="http://apache.org/xsp/form-validator/2.0"
  xmlns:xsp-request="http://apache.org/xsp/request/2.0"
>

<xsl:variable name="prefix">val-helper</xsl:variable>

<!-- Top level tag -->
<xsl:template match="xsp:page">
  <xsp:page>
    <xsl:apply-templates select="@*"/>
```

Listing 12.11 *(continued)*

```
    <xsp:logic>
     boolean notnew = true;
    </xsp:logic>
    <xsl:apply-templates/>
  </xsp:page>
</xsl:template>

<xsl:template match="val-helper:field">
   <xsp:logic>
    notnew = (<xsp-request:get-parameter name="visited"/> != null);
   </xsp:logic>

   <xsl:variable name="name">
     <xsl:call-template name="get-parameter">
       <xsl:with-param name="name">name</xsl:with-param>
       <xsl:with-param name="default">-1</xsl:with-param>
     </xsl:call-template>
   </xsl:variable>
   <xsl:variable name="dname">
     <xsl:call-template name="get-parameter">
       <xsl:with-param name="name">dname</xsl:with-param>
       <xsl:with-param name="default">-1</xsl:with-param>
     </xsl:call-template>
   </xsl:variable>
   <xsl:variable name="validate">
     <xsl:call-template name="get-parameter">
       <xsl:with-param name="name">validate</xsl:with-param>
       <xsl:with-param name="default">true</xsl:with-param>
     </xsl:call-template>
   </xsl:variable>

   <tr>
    <td align="right">
     <xsl:value-of select="string($dname)"/>:
    </td>

    <td align="left">
       <input type="text" name="fname">
        <xsp:attribute name="name">
         <xsl:value-of select="$name"/>
        </xsp:attribute>
```

Listing 12.11 *(continued)*

```
        <xsp:attribute name="value">
         <xsp-request:get-parameter default="">
          <xsl:attribute name="name">
           <xsl:value-of select="string($name)"/>
          </xsl:attribute>
         </xsp-request:get-parameter>
        </xsp:attribute>
       </input>
    </td>

    <xsl:if test="$validate = 'true'">
    <xsp:logic>
     if (notnew &amp;&amp; <xsp-formval:is-error>
      <xsl:attribute name="name">
       <xsl:value-of select="string($name)"/>
      </xsl:attribute></xsp-formval:is-error>)
     {
       <td><font color="red">
        <xsp:logic>
        if (<xsp-formval:is-null>
         <xsl:attribute name="name">
          <xsl:value-of select="string($name)"/>
         </xsl:attribute></xsp-formval:is-null>)
        {
         <xsp:text>Field must be filled in</xsp:text>;
        }
        if (<xsp-formval:is-toosmall>
         <xsl:attribute name="name">
          <xsl:value-of select="string($name)"/>
         </xsl:attribute></xsp-formval:is-toosmall>)
        {
         <xsp:text>Field is too small</xsp:text>;
        }
        if (<xsp-formval:is-toolarge>
         <xsl:attribute name="name">
          <xsl:value-of select="string($name)"/>
         </xsl:attribute></xsp-formval:is-toolarge>)
        {
         <xsp:text>Field is too large</xsp:text>;
        }
        if (<xsp-formval:is-nomatch>
```

Listing 12.11 *(continued)*

```
          <xsl:attribute name="name">
           <xsl:value-of select="string($name)"/>
          </xsl:attribute></xsp-formval:is-nomatch>)
         {
          <xsp:text>Field does not match the pattern</xsp:text>;
         }

         </xsp:logic>
        </font></td>
      } else {
        <td> </td>
      }

    </xsp:logic>
    </xsl:if>
   </tr>
</xsl:template>

<!-- Keep all unknown tags -->
<xsl:template match="@*|node()" priority="-1">
  <xsl:copy>
    <xsl:apply-templates select="@*|node()"/>
  </xsl:copy>
</xsl:template>

  <!-- Utility templates -->
  <xsl:template name="get-parameter">
    <xsl:param name="name"/>
    <xsl:param name="default"/>
    <xsl:param name="required">false</xsl:param>

    <xsl:variable name="qname">
      <xsl:value-of select="concat($prefix, ':param')"/>
    </xsl:variable>

    <xsl:choose>
      <xsl:when test="@*[name(.) = $name]">
        <xsl:value-of select="@*[name(.) = $name]"/>
      </xsl:when>
      <xsl:when test="(*[name(.) = $qname])[@name = $name]">
        <xsl:call-template name="get-nested-content">
```

Listing 12.11 *(continued)*

```
        <xsl:with-param name="content"
                        select="(*[name(.) = $qname])[@name = $name]"/>
      </xsl:call-template>
    </xsl:when>
    <xsl:otherwise>
      <xsl:choose>
        <xsl:when test="string-length($default) = 0">
          <xsl:choose>
            <xsl:when test="$required = 'true'">
              <xsl:call-template name="error">
                <xsl:with-param name="message">
                  [Logicsheet processor] Parameter
                  '<xsl:value-of select="$name"/>' missing in dynamic
                  tag &lt;<xsl:value-of select="name(.)"/>&gt;
                </xsl:with-param>
              </xsl:call-template>
            </xsl:when>
            <xsl:otherwise>""</xsl:otherwise>
          </xsl:choose>
        </xsl:when>
        <xsl:otherwise><xsl:copy-of select="$default"/></xsl:otherwise>
      </xsl:choose>
    </xsl:otherwise>
  </xsl:choose>
</xsl:template>

<xsl:template name="get-nested-content">
  <xsl:param name="content"/>
  <xsl:choose>
    <xsl:when test="$content/xsp:text">
      <xsl:value-of select="$content"/>
    </xsl:when>
    <xsl:when test="$content/*">
      <xsl:apply-templates select="$content/*|$content/text()"/>
    </xsl:when>
    <xsl:otherwise><xsl:value-of select="$content"/></xsl:otherwise>
  </xsl:choose>
</xsl:template>

<xsl:template name="error">
  <xsl:param name="message"/>
```

Listing 12.11 (continued)

```
    <xsl:message terminate="yes"><xsl:value-of select="$message"/></xsl:message>
  </xsl:template>

</xsl:stylesheet>
```

Our logicsheet actually has only one tag, `<val-helper:field>`. This tag takes three parameters: `name`, which specifies the field name; `dname`, for the display name; and `validate`, which tells the logicsheet whether to do any validation. The template for this tag starts by creating two table cells: one for the display name and one for the field. If the `validate` attribute was set to `true`, and if this is not the first time the form is being invoked, then the `xsp-formval` logicsheet is invoked to see whether the input is valid. If the input is not valid, a check is done to see which validation failed, and a corresponding error message is displayed.

Using the New Logicsheet

We'll put the new logicsheet in the `$CATALINA_HOME/webapps/cocoon/abc` directory. We must not forget to update `cocoon.xconf` with the following:

```
<builtin-logicsheet>
  <parameter name="prefix" value="val-helper"/>
  <parameter name="uri" value="http://samspublishing.com/val-helper/1.0"/>
  <parameter name="href" value="context://abc/formvalhelper.xsl"/>
</builtin-logicsheet>
```

Then we have to restart Cocoon's servlet container for the changes to take place.

> **Restarting Cocoon**
> There is another way to restart Cocoon, and that is to call any page with `?cocoon-reload` appended to the URL. This will cause the Cocoon servlet to restart everything. This little trick is controlled by an initialization parameter called `allow-reload` in `WEB-INF/web.xml`. It must be set to `yes` for this to work.

Revising newticket.xsp

Although the new logicsheet is somewhat long, look what happens to our `newtickets.xsp`, shown in Listing 12.12. (Be sure to note the namespace declaration for the `val-helper` logicsheet.)

Listing 12.12 *Revised New Ticket Form (newticket.xsp - Version 3)*

```
<?xml version="1.0"?>

<xsp:page language="java" xmlns:xsp="http://apache.org/xsp"
  xmlns:xsp-session="http://apache.org/xsp/session/2.0"
  xmlns:xsp-request="http://apache.org/xsp/request/2.0"
  xmlns:xsp-formval="http://apache.org/xsp/form-validator/2.0"
  xmlns:val-helper="http://samspublishing.com/val-helper/1.0"
>

<page>
 <page-title>New ticket form</page-title>
 <content>
  <title>New ticket submission form</title>
  <paragraph>
   Please fill out all fields as indicated.
  </paragraph>

  <xsp-formval:descriptor
    name="context://abc/content/defs/newticket-def.xml"
    constraint-set="add">

  <form Action="newticket" method="post">
   <input type="hidden" name="visited" value="true"/>
   <input type="hidden" name="customer_name">
     <xsp:attribute name="value">
      <xsp-session:get-attribute name="user"/>
     </xsp:attribute>
   </input>

   <table border="1">

     <val-helper:field name="user_name" dname="User name"/>
     <val-helper:field name="user_email" dname="User email"/>
     <val-helper:field name="user_phone" dname="User telephone"/>
     <val-helper:field name="product_name" dname="Product name"/>
     <val-helper:field name="product_version" dname="Product version"/>
     <val-helper:field name="product_os" dname="Product OS"/>
     <val-helper:field name="product_desc" dname="Product description"/>
     <val-helper:field name="problem_severity" dname="Severity (1, 2 or 3)"/>
```

Listing 12.12 *(continued)*

```
      <tr>
        <td align="center" colspan="2">
          <input type="submit" value="Submit"/>
        </td>
      </tr>

    </table>
   </form>

   </xsp-formval:descriptor>

 </content>
</page>

</xsp:page>
```

Much simpler! Now, all the messy code is encapsulated in the logicsheet, leaving the XSP much cleaner and more readable. Of course, this example is still quite rudimentary—a more well-developed logicsheet could be written to handle other form elements. One other problem is that the error messages are fairly generic and could be made more specific to the field in question. We'll leave that to the more adventuresome reader!

Adding the XSP with the sendmail Logicsheet

One of the requirements of a completed form was that the data be not only stored in the database but also emailed to a support account. We will therefore will make use of the `sendmail` logicsheet in `confirm.xsp`.

Defining the sendmail Logicsheet

The `sendmail` logicsheet is not defined in `WEB-INF/cocoon.xconf`, so we have to add it ourselves, as shown here:

```
<builtin-logicsheet>
  <parameter name="prefix" value="mail"/>
  <parameter name="uri" value="http://apache.org/cocoon/sendmail/1.0"/>
  <parameter name="href"
    value="resource://org/apache/cocoon/components/
      ➥language/markup/xsp/java/sendmail.xsl"/>
</builtin-logicsheet>
```

Adding Mail Jars

To use the `sendmail` logicsheet, Cocoon needs access to `mail.jar` and `activation.jar`, both from the JavaMail distribution. You can find this at `http://java.sun.com/products/javamail/`. You will also need the JavaBeans Activation Framework at `http://java.sun. com/beans/glasgow/jaf.html`. Both jars (`mail.jar` and `activation.jar`) go in `$CATALINA_HOME/webapps/cocoon/WEB_INF/lib`, and then you need to restart Cocoon (see the previous note) in order to load these jars as well as to reread `cocoon.xconf` and make the `sendmail` logicsheet available to XSPs.

Updating newticket-conf.xsp

The revised `newticket-conf.xsp` is shown in Listing 12.13.

Listing 12.13 *Revised New Ticket Confirmation Page (newticket-conf.xsp - Version 2)*

```
<?xml version="1.0"?>

<xsp:page language="java"
 xmlns:xsp="http://apache.org/xsp"
 xmlns:xsp-request="http://apache.org/xsp/request/2.0"
 xmlns:mail="http://apache.org/cocoon/sendmail/1.0"
>

<xsp:structure>
 <xsp:include>java.util.*</xsp:include>
</xsp:structure>

<page>
 <page-title>Confirmation</page-title>
 <content>
  <title>Hello!</title>
  <paragraph>
   Your ticket has been submitted with the following values:
  </paragraph>
  <table border="1">
   <xsp:logic>
     String emailBody = "";
     Enumeration e = request.getParameterNames();
     while (e.hasMoreElements()) {
         String name = (String)e.nextElement();
         String value = request.getParameter(name);
```

Listing 12.13 *(continued)*

```
          <xsp:element name="tr">
            <xsp:element name="td">
             <xsp:attribute name="align">right</xsp:attribute>
             <xsp:expr>name</xsp:expr>:
            </xsp:element>
            <xsp:element name="td">
             <xsp:expr>value</xsp:expr>
            </xsp:element>
          </xsp:element>

          emailBody += name + " = " + value + "\n";
      }
    </xsp:logic>
  </table>

  <mail:send-mail>
    <mail:charset>ISO-8859-1</mail:charset>
    <mail:smtphost>smtp.bigcorp.com</mail:smtphost>
    <mail:from>user@bigcorp.com</mail:from>
    <mail:to>support@bigcorp.com</mail:to>
    <mail:subject>New Trouble Ticket</mail:subject>
    <mail:body><xsp:expr>emailBody</xsp:expr></mail:body>
  </mail:send-mail>

 </content>
</page>

</xsp:page>
```

That's it. With a few simple tags each form submission will result in an email containing the contents of the request. (If you try this at home, remember to change the `<mail:smtphost>`, `<mail:from>`, and `<mail:to>` tags to something that works for you.) Of course, in a real-world situation we would probably want to make the contents more verbose and intelligible, but this example gets the point across. If the `sendmail` logicsheet encounters an error in the sending of the email, it will return an `<error>` tag, which we can catch in the XSL and do something intelligent with.

XMLForm

In the scratchpad area of 2.0.3, and in the main area of 2.1, you'll find something called `XMLForm`. In a nutshell, the `XMLForm` framework provides a way to implement constraint-driven multipart forms. Although you can do single page forms quite nicely with `XMLForm`, it excels at being able to handle wizard-type form processing, in which the results of one form determine the layout of the next one. `XMLForm` uses JavaBeans, a new `XMLFormTransformer`, and a new action, `AbstractXMLFormAction`. Although it's in alpha state, you might want to check it out if you have lots of form processing to implement in your application. It is highly recommended that you use the version in the latest 2.1 CVS, because you are guaranteed to get the latest bug fixes that way. You can read up on the subject on `http://xml.apache.org/cocoon/userdocs/concepts/xmlform.html` and `http://xml.apache.org/cocoon/howto/xmlform-wizard/howto-xmlform-wizard.html`.

Summary

We've really only just scratched the surface of what actions can do. There are two important things to remember about actions. First, actions make parameters available to the components that follow their definition in a pipeline. That is, everything within the `<map:act>` block will have access to the `Map` object returned by the object. There are many situations in which a component needs runtime information, and actions are a prime way of getting that information to the component. Second, if an action returns `null`, anything within the `<map:act>` block will be ignored. This allows you to implement simple `if-then` conditional processing with actions as we have seen in both the authentication and the form validation examples.

Besides these two features, actions also provide an efficient way to implement custom processing in a pipeline. Unlike XSPs, which mix logic and content, these components are pure Java objects that can do anything from simple database operations to complex calculations on incoming data. As you develop with Cocoon, you'll find that these components will often be the most important in your sitemap.

Cocoon handles forms fairly well, but what is really lacking, as we have seen, is a good form building process. Our `formvalhelper` logicsheet does something to help with this, but the real answer is going to be `XMLForm`, when it gets to a stable point in development. For now, using form validation with the `DatabaseAddAction` is a definite winner, and makes an otherwise complicated process much more manageable.

CHAPTER 13

Using Presentation Logic: Multi-Browser Support

One of the promises of Cocoon is the ease with which one can produce content for multiple browsers. We saw in Chapter 7, "Creating Static Pages," that it is relatively easy to present a simple page in WML, for example. You might have wondered, however, whether there is an easier way to provide browser-specific content without having to change the URIs. Why do we want to do this? It boils down to separating content from logic. If the URLs for an application differ based on browser type, we are still tied to how we get the data to our client. This might seem like a small thing, but if you want to access a site from your browser, and your WAP phone and your PDA, why should you have to remember three different URLs? Sure, you can prefix all the URIs with a literal like "wap" or "palm" but it is a bit contrived. A robust site, one that is able to support multiple browser types, should internally be able to recognize what browser is accessing it and serve up the appropriate content. This is what we'll explore in this chapter, in which we'll look at the `BrowserSelector` component and DELI.

BrowserSelector

One of the defined `Selectors` in Cocoon, operaters on the `user-agent` parameter in the request headers. The `BrowserSelector` allows a pipeline to switch on a set of literals that are based on the user-agent header. In the definition of the `BrowserSelector`, in the `<map:components>` section of the sitemap, various user-agent header values are mapped to these literals. The definition looks like this:

```
<map:selectors default="browser">
 <map:selector logger="sitemap.selector.browser"
    name="browser"
    src="org.apache.cocoon.selection.BrowserSelector">
  <browser name="explorer" useragent="MSIE"/>
  <browser name="pocketexplorer" useragent="MSPIE"/>
  <browser name="handweb" useragent="HandHTTP"/>
  <browser name="avantgo" useragent="AvantGo"/>
  <browser name="imode" useragent="DoCoMo"/>
  <browser name="opera" useragent="Opera"/>
  <browser name="lynx" useragent="Lynx"/>
  <browser name="java" useragent="Java"/>
  <browser name="wap" useragent="Nokia"/>
  <browser name="wap" useragent="UP"/>
  <browser name="wap" useragent="Wapalizer"/>
  <browser name="mozilla5" useragent="Mozilla/5"/>
  <browser name="mozilla5" useragent="Netscape6/"/>
  <browser name="netscape" useragent="Mozilla"/>
 </map:selector>
```

The order of these entries is important, because some words can be found in the user-agent header of more than one browser. When the `BrowserSelector` evaluates a request, it determines which literal matches the user-agent header. Using the literals, the correct steps in the pipeline are executed.

We are going to modify the definition of `BrowserSelector` and add an entry for Palm devices. A Palm Pilot has a user-agent header of `Mozilla/2.0 (compatible;Elaine/1.1)`, so we can add an entry like this:

```
<browser name="palm" useragent="Elaine"/>
```

We'll put this entry at the beginning of the `<browser>` tags and restart Cocoon.

The Palm Emulator

For our testing, we used the Palm Emulator, which you can find at `www.palmos.com/dev/tools/emulator/`. In addition to the software, you also need ROM images to actually do anything with the emulator. You'll need to follow the instructions on the preceding page for joining the program (it doesn't cost you anything except a bit of time) and getting access to the ROM images. Finally, if you are building Web clippings, you need to download the WCA Building. Check out `www.palmos.com/dev/tech/webclipping/gettingstarted.html` for more information.

In our few pipeline examples in earlier chapters, we defined two processing paths for the `main.xml` file according to the browser type. Using the `BrowserSelector`, however, we can create just one pipeline:

```
<map:match pattern="*.html">
 <map:generate type="file" src="content/{1}.xml"/>
 <map:select>
   <map:when test="palm">
    <map:transform src="style/index-palm.xsl"/>
    <map:serialize type="html"/>
   </map:when>
   <map:when test="wap">
    <map:transform src="style/index-wml.xsl"/>
    <map:serialize type="wml"/>
   </map:when>
   <map:when test="netscape">
    <map:transform src="style/index-html.xsl"/>
    <map:serialize/>
   </map:when>
   <map:when test="mozilla5">
    <map:transform src="style/index-html.xsl"/>
    <map:serialize/>
   </map:when>
   <map:otherwise>
    <map:serialize type="xml"/>
   </map:otherwise>
 </map:select>
</map:match>
```

Note the entry for `"palm"`. In this case, the stylesheets are actually identical, with the exception of the requisite `<meta>` tags needed by Palm devices:

```
<meta name="palmcomputingplatform" content="true">
<meta name="palmlauncherrevision" content="1.0">
```

Of course, this pipeline wouldn't be fair to Opera clients, unless their user-agent is already set to Mozilla or Netscape. Figures 13.1 through 13.3 show various outputs of our index page.

The Opera Browser

If you haven't met it yet, you might not know that the Opera browser is a fine alternative to the dueling Netscape and Microsoft browsers. Besides its MDI approach, skins, hotclick capabilities, and other neat GUI features, Opera is billed (and appears to be) the fastest browser available. You can learn more about Opera, and download it, from `www.opera.com`.

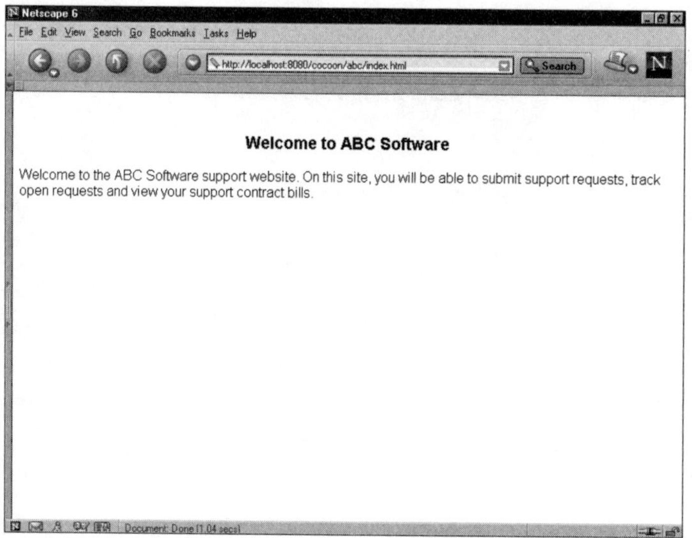

Figure 13.1

Output from Netscape.

Just for reference, there is an alternative to the `BrowserSelector`, the `HeaderSelector`. This `selector` allows you to construct pipeline switch statements based on the specified header. Because user-agent is such a header, one could use this as the determining factor in serving up the right XSL. Unfortunately, there are no wildcard capabilities with `<map:when>` tags, so you can use this selector only if you are prepared to specify full user-agent values. This makes the `BrowserSelector` a much better choice if you are supporting several different browser clients, but consider the `HeaderSelector` if you need to catch one particular client.

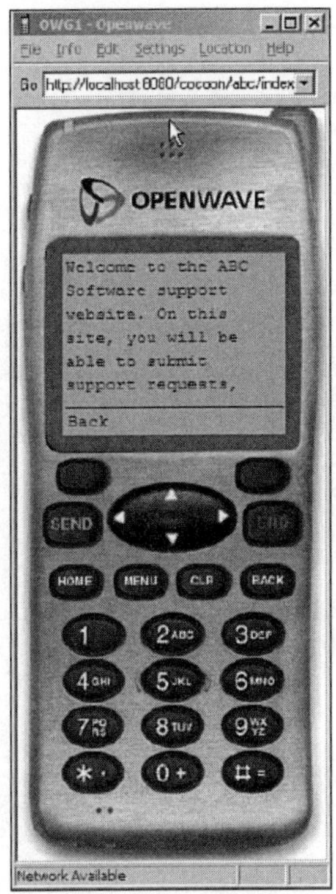

Figure 13.2
Output from UP SDK.

A pipeline using the `HeaderSelector` is shown here:

```
<map:match pattern="*.html">
 <map:generate src="content/{1}.xml"/>
 <map:select type="request-attribute">
   <map:parameter name="parameter-name" value="user-agent"/>
   <map:when test="SIE-C3I/1.0 UP/4.1.8c">
    <map:transform src="style/hello-wml-world.xsl"/>
    <map:serialize type="wml"/>
   </map:when>
   <map:when test="Mozilla/4.79-(Windows NT 5.0;U)">
    <map:transform src="style/hello-html-world.xsl"/>
    <map:serialize/>
   </map:when>
   <map:when test="Mozilla/6.01 (Windows; U; NT5.0; en-us)">
    <map:transform src="style/hello-html-world.xsl"/>
    <map:serialize/>
```

```
    </map:when>
    <map:otherwise>
     <map:transform src="style/hello-html-world.xsl"/>
     <map:serialize type="xml"/>
    </map:otherwise>
  </map:select>
</map:match>
```

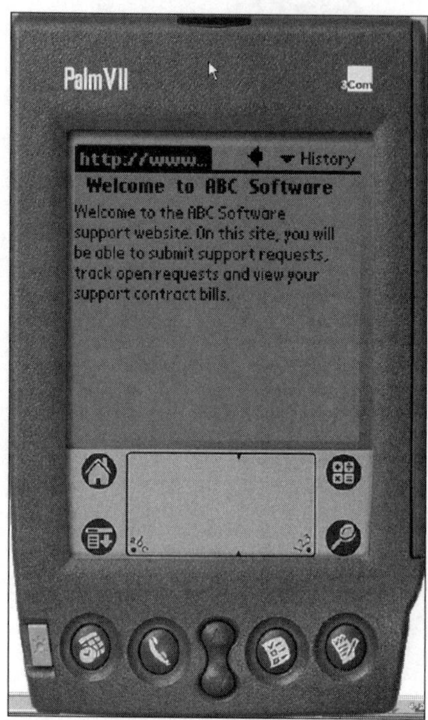

Figure 13.3
Output from Palm Pilot.

DELI

Now that we've covered the `BrowserSelector`, let's look at the other way in which Cocoon can internally switch on browser type, DELI. DELI stands for DElivery context LIbrary for CC/PP and UAProf. It is basically a library developed at HP labs that allows Java servlets to parse delivery context descriptions associated with browser clients. An excellent introduction can be found at `www.hpl.hp.co/uk/people/marbut/DeliUserGuideWEB.htm`.

DELI supports two compatible standards for describing delivery context information: CC/PP and UAProf. CC/PP stands for "Composite Capabilities/Preferences Profile" and is a W3C creation. You can get more information on CC/PP at `www.w3c.org/Mobile/CCPP`. UAProf stands for "User Agent Profile" and is being developed by the Wireless Application Forum (`www.wapforum.org`).

Both CC/PP and UAProf attempt to describe the capabilities of browser clients so that Web servers can determine what content the clients can accept. Both standards present their descriptions in Resource Description Framework (RDF) syntax.

> **More About RDF**
> RDF can be rather daunting to comprehend, and all the more so with some of the less-than-intelligible descriptions out there. The best introduction I could find is the documentation for Jena, a Java API for RDF from HP. You can find this at `www.hpl.hp.com/semweb/doc/tutorial/RDF_API/index.html`.

Cocoon implements DELI by means of the `TraxTransformer`. If the latter is passed a pipeline parameter `use-deli`, with the value set to `true`, Cocoon will use the DELI library to extract capability information from the client browser. If the browser does not have that information, DELI reads an RDF file containing description information that is associated with the browser type (more on how in a minute). Any capability information returned by DELI is then made available to the XSL file via the `TraxTransformer`. This information enables us to customize our output by taking into consideration the capabilities of our client browser. For example, if DELI tells us the screen size of our client, we can pick an appropriately sized image. Likewise, DELI provides information about whether the client supports such things as frames, tables, colors, and sound.

Configuring Cocoon for DELI

Because there are very few devices that provide capability information that DELI can read, we must rely on DELI's use of legacy device files to see it in action. To make things more interesting, we're going to configure DELI to recognize both Palm and our WAP simulator, neither of which is supported by default in Cocoon.

The first thing we have to do is enable DELI in Cocoon. We do this by first commenting out the original `<sitemap>` tag and uncommenting the one immediately below it:

```
<!--sitemap check-reload="yes" file="sitemap.xmap" logger="sitemap"
  reload-method="synchron"/-->

<sitemap logger="sitemap"/>
```

This new sitemap implementation is handled by a component called `TreeProcessor`. This interprets the sitemap, rather than compiling it into a Java object and executing it. The result is faster sitemap processing and no need to worry about recompiling on changes. On the downside, you must upgrade one component in the 2.0.3 distribution because of a bug in which sub-sitemaps don't inherit components from the parent sitemap. This issue is covered in Chapter 6.

Further down in the file, we must uncomment the `<deli>` tag.

```
<!-- Deli support -->
<!-- Uncomment this section to enable DELI -->
<deli class="org.apache.cocoon.components.deli.DeliImpl">
  <parameter name="deli-config-file"
    value="resources/deli/config/deliConfig.xml"/>
</deli>
<!-- -->
```

To implement the changes, we now have to restart Tomcat.

Manually Copying the DELI Config Files

If you are working with an out-of-the-box distribution of Cocoon, with all the samples intact, you can leave this definition as shown previously. However, if you have a stripped-down version without samples, you will have to manually copy the DELI files to your installation. Because these are configuration files, it makes sense to put them in the `WEB-INF` directory of the installation, rather than in the `resources` directory of the webapp as is done in the official distribution. To put the DELI files in the `WEB-INF` directory, simply copy the entire `deli` directory from the Cocoon source directory to `WEB_INF` as detailed next.

On Unix use

```
cp -r $COCOON_EXTRACT/src/webapp/resources/deli $CATALINA_HOME/webapps/
➥cocoon/WEB-INF
```

where `$COCOON_EXTRACT` refers to the source distribution directory. Make sure that the `webapp` directory is correct for your installation—`cocoon` is the default.

On Windows you'll have to use Windows Explorer to copy the directory.

We must edit `cocoon.xconf` to tell Cocoon where to find the DELI files:

```
<!-- Deli support -->
<!-- Uncomment this section to enable DELI -->
<deli class="org.apache.cocoon.components.deli.DeliImpl">
  <parameter name="deli-config-file"
```

```
      value="WEB-INF/deli/config/deliConfig.xml"/>
  </deli>
  <!-- -->
```

Let's look at the DELI configuration file, `deliConfig.xml`, in Listing 13.1.

Listing 13.1 *deliConfig.xml*

```
<?xml version="1.0"?>
<deli>
  <legacyDeviceFile>
   WEB-INF/deli/config/legacyDevice.xml
  </legacyDeviceFile>
  <debug>false</debug>
  <printDefaults>false</printDefaults>
  <printProfileBeforeMerge>false</printProfileBeforeMerge>
  <schemaVocabularyFile
    namespace="http://www.wapforum.org/UAPROF/ccppschema-20000405#">
   WEB-INF/deli/config/vocab/ccppschema-20000405.rdfs
  </schemaVocabularyFile>
  <schemaVocabularyFile
    namespace="http://www.wapforum.org/profiles/UAPROF/ccppschema-20010330#">
   WEB-INF/deli/config/vocab/ccppschema-20010330.rdfs
  </schemaVocabularyFile>
  <vocabularyFile>
   WEB-INF/deli/config/vocab/uaprof_vocab_30apr2001.xml
  </vocabularyFile>
</deli>
```

Let's look at the DELI configuration file, deliConfig.xml, in Listing 13.1 Note that we changed all references to files from "resources/deli/config" to "WEB-INF/deli/config". The main point of this file is to tell DELI where to find the legacy device file and the vocabulary information. The vocabulary files define the tag names and types used in the RDF descriptions. The legacy device file is what DELI will use to find the right legacy device descriptor file when a browser does not send any capability information. This file is shown in Listing 13.2.

Listing 13.2 *legacyDevice.xml*

```
<?xml version="1.0" encoding="UTF-8"?>
<devices>
  <legacyDevice>
    <useragentstring>Palm</useragentstring>
    <profileref>WEB-INF/deli/legacyProfiles/palm.rdf</profileref>
```

Listing 13.2 *(continued)*

```
    </legacyDevice>
    <legacyDevice>
      <useragentstring>UP</useragentstring>
      <profileref>WEB-INF/deli/legacyProfiles/nokia.rdf</profileref>
    </legacyDevice>
    <legacyDevice>
      <useragentstring>amaya</useragentstring>
      <profileref>WEB-INF/deli/legacyProfiles/amaya.rdf</profileref>
    </legacyDevice>
    <legacyDevice>
      <useragentstring>Nokia-WAP-Toolkit</useragentstring>
      <profileref>WEB-INF/deli/legacyProfiles/nokia.rdf</profileref>
    </legacyDevice>
    <legacyDevice>
      <useragentstring>Rainbow</useragentstring>
      <profileref>WEB-INF/deli/legacyProfiles/nokia.rdf</profileref>
    </legacyDevice>
    <legacyDevice>
      <useragentstring>Nokia-MIT-Browser</useragentstring>
      <profileref>WEB-INF/deli/legacyProfiles/nokia.rdf</profileref>
    </legacyDevice>
    <legacyDevice>
      <useragentstring>Opera</useragentstring>
      <profileref>WEB-INF/deli/legacyProfiles/opera.rdf</profileref>
    </legacyDevice>
    <legacyDevice>
      <useragentstring>Mozilla</useragentstring>
      <profileref>WEB-INF/deli/legacyProfiles/mozilla.rdf</profileref>
    </legacyDevice>
    <legacyDevice>
      <useragentstring>MSIE</useragentstring>
      <profileref>WEB-INF/deli/legacyProfiles/msie.rdf</profileref>
    </legacyDevice>
</devices>
```

The way this works is that DELI checks the content of the `user-agent` header for the text in each `<useragentstring>` tag. When it finds a match, it loads the appropriate definition file. The first two entries, for `palm` and `UP`, we've added ourselves; the rest come with Cocoon. You'll find an entry for IE, a couple of entries for WAP devices, one for the Opera browser, and one for Mozilla (Netscape). We moved the entry for IE to the bottom of the file so that it would not be confused with the Opera one.

The UP entry that we added points to an existing RDF description, `nokia.rdf`. The `palm` entry points to a new description, `palm.rdf`, that we have to create ourselves; it is found in Listing 13.3.

Listing 13.3 *palm.rdf*

```
<?xml version="1.0"?>

<rdf:RDF
  xmlns="http://www.w3.org/1999/02/22-rdf-syntax-ns#"
  xmlns:rdf="http://www.w3.org/1999/02/22-rdf-syntax-ns#"
  xmlns:prf="http://www.wapforum.org/profiles/UAPROF/ccppschema-20010430#"
>
  <rdf:Description rdf:ID="Palm">
    <prf:component>
      <rdf:Description rdf:ID="HardwarePlatform">
        <rdf:type rdf:resource="http://www.wapforum.org/profiles/UAPROF/
➥ccppschema-20010430#HardwarePlatform"/>
        <prf:ColorCapable>Yes</prf:ColorCapable>
        <prf:TextInputCapable>Yes</prf:TextInputCapable>
        <prf:ImageCapable>Yes</prf:ImageCapable>
        <prf:Keyboard>Qwerty</prf:Keyboard>
        <prf:Vendor>Palm</prf:Vendor>
        <prf:SoundOutputCapable>Yes</prf:SoundOutputCapable>
        <prf:StandardFontProportional>Yes</prf:StandardFontProportional>
      </rdf:Description>
    </prf:component>
    <prf:component>
      <rdf:Description rdf:ID="SoftwarePlatform">
        <rdf:type rdf:resource="http://www.wapforum.org/profiles/UAPROF/
➥ccppschema-20010430#SoftwarePlatform"/>
        <prf:AcceptDownloadableSoftware>No</prf:AcceptDownloadableSoftware>
        <prf:CcppAccept>
          <rdf:Bag>
            <rdf:li>image/gif</rdf:li>
            <rdf:li>image/jpeg</rdf:li>
            <rdf:li>text/html</rdf:li>
          </rdf:Bag>
        </prf:CcppAccept>
      </rdf:Description>
    </prf:component>
    <prf:component>
```

Listing 13.3 *(continued)*

```
      <rdf:Description rdf:ID="NetworkCharacteristics">
        <rdf:type rdf:resource="http://www.wapforum.org/profiles/UAPROF/
➥ccppschema-20010430#NetworkCharacteristics"/>
      </rdf:Description>
    </prf:component>
    <prf:component>
      <rdf:Description rdf:ID="BrowserUA">
        <rdf:type rdf:resource="http://www.wapforum.org/profiles/UAPROF/
➥ccppschema-20010430#BrowserUA"/>
        <prf:BrowserName>Palm</prf:BrowserName>
        <prf:FramesCapable>No</prf:FramesCapable>
        <prf:TablesCapable>Yes</prf:TablesCapable>
      </rdf:Description>
    </prf:component>
  </rdf:Description>
</rdf:RDF>
```

This file is merely a copy of the `opera.rdf` file, with the `BrowerName` and `Vendor` tags changed to say `Palm`. A more robust version should specify the screen size and probably some other things as well.

We also have to make one other change. That is to edit `WEB-INF/deli/legacyProfiles/nokia.rdf` and add a browser name to the `BrowserUA` section, which now looks like this:

```
      <rdf:Description rdf:ID="BrowserUA">
        <rdf:type rdf:resource="http://www.wapforum.org/profiles/UAPROF/ccppsche
ma-20010430#BrowserUA"/>
        <prf:BrowserName>WAP Device</prf:BrowserName>
        <prf:FramesCapable>No</prf:FramesCapable>
        <prf:TablesCapable>Yes</prf:TablesCapable>
      </rdf:Description>
```

The point of adding the `BrowserName` tag is simply so that our test, in the next section, will work. It is a valid tag, however, so you can leave it in.

Testing DELI

For our test, we'll use a simple XML file, shown in Listing 13.4, and an XSL, shown in Listing 13.5.

Listing 13.4 *DELI test XML (delitest.xml)*

```
<?xml version="1.0"?>

<page>
 <title>Test Page for DELI in Cocoon</title>
 <content>
  <para>Hi! Welcome! This dynamic page is brought to you by DELI.</para>
 </content>
</page>
```

Listing 13.5 *DELI test XSL (delitest.xsl)*

```
<?xml version="1.0"?>
<xsl:stylesheet xmlns:xsl="http://www.w3.org/1999/XSL/Transform" version="1.0">
  <xsl:param name="deli-capabilities"/>
  <xsl:param name="accept"/>
  <xsl:template match="/">
    <xsl:if test="normalize-space($accept)=''">
      <html>
      <head>
        <title><xsl:value-of select="title"/></title>
      </head>
      <body>
        <h1>DELI is switched off</h1>
      </body>
      </html>
    </xsl:if>
    <xsl:if test="contains($accept,'wml')
      and not(normalize-space($accept)='')">
      <xsl:call-template name="wmldevice"/>
    </xsl:if>
    <xsl:if test="not(contains($accept,'wml'))
      and not(normalize-space($accept)='')">
      <xsl:call-template name="htmldevice"/>
    </xsl:if>
  </xsl:template>
  <xsl:template name="wmldevice">
    <wml>
      <card id="init" newcontext="true">
        <p>
          <xsl:call-template name="welcome"/>
        </p>
```

Listing 13.5 *(continued)*

```
      </card>
    </wml>
  </xsl:template>
  <xsl:template name="htmldevice">
    <html>
      <head>
        <title>My First DELI Page</title>
      </head>
      <body>
        <xsl:call-template name="welcome"/>
      </body>
    </html>
  </xsl:template>
  <xsl:template name="welcome">
    <xsl:apply-templates select="//para"/>

    <xsl:if test="$deli-capabilities/browser/BrowserName">
      Your browser name is:
      <xsl:value-of select="$deli-capabilities/browser/BrowserName"/>
    </xsl:if>
  </xsl:template>

  <xsl:template match="//para">
   <p><xsl:apply-templates/></p>
  </xsl:template>
</xsl:stylesheet>
```

If you look at the top of this file, you'll see that we reference two parameters that will be set by the `TraxTransformer`: `deli-capabilities` and `accept`. The former holds a DOM document, which we can then reference as we do in the templates. Both of these are made available to the `TraxTransformer` by the DELI library.

As you can see, we aren't really doing anything complex here. All we actually want to do is see whether DELI finds the correct RDF file for each of the browsers in our test. Because the `BrowserName` tags are unique in the RDF files, that will tell us whether we got the right file.

We also need a sitemap entry, shown here:

```
<map:match pattern="deli.html">
 <map:generate src="delitest.xml"/>
 <map:transform src="delitest.xsl" type="xslt">
   <map:parameter name="use-deli" value="true"/>
```

```
  </map:transform>
  <map:select>
   <map:when test="wap">
    <map:serialize type="wml"/>
   </map:when>
   <map:otherwise>
     <map:serialize type="html"/>
   </map:otherwise>
  </map:select>
</map:match>
```

Again, we're using the `BrowserSelector` to pick the right `serializer`.

Let's see what we can do with this. First, we'll try our page with Opera, as shown in Figure 13.4.

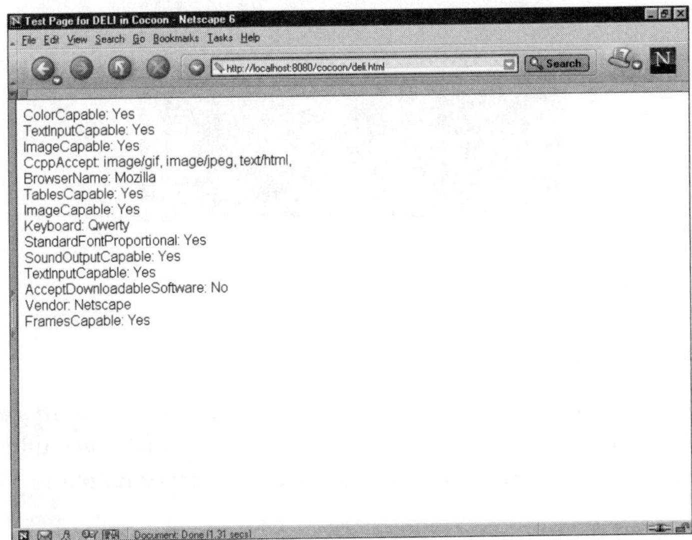

Figure 13.4
DELI test: Opera output.

It looks as though we got the `opera.rdf` file! Now let's try the Palm Pilot emulator and WAP emulator, whose outputs are shown in Figure 13.5 and Figure 13.6, respectively.

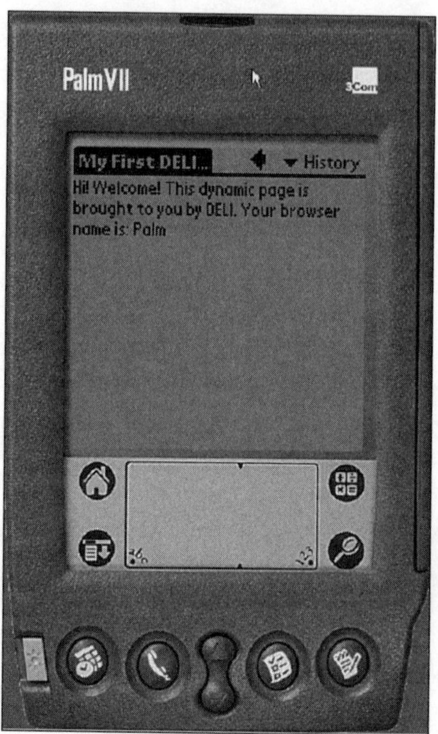

Figure 13.5
DELI test: Palm output.

Again, we get the right RDF files in each case.

As mentioned previously, a more robust use of DELI would be to customize content using the capability information that the DELI library returns to Cocoon. Such things as screen size, support fonts, and supported features all can be used to tailor output to your client.

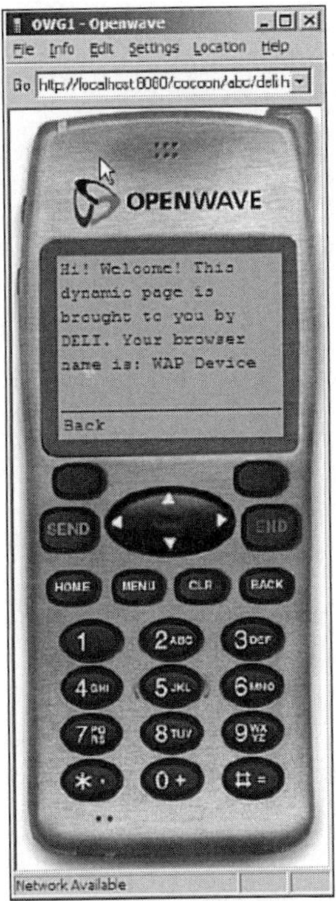

Figure 13.6
DELI test: WAP output.

Summary

If your application must support multiple browser types, and you want to customize output for each browser, consider the methods shown in this chapter. The advantage of both is that you need have only one pipeline to handle all possibilities. Using the `BrowserSelector` is an easy way to go, but it may involve having separate XSL files, as we did in our examples. Although a few browsers provide their own capability information, you can still use DELI, thank to its built-in support for legacy devices. The advantage of DELI is that you have access to detailed capability information. Rather than just knowing whether you should send HTML or WML back to the client, you can tweak the output to respect the restrictions of the client. As more and more devices become Web-enabled, we will soon be faced with dozens of different screen sizes that we have to deal with, rather than just the four or five that we have today. If you want to be ready to handle this situation, it is worth the learning curve to use DELI.

CHAPTER 14

Using Presentation Logic: Internationalization

Among the greatest challenges for the contemporary application developer are those associated with making the application usable by a global audience. Historically, to take an application written for one language group and make it available to another language group would involve a vast amount of work and usually result in another version of the application being developed. *Internationalization* and *Localization* are terms that have evolved to cover best practice that has been evolving over recent years to solve these issues and make software easier to make available to a wide range of language groups and locations.

What Do the Terms Mean?

Firstly, internationalization and localization are more commonly referred to using the acronyms *i18n* and *l10n*. This comes from the standards bodies not wanting to have to say or write the full terms—the best they could do was to work out how many letters are between the first and last letters and then use this number in between the first and last letters. Thus, *internationalization* has 20 letters in total, 18 between the first "i" and the last "n"—hence i18n. *Localization* has 10 letters in between the first and the last—hence l10n (some like to use a capital L to avoid confusion with a numeric one).

Another common phrase used is *locale*. A locale is generally used to refer to the combination of the language, country, and variant attributes that determine how an application is presented. The language and country are respectively represented with ISO639 and ISO3166 codes, and the variant is user-defined. So, `en_US` refers to English as spoken in the USA, `en_GB` refers to English as spoken in the United Kingdom, and `en_GB_scouse` could be used to refer to the colloquial English as spoken by the inhabitants of Liverpool in the United Kingdom.

In broad terms i18n is a design issue and l10n is an implementation issue. I18n really concerns how the application is designed to support multilingual capabilities—addressing how well the code copes with different locales, how easily the interface can be repurposed, and whether the data storage schema is compatible with the demands of different locales. L10n is about implementing the specifics for each locale—translating the interface, resource and documentation, customizing features, testing, and so on. In theoretical terms the minimal internationalized application consists of the internationalized software and the resources for a single, default locale.

Internationalization in Cocoon

Internationalization in Cocoon is achieved through the `I18nTransformer`. This transformer permits the application developer to identify many of the areas of the application that need internationalization and implement them using a method that keeps logic and content separate. What the `I18nTransformer` does not explicitly do is implement different application functionality for a given locale. For example, the transformer will handle the provision of translated text between an English and French version of an application but will not display a red interface on the English version and a blue interface on the French version. This would be up to the developer; however, many of the methods inherently used by the i18n transformation process can be used to provide this type of implementation functionality.

Usually this transformer would be used in conjunction with at least one other transformer, as shown in Figure 14.1.

The i18n transformer offers several features, including these:

- Pure text translation
- Attribute translation
- Parameter substitution
- Date internationalization

- Number internationalization
- Locale support
- Message catalog management support

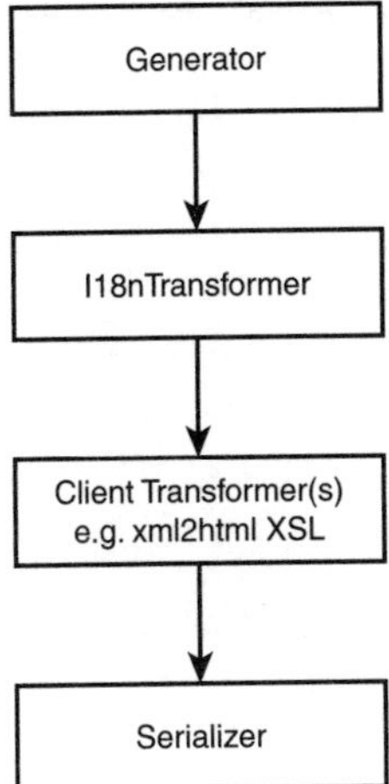

Figure 14.1
The i18n transformer in the pipeline.

Content that requires internationalization is identified in the source stream, thus enabling the transformer to pick up what needs to be translated. It then works out which message catalog to use, finds the message catalog, and looks up what the alternative rendering is and applies it, as illustrated in Figure 14.2.

A message catalog is a simple file that contains a list of key/value pairs expressed in XML. One message catalog needs to be created per locale that you want to support.

Using the I18nTransformer

The `I18nTransformer` is very powerful and covers a significant number of areas. This next section builds up the use of the transformer to cover these various areas, starting with enabling the transformer in the sitemap.

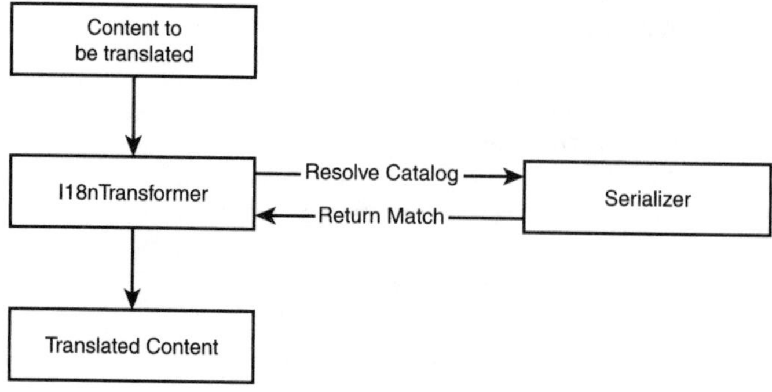

Figure 14.2
The basic translation process.

Configuring the I18nTransfomer in the Sitemap

Configuring the i18n transformer is a simple task. Within the sitemap you provide the following `<transformer>` element:

```
<map:transformer name="i18n"
  src="org.apache.cocoon.transformation.I18nTransformer" logger="sitemap.
  ➥transformer.i18n">
  <catalogue-name>messages</catalogue-name>
  <catalogue-location>translations</catalogue-location>
  <untranslated-text>untranslated</untranslated-text>
  <cache-at-startup>true</cache-at-startup>
</map:transformer>
```

The `catalogue-name` parameter refers to the name that the message catalogs take. In the preceding example the default message catalog would be called `messages.xml`, and a message catalog for the `fr` locale would be called `messages_fr.xml`. This is a mandatory parameter.

The `catalogue-location` parameter defines where the message catalogs are to be found. In the preceding example they would be found in the `translations` folder relative to the sitemap location. This too is a mandatory element.

The `untranslated-text` parameter defines text that will be used anywhere the transformer is unable to translate the text—that is, no match is found for a key. This parameter is optional, and if not supplied it defaults to using the wrapped-up text.

The `cache-at-startup` parameter defines whether the messages will be cached at startup. This, again, is an optional parameter and defaults to `false`. The default setting is fine during development, but for the best performance in a production environment you are best off making sure that this is set to `true`. It's also worth noting that when making changes to messages in a message catalog, you may need to restart Tomcat even if `cache-at-startup` is set to `false`, depending on your version of Cocoon.

When you want to use the transformer, you simply include it in the pipeline. For example:

```
<map:match pattern="*">
  <map:generate src="content/{1}.xml"/>
  <map:transform type="i18n"/>
  <map:transform src="stylesheets/document2html.xsl"/>
  <map:serialize/>
</map:match>
```

You can override the `catalogue-name`, `catalogue-location`, and `untranslated-text` parameters at the transformation stage by applying them as parameters to the transformer. You can also override the locale by adding the `locale` request parameter to the URL such as this:

```
http://localhost:8080/cocoon/somefile?locale=de
```

Configuring Message Catalogs

A message catalog is a very simple file that conforms to the following structure:

```
<?xml version="1.0" encoding="UTF-8"?>
<catalogue xml:lang="en">
  <message key="hello">Hello</message>
...
  <message key="goodbye">Goodbye</message>
</catalogue>
```

You build up as many message elements as you need to reflect the content that you want to provide translations for. Obviously, message catalogs must be created in the folder specified in the `catalogue-location` parameter. They must also follow a specific naming convention:

```
catalogue-name_language_country_variant.xml
```

The *`catalogue-name`* portion of the filename is the same as the one specified in the transformer catalogue-name parameter. The *`language`*, *`country`*, and *`variant`* portions reflect the specifics of the locale you are defining the message catalog for. Unless the locale information that specifies a message catalog will always be present, you must define a base message catalog, for example, `messages.xml`.

Message Catalogs and Dictionaries

The Cocoon 2.0.x documentation talks about a single file called a dictionary that contains all the language details. In fact, this has all been superceded and is not relevant. Message catalogs are how it is done!

When the transformer is determining which message catalog to use, it follows a set of logic that allows it to handle cases in which no explicit message catalog is defined. Figure 14.3 illustrates the process, assuming that the locale is set to `en_GB_scouse` and the message catalog *`catalogue-name`* is `messages`.

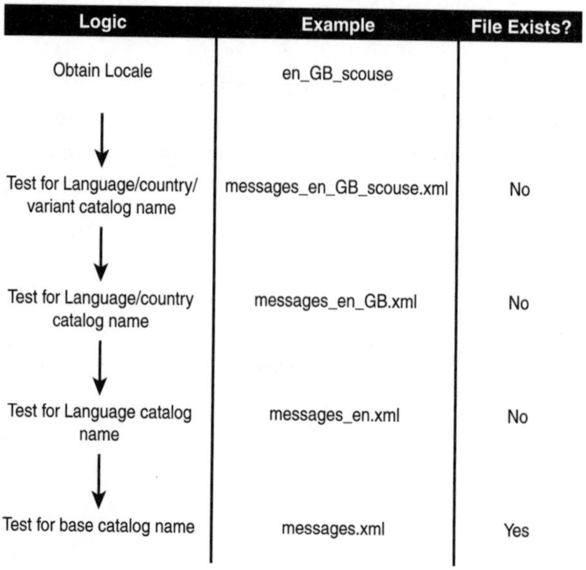

Logic	Example	File Exists?
Obtain Locale ↓	en_GB_scouse	
Test for Language/country/ variant catalog name ↓	messages_en_GB_scouse.xml	No
Test for Language/country catalog name ↓	messages_en_GB.xml	No
Test for Language catalog name ↓	messages_en.xml	No
Test for base catalog name	messages.xml	Yes

Figure 14.3

The message catalog resolution process.

The transformer works backward down the available locale settings until it finds a message catalog. If there is no message catalog, it will use the base message catalog. For example, you may have French and Swiss French message catalogs defined, named `messages_fr.xml` and `messages_fr_CH.xml`. The preceding process means that the `fr_CH` locale will use the `messages_fr_CH.xml` message catalog, but any other locale starting with `fr` will use the `messages_fr.xml` message catalog. A locale of just `de` (German) would not be found and the base message catalog used.

Translating Text

Text that requires translation is marked up using the <i18n:text> element. As a very simplistic example, let's consider how we might translate the word "Hello" into its French equivalent "Bonjour" (before I get flamed too much, let me say that I know that the literal translation is "salut"; however, culturally "bonjour" is more generally used). In its most simple form you could define the following:

```
<?xml version="1.0"?>
<page xmlns:i18n="http://apache.org/cocoon/i18n/2.0">
  <para><i18n:text>hello</i18n:text></para>
</page>
```

Here the root element (<page>) includes the i18n namespace declaration and then wraps up the text and requires translation within the <i18n:text> element. You would then define the corresponding entry in the French message catalog file:

```
<message key="hello">Bonjour</message>
```

When this is processed by the i18n transformer, the pure text ("hello") inside the <i18n:text> element will be taken as the key to look up into the relevant message catalog and matched. The transformer will find the match and replace the text with "Bonjour", passing that back for insertion in the SAX stream.

This method works well for short words, but what about sentences? In these cases you can use an i18n:key attribute to specify the key you want to use:

```
<i18n:text i18n:key="car1">car1 text</i18n:text>
```

Here, the key to use for the message catalog lookup is presented via an attribute in the <i18n:text> element. The pure text in the element is then used only if a match cannot be found. This presents clear advantages because in most real-world situations you would need to translate paragraphs of text, and it would not be practical to use these as the key.

You can also translate text with parameter substitution. This uses the <i18n:translate> element tag. This then can wrap up <i18n:param> elements that provide the text to replace placeholders with.

For example:

```
<i18n:translate>
  <i18n:text>My car is a {0}, 2.5 {1}.</i18n:text>
  <i18n:param>BMW</i18n:param>
  <i18n:param>litre</i18n:param>
</i18n:translate>
```

will result in the following output:

```
My car is a BMW, 2.5 litre.
```

Of course, the preceding example is using that entire string as a key; far better to use a separate key:

```
<i18n:translate>
  <i18n:text i18n:key="car2">car2 text</i18n:text>
  <i18n:param>BMW</i18n:param>
  <i18n:param>litre</i18n:param>
</i18n:translate>
```

Assuming that the English and French message catalogs have the respective messages, such as

```
<message key="car2">My car is a {0} 2.5 {1}.</message>
<message key="car2">Ma voiture est un {0} 2.5 {1}.</message>
```

then you would see this (again, English and French respectively):

```
My car is a BMW 2.5 litre.
Ma voiture est un BMW 2.5 litre.
```

You can translate the parameter as well. In the French version I want to use *litres* instead of *litre*. All that needs to happen is for the parameter text to be wrapped up with a simple `<i18n:text>` tag:

```
<i18n:translate>
  <i18n:text i18n:key="car2">car2 text</i18n:text>
  <i18n:param>BMW</i18n:param>
  <i18n:param><i18n:text>litre</i18n:text></i18n:param>
</i18n:translate>
```

If the appropriate entries are placed in the message catalogs like

```
<message key="litre">litre</message> (English)
<message key="litre">litres</message> (French)
```

then the output will change accordingly.

Attribute Translation

Element attributes can be translated as well as pure element text. This is achieved by adding in an `i18n:attr` to the element that contains the attribute you want to translate. The value of the `i18n:attr` is the name of attribute you want to translate. For example:

```
<input type="submit" value="processButton" i18n:attr="value"/>
```

will take the contents of the `value` attribute and use it as a key to look up into the message catalog.

Date, Time, and Number Formatting

The power of the internationalization transformer is not limited to text translation. It can also handle the formatting of dates, times, and numbers, including currencies. This is highly useful when you want to present these types of data in a locale-specific manner without having to worry about the nuances of every single permutation. The transformer neatly wraps up the work that has been done within core Java library classes and makes the work of the Cocoon developer much easier.

Date and Time

To format dates use the `<i18n:date>` tag. This will display a date (not date/time) and write it out dependent on supplied attributes. The attributes that it understands are defined in Table 14.1.

Table 14.1 *<i18n:date> Attributes*

Attribute	Description
`src-pattern`	Defines the pattern that the source date value adheres to. It can contain date formatting such as `"dd-mm-yyyy"` or the `"FULL"`, `"LONG"`, `"MEDIUM"` and `"SHORT"` strings.
`pattern`	Defines the output pattern. This accepts the same values as `src-pattern`.
`locale`	Defines the locale that the output date will use. This provides an easy way to translate month names.
`src-locale`	Defines the source locale of the date.
`value`	This is the date value to use. It can also be specified as a pure value between `<i18n:date>` start and end elements.

All the preceding attributes are optional. If they are not supplied, the default values from the current locale are used. If no value is supplied, the current date is used.

If you use a "real" value for `pattern` or `src-pattern`, this will override any locale settings, even if the `locale` or `src-locale` is also specified.

For example:

```
<i18n:date locale="de" pattern="FULL"
         src-locale="en_GB" src-pattern="SHORT"
         value="05/01/2001"/>
```

results in

```
Freitag, 5. Januar 2001,
```

because the UK format is *dd/MM/yyyy*, whereas

```
<i18n:date locale="de" pattern="FULL"
         src-locale="en_US" src-pattern="SHORT"
         value="05/01/2001"/>
```

results in

```
Dienstag, 1. Mai 2001
```

because the date value is being worked out to U.S. formatting standards rather than UK standards as in the first example.

The latter example could be overridden by using a real pattern as in

```
<i18n:date locale="de" pattern="FULL"
         src-locale="en_US" src-pattern="dd/MM/yyyy"
         value="05/01/2001"/>
```

resulting in

```
Freitag, 5. Januar 2001
```

Dates and times can be worked with using the `<i18n:date-time>` element, which works in the same way as `<i18n:date>` but extends the patterns to incorporate the display/formatting of time data. You can also use `<i18n:time>` to handle time values.

Numbers

Numbers are handled using the `<i18n:number>` element. It accepts several attributes, as described in Table 14.2 and Table 14.3.

Table 14.2 *<i18n:number> Attributes*

Attribute	Description
`type`	Specifies the type of the number. Table 14.3 describes the allowable types. If this attribute does not exist, the default is `number`.
`src-pattern`	Defines the pattern that the source number value adheres to. It can contain number formatting such as "`0`" and "`#`".
`pattern`	Defines the output pattern. This accepts the same values as `src-pattern`.
`locale`	Defines the locale that the output number will use.
`src-locale`	Defines the source locale of the number.
`fraction-digits`	Specifies the number of digits to express a fraction as.
`value`	Specifies the number value to use. This can also be specified as a pure value between `<i18n:number>` start and end elements.

Table 14.3 *<i18n:number type> Values*

Value	Description
`number`	Processes the number as a standard number.
`currency`	Processes the number as a currency.
`currency-no-unit`	Processes the number as a currency but does not output a unit indicator.
`percent`	Processes the number as a percentage.
`int-currency`	Forces the currency amount to be handled as an integer according to specific rules. If the currency does not have a sub-unit, no fractions will be displayed. Currencies with sub-units (for example, U.S. dollars/cents) will continue to have a fraction displayed.
`int-currency-no-unit`	Causes the same behavior as the preceding type without displaying a currency unit indicator.

Date, Time, and Numbers with Substitution Parameters

You can also use date, time, and number formatting with substitution parameters. To do this you need to add a `type` attribute to the `<i18n:param>` element that will specify the type of value being processed. Recognized values include `date`, `time`, `date-time`, `currency`, `currency-no-unit`, `int-currency`, `int-currency-no-unit` and `percent`. For example:

```
<i18n:translate>
  <i18n:text>You owe me {0}</i18n:text>
```

```
  <i18n:param type="currency" locale="en_GB">10</i18n:param>
</i18n:translate>
```

would display this:

```
You owe me £10.00
```

Beyond I18nTransformer

As you have seen thus far, `I18nTransformer` is a powerful piece of software, but it does not do everything. For example, it will not do anything like handle different front ends for different locales. This task requires the use of another part of the Cocoon armory: `LocaleAction`.

`LocaleAction` is a very useful piece of code. It makes locale information available via different methods such as the current request, cookies, and session variables. If another piece of code, such as `I18nTransformer`, needs local information, it will see whether the information is already available via one of these transports. If not, it will get what it can from the local system environment.

As previously mentioned, `I18nTransformer` uses `LocaleAction` itself to obtain the locale information, but this also means that this data becomes available to the rest of the pipeline. For example, if the locale data is kept as a request parameter, you can pick this up and use it to modify paths. This means you could place locale-specific content in locale-specific folders, resolving the correct path to use at runtime. You could prefix or suffix graphics with locale information and then get the right locale-specific graphic accordingly.

To enable this, `LocaleAction` needs to be placed in the sitemap. You do this with code similar to the following:

```
<map:action name="locale"
    logger="sitemap.action.locale"
    src="org.apache.cocoon.acting.LocaleAction">
  <store-in-session>false</store-in-session>
  <create-session>false</create-session>
  <store-in-request>true</store-in-request>
  <store-in-cookie>false</store-in-cookie>
  <locale-attribute>locale</locale-attribute>
  <language-attribute>language</language-attribute>
  <country-attribute>country</country-attribute>
  <variant-attribute>variant</variant-attribute>
</map:action>
```

The various parameters are described in Table 14.4.

Table 14.4 *LocaleAction Parameters*

Parameter	Description
`store-in-session`	Specifies whether the locale information should be stored in a session object.
`create-session`	If `store-in-session` is `true`, this creates a session if one is needed.
`store-in-request`	Specifies whether the locale information should be stored in request attributes.
`store-in-cookie`	Specifies whether the locale information should be stored in a cookie.
`local-attribute`	Defines the name of the attribute that will hold the current locale. If this is not supplied, it defaults to `locale`.
`language-attribute`	Defines the name of the attribute that will hold the current language from the locale data. If this is not supplied, it defaults to `language`.
`country-attribute`	Defines the name of the attribute that will hold the current country from the locale data. If this is not supplied, it defaults to `country`.
`variant-attribute`	Defines the name of the attribute that will hold the current variant field from the locale data. If this is not supplied, it defaults to `variant`.

When in the sitemap, a pipeline will need to include the relevant `<map:act>` element to bring `LocaleAction` into play:

```
<map:act type="locale">
  <map:match pattern="*">
    <map:generate src="content/{1}.xml"/>
    <map:transform type="i18n"/>
    <map:transform src="stylesheets/document2html.xsl">
      <map:parameter name="localeUsed" value="{../locale}"/>
    </map:transform>
    <map:serialize/>
  </map:match>
</map:act>
```

In this example the pipeline is passing the locale as a parameter (from the request attribute) to the rendering stylesheet. This can then be used by first defining an XSL parameter and then using it within the stylesheet:

```
<xsl:param name="localeUsed" />
...
<p>Locale is: <xsl:value-of select="$localeUsed"/></p>
```

This parameter could be used to modify paths and filenames as well. You could use something like

```
<xsl:element name="a">
  <xsl:attribute name="href">content/
➥<xsl:value-of select="$localeUsed"/>/menu.xml</xsl:attribute>
    a link
</xsl:element>
```

to get something like `href="content/en_GB/menu.xml"`, or use

```
<xsl:element name="link">
  <xsl:attribute name="rel">stylesheet</xsl:attribute>
  <xsl:attribute name="type">text/css</xsl:attribute>
  <xsl:attribute name="href">css/style-
➥<xsl:value-of select="$localeUsed"/>.css</xsl:attribute>
</xsl:element>
```

to get `<link rel="stylesheet type="text/css" href="css/style-en_GB.css">`.

Summary

Paying more than mere lip service to the issues of internationalization and localization is becoming a necessity for Web application designers everywhere, especially for those located in the native-English-speaking parts of world. Cocoon has benefited from its open source heritage and developed a truly global perspective within its code base. Core components, including `I18nTransformer` and `LocaleAction`, are mature pieces of software that provide a very comprehensive interface to the underlying capabilities of Java.

If I had to pick out just one part of Cocoon where the thinking behind the product is expertly demonstrated in a practical way, then I would pick internationalization. Principles such as separation of concerns and splitting logic, content, and presentation elements marry up precisely with architectural fundamentals like pipeline processing and the use of XML. In my (ever so humble) opinion, the only technologies that come close are pure content management systems that require a massive investment in money, infrastructure, and time.

When you are designing your applications, consider the likelihood of needing to add support for additional languages or locales. It does not cost much in time or performance to add in multi-locale support even in an application that only initially requires support for a single locale. The benefits of doing so will become very apparent after you start adding in other locales—it will be much smoother, require less code refactoring, and take less time.

Even if you need to support only a single locale it is worth looking at the internationalization components in Cocoon because they represent so much best practice when it comes to the design and implementation of Cocoon components. Whatever way you look at it, Cocoon's internationalization support is Cocoon at its best.

PART III

Advanced Cocoon Features

CHAPTER

CHAPTER 15
Extending Cocoon Components

As you have seen through the book so far, you can achieve a lot just through using Cocoon "out of the box." There will come a time, however, when you will not be able to make Cocoon do exactly what you would like it to do. Perhaps you want to use a data source for which there is no source or generator, or perhaps you want to develop an action so you can better handle the processing of a response. Cocoon offers the liberty to develop additional components such as generators, transformers, and serializers, augmenting the comprehensive set packaged with the distribution. In fact, pretty much everything inside Cocoon can be extended. This chapter provides the base information on how to extend Cocoon components. It concentrates on the most common types of components to be extended, such as actions and generators.

Principles of Extending Components

Each type of component inside Cocoon has its own particular nuances when it comes to extending them. All of them, however, do share an ancestry that provides a common foundation. This stems from the Avalon-based architecture that underpins Cocoon and gives Cocoon a set of predefined interfaces that can be reused and extended.

You can learn much about how to extend Cocoon components simply by looking at the source code already present in the distribution. After all, even the most fundamental of Cocoon components utilizes the same architecture that you need to use when building your own components. The core architectural building blocks are presented via Avalon as interfaces. So what are the constituent blocks that go into writing your own components?

Avalon Interfaces

Let's start by looking at a few of the Avalon classes and interfaces that are commonly used in Cocoon components.

Component

By default, all the components use the `Component` interface—they could not be Avalon components without it!

Loggable

Another almost de facto interface that is used is `Loggable`. This enables any component that implements it to gain access to a `Logger` component. Components normally use this interface via the `AbstractLoggable` helper class and then typically write log information with code such as this:

```
if ( getLogger().isDebugEnabled() )
{
  getLogger().debug( "some debug" );
}
```

The logger functionality is in the Avalon logkit class `org.apache.log.Logger`.

It is worth noting that much of the logging interface and functionality has been deprecated in more recent versions of Avalon. For example, the interface that should be used is now `org.apache.avalon.framework.logger.LogEnabled`, usually accessed via `org.apache.avalon.framework.logger.AbstractLogEnabled`. The task of updating all these deprecated implementations and calls is not a small one; however, it is very likely that this work will be completed for the release of Cocoon 2.1.

Composable

A composable component is one that can make use of other components. The principles of separation of concerns (SOC) and inversion of control (IOC) as exercised in Avalon mean that a component cannot directly use the implementation of another component. It must be done through a `ComponentManager`. Implementing the `Composable` interface allows a component to gain access to the `ComponentManager` and thus access implementations via the "role" method.

A component that implements the `Composable` interface will also implement the `compose()` method. This gets called as part of the component lifecycle and is where the component can gain access to the `ComponentManager` and from that to implementations of other components.

A typical use for component selection is illustrated by the `AbstractDatabaseAction` component. It needs to gain access to the implementation of the `DataSourceComponent` that will be used to handle connections to whatever data source has been configured. Its `compose()` implementation is as follows:

```
public void compose(ComponentManager manager)
throws ComponentException
{
  this.dbselector =
      (ComponentSelector)manager.lookup(
        DataSourceComponent.ROLE + "Selector");

  super.compose(manager);
}
```

The same type of functionality can be used in other scenarios. For example, in a particular application I wrote I needed to write a generator that worked directly on a data source. The `compose()` method did much the same as the preceding fragment, placing the `ComponentSelector` object in a variable called selector. The data source could then be accessed using the code

```
DataSourceComponent ds =
    (DataSourceComponent) this.selector.select( "xcpt" );
```

where `"xcpt"` was the name of the data source defined in the `<datasources>` block of `cocoon.xconf`.

Configurable

The `Configurable` interface is another common one to be implemented in Cocoon components. This is because many components need to be able to pick up configuration settings. To do this, the class must implement the `configure()` method along these lines:

```
public void configure( Configuration conf )
throws ConfigurationException
{
```

```
    super.configure( conf );
    if ( conf != null )
    {
      this.myValue = conf.getChild( "myValue" ).getValueAsInteger( 10 );
    }
}
```

A good example of how configuration data can be handled is in the `Database*Action` classes. These obtain the name of a configuration file, or descriptor, from the sitemap parameters and then use the `Configuration` class to read their data settings in an XML form.

Parameterizable

The `Parameterizable` interface provides slightly simpler name/value pair functionality than the XML-based `Configurable` interface/`Configuration` class.

The configuration of the `MRUMemoryStore` uses parameters, and this is how it handles them using the `Parameterize()` method:

```
public void parameterize(Parameters params)
throws ParameterException
{
  this.maxobjects =
    params.getParameterAsInteger("maxobjects", 100);
  this.persistent =
    params.getParameterAsBoolean("use-persistent-cache", false);
  if ((this.maxobjects < 1))
  {
    throw new ParameterException(
      "MRUMemoryStore maxobjects must be at least 1!");
  }

  this.cache = new Hashtable((int)(this.maxobjects * 1.2));
  this.mrulist = new LinkedList();
  this.storeJanitor.register(this);
}
```

The parameters that configure the `MRUMemoryStore` are held in `cocoon.xconf`.

Poolable

The `Poolable` interface is implemented by any component that wants to be pooled if required. Any `Poolable` component can have its pool settings configured using the `pool-max`, `pool-min`, and `pool-grow` parameters.

Other Avalon Interfaces

There are various other interfaces that Avalon-based components can use. These include `Runnable`, `Startable`, `ThreadSafe`, `Disposable`, and `Recyclable`. These are all found in various components, and it is worth investigating the source code to find out more. Of course, additional information can be found on the Avalon home page at `http://jakarta.apache.org/avalon`.

Cocoon Interfaces

Now that we've looked at a few of the key Avalon interfaces, there are also some regularly used Cocoon interfaces that are worthy of mention.

ObjectModelHelper

`ObjectModelHelper` is a highly useful class because it gives your classes, such as actions, access to the `Context`, `Request`, and `Response` objects. You can use it in the following manner:

```
import org.apache.cocoon.environment.ObjectModelHelper;
import org.apache.cocoon.environment.Context;
import org.apache.cocoon.environment.Request;

...

public Map act (Redirector redirector,
                  SourceResolver resolver,
                  Map objectModel,
                  String source,
                  Parameters parameters)
    throws Exception
{
  Request request =
      ObjectModelHelper.getRequest(objectModel);
  Context context =
      ObjectModelHelper.getContext(objectModel);

...
}
```

SitemapModelComponent

The `SitemapModelComponent` interface is implemented by (among other components) generators, readers, and transformers. It declares the `setup()` method that these components can override.

Generators

Generators are one of the components you are most likely to want to extend. The reason for this is that the content of your application has to come from somewhere, and has to be generated, and the likelihood is that a method such as XSP may not provide the neatest solution. The fact that XSPs are compiled to form generators simply adds drive to the choice to write your own generator. Of course, you may decide to use an action instead of a generator—the action framework does often allow for a more clear separation of logic and content—but do not underestimate the power of a simple generator to offer a significant level of "bang for the buck."

If you are writing your own generator, it almost certainly will either directly extend or be an eventual subclass of `AbstractGenerator`. This class implements the `Loggable`, `Poolable`, and `Recyclable` Avalon component interfaces. It is even more likely that your generator will end up being a subclass of `ComposerGenerator`. This direct subclass of `AbstractGenerator` adds the `Composable` and `Disposable` interfaces.

A good example of when to use a generator is when you are not likely to have a significant amount of application-specific business logic to have to contend with. For example, take the `DirectoryGenerator` class. All it has to do is read a directory structure and reflect the file contents, and this works as a generic utility for any application that may need it. This is easily extended to handle the specific requirements of image and MP3 files with the `ImageDirectoryGenerator` and `MP3DirectoryGenerator` classes. So as an example, let's follow suit and create another generator based on `DirectoryGenerator`. This one is going to handle ZIP files, and be called `ZipDirectoryGenerator`.

For reasons of space, it is not worth listing the whole class file in these pages, so if you want to look at the complete class, you can download the source code from the Web site. What we will do, however, is look at the key methods in the class, but before that let's consider what it is we need to extend from the base `DirectoryGenerator` class.

If you look at what the `DirectoryGenerator` class does, you will see two key methods: `setup()` and `generate()`. The `setup()` method is called to configure any specific settings before the main generation code is executed. It is here that the path to use and so on are configured. The `generate()` method is the entry point for the main code, and it goes through a file structure, creating `<directory>` and `<file>` nodes as appropriate. On each node, it sets up the attributes such as `name`, `lastModified`, and `date`, using a method called `setNodeAttributes()`. The `ZipDirectoryGenerator` needs to override this method so that it can place extra information about a ZIP file in the attribute list. The following code fragment shows the `ZipDirectoryGenerator.setNodeAttributes()` method that does this:

```
protected void setNodeAttributes(File path) throws SAXException
{

  // Call the DirectoryGenerator method to get all the basic
  // node attributes
  super.setNodeAttributes( path );

  // If we are looking at a directory then move on cos
  // there is nothing to see here...
  if (path.isDirectory())
  {
  return;
  }


  ZipFile zip = null;

  try
  {

    getLogger().debug(
        "Attempting to open ZIP file " + path );

    // Open the zip file
    zip = new ZipFile( path );

    // Add the number of entries as an attribute
    this.numEntries = zip.size();
    attributes.addAttribute( "",
          ZIP_FILE_NUM_ENTRIES_ATTR_NAME,
          ZIP_FILE_NUM_ENTRIES_ATTR_NAME, "CDATA",
          "" + this.numEntries );

    // Save the entries.  This is because otherwise
    // the entries appear before the parent node.
    this.entries = new Vector();

    for ( Enumeration e = zip.entries();
          e.hasMoreElements() ; )
    {
```

```
        this.entries.add( (ZipEntry)e.nextElement() );
      }

    }
    catch ( ZipException ze )
    {
      getLogger().debug(
          "ZIPException opening ZIP file " + path, ze );
    }
    catch ( IOException ioe )
    {
      getLogger().debug(
          "IOException opening ZIP file " + path, ioe );
    }
    finally
    {
      // Close the ZIP file if it was sucessfully opened
      if ( zip != null )
      {
        try
        {
          zip.close();
        }
        catch ( IOException ioe )
        {
          getLogger().debug(
              "IOException closing ZIP file " + path, ioe );
        }
      }

    }
}
```

The first thing that the method does is call the `setNodeAttributes()` method of its super (parent) class, `DirectoryGenerator`. This is so that all the same attributes are set up as for any other file. Assuming that the path is not a directory, it then uses the standard Java ZIP handling utilities to open the file.

Next, the method gets the number of entries in the ZIP file and uses this to set another attribute. The `attributes` variable is inherited from the parent class and is the same one that contains the rest of the attributes set there.

At this point the code saves details about all the entries in the ZIP file and closes it down.

The reason the details are saved away is that I also want to list all the entries in the ZIP file. Why can't this be done at this point? The reason is that doing this means adding another node (`<zipEntry>`) and the `setNodeAttributes()` call occurs before the parent node (`<file>`) is created. If the entries were listed to a node within the `setNodeAttributes()` method, you would end up with something that looked like

```
<zipEntry .../>
<zipEntry .../>
<file .../>
```

as opposed to this:

```
<file ...>
  <zipEntry .../>
  <zipEntry .../>
</file>
```

To resolve this issue, we need to churn out the `<zipEntry>` nodes after the beginning of the parent `<file>` node but before it is closed off. The way to do this is to override the `endNode()` method and list the entries before closing the `<file>` node:

```
protected void endNode(String nodeName)
throws SAXException
{

  // List any zip file entries and then clear them to
  // prevent them displaying on any irrelevant nodes.
  listEntries();

  this.entries.clear();
  super.endNode( nodeName );

}
```

The call is made to the `listEntries()` method, and then the super `endNode()` method is called to finish off the parent node. Of course, this code will get called whatever the node type is that is being finished off, so the entries are cleared to prevent their being unintentionally streamed.

The `listEntries()` method simply creates a whole new set of attributes for the entries inside the ZIP file and puts them in a `<zipEntry>` element node.

After the generator is compiled and made available to Cocoon, either in a JAR file or in `WEB-INF/classes`, it can be used inside a pipeline. The basic sitemap configuration is as follows:

```
<map:generator name="zipdirectory"
    logger="sitemap.generator.zipdirectory"
    src="com.pigbite.cdh.generation.ZipDirectoryGenerator"/>
```

Of course, because the class is ultimately inherited from `AbstractGenerator`, you could add pooling configuration data. You could also add to the class to accept further configuration setup parameters.

A simple pipeline entry to call the `ZipDirectoryGenerator` would be the following:

```
<map:match pattern="**zip.xml">
  <map:generate src="{1}" type="zipdirectory">
    <map:parameter name="depth" value="5"/>
    <map:parameter name="dateformat" value="dd-MMM-yyyy hh:mm:ss"/>
    <map:parameter name="root" value="cocoon"/>
    <map:parameter name="include" value=".zip$|.jar$"/>
    <map:parameter name="exclude" value="\.bak$"/>
  </map:generate>
  <map:serialize type="xml"/>
</map:match>
```

Note that the generator can accept exactly the same configuration data that the parent generator can—allowing us to filter the folder listing to look at only `.zip` and `.jar` files. A sample output is shown in Figure 15.1.

Transformers

Transformers are the middlemen of Cocoon. They sit right in the middle of the pipeline, receiving SAX events, doing stuff to them, and passing SAX events on. A generate-> transform->serialize process will have only one generator and one serializer but could have many transformers.

This behavior means that generally if you want to create a new transformer, you need to override the various content handling methods, such as `startDocument()` and `endElement()`. Obviously, because a transformer inherits from `AbstractTransformer`, you will have access to the same configuration, pooling, and logging functions, and so on, as other components.

In my experience, however, you can do a lot with the existing set of transformer classes, especially when you consider what can be done by incorporating one or more XSL stylesheets in the mix. To that end, this part of the chapter remains brief.

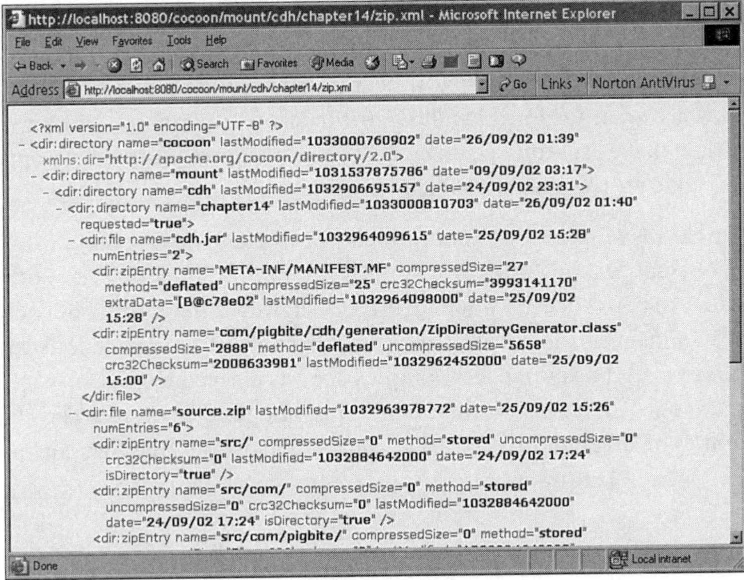

Figure 15.1

ZipDirectoryGenerator output showing details of the ZIP format files it has found.

Serializers

Serializers are at the end of the pipeline. They channel the incoming SAX event stream into something fit for consumption by the final client. A lot of content will get turned into HTML, but serializers exist for producing PDF files, RTF files, text files, a set of links, SVG files, and so on.

As with transformers, so much is provided for out of the box that the need to write a serializer raises its head less than for other components.

The core helper class is `AbstractSerializer`. This implements key component interfaces such as `Loggable` and `Poolable`, but not `Configurable`, `Cacheable`, or `Composable`. Any serializer that is handling text files will directly extend `AbstractTextSerializer`, which does implement `Configurable` and `Cacheable`.

The key method that is overridden by a serializer is the `setOutputStream()` method. It is this that configures the output stream where the final stream will be delivered. This is clearly what needs to change depending on the type of content being delivered.

Actions

Actions are key components because they are commonly used to handle logic within a Web application. They are great for form handling, for database interaction, and for implementing logic that at runtime changes the path a user takes through an application and therefore the pipeline entries that are called.

The base helper class is `AbstractAction`, which just implements the `Loggable` interface (aside from the obvious Avalon `Component` interface). From this class several other abstract and helper classes are derived, each implementing a slightly different mix of component interfaces. The two main subclasses are `ComposerAction` and `AbstractConfigurableAction`.`ComposerAction` has some less complex actions derived from it; `AbstractConfigurableAction`, on the other hand, has quite a complex class hierarchy sprouting from it. The diagram in Figure 15.2 helps to show the tree that comes directly from `AbstractConfigurableAction`.

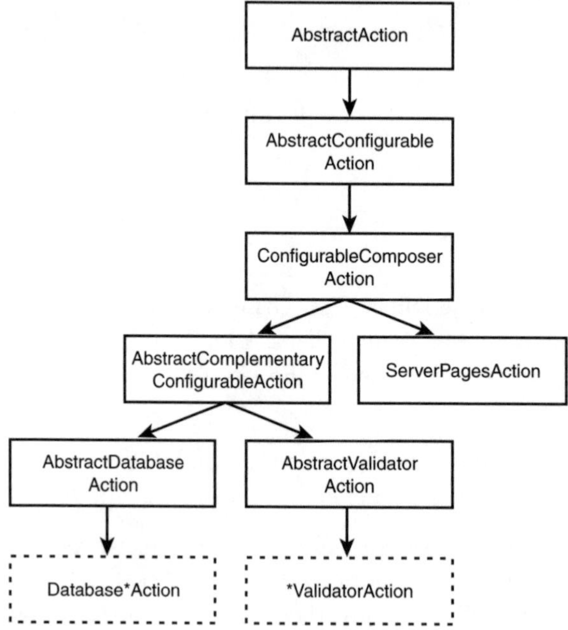

Figure 15.2
Class hierarchy from AbstractConfigurableAction.

The diagram shows the key classes that inherit from `AbstractConfigurableAction`. The route that develops down the left side of the tree is interesting because this benefits from having the Avalon `Configurable` component interface present. The `AbstractComplementaryConfigurableAction` adds capability for multiple actions to share a common configuration file, thereby providing the basis for the way all the database and form validation actions work. Any action you decide to write therefore can inherit at various levels in the tree, thereby benefiting from increasing levels of functional complexity.

As far as methods go, the prime method an action is likely to override is `act()`. This, like `generate()` with a generator, is the main hook for performing the specific functionality required.

Developing an action is easy and something that most Cocoon developers will get very used to doing. Actions can be written using XSP, via the `ServerPagesAction`, but we are going to look at a Java-based action as an example of what can be done. The example we are going to look at is an action that allows a file to be uploaded. Now Cocoon does include file upload capabilities out of the box, with its built-in multipart form handling. Where this action arose from, however, was the need to provide a little extra functionality—uploading to a user-specified folder. The action hangs off the existing file upload functionality that is called when it comes across multipart form data in a request. Cocoon will upload a file into a specific folder, configured via the `<upload-directory>` parameter in `web.xml`. The neat trick is that because the Cocoon upload process passes a serialized `FilePart` object up the request chain, an action can come along and use that object. So `FileUploadAction` is a little cheeky and checks the request again to see whether a serialized `FilePart` object is there, and if so manages placing the file into the user-specified upload folder. Listing 15.1 shows the whole of the class source.

Listing 15.1 *FileUploadAction.java*

```
package com.pigbite.cdh.acting;

/**
 * This action hooks into the multipart form processing offered by Cocoon and
 * uploads a file into the area specified in the <i>upload-dir</i> parameter.
 *
 * @author <a href="mailto:jez@pigbite.com">Jeremy Aston</a>
 * @version 1.00
 */

import org.apache.avalon.framework.configuration.Configurable;
import org.apache.avalon.framework.configuration.Configuration;
import org.apache.avalon.framework.configuration.ConfigurationException;
import org.apache.avalon.framework.parameters.Parameters;
import org.apache.avalon.framework.thread.ThreadSafe;
```

Listing 15.1 *(continued)*

```
import org.apache.cocoon.Constants;
import org.apache.cocoon.environment.Context;
import org.apache.cocoon.environment.ObjectModelHelper;
import org.apache.cocoon.environment.Redirector;
import org.apache.cocoon.environment.Request;
import org.apache.cocoon.environment.SourceResolver;
import org.apache.cocoon.acting.AbstractConfigurableAction;

import java.io.*;
import java.util.*;
import java.io.BufferedInputStream;
import org.apache.cocoon.components.request.multipart.*;

public class FileUploadAction
    extends AbstractConfigurableAction implements ThreadSafe
{

  /** Name of the parameter that holds the upload directory name to use **/
  private static final String UPLOAD_FOLDER_PARAMETER = "upload-dir";

  /**
   * Put an upload file into a specficed area
   * Requires that the upload directory is specified
   * as a parameter to the action called <i>upload-dir</i>
   */
  public Map act (Redirector redirector,
                  SourceResolver resolver,
                  Map objectModel,
                  String source,
                  Parameters parameters)
    throws Exception
  {
        Request request =
                ObjectModelHelper.getRequest(objectModel);
        Context context =
                ObjectModelHelper.getContext(objectModel);
    byte[] buffer = new byte[4096];
    HashMap results = new HashMap();

    if (request != null)
    {
```

Listing 15.1 *(continued)*

```
    // Loop through the parameter names
    // to find any file upload stuff
    getLogger().debug( "Request Parameters" );
    for ( Enumeration e = request.getParameterNames();
          e.hasMoreElements() ;)
    {
      String param = (String) e.nextElement();
      Object value = request.get( param );

      getLogger().debug(
            "[" + param +
            "] [" +
            value.getClass().getName() +
            "] : " + value );

     if ( value instanceof FilePart )
     {
        // Have got a File object
        // (or sub class - hence the casting )
        // which can be worked on...
        // Now get the filename and the real
        // path to form the file route.

        String filename =
               ( (FilePart)value ).getFileName();
        String uploadFolder =
               (String)parameters.getParameter(
                UPLOAD_FOLDER_PARAMETER );
        String realPath = context.getRealPath("/");

        // Do a sanity check on the upload folder

        if ( uploadFolder == null ||
             uploadFolder.length() == 0 )
        {
          getLogger().debug(
            "Missing " + UPLOAD_FOLDER_PARAMETER +
            " parameter or no upload folder specified in the " +
            UPLOAD_FOLDER_PARAMETER + " parameter" );

          return null;
        }
```

Listing 15.1 *(continued)*

```
// Concatenate the realPath
// folder to the upload folder

if ( realPath != null )
{
  uploadFolder = realPath + uploadFolder;
}

  getLogger().debug(
         "Uploading " + filename +
         " to " + uploadFolder );

// Create the upload folder if need be

File folder = new File( uploadFolder );
if ( !folder.exists() )
{
   folder.mkdir();
}

// Check to see if the object is a
// FilePartFile object as this can
// simply be renamed.

if ( value instanceof FilePartFile )
{

  getLogger().debug(
       "Renaming " + filename +
       " to " + uploadFolder +
       File.separator + filename );
  ( (FilePartFile)value ).getFile().renameTo(
      new File( uploadFolder +
          File.separator + filename) );
}
else
{

  getLogger().debug(
       "Streaming file to " + uploadFolder +
       File.separator + filename );
```

Listing 15.1 *(continued)*

```
          FileOutputStream out = new
               FileOutputStream( uploadFolder +
                   File.separator + filename );
          InputStream in = ( (FilePart)value ).getInputStream();

          int read = in.read( buffer );

          while ( read > 0 )
          {
            out.write( buffer, 0, read );
            read = in.read( buffer );
          }

          out.close();
        }

        request.setAttribute( "upload-file", filename );

      }
      else if ( value instanceof String )
      {
        getLogger().debug( "Skipping parameter: " + (String)value );
      }
      else
      {
        getLogger().debug("something else");
      }
    }

    String contentType = request.getContentType();
    getLogger().debug( "Content Type: " + contentType );

  }

  return Collections.unmodifiableMap(results);

  }

}
```

So what is happening in this action? For starters, notice that the action extends `AbstractConfigurableAction`. This is because, although it does not currently do so, it can then be extended to be configured via a configuration file.

A static `String` is declared that holds the name of a parameter that will be used to identify the upload folder:

```
private static final String UPLOAD_FOLDER_PARAMETER = "upload-dir";
```

You will see a little later how this is used by the calling form and pipeline.

In keeping with the tradition when writing actions, the only method in the whole class is `act()`. The first thing it does is to get the Cocoon `Request` and `Context` objects so that it can use them later.

Assuming that the request is not empty, the action then looks at the request parameters for anything that can be interpreted as a `FilePart` object. If it finds one, it then obtains the filename and sets up the user's upload folder.

This is done by getting the user-specified folder from a parameter and appending this to the root of the Cocoon context path. The context path is obtained by the following line:

```
String realPath = context.getRealPath("/");
```

This does mean that the storage location is relative to the context root. Of course, this could be changed or overridden. In fact, providing this type of flexibility via configuration parameters would be a logical development of the action. The code then checks that the upload folder exists, creating it if need be.

The next section of the code handles the storing of the uploaded file to the user-specified location. If the serialized object, interpreted as `FilePart`, is actually an instance of the subclass, then the process is a simple renaming of the existing file to the new name. If the object is a really a `FilePart`, it will be streamed as a new file in the user-specified folder. This is all done in the following fragment:

```
 if ( value instanceof FilePartFile )
 {

   ( (FilePartFile)value ).getFile().renameTo(
       new File( uploadFolder +
           File.separator + filename) );
   }
   else
   {
```

```
    FileOutputStream out = new
         FileOutputStream( uploadFolder +
             File.separator + filename );
    InputStream in = ( (FilePart)value ).getInputStream();

    int read = in.read( buffer );

    while ( read > 0 )
    {
      out.write( buffer, 0, read );
      read = in.read( buffer );
    }

    out.close();
  }

  request.setAttribute( "upload-file", filename );

}
else if ( value instanceof String )
{
  getLogger().debug( "Skipping parameter: " + (String)value );
}
else
{
  getLogger().debug("something else");
}
```

If there are any problems, the `act()` method returns `null`. This gets interpreted by the sitemap as a failure of the action, and thus processing stops; otherwise, processing will continue. The action also places a parameter on the request reflecting the name of the uploaded file.

The action can be tested using a couple of simple entries in the sitemap and a basic form. The form, presented in Listing 15.2, allows the user to browse for a file and then submits it as multipart form data, along with a hidden field (`upload-dir`) that contains the name of the upload folder. The pipeline entry that is called in response uses the action to copy the file. It also gets the name of the upload folder from the request and sets up a parameter for the action to grab hold of.

Listing 15.2 *upload-form.html*

```
<?xml version="1.0" encoding="UTF-8"?>
<html>
<head><title>This form allows you upload files</title></head>
<body>
  <form method="post"
        enctype="multipart/form-data"
        action="do-upload">
    <p>
      Please select the file that you wish to upload:<br/>
      File: <input type="file" name="uploaded-file" size="50" />
    </p>
    <p>
      <input type="submit" value="Upload File" />
      <input type="hidden" name="upload-dir" value="upload"/>
    </p>
  </form>
</body>
</html>
```

The sitemap contains the following three fragments that, respectively, configure the action, provide a pipeline entry to display the form, and handle the submission of the form:

```
<map:actions>
  <map:action
    logger="sitemap.action.fileuploadaction"
    name="fileupload"
    src="com.pigbite.cdh.acting.FileUploadAction"/>
</map:actions>

...

<map:match pattern="upload-form.html">
  <map:generate src="upload-form.html"/>
  <map:serialize type="html"/>
</map:match>

<map:match pattern="do-upload">
  <map:act type="request">
    <map:parameter name="parameters" value="true"/>
    <map:act type="fileupload">
      <map:parameter name="upload-dir" value="{upload-dir}" />
```

```
      <map:generate src="upload-form.html"/>
      <map:serialize type="html"/>
    </map:act>
  </map:act>
</map:match>
```

Any files uploaded using this form will be placed in a folder called `upload`, straight off the Cocoon context root, typically `$CATALINA_HOME/webapps/cocoon`.

Summary

In this chapter we have covered many of the key interfaces, classes, methods, and components that will enable you to make a strong start in extending Cocoon. We have examined the areas of Avalon that directly affect how you develop your extensions and what functionality can be inherited. The chapter also highlighted some parts of the Cocoon infrastructure that can be of use to the developer. After having looked at how to develop key sitemap components such as generators and actions, you should also be well equipped to start implementing your own code and making Cocoon do even more of what *you* want it to do.

CHAPTER 16

Cocoon Interfaces: Databases

One nice feature about Cocoon is the robustness of its interfaces. Modern-day application development almost always involves interfaces with various external resources such as databases, LDAP servers, and SOAP servers. In this and the next two chapters, we will explore some of the interfaces that Cocoon uses to talk to these resources. First, we will discuss database interfaces, both with traditional SQL databases, using JDBC, and with XML databases, using the XML:DB API.

Database Connectivity in Cocoon

Part II of this book, "Getting Started with Cocoon," has several examples of database connectivity. All told, there are three ways to interface with databases:

- XSPs via the ESQL logicsheet
- The `SQLTransformer`
- Actions

We will review these methods here, but this time we'll focus on the capabilities and limitations of each method for both selects and database update operations.

Enabling Database Access

Remember that database connectivity and pooling in Cocoon is handled by the Excalibur part of Avalon. To create a database pool, several steps are required. For details on these steps, refer to Chapter 8, "Using Content Logic: XSPs." Here are the necessary steps:

1. Make the JDBC JAR available to Cocoon—this means placing the JAR file someplace where Cocoon's classloader can find it.
2. Instruct Cocoon to preload the JDBC driver—here we edit Cocoon's `web.xml` so that Cocoon will know to load the driver.
3. Define the connection pool—this is done in Cocoon's `cocoon.xconf` and involves defining a pool name and providing the database URL, userid, password, and various optional attributes.

Database Select Examples

For our review, we'll assume that we have a simple table that lists some of the built-in Cocoon components (why not, because this is a Cocoon book—you'd have to know we would have the information listed somewhere on our servers!). The definition of this table is shown in Listing 16.1. Note that we're putting this table in the `abc` database that was created in Chapter 8.

Listing 16.1 *Simple Database Table (CocoonComponents.sql)*

```
use abc;

create table CocoonComponents (
ComponentType   varchar(20)     not null,
ComponentName   varchar(20)     not null,
ComponentClass  varchar(100)    not null
);

insert into CocoonComponents values ('Matcher', 'wildcard',
'org.apache.cocoon.matching.WildcardURIMatcher');
insert into CocoonComponents values ('Matcher', 'regexp',
'org.apache.cocoon.matching.RegexpURIMatcher');
insert into CocoonComponents values ('Matcher', 'request-parameter',
'org.apache.cocoon.matching.RequestParameterMatcher');
insert into CocoonComponents values ('Matcher', 'sessionstate',
'org.apache.cocoon.matching.WildcardSessionAttributeMatcher');
insert into CocoonComponents values ('Matcher', 'next-page',
```

Listing 16.1 *(continued)*

```
'org.apache.cocoon.matching.WildcardRequestParameterMatcher');
insert into CocoonComponents values ('Matcher', 'referer-match',
'org.apache.cocoon.matching.WildcardHeaderMatcher');
```

Note that for all the following examples we will use a `serializer` of type `xml` so that we can view the raw data. We'll take advantage of Internet Explorer's nifty XML presentation capabilities as well.

Simple Select Using the ESQL Logicsheet

Listing 16.2 shows a simple database `select` statement implemented using the ESQL logicsheet. In this case, we've chosen to define the tags for each column rather than use the ESQL default, which is the actual table column name.

Listing 16.2 *ESQL Logicsheet Select Example (simpleselect.xsp)*

```
<?xml version="1.0" encoding="ISO-8859-1"?>

<xsp:page language="java"
  xmlns:xsp="http://apache.org/xsp"
  xmlns:esql="http://apache.org/cocoon/SQL/v2"
>

  <page>

   <title>Simple select using ESQL logicsheet</title>

   <content>

   <esql:connection>
     <esql:pool>abc</esql:pool>
     <esql:execute-query>
       <esql:query>select * from CocoonComponents</esql:query>
       <esql:results>
        <components>
         <esql:row-results>
           <component>
            <type><esql:get-string column="ComponentType"/></type>
            <name><esql:get-string column="ComponentName"/></name>
            <class><esql:get-string column="ComponentClass"/></class>
           </component>
```

Listing 16.2 *(continued)*

```
          </esql:row-results>
        </components>
      </esql:results>
    </esql:execute-query>
  </esql:connection>

  </content>
 </page>
</xsp:page>
```

Our pipeline is as follows:

```
<map:match pattern="simpleselect.xsp">
 <map:generate type="serverpages" src="xsp/simpleselect.xsp"/>
 <map:serialize type="xml"/>
</map:match>
```

The raw output from this page is shown in Figure 16.1.

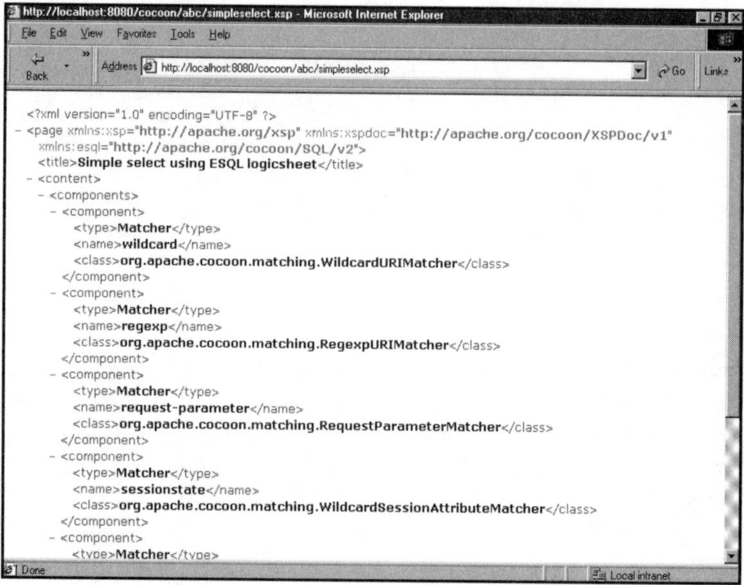

Figure 16.1
ESQL Logicsheet select example—output.

Simple Select Using the SQLTransformer

You first saw the `SQLTransformer` in action in Chapter 10, "Using Content Logic: Transformers." Here, in Listing 16.3, we can rewrite our database select command as an XML file that will be processed by the `SQLTransformer`.

Listing 16.3 *SQLTransformer Select Example (simpleselect.xml)*

```
<?xml version="1.0"?>

<page xmlns:sql="http://apache.org/cocoon/SQL/2.0">
 <title>Simple select using SQLTransformer</title>
 <content>
  <execute-query xmlns="http://apache.org/cocoon/SQL/2.0">
   <query>select * from CocoonComponents</query>
  </execute-query>
 </content>
</page>
```

The pipeline that handles this is shown here:

```
<map:match pattern="simpleselect.xml">
 <map:generate type="file" src="content/simpleselect.xml"/>
 <map:transform type="sql" label="raw">
  <map:parameter name="use-connection" value="abc"/>
 </map:transform>
 <map:serialize type="xml"/>
</map:match>
```

The output is shown in Figure 16.2.

Simple Select Using the DatabaseSelectAction

The final way to do a database select is by using the `DatabaseSelectAction`. The database actions (`DatabaseAddAction`, `DatabaseUpdateAction`, `DatabaseSelectAction`, and `DatabaseDeleteAction`) in the current 2.0.x versions of Cocoon are admittedly works in progress. (There are actually six objects, because there are two Oracle-specific actions: `OraAddAction` and `OraUpdateAction`.) The most robust of the four is the `DatabaseAddAction` action, which we have already encountered in Chapter 12, "Using Sitemap Logic: Actions and Forms." However, in some situations the others are certainly useful.

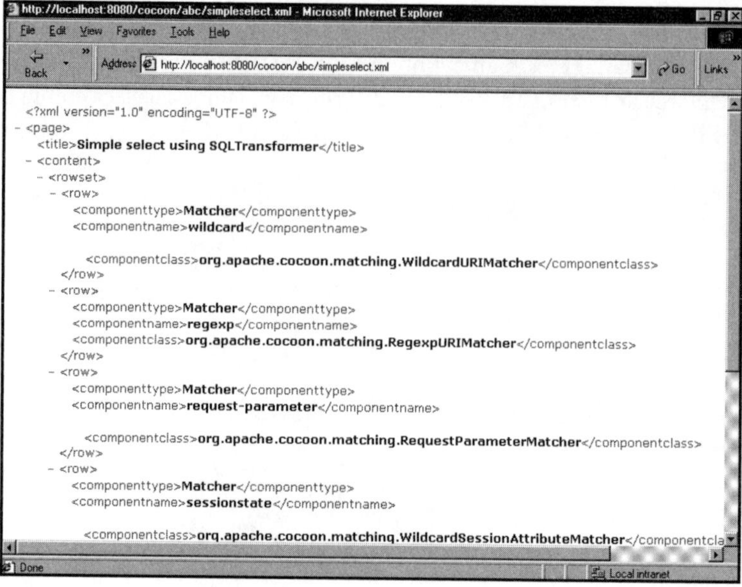
http://localhost:8080/cocoon/abc/simpleselect.xml - Microsoft Internet Explorer
File Edit View Favorites Tools Help
Back
Address http://localhost:8080/cocoon/abc/simpleselect.xml
Go
Links
<?xml version="1.0" encoding="UTF-8" ?>
- <page>
<title>Simple select using SQLTransformer</title>
- <content>
- <rowset>
- <row>
<componenttype>Matcher</componenttype>
<componentname>wildcard</componentname>
<componentclass>org.apache.cocoon.matching.WildcardURIMatcher</componentclass>
</row>
- <row>
<componenttype>Matcher</componenttype>
<componentname>regexp</componentname>
<componentclass>org.apache.cocoon.matching.RegexpURIMatcher</componentclass>
</row>
- <row>
<componenttype>Matcher</componenttype>
<componentname>request-parameter</componentname>
<componentclass>org.apache.cocoon.matching.RequestParameterMatcher</componentclass>
</row>
- <row>
<componenttype>Matcher</componenttype>
<componentname>sessionstate</componentname>
<componentclass>org.apache.cocoon.matching.WildcardSessionAttributeMatcher</componentcla
Done
Local intranet

Figure 16.2
SQLTransformer select example—output.

> **Future of Database Actions**
> In the scratchpad area of Cocoon 2.0.3 or in the main area of 2.1, you can find modular database actions. These are a redesign of the current set, and they include auto-increment and set features. For more information, consult `http://xml.apache.org/ cocoon/userdocs/actions/database-actions.html` and `http://xml.apache.org/cocoon/ userdocs/concepts/modules.html`.

Before we can use any of these actions to access our table, we need to do two things. First, let's add the definition for the `DatabaseSelectAction` to the `<map:actions>` section of the sitemap (remember, this section typically comes at the end of the `<map:components>` block). While we're at it, we'll show the definition for the `DatabaseAddAction` as well, because we'll need it later in the chapter. Note that if you followed along with Chapter 12, you would already have the `DatabaseAddAction` defined.

```
<map:actions>
 <map:action name="select" logger="sitemap.action.select"
   src="org.apache.cocoon.acting.DatabaseSelectAction"/>
 <map:action name="insert" logger="sitemap.action.insert"
   src="org.apache.cocoon.acting.DatabaseAddAction"/>
 <!-- other actions -->
</map:actions>
```

Now we need to create a definition file that describes the table structure, as shown in Listing 16.4.

Listing 16.4 *CocoonComponents Definition Table (simple.xml)*

```
<?xml version="1.0" encoding="UTF-8"?>

<components>
  <connection>abc</connection>
  <table name="CocoonComponents">
    <keys>
     <key param="type" dbcol="ComponentType" type="string" mode="form"/>
     <key param="name" dbcol="ComponentName" type="string" mode="form"/>
    </keys>
    <values>
     <value param="class" dbcol="ComponentClass" type="string"/>
    </values>
  </table>
</components>
```

Although we don't have any declarative statements in our table definition, we must provide the key information in this definition file. The columns contained in the `<keys>` block define the primary keys for the table. The `DatabaseSelectAction` will expect to find them, and will be unable to execute the `select` statement properly. Notice too the `mode` attribute in the `<key>` tags—this tells the actions that a form will provide the values for these keys.

The `DatabaseSelectAction` is really meant for single-row result sets. It creates a `select` statement based on the keys and the incoming request data. If one or more rows are returned, the values for the first or only row will be set in the `request` object as attributes. An empty `Map` object will be returned as well so that components inside the `<map:act>` statement can execute.

A simple pipeline to demonstrate this action is shown in the following text. Because the row results will be returned within the `Request` object as attributes, we need a way to view those attributes. There is a generator called the `RequestGenerator` that spits out details about the request object. However, it does not provide information on request attributes. Because it is a useful thing to know, we'll show you how to modify this `Generator` so that it does provide request attribute information. If you'd prefer to simply see what the output looks like, skip down to Figure 16.3.

To make the changes, edit the file `RequestGenerator.java` in the `src/java/org/apache/cocoon/generation` directory of the Cocoon source distribution. In the `generate()` method, after the request headers are printed, we'll add the following:

```
this.data("  ");
this.start("requestAttributes",attr);
this.data("\n");
Enumeration rattributes=request.getAttributeNames();
while (rattributes.hasMoreElements()) {
    String rattribute=(String)rattributes.nextElement();
    this.attribute(attr,"name",rattribute);
    this.data("    ");
    this.start("attribute",attr);
    this.data("\n");
    String value=(String)request.getAttribute(rattribute);
    if (value!=null) {
        this.data("      ");
        this.start("value",attr);
        if (form_encoding != null) {
            try {
                this.data(new String(value.getBytes(
                    container_encoding), form_encoding));
            } catch(java.io.UnsupportedEncodingException uee) {
                throw new RuntimeException("Unsupported
                        Encoding Exception: " + uee.getMessage());
            }
        } else {
            this.data(value);
        }
        this.end("value");
        this.data("\n");
    }
    this.data("    ");
    this.end("attribute");
    this.data("\n");
}
this.data("  ");
this.end("requestAttributes");
this.data("\n");
this.data("\n");
```

After you've done this, you'll need to compile Cocoon as described in Chapter 6, "Installing Cocoon." You do not need to redeploy the application—simply copy `cocoon-2.0.3.jar` from the `build/cocoon/webap/WEB-INF/lib` directory to the `WEB-INF/lib` directory of your Cocoon webapp. Besides restarting the servlet container, no other changes are required.

With our new `RequestGenerator` (or without, if you'd prefer), we can set up a pipeline for this example:

```
<map:match pattern="simpleselect.act">
  <map:act type="select">
   <map:parameter name="descriptor"
      value="context://abc/content/defs/simple.xml"/>

   <map:generate type="request"/>
   <map:serialize type="xml"/>
  </map:act>
</map:match>
```

As you can see, we reference the `DatabaseSelectAction` using the literal `select` that we assigned to this action in its definition previously. The output is shown in Figure 16.3.

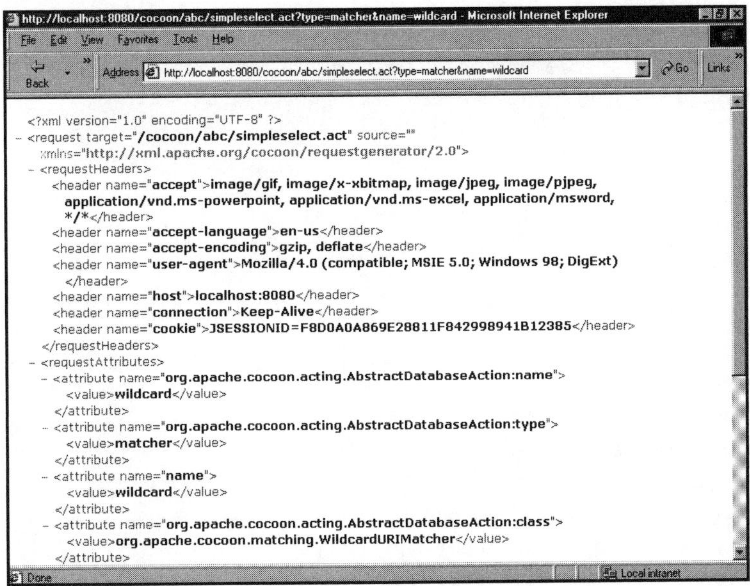

Figure 16.3
DatabaseSelectAction example—output.

We must provide values for each key defined in the definition file. Otherwise, the query will fail.

Database Insert Examples

Now that we've seen three ways to select from a database table, let's look at three ways to insert data into our table. As with the select examples, we'll cover use of the ESQL logicsheet, `SQLTransformer`, and a database action. For this example, we'll assume that we've created a form for users to add rows to our `CocoonComponents` table.

Simple Insert Using the ESQL Logicsheet

First, let's see how to do the insert using the ESQL logicsheet. Our XSP is shown in Listing 16.5.

Listing 16.5 *ESQL Logicsheet Insert Example (simpleinsert.xsp)*

```
<?xml version="1.0" encoding="ISO-8859-1"?>

<xsp:page language="java"
  xmlns:xsp="http://apache.org/xsp"
  xmlns:esql="http://apache.org/cocoon/SQL/v2"
  xmlns:xsp-request="http://apache.org/xsp/request/2.0"
>

  <page>

   <title>Simple insert using ESQL logicsheet</title>

   <content>

   <esql:connection>
     <esql:pool>abc</esql:pool>
     <esql:execute-query>
       <esql:query>
         insert into CocoonComponents values (
         '<xsp-request:get-parameter name="type"/>',
         '<xsp-request:get-parameter name="name"/>',
         '<xsp-request:get-parameter name="class"/>')        </esql:query>
       <esql:update-results/>
       <esql:error-results>
         <paragraph><esql:get-message/></paragraph>
       </esql:error-results>
     </esql:execute-query>
   </esql:connection>
```

Listing 16.5 *(continued)*

```
    </content>
  </page>
</xsp:page>
```

Again, we are expecting the column values to be stored in the request object. The `<esql:update-results/>` call is the guy that does the actual insert (by calling `executeUpdate()` on the `Statement` object).

The pipeline for this example is shown here:

```
<map:match pattern="simpleinsert.xsp">
 <map:generate type="serverpages" src="xsp/simpleinsert.xsp"/>
 <map:serialize type="xml"/>
</map:match>
```

Simple Insert Using the SQLTransformer

If we want to have a similarly dynamic insert using the `SQLTransformer`, we need to start with the XML file shown in Listing 16.6.

Listing 16.6 *SQLTransformer Insert Example—XML File (simpleinsert.xml)*

```
<?xml version="1.0"?>

<page>
 <title>Simple insert using SQLTransformer</title>
 <content>
   <query>
    insert into CocoonComponents values ('<type/>', '<name/>', '<class/>')
   </query>
 </content>
</page>
```

The tags `<type>`, `<name>`, and `<class>` are placeholders that denote the input parameters that will be provided by the request.

The XML file next needs to be transformed into something that can be handled by the `SQLTransformer`, using the stylesheet shown in Listing 16.7.

Listing 16.7 *SQLTransformer Insert Example—XSL File (simpleinsert-prep.xsl)*

```
<?xml version="1.0"?>

<xsl:stylesheet version="1.0"
```

Listing 16.7 *(continued)*

```
  xmlns:xsl="http://www.w3.org/1999/XSL/Transform"
  xmlns:sql="http://apache.org/cocoon/SQL/2.0"
>

 <xsl:param name="type"/>
 <xsl:param name="name"/>
 <xsl:param name="class"/>

 <xsl:template match="/">
  <xsl:apply-templates/>
 </xsl:template>

 <xsl:template match="query">
  <execute-query xmlns="http://apache.org/cocoon/SQL/2.0">
    <query><xsl:apply-templates/></query>
  </execute-query>
 </xsl:template>

 <xsl:template match="type">
  <xsl:value-of select="$type"/>
 </xsl:template>

 <xsl:template match="name">
  <xsl:value-of select="$name"/>
 </xsl:template>

 <xsl:template match="class">
  <xsl:value-of select="$class"/>
 </xsl:template>

 <xsl:template match="*" priority="-1">
  <xsl:element name="{local-name()}">
   <xsl:apply-templates select="@*|node()"/>
  </xsl:element>
 </xsl:template>

 <xsl:template match="@*" priority="-1">
  <xsl:copy/>
 </xsl:template>

</xsl:stylesheet>
```

The three <xsl:param> tags refer to the request parameters that will be accessible to this stylesheet. Essentially, we are customizing the query by replacing the placeholder tags with the actual values in the request. The last two templates handle all the other tags in the incoming file and pass them straight through. Whenever you are dynamically building an XML file using XSLT for the SQLTransformer to handle, you must have these two templates—don't be tempted to combine them or use the kind of template we have for other examples, because they will not work.

All this is hung together with the following pipeline:

```
<map:match pattern="simpleinsert.xml">
 <map:generate type="file" src="content/simpleinsert.xml"/>
 <map:transform type="xslt" src="style/simpleinsert-prep.xsl">
   <map:parameter name="use-request-parameters" value="true"/>
 </map:transform>
 <map:transform type="sql">
  <map:parameter name="use-connection" value="abc"/>
 </map:transform>
 <map:serialize type="xml"/>
</map:match>
```

Simple Insert Using the DatabaseAddAction

In this case, the DatabaseAddAction is the simplest of all. Using the definition file built earlier, all we need is a simple pipeline (remember that we already defined this action in the <map:actions> block):

```
<map:match pattern="simpleinsert.act">
  <map:act type="insert">
   <map:parameter name="descriptor"
      value="context://abc/content/defs/simple.xml"/>
   <map:serialize type="xml"/>
  </map:act>
</map:match>
```

Of course, a proper pipeline would give the user some sort of confirmation page or at least redirect to the original form.

The DatabaseAddAction has useful feature for automatically creating numeric ids. Suppose our table had a primary key called ComponentId and was an integer. If we defined the <keys> section in the definition file like

```
<keys>
 <key param="id" dbcol="ComponentId" type="int" mode="manual"/>
</keys>
```

then the action would automatically look up the highest value for `ComponentId` in that table, add 1 to it, and use that value for the insert statement.

Stored Procedures

Stored procedures, if your database supports them, can be a smart way of hiding database logic from your application and a good way to implement the Separation of Concerns that we talked about in Chapter 2, "Avalon." In Cocoon, stored procedures are supported by both the ESQL Logicsheet and the `SQLTransformer`. The details of the implementation are somewhat database dependent, so you'll have to consult the documentation carefully and expect to do some experimentation.

Stored Procedures with the ESQL Logicsheet

In the ESQL logicsheet, for example, the format for calling a stored procedures is something like this:

```
<xsp:logic>
  String componentType = "Matcher";
</xsp:logic>

<esql:connection>
  <esql:pool>abc</esql:pool>
  <esql:execute-query>
    <esql:call>{call GetComponents(<esql:parameter direction="in"
      type="String"><xsp:expr>componentType</xsp:expr></esql:parameter>)}
    </esql:call>
    <esql:results>
     <components>
      <esql:row-results>
        <component>
         <type><esql:get-string column="ComponentType"/></type>
         <name><esql:get-string column="ComponentName"/></name>
         <class><esql:get-string column="ComponentClass"/></class>
        </component>
      </esql:row-results>
     </components>
    </esql:results>
  </esql:execute-query>
</esql:connection>
```

In this example, all we've done is replaced the `<esql:query>` tag from the earlier example (Listing 16.2) with an `<esql:call>` tag. This tag invokes a stored procedure that takes a single input parameter, which provides the procedure with a component type. The procedure then queries our table with a `select` statement, thereby providing a result set for us to process. The result set can be handled with the `<esql:results>` and `<esql:row-results>` tags as was done before.

Sometimes, your stored procedure will return output parameters rather than a result set. The ESQL Logicsheet can handle this too, but the exact format will be dependent on your database. For example, if our previous stored procedure returned only three parameters, one for each column in the table (we'll assume that only one row is returned), we might have something like this:

```
<xsp:logic>
  String componentType = "Matcher";
</xsp:logic>

<esql:connection>
  <esql:pool>abc</esql:pool>
  <esql:execute-query>
    <esql:call>{call GetComponents(<esql:parameter direction="in"
      type="String"><xsp:expr>componentType</xsp:expr></esql:parameter>)}
    </esql:call>
    <esql:call-results>
      <component>
       <type><esql:get-string column="ComponentType" from-call="yes"/></type>
       <name><esql:get-string column="ComponentName" from-call="yes"/></name>
       <class><esql:get-string column="ComponentClass" from-call="yes"/></class>
      </component>
    </esql:call-results>
  </esql:execute-query>
</esql:connection>
```

Note the use of the `<esql:call-results>` tag instead of the `<esql:results>` tag. This tells Cocoon to expect output parameters instead of a result set. When specifying the `<esql:get-`*`xxx`*`>` tags, where *`xxx`* refers to the value type, we need to add the attribute `from-call="yes"` so that Cocoon knows to retrieve the values from the `CallableStatement` object instead of a result set.

Stored Procedures with the SQLTransformer

We can write the same query using the `SQLTransformer`. The following fragment shows how to access a stored procedure that returns a result set. This is an Oracle-specific example.

```
<page xmlns:sql="http://apache.org/cocoon/SQL/2.0">
  <execute-query xmlns="http://apache.org/cocoon/SQL/2.0">
```

```
    <query isstoredprocedure="true">
      begin GetComponents('Matcher'); end;
    </query>
    <out-parameter sql:nr="1" sql:name="resultset"
      sql:type="oracle.jdbc.driver.OracleTypes.CURSOR"/>
  </execute-query>
 </content>
</page>
```

Here, even though the stored procedure is returning a result set, we need to declare it as an output parameter of type `CURSOR`. With this declaration, the `SQLTransformer` will be able to return data with a `<rowset>` tag, as it did earlier.

Comparing Different Database Options

Now that we've reviewed these examples, let's look at the pros and cons for each approach.

ESQL Logicsheet

This logicsheet can be used only in XSPs. Because the XSP is the start of the pipeline, the database result set is available to all subsequent components. Within the XSP, the ESQL logicsheet allows you to create complex queries by nesting both connections and queries. Also advantageous is the fact that you can wrap result sets, rows, and columns in your own tags. In fact, you further customize output by changing output data as necessary.

One problem with this logicsheet is that when some database operations fail, they throw exceptions rather than the more appropriate `<esql:error-results>` tag. Another disadvantage to this logicsheet is maintainability. Although we users don't necessarily have to worry about editing it, the logicsheet implementation is rather complex and difficult to follow when debugging.

In general, use the ESQL logicsheet when you really need to customize output data tags, use complex queries, or combine the database operations with other Java logic. As an example, you might have a complex query form for a data warehousing application that will result in different database `select` statements depending on what values were filled out in the form. Using the XSP, we might first figure out the correct command inside an `<xsp:logic>` block and then reference a `String` variable containing that command when constructing the `<esql:query>` statement.

SQLTransformer

If you have a simple and straightforward SQL query, sometimes you can't beat the `SQLTransformer` for simplicity and elegance. This component is best suited for selects, however. Although you can do database update operations, as we have done here, it is difficult to trap failures. If it is important to know the outcome of such an operation, you're better off with the ESQL logicsheet and the `<esql:error-results>` tag.

Actions

Because actions can influence pipeline operation, by both what they return and whether they return anything, they can be useful when the result of a database operation can result in different pipeline processing. For example, we might query a user table and get the user's department. Based on the department name, we might use a different stylesheet or graphic.

Actions are also good for database operations because they can be placed anywhere in the pipeline and can be nested. Whereas the ESQL logicsheet can be used only in an XSP at the start of the pipeline, and the `SQLTransformer` must be used between `<map:generate>` and `<map:serialize>` tags, an action can go anywhere. The other nice thing about actions is that they rely on an external descriptor file that has been designed to hold database information for multiple uses so that developers do not have to create one file for each type of database operation.

A good rule for database actions is to use them either when you don't want to tie your database operations to a particular place in the pipeline or when the result of the database operations somehow will influence the pipeline. However, as we have seen, do not try to select multiple rows in an action: you'll only ever get one back!

Accessing Database Pools from Actions

There are cases when you need to write a custom action that interacts with a database. Thanks to the Avalon component framework, this is easy. Listing 16.8 shows an example of an action that retrieves customization settings for a user from a preferences table called `UserSettings`. The action will assume that the user has been authenticated and that the call to `request.getRemoteUser()` will return a valid user identifier. (This would happen, for example, if the servlet container performed authentication. You can see an example of this in Chapter 23, "Cocoon Administration.") If the user does not have any preferences saved in the table, some default values are added.

Listing 16.8 *Action Using Connection Pool Example (UserPrefsAction.java)*

```
package test;

import org.apache.avalon.excalibur.datasource.DataSourceComponent;
import org.apache.avalon.framework.component.ComponentException;
import org.apache.avalon.framework.component.ComponentManager;
import org.apache.avalon.framework.component.ComponentSelector;
```

Listing 16.8 *(continued)*

```
import org.apache.avalon.framework.parameters.Parameters;
import org.apache.avalon.framework.thread.ThreadSafe;
import org.apache.avalon.framework.component.Composable;
import org.apache.avalon.framework.activity.Disposable;
import org.apache.cocoon.Constants;
import org.apache.cocoon.environment.ObjectModelHelper;
import org.apache.cocoon.environment.Redirector;
import org.apache.cocoon.environment.Request;
import org.apache.cocoon.environment.SourceResolver;
import org.apache.cocoon.acting.AbstractAction;

import java.sql.Connection;
import java.sql.ResultSet;
import java.sql.Statement;
import java.sql.SQLException;

import java.util.Enumeration;
import java.util.HashMap;
import java.util.Map;

public class UserPrefsAction extends AbstractAction implements
 ThreadSafe, Composable, Disposable
{
    protected ComponentSelector dbselector;
    protected ComponentManager manager;

    public void compose(ComponentManager manager) throws ComponentException {
        this.dbselector = (ComponentSelector)
          manager.lookup(DataSourceComponent.ROLE + "Selector");

    }

    protected final DataSourceComponent getDataSource(String pool) throws
     ComponentException {
        return (DataSourceComponent) this.dbselector.select(pool);
    }

    public Map act( Redirector redirector, SourceResolver resolver,
            Map objectModel, String source, Parameters param )
        throws Exception
    {
```

Listing 16.8 *(continued)*

```
        Request request = ObjectModelHelper.getRequest(objectModel);
        Map map = new HashMap();
        DataSourceComponent dataSource = getDataSource("abc");
    Connection conn = null;

        try {
            conn = dataSource.getConnection();
            Statement stmt = conn.createStatement();
            String cmd = "select * from UserSettings where UserId = '" +
                request.getRemoteUser() + "'";
            ResultSet rs = stmt.executeQuery(cmd);

            if (rs.next()) {
                // If an entry was found, set the appropriate parameters
                map.put("user-name", rs.getString(1));
                map.put("user-dept", rs.getString(2));
                map.put("user-font-size", rs.getString(3));
                map.put("dept-image", rs.getString(4));
            } else {
                rs.close();
                // Otherwise, insert the defaults
                cmd = "insert into UserSettings values ('" +
                    request.getRemoteUser() + "', 'Default', '10pt', " +
                    "'images/default.gif')";
                stmt.executeUpdate(cmd);

                map.put("user-name", request.getRemoteUser());
                map.put("user-dept", "Default");
                map.put("user-font-size", "10pt");
                map.put("dept-image", "images/default.gif");
            }

            stmt.close();
     } catch (Exception e) {
         getLogger().error("Query failed: ", e);
     } finally {
         try {
            if (conn != null) conn.close();
            } catch (SQLException sqe) {
                getLogger().warn("Error closing the datasource", sqe);
            }
```

Listing 16.8 *(continued)*

```
        }

        return(map);
    }

    public void dispose() {
        this.manager.release(dbselector);
    }
}
```

The first thing to note is that this action is a `Composable` and `Disposable` component—that is, it implements these Avalon interfaces (refer to Chapter 2 for more on Avalon). All this means is that Cocoon will call the `compose()` method when the action is instantiated, and `dispose()` when it is decommissioned. When the former method is called, something called the `ComponentManager` is passed in. This object is used to retrieve a `ComponentSelector` that is then used to retrieve pool connections. It may seem like a lot of overhead with unfamiliar objects, but the net result is that you can retrieve a connection from the pool of your choice.

When the action retrieves the user customization settings from the table (or if it assigned defaults), it makes them available to the sitemap via a `Map` object. The sitemap can then have custom processing based on these values, or these parameters can be provided to the stylesheet for customization of the output.

If you want to try this example yourself, you'll need to create the `UserSettings` table in the `abc` database as shown here:

```
use abc;

create table UserSettings (
UserId         varchar(20)    not null,
UserName       varchar(50)    null,
UserDept       varchar(10)    null,
UserFontSize   varchar(10)    null,
UserDeptImage  varchar(50)    null
);
```

You will also have to compile the action as shown in Chapter 12. After it's compiled, we define this action in the `<map:actions>`:

```
<map:actions>
 <map:action name="userprefs" logger="sitemap.action.userprefs"
   src="test.UserPrefsAction"/>
 <!-- other actions go here -->
```

```
</map:actions>
```

Now we can use this action in a pipeline, as shown next. This is only a sample; you are encouraged to modify! Again, the real point here is in demonstrating how to access database connections from actions.

```
<map:match pattern="testpage">
 <map:act type="userprefs">
  <map:generate type="file" src="content/main.xml"/>
  <map:transform src="style/main.xsl">
   <map:parameter name="user-name" value="{user-name}"/>
   <map:parameter name="user-dept" value="{user-dept}"/>
   <map:parameter name="user-font-size" value="{user-font-size}"/>
   <map:parameter name="dept-image" value="{dept-image}"/>
  </map:transform>
  <map:serialize type="html"/>
 </map:act>

 <map:generate type="file" src="content/main.xml"/>
 <map:transform src="style/main.xsl"/>
 <map:serialize type="html"/>
</map:match>
```

As you can see, the four parameters that are retrieved by the action are made available to the `main.xsl` stylesheet. In this stylesheet, you can pull these in using `<param>` tags before any templates are defined. Then, in your templates, you can display a custom greeting for the user, display text in the user's preferred font size, and show the department logo somewhere in the page.

If you need database connections from a custom component such as your own `generator` or `transformer`, you'll be happy to hear that the method we just demonstrated in this action is the same for those components as well. Just be sure to implement the correct interfaces and don't leave a connection open longer than necessary.

Working with XML Databases

When it comes to dealing with XML databases, Cocoon is a nice fit. Because an XML database produces, well, XML, it is very easy to use the output from a database query as the input to a pipeline. And that is exactly how it works with Xindice.

Xindice is yet another Apache Software Foundation project and can be found at `http://xml.apache.org/xindice/`. Xindice is a native XML database, or NXD. What is a native XML database? It is simply a database that stores and retrieves XML documents according to a logical XML model. There is an initiative (you'd expect it, right?) called the "XML:DB Initiative" that seeks to standardize various aspects of XML databases: database API, update language, query language, and so on. You can read all about it at `http://www.xmldb.org`. Xindice implements the XML:DB XUpdate and XML:DB API specifications from this Initiative and uses XPath as its query language. The XML:DB API is implemented in Java, which is a good thing for us, because that is how Cocoon will talk to Xindice.

> **More About XML Databases**
> A good introduction to the subject of XML databases by Kimbro Staken can be found at http://www.xml.com/pub/a/2001/10/31/nativexmldb.html. An up-to-date list of XML databases and related products is maintained by Ronald Bourret at http://www.rpbourret.com/xml/XMLDatabaseProds.htm.

To use Xindice with Cocoon, we'll have to set up Xindice, add some data, and configure Cocoon.

Setting Up Xindice

First, download Xindice from `http://xml.apache.org/xindice/` in the archive format you prefer. Unpack it in the desired location. We'll refer to the Xindice directory as `$XINDICE_HOME`. In fact, you'll have to set that variable, add `$XINDICE_HOME/bin` to your `$PATH` variable, and add `Xindice.jar` to your `CLASSPATH`. On Windows, you can type the following, using the correct path, of course:

```
set XINDICE_HOME=c:\apps\xml-xindice-1.0
set PATH=%PATH%;%XINDICE_HOME%\bin
set CLASSPATH=%CLASSPATH%;%XINDICE_HOME\java\lib\xindice.jar
```

On Unix you type this:

```
export XINDICE_HOME=/opt/xml-xindice-1.0
export PATH=$PATH:$XINDICE_HOME/bin
export CLASSPATH=$CLASSPATH:$XINDICE_HOME%/java/lib/xindice.jar
```

After the environment is set up, you can `cd` to `$XINDICE_HOME` (or `%XINDICE_HOME%` on Windows) and type

```
startup
```

on Windows or

```
start
```

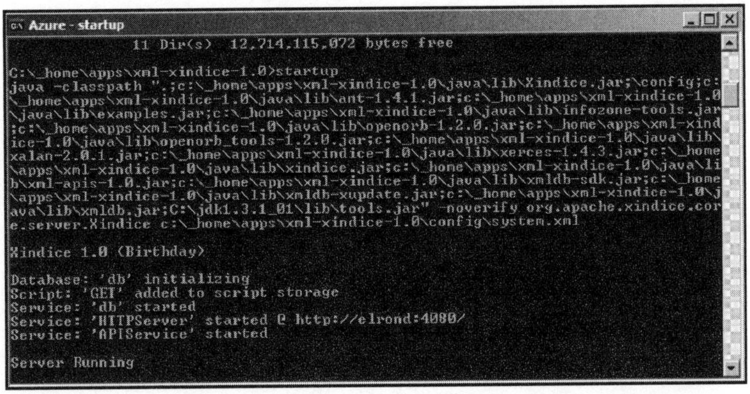

```
Azure - startup
               11 Dir(s)  12,714,115,072 bytes free

C:\_home\apps\xml-xindice-1.0>startup
java -classpath ".;c:\_home\apps\xml-xindice-1.0\java\lib\Xindice.jar;\config;c:
\_home\apps\xml-xindice-1.0\java\lib\ant-1.4.1.jar;c:\_home\apps\xml-xindice-1.0
\java\lib\examples.jar;c:\_home\apps\xml-xindice-1.0\java\lib\infozone-tools.jar
;c:\_home\apps\xml-xindice-1.0\java\lib\openorb-1.2.0.jar;c:\_home\apps\xml-xind
ice-1.0\java\lib\openorb_tools-1.2.0.jar;c:\_home\apps\xml-xindice-1.0\java\lib\
xalan-2.0.1.jar;c:\_home\apps\xml-xindice-1.0\java\lib\xerces-1.4.3.jar;c:\_home
\apps\xml-xindice-1.0\java\lib\xindice.jar;c:\_home\apps\xml-xindice-1.0\java\li
b\xml-apis-1.0.jar;c:\_home\apps\xml-xindice-1.0\java\lib\xmldb-sdk.jar;c:\_home
\apps\xml-xindice-1.0\java\lib\xmldb-xupdate.jar;c:\_home\apps\xml-xindice-1.0\j
ava\lib\xmldb.jar;C:\jdk1.3.1_01\lib\tools.jar" -noverify org.apache.xindice.cor
e.server.Xindice c:\_home\apps\xml-xindice-1.0\config\system.xml

Xindice 1.0 (Birthday)

Database: 'db' initializing
Script: 'GET' added to script storage
Service: 'db' started
Service: 'HTTPServer' started @ http://elrond:4080/
Service: 'APIService' started

Server Running
```

on Unix. If all goes well, you'll see something like what's shown in Figure 16.4.

Figure 16.4
The Xindice startup screen.

Adding Data to Xindice

Xindice comes with an AddressBook example you can install. To add data to it, you'll have to build and install the AddressBook Web applications. For our purposes, however, we'll create our own database and store in it information about Cocoon components, similar to what we used earlier in the chapter.

First, we need to create some XML files that store the information. Listing 16.9 shows one such file, holding information about a Cocoon component. (The other files, `data2.xml`, `data3.xml`, and `data4.xml`, are included in the code download for this chapter.) Because an XML database operates on XML documents, we will provide data as flat file XML files. We'll look at another insert option later.

Listing 16.9 *Sample Xindice Input File (data1.xml)*

```
<?xml version="1.0"?>

<cocoon-component>
 <component-type>matcher</component-type>
 <component-name>wildcard</component-name>
 <component-class>
  org.apache.cocoon.matching.WildcardURIMatcher
 </component-class>
</cocoon-component>
```

Before we can add this file, we need to create a collection. Briefly, a collection is a grouping of XML documents, and one or more collections belong to a database instance. Xindice comes already with one such instance, called db. Therefore, we can create our own collection like this:

```
xindiceadmin ac -c /db -n cocoon
```

Then it's a simple matter to add our file:

```
xindice ad -c /db/cocoon -f lajos/data1.xml
```

We continue like this until all the necessary files are added. Because the top-level tag of each file is <cocoon-component>, that will be the top-level content of the cocoon collection.

Configuring Cocoon for Xindice

Before we can create a pipeline using Xindice, we need to copy $XINDICE_HOME/java/lib/xindice.jar to $CATALINA_HOME/webapps/cocoon/WEB-INF/lib and restart Cocoon. Then we can create a pipeline like this:

```
<map:match pattern="xindiceselect/**">
 <map:generate type="file"
   src="xmldb:xindice://localhost:4080/db/cocoon/#/{1}"/>
 <map:serialize type="xml"/>
</map:match>
```

This bears some explanation. To start with, we are using the FileGenerator with the xmldb pseudo protocol. Remember, pseudo protocols are a shorthand for Cocoon to access resources via specific methods. The xmldb pseudo protocol defines a way for Cocoon to access XML databases via the XML:DB API. The URI after the xmldb: consists of the xindice protocol followed by the server host/port, in this case the default, and then the database instance, db; the collection, cocoon; and then the actual query after the #. Xindice uses XPath as the query language, so any kind of select involves an XPath statement of some sort. Generically, we can write the correct format for this kind of URI as shown here:

```
xmldb:xindice://<host>[:<port>]/[database-instance]/[collection]/#<XPath-query>
```

We can, of course, write our pipeline to allow dynamic passing in of database instance and collection identifiers, but it isn't necessary here.

Let's experiment. First, we'll query all the documents in the cocoon collection using the URL http://localhost:8080/cocoon/abc/xindiceselect/cocoon-component. In Figure 16.5, you can see we actually have four such documents. The main tag for the search results is the <collection-results> tag, which contains a <collection-result> block for each hit. Each of these in turn contains a <cocoon-component> tag, corresponding to one of the documents that were added to our earlier collection. You can see that the three child tags in each document, `<component-type>`, `<component-name>`, and `<component-class>`, are shown under each main tag.

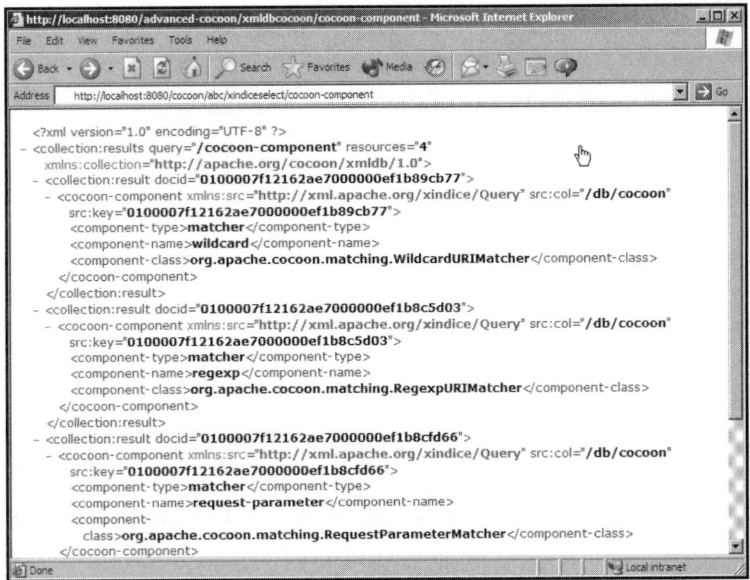

Figure 16.5
Xindice query #1.

Now let's try to find one of the documents using a bit more complicated XPath search string: `http://localhost:8080/cocoon/abc/xindiceselect/cocoon-component [component-name='regexp']`. Figure 16.6 shows the results.

Adding Documents to Xindice with Cocoon

If you think that adding new documents to Xindice using the flat file method is tedious, not to mention redundant, you are right. The AddressBook Web application that comes with Xindice allows you to add new context programmatically to that collection. However, because is this a Cocoon book, let's do it with a Cocoon component. And because there isn't one, we'll write our own and submit it to the Cocoon project! We'll choose an action, because we can use it anywhere in the pipeline. What we have to do is to take the results of a form, create an XML document, and insert it into Xindice.

It would be nice to make this action able to handle more than just the simple example used in this chapter. In fact, a robust component should be able to handle not just different

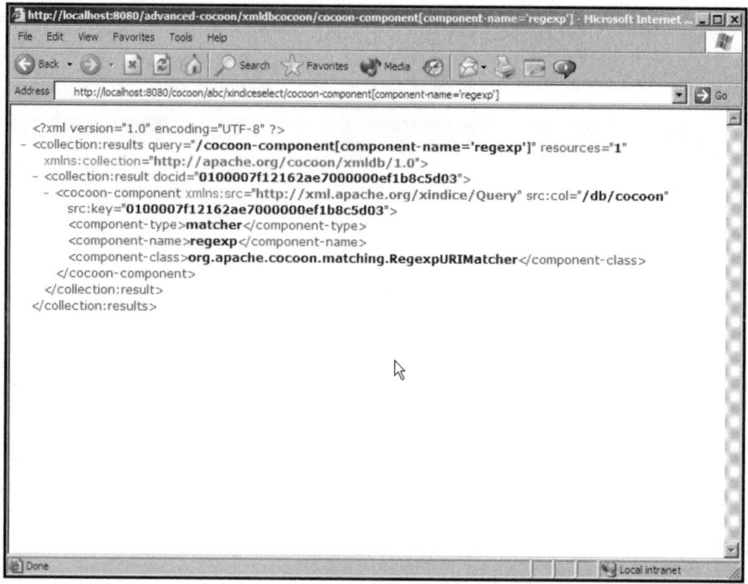

documents but different collection names, database names, and host information.

Figure 16.6
Xindice query #2.

There is a simple way to accomplish all these things, and that is with a descriptor or definition file similar to the one used by the database actions in Chapter 12. In that chapter, as well as earlier in this one, we used descriptor files to define tables, columns, and validation rules. The thing to understand about descriptor files is that they are really just XML documents that can contain any tags you want them to. They don't just have to describe database connection or table information; they can contain any valid XML. Typically, though, they are used to provide structured parameter data to a component. If you programmed in Java for any length of time, you are familiar with properties files, which provide a series of name/value pairs that can be automatically loaded into a `java.util.Properties` object. Such properties files have their use, but are limited in that they cannot represent structured settings. Descriptor files, on the other hand, can, and they are therefore extremely powerful little tools.

If you are envisioning writing a custom XML parser to handle your own descriptor file, stop worrying. Using descriptor files is easy in actions, thanks to something called the `AbstractComplementaryConfigurableAction` and an Avalon object, `Configuration`. This is the same action that forms the basis for the database actions. (If you look at the code for actions such as `DatabaseAddAction`, you'll see that each of them extends

AbstractDatabaseAction, which, in turn, extends AbstractComplementaryConfigurableAction.) This abstract action is able to take a descriptor file and return a Configuration object. This Configuration object represents all the settings in the file in the correct hierarchical order. It comes complete with methods that can be used to access individual configuration parameters or arrays of such parameters. Just like the database actions, our new action will expect that the path to the descriptor file will be provided via a sitemap input parameter. In the pipeline, this will show up as a <map:parameter> tag. We'll see this pipeline in a moment.

The descriptor file that will be expected by our new action is shown in Listing 16.10.

Listing 16.10 *XindiceInsertAction—Sample Descriptor File (xindice.xml)*

```
<?xml version="1.0" encoding="UTF-8"?>

<document-descriptor>
  <host>localhost</host>
  <port>4080</port>
  <database>db</database>
  <collection>cocoon</collection>

  <document name="cocoon-component">
   <element name="component-type"/>
   <element name="component-name"/>
   <element name="component-class"/>
  </document>
</document-descriptor>
```

As you can see, we expect this file to contain host, port, database, and collection information. The idea is that each file contains all the document definitions pertinent to a specific collection; in other words, the descriptor file is collection specific. In our example, we have only one document, called cocoon-component. The value of the name attribute of this tag will become the root element of the document we'll create during the insert process. For each <element> under the <document> tag, the action will attempt to extract a corresponding value from the Request object. In this version, no provision is made for required versus optional versus default values. That is easy enough to add in later.

Now let's look at the action itself, which we'll call XindiceInsertAction. You'll find it in Listing 16.11.

Listing 16.11 *XindiceInsertAction (XindiceInsertAction.java)*

```
package test;

import org.apache.avalon.framework.configuration.Configurable;
import org.apache.avalon.framework.configuration.ConfigurationException;
import org.apache.avalon.framework.configuration.Configuration;

import org.apache.avalon.framework.parameters.Parameters;
import org.apache.avalon.framework.thread.ThreadSafe;
import org.apache.cocoon.Constants;
import org.apache.cocoon.environment.ObjectModelHelper;
import org.apache.cocoon.environment.Redirector;
import org.apache.cocoon.environment.Request;
import org.apache.cocoon.environment.Context;
import org.apache.cocoon.environment.Session;
import org.apache.cocoon.environment.SourceResolver;
import org.apache.cocoon.util.Tokenizer;
import org.apache.cocoon.acting.AbstractComplementaryConfigurableAction;

import java.util.HashMap;
import java.util.Map;

import org.xmldb.api.DatabaseManager;
import org.xmldb.api.base.*;
import org.xmldb.api.modules.*;

public class XindiceInsertAction extends
   AbstractComplementaryConfigurableAction implements ThreadSafe
{
    protected static final String DEFAULT_XINDICE_HOST = "localhost";
    protected static final String DEFAULT_XINDICE_PORT = "4080";
    protected static final String DEFAULT_XINDICE_DB = "db";
    protected static final String DEFAULT_DESCRIPTOR = "xindice.xml";
    protected Database db = null;

    protected final Collection getDataCollection(String host, String port,
      String dbname, String coll) {
    Collection collection = null;

    try {
        if (db == null) {
            db = (Database)Class.forName("org.apache.xindice.client.xmldb.
➥DatabaseImpl").newInstance();
```

Listing 16.11 *(continued)*

```
      DatabaseManager.registerDatabase(db);
      }

          collection = DatabaseManager.getCollection("xmldb:xindice://" +
      host + ":" + port + "/" + dbname + "/" + coll);
  } catch (Exception e) {
      getLogger().warn("Error trying to get collection " + coll, e);
  }

  return collection;
  }

  public Map act (Redirector redirector, SourceResolver resolver,
    Map objectModel, String src, Parameters parameters) throws Exception {
      Request req = ObjectModelHelper.getRequest(objectModel);

      HashMap map = new HashMap();

      String documentName = parameters.getParameter("document");

         if (documentName == null || documentName.equals("")) {
          getLogger().error("No document name defined");
          return null;
      }

  try {
          Configuration conf = this.getConfiguration(parameters.getParameter
          ("descriptor", DEFAULT_DESCRIPTOR),
          resolver, true);

      String hostName = conf.getChild("host").getValue();
          if (hostName == null || hostName.equals(""))
             hostName = DEFAULT_XINDICE_HOST;
      String portNum = conf.getChild("port").getValue();
      if (portNum == null || portNum.equals(""))
      portNum = DEFAULT_XINDICE_PORT;
          String databaseName = conf.getChild("database").getValue();
             if (databaseName == null || databaseName.equals(""))
      databaseName = DEFAULT_XINDICE_DB;
      String collectionName = conf.getChild("collection").getValue();
```

Listing 16.11 *(continued)*

```
    if (collectionName == null || collectionName.equals("")) {
       getLogger().error("No collection name defined");
return null;
    }

getLogger().debug("Host is " + hostName);
getLogger().debug("Port is " + portNum);
getLogger().debug("Database is " + databaseName);
getLogger().debug("Collection is " + collectionName);
getLogger().debug("Document is " + documentName);

Collection coll = getDataCollection(hostName, portNum,
       databaseName, collectionName);

    if (coll == null) {
    getLogger().error("Unable to retrieve connection to " +
        collectionName);
    return null;
    }

    Configuration[] docs = conf.getChildren ("document");
String xmlContent = "";

for (int i = 0; i < docs.length; i++) {
if (docs[i].getAttribute("name").equals(documentName)) {
    Configuration[] elements = docs[i].getChildren ("element");
    xmlContent = buildContent(documentName, elements, req);
    break;
}
}

if (xmlContent.equals("")) {
getLogger().error("Unable to build document content");
return null;
}


getLogger().debug("About to add content: " + xmlContent);

    XMLResource resource = (XMLResource)
    coll.createResource( "", "XMLResource" );
```

Listing 16.11 (continued)

```
            resource.setContent(xmlContent);
            coll.storeResource(resource);
    } catch (Exception e) {
        getLogger().error("Unable to add cocoon-component", e);
    }

    return map;
    }

    private String buildContent(String documentName, Configuration[] elements,
      Request req) {
          String doc = "<" + documentName + ">";

    try {
            for (int i = 0; i < elements.length; i++) {
        String name = elements[i].getAttribute("name");
        String pvalue = req.getParameter(name);

        if (pvalue == null) pvalue = "";
        doc += "  <" + name + ">" + pvalue + "</" + name + ">";

            }
        } catch (Exception e) {
            getLogger().debug("Error building document content", e);
            return null;
        }

          doc += "</" + documentName + ">";
    return doc;
    }
}
```

Some points bear explaining.

```
String documentName = parameters.getParameter("document");
```

This line extracts a sitemap parameter called `document`. If the parameter is not present, the action will return null. You must provide this in the pipeline.

```
Configuration conf = this.getConfiguration(parameters.getParameter
("descriptor", DEFAULT_DESCRIPTOR),
resolver, true);
```

This line creates the `Configuration` object by called the `getConfiguration` method in the super-class. Note that this method expects a path to the descriptor file, which it expects to find as another sitemap parameter, and also a default value in case that sitemap parameter is missing. Our default value is simply `xindice.xml`.

```
String hostName = conf.getChild("host").getValue();
```

Here, the action pulls a child `Configuration` object from the parent for a tag called `host`. The `getValue()` method returns the text inside that tag.

```
Collection coll = getDataCollection(hostName, portNum,
       databaseName, collectionName);
```

The `Collection` object is part of the `org.xmldb.api` package and provides access to the collection itself. It requires host, port, database, and collection name parameters. This action does not necessarily need all of these defined in the descriptor file, because it has some default values set.

```
Configuration[] docs = conf.getChildren ("document");
```

From the parent `Configuration` object, we can get an array of child objects for each `<document>` tag in the definition file. The lines following this one loop through this array and find the right object whose `name` attribute matches the document name passed in from the sitemap. When found, the `buildContent` method is called to create a string representation of the XML content using the `<element>` tags to find the right values in the request.

```
XMLResource resource = (XMLResource)
coll.createResource( "", "XMLResource" );

resource.setContent(xmlContent);
coll.storeResource(resource);
```

This is where the actual insert takes place.

To use this action, it must be compiled. The classpath must include the following jars from the `WEB-INF/lib` directory: `xindice.jar`, `xml-apis.jar`, and `xmldb-api-20011111.jar`. The latter two files come as part of Cocoon, whereas the first file comes from the Xindice distribution.

Although we've covered action compilation in Chapter 12, it is worth showing the script for this action again. On Windows, you compile as shown in Listing 16.12.

Listing 16.12 *XindiceInsertAction Windows Build Script (build.bat)*

```
@echo off

set JAR_DIR=%CATALINA_HOME%\webapps\cocoon\WEB-INF\lib
set CLASS_DIR=%CATALINA_HOME%\webapps\cocoon\WEB-INF\classes

set CP=%JAR_DIR%\avalon-excalibur-vm12-20020705.jar
set CP=%CP%;%JAR_DIR%\avalon-framework-20020627.jar
set CP=%CP%;%JAR_DIR%\cocoon-2.0.3.jar
set CP=%CP%;%JAR_DIR%\logkit-20020529.jar
set CP=%CP%;%JAR_DIR%\xindice.jar
set CP=%CP%;%JAR_DIR%\xml-apis.jar
set CP=%CP%;%JAR_DIR%\xmldb-api-20011111.jar

javac -d %CLASS_DIR% -classpath %CP%;%CLASSPATH% XindiceInsertAction
```

This script on Unix is given in Listing 16.13.

Listing 16.13 *XindiceInsertAction Unix Build Script (build.sh)*

```
export JAR_DIR=$CATALINA_HOME/webapps/cocoon/WEB-INF/lib
export CLASS_DIR=$CATALINA_HOME/webapps/cocoon/WEB-INF/classes

export CP=$JAR_DIR/avalon-excalibur-vm12-20020705.jar
export CP=$CP:$JAR_DIR/avalon-framework-20020627.jar
export CP=$CP:$JAR_DIR/cocoon-2.0.3.jar
export CP=$CP:$JAR_DIR/logkit-20020529.jar
export CP=$CP:$JAR_DIR/xindice.jar
export CP=$CP:$JAR_DIR/xml-apis.jar
export CP=$CP:$JAR_DIR/xmldb-api-20011111.jar

javac -d $CLASS_DIR -classpath $CP:$CLASSPATH XindiceInsertAction
```

The action definition in `sitemap.xmap` looks like this:

```
<map:action name="xindice-insert" src="test.XindiceInsertAction"/>
```

Finally, we need a sample pipeline:

```
<map:match pattern="xindiceinsert">
 <map:act type="xindice-insert">
  <map:parameter name="descriptor"
     value="context://abc/content/defs/xindice.xml"/>
  <map:parameter name="document" value="cocoon-component"/>
```

```
  <map:generate type="file" src="content/confirm.xml"/>
  <map:transform src="style/main.xsl"/>
  <map:serialize type="html"/>
 </map:act>

 <map:generate type="file" file="content/failed.xml"/>
 <map:transform src="style/main.xsl"/>
 <map:serialize type="html"/>
</map:match>
```

Summary

This point cannot be emphasized enough: Cocoon often gives you many ways to do the same thing. This can be a disadvantage, because the options are often confusing to the beginner and dramatically increase the time it takes to comprehend Cocoon as a whole. On the other hand, we have seen in this chapter that although there are many ways to implement database operations, each has its own particular users. An application of any size can easily end up using all three methods. There are no global rules about choosing the method; rather, you must look at where you need the database operation and what you want to do with the result.

When it comes to XML databases, Cocoon makes access easy. As these databases grow in popularity, the number of Cocoon components dealing with them will grow as well. Already in the scratchpad area of Cocoon 2.0.3 is a `DbXMLAuthenticationAction` that validates login parameters against values stored in Xindice or a similar product. Watch as more show up and get moved into the main area.

CHAPTER 17

Cocoon Interfaces: SOAP

In this chapter we will talk about using Cocoon to interface with applications using the Simple Object Access Protocol, or SOAP. SOAP gives Cocoon the capability to interface with SOAP-enabled services made available on the Web. First, we'll provide a brief overview of SOAP. Then we'll look at using SOAP to interface with some well-known services, as well as a couple of our own. Finally, we'll discuss the future of Cocoon as a Web services platform.

Introduction to SOAP

SOAP, in case you are not familiar with it, is an XML-based protocol for distributed applications to exchange information. What gives SOAP the edge over other remote procedure protocols is the fact that it is designed to be transmitted over HTTP, which gets it by firewalls and into places binary protocols such as IIOP, ORPC, and JRMP can't go. SOAP can be used in two "modes": as an RPC mechanism and as a messaging mechanism.

For Cocoon developers, SOAP is a natural fit because SOAP messages are written in XML. The SOAP specification, available at `http://www.w3.org/TR/SOAP/`, defines the three major components of SOAP: the SOAP envelope, which describes the content; the SOAP encoding rules, used for exchanging data types; and the SOAP RPC representation, used to handle remote procedure calls and responses.

A SOAP message is nothing more than an XML message enclosed inside a `<SOAP-ENV:Envelope>` tag. Inside an `<envelope>` are optional `<SOAP-ENV:Header>` and required `<SOAP-ENV:Body>` tags.

More About SOAP

Besides the W3C specification, various introductory materials are available online. One quick start is the "Busy Developer's Guide to SOAP 1.1," available at `http://www.soapware.org/bdg`.

Another is an excellent four-part series published on JavaWorld.com called "Clean Up Your Wire Protocol with SOAP." The series starts at `http://www.javaworld.com/javaworld/jw-03-2001/jw-0330-soap_p.html`.

SOAP Logicsheet

SOAP is implemented in Cocoon via the SOAP logicsheet, part of the base package. The main tag is `<soap:call>`, which encloses the block of tags that constitute the content. Technically, you don't have to define any other tags, except those required by the SOAP service you are connecting to, because the SOAP logicsheet will automatically create them. The full list of supported tags is shown in Table 17.1.

Table 17.1 *SOAP Logicsheet Tags*

Tag	Description
`<soap:call>`	Root tag: must be present and must enclose all other soap: calls
`<soap:env>`	Envelope tag: if present, must enclose soap:header and soap:body tags
`<soap:header>`	Defines SOAP headers
`<soap:body>`	Defines the SOAP body
`<soap:enc>`	Defines the encoding style of the message

Accessing Google with SOAP

One of the more flashy examples of using Cocoon is a Google interface. This year, Google announced a SOAP interface to its search engine. Implementing this interface in Cocoon is a great way to get started in understanding how to use the protocol. There are four steps in getting it up and running:

1. Obtain license key and Google API.
2. Create the XSP.
3. Create the XSL.
4. Define the pipeline and test.

Obtaining Google API

You can download the Google API and apply for a key at `http://www.google.com/apis/`. The key usually comes via email within 24 hours. If you are following along with our examples, you don't necessarily need the kit; however, it contains all the documentation and various sample programs.

Creating the XSP

A quick and easy XSP to access the Google search service is shown in Listing 17.1.

Listing 17.1 *Google XSP (google.xsp)*

```
<?xml version="1.0" encoding="UTF-8"?>
<xsp:page language="java"
 xmlns:xsp="http://apache.org/xsp"
 xmlns:soap="http://apache.org/xsp/soap/3.0"
>

  <results>
    <xsp:logic>
      String query = "";
      try {
         query = request.getParameter("query");
      } catch (Exception e) { }
    </xsp:logic>

    <soap:call url="http://api.google.com:80/search/beta2"
            xmlns:xsi="http://www.w3.org/1999/XMLSchema-instance"
            xmlns:xsd="http://www.w3.org/1999/XMLSchema">
      <ns1:doGoogleSearch xmlns:ns1="urn:GoogleSearch">
        <key xsi:type="xsd:string">YOUR_KEY_GOES_HERE</key>
        <q xsi:type="xsd:string"><xsp:expr>query</xsp:expr></q>
        <start xsi:type="xsd:int">0</start>
        <maxResults xsi:type="xsd:int">10</maxResults>
```

Listing 17.1 *(continued)*

```
        <filter xsi:type="xsd:boolean">true</filter>
        <restrict xsi:type="xsd:string"></restrict>
        <safeSearch xsi:type="xsd:boolean">false</safeSearch>
        <lr xsi:type="xsd:string">lang_en|lang_de</lr>
        <ie xsi:type="xsd:string">latin1</ie>
        <oe xsi:type="xsd:string">latin1</oe>
      </ns1:doGoogleSearch>
    </soap:call>
  </results>
</xsp:page>
```

As we mentioned previously, the only SOAP tag you absolutely need is `<soap:call>`. The `url` attribute of this tag provides the URL of the target. Everything inside this tag is specific to the Google server. The main tag is `<ns1:doGoogleSearch>`, which contains child tags that provide the server key, search request (see the `<q>` tag), result set parameters, and various search restrictions. Note that you must replace the literal *`YOUR_KEY_GOES_HERE`* with your own key before you can run this example yourself. The search request string is set to the value of the `query` variable, which holds the contents of the request parameter of the same name.

Creating the XSL

Consult the Google API documentation in the kit you downloaded for detailed information about the tags used in the response. The actual search results are contained in an array of `<item>` tags that live under the tag `<resultElements>`. You can see one way to handle this information in the XSL in Listing 17.2.

Listing 17.2 *Google XSL (google.xsl)*

```
<?xml version="1.0"?>

<xsl:stylesheet version="1.0"
 xmlns:xsl="http://www.w3.org/1999/XSL/Transform"
 xmlns:ns1="urn:GoogleSearch"
>

 <xsl:template match="/">
  <html>
   <head>
    <title>Google search results via Cocoon</title>
```

Listing 17.2 (continued)

```
    </head>

    <body bgcolor="#ffffff">
     <center><h3>Google search via Cocoon</h3></center>
     <xsl:apply-templates/>
    </body>
   </html>
  </xsl:template>

  <xsl:template match="resultElements">
   <p>
    Your search for '<xsl:value-of select="//searchQuery"/>'
    found approximately <xsl:value-of select="//estimatedTotalResultsCounts"/>
    hits. These are results <xsl:value-of select="//startIndex"/> to
    <xsl:value-of select="//endIndex"/>.
   </p>
   <table width="100%" border="0">
    <xsl:apply-templates/>
   </table>
  </xsl:template>

  <xsl:template match="item">
   <tr>
    <xsl:apply-templates select="title"/>
   </tr>
   <xsl:if test="string(summary)">
    <tr>
     <td> </td>
     <xsl:apply-templates select="summary"/>
    </tr>
   </xsl:if>
   <tr>
    <td> </td>
    <xsl:apply-templates select="snippet"/>
   </tr>
   <tr><td colspan="3"> </td></tr>
  </xsl:template>

  <xsl:template match="snippet">
   <td><i>
```

Listing 17.2 *(continued)*

```
   <xsl:value-of select="." disable-output-escaping="yes"/>
  </i></td>
 </xsl:template>

 <xsl:template match="title">
  <td colspan="2">
   <a>
    <xsl:attribute name="href">
     <xsl:apply-templates select="../URL"/>
    </xsl:attribute>
    <xsl:value-of select="." disable-output-escaping="yes"/>
   </a>
  </td>
 </xsl:template>

 <xsl:template match="URL">
   <xsl:value-of select="." disable-output-escaping="yes"/>
 </xsl:template>

 <xsl:template match="summary">
  <td>
    Description:
    <xsl:value-of select="." disable-output-escaping="yes"/>
  </td>
 </xsl:template>

 <xsl:template match="text()">
 </xsl:template>

</xsl:stylesheet>
```

Defining the Pipeline

The pipeline to test this service is just like any other pipeline for an XSP:

```
<map:match pattern="google">
 <map:generate type="serverpages" src="xsp/google.xsp" label="raw"/>
 <map:transform src="style/google.xsl"/>
 <map:serialize type="html"/>
</map:match>
```

Let’s do a search for “Apache Cocoon” by pointing our browser to `http://localhost:8080/cocoon/abc/google?query=apache+cocoon`. (We have put our files and pipeline in the `abc` sub-sitemap; you can put them anywhere you want including the main sitemap.) The result is shown in Figure 17.1.

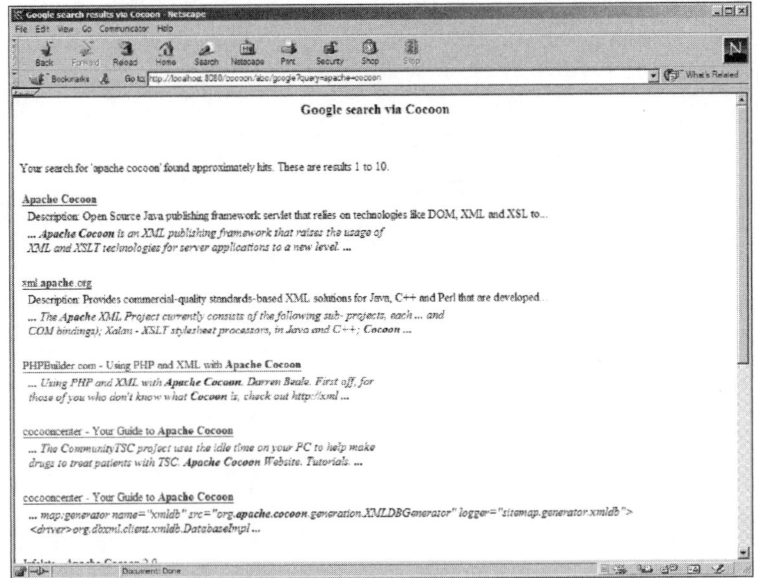

Figure 17.1

Google search via Cocoon.

Just for grins, we can see the actual SOAP response if we define a view called “raw” that does a simple serialization to XML. (If you need to see how to define this view, refer to Chapter 11, “Using Sitemap Logic: Matchers and Selectors.”) The result should look something like what’s shown in Figure 17.2.

Accessing Amazon.com with SOAP

While we’re on the subject, Amazon.com recently made its services available via SOAP. You can obtain a key and API kit at `https://associates.amazon.com/exec/panama/associates/join/developer/application.html`. Listing 17.3 shows the XSP to access the service, and Listing 17.4 shows a sample XSL. As with the earlier Google example, the only tag from the SOAP logicsheet that we need is `<soap:call>`. Within the enclosed `<KeywordSearchRequest>`, our query is represented by the `<keyword>` tag, which points to the `query` variable. It is worthwhile to consult the documentation that comes as part of the kit, because there are several options for searching and even the capability to add search results directly to shopping carts, wish lists, and wedding registries.

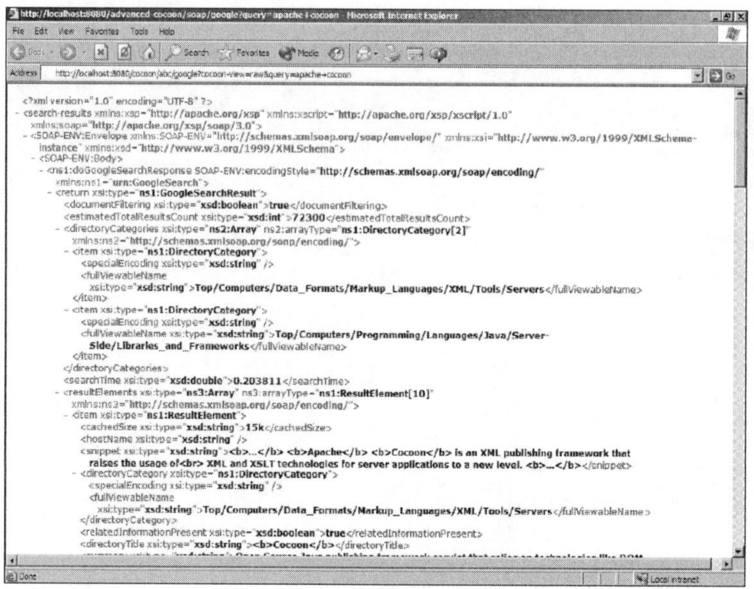

Figure 17.2

Google search—SOAP response.

Listing 17.3 *Amazon.com XSP (amazon.xsp)*

```
<?xml version="1.0" encoding="UTF-8"?>
<xsp:page
 language="java"
 xmlns:xsp="http://apache.org/xsp"
 xmlns:soap="http://apache.org/xsp/soap/3.0"
>

  <results>
    <xsp:logic>
      String query = "";
    try {
        query = request.getParameter("query");
    } catch (Exception e) { }
```

Listing 17.3 *(continued)*

```
    </xsp:logic>

    <soap:call url="http://soap.amazon.com:80/onca/soap"
            xmlns:xsi="http://www.w3.org/1999/XMLSchema-instance"
            xmlns:xsd="http://www.w3.org/1999/XMLSchema">

      <namesp1:KeywordSearchRequest
        xmlns:namesp1="urn:PI/DevCentral/SoapService">
         <KeywordSearchRequest xsi:type="namesp1:KeywordRequest">
           <keyword xsi:type="xsd:string"><xsp:expr>query</xsp:expr></keyword>
           <page xsi:type="xsd:string">1</page>
           <mode xsi:type="xsd:string">books</mode>
           <tag xsi:type="xsd:string">webservices-20</tag>
           <type xsi:type="xsd:string">heavy</type>
           <devtag xsi:type="xsd:string">YOUR_KEY_GOES_HERE</devtag>
           <format xsi:type="xsd:string">xml</format>
           <version xsi:type="xsd:string">1.0</version>
         </KeywordSearchRequest>
      </namesp1:KeywordSearchRequest>

    </soap:call>
  </results>
</xsp:page>
```

As with the Google example, you must put your own key where the *YOUR_KEY_GOES_HERE* literal is.

Listing 17.4 *Amazon.com XSL (amazon.xsl)*

```
<?xml version="1.0"?>

<xsl:stylesheet version="1.0"
 xmlns:xsl="http://www.w3.org/1999/XSL/Transform"
 xmlns:ns1="urn:GoogleSearch"
>

 <xsl:template match="/">
  <html>
   <head>
    <title>Amazon search results via Cocoon</title>
   </head>

   <body bgcolor="#ffffff">
```

Listing 17.4 *(continued)*

```
    <center><h3>Amazon search via Cocoon</h3></center>
    <xsl:apply-templates/>
   </body>
  </html>
 </xsl:template>

 <xsl:template match="return/Details">
  <table width="100%" border="0">
   <xsl:apply-templates/>
  </table>
 </xsl:template>

 <xsl:template match="Details">
  <tr>
   <td><a>
    <xsl:attribute name="href">
     <xsl:value-of select="Url"/>
    </xsl:attribute>
    <xsl:value-of select="ProductName"/>
   </a></td>
  </tr>
  <tr>
   <td><b>By:</b>
    <xsl:for-each select="Authors/Author">
     <xsl:value-of select="."/>
    </xsl:for-each>
    Lajos Moczar
   </td>
  </tr>
  <tr>
   <td><b>Release date:</b>  <xsl:value-of select="ReleaseDate"/></td>
  </tr>
  <tr>
   <td><b>Publisher:</b>  <xsl:value-of select="Manufacturer"/></td>
  </tr>
  <tr>
   <td><b>ISBN:</b>  <xsl:value-of select="Isbn"/></td>
  </tr>
  <tr>
   <td><b>Price:</b>  <xsl:value-of select="OurPrice"/> <i>
   (List price: <xsl:value-of select="ListPrice"/>)</i></td>
  </tr>
```

Listing 17.4 *(continued)*

```
 </xsl:template>

 <xsl:template match="text()">
 </xsl:template>

</xsl:stylesheet>
```

Amazon search results come in an array of `<Details>` tags, each of which contains data on title, author, price, description, ISBN, and so on.

To run this example, we need to define a new pipeline:

```
<map:match pattern="amazon">
 <map:generate type="serverpages" src="xsp/amazon.xsp" label="raw"/>
 <map:transform src="style/amazon.xsl"/>
 <map:serialize type="html"/>
</map:match>
```

So let's search for this book! If we point our browser to `http://localhost:8080/cocoon/abc/amazon?query=cocoon+handbook`, we'll get results similar to what is shown in Figure 17.3.

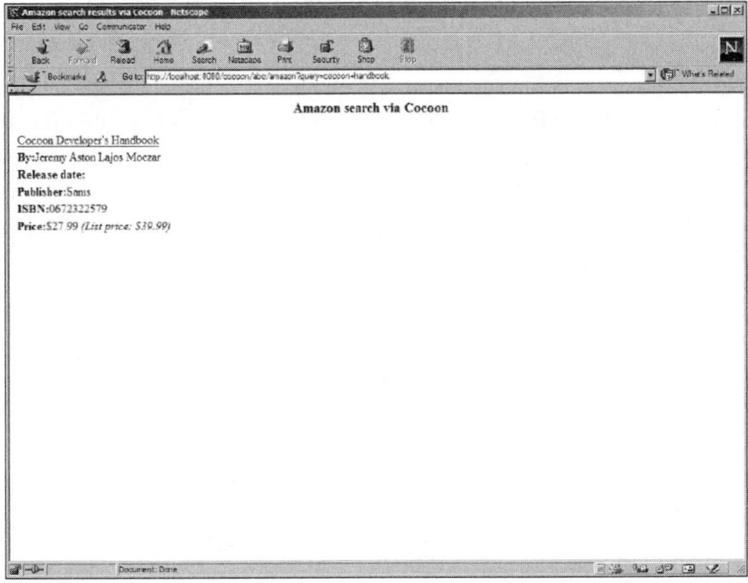

Figure 17.3
Amazon search for "cocoon handbook."

Accessing Custom SOAP Services

We can, of course, write our own SOAP service and access it from Cocoon. Cocoon version 2.0.x does not have the capability to act as a SOAP server; we'll look at Cocoon 2.1 for this function in the next section. However, if you are looking for an alternative, you have two SOAP engines available from the Apache Software Foundation: Apache SOAP and Apache AXIS. Apache SOAP originally came to life as IBM's SOAP4J, which was later gifted to Apache to become Apache SOAP. However, the current implementation has some limitations, notably, lack of WSDL support. Apache AXIS was started as a third-generation version of Apache SOAP. It features various improvements, such as a revamped architecture, speed, and WSDL support.

More About Apache SOAP

You can find Apache SOAP at `http://xml.apache.org/soap/`. The distribution includes several good examples to get you started. Another primer is available at `http://www.galatea.com/flashguides/tomcat-soap-win32.xml`.

The JavaWorld article series mentioned earlier, "Clean Up Your Wire Protocol with SOAP," is also extremely useful.

More About Apache AXIS

Apache AXIS lives at `http://xml.apache.org/axis/`. The 1.0 version was released in October, 2002. For an introduction see `http://www.galatea.com/flashguides/tomcat-axis-win32.xml` or `http://www.javaworld.com/javaworld/jw-01-2002/jw-0125-axis.html`.

Suppose we have our own SOAP service living on an Apache SOAP-enabled Tomcat server that handles newsletter registration requests. We'll assume that the registration request is processed in some custom way that is better served with a standalone Java program rather than inside Cocoon. The service deployment descriptor is shown in Listing 17.5, and the skeleton Java program is given in Listing 17.6.

Listing 17.5 *Registration Service Deployment Descriptor (descriptor.xml)*

```
<isd:service xmlns:isd="http://xml.apache.org/xml-soap/deployment"
             id="urn:registration" type="message">
  <isd:provider type="java"
                scope="Application"
                methods="register">
    <isd:java class="test.soap.Register" static="false"/>
  </isd:provider>

 <isd:faultListener>org.apache.soap.server.DOMFaultListener</isd:faultListener>
</isd:service>
```

Listing 17.6 *Registration Service (Register.java)*

```
package test.soap;

import java.io.*;
import org.apache.soap.*;
import org.apache.soap.rpc.SOAPContext;

public class Register {
  public void register (Envelope env, SOAPContext reqCtx,
                                           SOAPContext resCtx)
    throws MessagingException, IOException {
        <!-- Custom processing of the SOAP message goes here -->
        String msg = "<?xml version=\"1.0\"?>";
        msg += "<data>Got the registration</data>";
    resCtx.setRootPart(msg, "text/xml");
  }

}
```

After whatever processing is appropriate, we build up an XML message and send it back. Consult the Apache SOAP documentation for details on how to compile and deploy this service. The general procedure is as follows:

1. Make sure your `CLASSPATH` contains the following jars: `soap.jar`, `xerces.jar`, `mail.jar`, and `activation.jar`. It should also contain the `WEB-INF/classes` directory of your SOAP webapp.
2. Compile the Java file.
3. Deploy the compiled object to the `WEB-INF/classes` directory of the SOAP webapp.
4. Start the servlet container if you have not already done so, so that SOAP is running.
5. Deploy the service by calling the `org.apache.soap.server.ServiceManagerClient` and providing the path to the descriptor file (`descriptor.xml`).

Note that we are deploying this service as a messaging service. After it has been deployed, we can access it from Cocoon just as we did the Google and Amazon services. Listing 17.7 shows the XSP we'll use to access this service.

Listing 17.7 *Registration Service XSP (register.xsp)*

```
<?xml version="1.0" encoding="UTF-8"?>
<xsp:page
 language="java"
 xmlns:xsp="http://apache.org/xsp"
 xmlns:soap="http://apache.org/xsp/soap/3.0"
>

  <registration>

    <xsp:logic>
      String fname = request.getParameter("first-name");
      String lname = request.getParameter("last-name");
      String cname = request.getParameter("company-name");
      String tel = request.getParameter("tel");
      String email = request.getParameter("email");
    </xsp:logic>

    <soap:call url="http://localhost:8080/soap/servlet/messagerouter"
            xmlns:xsi="http://www.w3.org/1999/XMLSchema-instance"
            xmlns:xsd="http://www.w3.org/1999/XMLSchema">
      <reg:register xmlns:reg="urn:registration">
        <registrant>
          <first-name><xsp:expr>fname</xsp:expr></first-name>
          <last-name><xsp:expr>lname</xsp:expr></last-name>
          <company-name><xsp:expr>cname</xsp:expr></company-name>
          <telephone><xsp:expr>tel</xsp:expr></telephone>
          <email><xsp:expr>email</xsp:expr></email>
        </registrant>
      </reg:register>
    </soap:call>
  </registration>
</xsp:page>
```

We'll just define a simple pipeline for this example that returns XML:

```
<map:match pattern="register">
 <map:generate type="serverpages" src="xsp/register.xsp" label="raw"/>
<map:serialize type="xml"/>
</map:match>
```

And the result that is returned to Cocoon for processing is shown in Figure 17.4.

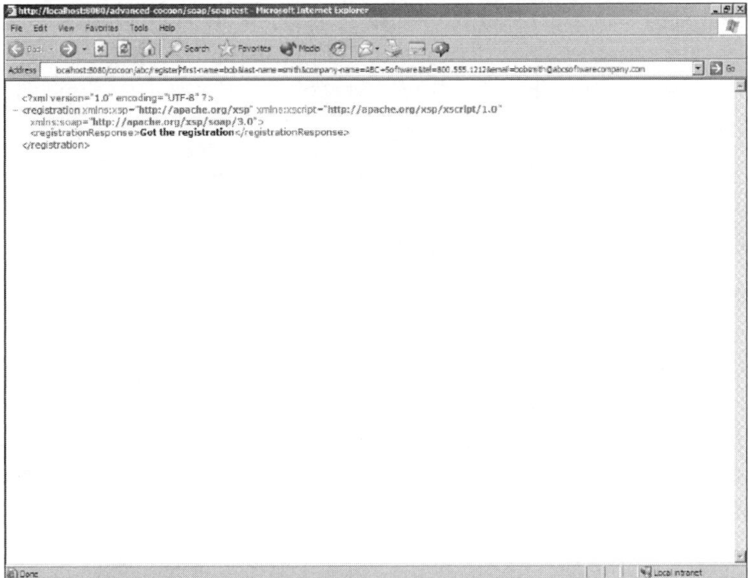

Figure 17.4
Registration service response.

Cocoon as a Web Services Platform

Web services is a growing trend in exposing distributed applications on the Web. Web services are provided by service providers and can be found by service brokers using the Universal Discovery, Description, and Integration (UDDI) specification. Normally, Web services are implemented as SOAP services. If you want to provide one or more Web services, you can publish the information about them using the Web Services Description Language (WSDL). A WSDL file enables applications to see which services you have and how each is accessed, that is, which input parameters each takes and what each returns.

> **More About Web Services**
> A good series of articles at IBM's developer works site can get you started. The series starts at `http://www-106.ibm.com/developerworks/library/ws-intwsdl/`.

As mentioned, Cocoon 2.0.x does not provide any built-in ways to provide either SOAP or Web services. However, this kind of functionality will be available in 2.1 in a number of ways. One is ability for pipelines to be exposed as Web Services by means of REST

(Representational State Transfer). Another is the availability of an Axis-based Reader that can serve SOAP responses based on SOAP requests. Yet a third enhancement is one that supports Web Site Syndication. Look for these features to get more developed as 2.1 approaches a release date.

Summary

SOAP, and Web services in general, is an ideal way to invoke custom applications written in various programming languages. Thanks to the fact that XML and the SOAP protocol are open standards (or will be, by SOAP version 1.2), SOAP has a much greater chance of widespread adoption than older protocols have. As a client, Cocoon is perfect for retrieving data from SOAP services. This data can simply be transformed to HTML, as we did in this chapter, or can be combined with other data through aggregation or portaling techniques.

CHAPTER 18

Cocoon Interfaces: J2EE

As you read the rest of this book, it is hopefully clear that Cocoon makes a very capable tool for building network applications. It can read from many sources and write to many destinations. Through technologies such as ESQL, relational database access is a breeze, and even the most basic use of XSP and logicsheets provides a good level of separation of concerns. The ever-increasing adoption of Cocoon is proof that developers can build maintainable, scalable, and well-architected solutions armed solely with a RDBMS, a servlet container, and Cocoon. This ever-increasing uptake also shows that this is not the only way Cocoon can be used and is being used. With its content aggregation capabilities, Cocoon is well suited to providing client-facing interfaces to all sorts of application, and—because Cocoon is Java based—many of these applications are developed using the Java 2 Enterprise Edition (J2EE) platform.

J2EE can be divided into two main areas: the distributed object technology of Enterprise JavaBeans (EJB) and the Web component technology of Servlets and Java Server Pages (JSP). Of course, behind all of this, J2EE covers areas such as messaging, authentication, transaction processing, resource management, and so on, but for the purposes of this chapter we will constrain the complexity to EJB and servlets/JSP. This chapter is intended to explain not how to develop EJBs, servlets, or JSP files, but rather how Cocoon interfaces with these technologies. If you want to find more information, including tutorials, on the specifics of J2EE, you can visit `http://java.sun.com` for more details.

Cocoon and J2EE Containers

A J2EE application server implements two runtime environments to control EJB and Web components, known as *containers*. The EJB container, naturally, controls EJBs, providing services such as transaction management, security, remote client interaction, database connectivity, and life-cycle management. Web components, basically servlets and JSP pages, are controlled in the Web container. When a J2EE-based application server implements a Web container, it is using the same JavaServer Pages and Java Servlet specifications that can be found in standalone servlet engines such as Tomcat and Jetty. By default, therefore, Cocoon (accessed via the `CocoonServlet` servlet) sits very comfortably within the J2EE architecture.

Figure 18.1 shows how Cocoon can sit within a Web container in a J2EE application server. Servers such as JRun, WebLogic, and JBoss (with Jetty) can be configured this way. If the Web container is on the same server as the EJB container, it is common that they are sharing the Java virtual machine space, and thus any JSP files or servlets can invoke EJBs directly without having to go through any remote object invocation mechanisms, and thus the network. Most J2EE application servers also provide HTTP server capabilities, again reducing network overhead.

It is also possible to run the Web container totally separately from the EJB container. This would be the case if, for example, you wanted to use a different servlet engine than the one provided by the J2EE server hosting the EJB container. Another scenario that may necessitate a similar architecture is when you want to access a third-party EJB container and you cannot host Cocoon within the Web container on the third-party infrastructure, or when only the EJB container has been deployed. Another occurrence of this type of configuration occurs when the containers has been deliberately split up, usually to split loads between two or more servers. Figure 18.2 illustrates how this architecture would appear. In this case, any calls to EJB take place using a remote object invocation protocol.

Cocoon and JSP

The easiest place to start examining how Cocoon can interface with J2EE technologies is by looking at the relationship between Cocoon and JSP. Over the past few years JSP has become one of the top server-side scripting languages, and thus many sites and applications make use of it. Cocoon offers functionality analogous to JSP through XSP, and no doubt many Cocoon users may want to migrate JSP applications without having to rewrite large amounts of code.

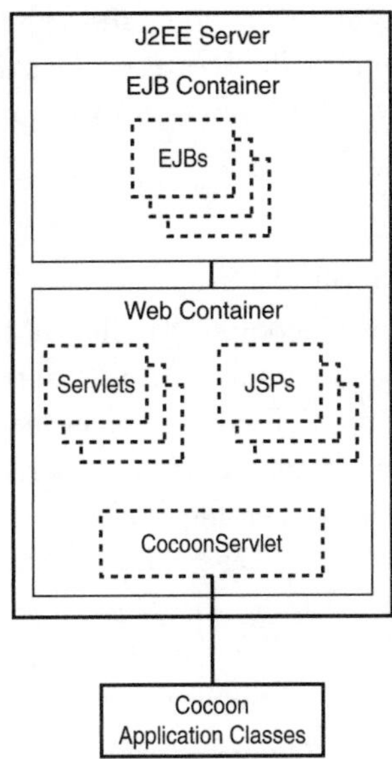

Figure 18.1
Cocoon within the J2EE architecture.

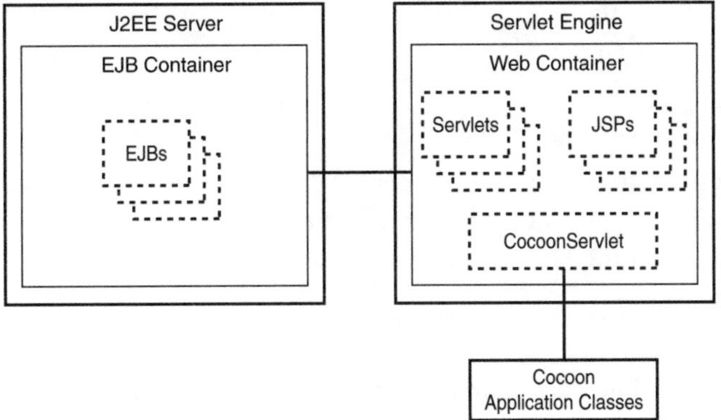

Figure 18.2
Cocoon operating in a separate Web container.

Cocoon contains two primary components that can help with this process: `JSPReader` and `JSPGenerator`. These components are supported by another component, `JSPEngine`. This provides the link to a servlet engine, such as Tomcat's engine Jasper. The servlet engine is called to compile and generate the JSP page; `JSPReader` just passes the results through the output stream, and `JSPGenerator` takes the results of the JSP compilation process and passes the results down the pipeline as a stream of SAX events.

Starting with a simple example, let's see how Cocoon can be configured to handle JSP files.

Configuring Servlet Engine Connectivity

The first step of the process to allow Cocoon to handle JSP files is to configure servlet engine connectivity. Because Cocoon is running within a servlet container, it is easy for Cocoon to gain access to the JSP compiler within whichever container it is using. By default, Cocoon is configured to use Tomcat's servlet engine, Jasper; however, this can be changed by overriding the settings in the `cocoon.roles` file. This file exists alongside the Cocoon Java classes inside the `org.apache.cocoon` package and is effectively not available unless you build Cocoon from the source or patch the `cocoon.jar` file. To do this is generally a bad idea because the `cocoon.roles` file could be overwritten or changed by a software upgrade. It is also feasible that as an application developer you may not have access to the relevant files on a production server. Cocoon does have a mechanism to allow additional roles to be added or existing ones overridden. You achieve this by building your own roles file and telling Cocoon to load it on startup.

Telling Cocoon about your own roles file is achieved by adding a setting to the `cocoon.xconf` (found in the `WEB-INF` folder) file. Right after the XML definition, there is the opening `<cocoon>` element:

```
<cocoon version="2.0">
```

You need to add a new attribute to the element, called `user-roles`. The value of the `user-roles` element defines the location of your roles file. It is standard practice to call the file `my.roles` and place it in the `WEB-INF` folder:

```
<cocoon version="2.0" user-roles="/WEB-INF/my.roles">
```

Note the leading slash. The documentation for version 2.0.3 indicates that the path should be minus the leading slash—that is, `WEB-INF/my.roles`. It has been noted that this does not work on all configurations of servlet container and JDK (for example, Tomcat 4.0.4_le and JDK 1.4.0); thus you may need to experiment to find the right setting.

The my.roles file follows exactly the same schema as cocoon.roles. Therefore, if you wanted to use the WebLogic JSP engine implementation, your file would look similar to the following:

```
<?xml version="1.0"?>
<role-list>
  <role name="org.apache.cocoon.components.jsp.JSPEngine"
        shorthand="jsp-engine"
        default-class="org.apache.cocoon.components.jsp.JSPEngineImplWLS"/>
</role-list>
```

After Cocoon has been configured for JSP execution, the next step is to consider how you want to handle your JSPs.

Straight JSP Execution

Running the JSP/Servlet Examples in This Chapter

All the JSP and servlet examples in this chapter are designed to be run using http://<server>:<port/cocoon/mount/cdh/chapter18/*. This means that the Chapter 18 code should be placed in $COCOON_HOME/mount/cdh/chapter18. The default Cocoon sitemap will automount the sitemap in cdh, the sitemap.xmap in the cdh folder automounting the chapter18 sitemap in turn. In this chapter the server and port are assumed to be localhost and 8080 respectively.

The most simple way of getting Cocoon to handle JSP files is to use JSPReader to handle calling the JSPEngine implementation and streaming the results straight to back to the requesting client. JSPReader is referenced within the <readers> element block in the sitemap in the following way:

```
<map:readers default="resource">
  ...
  <map:reader logger="sitemap.reader.jsp"
              name="jsp"
              src="org.apache.cocoon.reading.JSPReader"/>
  ...
</map:readers>
```

Note

The following examples are all based on Cocoon version 2.0.3. This is because there is a bug in JSPReader on previous versions of Cocoon. If you are using a version of Cocoon previous to this, you will need to patch the cocoon.jar file with the JSPReader from version 2.0.3.

Using `JSPReader`, the JSP can produce either XML or non-XML content. Consider Listing 18.1.

Listing 18.1 *currdate.jsp*

```
<html>
<head>
  <title>Current Date</title>
</head>

<body>
The current date is:<br>
<%= new java.util.Date() %>
</body>
</html>
```

What we have here is a simple JSP file that displays the current date within an HTML page. The generated HTML could not be considered as XHTML or well-formed XML because the `<br>` tag is not correctly closed with a trailing slash (`<br/>`). The file can be successfully handled, however, because all `JSPReader` is doing is passing the request to the `JSPEngine` and piping the response back to the client.

To simply generate the JSP file and stream it, the `JSPReader` would be matched in a similar way to the following sitemap entry:

```
<map:match pattern="*.jsp">
  <map:read type="jsp" src="{1}.jsp" mime-type="text/html" />
</map:match>
```

Any user-defined classes or beans need to be available on the servlet engine classpath. Typically, this would mean that they would exist in `WEB-INF/classes` or `WEB-INF/lib`.

This process is very simple to configure and enables the rapid redeployment of JSP files within a Cocoon environment.

SAX Generation from JSP Files

The next step up from simple piping of the JSP output is to use `JSPGenerator` to take the JSP output and pass it down the pipeline as a stream of SAX events. This stream can then be processed as any other generated stream in the pipeline: transformed, aggregated, serialized, and so on. The implicit requirement therefore is that the JSP output is valid, well formed XML, otherwise SAX errors will occur.

JSPGenerator is added to sitemap as shown here:

```
<map:generators default="file">
  ...
  <map:generator logger="sitemap.generator.jsp"
                 name="jsp"
                 src="org.apache.cocoon.generation.JspGenerator"/>
  ...
</map:generators>
```

Using the same currdate.jsp file shown previously, we can attempt to view the resultant XML stream using the following sitemap entry:

```
<map:match pattern="*.xml">
  <map:generate type="jsp" src="{1}.jsp"/>
  <map:serialize type="xml"/>
</map:match>
```

Requesting currdate.xml will fail because the <br> tag has not been closed off to form well-formed code. Changing the <br> tag to read <br/> and repeating the request should result in an XML file being displayed to the browser.

Integrating Servlets and Cocoon

The next part of the J2EE architecture we will look at are servlets. Servlets underpin JSP and XSP; therefore, you would expect that the integration of the two would be something quite easy. In principle this is true; however, as you will see from the following, various apparent limitations remain. The key point to remember, however, is that Cocoon is not meant to replace a servlet engine and should not be used to do so. In a Web environment, Cocoon and servlets should coexist, and this section should assist those integrating servlets and Cocoon together to do so with some success.

Running a Servlet from Cocoon

Of course, the simplest method of invoking a servlet from Cocoon is by referencing a URL from an XSP page (or equivalent) in the form http://*someserver*/*servletpath*/*servletname*. This, of course, is just calling an external URL like any other and shows no real integration.

Calling a servlet that is within the same Web application container as Cocoon is not difficult and can be achieved with a few basic steps:

1. Place the servlet class in the container file hierarchy.
2. Reference the servlet within Cocoon's Web application configuration file.
3. Match the servlet request within a pipeline.

The first of these steps involves placing the servlet class in one of two places: as a class file in `WEB-INF/classes` or within a JAR file in `WEB-INF/lib`. Generally, the class is placed in the `classes` folder during development and testing and then placed in a JAR file for deployment into the `WEB-INF/lib` folder for distribution and production use. Of course, the servlet needs to be placed inside a folder hierarchy representing the class package.

As an example, take the following simple servlet (Listing 18.2) that takes an entry from the user, multiplies it by 10, and displays the result. I know that this servlet can be broken very easily, but the code as is suffices for the example.

Listing 18.2 *CalculateValues.java*

```
package com.pigbite.calc;

import javax.servlet.*;
import javax.servlet.http.*;
import java.io.*;

/**
 * Multiply the specificed value by ten.
 * @author jez
 *
 */
public class CalculateValues extends HttpServlet
{

    private String amountParam;
    private int amount;

    /**
     * Handle the get request.
     * @see javax.servlet.http.HttpServlet#doGet(HttpServletRequest,
     *                            HttpServletResponse)
     */
```

Listing 18.2 (continued)

```
public void doGet( HttpServletRequest request,
                   HttpServletResponse response )
    throws ServletException, IOException
{

    // Check the incoming value
    amountParam = request.getParameter( "amount" );

    if ( amountParam == null )
    {
        amount = 0;
    }
    else
    {
        amount = Integer.valueOf( amountParam ).intValue();
    }

    // Prepare the response

    response.setContentType( "text/html" );

    PrintWriter out = response.getWriter();

    out.println( "<html>" );
    out.println( "<head>" );
    out.println( "<title>Calculate Example</title>" );
    out.println( "</head>" );

    out.println( "<body>" );
    out.println( "<form action=\"calcvalue\" method=\"get\">" );

    // If the amount is greater than zero then display the amount
    // multiplied by 10.

    if ( amount > 0 )
    {
        out.println( amount + " multiplied by 10 is " + amount * 10 );
        out.println( "<br>" );
    }
```

Listing 18.2 (continued)

```
        out.println( "<input type=\"text\" name=\"amount\" value=\""
➥+ amount + "\">" );
        out.println( "<br>" );
        out.println( "<input type=\"submit\" name=\"submit\"
➥value=\"Calculate Value\">" );
        out.println( "</form>" );
        out.println( "</body>" );
        out.println( "</html>" );

    }

    /**
     * Handle a post request
     * @see javax.servlet.http.HttpServlet#doPost(HttpServletRequest,
     * HttpServletResponse)
     */
    public void doPost( HttpServletRequest request,
                        HttpServletResponse response )
        throws ServletException, IOException
    {

        // Simply pass on to the get handler!
        doGet( request, response );

    }

}
```

When compiled to the `com.pigbite.calc.CalculateValues` class, this file can be placed in the `WEB-INF/classes/com/pigbite/calc` folder.

The next step is to tell the Web application about the servlet. This basically means that Cocoon's `web.xml` file (found in the `WEB-INF` folder) requires updating. The first step is to associate a servlet name to the servlet class using a construct as shown here:

```
<servlet>
  <servlet-name>CalculateValues</servlet-name>
  <servlet-class>com.pigbite.calc.CalculateValues</servlet-class>
</servlet>
```

This tells the Web application that there is a servlet named `CalculateValues` and its class file is in `com.pigbite.calc.CalculateValues`. The second construct inside `web.xml` maps the servlet to a URL:

```
<servlet-mapping>
    <servlet-name>CalculateValues</servlet-name>
    <url-pattern>/mount/cdh/chapter18/calcvalue</url-pattern>
</servlet-mapping>
```

This tells the Web application to check for a particular request and map that to a servlet. In this case, a call to `http://someserver/cocoon/mount/cdh/chapter18/calcvalue` will result in the `CalculateValues` servlet being called, which in turn is mapped to the `com.pigbite.calc.CalculateValues` class.

> **Note**
> Don't forget that if you make a change to `web.xml` you will need to restart Tomcat to effect the changes.

Transforming Servlet Output

These steps should be completely familiar to any servlet developer because they are exactly the same as what is done to deploy a servlet in any Web application container. As mentioned earlier, the preceding servlet is totally self-contained. If invoked with no parameters, it displays an HTML form and handles the processing of the form as well, displaying a response as appropriate. In many ways it reflects how servlets were used when they first appeared and demonstrates very clearly how logic and presentation can be mixed together in one unmaintainable lump. Of course, most modern-day servlets are not coded in this way because solutions have been found that help abstract presentation logic, markup, and business logic from one another. Nowadays, many Java-based Web applications will use servlets as marshalers, acting as an interface to data persistence layers, coordinating responses to user requests, and invoking presentation layers (typically JSP) for user interaction. Known as the JSP Model 2 approach, this reflects a reasonable implementation of the MVC paradigm, but because it is not always clear where to put specific logic, this can be prone to abuse.

A more robust servlet/JSP-based framework that reflects MVC is the Apache Jakarta subproject called Struts. Inside Struts, you have a controlling servlet that maps requests to actions and JSP files. Struts also encompasses a custom tag library that is used to simplify the JSP. For many Java-based Web application developers, Struts has been a very useful framework and one that potentially could be used instead of Cocoon.

Struts, however, is a very HTML- and Web-application–centric framework and is less capable when it comes to delivering multichannel content from a single source. Cocoon is also highly capable at bringing content in from multiple sources and passing it on for processing in a very neutral fashion, via XML. The usefulness of this cannot be underestimated. A "hot topic" in Java development circles continues to be the aggregation of data from multiple sources and the subsequent delivery to multiple channels. XML is an excellent method of describing this data in this context, and as such you see servlets that pass XML back for subsequent processing by a rendering engine. Here is where Cocoon can be used very effectively to transform the XML data.

If we take the servlet in Listing 18.2 and turn it into what is effectively a piece of business logic, we can illustrate this a little more. Listing 18.3 shows a modified version of the servlet that returns XML representing the amount and the result of the calculation.

Listing 18.3 *CalculateValuesXML.java*

```
package com.pigbite.calc;

import javax.servlet.*;
import javax.servlet.http.*;
import java.io.*;

/**
 * Multiply the specificed value by ten.
 * @author jez
 *
 */
public class CalculateValuesXML extends HttpServlet
{

    private String amountParam;
    private int amount;

    /**
     * Handle the get request.
     * @see javax.servlet.http.HttpServlet#doGet(
     * HttpServletRequest, HttpServletResponse)
     */
    public void doGet( HttpServletRequest request,
                       HttpServletResponse response )
        throws ServletException, IOException
    {
```

Listing 18.3 *(continued)*

```
        // Check the incoming value
        amountParam = request.getParameter( "amount" );

        if ( amountParam == null )
        {
            amount = 0;
        }
        else
        {
            amount = Integer.valueOf( amountParam ).intValue();
        }

        // Prepare the response

        response.setContentType( "text/plain" );

        PrintWriter out = response.getWriter();

        out.println( "<?xml version=\"1.0\"?>" );
        out.println( "<page>" );

        // If the amount is greater than zero then pass the amount
        // multiplied by 10.

        if ( amount > 0 )
        {
            out.println( "<amount>" + amount + "</amount>" );
            out.println( "<result>" + amount * 10 + "</result>" );
        }

        out.println( "</page>" );

    }

    /**
     * Handle a post request
     * @see javax.servlet.http.HttpServlet#doPost(
     * HttpServletRequest, HttpServletResponse)
     */
    public void doPost( HttpServletRequest request,
                        HttpServletResponse response )
```

Listing 18.3 *(continued)*

```
        throws ServletException, IOException
    {

        // Simply pass on to the get handler!
        doGet( request, response );

    }

}
```

The servlet is made available within the Web application container using the following entries in the `web.xml` file:

```
<servlet>
  <servlet-name>CalculateValuesXML</servlet-name>
  <servlet-class>com.pigbite.calc.CalculateValuesXML</servlet-class>
</servlet>

<servlet-mapping>
  <servlet-name>CalculateValuesXML</servlet-name>
  <url-pattern>/mount/cdh/chapter18/calcvaluexml</url-pattern>
</servlet-mapping>
```

Restarting Tomcat and making a subsequent request to `http://localhost:8080/cocoon/mount/cdh/chapter18/calcvaluexml` will result in the following XML stream being returned:

```
<?xml version="1.0" ?>
<page>
</page>
```

If a parameter with the name of `amount` and value of `15` is appended to the preceding request by using `?amount=15`, the stream of XML will look more like this:

```
<?xml version="1.0" ?>
<page>
  <amount>15</amount>
  <result>150</result>
</page>
```

This servlet is being served by the Cocoon Web application but *not* by a pipeline in the sitemap. Now that the servlet is returning XML, there is no reason why the result cannot be transformed, by making the call to the servlet from within a pipeline. The first task is to build a form that replicates the one displayed in the original servlet. This is done using a stylesheet, such as calcform.xsl, presented in Listing 18.4.

Listing 18.4 *calcform.xsl*

```
<xsl:stylesheet version="1.0" xmlns:xsl="http://www.w3.org/1999/XSL/Transform">
  <xsl:output indent="no" method="html"/>

  <xsl:template match="page">
    <html>
    <head>
      <title>Calculate Values</title>
    </head>

    <body>
    <form action="calcvaluexml" method="get">
      <xsl:apply-templates />
      <xsl:element name="input">
        <xsl:attribute name="name">amount</xsl:attribute>
        <xsl:attribute name="value">
            <xsl:value-of select="amount"/></xsl:attribute>
      </xsl:element>
      <br/>
      <input type="submit" name="submit" value="Calculate Value"/>
    </form>
    </body>
    </html>
  </xsl:template>

  <xsl:template match="amount">
    <xsl:value-of select="."/> multiplied by 10 is
  </xsl:template>

  <xsl:template match="result">
    <xsl:value-of select="."/><br/>
  </xsl:template>
</xsl:stylesheet>
```

The stylesheet generates the same HTML form that the original servlet does. When the matches on the <amount> and <result> elements are used, a message can be displayed showing the result. The previous amount value is placed back in the input box through the use of the <xsl:element> and <xsl:attribute> tags. This is required because you cannot use an `<xsl:value-of>` tag inside the `input`'s `value` attribute, as if you were constructing the HTML tag as normal inside the stylesheet. For example:

```
<input name="amount" value="<xsl:value-of select="amount"/>"/>
```

would cause XSL errors; therefore, `<xsl:element>` and `<xsl:attribute>` are used.

The next step is to enable the servlet to be called from within a pipeline. The following can be added to the sitemap:

```
<map:match pattern="servlet/calcvaluexml">
  <map:act type="request">
    <map:parameter name="parameters" value="true"/>
    <map:generate src="http://localhost:8080/cocoon/mount/
➥cdh/chapter18/calcvaluexml{requestQuery}"/>
    <map:transform src="calcform.xsl"/>
  </map:act>
  <map:serialize type="html"/>
</map:match>
```

There are various points to note here. First, take a look at the pattern that is being matched. To invoke the servlet you need to enter `http://localhost:8080/cocoon/mount/cdh/chapter18/servlet/calcvaluexml`. Of course, the `servlet/calcvaluexml` path and file does not physically exist but is used to build a different path to the one used as the servlet URL match in `web.xml`. If you simply used `calcvaluexml` as the pattern, the effect would be that the request URL would be
`http://localhost:8080/cocoon/mount/cdh/chapter18/calcvaluexml`, and exactly match what the servlet engine is looking for to invoke the servlet. In this case the servlet engine would resolve the request first, and it would never be passed to the pipeline. The generate step uses the URL that results in the servlet engine picking up the request and calling the servlet.

The second point is the use of the request action to pass the request query string to the servlet. This has to be done because any request parameters are not automatically passed on, and thus the servlet would never return the results of the calculation. The implication here is that the only HTTP method that can be used to pass request parameters to a servlet is `GET`.

The third and final point is the need to use a full URL, including the server and port references, in the generate source attribute. This is to ensure that the file generator uses HTTP to resolve the request URL and does not assume that it is a local file path. If it does the latter, the source will not be found because it is not a physical resource, but one that exists as a mapping entry in the servlet engine. To invoke this, HTTP must be used as the transport.

These points highlight some fairly fundamental limitations of calling servlets within Cocoon 2.0.3. Version 2.1 will likely include at least one additional generator that will ease the incorporation of XML-producing servlets into a Cocoon application. This will work along the lines of a Web service filter. This should further aid in the integration of servlets and Cocoon, maximizing the benefits of the respective technologies.

Integrating Cocoon and Enterprise JavaBeans

The most complex part of the J2EE platform concerns Enterprise JavaBeans. EJBs are at the heart of many applications, providing highly scalable, resilient, and robust services to all types of clients. EJB design and development is a skill all its own, and thus this section of the chapter concentrates on enabling the deployment of Cocoon within an EJB container rather then attempting to discuss in detail EJB development technicalities.

Choosing an EJB Container

Perhaps one of the most taxing parts of integrating Cocoon and EJBs is choosing the EJB container to use. There are many proven platforms out there from highly respected vendors, such as BEA, Oracle, IBM, and Macromedia. There are also open source options such as JBoss.

The factors that influence the final choice are many. The choice may already be made for you, or perhaps there is a corporate standard or you are working in an environment where the platform is already deployed. Cost is a consideration, the range going from free of charge (under public license conditions) to potentially hundreds of thousands of dollars. Support, consultancy, and development expertise will no doubt play a large part in the decision-making process, as will final project size.

Whatever the mix that determines the final choice, you can be certain that the cost of design and development will vastly outweigh the cost of licenses. In principle, EJBs really should be used only for applications in which a distributed environment will pay off. The inherent size and intricacy of these applications requires heavy investment in the application architecture design. If you're including Cocoon in this, experience shows there is even more reason for not skimping on this vital project stage.

Packaging Cocoon as an Enterprise Archive

A simple way to deploy Cocoon is to package it as an Enterprise Archive, or EAR, file. An EAR package allows you to combine Web application WAR files, Java class, bean, and EJB JAR files and other resources. You can then (usually) deploy the EAR file very simply.

If you are not using a large commercial EJB container with packaging toolsets, you can still get Cocoon packaged up. Cocoon can be packed into an EAR file using tools that come with the Sun J2EE SDK. You can download the latest version (1.3.1 at the time of writing) from `http://java.sun.com`. After it's installed, there are several tools that can be of use to the application developer, including the deploy tool. On Windows platforms you can find this in the `bin` folder of the SDK by running the `deploytool.bat` batch file. You will then see a Java application, as shown in Figure 18.3.

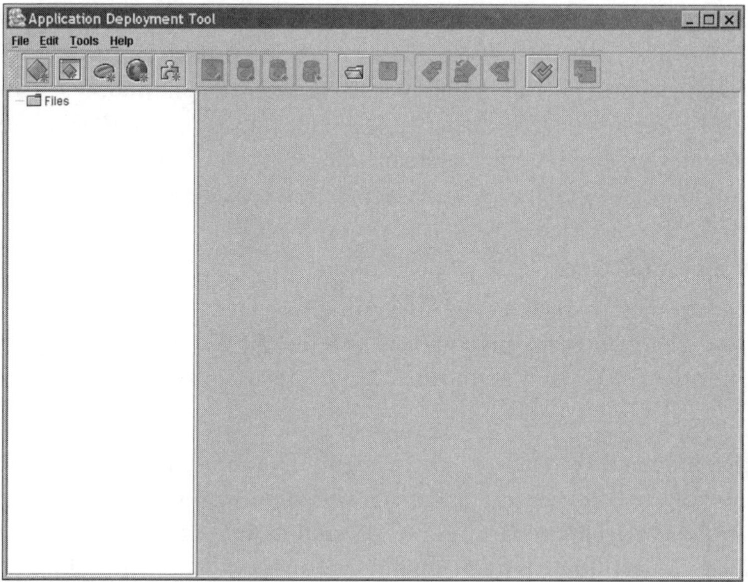

Figure 18.3

The Application Deployment Tool main screen.

Choose the File, New menu option and choose Application. You then will be presented with a dialog box requesting a path and name for your application, as well as a descriptive line of text. Choose a place where you would like to create the EAR file, followed by `cocoon.ear`, and enter something like Cocoon 2.0.3 as the name of the application, as shown in Figure 18.4.

The screen display will then change to show package information. The next step is to add in the existing Cocoon Web application archive file from the distribution—`cocoon.war`. Choose File, Add to Application and then choose Web WAR. The application will then present a File Open dialog box that will allow you to pick the `cocoon.war` file up from the source folder. Find the file (for example, `$COCOON_DISTRIBUTION/build/cocoon/cocoon.war`). The WAR will be added and the screen updated.

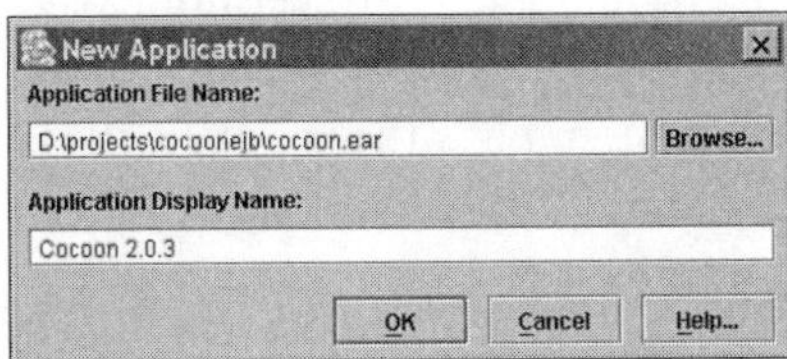

Figure 18.4
Choosing where to create the Cocoon enterprise archive.

The only thing you really need to do is ensure that the Web context is set correctly. The Web context specifies where Cocoon will sit relative to the Web server root. If you want to ensure that it sits at `/cocoon`, select the Web Context tab and enter `cocoon` into the Context Root field, as shown in Figure 18.5.

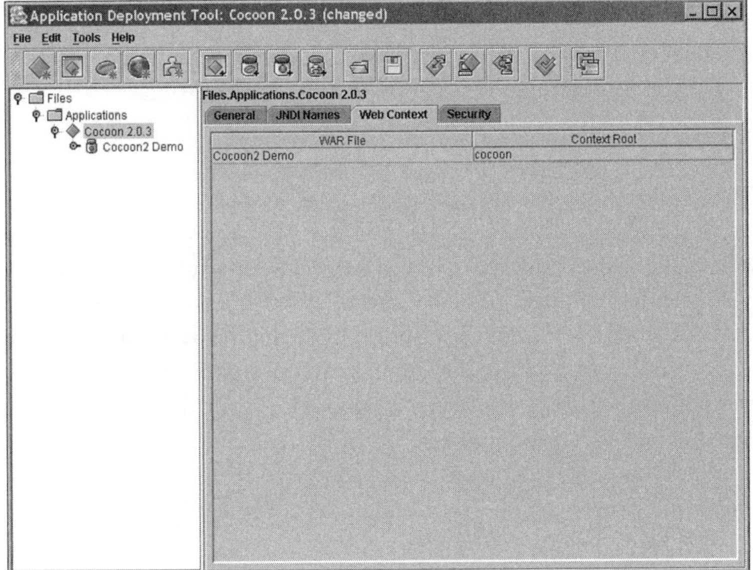

Figure 18.5
Entering the Cocoon Web context.

You can then choose the File, Save menu option and save the configured EAR file. This is now ready for deployment.

Deploying Cocoon with JBoss

As an open source J2EE server, JBoss is probably second to none and is well worth investigation. JBoss is available from the development project homepage at `www.jboss.org`. The Cocoon documentation includes instructions on how to configure Cocoon under version 2 of JBoss, but my recommendation is that you use JBoss 3.0.2 with Cocoon 2.0.3 and Java JDK 1.4.0 because the configuration is literally "plug and play."

After you have installed JBoss and built a `cocoon.ear` file as described in the previous subsection, simply copy the `cocoon.ear` file into `$JBOSS_HOME/server/default/deploy` and restart JBoss. It will automatically deploy Cocoon. After the JBoss server has started, call `http://localhost:8080/cocoon` (you did remember to force the Web context to be `cocoon`, didn't you? ;-)) from a browser and see Cocoon work out of the box!

Integrating EJBs with Cocoon

Integrating EJBs with Cocoon is something that has been successfully achieved many times. What is still expanding, however, is the capability of Cocoon to support EJB integration "out of the box" through having the required generators and source components to easily work with session and entity beans. Fully exploring this topic is beyond the scope of this chapter; however, for EJB developers who are getting into Cocoon, all the base information is available to enable you to develop your generators to aid integration.

Summary

Cocoon's Java heritage makes possible easy and powerful integration with the entire J2EE platform. JSP and servlets can be integrated into the Cocoon environment, thus aiding the migration of or coexistence with other Java-based Web applications. We have touched on how Cocoon can be integrated with EJBs, and it is certain that this facet of Cocoon's personality is something we are going to see a lot more of over the coming months as Cocoon matures further. What should be abundantly clear is that in the multitier world of Web application development, Cocoon is very well placed to act as an extremely powerful user interaction and interface engine, front-ending highly scalable back-office applications.

CHAPTER 19
Searching with Cocoon

It would be fair to say that pretty much any application you develop with Cocoon would benefit from having some kind of search capability. If the data of your application is persisted within a relational or object-oriented database, you will likely provide search capabilities by executing queries against the database. But what about application data that is held in XML files? In such cases you can add very powerful search functionality by using the Lucene search engine that has been integrated with Cocoon. In this chapter we are going to take a look at what the Lucene engine is, how it works, and how you can implement typical search functions using it.

What Is Lucene?

Lucene is a very powerful and flexible search engine written in Java. It is open source and has been incorporated into the Apache Jakarta project. If you want to keep up-to-date on all the latest news, documentation, and code for Lucene, then the place to go is `http://jakarta.apache.org/lucene`.

Lucene basically works by creating an *index* of words and their locations in source material. It does this by analyzing the content of the material based on rules specified in an *analyzer*. As an analyzer processes the source material, it builds *documents*. A document is a simple data object that represents the index data such as the word and location. The documents form the actual index that can then be searched. To search a Lucene index, you use a *searcher* class.

Integration of Lucene into Cocoon

Default Lucene integration into Cocoon is established through the classes present in the `org.apache.cocoon.components.search` package. Three interfaces are defined, as described in Table 19.1.

Table 19.1 *Cocoon Lucene Integration Interfaces*

Interface	Description
`LuceneCocoonIndexer`	Component interface for an indexer class.
`LuceneCocoonSearcher`	Component interface for a searching class.
`LuceneXMLIndexer`	Component that creates Lucene index documents based on XML files.

These interfaces then have implementation classes that provide the actual functionality. These classes are described in Table 19.2.

Table 19.2 *Cocoon Lucene Integration Classes*

Interface	Description
`SimpleLuceneCocoonIndexerImpl`	Actual indexing class. It crawls from a root URL, indexing XML documents.
`SimpleLuceneCocoonSearcherImpl`	Class that provides the capability to search a Lucene index from Cocoon.
`SimpleLuceneXMLIndexerImpl`	Class that indexes an XML file by producing Lucene `Document` objects from it. This class uses the `LuceneIndexContentHandler` class to do the core XML parsing and Lucene `Document` object creation.

Index Creation

The base Lucene functionality allows the indexing to take place on a specific source, such as an individual file. Cocoon, however, extends this to provide a comprehensive solution that can be used for most Web application search requirements.

The process of creating an index can be split into several stages:

- Crawl
- Fetch resource
- Index resource

These stages are illustrated in Figure 19.1.

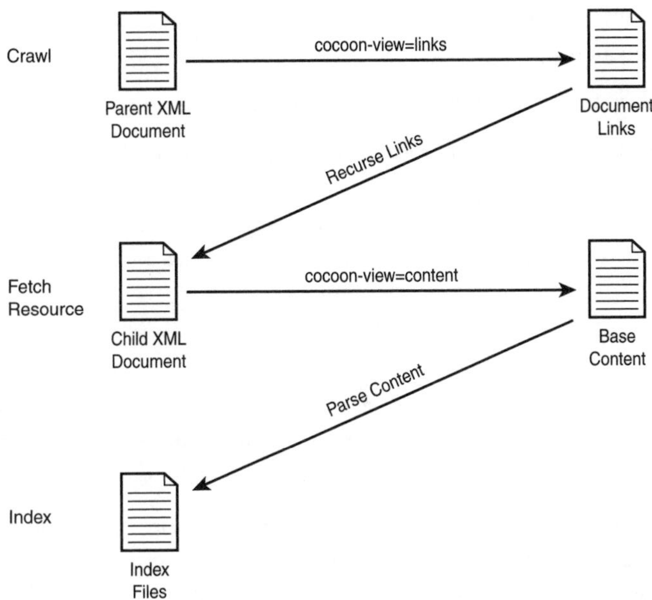

Figure 19.1
The Cocoon index creation process.

The indexing process starts by taking a top-level XML document and using this as the parent file for a crawler. The crawler, implemented in `org.apache.cocoon.components.crawler.SimpleCocoonCrawlerImpl`, takes the parent file and extracts all the links to other documents that are present inside it. To do this it uses a view, called the *links* view, to generate a simple list of every single link, via the `LinkSerializer`. This happens via the pipeline and a request appended with the `cocoon-view=links` parameter.

The next step of the process is to fetch resources for indexing. Using the list of links, the indexer class, `org.apache.cocoon.components.search.SimpleLuceneCocoon`

`IndexerImpl`, is then able to pass first the parent document and then its children (that is, the links found by the crawler) to the final part of the indexing process.

With each resource that requires indexing, the indexer class calls the `SimpleLuceneXMLIndexerImpl` class (in the `org.apache.cocoon.components.search` package) to generate the index files specific to the file. It does this by generating the document once again, but this time using the *content* Cocoon view. As with the link generation, a request is made via the pipeline with a parameter specifying `cocoon-view=content`. This view presents the basic content, which can then be parsed, generating the Lucene index documents. A final class, `LuceneIndexContentHandler`, is used to perform this task.

The whole process is then reiterated until all the links have been recursed.

The content indexer is able to create index entries for element text and attributes. Text that appears as pure text within XML elements is given a default index field name of `body`. XML elements are given an index field name that matches the element name. Element attribute values are also indexed and given a field name of *`element-name@attribute-name`*. The section "Search Phrases" elaborates on this topic.

Index Searching

Cocoon's integration with Lucene on the searching side is a little more simple than the index creation process. Cocoon includes examples of initiating a search through XSP or the `SearchGenerator`, but they work fundamentally in much the same way.

The key class is `SimpleLuceneCocoonSearcherImpl`, thus providing the integration with the Lucene query functionality. The key method `search()` returns a `Hits` object, replete with all the matches. This can then be processed as required.

Index Updating

Lucene is capable of updating an existing index with any changes that may have occurred. It can do this without the need to generate the index from scratch. Although the Cocoon/Lucene integration classes support this functionality, it is managed as an option on the index creation code. What this means is that to update an index you must crawl the document tree from the same place the index was originally created from. You cannot update a single file, although Lucene can do this if required. Naturally, you could write custom functionality to do this task; for example, if you have an application in which a user can alter files, you may want to have the index updated as the user changes the content.

The Cocoon Search Example

A good place to start examining how Lucene actually works with Cocoon, and how you can go about adding indexing and searching capabilities to your application, is with the Cocoon searching example. The search welcome page is linked to the main Cocoon welcome page, but for the record it can be found at `http://localhost:8080/cocoon/search/welcome`. As you will note from Figure 19.2, this page contains links that demonstrate the creation of an index and how to search the index using both XSP and the `SearchGenerator` component.

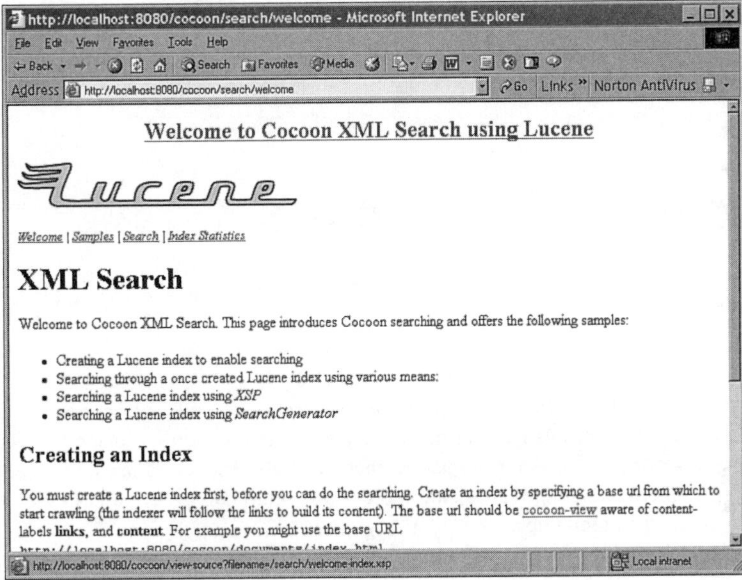

Figure 19.2
Cocoon search samples index page.

Creating an Index

The first thing to do is create an index. Clicking the Create link takes you to a page that allows you to create or update an index, as illustrated in Figure 19.3.

By default, the create index page uses the Cocoon documentation, physically located in `$TOMCAT_HOME/webapps/cocoon/documentation` and available from the default URL of `http://localhost:8080/cocoon/documentation/index.html`. This page also shows the configuration settings for the Cocoon/Lucene pairing. If you ensure that the Create radio button is selected and then click on the Create button, Cocoon will start to index. But what is it actually doing?

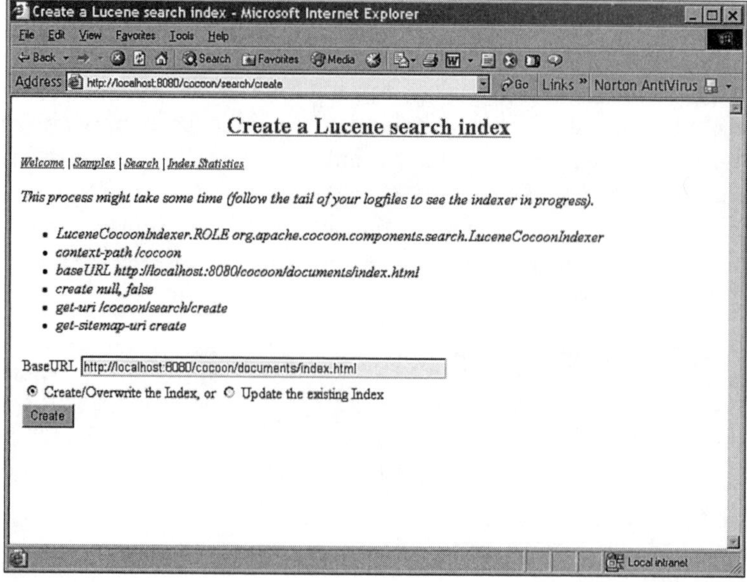

Figure 19.3

Creating an index of the Cocoon documentation.

> **Note**
>
> Note that if you attempt to do the index creation process on a Windows-based platform, you may experience problems. The most likely cause is that you are using the default `FilesystemStore` class for persisting cache objects. This class uses an object key as a filename when persisting the object, and the algorithm can generate keys that are too long to be used as filenames.
>
> The solution is to use the `JispFileSystemStore` class instead. This uses a single file with a B-Tree index and is a more scalable solution. You can change the persistence method by modifying the class used in the `<cache-persistent>` element found in `cocoon.xconf`. Having said this, as of release 2.0.3 there were still a few bugs with this method that may be manifest when indexing a relatively large tree such as the Cocoon documentation.
>
> Another possible problem may be caused by insufficient heap memory being available to the JVM. This can be cured by specifying the heapsize to use as part of the Web container configuration (for example, `catalina.bat/Catalina.sh` for Tomcat). The JVM setting to use is the `-Xmx` option. It is also recommended that you change the store janitor configuration in `cocoon.xconf` to reflect the JVM heapsize setting. See Chapter 23, "Cocoon Administration," for more on tuning and performance.

After the index has been created, of course it can be searched. The search samples include methods that demonstrate this, as you will see in the next section, "Searching an Index."

The creation of the index is initiated by the XSP that presents the preceding page. If you look at this file, found in `$TOMCAT_HOME/webapps/cocoon/search/create-index.xsp`, there are several points worthy of note.

First, look at the following extracts, based mainly on code from the `createIndex()` method:

```
LuceneCocoonIndexer lcii;
Analyzer analyzer = LuceneCocoonHelper.getAnalyzer(
    "org.apache.lucene.analysis.standard.StandardAnalyzer" );

...

lcii = (LuceneCocoonIndexer)this.manager.lookup( LuceneCocoonIndexer.ROLE );

Directory directory = LuceneCocoonHelper.getDirectory(
    new File( workDir, "index" ), create );

lcii.setAnalyzer( analyzer );
URL base_url = new URL( baseURL );
lcii.index( directory, create, base_url );
```

This code is where the indexer and analyzer get configured and the indexing code gets called. The `getDirectory()` method call sets up the folder that will hold the index files, creating it if it is not already there. The default place is in a folder called `index` under the context work area. The code fragment also uses the Lucene standard analyzer. An analyzer is used to configure the rules, or *policy*, that content will be subject to when being parsed for indexing. The analyzer includes a list of *stop words*, text that will be ignored because it is not useful for searches. The stop word list in the standard analyzer is based in English, but there is another stop word list for German and you could create your own for any other language, filtering, or other purpose you may have.

A URL object is then created using the `baseURL` string. This defaults to the documentation index document, although the sample form does allow this to be changed.

The call to `lcii.index()` finally gets things going, calling the code in the Cocoon indexer implementation pointed to from a lookup to the `LuceneCocoonIndexer`. This class is the `SimpleLuceneCocoonIndexerImpl` mentioned earlier, and if you examine the source code of that class, you will see how it initiates the crawling process, and the subsequent fetching and indexing of resources.

The previous code is the same code that is called if the index is being updated. The `create` variable is a boolean flag that indicates whether an index creation (`true`) or update (`false`) is taking place.

The following list summarizes the steps that are being taken by the Cocoon indexing example. When you are developing your own index creation functionality, you will need to emulate these steps:

1. Know the root folder where you want the index folder to be placed.
2. Know the index folder name.
3. Know whether you are creating or updating the index.
4. Declare and instantiate a Lucene `Analyzer` object.
5. Declare and instantiate the Cocoon indexer implementation object.
6. Use the Cocoon indexing helper methods to configure the folder that will be used to hold the index and obtain the associated object.
7. Configure the analyzer for the indexer.
8. Get a `URL` object that represents the base to be indexed from.
9. Call the indexer `index()` method, passing the index folder, create flag, and base URL.

Searching an Index

Cocoon allows the searching of an index in two preconfigured ways: via XSP and with a generator. Because both methods interface with Lucene in exactly the same way, let's look at how the examples demonstrate the integration and then consider the mechanics of the two methods.

Using either method, you will need to generate a search string that is simply the phrase being searched for. This search string then needs to be passed to the Lucene search methods for processing, and the result (hits) subsequently needs to be handled. Consider how this is handled by examining the following code fragments based on the examples:

```
LuceneCocoonSearcher lcs =
    (LuceneCocoonSearcher)this.manager.lookup( LuceneCocoonSearcher.ROLE );
Directory directory =
    LuceneCocoonHelper.getDirectory( new File( workDir, "index" ), false );
Analyzer analyzer =
    LuceneCocoonHelper.getAnalyzer(
        "org.apache.lucene.analysis.standard.StandardAnalyzer" );

lcs.setAnalyzer( analyzer );
lcs.setDirectory( directory );
Hits hits = lcs.search( query_string, LuceneXMLIndexer.BODY_FIELD );
```

The basic procedure here is as follows:

1. Set up a searcher, finding the implementation (`SimpleLuceneCocoonSearcherImpl`) from the role lookup on the `LucentCocoonSearcher` interface.
2. Set up an object that reflects the folder where the index has been created.
3. Create a reference to the analyzer.
4. Set the analyzer to use with the searcher.
5. Set the directory to use with the searcher.
6. Call the search and get back the hits.

The first few steps are very similar to what is required for creating the index, the main difference being the call to the search method. The two arguments are the actual query string and a default index field to use if none is specified in the query string. The index field is discussed further in this chapter when we look at search terms, but the default used here is the `body` field, representing pure text (as opposed to attribute values, for example) extracted from the source document.

Given that the previous fragments represent how both the XSP and `SearchGenerator` handle calling a search, what is handled differently? The answer is pretty simple; it's the result of the search—the hits that have been found. The `Hits` object is a collection of Lucene document objects, each of these containing index fields that reflect the location of the matches. Both methods manage the returning of hits to the user using a class called `LuceneCocoonPager`. This allows the "paging" of results so that large result sets can be examined in chunks, 10 at a time by default.

Handling Search Results with XSP

Looking in more detail at how the XSP file has been written to handle search results, take a look at the source file that can be found in `$TOMCAT_HOME/webapps/cocoon/search/search-index.xsp`. Examination of code shows that it handles the results coming back in the `Hits` object via the pager class as mentioned previously, but it then needs to handle the display of the hits directly. For each of the hits returned, it uses the following extract to display the data:

```
LuceneCocoonPager.HitWrapper hw = (LuceneCocoonPager.HitWrapper)i.next();
Document doc = hw.getDocument();
float score = hw.getScore();
String url = doc.get( LuceneXMLIndexer.URL_FIELD );
```

```
<xsp:content>
  <tr>
    <td> <xsp:expr>String.valueOf((int)(score * 100.0f))</xsp:expr>% </td>
    <td> <xsp:expr>String.valueOf(counter + 1)</xsp:expr> </td>
    <td>
      <a target="_blank">
        <xsp:attribute name="href"><xsp:expr>url</xsp:expr></xsp:attribute>
        <xsp:expr>url</xsp:expr>
      </a>
    </td>
  </tr>
</xsp:content>
```

The hit attributes are placed into variables and then used as expressions to fill a table. You may note the use of the `<xsp:attribute>` elements to enable the placing of the URL variable using `<xsp:expr>`.

The XSP file also uses hidden fields to maintain the query string, page length, and index values for the next and previous page (should they exist). It can then use these to handle the movement between pages. You will note that each time the XSP is called, it checks for the presence of these parameters so that the management of the results via the pager works correctly.

Handling Search Results with SearchGenerator

The `SearchGenerator` source can be found within the `org.apache.cocoon.generation` package. To initiate a search, you simply call the generator with a query string specified in a parameter called `queryString`. The subsequent results are presented as XML for handling in the pipeline.

The Cocoon search example (Cocoon 2.0.3) produces a URL along the lines of `http://localhost:8080/cocoon/search/findIt?queryString=lucene`.

This is handled by a very simple sitemap match:

```
<map:match pattern="findIt">
  <map:generate type="search"/>
  <map:transform type="log"/>
  <map:transform src="stylesheets/search2html.xsl"/>
  <map:serialize/>
</map:match>
```

This code block facilitates the logging of the results for debugging purposes and then uses a stylesheet to present the content. If you append "`&cocoon-view=content`" to the end of the previous request, you can see the resultant XML before any transformations are hit. In version 2.0.3 of Cocoon, the previous request produces an XML stream like this:

```
<?xml version="1.0" encoding="UTF-8" ?>
  <search:results date="1032258860636"
          query-string="lucene"
          start-index="0" page-length="10"
          xmlns:search=http://apache.org/cocoon/search/1.0
          xmlns:xlink="http://www.w3.org/1999/xlink">
    <search:hits total-count="2" count-of-pages="1">
      <search:hit rank="0"
              score="0.692587"
              uri="http://localhost:8080/cocoon/documents/
➥userdocs/concepts/xmlsearching.html" />
      <search:hit rank="1"
              score="0.16797704"
              uri="http://localhost:8080/cocoon/documents/
➥userdocs/generators/search-generator.html" />
    </search:hits>
    <search:navigation total-count="2" count-of-pages="1"
            has-next="false" has-previous="false"
            next-index="2" previous-index="0">
    <search:navigation-page start-index="0" />
  </search:navigation>
</search:results>
```

The hits are returned within `<search:hit>` elements within a `<search:hits>` block. You will note that this search has only two hits. No paging is occurring and this is reflected in the detail in the `<search:navigation>` element. What would the XML stream look like if paging were occurring? Examine the following XML:

```
<?xml version="1.0" encoding="UTF-8" ?>
<search:results date="1032262069951"
        query-string="cocoon" start-index="10" page-length="10"
        xmlns:search=http://apache.org/cocoon/search/1.0
        xmlns:xlink="http://www.w3.org/1999/xlink">
  <search:hits total-count="76" count-of-pages="8">
    <search:hit rank="10"
            score="0.24428736"
            uri="http://localhost:8080/cocoon/documents/doclist.html" />
    <search:hit rank="11"
            score="0.2402159"
            uri="http://localhost:8080/cocoon/documents/
➥userdocs/generators/script-generator.html" />
```

```
    <search:hit rank="12"
            score="0.23207298"
            uri="http://localhost:8080/cocoon/documents/plan/doc.html" />
    <search:hit rank="13"
            score="0.23071186"
            uri="http://localhost:8080/cocoon/documents/faq/faq-install.html" />
    <search:hit rank="14"
            score="0.22455841"
            uri="http://localhost:8080/cocoon/documents/
➥userdocs/transformers/xt-transformer.html" />
    <search:hit rank="15"
            score="0.2228913"
            uri="http://localhost:8080/cocoon/documents/
➥faq/faq-configure-environment.html" />
    <search:hit rank="16"
            score="0.21861102"
            uri="http://localhost:8080/cocoon/documents/
➥userdocs/xsp/xsp.html" />
    <search:hit rank="17"
            score="0.21849725"
            uri="http://localhost:8080/cocoon/documents/link/projects.html" />
    <search:hit rank="18"
            score="0.21171571"
            uri="http://localhost:8080/cocoon/documents/
➥userdocs/concepts/persistence.html" />
    <search:hit rank="19"
            score="0.20728469"
            uri="http://localhost:8080/cocoon/documents/plan/linkstatus.html" />
  </search:hits>
  <search:navigation total-count="76" count-of-pages="8"
          has-next="true" has-previous="true"
          next-index="20" previous-index="0">
    <search:navigation-page start-index="0" />
    <search:navigation-page start-index="10" />
    <search:navigation-page start-index="20" />
    <search:navigation-page start-index="30" />
    <search:navigation-page start-index="40" />
    <search:navigation-page start-index="50" />
    <search:navigation-page start-index="60" />
    <search:navigation-page start-index="70" />
  </search:navigation>
</search:results>
```

This is the second page of a search that returns 10 hits per page. Each of the 10 hits is there, with its respective ordinal ranking in the `rank` attribute of the `<search:hit>` element. The `<search-navigation>` block is a little more extensive here than for a single page of hits. It contains information about the total number of hits, the number of pages, whether there are previous or next pages for the current page and the indexes to use if there are, and then the starting indexes for each page. This final part allows the HTML transformer to display a "quick link" menu of each page, as shown in Figure 19.4.

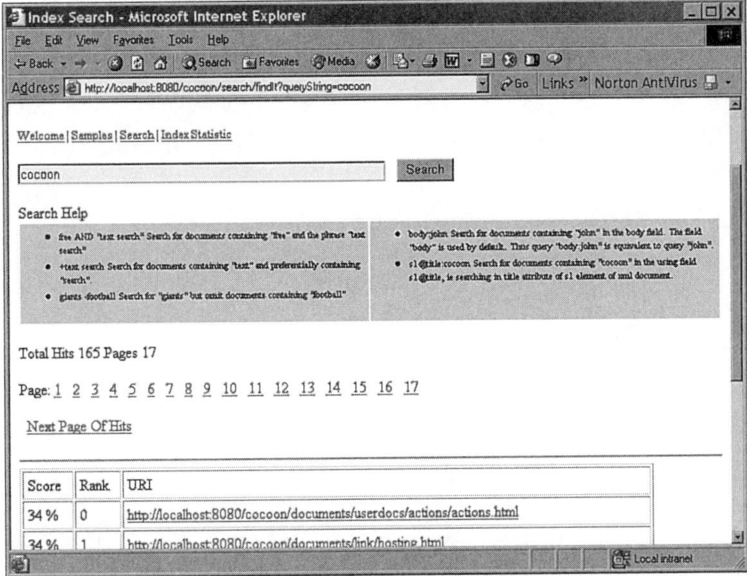

Figure 19.4
Search results from SearchGenerator, highlighting the "Quick Links" feature.

Search Phrases

Lucene offers powerful search capabilities. To understand how to use this feature effectively, it is worth looking at what is in a Lucene index a little more. Throughout this chapter we have looked at the mechanics of creating an index and performing a search, and have mentioned several Lucene objects, such as `Document` and `Field`. The `Document` object is the base unit that is created for indexing and searching. Each `Document` object has a collection of `Fields` that provide name-value pairings. When Cocoon indexes a file, it builds document objects for the constituent parts of the file—its pure text, elements, and attributes. For each of these parts several fields are built up. Pure text is tokenized and referenced using a field name of `body`. XML element contents are tokenized and referenced using a field name that matches the element. XML element attributes are tokenized and given a field name reference made up of *`element-name@attribute-name`*. In addition, fields are added that store the URL of the source document and a unique id. These two fields respectively allow the content to be linked to and index updates to be managed. You may have realized that because XML element text is also pure text in the source document, two fields are added, one with a name of `body` and one with the element name. Both contain the same tokenized data.

To make this point a little clearer, take the following XML element:

```
<link href="file.html">next</link>
```

The associated document object will have the fields as specified in Table 19.3.

Table 19.3 *Example Field Name/Value Pairs*

Name	Value
`body`	Token representing "next"
`link`	Token representing "next"
`link@href`	Token representing "`file.html`"
`URL`	URL of the source document
`UID`	Unique identifier

So what can Lucene do when it comes to searching for results? Obviously, it can search for single words, for example,

```
direct
```

This would do a case-insensitive search for all the instances of "direct". One point to note is that Lucene does not currently support *stemming*—that is, the preceding search will return only whole words and not partial matches such as "*direct*ory" or "in*direct*". To achieve this, you must use a wildcard such as "direct*". Again, Lucene does not support the use of a wildcard as the first character in a search.

You can search for text in a field by prefacing the word with *`field name:`*. In fact, if no field name is specified, the search mechanism automatically defaults to `body`; thus, searching for `direct` is the same as searching for `body:direct`.

As an example of this, take the following XML file:

```
<?xml version="1.0"?>
<page>
```

```
  <para>
    This is a paragraph of text.
    This file also has a link to a file - myfile.html
  </para>
  <link href="myfile.html">link to myfile.html</link>
</page>
```

Searching for `myfile.html` will match the instance in the `<para>` element and in the `<link>` element. Searching for `link:myfile.html` will match the instance in the `<link>` element. Searching for `link@href:myfile.html` will match the instance in the `href` attribute.

There are other ways of manipulating the search, such as using fuzzy and proximity searches. You can boost the relevance of one term over another. Boolean operators such as `AND` and `OR` can be used. Terms can be grouped using parentheses, and special characters can be escaped. For more details on this topic, see the Lucene documentation available from `http://jakarta.apache.org/lucene`.

Summary

In this chapter we have touched on how powerful Lucene is as a search engine. The built-in integration into Cocoon offers significant functionality that can be harnessed to index XML content and search that content using flexible search terms.

The samples included with Cocoon show how easy it is to hook into the Lucene engine and crawl through a hierarchy of content. But don't forget that these are just samples. The components supplied with Cocoon, as demonstrated in the samples, illustrate how you can add "on demand" indexing capabilities, along with multipage search interfaces. Take these samples and make them your own by extending them or even starting from scratch and developing your own bespoke code. You may also find that you want to index documents that do not fit into the predefined structure. Perhaps you will want to index single files. Perhaps you will want to automatically update an index as content is dynamically changed. Perhaps you will want to index content that is stored not as XML but as text or even in a database. This is all possible—all you have to do is learn from the base material provided and use Lucene as you need to use it.

CHAPTER 20
Building Portals with Cocoon

A big trend in Web application development is portals. Portals are defined in various ways, depending on your application (or what vendor you are talking to!). In general, a portal is a Web application that provides the user with various content areas within a single page. The content in each of these areas might come from different sources; a stock quote ticker, for example, might be pulled from an online service whereas a list of product offerings might come from a database.

Portal Overview

To start with, let's enumerate some of the key features of portals that may or may not be present in all implementations.

Content

Yes, of course a portal must include content! But what a portal has that an ordinary Web page doesn't is multiple content areas or panes. As just mentioned, these may contain data from multiple sources, such as Web applications, other Web sites, online services, discussion areas, and multimedia. Aggregating them in a way that is coherent from both a content and a presentation perspective can be a real challenge. A site can quickly become useless if there are simply too many content panes in front of the user.

Authentication

Obviously, authentication is a key component of most portal applications. What we're talking about is authentication that covers not just the Web server that the users point to, but the underlying applications or information sources required by the Web application as well. Often this is referred to as single-signon (a concept widely discussed but difficult to implement). Another part of authentication is when the content is dependent on the security level of the user. For example, a Web page for a software company might extol all the virtues of the product offerings to unauthenticated users while saving the extensive bug list for registered customers with support contracts.

Personalization

Another important part of designing portals is to provide the user with the option to customize the viewable content. This can concern either presentation customization, such as changing graphics for people from different companies, or the inclusion or exclusion of various content. In many cases, portal developers need to have rules over just what can be customized; some content panes may be essential to the site and thus cannot be excluded by the user from his window. Finally, if any personalization is done, a mechanism must exist to save the information for the user and retrieve on the next login or visit. In many cases, personalization is a critical part of one-to-one marketing, so it must be done well and should include anonymous users.

There are many other aspects important in designing portals, but that is not in the scope of this chapter. Because we are talking about Cocoon, we'll stick to the three main areas just discussed. However, be aware that if you want to start developing a portal, design is critical! We won't show you how to do it here, but you must pay attention to who your users are, what features/content they need (and which will keep them coming back), and, most especially, organization. Without a clear organization of the content areas, and a look and feel that keeps users focused on the areas you want them to pay attention to, you will end up with dissatisfied customers.

Using Cocoon to Build Portals

Cocoon is well-suited for building portals, thanks to such features as pipeline logic, aggregation mechanisms, SOAP, and the general XML-driven nature of the software. Out of the box, you can use these features to build quite sophisticated portal applications. In the scratchpad area of the latest version, 2.0.3, you will find the `sunShine` components that are specifically designed to help you build portals. We'll briefly discuss this topic at the end of the chapter.

The Cocoon Documentation Site

We have already seen in previous chapters several examples of techniques you can use to build portals. In this chapter, we'll present these in a more comprehensive fashion. We'll start with the end product: an application we'll call the "Cocoon Documentation Site." In designing this application, we've decided to include the following content:

- Various introductory paragraphs
- Links to other Cocoon resources
- Search results from Google for "cocoon"
- Search results from Amazon.com for books on Cocoon
- A list of all components from an Xindice database

For personalization, we'll want an optional authentication mechanism that can be used to store and retrieve customization parameters for various users. We'll let users decide, for example, what the first pane is that they want to view when they visit the site.

Creating the Main Panes

For the sake of simplicity, we'll stick to a three-pane layout. The header pane will contain the application and page titles and an application toolbar. This toolbar will not change as the user navigates through the site. We'll have a left-hand sidebar for the navigation of the site. This pane will have four categories: Home, Cocoon Links, Cocoon Components, and Cocoon Documentation. Cocoon Links will have two subcategories: Books and Web Links. Cocoon Components will have several subcategories, one for each type of Cocoon component. The final pane, the main content pane, will display content as determined by which navigation link the user has selected. Listing 20.1 shows the XML file for the header pane. Listing 20.2 shows the XML for the sidebar, or table of contents, and Listing 20.3 shows the XML for the home page of the site. Notice that in the first two listings, we are using our own namespace. This helps keep various tags separate and ensures that if by chance we use the same tag in other content, there will be no confusion.

Listing 20.1 *Header Pane (header.xml)*

```
<?xml version="1.0" encoding="ISO-8859-1"?>

<portal:header
 xmlns:portal="http://samspublishing.com/cocoon/portal"
>
```

Listing 20.1 *(continued)*

```
  <portal:header-title>
    Welcome to the Cocoon Documentation Site
  </portal:header-title>

  <portal:toolbar>
    <item href="login">Login</item>
    <item href="customize">Customize</item>
  </portal:toolbar>

</portal:header>
```

Listing 20.2 *Table of Contents Pane (contents.xml)*

```
<?xml version="1.0" encoding="ISO-8859-1"?>

<portal:sections
 xmlns:portal="http://samspublishing.com/cocoon/portal/1.0"
>

  <portal:section label="home" title="Home"/>
  <portal:section label="docs" title="Cocoon Documentation"/>

  <portal:section label="components" title="Cocoon Components">
    <portal:content href="components/matcher">Matchers</portal:content>
    <portal:content href="components/selector">Selectors</portal:content>
  </portal:section>

  <portal:section label="links" title="Cocoon Links">
    <portal:content href="links/books">Books</portal:content>
    <portal:content href="links/weblinks">Web Links</portal:content>
  </portal:section>

</portal:sections>
```

The table of contents is divided into sections, represented by the `<portal:section>` tags. Optionally, sections can have submenus or content panes, as the components and links sections do.

Listing 20.3 *Home Page (home.xml)*

```
<?xml version="1.0"?>

<page>
  <paragraph>
   This site provides resources and documentation for
   Apache Cocoon. Naturally, the site is powered by Cocoon.
   This site also illustrates how to use Cocoon to build portals.
  </paragraph>
</page>
```

Creating the Content Pipelines

The first thing we want to do is set up pipelines that will retrieve the various data sources we need. These pipelines each have an XSLT transformation defined and will all use the `XMLSerializer` so that we can more easily incorporate the pipelines into a single page via aggregation.

Listing 20.4 shows the first set of pipelines. We have defined the following:

- `portal-piece/page/*`: A pipeline that reads the XML file defined by the `{1}` parameter.
- `portal-piece/books`: A pipeline to access the `amazon.xsp` file we created in Chapter 17, "Cocoon Interfaces: SOAP."
- `portal-piece/weblinks`: A pipeline to access the `google.xsp` file we created in Chapter 17.
- `portal-piece/components/*`: A pipeline that retrieves a list of Cocoon components from an Xindice database based on the type of component as defined by the `{1}` parameter, as shown in Chapter 16, "Cocoon Interfaces: Databases."

Note that you must have already created the examples referenced; otherwise, these portal sections won't work. See Table 20.1, later in this chapter, for a list of all files belonging to this portal example and where they came from.

Listing 20.4 *Content Pipelines*

```
<map:pipeline>
 <map:match pattern="portal-piece/links/books">
  <map:generate type="serverpages" src="portal/amazon.xsp"/>
  <map:transform src="style/portal/amazon.xsl"/>
```

Listing 20.4 *(continued)*

```
  <map:serialize type="xml"/>
 </map:match>

 <map:match pattern="portal-piece/links/weblinks">
  <map:generate type="serverpages" src="portal/google.xsp"/>
  <map:transform src="style/portal/google.xsl"/>
  <map:serialize type="xml"/>
 </map:match>

 <map:match pattern="portal-piece/components/*">
  <map:generate src="xmldb:xindice://localhost:4080/db/cocoon/#/cocoon-compone
➥nt[component-type='{1}']"/>
  <map:transform src="style/portal/components.xsl"/>
  <map:serialize type="xml"/>
 </map:match>

 <map:match pattern="portal-piece/*">
  <map:generate src="portal/{1}.xml" type="file"/>
  <map:transform src="style/portal/page.xsl"/>
  <map:serialize type="xml"/>
 </map:match>

</map:pipeline>
```

Note that text for `components.xsl` can be found in Listing 20.15, and that for `page.xsl` can be found in Listing 20.16.

Implementing Authentication

In this example, authentication is optional; that is, users do not have to authenticate to use our site. But if users want to change things, we need to know who they are so that we can save their data and retrieve it when they come back. The top toolbar will have a Login link that users can use to bring up a simple form that asks for their email address and a password.

As we have seen before, there are several ways to handle the authentication itself: in an XSP, in a custom or built-in action, or even in the sitemap itself. We'll choose to use the `DatabaseAuthenticationAction` that we used before in Chapter 12, "Using Sitemap Logic: Actions and Forms." The definition file for our portal is shown in Listing 20.5.

Listing 20.5 *Definition File for DatabaseAuthenticationAction (auth-def.xml)*

```
<?xml version="1.0" encoding="UTF-8"?>

<auth-descriptor>
  <connection>abc</connection>
  <table name="UserPreferences">
    <select dbcol="UserUid" request-param="user" to-session="user"/>
    <select dbcol="UserPwd" request-param="pass"/>
  </table>
</auth-descriptor>
```

The `UserPreferences` table reference here is explained in the next section. Note that when the authentication succeeds, the `DatabaseAuthenticationAction` will populate the session object with the value of the request parameter called `user`. We'll rely on this attribute to retrieve the personalization.

The pipeline that implements this action is shown here:

```
<map:match pattern="portal/authenticate">
 <map:act type="authenticator">
  <map:parameter name="descriptor"
    value="context://cocoon/abc/portal/auth-def.xml"/>
  <map:redirect-to uri="../portal"/>
 </map:act>
</map:match>
```

If the authentication succeeds, the user is sent off to the portal entrance. Otherwise, he is returned to the login page.

Implementing Personalization

Because all we want to do is to illustrate the point, we'll only let the user provide a nickname to be used in a personalized greeting and let him decide which of the three main categories should be loaded when the site is accessed. This information will be stored in a database table called `UserPreferences`. Obviously, much more information could be stored as well. Listing 20.6 shows the definition of this table.

Listing 20.6 *UserPreferences Table (portal.sql)*

```
use abc;

drop table UserPreferences;
```

Listing 20.6 *(continued)*

```
create table UserPreferences (
UserUid         varchar(10)     not null,
UserPwd         varchar(10)     not null,
UserHomePage    varchar(20)     null,
UserNickName    varchar(50)     null
);

insert into UserPreferences values ('johnsonb', 'secret',
   'links', 'Bob Johnson');
insert into UserPreferences values ('smithm', 'lamb123',
   'components', 'Mary Smith');
```

We'll use a custom action, called `PortalPreferencesAction`, to retrieve user preferences and make them available to the sitemap. This action, shown in Listing 20.7, will be able to take the userid stored in a cookie and retrieve the preferences for the user.

Listing 20.7 *PortalPreferencesAction (PortalPreferencesAction.java)*

```
package test;

import org.apache.avalon.excalibur.datasource.DataSourceComponent;
import org.apache.avalon.framework.component.ComponentException;
import org.apache.avalon.framework.component.ComponentManager;
import org.apache.avalon.framework.component.ComponentSelector;
import org.apache.avalon.framework.configuration.Configurable;
import org.apache.avalon.framework.configuration.ConfigurationException;
import org.apache.avalon.framework.configuration.Configuration;
import org.apache.avalon.framework.parameters.Parameters;
import org.apache.avalon.framework.thread.ThreadSafe;
import org.apache.avalon.framework.component.Composable;
import org.apache.avalon.framework.activity.Disposable;
import org.apache.cocoon.Constants;
import org.apache.cocoon.environment.ObjectModelHelper;
import org.apache.cocoon.environment.Cookie;
import org.apache.cocoon.environment.http.HttpCookie;
import org.apache.cocoon.environment.Redirector;
import org.apache.cocoon.environment.Request;
import org.apache.cocoon.environment.Response;
import org.apache.cocoon.environment.Context;
import org.apache.cocoon.environment.Session;
import org.apache.cocoon.environment.SourceResolver;
```

Listing 20.7 *(continued)*

```
import org.apache.cocoon.util.Tokenizer;
import org.apache.cocoon.acting.AbstractAction;

import java.sql.Connection;
import java.sql.ResultSet;
import java.sql.Statement;
import java.sql.SQLException;
import java.util.HashMap;
import java.util.Map;

public class PortalPreferencesAction extends AbstractAction
   implements Composable, Disposable, ThreadSafe
{
    protected ComponentSelector dbselector;
    protected ComponentManager manager;

    public void compose(ComponentManager manager) throws ComponentException {
        this.dbselector = (ComponentSelector)
           manager.lookup(DataSourceComponent.ROLE + "Selector");

    }

    protected final DataSourceComponent getDataSource(String pool)
      throws ComponentException {
        return (DataSourceComponent) this.dbselector.select(pool);
    }

    public Map act (Redirector redirector, SourceResolver resolver, Map
objectModel,
      String src, Parameters parameters) throws Exception {
        HashMap map = new HashMap();
        Request req = ObjectModelHelper.getRequest(objectModel);
        Response resp = ObjectModelHelper.getResponse(objectModel);
        Context ctx = ObjectModelHelper.getContext(objectModel);
        Session ses = req.getSession(true);

    if (ses == null) {
        getLogger().error("Expected valid session - unable to run");
        return null;
    }

    Cookie cookie = null;
```

Listing 20.7 *(continued)*

```
String homePage = "home";
String nickName = "user";

Cookie[] cookies = req.getCookies();

if (cookies != null) {
        for (int i = 0; i < cookies.length; i++) {
        if (cookies[i].getName().equals("cocoonportaluser")) {
            getLogger().debug("Found cookie");
            cookie = cookies[i];
            break;
        }
        }
}

if (!ses.isNew()) {
    if (ses.getAttribute("homePage") != null
        && ses.getAttribute("nickName") != null) {
    // Pick up settings from session

    getLogger().debug("Preferences already set");
    homePage = (String)ses.getAttribute("homePage");
    nickName = (String)ses.getAttribute("nickName");
    } else {
    String userid = (String)ses.getAttribute("user");

    if (userid != null) {
        getLogger().debug("User in session is " + userid);
        HashMap prefs = retrievePreferences(userid, ses);

            if (prefs != null) {
            homePage = (String)prefs.get("homePage");
            nickName = (String)prefs.get("nickName");
            }

        cookie = new HttpCookie("cocoonportaluser", userid);
        cookie.setMaxAge(365*24*60*60);
        resp.addCookie(cookie);
    } else {
        getLogger().debug("No user in session");
    }
```

Listing 20.7 *(continued)*

```
        }
    } else {
        if (cookie != null) {
        getLogger().debug("Found a cookie");
        // Use the userid in the cookie to get prefs

        String userid = cookie.getValue();
        HashMap prefs = retrievePreferences(userid, ses);

        if (prefs != null) {
            homePage = (String)prefs.get("homePage");
            nickName = (String)prefs.get("nickName");
        }
        } else {
        getLogger().debug("No cookie");
        String userid = (String)ses.getAttribute("user");

        if (userid != null) {
            getLogger().debug("User in session is " + userid);
            HashMap prefs = retrievePreferences(userid, ses);

                if (prefs != null) {
                homePage = (String)prefs.get("homePage");
                nickName = (String)prefs.get("nickName");
                }

            cookie = new HttpCookie("cocoonportaluser", userid);
            resp.addCookie(cookie);
        } else {
            getLogger().debug("No user in session");
        }
        }
    }

    map.put("homePage", homePage);
    map.put("nickName", nickName);

    return map;
    }

    private HashMap retrievePreferences(String userid, Session ses) {
```

Listing 20.7 *(continued)*

```
        DataSourceComponent dataSource = null;
        Connection conn = null;
        HashMap prefs = null;

        try {
        dataSource = getDataSource("tutorial");
        conn = dataSource.getConnection();
            Statement stmt = conn.createStatement();

        String cmd = "select * from UserPreferences where UserUid = '" +
        userid + "'";
        ResultSet rs = stmt.executeQuery(cmd);

        if (rs.next()) {
        prefs = new HashMap();
        prefs.put("homePage", rs.getString(3));
        prefs.put("nickName", rs.getString(4));
            ses.setAttribute("homePage", rs.getString(3));
            ses.setAttribute("nickName", rs.getString(4));
        }

    } catch (Exception e) {
        getLogger().error("Unable to execute query", e);
    } finally {
        try {
            if (conn != null) conn.close();
            } catch (SQLException sqe) {
                getLogger().warn("Error closing datasource", sqe);
            }
        }

        this.dbselector.release(dataSource);

    return prefs;
    }

    public void dispose() {
        this.manager.release(dbselector);
    }
}
```

Briefly, the point of this action is to set two sitemap parameters, `nickName` and `homePage`. These are either retrieved from the database and put into the session, or retrieved right from the session. This means that the database is hit only once, per user, per session (except for the authentication itself, of course). To retrieve the preferences from the database, this action relies on the userid that is contained in either the cookie or the session. After the login, the value of the `user` request parameter is saved as a session attribute. If there is no cookie, but this attribute is present, then we can retrieve the values. For future reference, we then create and save a new cookie, containing the user's login name.

We compile this action as described in Chapter 12. The definition of the action, which goes inside the `<map:actions>` block in the sitemap, looks like this:

```
<map:action name="portal-prefs"
    src="test.PortalPreferencesAction"/>
```

Miscellaneous Files

To make all this work, we need a few more files. Listing 20.8 and Listing 20.9 show the login form and the customization form. Listings 20.10 through 20.12 show the XML files that constitute each of the main sections of our portal—Cocoon Links, Cocoon Components, and Cocoon Documentation. These pages are just placeholders; the real content will be provided by the portal pages we pull in via aggregation, as we'll see in a minute.

Listing 20.8 *Login Form (login.html)*

```
<page>
 <form action="authenticate" method="post">
  <center>

  <h3>Please enter your user id and password, so we can
   load your preferences</h3>
  <br/>

  <table>
   <tr>
    <td align="right">User:</td>
    <td align="left"><input type="text" name="user"/></td>
   </tr>
   <tr>
    <td align="right">Password:</td>
    <td align="left"><input type="password" name="pass"/></td>
   </tr>
```

Listing 20.8 *(continued)*

```
   <tr>
    <td colspan="2" align="center"><input type="submit" value="Login"/></td>
   </tr>
  </table>

  </center>
 </form>
</page>
```

Listing 20.9 *Customization Form (customize.xml)*

```
<page>
 <form action="update" method="post">
  <center>

  <h3>Select what you want to customize:</h3>
  <br/>

  <table width="100%">
   <tr>
    <td align="right">Nick name:</td>
    <td align="left"><input type="text" name="nickname"/></td>
   </tr>
   <tr>
    <td align="right">Home page:</td>
    <td align="left"><select name="home">
     <option value="home">Home</option>
     <option value="docs">Cocoon Documentation</option>
     <option value="components">Cocoon Components</option>
     <option value="links">Cocoon Links</option>
    </select></td>
   </tr>
   <tr>
    <td colspan="2" align="center"><input type="submit" value="save"/></td>
   </tr>
  </table>

  </center>
 </form>
</page>
```

Listing 20.10 *Cocoon Links Page (links.xml)*

```
<?xml version="1.0"?>

<page>
  <paragraph>Select link type from the left</paragraph>
</page>
```

Listing 20.11 *Cocoon Components Page (components.xml)*

```
<?xml version="1.0"?>

<page>
  <paragraph>
   Here you will find a list of all built-in components.
   Select a type from the list to the left, to view the members.
  </paragraph>
</page>
```

Listing 20.12 *Cocoon Documentation Page (docs.xml)*

```
<?xml version="1.0"?>

<page>
  <paragraph>
   Here, you can find Cocoon Documentation pulled from the Cocoon
   distribution.
  </paragraph>
</page>
```

Note that these files contain only the HTML necessary to build the forms, because they will be displayed inside the main content pane of the portal.

Putting It All Together: The Stylesheets

We're close to being done. First, let's look at the pipeline that will handle the portal. With all the complexity that we've built into this portal, we need only one pipeline:

```
<map:match pattern="portal/**">
 <map:act type="portal-prefs">
  <map:aggregate element="page">
   <map:part src="cocoon:/portal-piece/{../1}"/>
  </map:aggregate>
  <map:transform src="style/portal/main.xsl">
```

Listing 20.12 *(continued)*

```
    <map:parameter name="nick_name" value="{nickName}"/>
    <map:parameter name="home_page" value="{homePage}"/>
    <map:parameter name="section" value="{../1}"/>
  </map:transform>
  <map:serialize/>
 </map:act>
</map:match>
```

The first thing to note is that the entire pipeline is inside the `<map:act>` tag. That's because any and all portal pages need access to the sitemap parameters of `nickName` and `homePage` as set by our action. You can see that these parameters are passed to the XSL file in the `<map:transform>` step.

Remember the pipelines we defined for the content? Each of them is retrieved with the `<map:aggregate>` block. The output of those pipelines is HTML, because each has its own transformer already built in. The resulting HTML goes in the main content pane and is combined by `page.xsl` with the table of contents pane, `toc.xml`, and the header pane, `header.xml`. The two latter pages are identified by pipeline parameters passed to the XSL page, along with several other parameters—the user's nickname and default home page (from the `PortalPreferencesAction`), and a couple of parameters to help identify where we are URI-wise.

Let's look at the source for `main.xsl`, in Listing 20.13.

Listing 20.13 *Main Portal Stylesheet (main.xsl)*

```
<?xml version="1.0"?>

<xsl:stylesheet
 xmlns:xsl="http://www.w3.org/1999/XSL/Transform" version='1.0'
>

<xsl:import href="content.xsl"/>

<xsl:param name="section"/>
<xsl:param name="nick_name"/>

<xsl:template match="/page">
  <html>
  <head>
   <title><xsl:value-of select="//title"/></title>
```

Listing 20.13 *(continued)*

```
   <link rel="stylesheet" type="text/css" href="styles.css"/>
  </head>

  <body>

  <!-- first, bring in the header -->
  <xsl:apply-templates select="document('header.xml')/*"/>

  <!-- now, bring in the content -->
  <table border="0" cellpadding="10" cellspacing="0" height="100%">
   <tr>
    <td width="20%" bgcolor="lightGrey" valign="top">
     <xsl:apply-templates select="document('contents.xml')/*"/>
    </td>
    <td valign="top" width="80%">
     <table border="0" cellpadding="10" cellspacing="0">
      <tr>
       <td>
        <xsl:copy-of select="."/>
       </td>
      </tr>
     </table>
    </td>
   </tr>
  </table>

  </body>
</html>

</xsl:template>

</xsl:stylesheet>
```

So what's going on here? Well, first we pull in another stylesheet, called `content.xsl`, shown in Listing 20.14. This stylesheet is used to process the header and table of contents panes, both of which are pulled in by `<xsl:apply-templates select="document ('header.xml')/ *"/>` and `<xsl:apply-templates select="document ('contents.xml')/*"/>` instructions, respectively. This is a neat way to pull in XML content, but just be aware that it is an XSL-specific function. You can see that `main.xsl` defines the panes in terms of nested tables—a common and pragmatic way to implement them. The tags from the actual content, because they are already HTML, are simply copied into the output using the `<xsl:copy-of select="."/>` tag.

Listing 20.14 *Portal Content Stylesheet (content.xsl)*

```
<?xml version='1.0'?>

<xsl:stylesheet
 xmlns:xsl="http://www.w3.org/1999/XSL/Transform" version='1.0'
 xmlns:portal="http://samspublishing.com/cocoon/portal/1.0"
>

<!-- global variable -->
<xsl:variable name="url_base">/cocoon/abc/portal</xsl:variable>

<!-- site -->
<xsl:template match="portal:sections">
  <xsl:apply-templates/>
</xsl:template>

<!-- header -->
<xsl:template match="portal:header">
  <xsl:apply-templates/>
</xsl:template>

<xsl:template match="portal:header-title">
  <center>
   <h3>
    <font face="verdana, helvetica, sans serif">
     <xsl:choose>
      <xsl:when test="$nick_name != 'user'">
        Hi <xsl:value-of select="$nick_name"/>
      </xsl:when>
      <xsl:otherwise>
       <xsl:apply-templates/>
      </xsl:otherwise>
     </xsl:choose>
    </font>
   </h3>
  </center>
</xsl:template>
```

Listing 20.14 *(continued)*

```
<xsl:template match="portal:toolbar">
 <center>
  <table bgcolor="lightGrey" width="80%" border="0" cellspacing="0"
     cellpadding="10">
   <xsl:attribute name="cols">
    <xsl:value-of select="count(item)"/>
   </xsl:attribute>

   <tr>
    <xsl:apply-templates/>
   </tr>
  </table>
  <br/> 
 </center>
</xsl:template>

<xsl:template match="item">
 <td class="title-text">
  <a href="{$url_base}/{@href}"><xsl:apply-templates/></a>
 </td>
</xsl:template>

<!-- sections -->
<xsl:template match="portal:section">
  <!-- display section title -->
  <xsl:apply-templates select="portal:name"/>

  <p>
    <xsl:choose>
      <xsl:when test="contains($section,@label)">
       <b>
        <font face="verdana, helvetica, sans serif">
         <xsl:value-of select="@title"/>
        </font>
       </b>
      </xsl:when>
      <xsl:otherwise>
        <a href="{$url_base}/{@label}">
         <font face="verdana, helvetica, sans serif">
          <xsl:value-of select="@title"/>
         </font>
```

Listing 20.14 *(continued)*

```
        </a>
      </xsl:otherwise>
    </xsl:choose>
  </p>

  <xsl:if test="contains($section,@label)">
    <ul>
    <xsl:apply-templates select="portal:content"/>
    </ul>
  </xsl:if>
</xsl:template>

<!-- content pages -->
<xsl:template match="portal:content">
  <xsl:variable name="my_url" value="portal/$section"/>
  <li class="bold-base-text">
   <xsl:choose>
    <xsl:when test="$my_url=@href">
     <b>
      <font face="verdana, helvetica, sans serif">
       <xsl:apply-templates/>
      </font>
     </b>
    </xsl:when>
    <xsl:otherwise>
     <a href="{$url_base}/{@href}">
      <font face="verdana, helvetica, sans serif">
       <xsl:apply-templates/>
      </font>
     </a>
    </xsl:otherwise>
   </xsl:choose>
  </li>
</xsl:template>

</xsl:stylesheet>
```

The main point of this stylesheet is to process the content from the header and table of contents. A key part of its functionality is to figure out what section we are in (refer to the `section` sitemap parameter set in the pipeline) and, based on this, display the table of contents correctly. The current section is put in boldface in the sidebar, and any sublinks under it are then displayed.

We need two more stylesheets. The first is the one to process the Xindice search results for Cocoon components. Listing 20.15 shows this minimal XSL.

Listing 20.15 *Xindice Output XSL (components.xsl)*

```
<?xml version='1.0'?>

<xsl:stylesheet
 xmlns:xsl="http://www.w3.org/1999/XSL/Transform" version='1.0'
 xmlns:collection="http://apache.org/cocoon/xmldb/1.0"
>

<xsl:template match="collection:results">
 <table>
  <tr bgcolor="lightGrey" border="1">
    <td align="center">Type</td>
    <td align="center">Class</td>
  </tr>
  <xsl:apply-templates/>
 </table>
</xsl:template>

<xsl:template match="cocoon-component">
 <tr>
  <td><xsl:value-of select="component-class"/></td>
  <td><xsl:value-of select="component-name"/></td>
 </tr>
</xsl:template>

<xsl:template match="text()">
</xsl:template>

</xsl:stylesheet>
```

Finally, we need the stylesheet shown in Listing 20.16 to handle static pages. (This is the `page.xsl` stylesheet that we defined for our portal-pieces pipelines in Listing 20.4.)

Listing 20.16 *Static Page XSL (page.xsl)*

```
<?xml version='1.0'?>

<xsl:stylesheet
 xmlns:xsl="http://www.w3.org/1999/XSL/Transform" version='1.0'
>

<xsl:template match="/page">
  <xsl:apply-templates/>
</xsl:template>

<xsl:template match="paragraph">
 <p class="base-text"><xsl:apply-templates/></p>
</xsl:template>

<xsl:template match="@*|node()" priority="-1">
  <xsl:copy>
    <xsl:apply-templates select="@*|node()"/>
  </xsl:copy>
</xsl:template>
</xsl:stylesheet>
```

Accessing the Portal

Before trying out our little application, it might be helpful to double-check that all the right files are in place. Table 20.1 lists all the files belong to this example, and shows where they came from.

Table 20.1 *Portal Example Files*

File	Description	Source
abc/portal/amazon.xsp	Amazon SOAP example	Listing 17.3
abc/portal/auth-def.xml	Authentication definition file	Listing 20.5
abc/portal/components.xml	Intro page for Cocoon components	Listing 20.11
abc/portal/contents.xml	Portal table of contents	Listing 20.2
abc/portal/customize.xml	Customization page	Listing 20.9
abc/portal/docs.xml	Intro page for Cocoon documentation	Listing 20.12
abc/portal/google.xsp	Google SOAP example	Listing 17.1
abc/portal/header.xml	Header page	Listing 20.1
abc/portal/home.xml	Default portal page	Listing 20.3

Table 20.1 *(continued)*

File	Description	Source
abc/portal/links.xml	Intro page for Cocoon links	Listing 20.10
abc/portal/login.xml	Login page	Listing 20.8
abc/style/portal/amazon.xsl	Amazon SOAP example XSL	Listing 17.4
abc/style/portal/components.xsl	Xindice output XSL	Listing 20.15
abc/style/portal/content.xsl	Portal Content XSL	Listing 20.14
abc/style/portal/google.xsl	Google SOAP example XSL	Listing 17.2
abc/style/portal/main.xsl	Portal layout XSL	Listing 20.13
abc/style/portal/page.xsl	Static page XSL	Listing 20.16

Let's look at some examples. Figures 20.1 through 20.6 illustrate what we have been doing. First, let's browse to the main page at `http://localhost:8080/cocoon/abc/portal/home`. We should see the page shown in Figure 20.1.

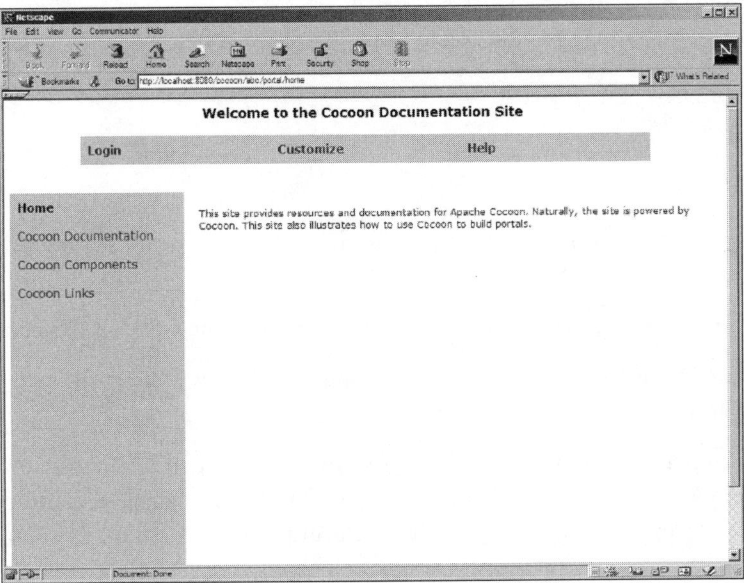

Figure 20.1
Portal home page.

Now, let's look at some books, by clicking on the Cocoon Links link to the left, and then selecting the menu item of Books. The resulting page is shown in Figure 20.2.

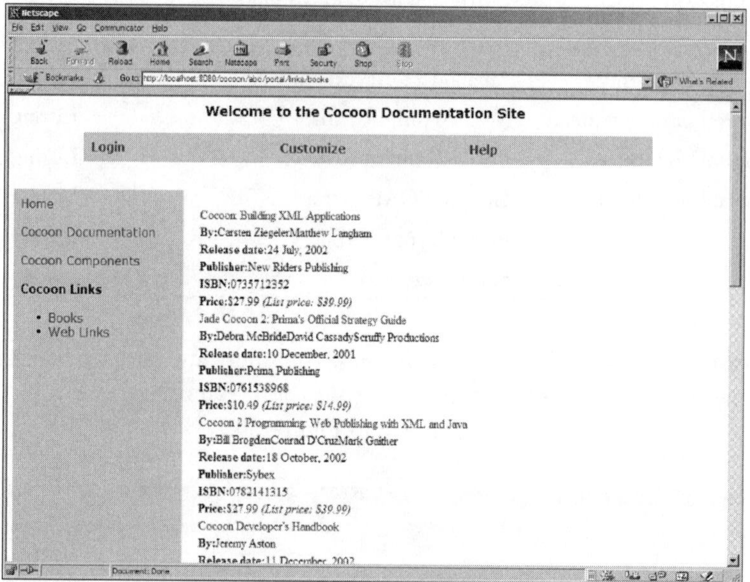

Figure 20.2
Cocoon books area.

We can also select the Web Links menu item in the same section and see what's shown in Figure 20.3.

Figure 20.4 shows the output from selecting Matchers from the Cocoon Components menu.

Finally, Figure 20.5 shows our login page, and Figure 20.6 shows the customized message we get after logging in as user `johnsonb`.

If you do this authentication, try this: Close your browser, reopen it, and surf to the site. You'll find (unless you have disabled cookies in your browser) that you retrieve the same personalization settings you had before without having to re-authenticate. Naturally, this is one of the important things you want to consider when designing real portals for your users.

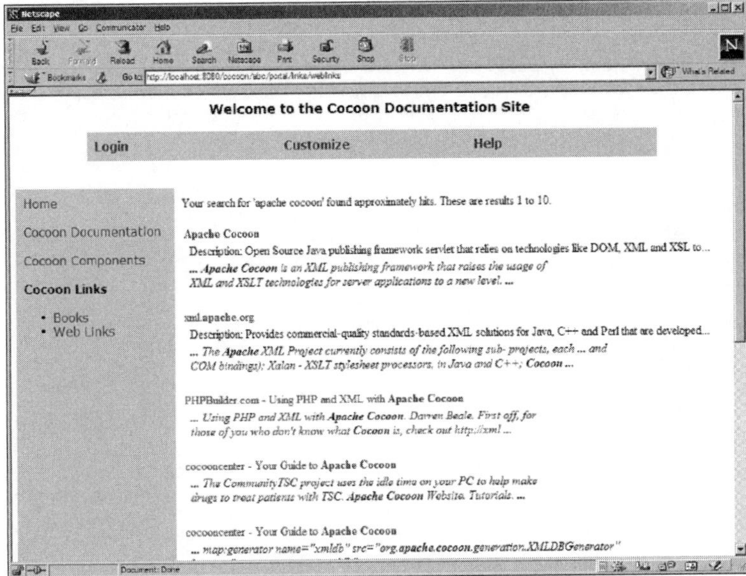

Figure 20.3

Cocoon Web Links area.

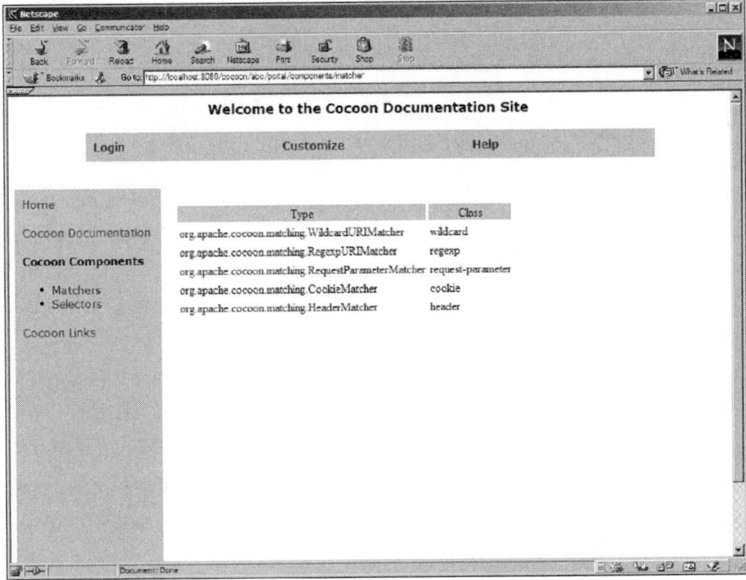

Figure 20.4

Cocoon components example.

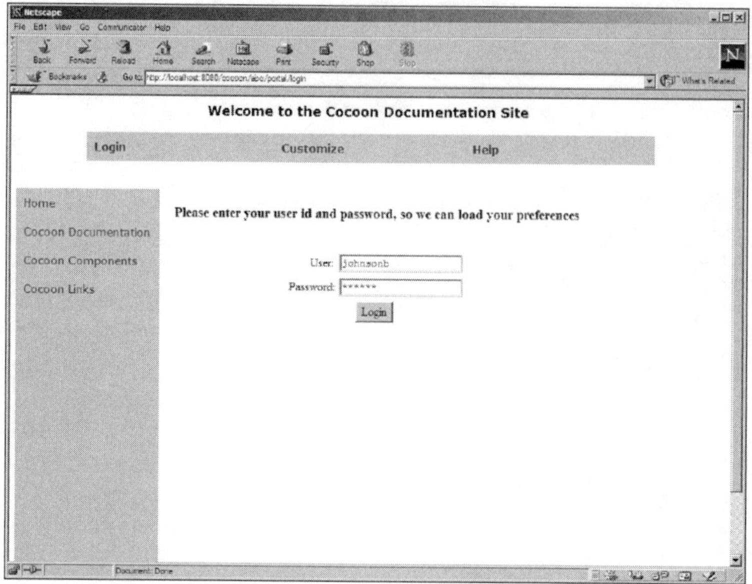

Figure 20.5

Login page.

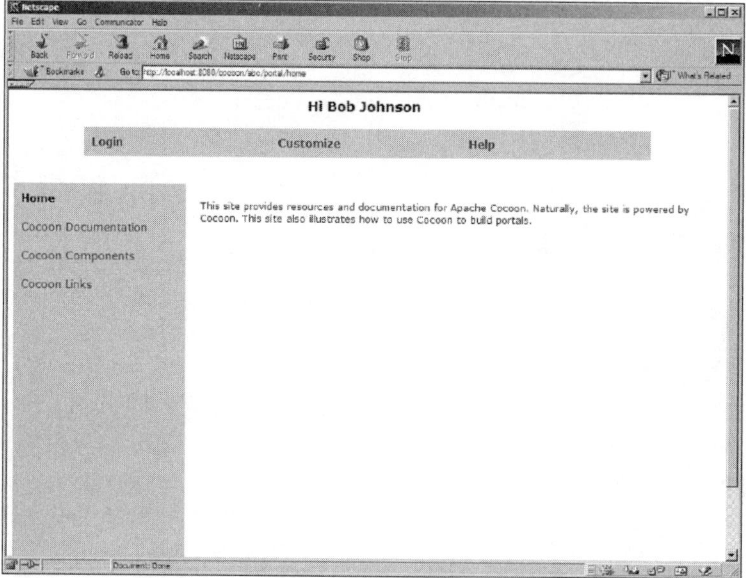

Figure 20.6

Home page with welcome message.

Cocoon Portal Engine

The scratchpad area of Cocoon 2.0.2/2.0.3 contains alpha versions of a set of components known as `sunShine`. These components are designed to facilitate the creation of portals and handling of authentication. If you are interested in them, we suggest you build Cocoon 2.1 from the latest CVS (as described in Chapter 6, "Installing Cocoon") and have a go at it. Just remember that until 2.1 is officially released, anything is subject to change! There are also a fair number of bugs left (as of this writing, summer 2002), which of course will slowly diminish as 2.1 gets closer to production release.

`sunShine` includes various components grouped into something called `sunSpot` and `sunRise`. In 2.1, the documentation has changed and the entire package is simply referred to as a portal engine (I prefer "portal framework"). The engine relies on XML definitions that describe the portals, their configuration options, and their content. The content areas of a portal are known as "coplets" (for *Co*coon *portlet*), a somewhat contrived term. What's nice about this framework is that you can highly customize the properties and capabilities of each portal. For example, you can define which coplets are optional and which are not. The definition of a portal is done through what is called "profiles," which are defined from generic to user-specific. In other words, you can define four "layers" or profiles, each of which builds on the preceding layer:

- The Base profile defines the portal capabilities, content areas, and customization possibilities.
- The Global profile constitutes the base "view" of the portal that all users inherit. This view can be changed, but should a user not have any customization, this is what he would be dealing with.
- The Role profile is the "view" of a portal as determined by a specific user role.
- The User profile represents the "view" of a portal as determined by a specific user. Remember, the extent to which a user can change the view is determined by the base profile.

Portal authentication is handled by something called the "Authentication Framework," also known as the `sunRise` components. This framework consists of a series of new actions that give you a more fine-grained control over authentication than something like the `DatabaseAuthenticationAction`. These actions can be used independently from the portal framework, though they are a nice fit.

Summary

This chapter has shown that it is actually very easy to build portals with Cocoon. Although this example has been rather simplistic, (for example, we don't have any show/hide/remove buttons on the panes), you can see how little code is actually necessary to build a decent portal. You can also see how the fact that Cocoon has many ways of doing the same thing works to our advantage. Look at the main pipeline for this portal example—simple! It is the same with the authentication/personalization code—by selecting the right method, we can first of all use existing components, and second of all keep things simple. This example did use one custom component, the `PortalAuthenticationAction`. But when you think about it, that is really not much code to have to add to Cocoon to create such a customized application. The bottom line is that Cocoon is great for building portals and will only get more so with the release of 2.1.

Part IV

Techniques for Building Cocoon Applications

Chapter

CHAPTER 21

Designing Cocoon Applications

Well, we've come a long way in learning what Cocoon can do. We've built some sample applications and tried an assortment of features. In Part IV, "Techniques for Building Cocoon Applications," we will now discuss some principles of designing, developing, deploying, and maintaining Cocoon-based applications. Some of these principles will inevitably pertain to Web-based applications in general. After all, developing with Cocoon is not that dissimilar to other kinds of Web applications.

This chapter covers principles of designing Cocoon-based projects. In the following chapters, we'll discuss development principles, development and deployment techniques, administration of Cocoon-based applications, and performance and tuning.

We've allocated design to its own chapter, because there are some important considerations to keep in mind when designing Cocoon applications as opposed to those based on other technologies. Cocoon's features give you more opportunities for creative solutions to design problems. On the flip side, they also pose potential pitfalls for the unwary.

Organizing Projects

One of the first decisions you'll have to make is whether to integrate your application with the main Cocoon sitemap or make it a subproject, with its own sitemap or even sub-sitemaps. The decision largely depends on the size and complexity of your application, as well as whether you are handling multiple applications with one Cocoon instance. If you have a single application, there is no technical reason why it can't live at the top of the webapp. The only downside to this is that your main sitemap will contain both the `<map:component>` definitions and your application-specific pipelines. In my own development, I always prefer to use a sub-sitemap for my application, even if it is the only one running in a particular installation. I view the main sitemap as a global definition file that contains pointers to the actual applications (via the `<map:mount>` tags), whereas the sub-sitemap is completely application-specific. This makes a nice clean break of functionality and helps keep administration simple.

If you have multiple applications on a single Cocoon instance, it is almost a given that you should put each application in its own directory with its own sitemap. Deployment can be as simple as copying a new jar file to the production instance and unpacking it. Another advantage of this practice is that the work of each application does not interfere with any others.

The one downside of running multiple applications on a single Cocoon instance is that you might have configuration conflicts in `cocoon.xconf`, `web.xml`, or `logkit.xconf`. If two or more applications need different settings for a configuration parameter, you might need to create a new instance for one of the applications. For example, one application might need the default XSLT processor (Xalan), and another needs Saxon or something else. The solution would be to define a second `<xslt-processor>` tag in `cocoon.xconf` for the second processor, and then define a second `TraxTransformer` component in the sitemap that uses this processor.

Another thing to keep in mind as you design your application is whether it naturally segments into sub-applications or tools. You might be able to create directories for each part of your webapp, each containing its own sitemap. This makes is easy to upgrade individual parts of the application without affecting everything else. It is also a nice way of having different developers work on different parts of the application without (necessarily) stepping on each other's toes.

Organizing Files and URIs

The importance of organizing files and URIs cannot be emphasized enough. Thanks to Cocoon's decoupling of URIs from the underlying organization of resources, you have the freedom to implement your own logic in the former. What do we mean by logic? Essentially, we mean that URIs can be used to reflect content and organization. Think back to your first Apache-based Web site (or Netscape FastTrack Server or IIS so we don't appear too heavily biased!). Basically, most early sites put all HTML pages in one directory, put all CGI scripts in another, told the server where to find them, and fired up the site. As sites became more complex, developers began separating content in directories, nesting them deeper and deeper. Sure the system worked, but it was also prone to inherent messiness, and directories filled up with files (and file versions!) and became hard to maintain.

With Cocoon our principle here is this: *Your file sources and URIs should be organized by separate principles*. In other words, have one set of rules for organizing your file resources and another for the URIs. Why? Not just because Cocoon allows you to, but because in fact file sources and URIs are apples and oranges. A design for one might not be the best choice for the other. And unlike with traditional servers, you get to choose the best design for both.

When designing the structure of your file resources, do it in such a way as to facilitate both your own management of it and that of your successors. Again, *do not* try to imagine how the paths will look in the browser, because *they don't have to be seen in the browser*. When thinking about management of your resources, you might group like files together: XSPs in one directory, XML files in another, stylesheets in another, and so on. Or you might segment the files by function, type of content, user grouping, and so on. If you have multiple developers on the project, you might segment the files by some sort of functional area or assignment. However you do it, make sure that the organization is logical and easy to maintain.

When you go to design your application, and you are doing flow charts or mock-ups, design the URLs in such a way as to help the user understand where he or she is in the application. You can look at the URLs as an additional piece of information. Think of it from the user's perspective—how do you want the user to understand the organization of the site? Perhaps it will be by major function, tool, or sub-application. If you implement personalization on your site, you can prefix each page name with the user's id. This will help distinguish user's pages from default or nonpersonalizable pages. It will also make the user feel as if the site is completely customized for his or her use.

Another aspect of this is how you might handle internationalization, localization, and branding issues. Internationalization is covered in more detail in Chapter 14, "Using Presentation Logic: Internationalization," but these are all variations on a theme. Basically, you will need to think of how far your application might be impacted by any one of these and then think how you might need to structure your resources accordingly. For example, if you are going to support multiple languages or customer branded sites, you will need to be able to specify graphics for the various sites. Again, how you structure these resources on the file system does not have to be how they are requested from the browser.

Dividing Up Data

When deciding how to handle the data in your application, Cocoon once again gives you a way to rethink the process. In a typical Web application, data is usually taken as a given. Of course, many times this is just the reality of the situation: You are given a database model and connection information, and are told to build a site that incorporates various database operations against that database. Often, data is available in a format that must be cleaned up or normalized before presentation. This too is often unavoidable.

With Cocoon, however, and with XML in general, we have the chance to start thinking of data in logical bites. Imagine a complex, portal-enabled site. What you have is data that is independent of the page: It may show up in another page, in another form, and under different circumstances. Users can pick and choose what data they actually want to see. On the back end, this can be a nightmare. With Cocoon, however, and all its ways of aggregation and data collection, much of the headache is removed. Rather than being tied to the data, pages can easily be made up as composites of data from different sources.

If possible, try to design your data in such a way as to facilitate its being used in different ways by different parts of your application. You can do this by thinking about the smallest logical "bite" or unit of data. In our ABC Software example, the client home page used database data to display contract information along with advertisements. We put each ad in a separate XML file, as each ad was its own standalone unit of data. The contract information also represented a unit of data—multiple rows, to be sure, but by putting the collection of that data in its own pipeline, we could reuse it in other pages.

Reuse

My opinion is that much too much is made of reuse. Not because the concept is a bad one, but because it is difficult to implement and in fact is rarely a success. But it is nonetheless important for you to consider reuse when designing Cocoon-based applications. As with data, you can save yourself much grief and make your application more flexible if you can design modularly.

The theory boils down to this: Look at your applications, and try to find patterns—data sets, functions, functional areas, and so on—that you can define and that can be used across different parts of your applications. Just as with data, look for units of functionality. When you develop, these units may turn into individual pipelines, actions, or custom components. The more you can identify these modules, the more opportunity you will have during development to put them into their own little packages, all ready for reuse. Equally important is that someone else dealing with your application has a better chance of understanding the atomic elements that are the base of the application. Think of it as a chemical compound: When you understand the particular elements involved, you can understand what the compound is. You can also rearrange the elements to get a new compound. It is the same with an application: If you have divided things up logically, you can reuse and reorganize them to fit any need.

As an example of this, consider a reporting application that uses a large corporate database. Suppose that different groups—marketing, sales, support, and so on—need to view customer and product information in different ways. Further, each group intends to implement its own look and feel for the application. If we are in charge of the first of these reporting tools, here is what we might look for. First, we'd see whether there are any common functions that all these applications will use—security, authentication, portals, and so forth. Perhaps our application will be using some action, such as a custom action that logs particular information about user activity, that might be applicable elsewhere. Because all tools will be working against a common database, we might design a dynamic query process using the `SQLTransformer` and XSL to build queries based on standard report names. This process could use a global definition file that maps report names to query definitions, and to which other application teams could add their own mapping. Again, the more we break down the process to its atomic units, the better chance we have of designing for reuse.

Deciding Where to Put the Logic

If you haven't noticed already, you have numerous ways of implementing logic in Cocoon: XSPs, generators, transformers, actions, and the sitemap. As you design, you may face decisions on where to put logic. Following are some guidelines.

When to Use What Logic

It is handy to think that actions and sitemap components in general are the best way to implement conditional processing logic, whereas generators (include XSPs) and transformers are best for implementing logic in the data. In our sample application, we saw many examples of implementing customization and security using pipeline components. Sitemap logic is great because you can accomplish all sorts of things in the pipeline, without writing any code. In general, when faced with a problem, think first whether there is any way you can implement the solution in the pipeline. If not with an existing component, how about an action?

When it comes to manipulating or working with the data stream, however, you do have to use the code. Here, you are faced with using an XSP, a custom component, or XSL. The real choice here depends on your personal preference and experience. Many people like to use the XSL files to manipulate the data, either because they are more familiar with XSLT or because you have the ability to chain `TraxTransformer` together to get a desired effect. XSPs are great if you have logic to implement at the start of the pipeline. They are fast (after the initial compilation) and with logicsheets are fairly easy to maintain. And you can't beat automatic compilation!

Databases: ESQL Versus SQLTransformer

You have really two choices for getting source data from a database: XSPs, with the ESQL logicsheet, and the `SQLTransformer`. (I'm not counting the database actions here, because that data does not go into the SAX event stream—it can be used only for implementing logic in the action.) In general, ESQL is faster, but also slightly more complex to implement. However, it does give you more options than the `SQLTransformer`, and you can implement custom Java logic in the XSP. On the other hand, the `SQLTransformer` can use incoming data to drive the query (or queries) and may better fit a model in which the database data is only part of the data going to the client. It also can go anywhere between the `<map:generate>` and `<map:serialize>` steps.

Logic: XSPs Versus Actions

Because XSPs mix content and logic, and are therefore dangerous, I recommend actions wherever possible. Actions are neat little units of work that you can use anywhere in the pipeline. XSPs can go only in the front (unless you are aggregating them together) and so are limited in that respect. If you do need to use XSPs, try to separate your logic from your content as much as possible. Think of your successor! Think of your worst JSP headache! Highly recommended is the use of logicsheets. Even if you use it for only a single XSP, it is worth considering when the custom code starts taking over the XSP. If you have trouble finding your data tags in the XSP, you should redesign!

Case Study: Data Warehousing Application

I did a Cocoon-based data warehousing application once. I was relatively new to Cocoon, and had recently done several JSP-based applications. So, because I could easily understand

XSPs, I designed my application in such a way that each report was served by its own XSP. Each XSP utilized the ESQL logicsheet to extract the data from the database. A couple of global XSLs served to handle all formatting for HTML and PDF.

Although the design was fairly easy to implement at first, I ran into problems as the application grew in scope and I added more and more reports. After more than a year, I had dozens of XSPs to maintain. Moreover, some of my XSPs were looking like my old JSPs—a mess of content and logic.

My solution was to totally redesign the application and use a more dynamic approach. In the new version, I used a custom action to dynamically build the database query based on the report type and input parameters. This action used an XML file that held report definitions. After the query was built, it was passed out of the action in a `Map` object and picked up by an XSP as a parameter and executed. The result? One XSP instead of 50! And a much more maintainable site, because all queries were stored in a single file and therefore could be changed easily.

The moral of the tale is that the more experience you gain with Cocoon, the more you will understand how best to use its many features. Consequently, when starting out as a novice, don't sweat it! Don't get paranoid about "doing it right." There really is no right way with Cocoon. If you can grasp the concept of XSPs, use them. If you are a pro at XSL and want to implement all your logic there, go ahead. The more you plunge in and experiment, the more you'll develop your own set of design guidelines and the more effective you will be with Cocoon.

You may also find that the implementation method within Cocoon changes over time as your experience grows, as user requirements change, or as other factors make you think again. Do not be afraid to learn from experience. You may find that a method you later had to improve for one project may be just the right thing to use when faced with another issue.

Summary

As you develop your Cocoon project, keep one thing in mind: Cocoon allows you to think in new ways about your application design. It is hard to put that into a formula or set of principles. Rather, as you gain experience with Cocoon, you will learn to ask the right questions during design time. If there is one principle, it is that Cocoon forces you to think atomically. That is, the more you think in terms of units of work, units of data, or units of logic, the more you can see that working with Cocoon is a matter of assembling these units to gain a desired effect. A pipeline is nothing more than an assemblage of these units. Your data may also be a group of units—maybe through aggregation, maybe through a series of

SQL queries, maybe through a series of transformations that bring in new data at each step. As you work with Cocoon, try to spend a bit of time laying out your application in terms of modules, starting from the overall big picture. If you can break it down into modules, and then each module into submodules or functions, you will start to see how you can implement the design units as work units in Cocoon. After you get the hang of it, you won't want to use any other application framework!

CHAPTER 22

Techniques for Developing Cocoon Applications

Now that we've looked at some design principles, let's discuss some development and deployment techniques that will help make your Cocoon project a success. As with the principles in the preceding chapter, these are not meant to be an exhaustive list. Rather, these are things that we have found to be useful in our own development experience and that we hope you will find useful as well.

Preparing for Development

The development process for a Cocoon-based application is much like any other. You must prepare a development environment, set up development applications, write your code, deploy, test, debug, and so forth. However, there are a few extra things to do along the way.

Sitemap or Sub-sitemap

One of the first things you will need to decide, and one that you may have already decided during your design phase (we all have a proper design phase, right?) is whether to build your Cocoon application as a top-level application, using the main sitemap, or as a subproject, using a sub-sitemap (or more than one, in fact). As mentioned in Chapter 21, "Designing Cocoon Applications," the key determining factor in making this decision is whether you have just one application to be deployed on a particular Cocoon instance or more than one. If one, go ahead and make it the main sitemap. If more than one, put your application in a subdirectory.

Preparing Cocoon and the Servlet Container

After you have figured out how you will ultimately deploy your application, you can configure your development environment. This includes configuring data sources, the servlet container, and, of course, Cocoon itself. It is *highly* recommended that you build yourself a clean version of Cocoon without all the samples and subdirectories that come with the official distribution. Instructions on how to do this are given in the next section. If you don't do this, you'll end up with an unnecessarily large application, as well as risking confusion on your part and that of your users.

As you prepare your servlet container and Cocoon instance, you may have to do a few things:

- Copy any special jars you need (such as JDBC, JSP compiler, or Xindice jars) into either the `lib` directory for your servlet container (like `$CATALINA_HOME/common/lib` if you are using Tomcat 4.x) or the `lib` directory of the Cocoon installation (`WEB-INF/lib`).
- Register all necessary JDBC drivers in `WEB-INF/web.xml`.
- Define all connection pools in `WEB-INF/cocoon.xconf`.
- Define all custom logicsheets in `WEB-INF/cocoon.xconf`.

One thing we will definitely need to do is to verify that all sitemaps are reloaded after any change and are done so synchronously. We discussed this in Chapter 6, "Installing Cocoon." Briefly, you'll need to edit `WEB-INF/cocoon.xconf` and make sure the entry for `<sitemap>` looks like this:

```
<sitemap check-reload="yes" file="sitemap.xmap" logger="sitemap"
  reload-method="synchron"/>
```

Similarly, make sure that any sub-sitemaps are defined with the `check-reload` attribute in the `<map:mount>` tag set to `true`.

Creating Development Directories

With the servlet container and Cocoon properly configured, you now need a development environment for the application. Strictly speaking, of course, you can develop right within the Cocoon Web application directory, but although this is sometimes fine for quick-and-dirty applications, it is not suitable for a regular development process. Unless you have a better mechanism, you can't go wrong with an Ant-based environment. Ant can be used for compilation, copying of files to different deployment targets (development, QA, production, and so on), packaging of application files, directory cleaning, and many other things. Go grab yourself a copy from `http://jakarta.apache.org/ant/` and check it out. As an example of an Ant-based Cocoon development environment, we'll go through that of the abc application we used earlier in the book.

If you recall, we originally deployed this application in a subdirectory of the Cocoon installation. For our development, we defined the directory structure shown in Table 22.1. For the sake of portability, we'll assume that the environment variable `$DEVEL_HOME` (`%DEVEL_HOME%` on Windows) points to our development area of our file system.

Table 22.1 *Sample Development Directory Structure*

Folder	Description
`$DEVEL_HOME/abc`	Root-level directory. Contains only subdirectories plus the ant build descriptor file (`build.xml`).
`$DEVEL_HOME/abc/db`	Directory for various database files—data definition language (DDL) files, sample data, and so on.
`$DEVEL_HOME/abc/docs`	Directory for various development documents and notes. Not meant to be deployed!
`$DEVEL_HOME/abc/etc`	Miscellaneous files. Contains primarily `sitemap.xmap` for our application. If this were a top-level Cocoon application, we might put `cocoon.xconf` and `web.xml` here as well.
`$DEVEL_HOME/abc/src`	Source directory for custom actions or other components.
`$DEVEL_HOME/abc/web`	Directory with all the content, stylesheets, scripts, and so on.
`$DEVEL_HOME/abc/web/content`	Contains the actual content files (static and dynamic).
`$DEVEL_HOME/abc/web/content/dynamic`	Used for XSPs.
`$DEVEL_HOME/abc/web/content/static`	Used for XML or HTML files.
`$DEVEL_HOME/abc/web/images`	Holds all application images.
`$DEVEL_HOME/abc/web/scripts`	Holds any scripting files, such as `*.js` files.
`$DEVEL_HOME/abc/web/style`	Holds XSL files and `*.css` files.

Listing 22.1 shows our `build.xml` file for the abc application. This is the file that tells ant what to do to build and deploy the application.

Listing 22.1 *ABC build.xml*

```
<project default="all" basedir=".">
  <property name="project.name" value="abc"/>
  <property name="catalina.home"
    value="c:/apps/jakarta-tomcat-4.0.4"/>
  <property name="cocoon.base"
    value="${catalina.home}/webapps/cocoon"/>
  <property name="deploy.home"
    value="${cocoon.base}/${project.name}"/>
  <property name="libdir"
    value="${cocoon.base}/WEB-INF/lib"/>

  <target name="prepare">
    <mkdir dir="${deploy.home}"/>
    <copy todir="${deploy.home}">
      <fileset dir="web"/>
    </copy>
    <copy file="etc/sitemap.xmap"
      tofile="${deploy.home}/sitemap.xmap"/>
  </target>

  <target name="compile" depends="prepare">
    <javac srcdir="src" destdir="${cocoon.base}/WEB-INF/classes"
     debug="on" optimize="off" deprecation="off">
      <classpath>
       <pathelement
          location="${libdir}/avalon-excalibur-vm12-20020705.jar"/>
       <pathelement location="${libdir}/avalon-framework-20020627.jar"/>
       <pathelement location="${libdir}/cocoon-2.0.3.jar"/>
       <pathelement location="${libdir}/logkit-20020529.jar"/>
      </classpath>
    </javac>
  </target>

  <target name="all" depends="prepare,compile"/>

</project>
```

This example is pretty simple. In Ant, each step or task is defined by a `<target>` tag. All we do here is to define a `prepare` task to copy files from the development directories to their deployment home, and a `compile` task to compile any `*.java` source files we might have. The `classpath` attribute for the `<javac>` tag must include all jars that you will be relying on to compile your application. For a typical action, it will be the four jars shown previously.

You'll see we set a few global variables at the top of the file so that we can find Catalina's home, Cocoon's home, and so on. A possible enhancement to this file is to include a properties file instead that sets these variables. Then all we have to do is to include that file with this command:

```
<property file="global.properties"/>
```

To deploy our application, we change to the directory `$DEVEL_HOME/abc` and type `ant`. That works on either Unix or Windows. The one thing that this process does not do is add a `<map:mount>` entry for our sub-sitemap to the parent `sitemap.xmap` of our Cocoon. This you can either do manually or, if you have a development project for the top-level Cocoon application, within that development project directory. Just remember that when you add a sub-sitemap to the main sitemap, it is a good idea to catch URIs that have the application name without a trailing slash. For our abc application, the entry in our main sitemap looks like this:

```
<map:match pattern="abc">
 <map:redirect-to uri="abc/"/>
</map:match>
<map:match pattern="abc/**>
  <map:mount uri-prefix="abc" src="abc/sitemap.xmap" check-reload="yes"/>
</map:match>
```

The first match will take a URI like `http://localhost:8080/cocoon/abc` and redirect it to `http://localhost:8080/cocoon/abc/`, which will then get properly directed to our application sitemap.

Building a Clean Cocoon

By "clean Cocoon," we mean a Cocoon that does not have all the samples and files that come with the distribution. If you want a clean version, you need to download the source distribution as described in Chapter 6, "Installing Cocoon." Next you need to create a new version of `sitemap.xmap` and edit the `build.xml` file in the root distribution directory.

Creating a New Main Sitemap

In the `src/webapp` directory of the Cocoon distribution (if you download the latest official release, the top-level directory will be called `cocoon-2.0.3`), you'll find the `sitemap.xmap` file. Copy this to a new file, called `sitemap-stripped.xmap`. Then edit this file, and remove everything between the `<map:pipelines>` and `</map:pipelines>` tags. You may also want to remove some or all of the actions between the `<map:actions>` and `</map:actions>` tags, if you don't plan on using them.

Editing build.xml

Now you can edit `build.xml` (again, it's in the root of the distribution), and add the following entry:

```
<target name="strip" depends="webapp" description="Strips the samples out">
    <copy file="./src/webapp/sitemap-stripped.xmap"
         tofile="./build/cocoon/webapp/sitemap.xmap"/>
    <jar jarfile="./build/cocoon/cocoon-clean.war"
          basedir="./build/cocoon/webapp"
          includes="sitemap.xmap,WEB-INF/**"/>
</target>
```

This target comes after the regular build is performed (that's why the `depends` attribute is set to `webapp`). The `webapp` target is the one that actually creates the `build` directory under the distribution root that contains the `cocoon.war` file along with an expanded version of the same file, residing in `build/cocoon/webapp`. Our new target then copies the `sitemap-stripped.xmap` file we created earlier over the `sitemap.xmap` file in the expanded version of webapp. It finally creates a new `cocoon-clean.war` file containing only `sitemap.xmap` and the contents of the `WEB-INF` directory.

Run this new build target on Unix as

```
./build.sh -Dinclude.webapp.libs=yes strip
```

and on Windows as

```
.\build.bat -Dinclude.webapp.libs=yes strip
```

In either case, of course, you run this command from the root distribution directory.

Building a Minimal Cocoon Distribution

If you are interested in making a small-as-possible Cocoon distribution, and you need only the most basic features of Cocoon, you can strip out quite a few jars from the build. Table 22.2 shows you which jars you can remove and which components will be affected. You can either take these jars out of your existing installation, along with all affected components, or remove them from the `lib/optional` directory of your Cocoon distribution before you build. It is understood that if you remove a component, you will have to remove not only any affected component definitions, but any pipelines that rely on those components as well.

Table 22.2 *Optional Jars for a Minimal Cocoon*

Jar	Description	Dependents
`batik-all-1.5b2.jar`	Graphics libraries	`SVGSerializer`, `FOPSerializer`
`bsf-2.2.jar`	Bean Scripting Framework	`ScriptGenerator`, `ScriptAction`
`commons-logging-1.0.jar`	Jakarta Commons logging package, required by POI library	`POIFSSerializer`
`deli-0.50.jar`	CC/P and UAProf support	DELI components, optionally used by `TraxTransformer`
`fop-0.20-3.jar`	XML:FO processor	`FOPSerializer`
`hsqldb-1.61.jar`	Hypersonic SQL database	HSQL `cocoon.xconf` entries
`jakarta-poi-1.5.0-dev-20020408.jar.jar`	APIs for working with Microsoft OLE 2 documents	`POIFSSerializer`
`jena-1.3.0.jar`	RDF Framework	DELI components
`jimi-1.0.jar`	Image library	`FOPSerializer`
`jisp_1_0_2.jar`	Java Indexed Serialization Package	`JispStore` component (replacement for `FilesystemStore`)
`jstyle.jar`	Java code formatter	Optionally used by Sitemap and XSP engine
`jtidy-04aug2000r7-dev.jar`	Cleans up HTML and makes it well-formed	`HTMLGenerator`
`lucene-1-2-rc2.jar`	Search engine	`SearchGenerator` and `cocoon.xconf` search components
`maybeupload_1-0-5pre3.jar`	File upload functions	
`pizza-1.1.jar`	Optional Java compiler	Change the Java compiler from Pizza to Javac in `cocoon.xconf`
`rdffilter.jar`	XML RDF Parser	DELI components
`resolver-20020130.jar`	Catalog Entity Resolver	Optionally used by `JaxpParser`
`rhino-1.5r3.jar`	Netscape Rhino support	XSP in JavaScript, `ScriptGenerator`, `ScriptAction`
`servlet_2_2.jar`	Servlet 2.2 API	`CocoonServlet`

Table 22.2 *(continued)*

Jar	Description	Dependents
velocity-1.2.jar	Velocity Engine	VelocityGenerator
xmldb-api-20011111.jar	XML:DB APIs	XMLDB protocol (and deprecated XMLDBGenerator and XMLDBCollection Generator)

Setting Up Basic Pipelines

Many Cocoon-based applications will have pages containing image files, `*.css` or `*.js` files. If you have such an application, you might want to include these handy pipelines at the beginning of the `<map:pipeline>` section of your `sitemap.xmap`:

```
<map:match pattern="*.css">
 <map:read mime-type="text/css" src="style/{1}.css"/>
</map:match>
<map:match pattern="**/*.css">
 <map:read mime-type="text/css" src="style/{2}.css"/>
</map:match>
<map:match pattern="*.gif">
 <map:read mime-type="image/gif" src="images/{1}.gif"/>
</map:match>
<map:match pattern="**/*.gif">
 <map:read mime-type="image/gif" src="images/{2}.gif"/>
</map:match>
<map:match pattern="*.jpg">
 <map:read mime-type="image/jpg" src="images/{1}.jpg"/>
</map:match>
<map:match pattern="**/*.jpg">
 <map:read mime-type="image/jpg" src="images/{2}.jpg"/>
</map:match>
<map:match pattern="*.js">
 <map:read mime-type="x-application/javascript" src="scripts/{1}.js"/>
</map:match>
<map:match pattern="**/*.js">
 <map:read mime-type="x-application/javascript" src="scripts/{2}.js"/>
</map:match>
```

You might recognize some of these pipelines from Chapter 11, "Using Sitemap Logic: `Matchers` and `Selectors`." There, we discussed how having two pipelines for each file type ensures that they will be caught no matter what the URI of the page they are referenced from. Of course, these examples assume you prefer to store your images in a directory called `images`, your `*.js` files in a directory called `scripts`, and your `*.css` files in a directory called `style`. If you don't, edit appropriately.

Another useful pipeline is one that handles `index.html` (or `index.htm`), as well as URIs that do not specify a page. The following pipelines do the trick:

```
<map:match pattern="">
 <map:redirect-to uri="index.html"/>
</map:match>

<map:match pattern="index.htm*">
 <map:read src="content/index.html" mime-type="text/html" />
</map:match>
```

Naturally, you might not have an actual `index.html` file, but rather a genuine pipeline to handle the URI.

One question that usually comes up with static files such as HTML pages and images is whether they should be served by Cocoon or a regular Web server. Undeniably, a Web server like Apache is going to be faster at serving static resources. However, performance is not the only consideration. If you like the idea of putting all your application files in one place, you might prefer to take the performance hit and use Cocoon to serve the static files. My own rule of thumb is to have the Web server serve up images or other resources only if they are used across the Cocoon applications I develop. For example, I often create a top-level `images` directory under the Web server document root to hold global images. I then prefix the image name with `/images` in the URLs so that they will be served by the Web server. The only downside of this is that it becomes slightly more difficult to maintain an application because the files are distributed into different directory structures.

Debugging

Although Cocoon does many things, it cannot make you write error-free code! And, unfortunately, you always have the stray bug or two in Cocoon itself to contend with. One of the more problematic areas of Cocoon is debugging. To help you, we'll review some of the places where errors can occur and where you might look for debugging information.

The two main places where you will find helpful information are in the Cocoon logs and in the source code for dynamically compiled components. Cocoon logs are kept in the `WEB-INF/logs` directory of the Cocoon Web application. The format and configuration of the log files are covered in Chapter 23, "Cocoon Administration." When Cocoon compiles dynamic components at runtime, such as XSPs and sitemaps, it puts both the source code and the class files in a directory structure under the servlet container's work directory. In Catalina, this work directory is `$CATALINA_HOME/work` (or `%CATALINA_HOME%\work` on Windows). Within this directory is an optional directory for the Tomcat service, a directory for the hostname, and then directories starting with the Web application name. On Tomcat 4.0.1 or 4.0.3, this directory is as follows:

```
$CATALINA_HOME/work/localhost/cocoon/cocoon-files/org/apache/cocoon/www
```

On Tomcat 4.0.4 and above, the directory is slightly different:

```
$CATALINA_HOME/work/Standalone/localhost/cocoon/cocoon-files/org/apache/
➥cocoon/wwwx
```

Here, `Standalone` refers to the Web server service within Catalina. For the sake of reference, we'll refer hereafter to this work directory as `$COCOON_WORK`. Subprojects within the main Cocoon application have their work files in subdirectories of the same name within `$COCOON_WORK`. To find the runtime Java files for the abc application, for example, we need to look in the `$COCOON_WORK/abc` directory.

XML Errors

Errors with the format of the input XML data are usually displayed to the screen. An example of this is shown in Figure 22.1.

XSP Errors

Recall that XSPs are compiled into Java programs and then executed. Both the source and the class files can be found in `$COCOON_WORK`, within the same directory structure the XSP itself is found in. For example, `login.xsp`, from Chapter 8, was put in `$CATALINA_HOME/webapps/cocoon/abc/xsp`. The source file for this XSP, after Cocoon creates it, is `$COCOON_WORK/abc/xsp/login_xsp.java`.

If we make an obvious mistake in `login.xsp`, such as not declaring a variable properly, we'll see an error page like the one shown in Figure 22.2.

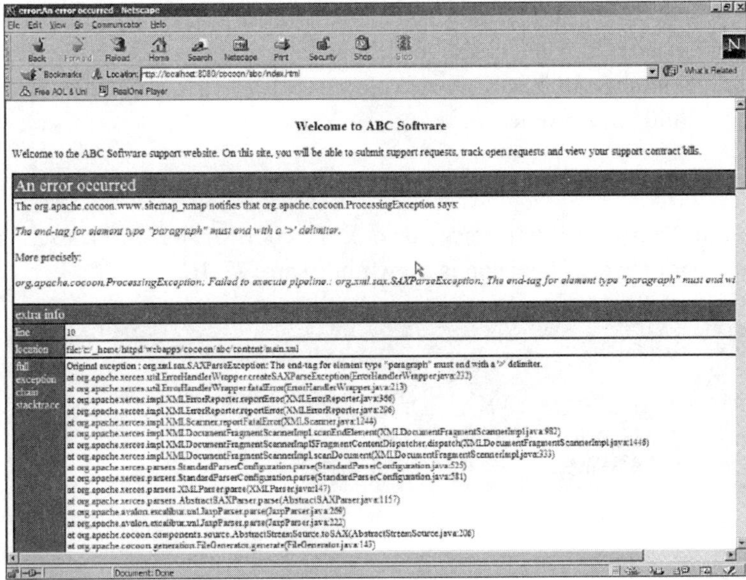

Figure 22.1
Example of an XML error.

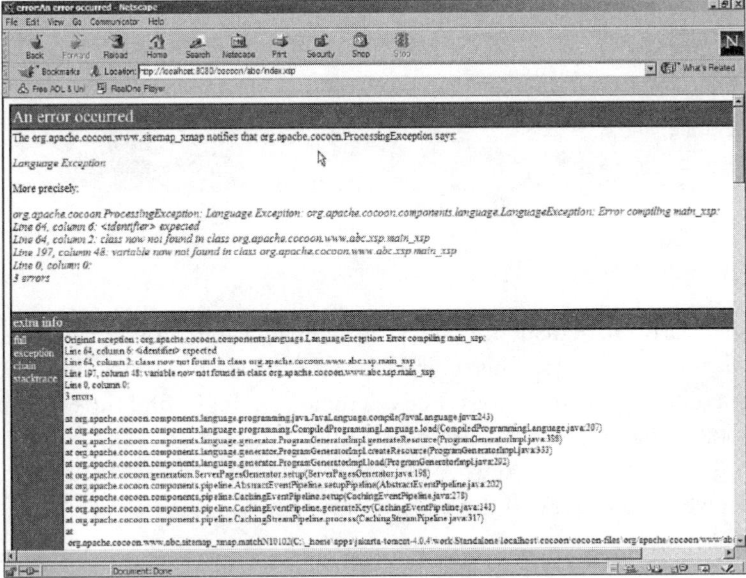

Figure 22.2
Example of an XSP error.

As you can see, Cocoon very kindly gives you a line number in the Java source so you can see where things went wrong. In some cases, you'll immediately recognize your error and fix it. However, in more complicated XSPs, or with more subtle errors, you'll have to poke around the source code to find your problem.

XSL Errors

XSL errors used to be frustrating to track down. In Cocoon versions prior to 2.0.3, the usual error page you get for such an occasion is shown in Figure 22.3.

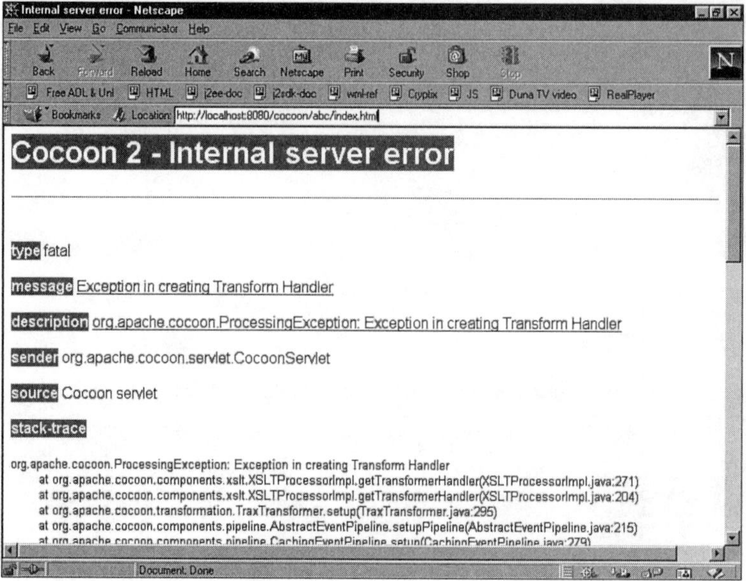

Figure 22.3

Example of an XSL error prior to 2.0.3.

Not much help, clearly. To actually find the error, you'll have to look at the error output from your servlet container logs. This might appear in the command window from which you started the container, or in the logs. For Catalina, you might find the error in a log file `$CATALINA_HOME/logs/catalina.out` or one called `$CATALINA_HOME/logs/localhost_log.`*`YYYY-MM-DD`*`.txt`, where *`YYYY-MM-DD`* refers to the current date. However, sometimes even when you check all these places, you won't find the error.

In Cocoon 2.0.3, however, XSL errors are now for the most part reported to the screen. Figure 22.4 shows an example.

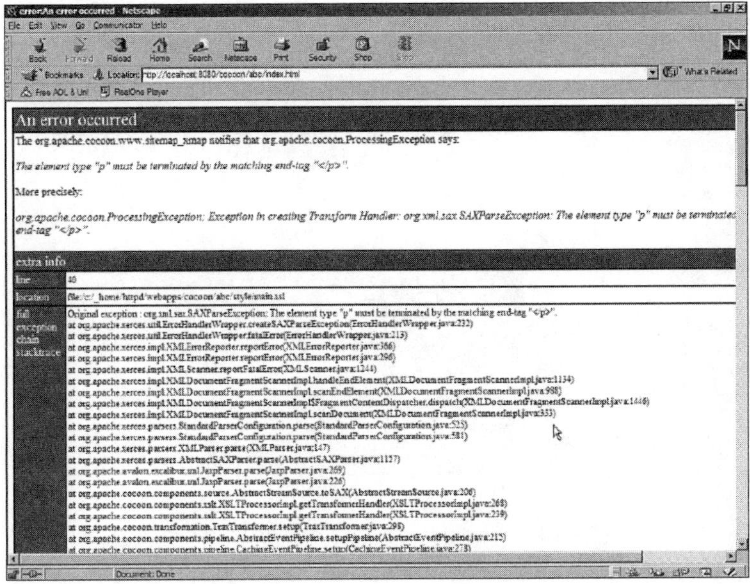

Figure 22.4

Example of an XSL error in 2.0.3.

Sitemap Errors

Sitemap errors are generally displayed to the screen as well. If we have a simple XML error in our sitemap, we get something like what's shown in Figure 22.5.

Figure 22.6 shows what happens when we try to use an action we haven't yet defined.

At some point in your time with Cocoon, you will find it necessary to look at the sitemap Java file to track down some problem or unexpected behavior (unless you are using the interpreted sitemap, which has no corresponding Java file). This file is called `sitemap_xmap.java` and is found in `$COCOON_WORK` at the root, for the main sitemap, or in the appropriate directory for a sub-sitemap. Of course, you won't want to edit the file, because it will be overwritten the next time the sitemap is compiled, but it can be very instrumental in seeing how Cocoon turns your pipeline into a method and what the method does.

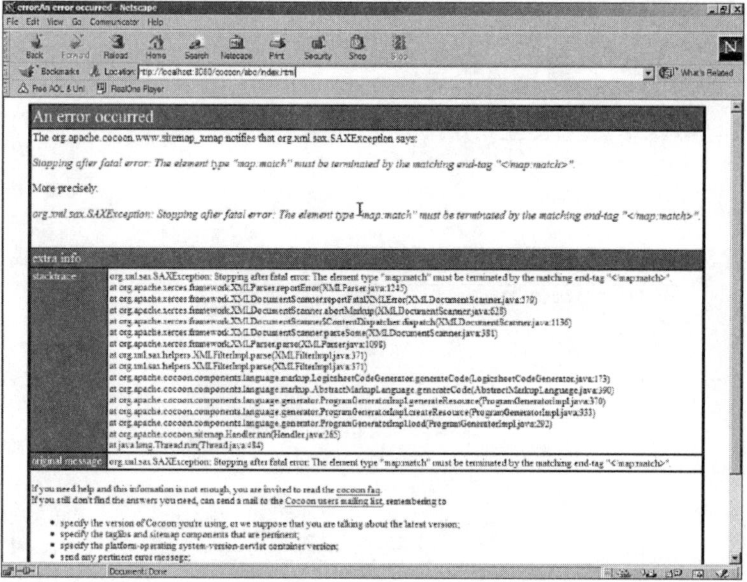

Figure 22.5
Example of an XML sitemap error.

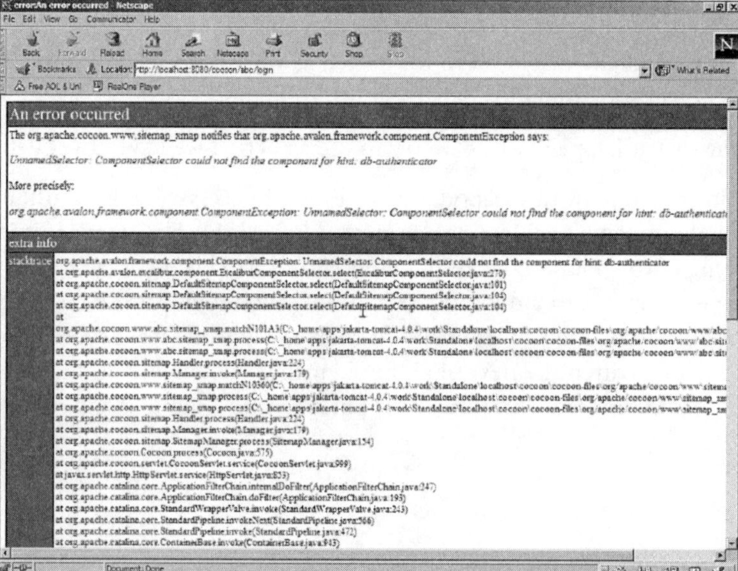

Figure 22.6
Example of an undefined-action sitemap error.

Using Views to Debug

As mentioned before, views can be extremely useful for debugging because they can be used to capture the XML at any stage of a pipeline. At the start of your sitemap, define a view that simply serializes output as XML:

```
<map:view from-label="raw" name="raw">
 <map:serialize type="xml"/>
</map:view>
```

Then, wherever you are having a problem, you can add an attribute such as `label="raw"` to any pipeline step you need and call the pipeline URI with `?cocoon-view=raw` appended. For example, you might find that your pipeline is producing unexpected results. Checking each step in the pipeline with a view might help uncover the place where the problem occurs. Just remember that if you have the same `label` attribute defined in multiple places within a pipeline, the first one that Cocoon encounters will be used as input to the view.

If you get tired of defining labels within pipelines, you might want to add the `label` attribute to one or more component definitions. For example, if you often need a view when debugging XSPs, edit the definition of the `ServerPagesGenerator` like this:

```
<map:generator label="raw"
  logger="sitemap.generator.serverpages"
  name="serverpages" pool-grow="2" pool-max="32" pool-min="4"
  src="org.apache.cocoon.generation.ServerPagesGenerator"/>
```

Now you can append `?cocoon-view=raw` to any URI that uses an XSP and you'll get the output directly from it.

Removing the Work Directory

Occasionally, Cocoon can get slightly confused and a restart is in order. At those times, it is a good idea to delete `$COCOON_WORK` to make sure that no old files get reused the next time Cocoon starts. This is especially recommended if you have just upgraded Cocoon.

Preparing for Deployment

So now you've finished your application, debugged it, and load-tested it, and you are ready to deploy on the production server. Before you get ready to just copy and paste, there are a few things to consider. Just as with any other application, things may change between development and deployment environments. This checklist can help you avoid unnecessary (and potentially embarrassing) errors in your new application.

Deployment Servlet Container

Make sure that your production servlet container is configured as your development copy. In particular, make sure that any custom jars are included. If you have made adjustments to the server configuration files that affect your application, be sure that these get copied over.

Deployment Cocoon Instance

An easy way of making sure that your production Cocoon webapp is the same as your development copy is to jar up the latter and copy it to the correct production directory. If you are installing your application into an existing Cocoon installation, however, run through this checklist:

- Is the Cocoon version the same? If not, don't deploy until you are running the same version for both development and production! Too many things change between versions to make this a good move. Always test on the same version you intend to deploy on.
- Assuming that the versions are the same, are they compiled the same? Does your application rely on scratchpad or even custom components that are built into your development instance but that may not be present in that of production?
- Does the main sitemap contain an entry for your new application?
- Does the main sitemap need additional definitions in the `<map:components>` section that your application relies on?
- Are there any jars that need to be copied to `WEB-INF/lib`?
- Are there any classes that need to be copied to `WEB-INF/classes`? These could be compiled actions or custom components.
- Do you have any changes to the Cocoon configuration files (`cocoon.xconf`, `web.xml`, and `logkit.xconf`—all discussed in greater detail in the next chapter) that need to be made in production? These include database connection pools, choice of the sitemap processor, XSLT processor, custom logicsheet definitions, container-managed security definitions, and so forth.

Data Sources

Make sure that any data source definitions are updated to production instances, if that is relevant for your project. Check things such as connection pool settings in `cocoon.xconf`, Xindice URLs, any `http://` resources used in pipelines, and email settings for the `sendmail` logicsheet or `SendmailAction`.

Debug Views

If you put in any views to help with your debugging, as described previously, remove them before your application reaches your users. No sense in leaving a back door open for someone to view your content in a way you hadn't intended.

Sitemap Compilation

By default, Cocoon is set to automatically recompile the sitemap after any change. In production, however, you might not want to do this. Typically, production installations are meant to be static, as far as sitemaps go, so make sure you have the `check-reload` attribute for the `<sitemap>` tag in `cocoon.xconf` set to `no`. Do the same for any `<map:mount>` entries in your sitemaps as well. Note that this does not apply if you are using the dynamically interpreted sitemap, discussed in Chapter 23, "Cocoon Administration."

Cocoon Logging

To improve performance in your production installation, it is a good idea to disable all logging except for messages of type `ERROR` and above. We'll show how in Chapter 23.

Deployment Issues

In some cases, your deployment environment is unavoidably different from your development environment. Two of the issues that we have had to deal with ourselves is taking the `cocoon` literal out of production URLs and running Cocoon on a headless UNIX server.

Removing the "Cocoon" String from Your Web Application

If you have a normal Cocoon installation, the URLs for your application will have the string `"cocoon"` in them, like `http://localhost:8080/cocoon/abc/login.html`. Because this word is really unnecessary, you can remove it in various ways. If you are using Tomcat, there are two ways to remove it. The first way is simply to rename the `cocoon` directory in the `$CATALINA_HOME/webapps` directory to `ROOT`. The `ROOT` webapp is the only webapp that does not need to be explicitly named in the URLs. Alternatively, you can edit `$CATALINA_HOME/conf/server.xml` and add an entry for the `cocoon` webapp like this:

```
<Context path="" docBase="/cocoon" debug="0"/>
```

What this does is effectively make the `cocoon` webapp the default or root webapp for Tomcat. If you do this, however, you MUST comment out any other `<context>` definition whose `path` attribute is set to `""`. By default, Tomcat comes with the `ROOT` context defined with this path. If you front Tomcat with Apache, you can also employ either URI rewriting, using `mod_rewrite`, or proxy settings, using `mod_proxy`. Consult Apache's documentation and the Cocoon FAQ for information on using these two modules.

Apache-Tomcat Connectivity
If you are using Apache with Tomcat, `mod_jk` is the recommended "glue," because `mod_webapp` is still rather buggy. Instructions for integrating Apache and Tomcat with either method can be found at `http://www.galatea.com/flashguides/index.html`.

Running on a Headless Server

It is possible that your production Cocoon installation will be on a headless Unix server; that is, a server without an Xserver running. The batik library in Cocoon, which relies on Java AWT graphics display, requires the use of an Xserver to render FOP-based output. The same library is also used for rendering SVG images. To run Cocoon on a headless server, you have at least four options.

First, if you aren't going to be using FOP or SVG at all, you can simply remove the batik jar (as of Cocoon 2.0.3 the jar name is `batik-all-1.5b2.jar`). Edit the main sitemap and remove all entries for the `FOPSerializer`, `SVGSerializer`, and anything that references either of those components. Then stop the servlet container, delete Cocoon's work directory (see the next chapter) and restart the container.

Probably the next best solution is to use Xvfb, available at `http://www.xfree86.org`. Xvfb is an open-source virtual Xserver that does not require a physical display to work with. Its main purpose is to provide X libraries for headless UNIX servers. Installation is fairly simple, but don't forget to configure Xvfb to start up when the machine boots. You can do so with an entry in a startup file (appropriate to your OS) like this:

```
Xvfb :1 -screen 0 800x600x8 &
export DISPLAY=:1
```

After Xvfb is running, you can start Cocoon's servlet container.

If you are running JDK 1.3, another solution is to use jars available at `http://www.eteks.com/pja/en` as replacements for the AWT libraries that require a display. PJA (Pure Java Toolit) is a graphic library developed by eTeks. After the PJA jars are installed, you need to edit the startup command for Tomcat by adding the options

```
-Djava.awt.Toolkit=com.eteks.awt.PJAToolkit
-Djava.awt.GraphicsEnvironment=com.eteks.java2d.PJAGraphicsEnvironment
-Djava.awt.fonts=$JAVA_HOME/jre/lib/fonts
```

where `$JAVA_HOME` refers to your JDK installation. You can set these options in the environment variable `$CATALINA_OPTS`, either in the shell or in `catalina.sh` (preferred). The `pja.jar` must be in the classpath, and you'll have to preload it by using the `-Xbootclasspath` option in Java, like

```
-Xbootclasspath=$PATH_TO/pja.jar
```

where `$PATH_TO` refers to the path to `pja.jar`.

The final way to run Cocoon on a headless UNIX server is to use JDK 1.4. We have not tested this kind of installation, but it appears to be stable, and more and more people are using it. The main advantage of JDK 1.4 is that it does not require a display. Hence, if you are using or planning to use this version of Java, it will solve your problem. Look at `http://xml.apache.org/cocoon/installing.html` for more details on this method.

Summary

In this chapter, we've discussed a few ways you can make your Cocoon development process easier. The most important thing is to be well organized. Take the time to lay out your development directories according to a scheme that makes sense to you. You might even want to build these directories slightly differently than you do for deployment. The main principle that should guide you is what works—for you, as well as for others who are collaborating with you or will inherit your work.

Also take the time to deploy your application carefully, especially if you're dealing with different server environments for development and production. Go through the deployment issues mentioned previously to be sure your application will run as expected in production. In a complex environment, make sure you document all the configuration changes in all environments so that you can quickly reconfigure the servers if need be. With careful planning, your Cocoon project will be a success.

CHAPTER 23

Cocoon Administration

In this chapter, we'll discuss several topics relating to Cocoon administration. Earlier, we learned how to install Cocoon and configure it in various ways to support our sample applications. Now, we'll take a comprehensive look at the Cocoon configuration files and see how different settings affect Cocoon's operation. We'll also deal with various administration tasks, including performance and tuning.

Cocoon Configuration

Cocoon has three configuration files, `web.xml`, `cocoon.xconf`, and `logkit.xconf`, all of which live in the `WEB-INF` directory of the webapp.

web.xml

Cocoon's `web.xml`, shown in Listing 23.1, is much like any other Web application descriptor file. It defines the Cocoon servlet, various `init` parameters, and mappings.

Listing 23.1 *web.xml*

```
<?xml version="1.0" encoding="ISO-8859-1"?>

<!DOCTYPE web-app
    PUBLIC "-//Sun Microsystems, Inc.//DTD Web Application 2.2//EN"
    "http://java.sun.com/j2ee/dtds/web-app_2_2.dtd">

<web-app>
  <display-name>Cocoon2 Demo</display-name>
  <description>Demo application for Cocoon2</description>
  <servlet>
    <servlet-name>Cocoon2</servlet-name>
    <display-name>Cocoon2</display-name>
    <description>The main Cocoon2 servlet</description>

    <servlet-class>org.apache.cocoon.servlet.CocoonServlet</servlet-class>

    <init-param>
      <param-name>configurations</param-name>
      <param-value>/WEB-INF/cocoon.xconf</param-value>
    </init-param>

    <init-param>
      <param-name>init-classloader</param-name>
      <param-value>false</param-value>
    </init-param>

    <init-param>
      <param-name>logkit-config</param-name>
      <param-value>/WEB-INF/logkit.xconf</param-value>
    </init-param>

    <init-param>
      <param-name>servlet-logger</param-name>
      <param-value>access</param-value>
    </init-param>

    <init-param>
      <param-name>cocoon-logger</param-name>
      <param-value>core</param-value>
    </init-param>

    <init-param>
```

Listing 23.1 *(continued)*

```
    <param-name>log-level</param-name>
    <param-value>DEBUG</param-value>
  </init-param>

  <init-param>
    <param-name>allow-reload</param-name>
    <param-value>yes</param-value>
  </init-param>

  <init-param>
    <param-name>load-class</param-name>
    <param-value>
      org.gjt.mm.mysql.Driver
    </param-value>
  </init-param>

  <init-param>
    <param-name>upload-directory</param-name>
    <param-value>/WEB-INF/work/upload-dir</param-value>
  </init-param>

  <!--
  <init-param>
    <param-name>cache-directory</param-name>
    <param-value>/WEB-INF/work/cache-dir</param-value>
  </init-param>
  -->

  <!--
  <init-param>
    <param-name>work-directory</param-name>
    <param-value>/WEB-INF/work</param-value>
  </init-param>
  -->

  <!--
  <init-param>
    <param-name>extra-classpath</param-name>
    <param-value>WEB-INF/extra-classes</param-value>
  </init-param>
  -->
```

Listing 23.1 *(continued)*

```
    <!--
    <init-param>
      <param-name>parent-component-manager</param-name>
      <param-value>org.apache.cocoon.samples.parentcm.ParentComponentManager/
➥org/apache/cocoon/samples/parentcm/ParentCMConfiguration</param-value>
    </init-param>
    -->

    <init-param>
      <param-name>request-factory</param-name>
      <param-value>org.apache.cocoon.components.request.
➥MultipartRequestFactoryImpl</param-value>
    </init-param>

    <!--
    <init-param>
      <param-name>show-time</param-name>
      <param-value>hide</param-value>
    </init-param>
    -->

    <init-param>
      <param-name>manage-exceptions</param-name>
      <param-value>true</param-value>
    </init-param>


    <load-on-startup>1</load-on-startup>
  </servlet>

  <servlet-mapping>
    <servlet-name>Cocoon2</servlet-name>
    <url-pattern>/</url-pattern>
  </servlet-mapping>

  <servlet-mapping>
    <servlet-name>Cocoon2</servlet-name>
    <url-pattern>*.jsp</url-pattern>
  </servlet-mapping>

  <servlet-mapping>
    <servlet-name>Cocoon2</servlet-name>
```

Listing 23.1 *(continued)*

```
    <url-pattern>*.html</url-pattern>
  </servlet-mapping>

  <mime-mapping>
    <extension>css</extension>
    <mime-type>text/css</mime-type>
  </mime-mapping>

</web-app>
```

As you can see, only one servlet is defined, `Cocoon2`. You might want to change the `<description>` tag in your own application, because the default says `Demo application for Cocoon2`. The servlet class is `org.apache.cocoon.servlet.CocoonServlet`. Another servlet is also available, `org.apache.cocoon.servlet.ParanoidCocoonServlet`, which uses its own class loader. You'd want to use this only if you find that your servlet container is somehow not making the right classes available to Cocoon, even though the classpath is correctly defined.

Table 23.1 lists all the initialization parameters defined in this file.

Table 23.1 *<web.xml> Initialization Parameters*

Parameter	Description
`configurations`	Points Cocoon to `cocoon.xconf`.
`init-classloader`	Set to `true` if you want Cocoon to use its own class loader (or use the `ParanoidCocoonServlet` class).
`logkit-config`	Points Cocoon to `logkit.xconf`.
`servlet-logger`	Category for the log messages coming from `CocoonServlet`. Default is `access`.
`cocoon-logger`	Category for the log messages coming from the Cocoon engine. This category becomes the default for any components that are defined in either `sitemap.xmap` or `cocoon.xconf` without a logger attribute. Default is `core`.
`log-level`	Sets the log level for messages coming out during the startup of Cocoon. Only those messages of this level and below will be logged. Default is `DEBUG`.
`allow-reload`	If this is set to yes, you can make Cocoon reload itself by calling a page with a request parameter of `cocoon-reload`.
`load-class`	Cocoon will load the classes defined here. You can separate the class names with spaces, commas, or returns. This is, of course, where you list JDBC driver classes.

Table 23.1 *(continued)*

Parameter	Description
`upload-directory`	Specifies where Cocoon should put files it uploads via the `upload` function. By default, this is commented out, and Cocoon uses the `cocoon-files/upload-dir` directory in the servlet's work directory.
`cache-directory`	Specifies where Cocoon should put cached files. By default, this is commented out and Cocoon uses the `cocoon-files/cache-dir` directory in the servlet container's work directory.
`work-directory`	Specifies where Cocoon should put its work files. By default, this is commented out and Cocoon uses the cocoon-files directory in the servlet container's work directory.
`extra-classpath`	Cocoon will add the directories, jars, or classes specified here to its `classpath`. If you use this, provide class information as you would when specifying the -classpath option when starting Java—that is, with the correct separator.
`parent-component-manager`	Specifies the parent component manager. This is commented out by default.
`request-factory`	Specifies either `org.apache.cocoon.components.request.MultipartRequestFactoryImpl` (the default) or `org.apache.cocoon.components.request.MaybeUploadRequestFactoryImpl`. The latter comes from `maybe-load.jar`, which is a product from `http://www.weft.co.uk/`. Both components react to requests whose content type is "multipart/form-data" and invoke the file upload process.
`show-time`	If this is set to `true` or `yes`, Cocoon will add processing time to each response returned to the client. If the value is `hide`, Cocoon will provide the processing time information as an HTML comment. To turn this off (you shouldn't need it in production), set the value to no.
`manage-exceptions`	If this is set to `true`, or not set at all, Cocoon will attempt to catch all exceptions and handle them itself. If it's set to anything else, Cocoon will rethrow them to the servlet container.
`load-on-startup`	If this is set to `1`, Cocoon will start immediately after the startup of the servlet container. Otherwise, it will start when the servlet is first executed.

Container Managed Security

Cocoon's `web.xml` follows the DTD of version 2.2 of the Java Servlet Specification. If you want to use container managed security, you should change this to reflect version 2.3 of the Specification, like this:

```
<!DOCTYPE web-app
    PUBLIC "-//Sun Microsystems, Inc.//DTD Web Application 2.3//EN"
    "http://java.sun.com/dtd/web-app_2_3.dtd">
```

With this DOCTYPE setting, you can now create a protected area like this:

```
<security-constraint>
 <web-resource-collection>
   <web-resource-name>ABC Security</web-resource-name>
   <url-pattern>/abc/*</url-pattern>
  </web-resource-collection>
 <auth-constraint>
  <role-name>tomcat</role-name>
 </auth-constraint>
</security-constraint>

<login-config>
 <auth-method>BASIC</auth-method>
 <realm-name>ABC</realm-name>
</login-config>
```

In this example, we're using Tomcat as the servlet container. These instructions tell Tomcat to authenticate any users who try to access the abc part of the Cocoon webapp using the BASIC login method. BASIC authentication is that which Tomcat handles itself, as opposed to FORM authentication, in which you supply Tomcat with a login form in a JSP. We've specified that only users with a role of tomcat can access our protected area. By default, Tomcat uses something called the MemoryRealm to authenticate, as defined in $CATALINA_HOME/conf/server.xml. This component implements authentication by checking the user credentials against a text file, $CATALINA_HOME/conf/tomcat-users. There is a login in this file with userid, password, and role of tomcat, which is what you can use if you want to test this example yourself. Figure 23.1 shows what the login form looks like if we put the preceding snippet into web.xml, restart Tomcat, and attempt to access a page within the abc project.

Another useful thing that is part of the 2.3 Java Servlet Specification is filters. Filters are a mechanism whereby you can preprocess requests before they reach the servlet, or post-process responses before they reach the client. The main aspect to note is that any filter declarations should come at the top of web.xml before the <servlet> tag. If you need more information on servlets, a good place to start is http://www.javaworld.com/javaworld/jw-06-2001/jw-0622-filters_p.html.

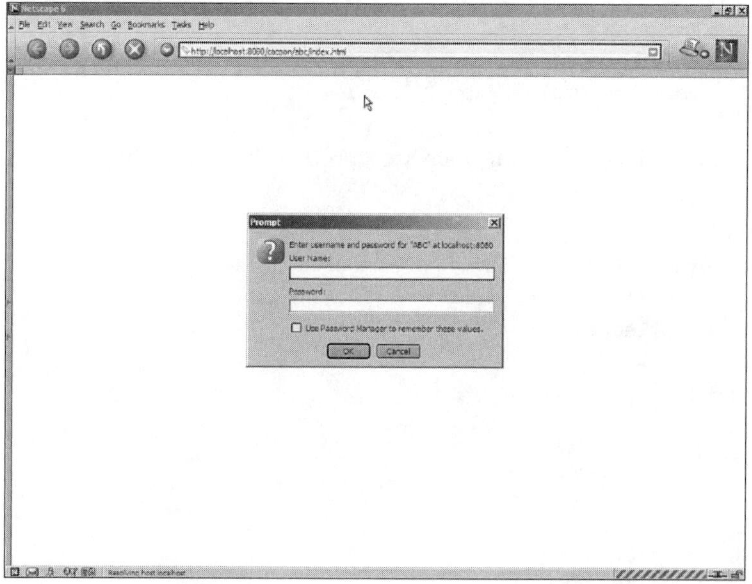

Figure 23.1
The Tomcat authentication screen.

cocoon.xconf

`cocoon.xconf` is the main Cocoon configuration file. We have already used it to define connection pools, logicsheets, and the reload settings for the sitemap. But there some other interesting configurables here as well.

Listing 23.2 shows the skeleton of `cocoon.xconf` from the 2.0.3 distribution.

Listing 23.2 *Skeleton Version of cocoon.xconf*

```
<?xml version="1.0" encoding="UTF-8"?>

<cocoon version="2.0">

  <hsqldb-server class="org.apache.cocoon.components.hsqldb.ServerImpl"
   logger="core.hsqldb-server" pool-max="1" pool-min="1">
   <!-- parameters go here -->
  </hsqldb-server>

  <xml-parser class="org.apache.avalon.excalibur.xml.JaxpParser"
   logger="core.xml-parser">
```

Listing 23.2 *(continued)*

```
  <!-- parameters go here -->
 </xml-parser>

 <cache-persistent class="org.apache.cocoon.components.store.FilesystemStore"
   logger="core.store.persistent">
  <!-- parameters go here -->
 </cache-persistent>

 <cache-transient class="org.apache.cocoon.components.store.MRUMemoryStore"
  logger="core.store.transient">
  <!-- parameters go here -->
 </cache-transient>

 <store-janitor class="org.apache.cocoon.components.store.StoreJanitorImpl"
  logger="core.store.janitor">
  <!-- parameters go here -->
 </store-janitor>

 <xslt-processor class="org.apache.cocoon.components.xslt.XSLTProcessorImpl"
  logger="core.xslt-processor">
  <!-- parameters go here -->
 </xslt-processor>

 <xpath-processor
  class="org.apache.avalon.excalibur.xml.xpath.XPathProcessorImpl"
  logger="core.xpath-processor"/>

 <url-factory logger="core.url-factory">
  <!-- parameters go here -->
 </url-factory>

 <source-handler logger="core.source-handler">
  <!-- parameters go here -->
 </source-handler>

 <program-generator logger="core.program-generator">
  <!-- parameters go here -->
 </program-generator>

 <jsp-engine logger="core.jsp-engine">
  <!-- parameters go here -->
```

Listing 23.2 *(continued)*

```
</jsp-engine>

<xscript logger="core.xscript">
 <!-- parameters go here -->
</xscript>

<programming-languages>
  <java-language logger="core.language.java" name="java">
    <!-- parameters go here -->
  </java-language>

  <js-language logger="core.language.js" name="js"/>
</programming-languages>

<classloader
 class="org.apache.cocoon.components.classloader.ClassLoaderManagerImpl"
 logger="core.classloader"/>

<markup-languages>
  <xsp-language logger="core.markup.xsp" name="xsp">
    <!-- parameters go here -->

    <target-language name="java">
      <!-- parameters go here -->

      <builtin-logicsheet>
        <!-- parameters go here -->
      </builtin-logicsheet>

      <!-- more logicsheets go here -->
    </target-language>

    <target-language name="js">
      <!-- parameters go here -->

      <builtin-logicsheet>
        <!-- parameters go here -->
      </builtin-logicsheet>

      <!-- more logicsheets go here -->
    </target-language>
  </xsp-language>
```

Listing 23.2 *(continued)*

```
  <sitemap-language logger="core.markup.sitemap" name="sitemap">
    <!-- parameters go here -->

    <target-language name="java">
      <!-- parameters go here -->
    </target-language>
  </sitemap-language>
</markup-languages>

<datasources>
  <jdbc logger="core.datasources.tutorial" name="tutorial">
    <!-- parameters go here -->
  </jdbc>
  <!-- more connection pools go here -->
</datasources>

<stream-pipeline
 class="org.apache.cocoon.components.pipeline.CachingStreamPipeline"
 logger="core.stream-pipeline" pool-grow="4" pool-max="32" pool-min="8"/>

<event-pipeline
 class="org.apache.cocoon.components.pipeline.CachingEventPipeline"
 logger="core.event-pipeline" pool-grow="4" pool-max="32" pool-min="8"/>

<xml-serializer
 class="org.apache.cocoon.components.sax.XMLByteStreamCompiler"
 logger="core.xml-serializer"/>

<xml-deserializer
 class="org.apache.cocoon.components.sax.XMLByteStreamInterpreter"
 logger="core.xml-deserializer"/>

<monitor logger="core.monitor">
  <!-- parameters go here -->
</monitor>

<sitemap check-reload="yes"
 class="org.apache.cocoon.sitemap.SitemapManager" file="sitemap.xmap"
 logger="sitemap" reload-method="synchron"/>

<deli class="org.apache.cocoon.components.deli.DeliImpl">
 <!-- parameters go here -->
```

Listing 23.2 *(continued)*

```
  </deli>

  <entity-resolver class="org.apache.cocoon.components.resolver.ResolverImpl"
    logger="core.resolver">
   <!-- parameters go here -->
  </entity-resolver>

  <cocoon-indexer logger="core.search.indexer"/>
  <cocoon-searcher logger="core.search.searcher"/>
  <cocoon-crawler logger="core.search.crawler"/>
  <lucene-xml-indexer logger="core.search.lucene"/>

  <input-modules logger="core.modules.input">
    <!-- component-instances go here -->
  </input-modules>

  <output-modules logger="core.modules.output">
    <!-- component-instances go here -->
  </output-modules>

  <autoincrement-modules logger="core.modules.auto">
    <!-- component-instances go here -->
  </autoincrement-modules>

  <!-- sunShine component definitions go here -->

</cocoon>
```

We'll review a few of the important sections here.

HSQLDB

The `<hsqldb-server>` block defines the Hypersonic SQL database used for the samples. This is the component responsible for those harmless but annoying HSQLDB error messages you see in your Tomcat startup window. Unless you plan on using HSQLDB, comment this section out.

XML Parser

The `<xml-parser>` block defines the JAXP 1.1 parser, required by Cocoon. By default, it is set to `JaxpParser`, which is found in the Avalon Excalibur package. The definition comes with several parameters that affect its operation, and several more you can add yourself. These parameters are shown in Table 23.2.

Table 23.2 *<xml-parser> Parameters*

Parameter	Description
`validate`	Set to either `true` or `false`. Default is false, which means that the XML parser will not attempt to validate XML against a DTD. Note that there is a bug (id #6200) that causes strange exceptions to be thrown during validation.
`namespace-prefixes`	Set to `true` if you want namespace declarations to be available as `xmlns` attributes (as in XSPs). Default is `false`.
`stop-on-warning`	If `true`, the default, XML parsing stops when a warning occurs.
`stop-on-recoverable-error`	If `true`, the default, XML parsing stops when a recoverable error occurs.
`reuse-parsers`	If `true`, Cocoon will attempt to reuse the parser for another parse. Default is false.
`sax-parser-factory`	Defines the name of the `SAXParserFactory` implementation class, as opposed to the default instance obtained by `SAXParserFactory.newInstance()`. This is useful if several implementations are available.
`document-builder-factory`	Defines the name of the `DocumentBuildingFactory` implementation class, as opposed to the default instance obtained by `DocumentBuildingFactory.newInstance()`. This is useful if several implementations are available.

Protocol Support

The classes responsible for handling the `resource:`, `file:`, and `xmldb:` pseudo-protocols are defined within the `<url-factory>` and `<source-handler>` blocks.

Caches

See the "Performance and Tuning" section for more information regarding the `<cache-persistent>`, `<cache-transient>`, and `<store-janitor>` blocks.

XSLT Processor

Cocoon's XSLT processor is defined in the `<xslt-processor>` block. The default processor is Xalan. If you want, you can use another processor such as Saxon, developed Michael Kay, which is actually faster than Xalan. You'll find Saxon at `http://saxon.sourceforge.net`. Be sure to use version 6.5.2, the current stable version. Version 7.2 is experimental and was compiled under JDK 1.4.

After you download Saxon, unpack the distribution and copy `saxon.jar` into the `WEB-INF/lib` directory of your Cocoon webapp folder. Remove the Xalan jar (in 2.0.3 the jar name is `xalan-2.3.1.jar`), stop your servlet container, delete the work directory, and start it back up.

Program Generator

The `<program-generator>` block defines some settings for the `ProgramGenerator`, which is responsible for turning XSPs into compiled objects. There are three parameters you can control. The `auto-reload` parameter (by default, set to `true`) causes Cocoon to recompile an XSP when it detects a change. The `root-package` parameter defines the package name for the compiled object. By default, this is `org.apache.cocoon.www`, but you can change it to whatever you like. The last parameter, `preload`, set to `true` by default, tells Cocoon whether to preload compiled XSP objects.

JSP Engine

The JSP engine to be used to process JSP files is defined in the `<jsp-engine>` block. The default class is the Jasper implementation from Apache (`org.apache.jasper.servlet.JspServlet`). Jasper comes as part of Tomcat, but you must copy `jasper-compiler.jar` from `$CATALINA_HOME/lib` to the `WEB-INF/lib` directory of the Cocoon webapp.

Programming Languages

In the `<programming-languages>` block is specified which programming languages are support by Cocoon for use in on-the-fly compilation. Both Java and JavaScript are defined. Also defined is the compiler that Cocoon uses for Java. The default is `org.apache.cocoon.components.language.programming.java.Pizza`, but you can also use a compiler such as Javac, from the JDK, or IBM's Jikes compiler.

Logicsheets

All Cocoon logicsheets for both the Java and JavaScript versions of XSPs are defined within the `<markup-languages>` block. We've already touched on some of these in previous chapters.

Connection Pools

All connection pools are defined inside the `<datasources>` block, one connection per `<jdbc>` block.

Sitemap

The sitemap engine is by default handled by `org.apache.cocoon.sitemap.SitemapManager`, as defined in the `<sitemap>` tag. Beginning with version 2.0.2, an interpreted version of the sitemap is available in `org.apache.cocoon.treeprocessor.TreeProcessor`. The advantage of this version is that it is faster, because it does not have to compile the sitemap. You'll also need it if you are using DELI, as discussed in Chapter 13, "Using Presentation Logic: Multi-Browser Support."

There is a bug in 2.0.3 in which using the `TreeProcessor` when you have sub-sitemaps will cause them not to inherit any components defined in the parent sitemap. This bug has been fixed in the `cocoon_2_0_3_branch` branch of CVS. If you need the `TreeProcessor` and you have sub-sitemaps, either wait for 2.0.4 or download `org.apache.cocoon.components.ExtendedComponentSelector.java` from CVS and rebuild your version of 2.0.3.

logkit.xconf

`logkit.xconf` is the configuration file for LogKit, the logging mechanism Cocoon borrows from Avalon. Here, you can control what is logged and how the log files are handled.

Listing 23.3 shows the skeleton of this file.

Listing 23.3 *Skeleton Version of logkit.xconf*

```
<?xml version="1.0"?>

<logkit>
  <factories>
    <!-- factories go here -->
  </factories>

  <targets>
    <cocoon id="core">
      <filename>${context-root}/WEB-INF/logs/core.log</filename>
      <format type="cocoon">
        %7.7{priority} %{time}   [%{category}] (%{uri}) %{thread}/
➥%{class:short}: %{message}\n%{throwable}
      </format>

      <append>false</append>
    </cocoon>
```

Listing 23.3 *(continued)*

```
    <cocoon id="sitemap">
      <filename>${context-root}/WEB-INF/logs/sitemap.log</filename>

      <format type="cocoon">
        %7.7{priority} %{time}   [%{category}] (%{uri}) %{thread}/
➥%{class:short}: %{message}\n%{throwable}
      </format>
      <append>false</append>
    </cocoon>

    <cocoon id="access">
      <filename>${context-root}/WEB-INF/logs/access.log</filename>
      <format type="cocoon">
        %7.7{priority} %{time}   [%{category}] (%{uri}) %{thread}/
➥%{class:short}: %{message}\n%{throwable}
      </format>
      <append>false</append>
    </cocoon>

    <priority-filter id="error" log-level="ERROR">
      <cocoon>
        <filename>${context-root}/WEB-INF/logs/error.log</filename>
        <format type="cocoon">
          %7.7{priority} %{time}   [%{category}] (%{uri}) %{thread}/
➥%{class:short}: %{message}\n%{throwable}
        </format>
        <append>false</append>
      </cocoon>
    </priority-filter>
  </targets>

  <categories>
    <category name="core" log-level="DEBUG">
      <!-- Startup component manager logger -->
      <category name="startup" log-level="DEBUG">
        <log-target id-ref="core"/>
        <log-target id-ref="error"/>
      </category>

      <category name="roles" log-level="DEBUG">
        <log-target id-ref="core"/>
```

Listing 23.3 *(continued)*

```
        <log-target id-ref="error"/>
      </category>

      <!-- Cocoon component manager logger -->
      <category name="manager" log-level="DEBUG">
        <log-target id-ref="core"/>
        <log-target id-ref="error"/>
      </category>

      <!-- Cocoon cache and stores logger -->
      <category name="store" log-level="DEBUG">
        <log-target id-ref="core"/>
        <log-target id-ref="error"/>
      </category>

      <log-target id-ref="core"/>
      <log-target id-ref="error"/>
    </category>

    <category name="sitemap" log-level="DEBUG">
      <log-target id-ref="sitemap"/>
      <log-target id-ref="error"/>
    </category>

    <category name="access" log-level="DEBUG">
      <log-target id-ref="access"/>
      <log-target id-ref="error"/>
    </category>
  </categories>
</logkit>
```

As we did with `cocoon.xconf`, let's review this file step-by-step.

Log Files

Log files are defined with the `<targets>` block. Each target has an id, which is used farther down in the file to map to various log message types. Currently, four target ids are defined, as shown in Table 23.3.

Table 23.3 *Cocoon Log Files*

Id	Description
`core`	Used primarily by the store janitor (see the "Performance and Tuning" section) to log memory conditions. Also serves as the default log file for any component that does have the `logger` attribute set in its definition.
`sitemap`	Is where most of the sitemap components do their logging.
`access`	Logs Cocoon's resolution of URIs and processing of pipeline resources.
`error`	Logs all error messages of type `ERROR` and `FATAL_ERROR`.

Each target definition sets the filename, format, append mode, and, optionally, rotation settings. By default, all log files are set to overwrite each time Cocoon starts up (set by the `<append>false</append>` line) and not to use rotation. Rotation settings, if you are interested, look like this:

```
<rotation type="revolving" init="1" max="30">
  <time>24:00:00</time>
</rotation>
```

These instructions tell Cocoon (or rather, LogKit) to keep a maximum of 30 logs files, rotating every 24 hours. We could also choose to rotate when the logs get to a certain size, using the following:

```
<size>100m</size>
```

In general, log rotation can be a bit of a pain because you can't immediately tell which file contains the latest error. You'll have to sort the files by date to find the right one. For more information on configuring rotation, or anything else in this file, see `http://jakarta.apache.org/avalon/logkit/` and `http://jakarta.apache.org/avalon/excalibur/logger/`.

Categories

The `<categories>` block associates log message types with files (or "targets"). Take, for example, the following:

```
<category name="sitemap" log-level="DEBUG">
 <log-target id-ref="sitemap"/>
 <log-target id-ref="error"/>
</category>
```

This entry says that log messages of type `"sitemap"` will be directed to both the `sitemap` and `error` targets, and will be logged with error type `"DEBUG"` and below. Because, however, the error target is earlier defined as getting only messages with error type "ERROR" and below, that rule takes precedence. Therefore, all log messages of type "sitemap" will go to the sitemap target, whereas only those with error level of "ERROR" and below will go to the error target.

If you're wondering how Cocoon indicates which category a log message should go to, all you have to do is check the logger attribute of the component definitions in sitemap.xmap (as well as those in cocoon.xconf). The TraxTransformer has, for instance, its logger defined as "sitemap.transformer.xslt". This definition says that the log message type is "sitemap" and its subtype is "transformer", while "xslt" is the specific source name. As we saw in the preceding paragraph, this means that the log messages from TraxTransformer will end up in the WEB-INF/logs/sitemap.log.

When you define custom components, such as actions, you can also define a logger attribute. In fact, if you would like to isolate your own error messages from Cocoon's, you might even want to define your own <target> and <category> entries in logkit.xconf.

Performance and Tuning

When we talk about performance and tuning in Cocoon, we are primarily talking about two things: Cocoon's memory usage and processing efficiency. How you control Cocoon's memory usage can be the difference between a happy Cocoon and one that regularly throws the dreaded OutOfMemoryException. Similarly, an out-of-the-box version of Cocoon can cause you all sorts of performance problems if you attempt to use it in a well-used production site without tuning it for maximum speed.

Memory Usage

When it comes to memory usage, Cocoon likes a lot. A small Cocoon application might be able to run under 64MB of RAM, but for most installations you'll want to use more than that. A good starting point, if you can afford the memory, is about 256MB. How do you allocate this to Cocoon? First, you need to allocate it to the servlet container's JVM. For Tomcat, you can do this by setting $CATALINA_OPTS as follows:

```
-Xmx300m
```

This tells the JVM that it can use up to 300MB of RAM, commonly referred to as "heap size." It is not a good idea to set this so high that the OS starts using virtual memory—the performance hit will be considerable. You can also specify a starting heap size, with the -Xms option, but there is not much point in doing that—Cocoon will grab as much as it needs when it starts.

Next you need to tell Cocoon what is the value of `-Xmx`. You do this by editing the `<store-janitor>` block in `cocoon.xconf`:

```
<store-janitor class="org.apache.cocoon.components.store.StoreJanitorImpl"
   logger="core.store.janitor">
   <parameter name="freememory" value="10000000"/>
   <parameter name="heapsize" value="300000000"/>
   <parameter name="cleanupthreadinterval" value="10"/>
   <parameter name="threadpriority" value="5"/>
   <parameter name="percent_to_free" value="10"/>
</store-janitor>
```

The `heapsize` parameter is the one that sets the maximum amount of RAM allocated to the JVM. The memory used by Cocoon (along with the servlet container itself and other applications in the servlet container) is referred to as the "heap in use." As this value grows, it slowly approaches the maximum set by `-Xmx` and the `heapsize` parameter. Cocoon watches this, and when it detects that the total JVM memory consumption has exceeded this maximum heap size setting, it will attempt to free up memory. The value of the `freememory` parameter is the difference that Cocoon will attempt to achieve between the total JVM heap size and the heap in use. In other words, Cocoon will free memory until there is at least the value of `freememory` difference between the two.

The value of `freememory` is something you have to figure out for your own application. You can watch the message from the `StoreJanitor` in `core.log`. If you find that it is freeing memory at a pretty good rate, you might want to increase the value of `freememory` so that it has less work to do. More likely, you'll need to increase your RAM because your application is memory intensive.

On some systems, such as Windows 98, you'll find that the JVM slowly uses up system memory and finally you start getting everyone's favorite `OutOfMemory` exception. Unfortunately, there is not much to be done, except buy more memory and/or restart periodically.

Improving Performance

Performance is obviously an important part of good design. Following are some things to keep in mind when designing, building, and maintaining your application.

Cacheability

One thing that affects performance is cacheability—the more of a pipeline you can get cached, the better. Obviously, pipelines that deal with dynamic elements can't be cached. In general, however, keep looking for opportunities for caching. If you are doing aggregation, for example, use CIncludeTransformer instead of XIncludeTransformer, if you can, because the former is cacheable. Unless absolutely necessary, don't use the use-request-parameters or use-session-info parameters for the TraxTransformer, because that will force Cocoon to redo the pipeline, rather than using the cache even when there is in reality no change to the pipeline elements.

Cocoon caches objects in memory, using something called the MRUMemoryStore, which is defined in cocoon.xconf in the <cache-transient> block. The definition allows you to specify how many objects the store will hold (the default is 100). If you have the memory, increase this value, but keep watching the memory messages in WEB-INF/logs/core.log in case you've increased it too much. After this store is used up, Cocoon utilizes a persistent storage, which is either a FileSystemStore, the default, or a new implementation, the JispFileSystemStore. The latter is newer and possibly less stable than the former. Both stores are defined inside <cache-persistent> blocks, but one must be commented out.

Precompiling XSPs

A neat trick with heavily used XSPs is to use the compiled classes directly as generators. To do this, access the XSP so that Cocoon creates and compiles it as a class. Then copy the resulting class file from $COCOON_WORK into the WEB-INF/classes directory. Don't forget to create all the necessary subdirectories. For example, if we wanted to do this with our login.xsp, the compiled class would be $COCOON_WORK/cocoon-files/org/apache/cocoon/www/abc/xsp/login_xsp.class. We would then copy that file into the WEB-INF/classes/org/apache/cocoon/www/abc/xsp directory (which we probably would have to create).

Then, you add a <map:generator> entry for the new generator, and you can use it throughout your sitemap. For this example, our entry would be this:

```
<map:generator name="login_xsp"
  logger="sitemap.generator.login_xsp"
  src="org.apache.cocoon.www.abc.xsp.login_xsp "/>
```

Now we can reference this generator by its name, login_xsp.

XSP Reloading

Another performance saver you might considering is turning off the auto-reloading of XSPs. By default, this is set to true in cocoon.xconf (via the auto-reload parameter in the <program-generator> block), which means that Cocoon will recompile XSPs when it detects a change. In a production environment in which your XSPs are static, set this parameter to false to save Cocoon time in checking for changes.

Pools

In Cocoon, many things are pooled besides database connections: `generators`, `transformers`, `serializers`, `readers`, and other components are pooled. The settings that control these pools are found in the component definitions, in the sitemap. Basically, what you need to think about here is how many simultaneous requests your application can have using a certain component. If, for example, you expect typically 50 concurrent requests, all accessing pipelines with a `TraxTransformer`, redefine its definition as shown here:

```
<map:transformer logger="sitemap.transformer.xslt" name="xslt"
  pool-grow="5" pool-max="100" pool-min="50"
  src="org.apache.cocoon.transformation.TraxTransformer"/>
```

Here, we are telling Cocoon to create 50 initial instances of this component, and allow that number to grow to 100, in increments of five. This ensures that each of the concurrent requests will get its own `TraxTransformer` component, rather than having to wait for another request to complete. Naturally, however, you must have the memory to support your requirements. As your application runs, watch the log files and make sure you are getting hits from the cache. Look for messages like this (found in `WEB-INF/logs/sitemap.log`):

```
DEBUG   (2002-08-19) 07:50.05:940   [sitemap](/cocoon/abc/count/blat) HttpProces
sor[8080][4]/LogKitLogger: Retrieving a org.apache.cocoon.transformation.TraxTra
nsformer from the pool
DEBUG   (2002-08-19) 07:50.05:940   [sitemap](/cocoon/abc/count/blat) HttpProces
sor[8080][4]/LogKitLogger: Returning a org.apache.cocoon.transformation.TraxTran
sformer to the pool
```

We can see that, when processing the URI `/cocoon/abc/count/blat`, Cocoon was able to retrieve a `TraxTransformer` instance from the pool and then return it after it was used.

The same philosophy of pool size applies to database connections. The other thing to keep in mind about these is that they will go stale if the database goes down while Cocoon is up. If you have any kind of cold backup happening with your database (that is, a backup in which the database goes offline), set up an automated task to bounce the servlet container after the backup completes; otherwise, the next user to hit your application will not get the intended results. If you use an Oracle database, make sure you have the `oradb` attribute set to `true` in the pool configuration in `cocoon.xconf`.

Log Messages

Logging is expensive, and in production you probably don't need all the `DEBUG` type messages. To allow only error messages through to the logs, edit `web.xml` and change the `log-level` initialization parameter to `ERROR`. This eliminates the `DEBUG` messages during startup. Then edit `logkit.xconf` and change the `log-level` attribute for all `<category>` tags to `ERROR` as well. After you restart your servlet container, you will notice a difference!

Sitemap Reloading

As mentioned before, don't deploy a production application with the `check-reload` attribute set to `yes` for your sitemaps, unless you have a very good reason. (This does not apply if you have changed to the interpreted sitemap implementation.) You will get a performance hit both to check for changes and to recompile. Similarly, if you had set your servlet container to reload the Cocoon webapp if it detected class changes (in Tomcat this is set via the `reloadable` attribute in the `<context>` tag), turn it off in production.

Static Files

Cocoon is noticeably slower in handling static files, such as HTML, CSS, and image files, via a `Reader`. If this is a concern, put that content into its own area and let either the servlet container serve it or, better yet, a front-end server like Apache handle it. The combination of Apache, Tomcat, and Cocoon is a popular one that allows you to utilize the strengths of each piece of software to efficiently deliver your application.

Summary

It is important to keep informed of new developments with Cocoon, because as various underlying parts get changed, fixed, or upgraded, principles of performance and tuning will change. These rules are probably valid for quite some time, but keep in mind that they will change. There are enough examples of Cocoon applications handling heavy loads and complex functionality to prove its robustness in a wide variety of situations. However, every application is different. If you find that the requirements of your application are causing unexpected performance problems, check with the mailing list and the official site to see whether anyone else has encountered this situation. Of course, you may find yourself debugging your problem and contributing a fix to the distribution. That's part of the open source process and the reason why Cocoon has matured and will continue to do so!

PART V

Reference

CHAPTER

CHAPTER 24

Sitemap Components

It should be 100% clear by now that the sitemap is one of the most important parts of Cocoon. If the sitemap is not configured correctly, requests cannot be properly processed and responses sent. The sitemap is at the heart of everything that Cocoon is asked to do, and therefore it is absolutely critical that Cocoon developers know what they can do with it. As you will no doubt have seen in other parts of this book, there is quite often more than one way to skin a cat. It should also be clear that there is not always a single correct way—some tasks can be achieved using different methods that have equal validity. Some problems, however, do have solutions that can be worked out more easily if the sitemap is used correctly, and to enable this it is imperative that a good understanding of what can be done in the sitemap is reached.

This chapter seeks to bring together much of the sitemap-related information that has been presented thus far and combine it with information about aspects of functionality that have not been covered in detail. In addition to reflecting some material that has been covered in the book thus far, the information contained in this chapter also may cover subjects you can find information on in the Cocoon documentation. You should not infer, however, that this is just a "stocking filler" chapter because there are many components that are not covered at all in the documentation or even as samples that you can hunt out. In addition, pains have been taken to check the source code to ensure that any configuration parameters and behavior are documented here that may not be included in either the distribution plain English or the API documentation.

We will first review the fundamental structure of the sitemap and then look at all the various available components, as well as considering some ways of handling request scenarios in the pipeline that have not been covered elsewhere in the book.

Sitemap Overview

The root sitemap, named `sitemap.xmap`, can be found in the root of the Cocoon Web application. The sitemap is organized into the following basic hierarchy:

```
<map:sitemap>
  <map:components>
    <map:generators>
    </map:generators>
    <map:transformers>
    </map:transformers>
    <map:readers>
    </map:readers>
    <map:serializers>
    </map:serializers>
    <map:matchers>
    </map:matchers>
    <map:selectors>
    </map:selectors>
    <map:actions>
    </map:actions>
  </map:components>
  <map:views>
  </map:views>
  <map:resources>
  </map:resources>
  <map:action-sets>
  </map:action-sets>
  <map:pipelines>
  </map:pipelines>
</map:sitemap>
```

Aside from the root sitemap, you can define sub-sitemaps that reside in folders off the root. These inherit components from parent sitemaps and can be used to keep sitemap configuration more simple and reduce the need to edit the root sitemap to deploy a new sub-application inside Cocoon.

Cocoon Components

Through the book as a whole, the purpose of each section of the sitemap has been covered, as well as the methods of using each of the parts. What we have not been able to cover is every single component that is available, so this part of the chapter provides a comprehensive list of all the generators, transformers, serializers, and so on that exist in Cocoon 2.0.3. You might find a way of performing a task you had not considered before. At the very least, you'll have a comprehensive reference of the vast number of components already in existence that you can use "out of the box." Note that most, if not all, of the components listed implement the `Poolable` interface and normally would have their pool configuration settings as part of their declaration element. For the sake of brevity, this has been removed. There are also no view-related labels for the same reason.

Generators

The first set of components we will look at are the generators. These components are used to build an input SAX event stream from a source such as a database or a file.

DirectoryGenerator

The `DirectoryGenerator` class creates a stream of XML that reflects a directory listing. It is defined in the sitemap using the following:

```
<map:generator
     logger="sitemap.generator.directory"
     name="directory"
     src="org.apache.cocoon.generation.DirectoryGenerator"/>
```

It is easily used in the pipeline, as the following example shows:

```
<map:match pattern="**dir.xml">
  <map:generate src="{1}" type="directory">
    <map:parameter name="depth" value="5"/>
    <map:parameter name="dateFormat" value="dd-MMM-yyyy hh:mm:ss"/>
    <map:parameter name="root" value="cocoon"/>
    <map:parameter name="include" value=".*"/>
    <map:parameter name="exclude" value="\.bak$"/>
```

```
  </map:generate>
  <map:serialize type="xml"/>
</map:match>
```

The <map:generate> element block can contain five optional parameters. The first, depth, sets the number of subfolders that the generator will recurse into. It defaults at 1. Note that there is no method for specifying that the directory generator should include all the subfolders.

The dateFormat parameter defines the format of the file modification date and time. This follows the same syntax as the Java SimpleDateFormat.

The root parameter uses a regular expression to define the root path to use for the folder hierarchy. For example, if this parameter is left off, the folder paths will be relative to the current folder. If it is used, the folder paths will be relative to the specified root. In the previous example, assuming that the pipeline is in a sitemap in /java/tomcat/webapps/cocoon/mount/cdh/chapter24, the hierarchy reflected in the XML stream will be cocoon/mount/cdh/chapter24.

The include parameter is a regular expression that indicates what file and folder names should be included. The ".*" pattern used previously means everything.

The exclude parameter is a regular expression that indicates what file and folder names should be excluded. The "\.bak$" pattern used previously will ignore any files with an extension of .bak. It will include a file with bak as part of its name, or even .bak, just as long as the latter is not the last part of the filename.

The resultant stream of XML will have <dir:directory> elements for the folders, and <dir:file> elements for the files. These elements share name, lastModified, and date attributes. The folder that is the original one specified also has an attribute called requested, set to a value of true, as per the following extract:

```
<?xml version="1.0" encoding="UTF-8" ?>
<dir:directory name="cocoon"
     lastModified="1032027000636"
     date="14/09/02 19:10"
     xmlns:dir="http://apache.org/cocoon/directory/2.0">
  <dir:directory name="mount"
       lastModified="1031537875786"
       date="09/09/02 03:17">
    <dir:directory name="cdh"
         lastModified="1032006482764"
         date="14/09/02 13:28">
      <dir:directory name="chapter24"
```

```
          lastModified="1032073348229"
          date="15/09/02 08:02
          requested="true">
        <dir:file name="sitemap.xmap"
            lastModified="1032073141142"
            date="15/09/02 07:59" />
        <dir:directory name="stylesheets"
            lastModified="1032027590684"
            date="14/09/02 19:19">
          <dir:file name="directory2html.xsl"
              lastModified="1028422980751"
              date="04/08/02 02:03" />
        </dir:directory>
      </dir:directory>
    </dir:directory>
  </dir:directory>
</dir:directory>
```

FileGenerator

The `FileGenerator` is probably the generator that is used most in Cocoon. It reads XML from a source and generates a SAX event stream. It is defined in the sitemap using the following:

```
<map:generator
     logger="sitemap.generator.file"
     name="file"
     src="org.apache.cocoon.generation.FileGenerator"/>
```

This generator has been used significantly through the book, so there is not much more that can be said about it here.

FragmentExtractorGenerator

This generator is little used and little known. It is typically used with the `FragmentExtractorTransformer` as a generator/transformer pair. The purpose of this pair of components is to extract a specific node for separate processing by another pipeline match.

The generator is configured in the sitemap as shown here:

```
<map:generator
    logger="sitemap.generator.extractor"
    name="extractor"
    src="org.apache.cocoon.generation.FragmentExtractorGenerator"/>
```

For more details on how this is used, see the FragmentExtractorTransformer details later in this chapter.

HTMLGenerator

The HTMLGenerator is used to convert a source HTML document to XHTML using the JTidy package. The benefit of doing this is that the subsequent stream is then well-formed XML and can be further processed, thus allowing the powerful manipulation of existing HTML resources.

The HTMLGenerator is configured in the sitemap in the following manner:

```
<map:generator
     logger="sitemap.generator.html"
     name="html"
     src="org.apache.cocoon.generation.HTMLGenerator"/>
```

HTMLGenerator is an optional component because the build process will include it only if it finds a Jtidy.jar file in the optional library folder of the distribution. This file, however, is by default in the distribution and therefore the generator is available from the start.

ImageDirectoryGenerator

The ImageDirectoryGenerator component extends the DirectorGenerator component detailed previously and adds an extra couple of attributes to the resultant stream: width and height. These obviously represent the width and height of the image. The class recognizes only JPEG and GIF formats. The sitemap configuration entry is as follows:

```
<map:generator
     logger="sitemap.generator.imagedirectory"
     name="imagedirectory"
     src="org.apache.cocoon.generation.ImageDirectoryGenerator"/>
```

The same configuration parameters that are used for DirectoryGenerator apply to ImageDirectoryGenerator.

JspGenerator

The JspGenerator allows the use of a JSP file as a generator. The details of this generator are covered in Chapter 18, "Cocoon Interfaces: J2EE," but it is set up in the sitemap with this:

```
<map:generator
     logger="sitemap.generator.jsp"
     name="jsp"
     src="org.apache.cocoon.generation.JspGenerator"/>
```

MP3DirectoryGenerator

This generator is another extension of the `DirectoryGenerator` class. It can be added to the sitemap using the following XML:

```
<map:generator
     logger="sitemap.generator.mp3directory"
     name="mp3directory"
     src="org.apache.cocoon.generation.MP3DirectoryGenerator"/>
```

The generator adds some additional attributes for MP3 files that it finds in the folder. These include the following:

- `frequency`—The frequency file in KHz.
- `bitrate`—The bitrate of the MP3 file in Kbps.
- `mode`—The mode of the MP3 file, one of the following: `Stereo`, `Joint stereo`, `Dual channel`, `Single channel`.
- `variable-rate`—This is an optional attribute and will have a value of `yes` if a variable bit rate (VBR) header is detected.
- `title`—The track title, if it is found in the MP3 ID tag.
- `artitst`—The track artist, if it is found in the MP3 ID tag.
- `album`—The album title, if it is found in the MP3 ID tag.
- `year`—The track year, if it is found in the MP3 ID tag.
- `comment`—Comments, if they are found in the MP3 ID tag.
- `track`—The track number on the album, if it is found in the MP3 ID tag.
- `genre`—The music genre type identifier, if it is found in the MP3 ID tag.

A sample node would look something like this:

```
<dir:file name="dOgs gO bOOm - demO cd - 03 - spiky.mp3"
     lastModified="1003799440141"
     date="23/10/01 02:10"
     frequency="44.1"
     mode="Joint stereo"
     bitrate="128"
     title="spiky"
     artist="dOgs gO bOOm"
     album="demO cd"
```

```
    track="3"
    genre="12" />
```

For more information about the `MP3DirectoryGenerator`, see Chapter 9, "Using Content Logic: Generators."

PHPGenerator

`PHPGenerator` allows you to use pages written in PHP language with Cocoon. This generator is optional, and before it can be used, it is necessary to download PHP servlet (it is part of PHP distribution) from `www.php.net/downloads.php` and recompile Cocoon with PHP servlet in the `lib/local` folder. After `PHPGenerator` is compiled, it can be added to the sitemap using this:

```
<map:generator
    logger="sitemap.generator.php"
    name="php"
    src="org.apache.cocoon.generation.PhpGenerator"/>
```

Before you start using this generator, you need to add a directory containing PHP native libraries to the system's path.

> **PHP**
> PHP recursively stands for PHP Hypertext Preprocessor and is a known scripting language well suited for Web development. Numerous resources on the Web are devoted to PHP. If you want to know more, start with `www.php.net/`. Read about PHP servlet at `www.php.net/manual/en/ref.java.php#java.servlet`.

ProfilerGenerator

`ProfilerGenerator` is intended to obtain collected profiler data. To get any results, first you need to have profiler components configured in `cocoon.xconf`. Profiler consists of the following three components:

```
<event-pipeline
  class="org.apache.cocoon.components.profiler.
  ➥ProfilingNonCachingEventPipeline"/>
<sax-connector
  class="org.apache.cocoon.components.profiler.ProfilingSAXConnector"/>
<profiler/>
```

One component, `ProfilingCachingEventPipeline`, replaces default event pipeline component `CachingEventPipeline`, and two others are additional components.

After configuration is done, `ProfilerGenerator` can be added to the sitemap:

```
<map:generator
    logger="sitemap.generator.profile"
    name="profile"
    src="org.apache.cocoon.components.profiler.ProfilerGenerator"/>
```

And can be used in the pipeline:

```
<map:match pattern="profile">
    <map:generate type="profile"/>
    <map:serialize type="xml"/>
</map:match>
```

Now everything is ready to use profiler. Restart Tomcat, and access several Cocoon sample pages to collect profiler data. Access profiler at `http://localhost:8080/cocoon/profile`. Profiler data will look similar to this:

```
<?xml version="1.0" encoding="UTF-8" ?>

<profilerinfo
    date="Sep 29, 2002 11:02:06 AM"
    xmlns="http://apache.org/cocoon/profiler/1.0">
  <pipeline uri="welcome" count="1" time="271">
    <average time="271">
      <element role="file" source="docs/samples/samples.xml" time="110" />
      <element role="xslt" source="stylesheets/simple-samples2html.xsl"
               time="20" />
      <element role="org.apache.cocoon.serialization.HTMLSerializer"
               time="141" />
    </average>
    <result time="271">
      <element role="file" source="docs/samples/samples.xml" time="110" />
      <element role="xslt" source="stylesheets/simple-samples2html.xsl"
               time="20" />
      <element role="org.apache.cocoon.serialization.HTMLSerializer"
               time="141" />
    </result>
  </pipeline>
  <pipeline uri="hello.html" count="2" time="100">
    <average time="50">
      <element role="file" source="docs/samples/hello-page.xml" time="20" />
      <element role="xslt" source="stylesheets/page/simple-page2html.xsl"
               time="10" />
```

```
      <element role="org.apache.cocoon.serialization.HTMLSerializer"
               time="20" />
    </average>
    <result time="70">
      <element role="file" source="docs/samples/hello-page.xml" time="20" />
      <element role="xslt" source="stylesheets/page/simple-page2html.xsl"
               time="10" />
      <element role="org.apache.cocoon.serialization.HTMLSerializer"
               time="40" />
    </result>
    <result time="30">
      <element role="file" source="docs/samples/hello-page.xml" time="20" />
      <element role="xslt" source="stylesheets/page/simple-page2html.xsl"
               time="10" />
      <element role="org.apache.cocoon.serialization.HTMLSerializer"
               time="0" />
    </result>
  </pipeline>
</profilerinfo>
```

Here, for each pipeline, profiler collects the time (in milliseconds) of every invocation, and the time taken by each step in the pipeline. Also, there is an element containing average times.

Cocoon has a simple stylesheet for the profiler data to convert it to readable HTML page. You can find it in `stylesheets/system/profile2html.xsl`.

RequestGenerator

The `RequestGenerator` component streams the content of the current request as XML. Having a match in the pipeline that uses the `RequestGenerator` component is very useful as a debugging tool to check what is being sent, such as on a form request. It can be incorporated into the sitemap by using the following notation:

```
<map:generator
     logger="sitemap.generator.request"
     name="request"
     src="org.apache.cocoon.generation.RequestGenerator"/>
```

When configuring the sitemap, there is no need to specify the source. Take the following simple example:

```
<map:match pattern="request">
  <map:generate type="request"/>
```

```
  <map:serialize type="xml"/>
</map:match>
```

ScriptGenerator

The `ScriptGenerator` is used to link Cocoon with the Bean Scripting Framework (BSF) library. The BSF library, part of the Apache Jakarta subproject, allows the integration of scripting languages, such as JavaScript, Python, and Perl, with Java. This means that a Java program can call a script, and a script can call Java code.

The `ScriptGenerator` can be configured in the sitemap with the following XML:

```
<map:generator
     logger="sitemap.generator.script"
     name="script"
     src="org.apache.cocoon.generation.ScriptGenerator"/>
```

The `ScriptGenerator` is examined in more detail in Chapter 9, "Using Content Logic: Generators."

SearchGenerator

This component is fully dealt with in Chapter 19, "Searching with Cocoon."

ServerPagesGenerator

The `ServerPagesGenerator` is the generator that is used for XSP files and is included in the sitemap using the following:

```
<map:generator
     logger="sitemap.generator.serverpages"
     name="serverpages"
     src="org.apache.cocoon.generation.ServerPagesGenerator"/>
```

Throughout the book, this generator has been used; however, the various configuration parameters have not been fully investigated. Three parameters can be specified in the generator configuration in the sitemap:

- `markup-language`—The markup language of the source file. This defaults to XSP.
- `autocomplete-documents`—This can be set to `true` or `false` and determines whether the generator will automatically close any elements that were not closed. By default, it is `false` to reduce processing overheads.

- programming-language—This determines the programming language that is used for logic in the server page. This defaults to java but can be set to js for JavaScript. The languages available are configured using the <programming-languages> block in cocoon.xconf.

The preceding configuration items would be set using a pipeline match such as this:

```
<map:generate src="file.xsp" type="serverpages">
  <map:parameter name="programming-language" value="js"/>
  <map:parameter name="autocomplete-documents" value="false"/>
  <map:parameter name="markup-language" value="xsp"/>
</map:generate>
```

SessionAttributeGenerator

SessionAttributeGenerator generates a document from a session attribute. The attribute may be a DOM node, an XMLizable object, or any other object, and is streamed using the same rules as for <xsp:expr> in XSPs (see the source of the XSPObjectHelper class for details, available in the source distribution). SessionAttributeGenerator can be added to the sitemap using the following:

```
<map:generator
     logger="sitemap.generator.session-attr"
     name="session-attr"
     src="org.apache.cocoon.generation.SessionAttributeGenerator"/>
```

When using it in the pipeline, two parameters can be specified:

- root-element—The root element to surround generated XML with. This parameter is optional if the session attribute contains a DOM node or XMLizable (no surrounding element will be generated), and is required for all other objects.
- attr-name—The name of the session attribute to generate XML from. This is a required parameter, and has no default.

Usage of this generator can look like this:

```
<map:generate type="session-attr">
  <map:parameter name="root-element" value="root"/>
  <map:parameter name="attr-name" value="my.attribute.name"/>
</map:generate>
```

StatusGenerator

`StatusGenerator` outputs the status of the Cocoon instance. This generator is declared in the sitemap using this:

```
<map:generator
    logger="sitemap.generator.status"
    name="status"
    src="org.apache.cocoon.generation.StatusGenerator"/>
```

And is used in the pipeline:

```
<map:match pattern="status">
    <map:generate type="status"/>
    <map:serialize type="xml"/>
</map:match>
```

`StatusGenerator` output looks similar to the following:

```
<statusinfo date="Sep 29, 2002 11:46:25 AM"
            host="vgritsenkopc"
            xmlns="http://apache.org/cocoon/status/2.0"
            xmlns:xlink="http://www.w3.org/1999/xlink">
  <group name="vm">
    <group name="memory">
      <value name="total">
        <line>25899008</line>
      </value>
      <value name="free">
        <line>5476032</line>
      </value>
    </group>
    <group name="jre">
      <value name="version">
        <line>1.3.1</line>
      </value>
      <value type="simple" href="http://java.sun.com/" name="java-vendor">
        <line>Sun Microsystems Inc.</line>
      </value>
    </group>
    <group name="operating-system">
      <value name="name">
        <line>Windows 2000</line>
      </value>
      <value name="architecture">
```

```
        <line>x86</line>
      </value>
      <value name="version">
        <line>5.0</line>
      </value>
    </group>
    <value name="classpath">
      <line>C:\Java\jdk1.3.1\lib\tools.jar</line>
      <line>C:\Apache\jakarta-tomcat-4.0.4\bin\bootstrap.jar</line>
    </value>
    <group name="Store-Janitor">
      <group name="org.apache.cocoon.components.store.MRUMemoryStore
➥ (hash = 0x94d48)">
        <value name="cached">
          <line>jar:file:C:/Apache/jakarta-tomcat-4.0.4/webapps/
➥cocoon/WEB-INF/lib/cocoon-2.0.3.jar!/org/apache/cocoon/
➥components/language/markup/sitemap/java/sitemap.xsl
➥ (class: [Ljava.lang.Object;)</line>
          <line>logicsheet:jar:file:C:/Apache/jakarta-tomcat-4.0.4/
➥webapps/cocoon/WEB-INF/lib/cocoon-2.0.3.jar!/org/apache/cocoon/
➥components/language/markup/sitemap/java/sitemap.xsl (class:
➥ org.apache.cocoon.components.language.markup.Logicsheet)</line>
        </value>
        <value name="size">
          <line>2 items in cache (0 are empty)</line>
        </value>
      </group>
    </group>
  </group>
</statusinfo>
```

StreamGenerator

`StreamGenerator` reads XML from a `POST` request's `InputStream` and generates SAX events. For `StreamGenerator` to work correctly, the request must have content length and content type headers. If the request has a mime-type of `application/x-www-form-urlencoded` (HTML form `POST`), then xml data is expected as the value of the posted parameter. If the request has a mime-type of `text/plain`, `text/xml`, or `application/xml`, then xml data is expected in the body of the request. `StreamGenerator` is declared in the sitemap using this:

```
<map:generator
    logger="sitemap.generator.stream"
```

```
    name="stream"
    src="org.apache.cocoon.generation.StreamGenerator"/>
```

It has the only one parameter:

- `form-name`—The name of the form input element containing XML data. This parameter is used only for HTML form `POST` requests. There is no default value.

`StreamGenerator` can be used like this:

```
<map:match pattern="request1">
  <map:generate type="stream">
    <map:parameter name="form-name" value="Foo"/>
  </map:generate>
  <map:serialize type="xml"/>
</map:match>
```

VelocityGenerator

Velocity is another Apache Jakarta project and is a Java-based templating technology. The `VelocityGenerator` component allows you to generate XML from a Velocity template. It is added to the sitemap using the following:

```
<map:generator
     logger="sitemap.generator.velocity"
     name="velocity"
     src="org.apache.cocoon.generation.VelocityGenerator"/>
```

For more information on using the `VelocityGenerator`, see Chapter 9.

Transformers

The next set of components to consider are the transformers. These take an input stream of SAX events and pass them through a transformation process to produce an output of SAX events.

CachingCIncludeTransformer

This is the cacheable version of the `CIncludeTransformer` described in the next subsection. It can be declared using this:

```
<map:transformer
    name="ccinclude"
    logger="sitemap.transformer.cinclude"
    src="org.apache.cocoon.transformation.CachingCIncludeTransformer"/>
```

Usage is similar to that for the `CIncludeTransformer`.

CIncludeTransformer

This transformer includes content of the other URLs or pipelines referenced by the `include` elements into the current pipeline. It is declared in the sitemap as shown here:

```
<map:transformer
    name="cinclude"
    logger="sitemap.transformer.cinclude"
    src="org.apache.cocoon.transformation.CIncludeTransformer"/>
```

This transformer does not have any configuration parameters. Here's an example of usage:

```
<map:match pattern="news/aggregate">
    <map:generate src="news.xml"/>
    <map:transform type="cinclude"/>
    <map:serialize type="xml"/>
</map:match>
```

`CIncludeTransformer` reacts on the `include` element in the namespace `http://apache.org/cocoon/include/1.0`:

```
<cinclude:include
    xmlns:cinclude="http://apache.org/cocoon/include/1.0"
    src="cocoon:/news/slashdot.xml"
    element="slashdot"
    prefix="slashdot"
    ns="http://foo.bar.com/slashdot"/>
```

This `include` element is replaced then with the content of the URL specified as the `src` attribute. `Element`, `prefix`, and `ns` attributes define optional element details to surround included content with.

EncodeURLTransformer

The `EncodeURLTransformer` transformer applies the `response.encodeURL()` method to URLs in the specified XML attributes. Encoding takes place only when a session exists. If no session is created, this transformer does nothing. You may want to use this transform to avoid doing `encodeURL` calls manually. `EncodeURLTransformer` can have the following parameters in its declaration:

- `include-name`—A regular expression specifying what attributes of what elements are to be encoded. The regular expression must match element name/attribute name pairs in the format *element-name/@attribute-name*. The default value is `.*/@href|.*/@action|frame/@src` (that is, all `href` and `action` attributes of any elements will be encoded, and `src` attributes of all frame elements will be encoded too).

- `exclude-name`—A regular expression specifying what attributes should not be encoded. This parameter has the same format. The default is `img/@src`.

A declaration may look like this:

```
<map:transformer
    name="encodeURL"
    logger="sitemap.transformer.encodeURL"
    src="org.apache.cocoon.transformation.EncodeURLTransformer">
    <include-name>.*/@href|.*/@action|frame/@src</include-name>
    <exclude-name>img/@src</exclude-name>
</map:transformer>
```

Both parameters can be overridden later when the transformer is used:

```
<map:transform type="encodeURL">
    <map:parameter name="include-name" value="*/@href|.*/@action|frame/@src"/>
    <map:parameter name="exclude-name" value="img/@src"/>
</map:transform>
```

FilterTransformer

`FilterTransformer` allows you to divide incoming XML streams containing too many repetitions of the particular elements on multiple "blocks." This is similar to paging results obtained from the database: Only one page of the rows is shown at a time. `FilterTransformer` is declared in the sitemap using the following:

```
<map:transformer
    name="filter"
    logger="sitemap.transformer.filter"
    src="org.apache.cocoon.transformation.FilterTransformer"/>
```

It has the following parameters:

- `element-name`—The name of the element constituting block.
- `count`—The amount of the elements with the specified name in one block.
- `blocknr`—The number of the block to output. Elements from the other blocks will be omitted.

`FilterTransformer` can be used in the pipeline with this:

```
<map:transform type="filter">
    <map:parameter name="element-name" value="data"/>
    <map:parameter name="count" value="5"/>
    <map:parameter name="blocknr" value="2"/>
</map:transform>
```

Let's suppose that we are transforming an XML document similar to this:

```
<?xml version="1.0" encoding="UTF-8"?>

<page>
  <data>element  1</data>
  <data>element  2</data>
  <data>element  3</data>
  ...
  <data>element 20</data>
</page>
```

Then, with the preceding transformer configuration, the result will look like the following:

```
<?xml version="1.0" encoding="UTF-8" ?>
  <page>
    <block id="1"/>
    <block id="2">
      <data>element 6</data>
      <data>element 7</data>
      <data>element 8</data>
      <data>element 9</data>
      <data>element 10</data>
    </block>
    <block id="3"/>
    <block id="4"/>
  </page>
```

FragmentExtractorTransformer

This transformer is used with the `FragmentExtractorGenerator` mentioned previously. The purpose of this transformer is to extract a specific node for separate processing by another pipeline starting with `FragmentExtractorGenerator`.

`FragmentExtractorTransformer` can have the following configuration elements in its declaration:

- extract-uri—The namespace of the element to extract. The default value is http://www.w3.org/2000/svg.
- extract-element—The name of the element to extract. The default value is svg.

The transformer is configured in the sitemap as shown here:

```
<map:transformer
    name="extractor"
    logger="sitemap.transformer.extractor"
    src="org.apache.cocoon.transformation.FragmentExtractorTransformer">
    <extract-uri>http://www.w3.org/2000/svg</extract-uri>
    <extract-name>svg</extract-name>
</map:transformer>
```

With the default configuration, this transformer will extract all SVG graphics embedded into the XML and replace them with the IDs of the extracted fragments, and these fragments can be picked up by the FragmentExtractorGenerator. Here's an example of such a setup:

```
<map:match pattern="extract">
    <map:generate src="extract.xml"/>
    <map:transform type="extractor"/>
    <map:transform src="extract.xsl"/>
    <map:serialize/>
</map:match>
<map:match pattern="extract-image-*.png">
    <map:generate type="extractor" src="{1}"/>
    <map:serialize type="svg2png"/>
</map:match>
```

The first pipeline uses the extract.xsl XSLT transformation to replace fragments with image elements:

```
<?xml version="1.0"?>

<xsl:stylesheet version="1.0"
    xmlns:xsl="http://www.w3.org/1999/XSL/Transform"
    xmlns:fe="http://apache.org/cocoon/fragmentextractor/2.0">

    <xsl:template match="//fe:fragment">
        <img src="extract-image-{@fragment-id}.png" border="0"/>
    </xsl:template>

    <xsl:template match="@*|*|text()|processing-instruction()"
```

```
                priority="-1">
        <xsl:copy>
            <xsl:apply-templates
                select="@*|*|text()|processing-instruction()"/>
        </xsl:copy>
    </xsl:template>
</xsl:stylesheet>
```

Fragment IDs here are used to create image URLs that will match the second matcher.

I18nTransformer

This transformer is used to support internationalization features and is fully covered in Chapter 14, "Using Presentation Logic: Internationalization."

LDAPTransformer

This transformer executes LDAP queries and replaces query elements with query results. This transformer is optional and is compiled into the application only when Java Naming and Directory Interface (JNDI) classes are present. The transformer can be then configured in the sitemap as shown here:

```
<map:transformer
    name="ldap"
    logger="sitemap.transformer.ldap"
    src="org.apache.cocoon.transformation.LDAPTransformer"/>
```

`LDAPTransformer` has many configuration parameters:

- `initializer`—The class name of the `InitialDirContext` class implementation to use. The default value is `com.sun.jndi.ldap.LdapCtxFactory`.
- `version`—The value for the `java.naming.ldap.version` parameter passed to `InitialDirContext`. The default value is `2`.
- `serverurl`—The hostname of the directory server. The value should be in the form of `ldap://`*`somehost`*.
- `port`—The port of the directory server. The default is `389`.
- `authentication`—The value for the `Context.SECURITY_AUTHENTICATION` parameter passed to `InitialDirContext`. The default value is `simple`. This parameter is used only when `rootdn` and `password` are specified.

- rootdn—The value for the Context.SECURITY_PRINCIPAL parameter passed to InitialDirContext. This parameter is optional. When specifying this parameter, provide the password parameter also.
- password—The value for the Context.SECURITY_CREDENTIAL parameter passed to InitialDirContext. This parameter is optional. When specifying this parameter, provide the rootdn parameter also.
- searchbase—The name of the base context for the query. The default is an empty string ("").
- filter—The filter expression to use for the query. The default is an empty string ("").
- scope—The scope of the query. Possible values are OBJECT_SCOPE, SUBTREE_SCOPE, and ONELEVEL_SCOPE (the default).
- doc-element—The element name to wrap the query result into. The default value is doc-element. If the value is empty, no element will be produced.
- row-element—The element name to wrap a single result into. The default value is row-element. If the value is empty, no element will be produced.
- sax-error—If the value is true, the transformer will throw an exception when an error is encountered. Otherwise, it will produce an error element. The default value is false.
- error-element—The name of the error element, produced on exception. The default value is ldap-error.
- deref-link—A true value will enable dereferencing during a search. The default value is false.
- count-limit—Sets the maximum number of entries in the result. The default value is 0 (no limit).
- time-limit—Sets the maximum amount of time (in milliseconds) for the search. The default value is 0 (no limit).
- debug—Outputs additional debug info to the log files when set to true. The default value is false.

LDAPTransformer can be used in the sitemap using the following:

```
<map:transform type="ldap">
    <map:parameter name="serverurl" value="ldap://localhost"/>
    <map:parameter name="doc-element" value="entries"/>
    <map:parameter name="row-element" value="entry"/>
</map:transform>
```

LogTransformer

`LogTransformer` is used for debugging purposes. It can be placed in anywhere between the generator and the serializer, and it will capture all the events going down the SAX pipeline into a log file. It is declared in the sitemap using this:

```
<map:transformer
    name="log"
    logger="sitemap.transformer.log"
    src="org.apache.cocoon.transformation.LogTransformer"/>
```

`LogTransformer` has two parameters:

- `append`—When this is set to `false`, the log file is overwritten on every request. The default is `false`.
- `logfile`—The name for the log file. This must resolve to the file—no `http:`, `cocoon:`, or other protocol allowed here.

Here's an example of usage:

```
<map:transform type="log">
    <map:parameter name="logfile" value="my.log"/>
</map:transform>
```

ReadDOMSessionTransformer

This transformer reacts on some configured "trigger" element and adds before, inserts into, or appends after it XML from the DOM node stored as a session attribute. This transformer is similar to `SessionAttributeGenerator`, but there is a difference: It supports only DOM node objects; no other objects can be used with it. This transformer needs the presence of a session object to do its work, and when there is no session, it does not alter the XML stream.

`ReadDOMSessionTransformer` is declared in the sitemap using the following:

```
<map:transformer
    name="readDOMsession"
    logger="sitemap.transformer.readDOMsession"
    src="org.apache.cocoon.transformation.ReadDOMSessionTransformer"/>
```

These are the parameters:

- `dom-name`—The name of the session attribute to use.
- `trigger-element`—The name of the trigger element.
- `position`—The insertion position—`before`, `in`, or `after`. The default is `in`.

The transformer can be used in the pipeline as shown here:

```
<map:transform type="readDOMsession">
    <map:parameter name="dom-name" value="my.session.attribute"/>
    <map:parameter name="trigger-element" value="placeholder"/>
</map:transform>
```

See also "WriteDOMSessionTransformer"—the counterpart to this transformer.

RoleFilterTransformer

`RoleFilterTransformer` can be used to restrict access to certain parts of the XML data based on the user's role. Role information is obtained from the servlet container, using the request method `isUserInRole`. In Tomcat, users and roles are defined in the file `tomcat-users.xml`, in the `config` folder of the Tomcat installation. This transformer can be added to the sitemap using this:

```
<map:transformer
    name="role-filter"
    logger="sitemap.transformer.role-filter"
    src="org.apache.cocoon.transformation.RoleFilterTransformer"/>
```

`RoleFilterTransformer` does not have any parameters, so usage in the pipeline is always as follows:

```
<map:transform type="role-filter"/>
```

`RoleFilterTransformer` reacts on the two attributes in the input document: `restricted` and `read-only`. These attributes must be in the `http://apache.org/cocoon/role-filter/1.0` namespace. Given input XML like

```
<root xmlns:roles="http://apache.org/cocoon/role-filter/1.0">
    <textbox name="identifier" roles:restricted="admin"/>;
    <textbox name="name" roles:read-only="admin,boss"/>
    <textbox name="email"/>
</root>
```

output will depend on whether the current user is in `admin`, `boss`, or some other role. Assuming that the user is in the role `boss`, the output will be as shown here:

```
<root xmlns:roles="http://apache.org/cocoon/role-filter/1.0">
    <textbox name="name" roles:read-only=""/>
    <textbox name="email"/>
</root>
```

Note that the restricted element containing the identifier is filtered out, and the `read-only` attribute is passed with the empty value. This `read-only` attribute can be used later by the application.

SQLTransformer

`SQLTransformer` is used to execute SQL queries. It converts the resulting SQL rowset to the XML elements, replacing the query element. It supports the following configuration elements:

- `old-driver`—Is `true` if the JDBC driver you are using is a JDBC 2.0 driver or newer.
- `connect-attempts`—Specifies the number of connect attempts to make if the database is not available. The default value is `5`.
- `connect-waittime`—The waiting time between connection attempts in milliseconds. The default is `5000` (5 seconds).

The declaration in the sitemap looks like this:

```
<map:transformer
    name="sql"
    logger="sitemap.transformer.sql"
    src="org.apache.cocoon.transformation.SQLTransformer"/>
```

For a detailed description of `SQLTransformer` parameters and input XML format, see Chapter 10, "Using Content Logic: Transformers," and Chapter 16, "Cocoon Interfaces: Databases."

TraxTransformer

`TraxTransformer` is the most used transformer of all. It allows you to run an XSLT transformation on the input XML stream. `TraxTransformer` has several configuration elements:

- `use-request-parameters`—When set to `true`, this indicates that the request parameters should be passed to the XSLT stylesheet. You just need to declare top-level `xsl:param` elements to get the request parameter values into the stylesheet. The default value is `false`.
- `use-cookies`—Similar to request parameters, all cookies' values can be made accessible to the stylesheet. The default value is `false`.
- `use-browser-capabilities-db`—When set to `true`, the transformer makes the following parameters accessible from the stylesheet: `accept`, `user-agent`, `browser`

(the value of this parameter is a `Map`), `browser-media`, and `ua-capabilities` (the value is a DOM document). The default is `false`.

- `use-session-info`—Session information that can be made available to the stylesheet is `session-available`, `session-is-new`, `session-id-from-cookie`, `session-id-from-url`, `session-valid`, and `session-id` parameters. The default value is `false`—no session information is provided.
- `xslt-processor-role`—Indicates the role of the XSLT processor to use. If you have several XSLT processors (with different role names, of course) configured in the `cocoon.xconf`, you can choose which one this `TraxTransformer` should pick. The default is `org.apache.cocoon.components.xslt.XSLTProcessor`.

Taking into account all these parameters, `TraxTransformer` can be declared in the sitemap using the following:

```
<map:transformer
        name="xslt"
        logger="sitemap.transformer.xslt"
        src="org.apache.cocoon.transformation.TraxTransformer">
    <use-request-parameters>false</use-request-parameters>
    <use-browser-capabilities-db>false</use-browser-capabilities-db>
    <use-deli>false</use-deli>
</map:transformer>
```

When it comes to usage of the transformer in the pipeline, all parameters (with the exception of `xslt-processor-role`) could be overwritten like this:

```
<map:transform type="xslt" src="mystyle.xsl">
    <map:parameter name="use-cookies" value="true"/>
    <map:parameter name="use-session-info" value="true"/>
    <map:parameter name="myparameter" value="myvalue"/>
</map:transform>
```

Note that in addition to request parameters, cookies, and session-related parameters, it is possible to pass any other parameter into the stylesheet. Here we just passed our own `myparameter`. To get the value of this parameter—or any other parameter—simply define the appropriate `xsl:param` element in the stylesheet as shown here:

```
<?xml version="1.0"?>

<xsl:stylesheet version="1.0" xmlns:xsl="http://www.w3.org/1999/XSL/Transform">
    <xsl:param name="myparameter"/>
    <xsl:param name="session-available"/>
```

```
    <xsl:template match="/">
        <page>Your XSL code goes here...</page>
    </xsl:template>
</xsl:stylesheet>
```

WriteDOMSessionTransformer

This transformer is a counterpart to the `ReadDOMSessionTransformer`. It reacts on some configured "trigger" element, and stores all its content (including the trigger node itself) in a session, as a session attribute. This transformer does not modify the XML stream. The `Session` object must exist for this transformer to work; it will not create `Session` if it does not exist.

`WriteDOMSessionTransformer` is declared in the sitemap using the following:

```
<map:transformer
    name="writeDOMsession"
    logger="sitemap.transformer.writeDOMsession"
    src="org.apache.cocoon.transformation.WriteDOMSessionTransformer"/>
```

These are the parameters:

- `dom-name`—The name of the session attribute to use.
- `dom-root-element`—The name of the trigger element.

The transformer can be used in the pipeline as shown here:

```
<map:transform type="writeDOMsession">
    <map:parameter name="dom-name" value="my.session.attribute"/>
    <map:parameter name="dom-root-element" value="content"/>
</map:transform>
```

XIncludeTransformer

`XIncludeTransformer` is an implementation of the XInclude specification (see `www.w3.org/TR/xinclude/`). It differs from the `CIncludeTransformer` in syntax, and it has the capability to include only the parts of the source specified by the XPath expression. It is declared in the sitemap using the following:

```
<map:transformer
    name="xinclude"
    logger="sitemap.transformer.xinclude"
    src="org.apache.cocoon.transformation.XIncludeTransformer"/>
```

`XIncludeTransformer` does not have any configuration parameters, and thus can be used in the pipeline simply as shown here:

```
<map:transform type="xinclude"/>
```

XTTransformer

`XTTransformer` is a transformer that uses the XT processor to perform XSLT transformation. This transformer is deprecated in favor of `TraxTransformer` and will be removed from the Cocoon starting with version 2.1.

Serializers

Serializers are used to turn the generated and transformed SAX event stream into an output suitable for delivery to the final client environment.

FOPSerializer

`FOPSerializer` performs conversion of the XSL formatting objects (XSL-FO) document into the PDF (or PCL, PS, SVG, and other formats) stream. This is done with the help of the FOP processor. `FOPSerializer` has the following configuration elements:

- `user-config`—Attribute `src` of this element should point to the FOP user configuration file. It usually contains font definitions you want to use in your PDF. Refer to the FOP user documentation for details.
- `set-content-length`—Indicates to Cocoon that the response should have the `Content-Length` header set. This header is required for the Acrobat Reader browser plug-in to work correctly. The default is `true`.

Usually, several instances of `FOPSerializer` are declared in the sitemap, one for every desired output type:

```
<map:serializer
    name="fo2pdf"
    mime-type="application/pdf"
    src="org.apache.cocoon.serialization.FOPSerializer"/>
<map:serializer
    name="fo2ps"
    mime-type="application/postscript"
    src="org.apache.cocoon.serialization.FOPSerializer"/>
<map:serializer
    name="fo2pcl"
    mime-type="vnd.hp-PCL"
    src="org.apache.cocoon.serialization.FOPSerializer"/>
```

`FOPSerializer` can be used to finish your pipeline-generating XSL formatting objects document:

```
<map:serialize type="fo2pdf"/>
```

The response will contain PDF.

> **FOP**
> FOP, which stands for Formatting Objects Processor, is an Apache XML project. The home of the FOP project is `http://xml.apache.org/fop/`. The goals of the Apache XML FOP project are to deliver an XSL-FO to a PDF formatter that is compliant to at least the Basic conformance level described in the W3C Recommendation from October 15, 2001, and that complies with the March 11, 1999, Portable Document Format Specification (Version 1.3) from Adobe Systems.
>
> Read more about XSL-FO on the W3C site, at `www.w3.org/TR/xsl/`.

HSSFSerializer

`HSSFSerializer` produces HSSF (Horrible Spread Sheet Format) documents, also known as Microsoft Excel Spreadsheets (XLS). It does not require any configuration, and works on Gnumeric XML documents. It uses the POI project to produce its output.

Here's an `HSSFSerializer` declaration:

```
<map:serializer
    name="xls"
    mime-type="application/vnd.ms-excel"
    logger="sitemap.serializer.xls"
    src="org.apache.cocoon.serialization.HSSFSerializer"/>
```

Usage is as simple as this:

```
<map:serialize type="xls"/>
```

> **POI**
> The POI project is an Apache Jakarta project, consisting of APIs for manipulating various file formats based on Microsoft's OLE 2 Compound Document format using pure Java. The POI project can be found at `http://jakarta.apache.org/poi/`.

HTMLSerializer

`HTMLSerializer` serializes input in an HTML document. It converts `<br/>` to `<br>`, `<img src="picture.jpg"/>` to `<img src="picture.jpg">`, and so forth. It does the work with the help of the XSLT processor. Configuration includes the following parameters passed to the XSLT processor:

- `buffer-size`—Specifies the size of the output buffer; must be greater than 0. The default is 8192 bytes.
- `cdata-section-elements`—Specifies a whitespace-delimited list of the names of elements whose text node children should be output using CDATA sections.
- `doctype-public`—Specifies the public identifier to be used in the document type declaration.
- `doctype-system`—Specifies the system identifier to be used in the document type declaration.
- `encoding`—Specifies output encoding.
- `indent`—Specifies whether additional whitespace may be added. The value must be `yes` or `no`.
- `omit-xml-declaration`—Specifies whether an XML declaration should be present.

The `HTMLSerializer` declaration in the sitemap for the HTML 4.01 (loose DTD) looks like this:

```
<map:serializer
        name="html"
        mime-type="text/html"
        src="org.apache.cocoon.serialization.HTMLSerializer">
    <buffer-size>1024</buffer-size>
    <indent>no</indent>
    <omit-xml-declaration>yes</omit-xml-declaration>
    <doctype-public>-//W3C//DTD HTML 4.01 Transitional//EN</doctype-public>
    <doctype-system>http://www.w3.org/TR/html4/loose.dtd</doctype-system>
</map:serializer>
```

LinkSerializer

`LinkSerializer` generates a list of the URLs referenced in the XML. It is used by Cocoon's command line and search components to traverse the site structure. The result is plain text with links, one link per line.

`LinkSerializer` is declared in the sitemap as shown here:

```
<map:serializer
    name="links"
    src="org.apache.cocoon.serialization.LinkSerializer"/>
```

Usually it is used from the views:

```
<map:view from-position="last" name="links">
    <map:serialize type="links"/>
</map:view>
```

`LinkSerializer` recognizes links in `href`, `src`, and `background` attributes. In addition to that, it understands two types of XLink elements: simple link and XLink locator.

Links to resources with `mailto:`, `news:`, `javascript:` protocols are ignored.

POIFSerializer

`POIFSerializer` can produce an OLE 2 Compound Document format stream. This is an abstract class on top of which XLS or DOC serializers can be written. See "HSSFSerializer," earlier in this chapter.

SVGSerializer

`SVGSerializer` can serialize JPG and PNG images given SVG input XML. Batik stands behind the serializer to do this work. The sitemap has two instances of `SVGSerializer` declared, one for serializing JPEG images and another for PNG:

```
<map:serializer
        name="svg2jpeg"
        mime-type="image/jpeg"
        src="org.apache.cocoon.serialization.SVGSerializer">
    <parameter name="quality" type="float" value="0.9"/>
</map:serializer>
<map:serializer
        name="svg2png"
        mime-type="image/png"
        src="org.apache.cocoon.serialization.SVGSerializer"/>
```

JPEG serializer accepts one parameter, `quality`, and PNG serializer can have two parameters, `gamma` (of type float) and `force_transparent_white` (boolean).

Sitemap usage is simply as follows:

```
<map:serialize type="svg2jpeg"/>
```

> **Batik**
> Batik is an Apache XML project, a toolkit for applications or applets that want to use images in the SVG format for various purposes, such as viewing, generation, or manipulation. Its homepage is located at `http://xml.apache.org/batik/`.

SVG
SVG is Scalable Vector Graphics format from the W3C. The SVG 1.0 standard specification is available at `www.w3.org/TR/SVG/`.

TextSerializer

`TextSerializer` omits all the tags from the XML and outputs only text nodes. It uses the same base class as `HTMLSerializer`, and shares with it two configuration parameters: `buffer-size` and `encoding`. It is declared in the sitemap as shown here:

```
<map:serializer
    name="text"
    mime-type="text/text"
    logger="sitemap.serializer.text"
    src="org.apache.cocoon.serialization.TextSerializer"/>
```

Usage of the serializer is simple:

```
<map:serialize type="text"/>
```

XMLSerializer

`XMLSerializer` is intended to serialize SAX events into an XML stream. It reuses the same base class as `HTMLSerializer`, and shares with it most of the configuration parameters: `cdata-section-elements`, `buffer-size`, `doctype-public`, `doctype-system`, `encoding`, `indent`, and `omit-xml-declaration`. `XMLSerializer` is used to output all types of XML content: WML, SVG, XHTML, and any other XML. Declarations for generic XML serializer, WML, and XHTML look like this:

```
<map:serializer
        name="xml"
        mime-type="text/xml"
        logger="sitemap.serializer.xml"
        src="org.apache.cocoon.serialization.XMLSerializer"/>
<map:serializer
        name="wml"
        mime-type="text/vnd.wap.wml"
        logger="sitemap.serializer.wml"
        src="org.apache.cocoon.serialization.XMLSerializer">
    <doctype-public>-//WAPFORUM//DTD WML 1.1//EN</doctype-public>
    <doctype-system>http://www.wapforum.org/DTD/wml_1.1.xml</doctype-system>
    <encoding>ASCII</encoding>
    <omit-xml-declaration>yes</omit-xml-declaration>
```

```
</map:serializer>
<map:serializer
        name="xhtml"
        mime-type="text/html"
        logger="sitemap.serializer.xhtml"
        src="org.apache.cocoon.serialization.XMLSerializer">
    <doctype-public>-//W3C//DTD XHTML 1.0 Strict//EN</doctype-public>
    <doctype-system>http://www.w3.org/TR/xhtml1/DTD/xhtml1-strict.dtd
➥</doctype-system>
    <encoding>UTF-8</encoding>
</map:serializer>
```

Using `XMLSerializer` in the pipeline looks like this:

```
<map:serialize type="xml"/>
```

Readers

Readers are used to produce non-XML (binary) output from the non-XML input. They can be thought of as a whole Cocoon pipeline combined into one component. They work as generator and serializer at once.

Mostly, readers are used to serve content that does not need to be modified. It can be static images, HTML files, Flash animations, Java applets, and other content usually served by the ordinary Web server.

Readers are more performant than complete pipeline with generation and serialization steps, but they are slower comparing to a Web server. If you have a significant amount of static resources, always consider using a Web server, such as Apache, to improve the performance of your site.

DatabaseReader

`DatabaseReader` allows you to serve content right from the `BLOB` objects stored in the relational database. To work, it should be configured:

- `use-connection`—Specifies the name of the JDBC connection pool to use.
- `invalidate`—Specifies what to do if the reader cannot determine the timestamp of the resource. If set to `always`, the result will never be cached. The default is `never`.

Thus, the declaration might be as follows:

```
<map:reader
        name="db"
        logger="sitemap.reader.db"
        src="org.apache.cocoon.reading.DatabaseReader">
    <use-connection>personnel</use-connection>
</map:reader>
```

Make sure you have configured the `personnel` data source in the `cocoon.xconf` file.

When using `DatabaseReader`, you must specify several parameters:

- `table`—The table name. This is a mandatory parameter.
- `image`—The column name where the content is stored. This is a mandatory parameter. The column must be of type `BLOB`.
- `key`—The key column name. This is a mandatory parameter.
- `where`—An additional `where` clause to the SQL query.
- `order-by`—An `order by` clause in the SQL query.
- `last-modified`—The column name where the last modification time of the content is stored. This parameter is optional.
- `content-type`—The content type of the content.
- `expires`—The expiration time, in milliseconds. When this parameter is set, the reader will add an `Expires` header to the response.

If we have a table IMAGES with the columns NAME, LAST_MODIFIED, and IMAGE, then serving the image from the database by its name can be done by using this:

```
<map:read type="db" src="mypicture">
    <map:parameter name="table" value="IMAGES"/>
    <map:parameter name="image" value="IMAGE"/>
    <map:parameter name="key" value="NAME"/>
    <map:parameter name="last-modified" value="LAST_MODIFIED"/>
    <map:parameter name="content-type" value="image/jpeg"/>
</map:read>
```

The name of the image is provided to the reader as an `src` attribute on the `map:read` tag. The SQL statement constructed by the `DatabaseReader` will be

```
SELECT IMAGE, LAST_MODIFIED FROM IMAGES WHERE NAME = ?
```

where the question mark is substituted with the value from the `src` attribute—`mypicture`.

JSPReader

The JSPReader component allows the simple passing through of JSP content and is covered fully in Chapter 18, "Cocoon Interfaces: J2EE."

ResourceReader

ResourceReader reads any resource specified by the src parameter and serves it to the client. The most common usage of the reader is to serve static files: images, pages, archives, anything else. It can also serve remote resources, available via the http protocol, or resources stored inside an application's JAR archive, using the resource protocol. ResourceReader does not have configuration parameters:

```
<map:reader
    name="resource"
    logger="sitemap.reader.resource"
    src="org.apache.cocoon.reading.ResourceReader"/>
```

When using ResourceReader, you can specify when content should expire from the browser cache, via a parameter:

- expires—This parameter sets the expiration time, in milliseconds. This is optional, but when specified it should be greater than 0.

In the pipeline it will look like this:

```
<map:read type="resource" src="picture.jpg" mime-type="image/jpg">
    <map:parameter name="expires" value="86400000"/>
</map:read>
```

This tells ResourceReader to set the expiration time to 24 hours from now.

Usually, ResourceReader is set as the default reader in the sitemap, and thus usage is simplified to the following:

```
<map:read src="http://images.slashdot.org/topics/topicmoney.gif"
         mime-type="image/gif"/>
```

(This will read GIF resource from the remote server.)

Matchers

It should come as no surprise by now to realize that matchers are the components that determine which bit of the pipeline handles a specific request. Through the following listing you will note that many of the matchers fall into two camps: Regexp* and Wildcard*.

Wildcard matchers are limited to pattern matches that use basic wildcard features: * matches any symbols but not the path separator / (just like in a file system search), and ** matches everything. The Regexp matchers, however, offer the full power of regular expressions.

Matchers that use regular expressions (regexp) can be very useful and powerful alternatives to wildcard matches. For example:

```
<map:match type="regexp" pattern="^(en|de|fr)-(.*)$">
       <map:generate type="file" src="{1}/{2}.xml"/>
       <map:transform type="xslt" src="stylesheets/xml2html.xsl"/>
       <map:serialize type="html"/>
</map:match>
```

will match requests starting with en, de, or fr, followed by the - character, followed by any string of characters to the end of the line. The generator will then take the result of the first expression ((en|de|fr)) to form a folder name, and then append .xml to the result of the second expression ((.*)) to form its source filename. So a request for en-login would resolve to en/login.xml.

> **Regular Expressions**
> A whole chapter could be devoted to regular expressions, but because this is a book on Cocoon, this is as far as a regexp tutorial will go. If you want to know more, you can check out loads of sites that cater to all levels. A great tutorial can be found at www.zvon.org/other/PerlTutorial/Output/index.html.

So let's consider each matcher in a little more detail.

CookieMatcher

CookieMatcher compares a pattern with all available cookie names and when a cookie is found, its value is returned to the sitemap as variable 1.

Here's a declaration:

```
<map:matcher
    name="cookie"
    logger="sitemap.matcher.cookie"
    src="org.apache.cocoon.matching.CookieMatcher"/>
```

And here's an example of usage:

```
<map:match type="cookie" pattern="id">
    <!-- {1} contains value of the "id" cookie -->
</map:match>
```

HeaderMatcher

`HeaderMatcher` matches when there is a request header named as a pattern value. The header value is returned to the sitemap as variable `1`.

Here's a declaration:

```
<map:matcher
    name="header"
    logger="sitemap.matcher.header"
    src="org.apache.cocoon.matching.HeaderMatcher"/>
```

And here's an example of usage:

```
<map:match type="header" pattern="referer">
    <!-- {1} contains value of the "referer" header -->
</map:match>
```

ParameterMatcher

`ParameterMatcher` matches when there is a sitemap parameter defined with a specified name. The parameter's value is returned to the sitemap as variable `1`.

Here's a declaration:

```
<map:matcher
    name="parameter"
    logger="sitemap.matcher.parameter"
    src="org.apache.cocoon.matching.ParameterMatcher"/>
```

And here's an example of usage:

```
<map:match type="parameter" pattern="dest">
    <!-- {1} contains value of the "dest" header -->
</map:match>
```

RegexpHeaderMatcher

`RegexpHeaderMatcher` matches the value of the configured header name against a regular expression pattern. It has only one configuration element:

- `header-name`—Specifies the header name to use. This is optional (if a parameter is present).

Here's a declaration:

```
<map:matcher
    name="regexp-header"
    logger="sitemap.matcher.regexp-header"
    src="org.apache.cocoon.matching.RegexpHeaderMatcher">
    <header-name>accept</header-name>
</map:matcher>
```

The header name can be overridden by a parameter:

- `header-name`—Overrides the default header name. This is optional.

Here's an example of usage:

```
<map:match type="regexp-header" pattern="^http://www.host.com/(.*)(\?.*)+$">
    <map:parameter name="header-name" value="referer"/>
    <!-- {1} contains request path, {2} contains query string (optionally) -->
</map:match>
```

RegexpHostMatcher

`RegexpHostMatcher` works exactly like the `RegexpHeaderMatcher` matcher, but only on a host request header. It does not have configuration parameters.

RegexpParameterMatcher

`RegexpParameterMatcher` matches the value of a sitemap parameter against a regular expression pattern. There is one configuration element:

- `parameter-name`—Specifies the sitemap parameter to use. This is optional (if a parameter is present).

Here's a declaration:

```
<map:matcher
    name="regexp-parameter"
    logger="sitemap.matcher.regexp-parameter"
    src="org.apache.cocoon.matching.RegexpParameterMatcher">
    <header-name>accept</header-name>
</map:matcher>
```

The header name can be overridden by a parameter:

- parameter-name—Overrides the default parameter name. This is optional.

Here's an example of usage:

```
<map:match type="regexp-parameter" pattern="any-(.*)-regexp">
    <map:parameter name="parameter-name" value="referer"/>
    <!-- {1} contains value from (.*) -->
</map:match>
```

RegexpRequestAttributeMatcher

RegexpRequestAttributeMatcher matches the value of a request attribute against a regular expression pattern. There is one configuration element (which can be overridden by a parameter):

- attribute-name—Specifies the request attribute name to use. This is optional (if a parameter is present).

Here's a declaration:

```
<map:matcher
    name="regexp-req-attr"
    logger="sitemap.matcher.regexp-req-attr"
    src="org.apache.cocoon.matching.RegexpRequestAttributeMatcher">
    <attribute-name>data</attribute-name>
</map:matcher>
```

Usage is similar to the usage of RegexpParameterMatcher.

RegexpRequestParameterMatcher

RegexpRequestParameterMatcher is similar to RegexpRequestAttributeMatcher, with two differences: It matches against request parameters, and the configuration parameter is different:

- parameter-name—Specifies the name of the request parameter to use.

RegexpSessionAttributeMatcher

RegexpSessionAttributeMatcher works the same way on session attributes as RegexpRequestAttributeMatcher works on request attributes. It uses the same configuration parameter, attribute-name.

RegexpTargetHostMatcher

This matcher is deprecated in favor of `RegexpHostMatcher`.

RegexpURIMatcher

`RegexpURIMatcher` matches the request URI against a regexp pattern.

Here's a declaration:

```
<map:matcher
    name="regexp"
    logger="sitemap.matcher.regexp"
    src="org.apache.cocoon.matching.RegexpURIMatcher"/>
```

And here's an example of usage:

```
<map:match type="regexp" pattern="^(en|de|fr)-(.*)$">
    <!-- {1} contains "en", or "de", or "fr".
        {2} contains everything after "-"
    -->
</map:match>
```

RequestAttributeMatcher

`RequestAttributeMatcher` checks for the existence of the request attribute. If it exists, its value is returned as variable `1`. Declaration and usage are similar to those for `ParameterMatcher`.

RequestParameterMatcher

`RequestParameterMatcher` checks for the existence of the request parameter. If it exists, its value is returned as variable `1`. Declaration and usage are similar to those for `ParameterMatcher`.

SessionAttributeMatcher

`SessionAttributeMatcher` checks for the existence of the session attribute. If it exists, its value is returned as variable `1`. Declaration and usage are similar to those for `ParameterMatcher`.

WildcardHeaderMatcher

`WildcardHeaderMatcher` matches the value of the configured header name against a wildcard expression pattern. It has only one configuration element:

- `header-name`—Specifies the header name to use. This is optional (if a parameter is present).

Here's a declaration:

```
<map:matcher
    name="wildcard-header"
    logger="sitemap.matcher.wildcard-header"
    src="org.apache.cocoon.matching.WildcardHeaderMatcher">
    <header-name>accept</header-name>
</map:matcher>
```

The header name can be overridden by a parameter:

- `header-name`—Overrides the default header name. This is optional.

And here's an example of usage:

```
<map:match type="wildcard-header" pattern="http://www.host.com/**/*">
    <map:parameter name="header-name" value="referer"/>
    <!-- {1} contains request path up to last "/", {2} contains reminder -->
</map:match>
```

`WildcardHeaderMatcher` is a wildcard counterpart of Regexp `HeaderMatcher`.

WildcardHostMatcher

`WildcardHostMatcher` matches the host header against a wildcard expression. It is similar to `WildcardHeaderMatcher`, and is a wildcard counterpart of `RegexpHeaderMatcher`.

WildcardParameterMatcher

`WildcardParameterMatcher` is a wildcard counterpart of `RegexpParameterMatcher`, and differs only in pattern syntax.

WildcardRequestAttributeMatcher

`WildcardRequestAttributeMatcher` is a wildcard counterpart of `RegexpRequestAttributeMatcher`.

WildcardRequestParameterMatcher

`WildcardRequestParameterMatcher` is a wildcard counterpart of `RegexpRequestParameterMatcher`.

WildcardSessionAttributeMatcher

`WildcardSessionAttributeMatcher` is a wildcard counterpart of `RegexpSessionAttributeMatcher`.

WildcardURIMatcher

`WildcardURIMatcher` is a wildcard counterpart of `RegexpURIMatcher`. This matcher is the most commonly used one, and that's why it is usually declared as the default matcher. Thus, it can be used simply as shown here:

```
<map:match pattern="*.html">
</map:match>
```

Selectors

Whereas matchers are the components that are similar to the `if-then` construct in the programming languages, selectors are the `switch-case` type construct. Selectors are used to select one among several possible options, and you can provide a default when none of the options is suited. The selector syntax is as follows:

```
<map:select type="name-of-selector">
    <map:when test="value1">
    ...
    </map:when>
    <map:when test="value2">
    ...
    </map:when>
    ...
    <map:otherwise>
    ...
    </map:otherwise>
</map:select>
```

Depending on the type of selector, it compares the value against test attributes until it finds a match. The type of comparison depends on the selector type: it can be an exact match, or a substring search, or some other way of matching. When a match is found, the selector gives control to the `found when` section, and stops further comparison. If no match is found, the selector falls into the `otherwise` section. If no `otherwise` is specified, the selector will do nothing.

Let's go over the selectors available in Cocoon.

BrowserSelector

`BrowserSelector` allows you to build a pipeline depending on the type of browser a client uses. It compares a User-Agent request header with a named set of preconfigured browsers and selects the first one that matches. Browsers are configured via a browser element when declaring the selector:

```
<map:selector
        name="browser"
        logger="sitemap.selector.browser"
        src="org.apache.cocoon.selection.BrowserSelector">
    <!-- NOTE: The appearance indicates the search order. This
         is very important since some words may be found in
         more than one browser description. (MSIE is presented
         as "Mozilla/4.0 (Compatible; MSIE 4.01; ...") -->
    <browser name="explorer" useragent="MSIE"/>
    <browser name="pocketexplorer" useragent="MSPIE"/>
    <browser name="handweb" useragent="HandHTTP"/>
    <browser name="avantgo" useragent="AvantGo"/>
    <browser name="imode" useragent="DoCoMo"/>
    <browser name="opera" useragent="Opera"/>
    <browser name="lynx" useragent="Lynx"/>
    <browser name="java" useragent="Java"/>
    <browser name="wap" useragent="Nokia"/>
    <browser name="wap" useragent="UP"/>
    <browser name="wap" useragent="Wapalizer"/>
    <browser name="mozilla5" useragent="Mozilla/5"/>
    <browser name="mozilla5" useragent="Netscape6/"/>
    <browser name="netscape" useragent="Mozilla"/>
</map:selector>
```

Every browser is given a name, and a string that must be found in the User-Agent header to identify this browser. When declared, a selector can be used to customize your output depending on the user agent:

```
<map:select type="browser">
    <map:when test="wap">
        <map:transform src="document2wml.xsl"/>
    </map:when>
    <map:when test="netscape">
        <map:transform src="document2html-netscape.xsl"/>
    </map:when>
    <map:when test="lynx">
        <map:transform src="document2html-simple.xsl"/>
```

```
    </map:when>
    <map:otherwise>
        <map:transform src="document2html-default.xsl"/>
    </map:otherwise>
</map:select>
```

CookieSelector

`CookieSelector` allows you to select based on the value of the specified cookie. Unlike `BrowserSelector`, `CookieSelector` tries to find an exact match. It has one configuration element:

- `cookie-name`—Specifies the cookie to use. This is required.

Here's a declaration in the sitemap:

```
<map:selector
        name="cookie"
        logger="sitemap.selector.cookie"
        src="org.apache.cocoon.selection.CookieSelector">
    <cookie-name>layout</cookie-name>
</map:selector>
```

Here's a usage example:

```
<map:select type="cookie">
    <map:when test="tables">
        <map:transform src="document2tables.xsl"/>
    </map:when>
    <map:when test="lists">
        <map:transform src="document2lists.xsl"/>
    </map:when>
    <map:otherwise>
        <map:redirect-to uri="preferences"/>
    </map:otherwise>
</map:select>
```

HeaderSelector

`HeaderSelector` is similar to `CookieSelector`: It selects on a specified header's value. The configuration element is named obviously:

- `header-name`—Specifies the header to use. This is required.

It also, as does `CookieSelector`, compares the header value to the test attribute on equality.

HostSelector

`HostSelector` is used to choose the processing path depending on the Host header. It is intended for use in an environment with multiple virtual hosts configured. It works like `BrowserSelector`: You need to configure a set of named hosts, one of which will be selected using a substring search.

Here's a sample declaration:

```
<map:selector
        name="host"
        logger="sitemap.selector.host"
        src="org.apache.cocoon.selection.HostSelector">
    <host name="www" value="www.apache.org"/>
    <host name="jakarta" value="jakarta.apache.org"/>
    <host name="xml" value="xml.apache.org"/>
</map:selector>
```

Now, to serve multiple static Web sites you simply do this:

```
<map:match pattern="**/*.html">
    <map:select type="host">
      <map:when test="www">
          <map:read mime-type="text/html" src="www/{1}/{2}.html"/>
      </map:when>
      <map:when test="jakarta">
          <map:read mime-type="text/html" src="jakarta/{1}/{2}.html"/>
      </map:when>
      <map:when test="xml">
          <map:read mime-type="text/html" src="xml/{1}/{2}.html"/>
      </map:when>
    </map:select>
</map:match>
```

NamedPatternsSelector

`NamedPatternsSelector` is an abstract selector that is the base for `BrowserSelector` and `HostSelector`. You can use it to create your own selector.

ParameterSelector

The purpose of `ParameterSelector` is to select based on the value provided via a parameter to the selector. It is declared as shown here:

```
<map:selector
        name="parameter"
        logger="sitemap.selector.parameter"
        src="org.apache.cocoon.selection.ParameterSelector"/>
```

`ParameterSelector` has one parameter:

- `parameter-selector-test`—Specifies the value to compare with. When this parameter is omitted, the `otherwise` section is always selected.

Here's some sample usage:

```
<map:match pattern="**.*">
    <map:select type="parameter">
      <map:parameter name="parameter-selector-test" value="{2}"/>
      <map:when test="html">
          <map:read mime-type="text/html" src="{1}.html"/>
      </map:when>
      <map:when test="jpg">
          <map:read mime-type="image/jpeg" src="{1}.jpg"/>
      </map:when>
    </map:select>
</map:match>
```

RequestAttributeSelector

`RequestAttributeSelector` is similar to the `ParameterSelector`, but it works on the value of the request attribute.

Here's a declaration:

```
<map:selector
        name="request-attribute"
        logger="sitemap.selector.request-attribute"
        src="org.apache.cocoon.selection.RequestAttributeSelector"/>
```

`RequestAttributeSelector` has one parameter:

- `attribute-name`—Specifies the name of the request attribute whose value is used to compare with. When this parameter is omitted, the `otherwise` section is always selected.

RequestMethodSelector

`RequestMethodSelector` selects on a request method (that is, `GET`, `POST`).

Here's a declaration:

```
<map:selector
        name="request-method"
        logger="sitemap.selector.request-method"
        src="org.apache.cocoon.selection.RequestMethodSelector"/>
```

RequestParameterSelector

`RequestParameterSelector` selects on the value of the request parameter.

Here's a declaration:

```
<map:selector
        name="request-parameter"
        logger="sitemap.selector.request-parameter"
        src="org.apache.cocoon.selection.RequestParameterSelector"/>
```

`RequestParameterSelector` has one parameter:

- `parameter-name`—Specifies the name of the request parameter whose value is used to compare with. When this parameter is omitted, the `otherwise` section is always selected.

SessionAttributeSelector

`SessionAttributeSelector` selects on the value of the session attribute. Declaration and usage are the same as those of `RequestAttributeSelector`.

SessionStateSelector

`SessionStateSelector` is deprecated in favor of `SessionAttributeSelector`. Don't use it—it will be removed soon.

Actions

Actions are the components in the pipeline that are intended to contain all your custom business logic. Java code in actions can connect to databases, communicate to EJBs in J2EE servers, and make decisions on how the request should be processed. Actions return their decision to the sitemap in the form of sitemap variables, in the same way matchers return their variables. Unlike matchers, actions can return sitemap variables with any convenient name, and are not limited to numbers. If an action fails, it can return null instead of a map of variables, and then the sitemap will skip processing of nested into the action part of the pipeline, and will continue sitemap execution with the pipeline component next after the action.

Cocoon has several generic enough actions you can use to quickly build a database-driven site, with form validation, and you can quickly write your own actions in a scripting language or XSP.

DatabaseAddAction

`DatabaseAddAction` can be used to add a record into the relational database. The configuration it supports includes the following:

- `descriptor`—The filename or the URL of the database table descriptor file.
- `reloadable`—When this is `true`, the action will reload the descriptor file when it is modified. The default is `true`.

This is declared in the sitemap as shown here:

```
<map:action
    name="db-add"
    logger="sitemap.action.db-add"
    src="org.apache.cocoon.acting.DatabaseAddAction">
    <reloadable>false</reloadable>
</map:action>
```

`DatabaseAddAction`'s configuration can be overridden by parameters when using the action. Here's an example of usage:

```
<map:act type="db-add">
    <map:parameter name="descriptor" value="employees.xml"/>
</map:act>
```

This action and other database-related actions are covered in more detail in Chapter 16, "Cocoon Interfaces: Databases."

DatabaseAuthenticatorAction

`DatabaseAuthenticatorAction` can be used to authenticate a user against a users table in the database, containing at least user name and password columns. The configuration it supports includes the following:

- `descriptor`—The filename or the URL of the database table descriptor file.
- `reloadable`—When this is `true`, the action will reload the descriptor file when it is modified. The default is `true`.

- `create-session`—When this is `true`, the action will create a session upon successful authentication. The default is `true`.

This is declared in the sitemap as shown here:

```
<map:action
    name="db-auth"
    logger="sitemap.action.db-auth"
    src="org.apache.cocoon.acting.DatabaseAuthenticatorAction">
    <reloadable>false</reloadable>
</map:action>
```

`DatabaseAuthenticatorAction`'s configuration can be overridden by parameters when using the action. Here's an example of usage:

```
<map:act type="db-auth">
    <map:parameter name="descriptor" value="employees.xml"/>
</map:act>
```

DatabaseDeleteAction

`DatabaseDeleteAction` can be used to delete a record from the relational database. Configuration and usage are the same as those of `DatabaseAddAction`.

DatabaseSelectAction

`DatabaseSelectAction` can be used to retrieve a single record from the relational database. The record's values are stored then as request attributes. If some of the request parameters are present, they override values from the database. Configuration and usage are same as those of `DatabaseAddAction`.

DatabaseUpdateAction

`DatabaseUpdateAction` can be used to update one or several records in the relational database. Configuration and usage are the same as those of `DatabaseAddAction`.

FormValidatorAction

`FormValidatorAction` is used to validate request parameters (the result of submitting a form) against a set of given rules. Form and constraints are defined in the descriptor file (the syntax is different from the descriptor file for database actions). `FormValidatorAction` has the following configuration:

- `descriptor`—The filename or the URL of the form descriptor file.

- `reloadable`—When this is `true`, the action will reload the descriptor file when it is modified. The default is `true`.
- `validate`—A list of form fields to validate. The default is `true`.
- `validate-set`—Validates a set of parameters specified in the named `constraint-set` in the descriptor file.

Both parameters `validate` and `validate-set` are optional. When none of them is specified, this action always succeeds.

Here's a declaration in the sitemap:

```
<map:action
    name="validator"
    logger="sitemap.action.validator"
    src="org.apache.cocoon.acting.FormValidatorAction">
    <reloadable>false</reloadable>
</map:action>
```

Here's an example of usage in the pipeline:

```
<map:act type="validator">
    <map:parameter name="validate" value="phone"/>
</map:act>
```

If the action validation is successful, the action returns all validated parameters to the sitemap.

An example of the descriptor file is as shown here:

```
<?xml version="1.0"?>
<root>
   <parameter name="persons" type="long" min="2" default="9" nullable="yes"/>
   <parameter name="deposit" type="double" min="10.0" max="999.99"/>
   <parameter name="email" type="string" max-len="50"
              matches-regex="^[\d\w][\d\w\-_\.]*@([\d\w\-_]+\.)\w\w\w?$"/>
   <constraint-set name="car-reservation">
       <validate name="persons"/>
       <validate name="deposit" min="50.0"/>
       <validate name="email"/>
    </constraint-set>
</root>
```

HttpHeaderAction

This action simply adds a header to the response. You can configure headers you want to set by default, and it is possible to override defaults later.

This is declared as shown here:

```
<map:action
    name="header"
    logger="sitemap.action.header"
    src="org.apache.cocoon.acting.HttpHeaderAction">
    <x-my-header>default</x-my-header>
</map:action>
```

Here's an example of usage in the pipeline:

```
<map:pipeline>
    <map:act type="header">
        <map:parameter name="x-my-header" value="override"/>
        <map:parameter name="Pragma" value="no-cache"/>
        <map:parameter name="Expires" value="-1"/>
        <map:parameter name="Cache-Control" value="no-cache"/>
    </map:act>
    ...
</map:pipeline>
```

This example sets one custom header, and disables caching of all resources served by Cocoon in the Internet browser's cache, and in all proxies along the path.

LocaleAction

`LocaleAction` obtains locale information from the request object. Information includes language, country, and variant.

The following search criteria are used when obtaining locale values: first, the request parameter `locale` is examined; second, the session attribute `locale` is tested; third, the action tries to obtain the locale from the `locale` cookie; and last, the locale is obtained from the request object.

When the locale information is determined, it can be stored in the request, in the session attribute, and in the cookie. In addition to that, the variables `lang`, `country`, `variant`, and `locale` are returned to the sitemap. Note that the `country` and `variant` variables can be empty, but `land` and `locale` always will contain a valid value.

`LocaleAction` has the following configuration:

- `store-in-request`—When this is `true`, obtained locale information will be stored in the request attributes. The default is `false`.
- `create-session`—When this is `true`, the action will create a session object. The default is `false`.
- `store-in-session`—When this is `true`, obtained locale information will be stored in the session attributes (only if the session object is available or `create-session` is `true`). The default is `false`.
- `store-in-cookie`—When this is `true`, obtained locale information will be stored in the cookie. The default is `false`.
- `language-attribute`—The name for the `language` attribute. The default is `lang`.
- `country-attribute`—The name for the `country` attribute. The default is `country`.
- `variant-attribute`—The name for the `variant` attribute. The default is `variant`.
- `locale-attribute`—The name for the `locale` attribute. The default is `locale`.

`LocaleAction` can be declared in the sitemap as shown here:

```
<map:action
    name="locale"
    logger="sitemap.action.locale"
    src="org.apache.cocoon.acting.LocaleAction">
    <store-in-cookie>true</store-in-cookie>
</map:action>
```

A sample action usage is as follows:

```
<map:match pattern="*.html">
  <map:act type="locale">
    <map:generate src="{../1}_{lang}{country}.xml"/>
  </map:act>
</map:match>
```

RequestParamAction

`RequestParamAction` makes available to the sitemap some information about the request. This information includes request URI, query string, and context path.

This is declared as shown here:

```
<map:action
    name="request"
    logger="sitemap.action.request"
    src="org.apache.cocoon.acting.RequestParamAction"/>
```

`RequestParamAction` has parameters:

- `parameters`—When this is `true`, it returns the values of all request parameters as sitemap variables. The default is `false`.
- `default.*`—Parameters starting with `default.` set default values for the parameters, so for these parameters you always will have some value in the sitemap.

Here's an example of usage:

```
<map:act type="request">
    <map:parameter name="parameters" value="true"/>
    <map:parameter name="default.color" value="green"/>
    <map:read mime-type="text/css" src="{color}.css"/>
</map:act>
```

RequestParameterExistsAction

This action checks for the existence of request parameters specified in the action's parameters or configuration. If parameters are present, it returns their values to the sitemap.

Here's an example of a declaration:

```
<map:action
    name="parameter-exists"
    logger="sitemap.action.parameter-exists"
    src="org.apache.cocoon.acting.RequestParameterExistsAction">
    <one>param1</one>
    <two>param2</two>
</map:action>
```

In this sample configuration, the action is configured to check for request parameters `param1` and `param2`, specified as values of configuration elements. The names of the configuration elements do not matter (for example, instead of `one` you can use `anything` to the same effect).

In addition to the default parameters, more parameters can be added when the action is used in the pipeline. Here is an example:

```
<map:match pattern="require-params">
    <map:act type="parameter-exists">
        <map:parameter name="parameters" value="param3 param4"/>
        <map:generate type="file" src="content.xml"/>
        <map:serialize type="html"/>
    </map:act>
    <map:redirect-to uri="error.html"/>
</map:match>
```

With this configuration, the action will succeed only when the request has all four parameters: `param1`, `param2`, `param3`, and `param4`.

ResourceExistsAction

`ResourceExistsAction` checks for the existence of a specified (via the `url` parameter) resource. The resource can be a reference to a file, or a URL. All Cocoon protocols are supported. The action does not return any variables to the sitemap.

This can be declared as shown here:

```
<map:action
    name="resource-exists"
    logger="sitemap.action.resource-exists"
    src="org.apache.cocoon.acting.ResourceExistsAction"/>
```

Here's an example of usage:

```
<map:match pattern="*.html">
    <map:act type="resource-exists">
        <map:parameter name="url" value="{1}.html"/>
        <map:read mime-type="text/html" src="{../1}.html"/>
    </map:act>
    <map:redirect-to uri="error.html"/>
</map:match>
```

ScriptAction

`ScriptAction` allows you to write actions in any scripting language supported by the BSF (make sure you have the interpreter of the language you want to use).

Declare it in the sitemap using this:

```
<map:action
    name="script"
    logger="sitemap.action.script"
    src="org.apache.cocoon.acting.ScriptAction"/>
```

Now you can use it in the pipeline:

```
<map:act type="script" src="hello.js">
    <map:parameter name="myparameter" value="myvalue"/>
</map:act>
```

Here, `hello.js` is an action in JavaScript (requires the Rhino JavaScript interpreter, which is shipped with Cocoon).

The action written in a script language will have access to the following preconfigured beans:

- `resolver`—The Cocoon source resolver.
- `objectModel`—The current object model.
- `parameters`—Parameters passed to the action (in this example it will have one parameter, `myparameter`).
- `actionMap`—The hash map to store the result of this action.
- `logger`—An instance of the logger.
- `request`—The request object.
- `scriptaction`—An instance of the `ScriptAction`.
- `manager`—The component manager.

A simple "Hello, World!" script action looks like this:

```
// Step 1 - Retrieve helper "beans" from the BSF framework
request      = bsf.lookupBean( "request" )
logger       = bsf.lookupBean( "logger" )
actionMap    = bsf.lookupBean( "actionMap" )

// Step 2 - Perform the action
logger.debug( "START hello.js" )

// Hello action always succeeds, and returns message
actionMap.put( "scriptaction-continue", "" )
actionMap.put( "message", "Hello, World!" )
logger.debug( "END hello.js" )
```

Note that the action indicates success to the `ScriptAction` by returning a non-null value for the `scriptaction-continue` entry in the `actionMap` hash map.

BSF

BSF is a Bean Scripting Framework, open source project by IBM. It provides a unified interface to several scripting languages, such as Netscape Rhino (JavaScript), VBScript, Perl, Tcl, Python, NetRexx, and Rexx. The project homepage is `http://oss.software.ibm.com/developerworks/projects/bsf`.

ServerPagesAction

`ServerPagesAction` allows for writing actions using Cocoon's XSP engine and XSP logicsheets (see Chapter 8, "Using Content Logic: XSPs," for more information on XSP). In addition to standard logicsheets (request, response, and so on), `ServerPagesAction` provides the action logicsheet for features specific to actions. If you developed your own logicsheets for XSP pages, you can now reuse them to write actions too.

You can declare the action in the sitemap like this:

```
<map:action
    name="serverpages"
    logger="sitemap.action.serverpages"
    src="org.apache.cocoon.acting.ServerPagesAction"/>
```

`ServerPagesAction` has a single parameter:

- `output-attribute`—Indicates the request attribute name that will store the document generated by the XSP action. This parameter is optional, and when it is omitted, the generated document is ignored.

Now you can use it in the pipeline:

```
<map:act type="serverpages" src="hello.xsp">
</map:act>
```

Here, `hello.xsp` is an action in XSP. A simple "Hello, World!" XSP action looks like this:

```
<?xml version="1.0" encoding="ISO-8859-1"?>

<xsp:page language="java"
          xmlns:xsp="http://apache.org/xsp"
          xmlns:xsp-action="http://apache.org/cocoon/action/1.0">
  <page>
    <xsp:logic>
        // Do stuff
    </xsp:logic>
    <xsp-action:set-result name="message" value="Hello, World!"/>
```

```
    <xsp-action:set-success/>
  </page>
</xsp:page>
```

Note that to indicate success and return a result action a logicsheet is used.

SessionInvalidatorAction

This action simply invalidates the session (if present).

It is declared in the sitemap as shown here:

```
<map:action
    name="session-invalidate"
    logger="sitemap.action.session-invalidate"
    src="org.apache.cocoon.acting.SessionInvalidatorAction"/>
```

And it is used in the pipeline in this way:

```
<map:act type="session-invalidate"/>
```

SessionIsValidAction

This action succeeds only when a session is present and is valid.

This is declared in the sitemap as shown here:

```
<map:action
    name="session-isvalid"
    logger="sitemap.action.session-isvalid"
    src="org.apache.cocoon.acting.SessionIsValidAction"/>
```

It is used in the pipeline like this:

```
<map:act type="session-isvalid">
  <!-- Success: session is valid -->
</map:act>
```

SessionPropagatorAction

`SessionPropagatorAction` populates the session with specified (via configuration or parameters) values. It also returns these values back to the sitemap. The action fails if no session object is present.

Here's an example of a declaration:

```
<map:action name="session-propagator"
            logger="sitemap.action.session-propagator"
            src="org.apache.cocoon.acting.SessionPropagatorAction">
    <my-parameter>default</my-parameter>
</map:action>
```

When using the action in the pipeline, it is possible to add more values and override defaults:

```
<map:act type="session-propagator">
    <map:parameter name="my-parameter" value="value"/>
    <map:parameter name="another-parameter" value="another-value"/>
</map:act>
```

SessionStateAction

`SessionStateAction` is used to store the application's "state" as session attributes with a configured prefix. State can have several levels of nested sub-states as well. Configuration elements (which can be modified later by parameters) are listed here:

- `state-key-prefix`—The prefix for session state variables. The suffix will be a number indicating the sub-state level, starting with `1` for top-level state.
- `sub-levels`—The count of sub-levels. A `0` means no sub-levels.
- `state-level`—Indicates what level to modify when `new-state` is provided.
- `new-state`—A new value for the state.

Here's a sample declaration:

```
<map:action name="session-state"
            logger="sitemap.action.session-state"
            src="org.apache.cocoon.acting.SessionStateAction">
    <state-key-prefix>myState</state-key-prefix>
    <sub-levels>2</sub-levels>
</map:action>
```

Here's an example of using the action to set the state:

```
<map:act type="session-state">
    <map:parameter name="state-level" value="1"/>
    <map:parameter name="new-state" value="StateA"/>
</map:act>
```

This shows using the action to set the sub-state:

```
<map:act type="session-state">
    <map:parameter name="state-level" value="2"/>
    <map:parameter name="new-state" value="SubStateA"/>
</map:act>
```

SessionValidatorAction

This action is analogous to `FormValidatorAction`, but it works not on request parameters (form data), but on session attributes. Thus, it validates the current session's state against a set of given rules. This action has the same configuration and usage as those of `FormValidatorAction`.

SetCharacterEncodingAction

When the browser submits the form and the application picks up values from the form, the default servlet container encoding is used. When you deal with forms in other than default encoding, this action comes in handy. Use this action before any other access to the request object to set the encoding used to submit the form. Encoding can be specified globally, in the action configuration, and it can be overridden later when the action is used in the pipeline.

Here's a sample declaration:

```
<map:action
    name="set-encoding"
    logger="sitemap.action.set-encoding"
    src="org.apache.cocoon.acting.SetCharacterEncodingAction">
    <parameter name="form-encoding" value="UTF-8"/>
</map:action>
```

`SetCharacterEncodingAction` never returns success to the sitemap; thus, when it's used, nothing should be nested within this action.

Here's an example of usage:

```
<map:pipeline>
  <map:act type="set-encoding">
    <map:parameter name="form-encoding" value="windows-1251"/>
  </map:act>
  <!-- the rest of the pipeline goes here -->
</map:pipeline>
```

Summary

This chapter has provided a comprehensive reference to the usage of all the sitemap components that are provided in the Cocoon distribution. This should enable you to make the right choice for your application when determining what combination of components to use when attempting to solve a particular problem. Remember that there is not always a right way or a wrong way to perform a task; your choice will be influenced by many determining factors. The key is that you have sufficient knowledge to understand to what level the Cocoon components can help you and thus where they fit in the decision-making jigsaw.

CHAPTER 25

Entity Catalogs

You do not have to work with XML for long to realize how much you rely on a multitude of resources to ensure that documents are created and parsed correctly. Logically, your XML document is made up of elements. How the XML parser determines the physical structure of the XML document, however, depends on the aggregation of resources that may be located in the same folder, on the same machine, or even across a network or the Internet. Document types definitions (DTDs) are a classic example of where an external resource is required by the parser. A DTD constrains the XML that is used inside the file to a known type and allows the parser to ensure that the XML file is valid. A typical DTD definition would be something like this:

```
<!DOCTYPE html PUBLIC "html"
    "http://www.w3.org/TR/xhtml1/DTD/xhtml1-transitional.
    ➥dtd">
```

Character entity sets are another example of external resources. This construct allows the mapping of hexadecimal or decimal character codes to be mapped to a textual "entity reference." For example,

```
<!ENTITY pound "&#163;">
```

enables you to use `£` in your XML file to insert the British pound sterling symbol, which is decimal code 163. An entity reference like this must be placed inside a DTD, thus further highlighting the physical dependencies inside a logical XML file. Because the desire to map the many and varied character sets to more meaningful text is not a new one, you can now find files that contain entire lists of entity references for inclusion inside a DTD. It would not make sense for you to have to cut and paste the list into your DTD, so it is possible to embed the file inside your DTD using a slightly different format of the ENTITY keyword. By way of example, the previously used HTML DTD contains the following lines:

```
<!ENTITY % HTMLspecial PUBLIC "-//W3C//ENTITIES Special for XHTML//EN"
   "xhtml-special.ent">
%HTMLspecial;
```

Here, the DTD is using two methods (more on these in a moment) to refer to a file (xhtml-special.ent) that contains special character entity references and giving a reference of HTMLspecial. The subsequent %HTMLspecial; line instructs the parser to include the entity file in the DTD.

Similar entity references can be used to refer to and embed other types of resources such as images or sub XML files.

So what are the problems that these fundamental instructions cause, and what is the need for entity catalogs?

Issues in Resolving Entities

As alluded to previously, external entities can be referred to in two ways, indicated by the SYSTEM and PUBLIC keywords. Take the following XML file extract:

```
<?xml version="1.0"?>
<!DOCTYPE mydtd SYSTEM "mydtd.dtd">
```

Here, a DTD is being referred to using the SYSTEM keyword. Following the SYSTEM keyword is a *system identifier* that determines the physical location of the DTD file, using a URI. Because the URI has no scheme or path components, the XML parser would look for mydtd.dtd in the same folder location as the XML file. In this scenario, a physical *address* is being used to locate the desired resource and, in this case, would always work as long as the DTD was always named the same and in the same folder location as the XML file.

What would be the case, though, if a path to the DTD were added? For example:

```
<?xml version="1.0"?>
<!DOCTYPE mydtd SYSTEM "c:\dtd\mydtd.dtd">
```

As long as `mydtd.dtd` always existed in the `c:\dtd folder`, there would be no problem. The XML parser would find the resource and be able to successfully parse the file. To do this in practice, however, would be a very risky prospect. When this file is distributed to a third party, they must have the DTD in exactly the same place, and of course this is highly unlikely, especially if this file was being delivered to different operating-system platforms.

Needless to say, in real life you very rarely see this sort of construct. System identifiers tend to use a full URL, so you may see something more like this:

```
<?xml version="1.0"?>
<!DOCTYPE mydtd SYSTEM "http://www.pigbite.com/dtd/mydtd.dtd">
```

This would appear to solve the problem—cause the DTD to be referenced over the network using a highly transportable protocol such as HTTP and everything should be great. Not at all! Several issues could occur. What if you, as the DTD owner, decide to move the location of the DTD or rename it? Suddenly, everyone who references your DTD using the old address is going to have problems. What if the machine that the XML file is on is not connected to the network or cannot reach the machine with the resource on it? What happens if there is a copy of the resource held locally to the XML file—how can it be reached?

These issues of resolution do not just affect parsing, but can have a direct impact on system performance. When the parser hits a reference to an external entity, it will resolve the location and get the entity. This entity may contain references to other external entities, all of which need resolution and parsing. These entities may be located in different places on a global network and need resolution each time the file is requested. All this network traffic and time taken to pull all the data together by the parser clearly will have an adverse effect on performance. Add in the compounding effect of multiple requests from many users, and the overhead could be significantly large. In these circumstances it is vital that as many of the resources as possible be located locally, but without compromising flexibility.

Referring to a Named Resource

There are two alternative ways to refer to a resource: using a *Uniform Resource Name (URN)* or a *Public Identifier*. Both of these methods basically associate a resource with an identifier that does not change. A registry, or catalog, can then be used to maintain the associations of identifiers with physical locations. If the location changes, the identifier stays the same, so no one's XML files break. Ultimately, instead an *address* being used to reference an external entity, a *name* can be used.

A URN looks something like `urn:x-pigbite:mydtd`. The first part of the URN—the prefix `urn:`—always exists. The second part is known as the *Namespace Identifier (NID)*. Official NIDs are assigned by the Internet Assigned Numbers Authority (IANA) and include namespaces such as IEEE and OASIS. If the NID is preceded by an "`x-`" this indicates an experimental NID, one that has not been registered by the IANA. Experimental NIDs are not guaranteed to be unique and therefore should be used with caution. The final part of the URN is the *Namespace Specific String*, or *NSS*. The NSS is determined by the NID owner.

Public identifiers were instigated as part of SGML, where they are called Formal Public Identifiers, or FPIs. An FPI must conform to the following syntax:

```
regid//owner//class description//language
```

In this syntax:

`regid` is either + or -. This indicates whether the owner information is registered.

`owner` specifies the owner of the FPI.

`class` indicates the type of information in the resource. This might typically be something like `DTD`, `ELEMENT`, or `ENTITIES`.

`description` is a short description of the resource.

`language` is the ISO two-character code that defines the native language for the resource.

A sample public identifier is as follows:

```
-//W3C//ENTITIES Special for XHTML//EN
```

In this case the owner is the World Wide Web Consortium. They are not registered. The resource contains `ENTITIES` that are special for XHTML, and the default language is English.

The only exception to this format occurs if the FPI is issued by ISO. If so, the *`regid`* and *`owner`* components would be replaced by *`ISO nnnn:yyyy`*, where *nnnn* represents the ISO standard reference number and *yyyy* represents the year of issue.

Mapping Names to Addresses Using a Catalog

The benefit of referring to a resource using a name is that you can then map the name to an address, just as a domain name server maps a server and domain name to an IP address. You are then at liberty to update the physical location of a resource, having to change only the mapping. In the world of external resources, considerable work has been done on standardizing the definition of *entity resolution catalogs*, files that contain the mapping data needed for entity resolution.

The prime driver of this work has been the Entity Resolution Technical Committee (TC) of the Organization for the Advancement of Structured Information Standards (OASIS—`http://www.oasis-open.org`). The official definition for entity resolution catalog files can be found in Technical Resolution TR9401.

Entity Resolution Catalog Format

OASIS TR9401 specifies the format of an entity resolution catalog, simply referred to as a catalog from now on, as a simple whitespace-delimited text file. Inside this file are keywords that define the mappings between a name and an address. The main keywords to consider are outlined in Table 25.1.

Table 25.1 *Primary Catalog Keywords*

Keyword	Description
`--`	Comment. A comment must start and end with the `--` character sequence.
`PUBLIC`	Maps a public identifier with the given address.
`SYSTEM`	Maps a system identifier to the given address.
`OVERRIDE`	Allows the choice of whether to use an explicit system identifier.
`BASE`	Sets the base URI from which subsequent addresses should be resolved relative to.

Listing 25.1 illustrates a sample catalog file (`local.catalog`) we can use to demonstrate the key features mentioned previously.

Listing 25.1 *local.catalog*

```
-- Cocoon Developer's Handbook --
-- Example Local Entity Catlog --

BASE "entities/"

OVERRIDE YES
PUBLIC "-//PIGBITE//TEXT neil//EN"                "neil.inc"
PUBLIC " -//PIGBITE//TEXT joe V1.0//EN"           "joe.inc"
SYSTEM "urn:x-pigbite:neil"                       "neil.inc"
```

Listing 25.1 *(continued)*

```
SYSTEM "http://www.pigbite.com/entities/richie.inc" "richie.inc"

OVERRIDE NO
PUBLIC "-//PIGBITE//TEXT phil V1.0//EN"              "phil.inc"
```

The first couple of lines are simply comments, delimited with -- characters. The first keyword is BASE, signifying that all resources resolved to a local file store should be relative to this path. If the base path is relative itself (as in this case), the path will be constructed relative to the location of the catalog.

Next come the keyword mapping commands. These follow a simple format, with the keyword followed by the external identifier and then the resource that the identifier is mapped to. Each component of the map can be separated by tabs, spaces, or even a new line.

Configuring Catalog Files in Cocoon

Catalog files are configured in various ways in Cocoon. First, there is the default catalog file that defines some core mappings to local resources. Second, you can add in your own local catalogs to supplement the default catalog.

Default Catalog Configuration

Because Cocoon regularly uses DTDs and other entities, some of these have been pulled into the distribution and are referenced using the default catalog. This file and the associated entity files can be found in `$CATALINA_HOME/webapps/cocoon/resources/entities`. The default catalog itself is called `catalog` and is not too large.

The default catalog is automatically loaded when Cocoon starts and is configured using a combination of `cocoon.xconf` and a properties file—`CatalogManager.properties`—which can be found in `$CATALINA_HOME/webapps/cocoon/WEB-INF/classes`.

The section that controls the entity catalog configuration in `cocoon.xconf` is `<entity-resolver>`. It will typically look something like this:

```
<entity-resolver
    class="org.apache.cocoon.components.resolver.ResolverImpl"
    logger="core.resolver">
  <parameter name="catalog" value="/resources/entities/catalog"/>
  <parameter name="verbosity" value="1"/>
</entity-resolver>
```

The attributes of the main tag tell Cocoon what the resolving class is and the logger details. There are then parameters that determine the location of the default catalog and a logging verbosity level. The default settings here are built from the `resolver.xconf` file that can be found in `org/apache/cocoon/components/resolver` under the `src` source folder. Raising the verbosity level will increase the number of logging messages sent. An additional parameter can be used to define a local catalog (see the next section for more details).

The other file that completes the configuration of the catalog is the `CatalogManager.properties` file. The build process places this file in the `WEB-INF/classes` folder. Among other things, settings in this file also control the logging verbosity level and additional catalogs.

It is worth noting that the logging verbosity level is shared by both `cocoon.xconf` and `CatalogManager.properties` and that the settings in `cocoon.xconf` take priority.

Local Catalog Configuration

It is possible to add your own mapping to the default catalog; however, best practice determines that you set up at least one separate local catalog. This way there are fewer issues in modifying default distribution files.

There are two ways to configure the loading of local catalogs into your application. Firstly, you can load a single local catalog using `cocoon.xconf`. You can supply the path and filename as a `local-catalog` parameter element within the `<entity-resolver>` element block:

```
<entity-resolver
    class="org.apache.cocoon.components.resolver.ResolverImpl"
     logger="core.resolver">
  <parameter name="catalog" value="/resources/entities/catalog"/>
  <parameter name="verbosity" value="1"/>
  <parameter name="local-catalog"
   ➥value="/java/tomcat4.0.4_le/webapps/cocoon/mount/cdh/chapter25/
   ➥local.catalog"/>
</entity-resolver>
```

Secondly, you can load one or more local catalogs through the `CatalogManager.properties` file. One of the properties in this file is called `catalogs`; supplying one or more full paths, separated by a semicolon (`;`) will load the catalogs. For example:

```
catalogs=/java/tomcat4.0.4_le/webapps/cocoon/mount/cdh/chapter25/
➥/pigbite.catalog;/java/tomcat4.0.4_le/webapps/cocoon/mount/cdh/
➥chapter25/local.catalog
```

will load two catalogs. Note the use of full paths and the forward slash character as the folder separator. The latter is always used, regardless of the operating system.

If you want to know whether the catalog is being loaded properly, you can check by raising the verbosity level to 10 and then checking the output to `stdout`. If you are using a servlet container such as Tomcat, you can check the `stdout.log` file in the Tomcat (not Cocoon) `logs` folder and you will see various messages. As a snippet you may see something like this:

```
Parse catalog:
➥/java/tomcat4.0.4_le/webapps/cocoon/mount/cdh/chapter25/local.catalog
Loading catalog:
➥/java/tomcat4.0.4_le/webapps/cocoon/mount/cdh/chapter25/pigbite.catalog
Default BASE:
➥file:/java/tomcat4.0.4_le/webapps/cocoon/mount/cdh/chapter25/
➥pigbite.catalog
BASE CUR:
➥file:/java/tomcat4.0.4_le/webapps/cocoon/mount/cdh/chapter25/
➥pigbite.catalog
BASE STR: dtd/
BASE NEW: file:/java/tomcat4.0.4_le/webapps/cocoon/mount/cdh/chapter25/dtd/
OVERRIDE: YES
PUBLIC: -//PIGBITE//DTD fred v1//EN
    file:/java/tomcat4.0.4_le/webapps/cocoon/mount/cdh/chapter25/dtd/person.dtd
Parse catalog: D:\java\Tomcat4.0.4_le\webapps\cocoon\resources\entities\catalog
Parse catalog:
➥/java/tomcat4.0.4_le/webapps/cocoon/mount/cdh/chapter25/local.catalog
Loading catalog:
➥/java/tomcat4.0.4_le/webapps/cocoon/mount/cdh/chapter25/local.catalog
Default BASE:
➥file:/java/tomcat4.0.4_le/webapps/cocoon/mount/cdh/chapter25/
➥local.catalog
BASE CUR:
➥file:/java/tomcat4.0.4_le/webapps/cocoon/mount/cdh/chapter25/
➥local.catalog
BASE STR: dtd/
BASE NEW: file:/java/tomcat4.0.4_le/webapps/cocoon/mount/cdh/chapter25/dtd/
OVERRIDE: YES
SYSTEM: person.dtd
    file:/java/tomcat4.0.4_le/webapps/cocoon/mount/cdh/chapter25/dtd/person.dtd
SYSTEM: http://www.pigbite.com/dtd/jez.txt
    file:/java/tomcat4.0.4_le/webapps/cocoon/mount/cdh/chapter25/dtd/jez.txt
SYSTEM: urn:x-pigbite:person
    file:/java/tomcat4.0.4_le/webapps/cocoon/mount/cdh/chapter25/dtd/person.dtd
```

```
SYSTEM: http://www.pigbite.com/dtd/person.dtd
    file:/java/tomcat4.0.4_le/webapps/cocoon/mount/cdh/chapter25/dtd/person.dtd
PUBLIC: -//PIGBITE//DTD Person V1.0//EN
    file:/java/tomcat4.0.4_le/webapps/cocoon/mount/cdh/chapter25/dtd/person.dtd
```

If your catalog file is not being found, you will get a message in this log file to tell you that is the case.

So which method should you use? Well, if you have multiple local catalogs, there is only one method you can use: `CatalogManager.properties`. If you have only a single local catalog, the choice is yours; however, it is worth bearing in mind that not only does `cocoon.xconf` override settings from `CatalogManager.properties` but restricting application-specific modifications to `cocoon.xconf` could help simplify maintenance and deployment of your application.

> **Tip**
> If you do change your catalog file, you must restart the Web application, because the catalogs are loaded only at startup.

Regardless, the crux of this technology is to provide a resolution mechanism, so let's look at some examples of how you can make catalogs work for you.

Resolving Public Identifiers

In many cases you will want to provide a way of resolving a public identifier because this method results in the most portable solution. Because a public identifier is a *name* and not an *address*, it must be resolved in some way, and entity catalogs are a great way of performing this task.

Let's start by looking at a simple XML hierarchy and examining how a DTD can be added to it and then resolved using a local catalog:

```
<person>
  <name>
    <firstname>Jeremy</firstname>
    <surname>Aston</surname>
  </name>
  <profession>Software Developer</profession>
</person>
```

If the preceding extract was preceded by the `<?xml version="1.0">` header and then saved as an XML file, it could be rendered using the simple stylesheet shown in Listing 25.2.

Listing 25.2 *people2html.xsl*

```
<?xml version="1.0"?>
<xsl:stylesheet version="1.0" xmlns:xsl="http://www.w3.org/1999/XSL/Transform">
  <xsl:output indent="no" method="html"/>

  <xsl:template match="/">
    <html>
    <head>
      <title>People</title>
    </head>

    <body>

      <xsl:apply-templates />

    </body>
    </html>
  </xsl:template>

  <xsl:template match="person">
    <xsl:apply-templates />
  </xsl:template>

  <xsl:template match="name">
    <h1><xsl:value-of select="surname"/>, <xsl:value-of select="firstname"/>
    ➥</h1>
  </xsl:template>

  <xsl:template match="profession">
    <h2><xsl:value-of select="text()"/></h2>
  </xsl:template>

</xsl:stylesheet>
```

Rendering this file would result in a simple HTML page, as illustrated in Figure 25.1.

What would be nice, of course, would be to provide a DTD so that the `<person>` XML hierarchy can be properly formed and validated. We know that `<person>` is made up of a `<name>` and at least one `<profession>` sub-element. We also know that the `<name>` element is in turn made up of `<firstname>` and `<surname>` elements. This hierarchy can be represented using the `person.dtd` file as shown in Listing 25.3.

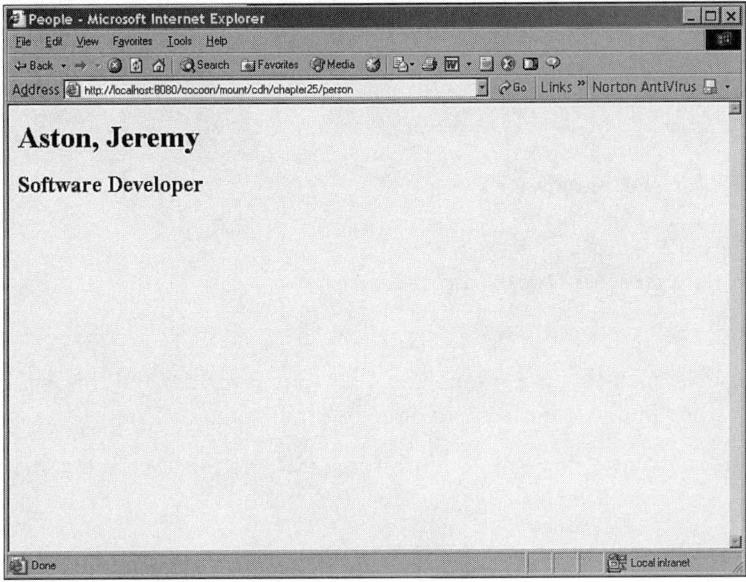

Figure 25.1

The result of rendering simple personal details.

Listing 25.3 *person.dtd*

```
<!ELEMENT person (name, profession?)>
<!ELEMENT name (firstname, surname)>
<!ELEMENT firstname (#PCDATA)>
<!ELEMENT surname (#PCDATA)>
<!ELEMENT profession (#PCDATA)>
```

To attach this DTD to the previous XML file requires that we add a `DOCTYPE` tag. This will tell the parser where the DTD can be found. The simplest method would be to place the DTD in the same folder as the XML file and use a system identifier:

```
<!DOCTYPE person SYSTEM "person.dtd">
```

This, however, is using a physical address to locate the DTD, and as already explained, this could quite easily change. A better way would be to use a public identifier, which, because this is not a public DTD, can be pretty much made up. The resultant file, `person.xml`, can be examined in Listing 25.4.

Listing 25.4 *person.xml*

```
<?xml version="1.0"?>
<!DOCTYPE person PUBLIC "-//PIGBITE//DTD Person V1.0//EN" "person.dtd">
<person>
  <name>
    <firstname>Jeremy</firstname>
    <surname>Aston</surname>
  </name>
  <profession>Software Developer</profession>
</person>
```

Following the public identifier is a system identifier (`person.dtd`), but this will be used by the parser only if the public identifier cannot be resolved.

Using the `local.catalog` file presented in Listing 25.1, we can see the line that provides the mapping:

```
PUBLIC "-//PIGBITE//DTD Person V1.0//EN" "person.dtd"
```

Assuming that we are working in the `$CATALINA_HOME/webapps/cocoon/mount/cdh/chapter25` folder, we can place the `person.xml` and `local.catlog` files in that folder and the `person.dtd` in a subfolder called `entities`. The use of the `BASE` keyword in the catalog to specify that all subsequent local sources should be prefaced with `entities/` shows that we need to do this last step. Of course, the local catalog must be configured for loading by using one of the two methods specified in the preceding section.

Attempting to render the `person.xml` file should result in a screen exactly as shown in Figure 25.1. If you have set the resolver logging verbosity to a high level, you can check the servlet container's `stdout` log to see that the resolution has been done. You should see something like this:

```
resolvePublic(-//PIGBITE//DTD Person V1.0//EN,null)
Resolved public: -//PIGBITE//DTD Person V1.0//EN
    ➥file:/java/tomcat4.0.4_le/webapps/cocoon/mount/cdh/chapter25/
    ➥entities/person.dtd
```

This shows that the public identifier has been resolved to the local file.

Resolving System Identifiers

Having discussed how to resolve public identifiers, let's examine how system identifiers can be resolved. The method is effectively the same; however, as of Cocoon 2.0.3, there is a slight difference. Due to a known bug in Xerces 2.0.0, system identifier resolution works properly only when the system identifier is used to reference an entity defined with the `ENTITY` keyword. If you specify a system identifier either as a standalone reference or subsequent to a public identifier, for a keyword such as `DOCTYPE`, then it will not get successfully resolved by the catalog resolver. You can see this in action if you look at the log message in the earlier successful public identifier resolution example. Note that the call to the `resolvePublic()` method has a null argument. This should contain the system identifier that was specified, along with the public identifier. If you are using a version of Xerces above or below 2.0.0 (it was okay in 1.4.x), then when using `DOCTYPE`, just be sure to stick with public identifiers.

Looking at system identifier resolution in more detail, let's see how this works with the `ENTITY` keyword. Look at an extension of the `person.xml` file, `people.xml`, as shown in Listing 25.5.

Listing 25.5 *people.xml*

```
<?xml version="1.0"?>
<!DOCTYPE people PUBLIC "-//PIGBITE//DTD Person V1.0//EN" "person.dtd"
[
  <!ELEMENT people (person+)>
  <!ENTITY neil SYSTEM "urn:x-pigbite:neil">
  <!ENTITY richie SYSTEM "http://www.pigbite.com/entities/richie.inc">
  <!ENTITY joe PUBLIC "-//PIGBITE//TEXT joe V1.0//EN" "joe.inc" >
  <!ENTITY phil PUBLIC "-//PIGBITE//TEXT phil V1.0//EN" "phil.inc" >
]>
<people>
  <person>
    <name>
      <firstname>Jeremy</firstname>
      <surname>Aston</surname>
    </name>
    <profession>Software Developer</profession>
  </person>
  &neil;
  &richie;
  &phil;
</people>
```

This file extends the person.xml file into a collection of people. Instead of having its own DTD, it takes the internal DTD to extend the person DTD, wrapping it in a <people> container element. In addition, it specifies some external entities. Each of these files is a <person> node included using an entity reference; for example:

```
<person>
  <name>
    <firstname>Neil</firstname>
    <surname>Hodgson</surname>
  </name>
  <profession>Motorcycle Racer</profession>
</person>
```

The same stylesheet can be used to render this file; however, the output will look a little different because the parser will throw an error attempting to resolve the final entity (&phil;). Going through each of the samples in turn will shed a little more light onto what is happening.

First, let's see what entries need to be added to the local catalog file to provide the mapping:

```
SYSTEM "urn:x-pigbite:neil"                              "neil.inc"
PUBLIC "-//PIGBITE//TEXT joe V1.0//EN"                  "joe.inc"
SYSTEM "http://www.pigbite.com/entities/richie.inc" "richie.inc"
OVERRIDE NO
PUBLIC "-//PIGBITE//TEXT phil V1.0//EN"                  "phil.inc"
```

The first entity uses an URN in the system identifier. When the parser attempts to resolve the reference to &neil; in the code, it will find the matching urn:x-pigbite:neil entry and use entities/neil.inc.

The second entity uses an HTTP-based system identifier. This gets resolved in exactly the same way as the urn:x-pigbite:neil entry, this time resulting in the entities/richie.inc file being used.

The third entry illustrates an entity that is has both a public and a system identifier. Due to the default search mode (see the next section), this gets matched using the public identifier as the key.

The fourth entry illustrates what happens when the OVERRIDE keyword is set to NO. From this point on in the catalog, if a public identifier is matched, the match will be ignored if a system identifier is also provided in the source file. In this example there is a match for the public "-//PIGBITE//TEXT phil V1.0//EN" identifier used for the phil entity. The source file, however, also specifies a system identifier—"phil.inc". There is no match for this in the catalog, and, because the override is set to NO, the original system identifier is used. Because there is no `phil.inc` file in the same folder as the XML source, the resolution fails and an exception is thrown.

Catalog Search Modes

The catalog can be searched in two ways: One is by giving preference to public identifiers and the other is by giving preference to system identifiers. The default mode is for public identifiers to have preference, and this is the mode the previous examples are to be run against.

You can change the preference by looking at the `prefer` setting in `CatalogManager.properties`. This will, by default, be set to equal `public` but it can be changed to `system`. If you change it to prefer system identifiers, it means that the supplied public identifier will be ignored if there is no match for the system identifier.

To make more sense of this, change the search mode preference to `system`, and also comment out (or remove) the `OVERRIDE YES` command. Restart your Web server and then attempt to render `people.xml` again. You should find that an exception is thrown when trying to sort out the `joe` entity. This is because even though the public identifier has a match, the system identifier is preferred and there is no override. Therefore, the original system identifier is being used, which does not exist and has no match in the catalog.

Catalog Resources

There are several other catalog keywords, including `DELEGATE`, `CATALOG`, `DOCTYPE`, `LINKTYPE`, and `NOTATION`. The `DELEGATE` keyword is one you might use because it allows the routing of matches to another catalog. You can specify a partial public identifier and the catalog file that is used to resolve the entities. The `CATALOG` directive is similar in that it allows the inclusion of subcatalogs.

The previous descriptions refer to a catalog file that is configured as per the OASIS Technical Resolution 9401:1997 specification. This can be found at `http://www.oasis-open.org/specs/a401.html`. Since this standard was released, it has become possible to specify catalog files using an XML format. The XML Catalog format has a draft specification available at `http://home.ccil.org/~cowan/XML/XCatalog.html`. Be aware that this is still a draft specification and that it does not yet completely support equivalents to all the keywords that TR9401 makes available.

Of course, the Cocoon distribution documentation includes a helpful discussion on entity resolution. This is found in `cocoon/docs/userdocs/concepts/catalog.html`. This page also includes several links to other backup resources. One of the resources it does point to is a really good explanation of why entity resolution is a hot topic, written by one of the leading lights of this subject, Mr. Norman Walsh. The article can be found at `http://www.arbortext.com/Think_Tank/XML_Resources/Issue_Three/issue_three.html`. Mr. Walsh basically wrote most of Sun's XML resolver code, the home page of which can be found at `http://www.sun.com/software/xml/developers/resolver`. Downloading the code and examples from here is useful because you'll get a lot of background information and tools. This code also fed into the Apache xml-commons project. It is this area that has taken this code and implemented its code core to various Apache projects. You can find out more by visiting the xml-commons distribution page at `http://xml.apache.org/dist/commons/`. There are links here to join a development mailing list, access archives, and download the distribution and source files.

The final resource is the Cocoon entity resolving sample. It is well worth looking at because it provides alternative demonstrations of the principles we have covered in this chapter.

Summary

This chapter has explained the need for catalogs to support the resolution of entity references to known resources without compromising performance and robustness. It has also shown how this is possible using Cocoon and how you can create and manage your own catalog for entity resolution.

CHAPTER 26

Parent Component Manager

Any software based on Avalon's component architecture needs to supply a component manager that will handle the job of resolving which actual component object to use for a particular role. The `org.apache.components.CocoonComponentManager` class does this job for Cocoon. The `cocoon.roles` file configures the role to class relationships for all the core components that are contained in the distribution and, because it is found in the `src/org/apache/cocoon` folder, gets packaged up into the main Cocoon jar file. If you want to configure additional components, you can do this through the `user.roles` file. For further details on this topic, see Chapter 2, "Avalon."

At times, however, you might want to access a component from a source other than `user.roles`, or you might even want to have a single component manager for several Web applications. You can achieve this by using the parent component manager functionality present in Cocoon. This allows for another component manager to be "attached" to the application and for this to handle role and component resolution for particular components.

So how does all this happen? The Cocoon distribution includes an example that provides all the raw material needed to explain the process. The source code for this can be found in the `src/java/org/apache/cocoon/samples/parentcm` folder within the source distribution. Let's start by providing an overview of the process that is required to create and use a parent component manager.

Coding a Parent Component Manager—Overview

Several steps need to be taken to create and use a parent component manager. These can be summarized in the following way:

1. Make sure that the component(s) you want to have managed by the parent component manager are available. This may mean they need to be developed.
2. Create a configuration class. The resultant object creates the role definitions and binds the configuration to the core initial context.
3. Develop the actual parent component manager class.
4. Configure Cocoon to execute the initialization code within the configuration object. This is done via the application `web.xml` configuration file.
5. Configure Cocoon to use the parent component manager class. Again, this is achieved by modifying `web.xml`.
6. Use the component.

Using the supplied sample code, let's go through these steps in more detail.

Obtain the Component Classes

The first step of the preceding process is to obtain the components we want to manage with the parent component manager. You may already have these components, but in the sample code we want to develop a new component. This component simply returns the current date and time, thereby allowing us to use it in any suitable manner.

In the previously mentioned parent component manager sample code folder, you will find two files, `Time.java` and `TimeComponent.java`. `Time.java`, as shown in abbreviated form in Listing 26.1, is the interface class; `TimeComponent.java`, again shown in abbreviated form in Listing 26.2, is the actual component class that implements the `Time` interface.

Listing 26.1 *Time.java*

```
package org.apache.cocoon.samples.parentcm;


import org.apache.avalon.framework.component.Component;
import java.util.Date;
```

Listing 26.1 *(continued)*

```
/**
 * Interface for a simple time-keeping component.
*/
public interface Time extends Component {
    String ROLE = "org.apache.cocoon.samples.parentcm.Time";
    /**
     * Gets the current time.
     */
    Date getTime ();
}
```

Listing 26.2 *TimeComponent.java*

```
package org.apache.cocoon.samples.parentcm;

import org.apache.avalon.framework.component.Component;
import org.apache.avalon.framework.thread.ThreadSafe;
import java.util.Date;

/**
 * Implementing class for the parent component manager sample's
 * <code>org.apache.cocoon.samples.parentcm.Time</code> component.
*/
public class TimeComponent implements Component, Time, ThreadSafe {
    public Date getTime () {
        return new Date();
    }
}
```

We now have the component classes that we need in order to continue to the next step.

Create a Configuration Class

The next item on the list is creating a configuration object. What this code does is initialize the parent component manager and bind it to the initial Cocoon context, thus making it available.

The sample folder contains a file called `Configurator.java`, as shown in abbreviated form in Listing 26.3, that performs this task.

Listing 26.3 *Configurator.java*

```
package org.apache.cocoon.samples.parentcm;

import org.apache.avalon.excalibur.naming.memory.MemoryInitialContextFactory;
import org.apache.avalon.framework.configuration.DefaultConfiguration;

import javax.naming.Context;
import javax.naming.InitialContext;
import java.util.Hashtable;

/**
 * This class sets up the configuration
 * used by the ParentComponentManager sample.
 * The class also holds a reference to
 * the initial context in which the configuration
 * is available.
 * <p>
 * The configuration is bound to
 * <code>org/apache/cocoon/samples/parentcm/ParentCMConfiguration</code>.
 *
*/
public class Configurator  {

    /**
     * The Excalibur in-memory JNDI directory. Since the directory doesn't
     * provide any persistence we must keep a reference to the initial context
     * as a static member to avoid passing it around.
     */
    public static Context initialContext = null;

    static {
        try {
            //
            // Create a new role.
            //
            DefaultConfiguration config = new DefaultConfiguration("roles", "");
            DefaultConfiguration timeComponent =
                   new DefaultConfiguration("role", "roles");
            timeComponent.addAttribute("name", Time.ROLE);
            timeComponent.addAttribute("default-class",
                   TimeComponent.class.getName());
            timeComponent.addAttribute("shorthand", "samples-parentcm-time");
```

Listing 26.3 (continued)

```
            config.addChild(timeComponent);

            //
            // Bind it - get an initial context.
            //
            Hashtable environment = new Hashtable();
            environment.put(Context.INITIAL_CONTEXT_FACTORY,
                    MemoryInitialContextFactory.class.getName());
            initialContext = new InitialContext(environment);

            //
            // Create subcontexts and bind the configuration.
            //
            Context ctx = initialContext.createSubcontext("org");
            ctx = ctx.createSubcontext("apache");
            ctx = ctx.createSubcontext("cocoon");
            ctx = ctx.createSubcontext("samples");
            ctx = ctx.createSubcontext("parentcm");
            ctx.rebind("ParentCMConfiguration", config);
        } catch (Exception e) {
            e.printStackTrace(System.err);
        }
    }
}
```

Note the section of code that creates the new role configuration data. This is building directly in code the same configuration information that would be found in `user.roles` or `cocoon.roles` if the component were being configured for management by the base Cocoon component manager.

The last section of the code creates the naming subcontext data and binds a JNDI identifier for the configuration data built earlier, the name in this case being `ParentCM Configuration`. This will be used in the construction of the runtime parent component manager object.

Create the Parent Component Manager Class

The next step is to write the parent component manager code. Listing 26.4 shows the abbreviated version of the sample code found in the `ParentComponentManager.java` file.

Listing 26.4 *ParentComponentManager.java*

```
package org.apache.cocoon.samples.parentcm;

import org.apache.avalon.excalibur.component.ExcaliburComponentManager;
import org.apache.avalon.excalibur.naming.memory.MemoryInitialContextFactory;
import org.apache.avalon.framework.activity.Initializable;
import org.apache.avalon.framework.component.Component;
import org.apache.avalon.framework.component.ComponentException;
import org.apache.avalon.framework.component.ComponentManager;
import org.apache.avalon.framework.configuration.Configuration;
import org.apache.avalon.framework.context.DefaultContext;
import org.apache.avalon.framework.logger.Loggable;
import org.apache.log.Logger;

import javax.naming.Context;
import java.util.Hashtable;

/**
 * A sample parent component manager.
 * This manager will look up the configuration object
 * given by the initialization parameter in JNDI,
 * use it to configure an ExcaliburComponentManager
 * and delegate any requests to it.
*/
public class ParentComponentManager
implements ComponentManager, Loggable, Initializable {

    /**
     * Our logger.
     */
    private Logger logger;

    /**
     * The JNDI name where the component manager configuration can be found.
     */
    private final String jndiName;

    /**
     * The delegate that will be configured and provide the
     * functionality for this component manager.
     */
    private final ExcaliburComponentManager delegate;
```

Listing 26.4 *(continued)*

```
public ParentComponentManager(final String jndiName) {
    this.jndiName = jndiName;

    // Initialize it here so we can let it be final.
    this.delegate = new ExcaliburComponentManager();
}

public boolean hasComponent(final String role) {
    return delegate.hasComponent(role);
}

/**
 * Initializes the CM by looking up the configuration object and using it to
 * configure the delegate.
 */
public void initialize() throws Exception {
    this.logger.debug("Looking up component manager configuration at : "
         + this.jndiName);

    Hashtable environment = new Hashtable();
    environment.put(Context.INITIAL_CONTEXT_FACTORY,
    MemoryInitialContextFactory.class.getName());

    //
    // Yes, this is cheating, but the Excalibur in-memory naming provider
    // is transient. That is, it doesn't store objects persistently and
    // is more like a HashMap.
    //
    // Should be:
    // Context initialContext = new InitialContext(environment);
    //
    Context initialContext = Configurator.initialContext;

    Configuration config =
         (Configuration) initialContext.lookup(this.jndiName);

    // We ignore the setRoleManager call,
    // as ExcaliburComponentManager handles that
    // in configure().
    this.delegate.setLogger(logger);
    this.delegate.contextualize(new DefaultContext());
```

Listing 26.4 *(continued)*

```
        this.delegate.configure(config);
        this.delegate.initialize();

        this.logger.debug("Component manager successfully initialized.");
    }

    public Component lookup(final String role) throws ComponentException {
        return this.delegate.lookup(role);
    }

    public void release(final Component component) {
        this.delegate.release(component);
    }

    public void setLogger(final Logger logger) {
        this.logger = logger;
    }
}
```

So what exactly is this code doing? The first area to look at is the class declaration. A parent component manager must implement (remarkably enough) `ComponentManager` but can choose whether it will implement `Loggable` and `Initializable`. In this case, both interfaces are implemented.

Next, take a look at the constructor:

```
public ParentComponentManager(final String jndiName) {
    this.jndiName = jndiName;
    // Initialize it here so we can let it be final.
    this.delegate = new ExcaliburComponentManager();
}
```

The constructor takes the JNDI name as a `String` parameter, storing it in a local property, `jndiName`. It also sets up a local property called `delegate` that will contain an `ExcaliburComponentManager` object. This object will then handle the actual work of role/component resolution, logging, initialization, and so on. Some or all of this work could be handled in the component manager class, but in this sample case it is not needed.

The final area to look at is the initialize method. Here is where the configuration data for the delegate `ExcaliburComponentManager` is looked up using the value, supplied via the constructor, in `jndiName`:

```
Configuration config = (Configuration) initialContext.lookup(this.jndiName);
```

Another, slightly cheeky, aspect of the sample code is the fact that it does an in-memory lookup of the initial context. This does not really matter in this case, but beware of this if you are developing a parent component manager that might not be running in the same memory space as the application context. The comments inside the code illustrate what the longer-winded (in performance terms) approach is.

We now have the component, the configurator, and the parent component manager. All is set to next configure Cocoon.

Configure Cocoon

There are two items to configure in Cocoon to get the parent component manager loaded, and both involve `web.xml`. The first is to force the initialization code to be run, and the second is an initialization parameter.

Forcing the initialization code to be run is achieved by adding a line to the `<load-class>` element that tells Cocoon to load specific classes such as JDBC database drivers. Fortunately, the distribution has the required parameter within `web.xml`; all that is needed is for it to be uncommented. When done, the `<load-class>` element should look similar to the following:

```
<init-param>
  <param-name>load-class</param-name>
  <param-value>
    <!-- For IBM WebSphere:
    com.ibm.servlet.classloader.Handler -->

    <!-- For Database Driver: -->
    org.hsqldb.jdbcDriver

    <!-- For parent ComponentManager sample: -->
    org.apache.cocoon.samples.parentcm.Configurator
  </param-value>
</init-param>
```

This is forcing Cocoon to load the `Configurator` class defined previously, which will in turn automatically execute the static code contained within it.

The second area of `web.xml` that requires modification is the configuration of an initialization parameter called `parent-component-manager`. This parameter has a value that defines the class and the JNDI name that will be used to locate the configuration data. Again, the distribution contains the required settings for the sample code; all you need to do is uncomment the relevant area. After you have done this, you should have a block that looks similar to this:

```
<init-param>
  <param-name>parent-component-manager</param-name>
  <param-value>org.apache.cocoon.samples.parentcm.ParentComponentManager
➥/org/apache/cocoon/samples/parentcm/ParentCMConfiguration</param-value>
</init-param>
```

Note here that because the parameter can have only a single value there is a convention that is used to signify both the parent component manager class name and the configuration JNDI name. The first part of the value string is the parent component manager class name (`org.apache.cocoon.samples.parentcm.ParentComponentManager`). The first forward slash is then used as a separator for the JNDI name (`org/apache/cocoon/samples/parentcm/ParentCMConfiguration`) to follow.

When Cocoon processes all of this configuration data, it will first load the `Configurator` class and execute the configuration code. This sets up the configuration data, binding it to a JNDI name of `org/apache/cocoon/samples/parentcm/ParentCMConfiguration`. When the `parent-component-manager` initialization parameter is processed, Cocoon will separate the class name and JNDI name held within the parameter value and load the `org.apache. cocoon.samples.parentcm.ParentComponentManager` class, passing the JNDI name to the constructor. The initialize method in this class will be called, causing the configuration data to be looked up using the JNDI name and a delegate component manager to be instantiated.

Now that the parent component manager is ready to use, all that remains is for some code to be put in place to use the component.

Use the Component

The only thing that is not in place is something that will actually use the component. The parent component manager sample code includes something that does this for us in the form of the generator in `Generator.java`, abbreviated in Listing 26.5.

Listing 26.5 *Generator.java*

```
package org.apache.cocoon.samples.parentcm;

import org.apache.avalon.excalibur.pool.Poolable;
import org.apache.avalon.framework.component.ComponentException;
import org.apache.avalon.framework.parameters.Parameters;
import org.apache.cocoon.ProcessingException;
import org.apache.cocoon.environment.SourceResolver;
import org.apache.cocoon.generation.ComposerGenerator;
import org.xml.sax.SAXException;
```

Listing 26.5 *(continued)*

```
import org.xml.sax.helpers.AttributesImpl;

import java.io.IOException;
import java.util.Date;
import java.util.Map;

/**
 * Generator for the parent component manager sample. The generator outputs
 * a single tag <code>&lt;time&gt;<i>current time</i>&lt;/time&gt;</code>.
 * Where <code><i>current time</i></code>
 * is the current time as obtained from the
 * <code>Time</code> component.
 *
*/
public class Generator extends ComposerGenerator implements Poolable {

    /**
     * Current time.
     */
    private Date time;

    /**
     * Looks up a <code>Time</code> component and obtains the current time.
     */
    public void setup(SourceResolver resolver,
               Map objectModel, String src, Parameters par)
        throws ProcessingException, SAXException, IOException {

        Time timeGiver = null;
        try {
            timeGiver = (Time) manager.lookup(Time.ROLE);
            this.time = timeGiver.getTime ();
        } catch (ComponentException ce) {
            throw new
               ProcessingException("Could not obtain current time.", ce);
        } finally {
            manager.release(timeGiver);
        }
    }

    /**
```

Listing 26.5 *(continued)*

```
     * Generate XML data.
     */
    public void generate() throws SAXException, ProcessingException {
        AttributesImpl emptyAttributes = new AttributesImpl();
        contentHandler.startDocument();
        contentHandler.startElement("", "time", "time", emptyAttributes);

        char[] text = this.time.toString().toCharArray();

        contentHandler.characters(text, 0, text.length);

        contentHandler.endElement("", "time", "time");
        contentHandler.endDocument();
    }

    /**
     * Prepare this object for another cycle.
     */
    public void recycle () {
        this.time = null;
    }
}
```

This is a simple generator component that looks up the component referenced by the `Time.ROLE`, using the parent component manager, and queries the current time. The resultant time value is then wrapped in an XML element called `<time>`.

To use this we need to add a couple of settings into a sitemap. The first is the reference to the generator, which needs to sit in the `<generators>` block.

```
<map:generators default="file">
...
  <map:generator name="time" pool-grow="4" pool-max="32" pool-min="8"
➥src="org.apache.cocoon.samples.parentcm.Generator"/>
...
</map:generators>
```

A simple test of the generator is to write a pipeline entry that will stream the result of the generator as XML to the browser. This can be achieved with a block such as the following:

```
<map:match pattern="time">
  <map:generate type="time"/>
```

```
  <map:serialize type="xml"/>
</map:match>
```

Running the Parent Component Manager Sample

To get all this running does require that Cocoon has been built with the JNDI classes available, basically what is in the `javax.naming` package. If you have JDK1.4, you can make sure that the `jre/lib/rt.jar` library is on your classpath because this contains the JNDI package files. Alternatively, you can download the JNDI 1.2.1 library files from `http://java.sun.com` and place `jndi.jar` into the source `lib/local` folder. Performing a build will then pick up the fact that `javax.naming` is available and compile the `org/apache/cocoon/samples/parentcm` files into the build `WEB-INF/classes` folder. Redeploying the `cocoon.war` file or simply copying the relevant files into an existing Cocoon Web application will make the classes available.

The sample code for this chapter contains a sitemap that, if correctly deployed under `cocoon/mount`, will cause a request to `http://localhost:8080/cocoon/mount/cdh/chapter26/time` to present the screen shown in Figure 26.1.

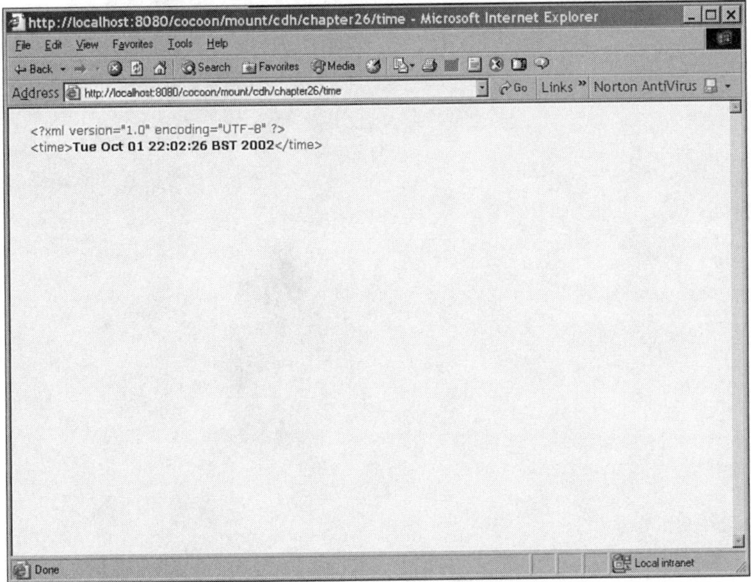

Figure 26.1
The result of the parent component manager example.

Summary

In this chapter we have reviewed the benefits of using a parent component manager and discussed when you might want to do so. Using the sample files distributed with Cocoon, we have looked at how you can develop a parent component manager that will manage a new component. We have also discussed how to configure both the parent component manager and Cocoon so that a successful implementation can take place.

CHAPTER 27

Cocoon Resources

As an open source project, Cocoon is dependent on the support of an active user base. In the early stages of a project when there is a small but dedicated team of developers, it is not too difficult for people to work without significant amounts of external support. As the user population grows, however, it is important that these people be able to get going quickly. This encourages use of the software and proactive contribution to the project. So what resources are available to users of and prospective contributors to Cocoon?

Core Cocoon Documentation

The best place to start is the Cocoon documentation. Historically, however, it perhaps has been one of the most painful places—one of the most common issues that users new to Cocoon seem to have is with the supplied documentation. Cocoon is a highly extendable and configurable platform, but some of the concepts behind Cocoon are perhaps not well understood by those recently exposed to it. In the past, many users have struggled to come to grips with even some of the most seemingly simple tasks, such as writing an XSP page and configuring the sitemap to get it displayed.

The Cocoon documentation is included as part of the distribution and is becoming increasingly more comprehensive. Some time ago, it was recognized that the documentation available was disjointed and incomplete, and in recent months a concerted effort has been made to coordinate efforts so that the documentation is far more comprehensive, structured, and easy to navigate. There is a mailing list (see the "Mailing Lists" section, later in the chapter) specifically for the discussion of documentation-related matters, and all contributors, direct or indirect, are encouraged to support their code with comprehensive Javadoc and written documentation as appropriate.

The documentation is split into several distinct areas, each geared to particular audiences, as shown as an overview in Table 27.1.

Table 27.1 *Cocoon Documentation Overview*

Topic	Description
Introduction	Description of what Cocoon is about and why it is of value
Installing	Instructions on how to obtain, install, and configure Cocoon on various platforms
User Guide	Documentation on concepts behind Cocoon and the sitemap components
Dev Guide	Documentation on how to extend Cocoon and develop Web applications
Tutorials	Internal and external tutorials on various aspects of Cocoon application development
FAQs	Frequently Asked Questions on numerous Cocoon topics
How Tos	Various process-oriented documents that cover how to perform various tasks, both programming and project oriented
Performance	Hints and tips along with background information that can help you configure your Cocoon application for the best possible performance
Snippets	Small pieces of code examples
Table of Contents (ToC)	Comprehensive list of all the documentation available

So, given all this material, where should you start? How do you find what you need? Clearly there are some obvious places to go if you are interested, for example, in installing Cocoon. But what are you going to find in some of the other areas of the core documentation? Let's look in more detail at some of the resources available.

User Guide

This is the area to go to if you are interested in the key material for understanding how Cocoon works and basic application configuration. For starters, there is a great section on the *concepts* of how Cocoon works that explains document processing mechanisms, pipeline processing, and application architecture. It also covers key points of core components such as generators, transformers, and serializers. From here you can also see details about many of the underlying technology "gubbins" that make up Cocoon, including entity catalogs, caching, the StoreJanitor, and so on.

The User Guide area also covers the sitemap components, detailing the various Generators, Transformers, Serializers, `Matchers`, and so on that are all included in the core distribution.

Dev Guide

The Dev (or Developers) Guide area introduces some of the more advanced configuration information that is required to be able to add new functionality to Cocoon and successfully manage any Web applications you develop. It explains the role of the sitemap and `cocoon.xconf`, along with how requests are managed and details of the component-based architecture.

This section of the documentation also explains how Cocoon can be extended, details the relationship between Cocoon and Avalon, and presents methods for the development of Web applications, such as session management, user authentication, and form handling.

Tutorials

The section on tutorials points to mostly external resources that can take you on a step-by-step journey through various exercises. The good thing about many of these is that they are not all just about how to generate XSP pages but cover a range of topics including information on request parameters, navigation menus, and database integration.

FAQs

The FAQs are an excellent resource that presents hints and tips on numerous aspects of Cocoon. There are sections on configuration, XSP, and XSLT, as well as lots of specific help with components.

How Tos

In some ways the How Tos area could easily overlap the tutorial and FAQ areas; however, it primarily offers advice on how to add to the documentation and contribute bug reports. There is some more programming-oriented material in here as well, but this may move over time.

Samples

Another key part of the Cocoon learning experience involves looking at the many samples. There is sample code for almost all scenarios you may come across, and this code provides an extremely valuable resource.

Examination of the sitemaps can provide real-life examples of how to achieve specific tasks such as aggregation, standalone publishing, and action handling. Not too long ago, this was really the only way of learning some of the details, but now you can work along with much of the documentation to gain a depth of practical understanding.

Code is also available as part of the samples and the Cocoon source itself that provides a practical demonstration of how to develop new components and common ways of solving a problem.

Keeping an eye on the scratch pad is another good way of seeing what is happening with Cocoon and being able to feed your knowledge. The scratch pad is the "R&D" area of Cocoon, where code that is likely to become part of the core can be made available for all to see and try out. Many parts of Cocoon started life in the scratch pad, and the code within benefits from a collaborative development environment.

Mailing Lists

At time of writing three main mailing lists are associated with Cocoon: `cocoon-users`, `cocoon-dev`, and `cocoon-docs`. Information and subscription instructions are available as part of the Cocoon documentation, but it is worth summarizing each one here.

cocoon-users

The `cocoon-users` list is the core list for any person who uses Cocoon. If you develop applications using Cocoon or have to support Cocoon, then it is very definitely worth subscribing to and participating in this list. Its purpose is to ask for and provide help with problems, report possible bugs, and offer general Cocoon community news and information. You subscribe to this list by sending a blank email to `cocoon-users-subscribe@xml.apache.org`.

This list gets a lot of traffic, and it is worth considering the next few points with the aim of reducing traffic and making sure that your question or point gets the attention it deserves:

- Do not use the list as a place to ask general XML/XSLT/Java questions. Use one of the more specific lists mentioned later.

- Always check the documentation, especially the FAQs, first. Certain questions come up time and time again, particularly from new users, and these have typically been dealt with not just in the list but in the documentation as well. Please check this resource first because that will speed things up for everyone.
- Check the archives first. Again, there is a good chance that your question has been dealt with in a previous thread. Use the list archives to check things out first.
- Keep your eye on the list. Somebody else may have recently asked the same or a similar question, and there is no point in asking it again. This is especially important if there is some problem that affects a large number of users. There is no point in having 100 people tell the whole list that the latest distribution file is corrupt (or whatever).

cocoon-dev

This list is for those who are working or want to work on Cocoon itself, as opposed to building a solution with Cocoon. Typical threads on this list revolve around bug fixes, code patches, brainstorming development issues, and so on. The same general rules as were previously discussed apply to subscribers wanting to post: always check the archives for duplicate threads and check the documentation first. You subscribe to this list by sending a blank email to `cocoon-users-subscribe@xml.apache.org`.

cocoon-docs

This email list is for those wanting to work on the Cocoon documentation. The whole purpose of this list is to discuss documentation matters, and therefore there is no point in sending these messages to the `users` or `dev` lists. You subscribe to this list by sending a blank email to `cocoon-docs-subscribe@xml.apache.org`.

List Archives

Various sites on the Web maintain archives of all the previous lists. These archives are referenced in the project documentation; however, the two most useful are the Aims group (`http://marc.theaimsgroup.com`) and mail-archive.com (`http://www.mail-archive.com`) because they offer comprehensive search capabilities. If you have a problem or want to know how to do something, there is a very good chance that the subject will have been discussed already; therefore, searching the archives really is a prerequisite before posting a query.

Related Lists

There are other email lists that those who are using and developing with Cocoon may find useful. For starters, there is the `cocoon-cvs` list. (Send a blank email to `cocoon-cvs-subscribe@xml.apache.org`.) This is a read-only list that sends a message anytime a CVS repository change is made.

The documentation, in both the mail list and the Cocoon Links sections, mentions several resources such as lists, newsgroups, and online help for matters such as XML/XSLT, Java, servlet engine help, and the other Apache XML projects.

Third-Party Resources

The Cocoon Links section of the Cocoon documentation provides links to numerous resources. These include tips, books, training, Cocoon-related sites, Cocoon-based projects, and background resources.

Key tutorial Web sites include `cocooncenter.de` and `galatea.com` (run by one of this book's authors), which both provide numerous articles and help documentation.

Another very useful part of this section of the documentation is the set of links under Related Topics. Because Cocoon relies on so many other standard technologies, there are lots of links to Web sites, mail lists, and newsgroups on XML, XSLT, and DTD/Schema support. This material is very important, because much of a developer's ability to produce a well-designed and well-implemented solution using Cocoon comes down to her understanding of these subjects. The more background knowledge one can have in this, the better.

The rest of the Apache site, especially the XML-related projects (`http://xml.apache.org`) and the Java-related projects (`http://jakarta.apache.org`), also provide important resources, especially to a developer working on Cocoon itself. The Avalon and xml-commons subprojects are two of the many important areas that are closely related to Cocoon.

Contributing

One of the best ways of making sure Cocoon has the right resources for you as a developer is to get involved with contributing to the Cocoon project. You can do this in various ways, such as these:

- *Practicing advocacy.* The simplest way of contributing to the project is to advocate Cocoon among the larger development community. Tell people about it and get them interested!
- *Responding to queries on the mail lists.* If you have solved a problem or want to help solve a problem that you see on a list, it normally does not take much effort to put the information into an email and move the issue toward a conclusion. This adds to the

overall knowledge base and, in all the best holistic fashions, puts something back into the project. After all, if you are asking questions, someone has to volunteer a little of his time to lead you to the answers.

- *Contributing links.* If you have found a resource that really helps you with your Cocoon development experience and it is not already mentioned, follow the instructions in the documentation and add that resource to the growing list.
- *Adding to the documentation.* This is a fine way to move the project along because this is the one area in which almost anyone can help. There are always more How Tos, FAQs, and so on. Perhaps you can contribute a little more. One of the authors of this book contributed an "idiots guide" tutorial and has had lots of positive feedback from other users who have benefited.
- *Testing.* Some parts of the Cocoon codebase are quite new or have recently changed. Although the code will have had a certain level of testing applied to it, it may be that your use of that code in your application is the most challenging real-world environment it has been used in. The code may not operate in the way you expect. If so, why not fix the issue and send in the fixes as a patch (via Bugzilla), or at the very least let the development team know of your experiences.
- *Committing code.* If you have fixed a bug or developed a new feature, please commit it to the project. The instructions for doing this are in the Contributing section of the documentation. Committing code really does add to the collaborative effort of an open source project like Cocoon.

However you decide to contribute to Cocoon, you can be sure that your contribution is appreciated, and the more involved you get the more reward you see!

Summary

This chapter has provided an overview of the Cocoon documentation and other material that furnish the Cocoon user with a wealth of resources to support their development of solutions using Cocoon. It has also highlighted the opportunities for becoming involved in the Cocoon project and the ways of contributing to the advancement of the software.

PART VI

Appendices

APPENDIX A

XSP Commands

XSP is Cocoon's dynamic template language. XSP, which stands for eXtensible Server Pages, is one of the core technologies included with Cocoon. XSP provides a way to do dynamic templating in Cocoon, and it is normally used to implement the front-end display of a Web application.

XSP Imports

When you're creating XSP pages, it is important to know that certain Java packages are imported automatically for you. The import section of an XSP generated source file looks like this:

```
import java.io.File;
import java.io.IOException;
import java.io.StringReader;
//import java.net.*;
import java.util.Date;
import java.util.List;
import java.util.Stack;

//import org.w3c.dom.*;
import org.xml.sax.InputSource;
import org.xml.sax.SAXException;
import org.xml.sax.helpers.AttributesImpl;
```

```
//import org.apache.avalon.framework.*;
import org.apache.avalon.framework.component.Component;
import org.apache.avalon.framework.component.ComponentException;
import org.apache.avalon.framework.component.ComponentManager;
import org.apache.avalon.framework.component.ComponentSelector;
import org.apache.avalon.framework.context.Context;
import org.apache.avalon.excalibur.datasource.DataSourceComponent;
//import org.apache.avalon.framework.util.*;

import org.apache.cocoon.Constants;
import org.apache.cocoon.ProcessingException;
import org.apache.cocoon.components.parser.Parser;
import org.apache.cocoon.generation.Generator;
//import org.apache.cocoon.util.*;

import org.apache.cocoon.components.language.markup.xsp.XSPGenerator;
import org.apache.cocoon.components.language.markup.xsp.XSPObjectHelper;
import org.apache.cocoon.components.language.markup.xsp.XSPRequestHelper;
import org.apache.cocoon.components.language.markup.xsp.XSPResponseHelper;
import org.apache.cocoon.components.language.markup.xsp.XSPSessionHelper;
```

All the classes in these packages are available for use automatically in XSP. You can also import any other classes you may need. XSP also automatically provides access to certain Java objects:

- **`servletContext`**—An object mapped to the `ServletContext`
- **`request`**—Mapped to `org.apache.cocoon.environment.Request`
- **`response`**—Mapped to `org.apache.cocoon.environment.Response`
- **`session`**—Mapped to the `HttpSession` object
- **`document`**—Mapped to an `org.w3c.Document` object representing the XSP page
- **`xspNodeStack`**—An instance of `java.util.Stack` used to control element nesting in XSP
- **`xspCurrentNode`**—An instance of an `org.w3c.Node` object referencing the current node
- **`xspParentNode`**—An instance of an `org.w3c.Node` object referencing the parent node of the current node
- **`xspParser`**—Mapped to a DOM parser that can be used to create and parse XML documents

Using these objects, you can access the environment parameters. The request, context, and response objects are the same as the Servlet ones used in JSP.

XSP Tag List

Following is a basic listing of the XSP tags. All of these tags can be used in an XSP stylesheet.

<xsp:page>

This is the root tag for all XSP pages. In this tag, you can declare the page language and import namespaces for logicsheets.

<xsp:structure>

This tag is a container for top-level instruction tags. For example, you would nest `<xsp:include>` inside `<xsp:structure>` tags.

<xsp:include>

This tag allows you to import other external packages in the language you are using. It is the same thing as using an `import` in Java.

<xsp:logic>

This tag is used to embed programming logic in an XSP page. Other XSP tags can be nested inside this tag.

<xsp:content>

This tag is used to embed content inside an `<xsp:logic>` tag so that you avoid having to nest `<xsp:logic>` tags. For example:

```
<ul>
    <xsp:logic>
      <![CDATA[
      for (int i=0; i<3; i++) {
      ]]>
        <li>
          <xsp:content>Some content here</xsp:content>
        </li>
      <![CDATA[
      }
      ]]>
    </xsp:logic>
  </ul>
```

<xsp:expr>

This tag outputs a programmatic expression as text. When used in another XSP tag, the `<xsp:expr>` tag contents are output as an expression. To output an `<xsp:expr>` tag as a node inside an XSP tag, you wrap it in an `<xsp:content>` element.

<xsp:element>

This tag is used to dynamically build an element when its attributes need to be determined at runtime.

<xsp:attribute>

This tag is used to provide attributes for an element whose values are not known until runtime. This tag is typically used with `<xsp:element>`.

<xsp:pi>

This tag is used to create a processing instruction. This tag requires a target attribute to specify the processing instruction's name. For example:

```
<xsp:pi target="xml-stylesheet">
  href="http://server.com/docs/stylesheet.xsl"
  type="text/xsl"
</xsp:pi>
```

<xsp:comment>

This tag is used to create XML comments. The XML comments may be ignored or removed in additional processing by Cocoon.

XSPUtil Java Class Functions

XSP provides a Java class `XSPUtil` that contains several helper functions. These include `DOM`, `HTTP`, `File`, and `String` utilities. More information on the helper functions can be found in the Cocoon Javadocs located at

```
http://xml.apache.org/cocoon/apidocs/org/apache/cocoon/
components/language/markup/xsp/XSPUtil.html
```

DOM Utilities

The DOM utilities allow the programmer to manipulate the underlying XML document represented as a `DOM` tree.

`Node cloneNode(Node node, Document factory)`

This method copies a `Node` from an XML document to the current XSP document.

`String toMarkup(Node node)`

This method outputs a `Node` as a `String`.

HTTP Utility Methods

These methods provide utility functions to URL encode and URL decode strings so that they are safe to use in a URL query string. There is also a method for replacing HTML characters with entity tags that are considered special characters in XML.

`String encodeMarkup(String string)`

This method replaces markup characters `<`, `>`, and `&` with `<`, `>`, `&`, respectively, in the given string.

`String formEncode(String text)`

This method wraps `java.net.URLEncoder.encode`.

`String formDecode(String text)`

This method wraps `java.net.URLDecoder.decode`.

File Utilities

These methods provide utilities for accessing and modifying filenames and file paths.

`String baseName(String filename)`

This method extracts the filename from a path, excluding the file extension.

`String baseName(String filename, String suffix)`

This method extracts the filename from a path, excluding the last occurrence of the file extension specified in `suffix`.

`String fileComponent(String path)`

This method extracts the filename from a path.

`String normalizedBaseName(String filename)`

This method extracts the filename from a path, excluding the file extension. Any non-alphanumeric characters are replaced by an underscore.

`String pathComponent(String path)`

This method extracts the directory path from a path.

`String relativeFilename(String filename, HttpServletRequest request, ServletContext context)`

This method builds a path for a filename relative to the request URI.

`String relativeFilename(String filename, HttpServletRequest request)`

This method builds a path for a filename relative to the request URI. This method is provided only for compatibility with older JDKs.

String Utilities

These methods provide string utilities such as checking whether a character is alphanumeric, and splitting strings based on a whitespace delimiter.

`boolean isAlphaNumeric(char c)`

This method checks `char c` to see whether it is alphanumeric. This includes A-Z, a-z, 0-9, and _ (underscore).

`String[] split(String line)`

This method splits a `String` using whitespace as the delimiter.

`String[] split(String line, String delimiter)`

This method splits a `String` using the specified delimiter.

APPENDIX B

Session Logicsheet Commands

The session logicsheet is an XSP logicsheet that wraps XML tags around the Java Servlet API class `HttpSession`.

The session logicsheet provides similar functionality to Cocoon as exists in other popular application servers. Examples of these include Apache Tomcat and the session object from Microsoft's Active Server Pages.

The session logicsheet can be used only in an XSP page, and the session namespace must first be imported before it can be used.

```
<xsp:page
  xmlns:xsp="http://apache.org/xsp"
  xmlns:xsp-session="http://apache.org/xsp/session/2.0"
  create-session="true">

</xsp:page>
```

In the preceding example, the `xsp-session` name is mapped to `http://apache.org/xsp/session/2.0`. The namespace declaration takes a `create-session` parameter. This can be set to either `true` or `false`. When this parameter is set to `true`, the existing session is retrieved, or if that doesn't exist, a new session is created. If it's set to `false`, the session will be retrieved only if it already exists.

One of the most common uses for a session object is to persist information between http requests. This is accomplished by using the <xsp-session:set-attribute> tag to set the session variable and <xsp-session:get-attribute> to retrieve the session variable. These tags take a name attribute that specifies the variable name. An example of this would be as follows:

```
<xsp-session:set-attribute name="username">Joe User</xsp-session:set-attribute>
```

The preceding example sets a session variable named username with the value of `Joe User`.

Following is an example of using the session logicsheet to set and get variables:

```
<xsp:page
  xmlns:xsp="http://apache.org/xsp"
  xmlns:xsp-session="http://apache.org/xsp/session/2.0"
  create-session="true">

  <page>
    <xsp-session:set-attribute name="username">Joe User
     </xsp-session:set-attribute>
    <username>
        <xsp-session:get-attribute name="username"/>
    </username>
  </page>
</xsp:page>
```

The preceding example sets a session variable named `username` and then immediately prints that value in a `username` node.

Some <xsp-session> tags can be output as an XML node, or an object instead of text. This is accomplished by adding the `as` attribute. The `as` attribute can have the value of `xml` and `object` in most cases.

```
<xsp-session:get-attribute as="xml" name="username"/>
```

This would evaluate to the following:

```
<xsp-session:attribute>Joe User</xsp-session:attribute>
```

The `as` attribute options for each function are discussed later in the function listing.

Returning output as an XML node can be useful when a tag returns several values, and these values need to be available for further processing.

The session object can also be accessed directly from Java because it is a thin wrapper over the Java `HttpSession` object. For example:

```
<xsp:page
  xmlns:xsp="http://apache.org/xsp"
  xmlns:xsp-session="http://apache.org/xsp/session/2.0"
  create-session="true">

<page>
<xsp:logic>session.setAttribute("username", "Joe User");</xsp:logic>
<username>
<xsp:expr>session.getAttribute("username")</xsp:expr>
</username>
</page>

</xsp:page>
```

Session Logicsheet Functions

Following is a list of all the supported XSP session logicsheet functions.

xsp-session:get-attribute

This function retrieves a variable from the session. The function takes a `name` parameter, an optional `as` parameter, and a default parameter. This function can be output as an XML node, a string, or an object. If the `as` parameter is set to `xml`, the return value will be wrapped in an XML node. For example:

```
<xsp-session:get-attribute name="testvalue" as="xml"/>
```

would return

```
<xsp-session:attribute>Test</xsp-session:attribute>
```

The item returned from the session is a Java object. The object is output by calling its `toString` method. The object may also be accessed directly by specifying `as="object"` as an attribute. For example:

```
<xsp-session:get-attribute default="none" name="testvalue" as="object"/>
```

would return

```
<xsp:expr>
XSPSessionHelper.getSessionAttribute(session,"testvalue","none")
</xsp:expr>
```

This example shows how you can retrieve a named value from the session as an object, and supply a default value if one is needed.

xsp-session:get-attribute-names

This function returns all the attribute names stored in the session. The function can take an optional `as` parameter to specify whether the output should be as XML or a Java array. The default is as an array.

```
<xsp-session:get-attribute-names as="xml"/>
```

would return

```
<xsp-session:attribute-names>
<xsp-session:attribute-name>attribute 1</xsp-session:attribute-name>
</xsp-session:attribute-names>
```

Using `as="array"` would output a comma-separated list of strings. You could also access the array in Java code and manipulate it.

xsp-session:get-creation-time

This function returns the session's creation time. The `as` attribute for this element can have three values: `long`, `string`, and `xml`. If the `as` attribute is specified as `long`, the element returns a Java long that represents a date value. If the `as` attribute is specified as `string`, the literal date time string is returned. If `xml` is specified, an XML node is returned containing the Java long representation. For example:

```
<xsp-session:get-creation-time as="string"/>
```

would return

```
Wed Jun 12 15:57:06 EDT 2002
```

and

```
<xsp-session:get-creation-time as="xml"/>
```

would return

```
<xsp-session:creation-time>Wed Jul 31 22:24:50 EDT 2002
</xsp-session:creation-time>
```

xsp-session:get-id

This function returns the session ID. The session ID is given by the Servlet container. This function can take an optional as parameter to specify the output type. The as parameter can have the value xml. For example:

```
<xsp-session:get-id/>
```

would return

```
63BEF57303FFF982EB0515D1334D75B5
```

and

```
<xsp-session:get-id as="xml"/>
```

would return

```
<xsp-session:id>63BEF57303FFF982EB0515D1334D75B5</xsp-session:id>
```

xsp-session:get-last-accessed-time

This function returns the last time the session was accessed. This function can take an optional as parameter to determine the output type. The as parameter can have the value xml or long. For example:

```
<xsp-session:get-last-accessed-time as="xml"/>
```

would return

```
<xsp-session:last-accessed-time>Wed Jul 31 22:24:50 EDT 2002
</xsp-session:last-accessed-time>
```

and

```
<xsp-session:get-last-accessed-time/>
```

would return

```
1028168690178
```

If the as parameter is set to long, the Java long representation of the time is returned.

xsp-session:get-max-inactive-interval

This function returns the amount of time in seconds that the server will keep a session alive. Every time there is a new request, the timer is reset. This function can take an optional as parameter. If the as parameter is set to xml, an XML node will be output. For example:

```
<xsp-session:get-max-inactive-interval/>
```

would return

```
500
```

and

```
<xsp-session:get-max-inactive-interval as="xml"/>
```

would return

```
<xsp-session:max-inactive-interval>500
</xsp-session:max-inactive-interval>
```

The as parameter can also be set to int. This will return a Java int representing the inactive time.

xsp-session:invalidate

This function invalidates the current session and destroys any stored values.

xsp-session:is-new

This function allows developers to determine whether the session has just been created. This function can take an optional as parameter that can have the value of xml or boolean. If the as parameter has the value of xml, an XML node is returned. Setting the as parameter to boolean will return the Boolean value. For example:

```
<xsp-session:is-new as="xml"/>
```

would return

```
<xsp-session:is-new>true</xsp-session:is-new>
```

xsp-session:remove-attribute

This function removes the named value from the session. This function takes a name parameter, which is the name of the object to remove from the session. For example:

```
<xsp-session:remove-attribute name="username"/>
```

xsp-session:set-attribute

This function stores a named attribute in the session. This function takes a `name` parameter that specifies the name that will be stored in the session. For example:

```
<xsp-session:set-attribute name="username">Joe User
</xsp-session:set-attribute>
```

xsp-session:set-max-inactive-interval

This function sets the time in seconds that a session can remain active between requests. This function takes an interval parameter that is a numeric value that represents the time in seconds. The interval parameter can be provided either as an attribute or as a child node `<xsp-session:interval>`. For example:

```
<xsp-session:set-max-inactive-interval interval="1200"/>
```

APPENDIX C

Request Logicsheet Commands

The Request logicsheet provides access in XSP to all the properties of the HTTP request object.

The following entry is used within `cocoon.xconf` to declare the Request logicsheet as a built-in logicsheet:

```
<builtin-logicsheet>
  <parameter name="prefix" value="xsp-request "/>
  <parameter name="uri"
➥value="http://apache.org/xsp/request/2.0"/>
  <parameter name="href"
    value="resource://org/apache/cocoon/components/
➥language/markup/xsp/java/request.xsl"/>
</builtin-logicsheet>
```

The following code is required in any XSP file that needs to use the Cookie logicsheet:

```
<xsp:page language="java"
  xmlns:xsp="http://apache.org/xsp"
  xmlns:xsp-request="http://apache.org/xsp/request/2.0"
...>
```

Elements

<xsp-request:get-uri>

`<xsp-request:get-uri>` returns the request URI. It can send this back as a string or wrapped within an XML element (`<xsp-request:uri>`). The `as` attribute determines how the response will be returned.

Attributes

Name	Value	Description
as	"string" | "xml"	Indicates how the response is to be returned. The default is "string".

Example

Return the request URI as a string:

```
<xsp-request:get-uri/>
```

<xsp-request:get-sitemap-uri>

`<xsp-request:get-sitemap-uri>` returns the URI of the sitemap that is being used to match and serve the current request. The URI is relative to either the Web application root (in the case of the root sitemap) or the mounting sitemap URI (in the case of a mounted sub-sitemap). The response can be returned as a string or XML, based on the `as` attribute.

Attributes

Name	Value	Description
as	"string" | "xml"	Indicates how the response is to be returned. The default is "string".

Example

Return the sitemap URI, wrapped with an XML element:

```
<xsp-request:get-sitemap-uri as="xml"/>
```

<xsp-request:get-scheme>

`<xsp-request:get-scheme>` returns the name of the scheme used to make the request. This would usually equate to the protocol identifier, such as HTTP or FTP.

Attributes

Name	Value	Description
as	"string" | "xml"	Indicates how the response is to be returned. The default is "string".

Example

Return the scheme as a string:

```
<xsp-request:get-scheme as="string"/>
```

<xsp-request:get-character-encoding>

`<xsp-request:get-character-encoding>` returns the type of character encoding used in this request, assuming that one has been specified.

Attributes

Name	Value	Description
as	"string" | "xml"	Indicates how the response is to be returned. The default is "string".

Example

Return the character encoding as a string:

```
<xsp-request:get-character-encoding as="string"/>
```

<xsp-request:get-content-length>

`<xsp-request:get-content-length>` returns the length of the request body in bytes. This would typically contain a positive value only if a post method has been used.

Attributes

Name	Value	Description
as	"string" | "xml"	Indicates how the response is to be returned. The default is "string".

Example

Return the content length, wrapped in an XML element:

```
<xsp-request:get-content-length as="xml"/>
```

<xsp-request:get-content-type>

`<xsp-request:get-content-type>` returns the MIME type of the request.

Attributes

Name	Value	Description
as	"string" | "xml"	Indicates how the response is to be returned. The default is "string".

Example

Return the content MIME type as a string:

```
<xsp-request:get-content-type/>
```

<xsp-request:get-locale>

`<xsp-request:get-locale>` returns the preferred locale that the client can accept content in. This is based on the contents of the Accept-Language header in the HTTP request. This can be returned as a string, can be wrapped in an XML element, or can be returned as an object. If the client does not provide or accept the Accept-Language HTTP header, the default locale for the server is returned.

Attributes

Name	Value	Description
as	"string" | "xml" | "object"	Indicates how the response is to be returned. The default is "string".

Example

Return the locale as an object:

```
<xsp-request:get-locale as="object"/>
```

<xsp-request:get-locales>

`<xsp-request:get-locales>` returns a list of locales that are acceptable to the client. The order of this list is decreasing, with the most preferred locale first. This list is based on the contents of the Accept-Language HTTP header. As with `<xsp-request:get-locale>`, this command will return the server information if the client does not accept or pass anything in the Accept-Language HTTP header. The list is returned either as an array of `Locale` objects or as an XML list.

Attributes

Name	Value	Description
`as`	`"array"` | `"xml"`	Indicates how the response is to be returned. The default is `"xml"`.

Example

Return the locales, wrapped in an XML list:

```
<xsp-request:get-locales as="xml"/>
```

<xsp-request:get-parameter>

`<xsp-request:get-parameter>` returns the contents of a parameter. The parameter name is specified in the `name` attribute. A default value to use if the parameter is null or does not exist can be specified using the `default` attribute. The response can be returned as a string or wrapped in an XML element.

Attributes

Name	Value	Description
`name`	*`text`*	Name of the parameter to return.
`default`	*`text`*	Optional value to use if the parameter is null or not found.
`as`	`"string"` | `"xml"`	Indicates how the response is to be returned. The default is `"string"`.

Example

Return the value, as a string, of the `"country"` parameter, using the value `"United Kingdom"` if the parameter does not exist:

```
<xsp-request:get-parameter name="country" default="United Kingdom" as="string"/>
```

<xsp-request:get-parameter-values>

`<xsp-request:get-parameter-values>` returns the values of all the parameters in the request.

Attributes

Name	Value	Description
as	"array" | "xml"	Indicates how the response is to be returned. The default is "xml".

Example

Return the parameter values as an array:

```
<xsp-request:get-parameter-values as="array"/>
```

<xsp-request:get-parameter-names>

`<xsp-request:get-parameter-names>` returns the names of all the parameters in the request.

Attributes

Name	Value	Description
as	"array" | "xml"	Indicates how the response is to be returned. The default is "xml".

Example

Return the parameter names as an array:

```
<xsp-request:get-parameter-names as="array"/>
```

<xsp-request:get-header>

`<xsp-request:get-header>` returns the value of a specified request header.

Attributes

Name	Value	Description
name	*text*	Name of the header to return.
as	"string" | "xml"	Indicates how the response is to be returned. The default is "string".

Example

Return the value of the "accept" header wrapped in an XML element:

```
<xsp-request:get-header name="accept" as="xml"/>
```

<xsp-request:get-header-names>

`<xsp-request:get-header-names>` returns the names of all the headers in the request.

Attributes

Name	Value	Description
`as`	`"array" | "xml"`	Indicates how the response is to be returned. The default is "xml".

Example

Return all the headers as an array:

```
<xsp:expr>
  String.valueOf(<xsp-request:get-header-names as="array"/>)
</xsp:expr>
```

<xsp-request:get-headers>

`<xsp-request:get-headers>` returns all the header settings for a specified HTTP header as an array or as an XML element list.

Attributes

Name	Value	Description
`name`	*text*	Name of the header to return.
`as`	`"array" | "xml"`	Indicates how the response is to be returned. The default is "xml".

Example

Return the value of the "accept" header wrapped in an XML element:

```
<xsp-request:get-headers name="accept" as="xml"/>
```

<xsp-request:get-attribute>

`<xsp-request:get-attribute>` returns the value of an attribute.

Attributes

Name	Value	Description
`name`	*`text`*	Name of the attribute to return.
`as`	`"object"` | `"string"` | `"xml"`	Indicates how the response is to be returned. The default is `"object"`.

Example

Return the value of the `"location"` attribute wrapped in an XML element:

```
<xsp-request:get-attribute name="location" as="xml"/>
```

<xsp-request:set-attribute>

`<xsp-request:set-attribute>` allows the setting of an attribute in the request.

Attributes

Name	Value	Description
`name`	*`text`*	Name of the attribute to set.
`content`	*`text`*	Content to use as the value of the attribute.

Example

Set the value of the `"location"` attribute to `"Royston Vasey"`:

```
<xsp-request:set-attribute name="location" content="Royston Vasey"/>
```

<xsp-request:get-attribute-names>

`<xsp-request:get-attribute-names>` gets a list of the names of all the attributes in the request.

Attributes

Name	Value	Description
`as`	`"array"` | `"xml"`	Indicates how the response is to be returned. The default is `"xml"`.

Example

Return the value of all the attribute names as an array:

```
<xsp:expr>
  String.valueOf(<xsp-request:get-attribute-names as="array"/>)
</xsp:expr>
```

<xsp-request:remove-attribute>

`<xsp-request:remove-attribute>` removes an attribute from the request.

Attributes

Name	Value	Description
`name`	*`text`*	Name of the attribute to remove.

Example

Remove the `"location"` attribute:

```
<xsp-request:remove-attribute name="location"/>
```

<xsp-request:get-requested-url>

`<xsp-request:get-requested-url>` returns the full URL of the request.

Attributes

Name	Value	Description
`as`	`"string"` | `"xml"`	Indicates how the response is to be returned. The default is `"string"`.

Example

Return the requested URL:

```
<xsp-request:get-requested-url/>
```

<xsp-request:get-remote-address>

`<xsp-request:get-remote-address>` returns the IP address of the requesting client.

Attributes

Name	Value	Description
as	"string" | "xml"	Indicates how the response is to be returned. The default is "string".

Example

Return the IP address of the requesting client:

```
<xsp-request:get-remote-address/>
```

<xsp-request:get-remote-user>

`<xsp-request:get-remote-user>` returns the login name of the requesting user if the user has been authenticated.

Attributes

Name	Value	Description
as	"string" | "xml"	Indicates how the response is to be returned. The default is "string".

Example

Return the remote user, wrapped in an XML element:

```
<xsp-request:get-remote-user as="xml"/>
```

<xsp-request:get-context-path>

`<xsp-request:get-context-path>` returns the part of the URL that represents the context. For example, a request to `http://localhost/cocoon/xsp/login` would return `/cocoon`.

Attributes

Name	Value	Description
as	"string" | "xml"	Indicates how the response is to be returned. The default is "string".

Example

Return the context path as a string:

```
<xsp-request:get-context-path/>
```

<xsp-request:get-path-info>

`<xsp-request:get-path-info>` returns any extra path information that was on the request path.

Attributes

Name	Value	Description
as	"string" | "xml"	Indicates how the response is to be returned. The default is "string".

Example

Return extra path information:

```
<xsp-request:get-path-info/>
```

<xsp-request:get-server-name>

`<xsp-request:get-server-name>` returns the hostname of the server from the URL.

Attributes

Name	Value	Description
as	"string" | "xml"	Indicates how the response is to be returned. The default is "string".

Example

Return the server hostname wrapped in an XML element:

```
<xsp-request:get-server-name as="xml"/>
```

<xsp-request:get-server-port>

`<xsp-request:get-server-port>` returns the server port number (for example, 80 or 8080) that the request was made to.

Attributes

Name	Value	Description
as	"string" | "xml"	Indicates how the response is to be returned. The default is "string".

Example

Return the server IP port as a string:

```
<xsp-request:get-server-port as="string"/>
```

<xsp-request:get-method>

`<xsp-request:get-method>` returns the HTTP request method used. This would normally be `GET`, `POST`, or `PUT`.

Attributes

Name	Value	Description
as	"string" | "xml"	Indicates how the response is to be returned. The default is "string".

Example

Return the request method:

```
<xsp-request:get-method as="string"/>
```

<xsp-request:get-query-string>

`<xsp-request:get-query-string>` returns the query string that is contained in the URL after the path information (everything after the "?").

Attributes

Name	Value	Description
as	"string" | "xml"	Indicates how the response is to be returned. The default is "string".

Example

Return the request query string wrapped in an XML element:

```
<xsp-request:get-query-string as="xml"/>
```

<xsp-request:get-protocol>

`<xsp-request:get-protocol>` returns the name and version number of the protocol being used by the request. This is returned in the form of *`protocol/major_version.minor_version`*. Therefore, an HTTP 1.1 request would manifest the return string of `HTTP/1.1`.

Attributes

Name	Value	Description
as	"string" | "xml"	Indicates how the response is to be returned. The default is "string".

Example

Return the request protocol:

```
<xsp-request:get-protocol as="string"/>
```

<xsp-request:get-remote-host>

`<xsp-request:get-remote-host>` returns the hostname of the calling client.

Attributes

Name	Value	Description
as	"string" | "xml"	Indicates how the response is to be returned. The default is "string".

Example

Return the request method:

```
<xsp-request:get-remote-host as="string"/>
```

<xsp-request:is-secure>

<xsp-request:is-secure> returns "true" or "false" depending on whether the request was made through a secure protocol such as HTTPS.

Attributes

Name	Value	Description
as	"boolean" | "string" | "xml"	Indicates how the response is to be returned. The default is "boolean".

Example

Return a flag indicating whether the request is secure:

```
<xsp-request:is-secure as="string"/>
```

<xsp-request:get-servlet-path>

<xsp-request:get-servlet-path> returns the part of the request URL that calls the servlet. For example, querying this value on the URL http://localhost:8080/cocoon/xsp/request will return /xsp/request.

Attributes

Name	Value	Description
as	"string" | "xml"	Indicates how the response is to be returned. The default is "string".

Example

Get the servlet path:

```
<xsp-request:get-servlet-path as="string"/>
```

<xsp-request:get-user-principal>

<xsp-request:get-user-principal> returns the login of the user making the request if the user has been authenticated.

Attributes

Name	Value	Description
as	"string" | | "xml"	Indicates how the response is to be returned. The default is "string".

Example

Get the user login information:

```
<xsp-request:get-user-principal as="string"/>
```

<xsp-request:get-auth-type>

<xsp-request:get-auth-type> returns the name of the authentication scheme (if any) used to secure the request.

Attributes

Name	Value	Description
as	"string" | | "xml"	Indicates how the response is to be returned. The default is "string".

Example

Get the authentication scheme, wrapping it in an XML element:

```
<xsp-request:get-auth-type as="xml"/>
```

<xsp-request:is-user-in-role>

<xsp-request:is-user-in-role> indicates whether the user is in the specified role.

Attributes

Name	Value	Description
role	*text*	Name of the role.
as	"boolean" | "string" | | "xml"	Indicates how the response is to be returned. The default is "boolean".

Example

Establish whether the user is in the "admin" role:

```
<xsp-request:is-user-in-role role="admin"/>
```

<xsp-request:get-requested-session-id>

`<xsp-request:get-requested-session-id>` returns the session identifier.

Attributes

Name	Value	Description
as	"string" | | "xml"	Indicates how the response is to be returned. The default is "string".

Example

Get the session identifier:

```
<xsp-request:get-requested-session-id as="string"/>
```

APPENDIX D

Response Logicsheet Commands

The Response logicsheet that is shipped with Cocoon allows the developer to manipulate the response stream of the application. The Response logicsheet is provided as a wrapper around the Java Servlet `HttpServletResponse` class. As such, the Response logicsheet mirrors the Java Servlet functionality and provides an interface that will be familiar to programmers who have experience with other popular Web application environments such as JSP or Microsoft's ASP.

The Response logicsheet is an XSP page, and as such can be used only in an XSP page. Before the logicsheet can be used, the `xsp:response` namespace must be declared. This is done in the `xsp:page` declaration as shown here:

```
<xsp:page
    xmlns:xsp="http://apache.org/xsp"
    xmlns:xsp-response="http://apache.org/xsp/response/
    ➥2.0"
>
</xsp:page>
```

After this is done, the `xsp:response` functions are available for use in the XSP page.

The Response logicsheet has functions for sending cookies to the calling Web browser, adding headers to the response stream, encoding URLs with the current session ID, setting the character encoding scheme, and setting the locale.

Following is a list of all the `xsp-response` functions.

xsp-response:get-character-encoding

This function returns a string representing the name of the current character set in the MIME body of the response. For example, English is represented in the ISO-8859-1 or Latin 1 character set. English can also be represented as US-ASCII. Here's a sample usage of this function:

```
<xsp-response:get-character-encoding/>
```

This function can take an optional `as` parameter. The value of this parameter can be either `string` or `xml`. If it's set to `string`, the function returns a string representation of the character set. If it's set to `xml`, as in

```
<xsp-response:get-character-encoding as="xml"/>
```

the function will return an XML node with the string value contained in it. For example, the preceding example would return this:

```
<xsp-response:get-character-encoding>
    ISO-8859-1
</xsp-response:get-character-encoding>
```

xsp-response:get-locale

This function allows the developer to retrieve the current locale from the browser. By default, the function will return the language and country codes. The function can take an optional `as` parameter. If the `as` parameter is supplied, the function returns an XML fragment containing the information. For example

```
<xsp-response:get-locale/>
```

would return

```
en_US
```

and

```
<xsp-response:get-locale as="xml"/>
```

would return

```
<xsp-response:locale>
<xsp-response:language>en</xsp-response:language>
<xsp-response:country>US</xsp-response:country>
```

```
<xsp-response:variant/>
</xsp-response:locale>
```

xsp-response:set-locale

This function allows the developer to set the current `Locale` of the response. Values can be any of the `Locale` constants located in `java.util.Locale`. For example

```
<xsp-response:set-locale><xsp:expr>java.util.Locale.ITALY</xsp:expr>
➥</xsp-response:set-locale>
```

This example would set the current `Locale` to `Italy`.

xsp-response:add-cookie

This function allows the developer to send a cookie to the calling browser. The function takes a Java `org.apache.cocoon.environment.http.HttpCookie` object and then adds this to the response stream. For example

```
<xsp:logic>org.apache.cocoon.environment.http.HttpCookie c = new
➥org.apache.cocoon.environment.http.HttpCookie
➥("testcookie","testvalue");</xsp:logic>

<xsp-response:add-cookie><xsp:expr>c</xsp:expr></xsp-response:add-cookie>
```

The Apache Cocoon `HttpCookie` class wraps the Java Servlet `Cookie` class. For more information on the Java `Cookie` class, see the Javadocs for your version of the Java Servlet classes.

xsp-response:add-date-header

This function allows the developer to set a date value to a named header. This function allows a header to have multiple values. If the named header already exists, a new header is added to the collection, but not replacing the old one. The function takes a `name` parameter, a `date` parameter, and an optional `format` parameter. The `format` parameter can be any valid `java.text.DateFormat` format. This function uses the `XSPResponseHelper` java class to add the headers to the response object. The `date` parameter can be specified as an attribute of the XSP tag, or as an `xsp-response:date` sub-element. The `format` parameter can be specified as an attribute of the XSP tag, or as an `xsp-response:format` sub-element. If the `date` parameter is supplied as an attribute, it is assumed to be a string constant. The `format` parameter needs to be supplied if the date value is a string constant. You will also need to catch any `java.text.ParseException` exceptions that may be thrown. For example

```
<xsp:logic>try{</xsp:logic>
<xsp-response:add-date-header name="testdate"
```

```
    date="01.02.2002" format="dd.MM.yyyy"/>
<xsp:logic>}catch(Exception e){//do something here};</xsp:logic>
```

xsp-response:add-header

This function allows the developer to set a value for a named header in the response header collection. If the named header already exists, a new header is added to the collection, but not replacing the old value. This allows headers to have multiple values. This function takes a `name` parameter and a `value` parameter. The `value` parameter can be specified as an attribute or as an `xsp-response:value` child element. For example

```
<xsp-response:add-header name="testheader" value="test"/>
```

and

```
<xsp-response:add-header name="testheader">
    <xsp-response:value>test</xsp-response:value>
</xsp-response:add-header>
```

are equivalent.

xsp-response:add-int-header

This function allows the developer to set a value as an Integer for a named header in the response header collection. If the named header already exists, a new header is added to the collection, but not replacing the old value. This allows headers to have multiple values. This function takes a `name` parameter and a `value` parameter. The `value` parameter can be specified as an attribute or as an `xsp-response:value` child element. For example

```
<xsp-response:add-int-header name="testheader" value="1000"/>
```

and

```
<xsp-response:add-int-header name="testheader">
    <xsp-response:value>1000</xsp-response:value>
</xsp-response:add-int-header>
```

are equivalent.

xsp-response:contains-header

This function searches the header collection for the supplied header name in the required `name` parameter. This function can take the optional parameter `as`. The `as` parameter can be `boolean`, `string`, or `xml`. If the `as` parameter is set to `string`, the function returns a string representation of the Boolean return value. For example

```
<xsp-response:contains-header name="NoHeader"/>
```

would return the string value `false`.

If the `as` parameter is set to `xml`, an XML node is returned. For example

```
<xsp-response:contains-header name="NoHeader" as="xml"/>
```

would return

```
<xsp-response:contains-header>
<xsp:expr>
    response.containsHeader(String.valueOf("NoHeader"))
</xsp:expr>
</xsp-response:contains-header>
```

which would further evaluate to

```
<xsp-response:contains-header>false</xsp-response:contains-header>
```

If the `as` parameter is set to `boolean`, an `xsp:expr` is returned to get the Boolean value. For example

```
<xsp-response:contains-header name="NoHeader" as="boolean"/>
```

would return

```
<xsp:expr>
    response.containsHeader(String.valueOf("NoHeader"))
</xsp:expr>
```

xsp-response:encode-url

This function allows the developer to encode a URL with the current session ID. This is useful for applications that have to maintain state without using cookies. This function takes a required `url` parameter that specifies the URL to encode. This parameter can be supplied as an attribute or as a subnode. For example

```
<xsp-response:encode-url url="http://www.w3.org"/>
```

and

```
<xsp-response:encode-url>
    <xsp-response:url>http://www.w3.org</xsp-response:url>
</xsp-response:encode-url>
```

are equivalent.

The function can also take an optional as parameter. The as parameter can have the value string or xml. If the value is string, the encoded URL is returned as a string. If the parameter value is xml, an xsp:expr is returned. For example

```
<xsp-response:encode-url url="http://www.w3.org" as="xml"/>
```

would return

```
<xsp-response:encode-url>
<xsp:expr>response.encodeURL(String.valueOf("http://www.w3.org"))</xsp:expr>
</xsp-response:encode-url>
```

xsp-response:set-date-header

At the time of writing, this function was not working properly.

This function allows the developer to set a date value to a named header. If the header already exists, the value is replaced by the new one. The function takes a name parameter, a date parameter, and an optional format parameter. The format parameter can be any valid java.text.DateFormat format. This function uses the XSPResponseHelper java class to add the headers to the response object. The date parameter can be specified as an attribute of the XSP tag, or as an xsp-response:date sub-element. The format parameter can be specified as an attribute of the XSP tag, or as an xsp-response:format sub-element. If the date parameter is supplied as an attribute, it is assumed to be a string constant. The format parameter needs to be supplied if the date value is a string constant. For example

```
<xsp-response:set-date-header name="testdate"
➥date="01.02.2002" format="dd.MM.yyyy"/>
```

xsp-response:set-header

This function allows the developer to set a value for a named header in the response header collection. If the named header already exists, the value is replaced by the new one. This function takes a name parameter and a value parameter. The value parameter can be specified as an attribute or as the text in the element. For example

```
<xsp-response:set-header name="testheader" value="test"/>
```

and

```
<xsp-response:set-header name="testheader">test</xsp-response:set-header>
```

are equivalent.

xsp-response:set-int-header

This function allows the developer to set a value as an Integer for a named header in the response header collection. If the named header already exists, the value is replaced by the new one. This function takes a `name` parameter and a `value` parameter. The `value` parameter can be specified as an attribute or as the text in the element. For example

```
<xsp-response:set-int-header name="testheader" value="1000"/>
```

and

```
<xsp-response:set-int-header name="testheader">1000
➥</xsp-response:set-int-header>
```

are equivalent.

APPENDIX E
ESQL Logicsheet Commands

The ESQL logicsheet provides an easy way for developers to include database support in their applications. The ESQL logicsheet allows developers to issue SQL queries to a database, and receive the results back as XML for processing in Cocoon.

The ESQL logicsheet is implemented as a wrapper around Java's JDBC. Because of this, the ESQL logicsheet can support any of the SQL syntax that the JDBC driver can support. ESQL supports SQL queries, parameterized SQL queries, stored procedures, and, if the JDBC driver supports it, multiple result sets from one statement.

To use the ESQL logicsheet, you must first see whether it has been enabled in the `cocoon.xconf` file. Open this file and check for this:

```
<!-- The ESQL logicsheet is an XSP logicsheet that
➥performs sql queries and serializes
 their results as XML. This allows you to work with data
➥from a wide variety of
different sources when using Apache Cocoon. -->

<builtin-logicsheet>
<parameter name="prefix" value="esql"/>
       <parameter name="uri"
➥value="http://apache.org/cocoon/SQL/v2"/>
       <parameter name="href"
```

```
➥value="resource://org/apache/cocoon/components/
        language/markup/xsp/Java/esql.xsl"/>
</builtin-logicsheet>
```

This tells Cocoon to load the ESQL logicsheet and have it available for use in applications. The prebuilt installation of Cocoon usually comes with ESQL enabled, but it's a good idea to check just to be sure.

To use the ESQL logicsheet in your application, you must first declare the namespace in the `xsp:page` tag as in the following example:

```
<xsp:page
      language="Java"
      xmlns:xsp="http://apache.org/xsp"
      xmlns:esql="http://apache.org/cocoon/SQL/v2"
>
</xsp:page>
```

ESQL Datasources

Before you can start making SQL queries, you must have a data source set up in your `cocoon.xconf` file to query against.

Cocoon ships with a sample data source in the default `cocoon.xconf` file:

```
<!-- Datasources: -->
  <datasources>
    <jdbc logger="core.datasources.personnel" name="personnel">
      <!--
      If you have an Oracle database, and are using the
      pool-controller below, you should add the attribute
      "oradb" and set it to true.

      <pool-controller min="5" max="10" oradb="true"/>

      That way the test to see if the server has disconnected
      the JdbcConnection will function properly.
      -->
      <pool-controller max="10" min="5"/>
      <!--
```

```
        If you need to ensure an autocommit is set to true or
    false, then create the "auto-commit" element below.

    <auto-commit>false</auto-commit>

    The default is true.
    -->
    <dburl>jdbc:hsqldb:hsql://localhost:9002</dburl>
    <user>sa</user>
    <password/>
  </jdbc>
</datasources>
```

The sample data source setup in the `cocoon.xconf` file uses Hypersonic SQL as the database. Hypersonic is an open source lightweight database server implemented in Java. Cocoon ships with Hypersonic, but if you want to get the source code, you can download a copy of Hypersonic from `http://hsqldb.sourceforge.net/index.html`. If you want to use another database server, you need to specify the JDBC URL for your server in the `dburl` section.

In the preceding example, a JDBC data source is created with the name `personnel`. This data source has a connection pool, specified by the pool-controller tag, which will have between 5 and 10 connections open. The `auto-commit` tag specifies that the connection will auto-commit transactions. The data source tag also includes the `dburl` tag that specifies the JDBC URL, and a `user` and `password` tag to specify the login credentials to the database.

ESQL Syntax

Now that the data source has been set up, lets look at a sample ESQL query. Cocoon ships with a simple ESQL sample in the `/docs/samples/xsp` directory. Open the file `esql.xsp` and you should see the following:

```
<?xml version="1.0" encoding="ISO-8859-1"?>

<xsp:page language="Java"
          xmlns:xsp="http://apache.org/xsp"
          xmlns:esql="http://apache.org/cocoon/SQL/v2">

  <page>
   <title>A Database Driven XSP Page</title>
```

```
    <content>

    <esql:connection>
      <esql:pool>personnel</esql:pool>
      <esql:execute-query>
        <esql:query>select * from department</esql:query>
        <esql:results>
          <esql:row-results>
            <para><esql:get-string column="name"/></para>
            <esql:get-columns/>
          </esql:row-results>
        </esql:results>
      </esql:execute-query>
    </esql:connection>

    </content>
  </page>
</xsp:page>
```

In this ESQL example, a basic query is executed and the results are placed in `<para>` tags for further processing by Cocoon.

ESQL tags are nested in a hierarchy of operations. For example, an executable query is specified inside a data source connection, as is the results output. The first tag in the preceding example is the `<esql:connection>` tag. This tag defines the connection to the database, and all the other ESQL tags are nested under this one. The first nested tag is `<esql:pool>`. This tag tells the system which data source this query should use. The preceding example uses the `personnel` data source that was defined previously. The data source attributes can also be specified as child elements to the connection tag if you do not want to set up a connection in the `cocoon.xconf` file. An example of this syntax would be this:

```
<esql:connection>
    <esql:autocommit>true</esql:autocommit>
    <esql:driver>org.hsqldb.jdbcDriver</esql:driver>
    <esql:dburl>jdbc:hsqldb:hsql://localhost:9002</esql:dburl>
    <esql:username>sa</esql:username>
    <esql:password></esql:password>
</esql:connection>
```

The next tag is the `<esql:execute-query>` tag, which contains, as sub-elements, the tags that define the query to execute, as well as the results of that query. Nested within the

`<esql:execute-query>` tag are the `<esql:query>`, `<esql:results>`, and `<esql:row-results>` tags.

The `<esql:query>` tag contains the SQL statement to be executed—in this case a simple `select *` from the table.

Next is the `<esql:results>` tag. This tag contains sub-elements that will be processed if there are results from the query. In the case of the preceding example, the `<esql:row-results>` tag is used to loop over the result set. For each row, the value of the `name` column is output between a `<para>` tag using the `<esql:get-string>` tag. This tag takes a `column` attribute to specify the name of the column to get.

An `<esql:no-results>` tag can also be included that will be processed if there are no results from the query. For example:

```
<esql:connection>
     <esql:pool>personnel</esql:pool>
     <esql:execute-query>
       <esql:query>select * from department</esql:query>
       <esql:results>
         <esql:row-results>
           <para><esql:get-string column="name"/></para>
           <esql:get-columns/>
         </esql:row-results>
       </esql:results>
    <esql:no-results>
             <p>Sorry, no results!</p>
      </esql:no-results>
     </esql:execute-query>
   </esql:connection>
```

If there were no results from the database query, `<p>Sorry, no results!</p>` would be returned.

You may also use the `<esql:error-results>` to process an error condition. Within the `<esql:error-results>`, you may use `<esql:to-string>`, `<esql:get-stacktrace>`, and `<esql:get-message>` tags to get more information about the exception. For example:

```
<esql:connection>
     <esql:pool>personnel</esql:pool>
     <esql:execute-query>
       <esql:query>select * from department</esql:query>
       <esql:results>
         <esql:row-results>
```

```
            <para><esql:get-string column="name"/></para>
            <esql:get-columns/>
          </esql:row-results>
        </esql:results>
    <esql:no-results>
                <p>Sorry, no results!</p>
          </esql:no-results>
    <esql:error-results>
         <p>An error has occurred</p>
         <esql:to-string/>
         <esql:get-stacktrace/>
    </esql:error-results>
     </esql:execute-query>
   </esql:connection>
```

ESQL also has the capability to limit the amount of results that are returned. This is accomplished using the `<esql:use-limit-clause>`, `<esql:skip-rows>`, and `<esql:max-rows>` tags. The following example illustrates this:

```
<esql:connection>
     <esql:pool>personnel</esql:pool>
     <esql:execute-query>
       <esql:query>select * from department</esql:query>
    <esql:use-limit-clause>auto</esql:use-limit-clause>
         <esql:skip-rows>10</esql:skip-rows>
         <esql:max-rows>10</esql:max-rows>

       <esql:results>
          <esql:row-results>
            <para><esql:get-string column="name"/></para>
            <esql:get-columns/>
          </esql:row-results>
       </esql:results>
    <esql:no-results>
                <p>Sorry, no results!</p>
          </esql:no-results>
    <esql:error-results>
         <p>An error has occurred</p>
         <esql:to-string/>
         <esql:get-stacktrace/>
    </esql:error-results>
     </esql:execute-query>
   </esql:connection>
```

The <esql:use-limit-clause> is set to auto so that if the underlying database supports it, a limits clause will be used. The <esql:skip-rows> tag tells the database to skip the first 10 rows, and the <esql:max-rows> tag tells the database to return at most 10 rows.

Limiting the results that are returned from a query is most often used in an application to create a paged view of the database so that you don't overwhelm the end user with lots of data at one time, and for speed reasons. It is very intensive to send the entire result set of a query over the network each time it is requested.

Update Queries

To run queries that add or modify data in the database, you must replace the <esql:results> tags with the <esql:update-results> tag. The <esql:get-update-count> tag can be nested within the <esql:update-results> tag. This tag allows you to retrieve the number of rows affected by the update. Any code that relies on this number must also be included in the <esql:update-results> tag block. The following example demonstrates this point:

```
<esql:connection>
  <esql:pool>connectionName</esql:pool>
  <esql:execute-query>
    <esql:query>update users set active = 1</esql:query>
    <esql:error-results>An error occurred</esql:error-results>
    <esql:update-results>
       <p><esql:get-update-count/> users adjusted.</p>
    </esql:update-results>
    <esql:no-results>
       <p>Sorry, no users were adjusted!</p>
    </esql:no-results>
  </esql:execute-query>
</esql:connection>
```

Group Queries

ESQL supports a feature called group queries. This is a useful feature when you want to "watch" the value of one column and change the header information when that value changes. An example of this would be printing a list of company employees by office location. By using a group query, you could print a header and list of employees for each office very easily. For example:

```
<esql:execute-query>
  <esql:query>
    SELECT OfficeID, OfficeName, OfficeLocation, firstName, lastName
    FROM offices, employees
    WHERE offices.OfficeID = employees.OfficeID
  </esql:query>
  <esql:results>
    <esql:row-results>
      <esql:group group-on="OfficeName">
        <b><esql:get-string column="OfficeName"/> Employees</b><br/>
          <esql:member>
              <esql:get-string column="lastName"/>,
              <esql:get-string column="firstName"/>
            <br/>
          </esql:member>
      </esql:group>
    </esql:row-results>
  </esql:results>
</esql:execute-query>
```

The preceding example uses the `<esql:group>` tag inside the `<esql:row-results>` tag to set the field name to group by. This field is what ESQL "watches" for a changed value. Nested within the `<esql:group>` tag is the `<esql:member>` tag that specifies the output for the rows that match the group column's value. Output for the preceding example would look like this:

```
<b>New York Office Employees</b>
John Doe<br/>
Mary jane<br/>

<b>London Office Employees</br/>
George Guern<br/>
Henry Li<br/>
```

Stored Procedures

To use stored procedures in ESQL, you replace the `esql:query` tag with the `esql:call` tag. The query syntax in the `esql:call` tag is the same as JDBC. For example:

```
<esql:call>{? = updateEmployee}</esql:call>
```

This example would call the stored procedure `updateEmployee`.

If your database JDBC drivers expect you to call `ExecuteQuery` and not `Execute`, you can set the `needs-query="true"` attribute.

If your stored procedure returns a result set, you can set the `resultset-from-object` attribute equal to `1` in the `esql:call` tag. This will set the single `resultset` as the default.

Most stored procedures can take parameters as input and output. To specify a stored procedure parameter, you use the `esql:parameter` tag. This tag takes a direction attribute that specifies an `in`, `inout`, or `out` parameter, and a `type` parameter that specifies the primitive type of the parameter such as `int` or `string`. The body of the parameter statement takes an `<xsl:expr>`, which is the variable that holds the parameter value. An example of this would be as follows:

```
<esql:parameter direction="in" type="Int">
    <xsp:expr>my_int_var</xsp:expr>
</esql:parameter>
```

A full example of a callable stored procedure with parameters would look like this:

```
<esql:call>{? = updateEmployee(<esql:parameter direction="in"
  type="Int"><xsp:expr>emp_number</xsp:expr></esql:parameter>)}
</esql:call>
```

This statement would call a stored procedure and pass in an integer specifying the employee number to update.

Next you must define an `esql:call-results` tag. This tag block can contain code that is run whether or not the stored procedure returned results. In this block, you can access the values of the output parameters. You can use the `<esql:get-xxx>` tags, where *xxx* is the type you want to retrieve, for example, `<esql:get-string>` or `<esql:get-int>`. You then specify the column you want to access and specify that you are accessing results from the `esql:call` block.

Here's a full example of a stored procedure in Oracle returning output parameters:

```
<esql:execute-query>
    <esql:call>
        begin Uman.Logon(
         'manager',
         'manage',
         <esql:parameter direction="out" type="String"/>,
         <esql:parameter direction="out" type="String"/>,
         <esql:parameter direction="out" type="String"/>,
         <esql:parameter direction="out" type="String"/>,
         <esql:parameter direction="out" type="Int"/>
```

```
        );
        end;
    </esql:call>

        <esql:call-results>
            <esql:get-string column="1" from-call="yes"/>
            <esql:get-string column="2" from-call="yes"/>
            <esql:get-string column="3" from-call="yes"/>
            <esql:get-string column="4" from-call="yes"/>
            <esql:get-int column="4" from-call="yes"/>
    </esql:call-results>

</esql:execute-query>
```

Tag Reference

Listed here are all the ESQL tags that operate on row data returned from a query. These tags are nested inside the tags described previously. The parent element of the tag is specified in the following listings. For example, `esql:row-results//esql:get-columns` notes that the `<esql:get-columns>` tag is nested inside the `<esql:row-results>` tag.

Error Tags

`esql:error-results//esql:get-message`

This function returns the string message of the current exception.

`esql:error-results//esql:to-string`

This function returns the current exception as a string.

`esql:error-results//esql:get-stacktrace`

This function returns the stacktrace of the current exception.

Grouping Tags

`esql:group`

This tag allows a developer to perform looping based on watched values. This is something that is very handy when you want to display a list and add a new header when a column value changes. For example, you may want to output a list of company employees by location. You can use `esql:group` to group on the location column, and when that value changes, a new header row would be inserted. This tag has a `group-on` attribute that specifies the column to group on.

`esql:member`

This tag is used along with `esql:group`. The `esql:member` tag holds the formatting for each row in the group. This could be specific HTML formatting for the list, such as a table or an unordered list.

An example of these tags is as follows:

```
<esql:group group-on="OfficeName">
        <b><esql:get-string column="OfficeName"/> Employees</b><br/>
          <esql:member>
              <esql:get-string column="lastName"/>,
              <esql:get-string column="firstName"/>
            <br/>
          </esql:member>
</esql:group>
```

Results Tags

`esql:results/esql:get-metadata`

This function returns the current result set's metadata.

`esql:results/esql:get-resultset`

This function returns the current result set.

Row Results Tags

`esql:row-results//esql:get-array`

This function returns the value of a specified column as a `Java.sql.array`. This function takes a `column` attribute specifying the column to return. For example:

```
<esql:get-array column="1"/>
```

`esql:row-results//esql:get-ascii`

This function returns the value of a specified column as a CLOB. This function takes a `column` attribute specifying the column to return. For example:

```
<esql:get-ascii column="1"/>
```

esql:row-results//esql:get-boolean

This function returns the value of a specified column as a Boolean value. This function takes a `column` attribute specifying the column to return. For example:

```
<esql:get-boolean column="1"/>
```

esql:results//esql:get-column-count

This function returns an `xsp:expr` that evaluates to the number of columns in a result set.

esql:row-results//esql:get-column-label

This function returns the label of the specified column. This is similar to the value you would get from `esql:get-column-name`. The function takes a required `column` attribute that specifies the column you want the name of. The `column` attribute must be a number. For example:

```
<esql:get-column-label column="1"/>
```

esql:row-results//esql:get-column-name

This function returns the name of the specified column. The function takes a required `column` attribute that specifies the column you want the name of. The `column` attribute must be a number. For example:

```
<esql:get-column-name column="1"/>
```

esql:row-results//esql:get-column-type-name

This function returns the name of the type of the specified column. The return values could be `Integer`, `Varchar`, `Boolean`, or whatever your database supports. The function takes a required `column` attribute that specifies the column you want to get the type of. The `column` attribute must be a number. For example:

```
<esql:get-column-type-name column="1"/>
```

esql:row-results//esql:get-columns

This function returns a set of XML elements that represent the columns in the database query. The nodes will be named the same as the column name, and will contain the column value. For example, the personnel example would return this:

```
<esql:get-columns/>
```

```
<ID>1</ID>
<NAME>Development</NAME>
```

esql:row-results//esql:get-date

This function returns the value of a specified column as a date. This function takes a `column` attribute specifying the column to retrieve, as well as an optional `format` attribute. The `format` attribute can be any valid Java date format. For example:

```
<esql:get-date column="1" format="dd/mm/yyyy"/>
```

esql:row-results//esql:get-double

This function returns the value of a specified column as a Java double. This function takes a `column` attribute specifying the column to retrieve, as well as an optional `format` attribute. The `format` attribute can be any valid Java decimal format. For example:

```
<esql:get-double column="1" format="###,###.###"/>
```

esql:row-results//esql:get-float

This function returns the value of a specified column as a Java float. This function takes a `column` attribute specifying the column to retrieve, as well as an optional `format` attribute. The `format` attribute can be any valid Java decimal format. For example:

```
<esql:get-float column="1" format="###,###.###"/>
```

esql:row-results//esql:get-int

This function returns the value of a specified column as an integer. This function takes a `column` attribute specifying the column to return. For example:

```
<esql:get-int column="1"/>
```

esql:row-results//esql:is-null

This function tests to see whether the specified column is null. The function takes a `column` attribute that specifies the column to check by number. The function returns an `xsp:expr` that evaluates to a Boolean value. The result will be `true` if the column is null. For example:

```
<esql:is-null column="1"/>
```

esql:row-results//esql:get-long

This function returns the value of a specified column as a Java long. This function takes a `column` attribute specifying the column to return. For example:

```
<esql:get-long column="1"/>
```

esql:row-results//esql:get-object

This function returns the value of a specified column as a Java object. This function takes a `column` attribute specifying the column to return. For example:

```
<esql:get-object column="1"/>
```

esql:row-results//esql:get-row-position

esql:results//esql:get-row-position

These functions return the position of the current row in the result set.

esql:row-results//esql:get-string

This function returns the value of a specified column as a string. This function takes a `column` attribute specifying the column to return. For example:

```
<esql:get-string column="1"/>
```

esql:row-results//esql:get-time

This function returns the value of a specified column as a time. This function takes a `column` attribute specifying the column to retrieve, as well as an optional `format` attribute. The `format` attribute can be any valid Java date format. For example:

```
<esql:get-time column="1" format="hh:mm:ss"/>
```

esql:row-results//esql:get-timestamp

This function returns the value of a specified column as a timestamp. This function takes a `column` attribute specifying the column to retrieve, as well as an optional `format` attribute. The `format` attribute can be any valid Java date format. For example:

```
<esql:get-timestamp column="1" format="dd/mm/yyyy hh:mm:ss"/>
```

esql:row-results//esql:get-short

This function returns the value of a specified column as a short. This function takes a `column` attribute specifying the column to return. For example:

```
<esql:get-short column="1"/>
```

esql:row-results//esql:get-struct

This function returns the value of a specified column as a `Java.sql.Struct`. This function takes a `column` attribute specifying the column to return. For example:

```
<esql:get-struct column="1"/>
```

esql:row-results//esql:get-xml

This function returns the value of a column as an XML fragment. This function takes a `column` attribute and a `root` attribute. The `column` attribute specifies the column that should be returned. The `root` attribute specifies the root node to wrap around the `column` value. For example:

```
<esql:get-xml column="1" root="ColumnOneValue"/>
```

APPENDIX F

Cookie Logicsheet Commands

The `Cookie` logicsheet provides the XSP developer with various functions that will handle cookies.

Declaration

The following entry can be used within `cocoon.xconf` to declare the `Cookie` logicsheet as a built-in logicsheet:

```
<builtin-logicsheet>
  <parameter name="prefix" value="xsp-cookie"/>
  <parameter name="uri"
value="http://apache.org/xsp/cookie/2.0"/>
  <parameter name="href"
value="resource://org/apache/cocoon/components/
➥language/markup/xsp/java/cookie.xsl"/>
</builtin-logicsheet>
```

Usage

The following code is required in any XSP file that needs to use the `Cookie` logicsheet:

```
<xsp:page language="java"
  xmlns:xsp="http://apache.org/xsp"
```

```
  xmlns:xsp-cookie="http://apache.org/xsp/cookie/2.0"
...>
```

Elements

<xsp-cookie:create-cookies>

<xsp-cookie:create-cookies> wraps one or more <xsp-cookie:cookie> elements.

<xsp-cookie:cookie>

<xsp-cookie:cookie> is used to create a cookie. It wraps several child elements:

- <xsp-cookie:name>
- <xsp-cookie:value>
- <xsp-cookie:setComment>
- <xsp-cookie:setDomain>
- <xsp-cookie:setMaxAge>
- <xsp-cookie:setPath>
- <xsp-cookie:setSecure>
- <xsp-cookie:setVersion>

<xsp-cookie:name> and <xsp-cookie:value> can be supplied as attributes of the <xsp-cookie:cookie> element.

Attributes

Name	Value	Description
name	*text*	Name of the cookie. This can be also supplied as a child element using <xsp-cookie:name> element.
value	*text*	Value to be stored in the cookie. This can be also supplied as a child element using the <xsp-cookie:value> element.

Example

The following example creates a cookie called "foo" with a value of bar. It will last until the browser is shut down. All the cookie properties that have not been specified will be set to defaults. It also demonstrates the name property being set using an attribute and the value property being set using a child element.

```
<xsp-cookie:cookie name="foo">
  <xsp-cookie:value>bar</xsp-cookie:value>
  <xsp-cookie:setMaxAge><xsp:expr>-1</xsp:expr></xsp-cookie:setMaxAge>
</xsp-cookie:cookie>
```

<xsp-cookie:name>

<xsp-cookie:name> is a child element of <xsp-cookie:cookie>. It can be used instead of supplying a name attribute to the <xsp-cookie:cookie> element.

The element value specifies the cookie name.

Example

Create a cookie with a name of "foo":

```
<xsp-cookie:cookie>
  <xsp-cookie:name>foo</xsp-cookie:name>
  <xsp-cookie:value>bar</xsp-cookie:value>
  <xsp-cookie:setMaxAge><xsp:expr>-1</xsp:expr></xsp-cookie:setMaxAge>
</xsp-cookie:cookie>
```

<xsp-cookie:value>

<xsp-cookie:value> is a child element of <xsp-cookie:cookie>. It can be used instead of supplying a value attribute to the <xsp-cookie:cookie> element.

The element value specifies the cookie value.

Example

Create a cookie with a value of bar:

```
<xsp-cookie:cookie>
  <xsp-cookie:name>foo</xsp-cookie:name>
  <xsp-cookie:value>bar</xsp-cookie:value>
  <xsp-cookie:setMaxAge><xsp:expr>-1</xsp:expr></xsp-cookie:setMaxAge>
</xsp-cookie:cookie>
```

<xsp-cookie:setComment>

<xsp-cookie:setComment> is a child element of <xsp-cookie:cookie>. The element value specifies a comment that is associated with the cookie. This is an optional element and

is relevant only to cookies that are stored in accordance with the RFC 2109 specification. Cookies that are stored in accordance with the original Netscape specification cannot maintain comments. Note that the RFC 2109 specification may not be fully supported on the client platform and thus should not be relied on within a production environment.

Example

Create a cookie with a comment specifying a test purpose:

```
<xsp-cookie:cookie>
  <xsp-cookie:name>foo</xsp-cookie:name>
  <xsp-cookie:value>bar</xsp-cookie:value>
  <xsp-cookie:setMaxAge><xsp:expr>-1</xsp:expr></xsp-cookie:setMaxAge>
  <xsp-cookie:setComment>Test Cookie</xsp-cookie:setComment>
  <xsp-cookie:setVersion><xsp:expr>1</xsp:expr></xsp-cookie:setVersion>
</xsp-cookie:cookie>
```

<xsp-cookie:setDomain>

`<xsp-cookie:setDomain>` is a child element of `<xsp-cookie:cookie>`. The element value specifies the domain that the cookie refers to. Note that full support for this may vary depending on the Web server/browser combination.

Example

Create a cookie, specifying the domain:

```
<xsp-cookie:cookie>
  <xsp-cookie:name>foo</xsp-cookie:name>
  <xsp-cookie:value>bar</xsp-cookie:value>
  <xsp-cookie:setMaxAge><xsp:expr>-1</xsp:expr></xsp-cookie:setMaxAge>
  <xsp-cookie:setDomain>"myhost.com"</xsp-cookie:setDomain>
</xsp-cookie:cookie>
```

<xsp-cookie:setMaxAge>

`<xsp-cookie:setSetMaxAge>` is a child element of `<xsp-cookie:cookie>`. The element value specifies the maximum length of time that the cookie will be available, specified in seconds. A value of `-1` indicates that the cookie should expire when the browser closes down. This value is an integer and needs to be configured as an expression to ensure the correct operation of the template.

Example

Create a cookie, specifying that the cookie will expire in 24 hours:

```
<xsp-cookie:cookie>
  <xsp-cookie:name>foo</xsp-cookie:name>
  <xsp-cookie:value>bar</xsp-cookie:value>
  <xsp-cookie:setMaxAge><xsp:expr>24*60*60</xsp:expr></xsp-cookie:setMaxAge>
</xsp-cookie:cookie>
```

<xsp-cookie:setPath>

`<xsp-cookie:setSetPath>` is a child element of `<xsp-cookie:cookie>`. The element value specifies the path that must be used by the requesting client to trigger the sending of the cookie. Note that full support for this may vary depending on the Web server/browser combination.

Example

Create a cookie and set the path so that the cookie is returned only when `/myfolder` or its subfolders are within the requesting path:

```
<xsp-cookie:cookie>
  <xsp-cookie:name>foo</xsp-cookie:name>
  <xsp-cookie:value>bar</xsp-cookie:value>
  <xsp-cookie:setMaxAge><xsp:expr>-1</xsp:expr></xsp-cookie:setMaxAge>
  <xsp-cookie:setPath>/myfolder</xsp-cookie:setPath>
</xsp-cookie:cookie>
```

<xsp-cookie:setSecure>

`<xsp-cookie:setSecure>` is a child element of `<xsp-cookie:cookie>`. The element value specifies whether the cookie should be sent only if a secure protocol such as SSL is being used. The default value is `false` and only when the value is set to `true` will the secure setting be initiated.

Example

Create a cookie, specifying that it is secure:

```
<xsp-cookie:cookie>
  <xsp-cookie:name>foo</xsp-cookie:name>
  <xsp-cookie:value>bar</xsp-cookie:value>
  <xsp-cookie:setMaxAge><xsp:expr>-1</xsp:expr></xsp-cookie:setMaxAge>
  <xsp-cookie:setSecure>true</xsp-cookie:setSecure>
</xsp-cookie:cookie>
```

<xsp-cookie:setVersion>

`<xsp-cookie:setVersion>` is a child element of `<xsp-cookie:cookie>`. The element value specifies whether the cookie conforms to the Netscape cookie standard or to RFC 2109. Use `0` to specify Netscape (the default) and `1` to specify RFC 2109. This value is an integer and needs to be configured as an expression to ensure the correct operation of the template. Note that this may not work on all Web server/browser combinations because they may not implement RFC 2109.

Example

Create a cookie, specifying that the cookie will use RFC 2109:

```
<xsp-cookie:cookie>
  <xsp-cookie:name>foo</xsp-cookie:name>
  <xsp-cookie:value>bar</xsp-cookie:value>
  <xsp-cookie:setMaxAge><xsp:expr>-1</xsp:expr></xsp-cookie:setMaxAge>
  <xsp-cookie:setVersion><xsp:expr>1</xsp:expr></xsp-cookie:setVersion>
</xsp-cookie:cookie>
```

<xsp-cookie:getCookies>

`<xsp-cookie:getCookies>` returns all the cookies applicable for the path and domain for the request.

Attributes

Name	Value	Description
`as`	`"cookie" | "xml"`	The `as` attribute determines whether the cookies are to be returned as a cookie object or as a stream of XML.

Example

Call the `xsp-cookie:getCookies` function, returning the cookies as a stream of XML:

```
<xsp-cookie:getCookies as="xml"/>
```

<xsp-cookie:getCookie>

`<xsp-cookie:getCookie>` returns a cookie as a stream of XML or a cookie object. The cookie can be referred to by name or an index number.

Attributes

Name	Value	Description
`as`	`"cookie" | "xml"`	The `as` attribute determines whether the cookie is returned as a cookie object or as a stream of XML.
`name`	*`text`*	Specifies the name of the cookie to return. This can be used instead of the `index` attribute.
`index`	*`text`*	Specifies the index number of the cookie to be returned. This can be used instead of the `name` attribute. The range of this is from 0 to (number of cookies – 1).

Example

Get the `"foo"` cookie as a cookie object:

```
<xsp-cookie:getCookie name="foo" as="cookie"/>
```

<xsp-cookie:getName>

`<xsp-cookie:getName>` returns the name of a specified cookie. The cookie can be referred to by name or an index number.

Attributes

Name	Value	Description
`name`	*`text`*	Specifies the name of the cookie to return. This can be used instead of the `index` attribute.
`index`	*`text`*	Specifies the index number of the cookie to be returned. This can be used instead of the `name` attribute. Once again, this is from 0 to (number of cookies – 1).

Example

Get the name of the `"foo"` cookie:

```
<xsp:expr><xsp-cookie:getName name="foo"/></xsp:expr>
```

<xsp-cookie:getComment>

`<xsp-cookie:getComment>` returns the comment of a specified cookie. The cookie can be referred to by name or an index number.

Attributes

Name	Value	Description
`name`	*text*	Specifies the name of the cookie to return. This can be used instead of the `index` attribute.
`index`	*text*	Specifies the index number of the cookie to be returned. This can be used instead of the `name` attribute.

Example

Get the comment associated with the "`foo`" cookie:

```
<xsp:expr><xsp-cookie:getComment name="foo"/></xsp:expr>
```

<xsp-cookie:getDomain>

`<xsp-cookie:getDomain>` returns the domain of a specified cookie. The cookie can be referred to by name or an index number.

Attributes

Name	Value	Description
`name`	*text*	Specifies the name of the cookie to return. This can be used instead of the `index` attribute.
`index`	*text*	Specifies the index number of the cookie to be returned. This can be used instead of the `name` attribute.

Example

Get the domain of the "`foo`" cookie:

```
<xsp:expr><xsp-cookie:getDomain name="foo"/></xsp:expr>
```

<xsp-cookie:getMaxAge>

`<xsp-cookie:getMaxAge>` returns the `MaxAge` property of a specified cookie. The cookie can be referred to by name or an index number.

Attributes

Name	Value	Description
`name`	*`text`*	Specifies the name of the cookie to return. This can be used instead of the `index` attribute.
`index`	*`text`*	Specifies the index number of the cookie to be returned. This can be used instead of the `name` attribute.

Example

Get the `MaxAge` of the `"foo"` cookie:

```
<xsp:expr><xsp-cookie:getMaxAge name="foo"/></xsp:expr>
```

<xsp-cookie:getPath>

`<xsp-cookie:getPath>` returns the path of a specified cookie. The cookie can be referred to by name or an index number.

Attributes

Name	Value	Description
`name`	*`text`*	Specifies the name of the cookie to return. This can be used instead of the `index` attribute.
`index`	*`text`*	Specifies the index number of the cookie to be returned. This can be used instead of the `name` attribute.

Example

Get the path of the `"foo"` cookie:

```
<xsp:expr><xsp-cookie:getPath name="foo"/></xsp:expr>
```

<xsp-cookie:getSecure>

`<xsp-cookie:getSecure>` returns the secure attribute of a specified cookie. The cookie can be referred to by name or an index number. This will typically be `false` unless you are using a secure protocol such as HTTPS.

Attributes

Name	Value	Description
`name`	*text*	Specifies the name of the cookie to return. This can be used instead of the `index` attribute.
`index`	*text*	Specifies the index number of the cookie to be returned. This can be used instead of the `name` attribute.

Example

Get the secure attribute of the `"foo"` cookie, first to a variable and then wrap that up in an XML element:

```
<xsp:logic>
  String cookieSecure = <xsp-cookie:getSecure name="foo"/>;
</xsp:logic>
<cookiesecure>
  <xsp:expr>cookieSecure</xsp:expr>
</cookiesecure>
```

<xsp-cookie:getValue>

`<xsp-cookie:getValue>` returns the value of a specified cookie. The cookie can be referred to by name or an index number.

Attributes

Name	Value	Description
`name`	*text*	Specifies the name of the cookie to return. This can be used instead of the `index` attribute.
`index`	*text*	Specifies the index number of the cookie to be returned. This can be used instead of the `name` attribute.

Example

Get the value of the "foo" cookie:

```
<xsp:expr><xsp-cookie:getPath name="foo"/></xsp:expr>
```

<xsp-cookie:getVersion>

`<xsp-cookie:getVersion>` returns the version of a specified cookie. The cookie can be referred to by name or an index number. Note again that you may find you always get `0` returned because the Web server/browser combination may not support RFC 2109 properly.

Attributes

Name	Value	Description
`name`	*`text`*	Specifies the name of the cookie to return. This can be used instead of the `index` attribute.
`index`	*`text`*	Specifies the index number of the cookie to be returned. This can be used instead of the `name` attribute.

Example

Get the version of the "foo" cookie:

```
<xsp:expr><xsp-cookie:getVersion name="foo"/></xsp:expr>
```

APPENDIX G

Log Logicsheet Commands

The log logicsheet provides a standard interface to logging functions in Cocoon. It is a wrapper around the logkit logger class that Cocoon uses for all its logging needs. The log logicsheet allows you to print log messages of several kinds, including debug, info, warn, error, fatal, and log.

The log logicsheet can be used only in an XSP page, and the log namespace must first be imported before it can be used:

```
<xsp:page
  xmlns:xsp="http://apache.org/xsp"
  xmlns:log="http://apache.org/xsp/log/2.0">

</xsp:page>
```

The first thing you must do to use the logging functionality is to create a Logger. This is accomplished by using the following tag:

```
<log:logger name="my-log"/>
```

The <log:logger> tag can take two attributes: name and level. The name is the log category, set up in logkit.xconf, that you want to write to. The logging formats are also set up in logkit.xconf. The level attribute specifies the level of logging. Valid values for this attribute are DEBUG, INFO, WARN, ERROR, and FATAL-ERROR. If not specified, the level attribute will default to DEBUG.

After you have a valid logger, you can write logging statements.

The `log` logicsheet has several print methods that can log to the different log levels. These are the methods:

```
<log:debug>Debug message goes here</log:debug>
<log:info>Info message goes here</log:info>
<log:warn>Warning message goes here</log:warn>
<log:error>Error message goes here</log:error>
<log:fatal-error>Fatal Error message goes here</log:fatal-error>
```

A full example of using a log function would be as follows:

```
<xsp:page
  xmlns:xsp="http://apache.org/xsp"
  xmlns:log="http://apache.org/xsp/log/2.0">

<log:logger name="sitemap"/>
<log:debug>Processing the beginning of the page</log:debug>

<para>A test page for the log logicsheet</para>

<log:debug>Processing the end of the page</log:debug>
</xsp:page>
```

This would insert the following lines in the `sitemap.log` file under `WEB-INF/logs`. Some of the information may be different depending on where you saved the file, and how your sitemap is set up.

```
DEBUG   (2002-06-14) 00:20.59:778   [sitemap.generator.serverpages]
➥(/cocoon/xsp/test) HttpProcessor[8080][4]/test_xsp:
➥Processing the beginning of the page

DEBUG   (2002-06-14) 00:20.59:778
➥[sitemap.generator.serverpages](/cocoon/xsp/test)
➥HttpProcessor[8080][4]/test_xsp: Processing the end of the page
```

APPENDIX H

Util Logicsheet Commands

The util logicsheet provides a standard interface for commonly used utility functions. These include functions for including files, date formatting, and counters.

The util logicsheet can be used from XSP, and must be declared before it can be used. This is done like so:

```
<xsp:page
  xmlns:xsp="http://apache.org/xsp"
  xmlns:util="http://apache.org/xsp/util/2.0">

</xsp:page>
```

Util Logicsheet Functions

util:include-uri

This function includes a URL as SAX. It takes a parameter href that specifies the URL to include.

```
<xsp:page
  xmlns:xsp="http://apache.org/xsp"
  xmlns:util="http://apache.org/xsp/util/2.0">
```

```
<extra-content>
<util:include-uri href="http://www.company.com/someXMLgenerator.xsp"/>
</extra-content>
</xsp:page>
```

The preceding example would include the contents of the specified URL as SAX.

util:include-file

This function includes a file as SAX. It takes a parameter `name` that specifies the filename to include.

The filename is relative to the location of the calling page. An example of usage would be `<util:include-file name="myfile.xml"/>`.

util:include-expr

This function includes the value of an expression as SAX. It takes a parameter `expr` that specifies the expression to include. Using this function, you can include an XML fragment stored in a scalar variable. For example:

```
<xsp:logic>
String xmlString = "<test>A test value</test>";
<util:include-expr><util:expr>xmlString</util:expr></util:include-expr>
</xsp:logic>
```

This would take the value of `xmlString` and include it as SAX.

util:get-file-contents

This function includes the contents of a file as text. It takes a parameter `name` that specifies the file to include.

```
<xsp:page
  xmlns:xsp="http://apache.org/xsp"
  xmlns:util="http://apache.org/xsp/util/2.0">

<html>
<head><title>Test Page</title></head>
<body>
<util:get-file-contents href="body-include.html"/>
</body>
</html>
</xsp:page>
```

The preceding example would take the contents of `body-include.html` and insert them into the document as text.

util:time

This function returns a new `Time` object formatted as specified by the `format` attribute. It takes a parameter `format` that can be a valid java time format.

```
<util:time format="hh:mm:ss"/> would return

<xsp:expr>
  SimpleDateFormat.getInstance().format(new Date(), "hh:mm:ss")
</xsp:expr>
```

util:counter

This function returns a counter. It takes an optional parameter `scope` that specifies the scope of the counter you want. Currently, the only value allowed for scope is `session`. Adding the `scope="session"` parameter will limit the counter scope to the current session. You must use the session logicsheet to set up a session before you use this.

One example of using `util:counter` would be to implement a page counter. For example:

```
<xsp:page
  xmlns:xsp="http://apache.org/xsp"
  xmlns:util="http://apache.org/xsp/util/2.0">

<html>
<head><title>Test Page</title></head>
<body>
This page has been called <util:counter/> times.
</body>
</html> </xsp:page>
```

APPENDIX I

Form Validation Logicsheet Commands

Apache Cocoon provides a robust and easy-to-use mechanism for form validation in the form logicsheet.

The form logicsheet can be used only from XSP and must be imported in the usual way before use:

```
<xsp:page
  xmlns:xsp="http://apache.org/xsp"
  xmlns:xsp-formval="http://apache.org/xsp/form
➥validator/2.0">

</xsp:page>
```

The form validation logicsheet also requires a descriptor file that describes the parameters and constraints that apply to the items from the input form. This file is an XML file; more details about its format can be found in the Cocoon Javadocs under `FormValidatorAction`. An example of the form validation logicsheet can be found in your Cocoon `samples` directory. If your `cocoon.war` file has not been extracted by your Servlet container, you can unzip it to your file system by using a zip utility. After it's extracted, you will see three files in your `COCOON_ROOT\docs\ samples\formvalidation` folder: `ERROR.xsp`, `OK.xsp`, and `descriptor.xml`.

To use the form validation logicsheet, you should create a page to hold the form to be validated, a success page, and the descriptor file.

The Cocoon form validation can be seen by running your JSP server, and navigating to the `/cocoon/samples/formvalidation/test` directory. The full URL path on my machine is `http://localhost:8080/cocoon/formvalidation/test`.

This assumes you have the samples installed and have the default sitemap.

When you navigate to this page, you will see three form fields that can be validated: `persons`, `deposit`, and `email`. Let's examine the `descriptor.xml` file first.

Descriptor.xml

This is where you set the field names and the validation rules for each item you want to validate. The contents of this file are as shown here:

```
<?xml version="1.0"?>
<root>

   <parameter name="persons" type="long" min="2" default="9" nullable="yes"/>
   <parameter name="deposit" type="double" min="10.0" max="999.99"/>
   <parameter name="email" type="string" max-len="50"
       matches-regex="^[\d\w][\d\w\-_\.]*@([\d\w\-_]+\.)\w\w\w?$"/>

   <constraint-set name="car-reservation">
       <validate name="persons"/>
       <validate name="deposit" min="50.0"/>
       <validate name="email"/>
    </constraint-set>

</root>
```

First, the three parameters are declared, along with their attributes. The `persons` parameter is declared as a Java along with a minimum value of `2` and a default value of `9`. `persons` can also be null. The `deposit` parameter is a Java double with a minimum value of `10.0` and a maximum of `999.99`. The `email` parameter is a Java string with a maximum length of 50 that must match the supplied regular expression.

The second part of the file creates a named constraint-set that holds the items to be validated. This allows you to set up multiple forms in one descriptor file. Now that the descriptor is in place, let's examine the main page.

Form Logic Page

In the Cocoon sample, this is `ERROR.xsp`. The contents of this page are shown here:

```
<?xml version="1.0" encoding="ISO-8859-1"?><!-- -*- sgml -*- -->
<xsp:page
   language="java"
   xmlns:xsp="http://apache.org/xsp"
   xmlns:xsp-formval="http://apache.org/xsp/form-validator/2.0"
   xmlns:xsp-request="http://apache.org/xsp/request/2.0"
>

   <page>

      <title>Car Reservation</title>
      <content>

      <para>
        Informal validation results <xsp:expr><xsp-formval:results/></xsp:expr>
      </para>

       <form action="test" method="POST">
       <!-- use this to get a clue if the user had a chance to fill in
            any date already -->
       <input type="hidden" name="visited" value="true"/>
       <xsp:logic>
          boolean userHasSeenForm = (
               <xsp-request:get-parameter name="visited"/>!=null);
       </xsp:logic>
      <para>
      How many persons should the car seat?
      <input type="TEXT" name="persons" size="2">
         <xsp:attribute name="value">
               <xsp-request:get-parameter name="persons" default=""/>
        </xsp:attribute>
      </input>
      <xsp-formval:descriptor
            name="context:///docs/samples/formvalidation/descriptor.xml"
            constraint-set="car-reservation">
         <xsp:logic>
             if (userHasSeenForm) {
           if (<xsp-formval:is-toosmall name="persons"/> ) {
             <b> The smallest available car seats
```

```
          <xsp-formval:get-attribute parameter="persons" name="min"/>
       </b>
         } else if ( <xsp-formval:is-toolarge name="persons"/> ) {
      <b> The largest available car seats
          <xsp-formval:get-attribute parameter="persons" name="max"/>
      </b>
         } else if (<xsp-formval:is-error name="persons"/> ) {
       <b> Some error occurred. Your input is not correct. </b>
            };
  };
  </xsp:logic>
</xsp-formval:descriptor>
</para>

<xsp-formval:descriptor
  name="context:///docs/samples/formvalidation/descriptor.xml"
  constraint-set="car-reservation">
<para>
   <xsp-formval:validate name="deposit">
       Please enter your deposit EUR
  <input type="TEXT" name="deposit" size="10">
      <xsp:attribute name="value">
      <xsp-request:get-parameter name="deposit" default=""/>
      </xsp:attribute>
  </input>
  <xsp:logic>
       if (userHasSeenForm) {
      if ( <xsp-formval:is-null/>) {
        <b> You need to specify a deposit </b>
          } else if ( <xsp-formval:is-toosmall/> ) {
        <b> The deposit has to be at least EUR
          <xsp-formval:get-attribute name="min"/></b>
          } else if ( <xsp-formval:is-toolarge/> ) {
        <b> The deposit has to be at most EUR
         <xsp-formval:get-attribute name="max"/></b>
          } else if (<xsp-formval:is-notpresent/> ) {
        <b></b>
          } else if ( <xsp-formval:is-error/>) {
        <b> Some error occurred. Your input is not correct. </b>
            };
  };
  </xsp:logic>
```

```
        </xsp-formval:validate><br/>
    </para>

    <para>
        <xsp-formval:validate name="email">
            Please enter your email
      <input type="TEXT" name="email" size="50">
        <xsp:attribute name="value">
          <xsp-request:get-parameter name="email" default=""/>
        </xsp:attribute>
      </input>

      <xsp:logic>
            if (userHasSeenForm) {
          if ( <xsp-formval:is-null/>) {
            <b> You need to specify an email </b>
          } else if ( <xsp-formval:is-nomatch/> ) {
            <b> This does not seem to be a valid email
          address. Expected <pre><xsp-formval:get-attribute
          parameter="email" name="matches-regex"/></pre></b>
              } else if ( <xsp-formval:is-toolarge/> ) {
            <b> Only addresses with up to
          <xsp-formval:get-attribute parameter="email" name="max-len"/>
           characters are accepted</b>
              } else if (<xsp-formval:is-notpresent/> ) {
            <b></b>
              } else if ( <xsp-formval:is-error/>) {
            <b> Some error occurred. Your input is not correct. </b>
                 };
               };
        </xsp:logic>
        </xsp-formval:validate><br/>
    </para>

    </xsp-formval:descriptor>
    <input type="submit" name="submit" value="submit"/>
    </form>

    </content>
  </page>
</xsp:page>
```

The first thing to notice is the declaration of the `xsp-formval` namespace. Let's examine each `xsp-formval` section in detail.

The first one deals with validating the `persons` field:

```
<input type="TEXT" name="persons" size="2">
     <xsp:attribute name="value">
<xsp-request:get-parameter name="persons" default=""/></xsp:attribute>
</input>
      <xsp-formval:descriptor
        name="context:///docs/samples/formvalidation/descriptor.xml"
        constraint-set="car-reservation">
         <xsp:logic>
             if (userHasSeenForm) {
           if (<xsp-formval:is-toosmall name="persons"/> ) {
             <b> The smallest available car seats
        <xsp-formval:get-attribute parameter="persons" name="min"/></b>
               } else if ( <xsp-formval:is-toolarge name="persons"/> ) {
             <b> The largest available car seats
        <xsp-formval:get-attribute parameter="persons" name="max"/></b>
               } else if (<xsp-formval:is-error name="persons"/> ) {
             <b> Some error occurred. Your input is not correct. </b>
                   };
         };
         </xsp:logic>
      </xsp-formval:descriptor>
```

In the preceding example, a validator has been set up for the `persons` input text box. First the `xsp-formval:descriptor` tag is used to tell the Cocoon which descriptor you are using and the constraint-set used within. The `xsp-formval:descriptor` has an `xsp:logic` sub-element that contains the validation code. The code checks to see whether the user has seen the form and then includes three validation options. By using `xsp-formval:is-toosmall`, the Cocoon checks to make sure that the `persons` value is greater than `2`, the limit set up in the descriptor file. If the value is too small, an error message is displayed. The code then checks `xsp-formval:is-toolarge`. If the value is too large, another error is displayed. Finally, the code includes a default case to catch any unspecified errors with `xsp-formval:is-error`.

The next validator deals with the `deposit` field:

```
<xsp-formval:descriptor
    name="context:///docs/samples/formvalidation/descriptor.xml"
    constraint-set="car-reservation">
```

```
<para>
   <xsp-formval:validate name="deposit">
       Please enter your deposit EUR
  <input type="TEXT" name="deposit" size="10">
      <xsp:attribute name="value">
      <xsp-request:get-parameter name="deposit" default=""/>
      </xsp:attribute>
  </input>
  <xsp:logic>
       if (userHasSeenForm) {
      if ( <xsp-formval:is-null/>) {
        <b> You need to specify a deposit </b>
          } else if ( <xsp-formval:is-toosmall/> ) {
        <b> The deposit has to be at least EUR
          <xsp-formval:get-attribute name="min"/></b>
          } else if ( <xsp-formval:is-toolarge/> ) {
        <b> The deposit has to be at most EUR
          <xsp-formval:get-attribute name="max"/></b>
          } else if (<xsp-formval:is-notpresent/> ) {
        <b></b>
          } else if ( <xsp-formval:is-error/>) {
        <b> Some error occurred. Your input is not correct. </b>
              };
   };
   </xsp:logic>
   </xsp-formval:validate>
```

Just as in the earlier example, the `xsp-formval:descriptor` tag is defined first to tell Cocoon the name of the descriptor file and the constraint-set to use in the file.

This `validator` uses the `xsp-formval:validate` sub-element to declare which parameter to validate against. The `xsp-formval:validate` tag takes a `name` attribute that contains the name of the parameter.

In the `xsp:logic` section, the code performs five validation checks. The first one uses `xsp-formval:is-null` to check for a null value. If a null value is found, an error message is displayed. The second and third use `xsp-formval:is-toosmall` and `xsp-formval:is-toolarge`, respectively. If either is true, an error message is displayed. The fourth test uses `xsp-formval:is-notpresent` to see whether the value exists. The fifth test uses `xsp-formval:is-error` to catch any unhandled error.

The third `validator` deals with validating the `email` text box:

```
<xsp-formval:validate name="email">
            Please enter your email
        <input type="TEXT" name="email" size="50">
          <xsp:attribute name="value">
<xsp-request:get-parameter name="email" default=""/></xsp:attribute>
        </input>

        <xsp:logic>
             if (userHasSeenForm) {
            if ( <xsp-formval:is-null/>) {
              <b> You need to specify an email </b>
            } else if ( <xsp-formval:is-nomatch/> ) {
              <b> This does not seem to be a valid email
            address. Expected <pre><xsp-formval:get-attribute
            parameter="email" name="matches-regex"/></pre></b>
                } else if ( <xsp-formval:is-toolarge/> ) {
              <b> Only addresses with up to
            <xsp-formval:get-attribute parameter="email" name="max-len"/>
            characters are accepted</b>
                } else if (<xsp-formval:is-notpresent/> ) {
              <b></b>
                } else if ( <xsp-formval:is-error/>) {
              <b> Some error occurred. Your input is not correct. </b>
                    };
                  };
         </xsp:logic>
         </xsp-formval:validate>
```

This third validator uses the `xsp-formval:validate` tag to name the value to validate. This validator is still under the `xsp-formval:descriptor` defined for the second item, so we don't have to declare one here. In the `xsp:logic` section, the code defines five validation tests. The first one uses `xsp-formval:is-null` and checks for a null value. The second one uses `xsp-formval:is-nomatch` to see whether the e-mail address matches the regular expression defined in the descriptor file. If it doesn't, an error is displayed showing the proper regular expression. This uses the `xsp-formval:get-attribute` tag to retrieve information from the descriptor file. This tag has a `parameter` attribute that defines the parameter in the descriptor file you want to access, and a `name` attribute that defines the value of the named parameter in the descriptor file you want to access. The third test checks to see whether the value entered in the field is too large. If it is, an error is displayed showing the maximum length. The fourth uses `xsp-formval:is-notpresent` to see whether the value exists, and the fifth uses `xsp-formval:is-error` to check for an unhandled error.

You can also access the raw results values by using the `xsp-formaval:results` tag. This returns a `java.util.Map` object you can iterate over to get the results.

The final step for setting up your form validation is to add a pipeline to the sitemap to define the page with the form input, and the actions to take when the file passes all the validation tests.

In the Cocoon form validation example, the following would be added to the sitemap to set up the pipeline:

```
<map:match pattern="formvalidation/test">
    <map:act type="form-validator">
      <map:parameter name="descriptor"
          value="context:///docs/samples/formvalidation/descriptor.xml"/>
      <map:parameter name="validate-set" value="car-reservation"/>
      <map:call resource="dynamic-page">
        <map:parameter name="target" value="docs/samples/formvalidation/OK"/>
      </map:call>
    </map:act>
    <map:call resource="dynamic-page">
      <map:parameter name="target" value="docs/samples/formvalidation/ERROR"/>
    </map:call>
  </map:match>
```

The preceding sitemap entry matches for the `formvalidation/test` string in the URL and then applies the pipeline. The map sets up the descriptor and validation set, and also specifies that the OK page is the target when everything goes well. It then tells Cocoon that `formvalidation/ERROR` is the page to return for this pipeline. The ERROR and OK pages are set up as resources in this example. A resource is a descriptor that can be set up in the sitemap that describes a series of actions for the server to take when the named resource is requested. In this case, the sitemap would contain a section like the following:

```
<map:resource name="dynamic-page">
    <map:generate src="{target}.xsp" type="serverpages"/>
    <map:transform src="stylesheets/dynamic-page2html.xsl">
      <map:parameter name="view-source" value="{target}.xsp"/>
    </map:transform>
    <map:serialize/>
  </map:resource>
```

When the validation script calls the `dynamic-page` resource, the target parameter is expanded to the XSP page it represents, and the `dynamic-page2html.xsl` style sheet is used to process the XSP page. Finally, the result is serialized to HTML.

XSP Form Validation Logicsheet Functions

`xsp-formval:is-ok`

No error occurred, and the parameter was successfully checked.

`xsp-formval:is-error`

An unforeseen error has occurred.

`xsp-formval:is-null`

A parameter is null that should contain data.

`xsp-formval:is-toosmall`

The value or length of the object is too small.

`xsp-formval:is-toolarge`

The value or length of the object is too large.

`xsp-formval:is-nomatch`

The value of the parameter did not match the specified regular expression.

`xsp-formval:is-notpresent`

A required parameter was not present.

APPENDIX J

Capture Logicsheet Commands

The capture logicsheet provides a way for you to capture parts of the generated XML as an XMLFragment object containing serialized SAX events (using XMLByteStreamCompiler), or as a DOM node. This can be very helpful if you want to hold XML data for later processing instead of outputting it. The capture logicsheet is also part of the ServerPagesAction and associated "action" logicsheet that allow actions to be written in XSP.

The capture logicsheet can be used only from an XSP page and must be declared before use like this:

```
<xsp:page
  xmlns:xsp="http://apache.org/xsp"
  xmlns:capture="http://apache.org/cocoon/capture/1.0">

</xsp:page>
```

The capture logicsheet can perform four functions: storing an XML fragment in a variable, storing an XML fragment in a request attribute, storing a DOM node in a variable, and storing a DOM node in a request variable.

Capture Logicsheet Functions

capture:fragment-variable

This function takes a name attribute that is the name of the variable to store the XML fragment in.

```
<xsp:page
  xmlns:xsp="http://apache.org/xsp"
  xmlns:capture="http://apache.org/cocoon/capture/1.0"
 >
<capture:fragment-variable name="myVar">
<sample>A sample value</sample>
</capture:fragment-variable>
</xsp:page>
```

The preceding example would store the XML as an XMLFragment in the variable myVar.

capture:fragment-request-attr

This function takes a name attribute that is the name of the request attribute to store the XML fragment in.

```
<xsp:page
  xmlns:xsp="http://apache.org/xsp"
  xmlns:capture="http://apache.org/cocoon/capture/1.0"
  xmlns:xsp-request="http://apache.org/xsp/request/2.0">

<capture:fragment-request-attr name="myVar">
<sample>A sample value</sample>
</capture:fragment-request-attr>

</xsp:page>
```

The preceding example would store the XML in the request attribute myVar as an XMLFragment, which can later be retrieved and processed.

capture:dom-request-attr

This function takes a name attribute that is the name of the request attribute to store the DOM node in.

```
<xsp:page
```

```
  xmlns:xsp="http://apache.org/xsp"
  xmlns:capture="http://apache.org/cocoon/capture/1.0"
  xmlns:xsp-request="http://apache.org/xsp/request/2.0">

<capture:dom-request-attr name="myVar">
<sample>A sample value</sample>
</capture:dom-request-attr>

</xsp:page>
```

The preceding example would store the XML in the `request` attribute `myVar` as a `node` object that can later be retrieved and processed.

capture:dom-variable

This function takes a `name` attribute that is the name of the variable to store the DOM node in.

```
<xsp:page
  xmlns:xsp="http://apache.org/xsp"
  xmlns:capture="http://apache.org/cocoon/capture/1.0"
  xmlns:xsp-request="http://apache.org/xsp/request/2.0">

<capture:dom-variable name="myVar">
<sample>A sample value</sample>
</capture:dom-variable>

</xsp:page>
```

The preceding example would store the XML in the variable `myVar` as a `node` object.

Index

Symbols

A

B

C

D

E

F

G

H

I

J

K-L

M

N

O

P

Q-R

S